THE OTHER HOLLYWOOD

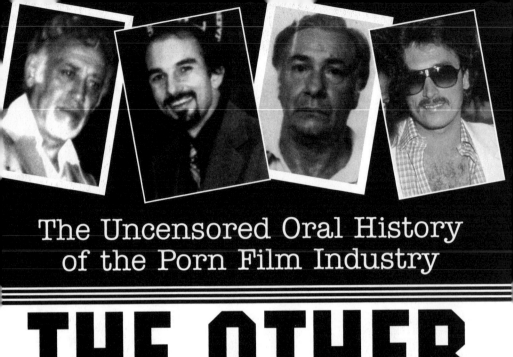

The Uncensored Oral History
of the Porn Film Industry

THE OTHER

HOLLYWOOD

BY LEGS McNEIL & JENNIFER OSBORNE
WITH PETER PAVIA

ReganBooks
Celebrating Ten Bestselling Years
An Imprint of HarperCollins Publishers

TITLE PAGE SPREAD:
Left page: Top row, *left to right:* Gerard Damiano, Pat Livingston, Michael "Mickey" Zaffarano, Marc Carriere. Bottom row, left to right: Nina Hartley, Savannah, Jenna Jameson.

Right page: *Left to right:* John Holmes, Ginger Lynn, Harry Reems.

HarperCollins books may be purchased for educational, business, or sales promotional use. For information please write: Special Markets Department, HarperCollins Publishers, Inc., 10 East 53rd Street, New York, NY 10022.

FIRST EDITION

Designed by Kris Tobiassen

Part openers designed by Kristina Berg

All photos courtesy of Tim Connelly/*Adult Video News*, except: *Title spread:* Pat Livingston courtesy of Pat Livingston. Michael "Mickey" Zaffarano from the author's collection. *Prologue:* Bettie Page and Bunny Yeager courtesy of Bunny Yeager. *Part I: Left page:* Linda Lovelace courtesy of Bettmann/Corbis. Chuck Traynor courtesy of Dave Patrick. Louis "Butchie" Peraino from the author's collection. *Right page:* Lenny Camp from the author's collection. *Part 2: Left page:* Reuben Sturman, Robert 'DiBe' DiBernardo from the author's collection. *Right page:* Jim and Artie Mitchell courtesy of Dave Patrick. *Part 3:* Annie Sprinkle courtesy of Annie Sprinkle. *Part 4: Left page:* All photos from the author's collection except Pat Livingston and Bruce Ellavsky courtesy of Pat Livingston. *Right page:* All photos courtesy of Pat Livingston. *Part 5: Left page:* Gordon McNeil and Pat Livingston courtesy of Pat Livingston. Joel Steinberg and Andre D'Apice from the author's collection. *Part 6: Left page:* All photos from the author's collection. *Right page:* John Holmes courtesy of AP/Wide World Photos. Eddie Nash courtesy of Boris Yaro, Copyright 1988, *Los Angeles Times.* Reprinted with permission. *Part 7:* All photos from the author's collection except John Holmes courtesy of AP/Wide World Photos. *Part 8: Left page:* Reuben Sturman from the author's collection. *Part 10:* Photo of Edwin Meese and Ronald Reagan courtesy of Bettmann/Corbis.

Library of Congress Cataloging-in-Publication Data

McNeil, Legs.
 The other Hollywood : the uncensored oral history of the porn film industry / Legs McNeil, Jennifer Osborne, and Peter Pavia.— 1st ed.
  p. cm.
 Includes bibliographical references.
 ISBN 0-06-009659-4
 1. Erotic films—United States—History and criticism. 2. Sex in motion pictures. 3. Oral history. I. Osborne, Jennifer, 1973- II. Pavia, Peter, 1959- III. Title.

PN1995.9.S45M36 2004
791.43'6538'0973—dc22   2004051048

05 06 07 08 09 ❖/RRD 10 9 8 7 6 5 4 3 2

Authors' Note

The overwhelming majority of the material in *The Other Hollywood* is the result of hundreds of interviews conducted by the authors. In some cases, interviews and text were excerpted from other sources, including anthologies, magazines, newspapers, journals, federal wire taps, police reports, FBI 302s, coroners' reports, psychiatric records, court records and testimony, published and unpublished interviews, and other books. A list of these sources appears on page 591. We wish to acknowledge the contributions of these sources, which have enriched the content of our book.

Because I miss her and love her more
every day, this book is dedicated to:

Shannon McNamara

May 9, 1974–January 26, 2001

"Everyone gets everything they want.
Absolutely goddamn right."

—Captain Willard, *Apocalypse Now*

Contents

INTRODUCTION xv

PROLOGUE: NUDIE-CUTIES xviii

PART ONE: THE SWORD SWALLOWER

The Turkey Raffle **15**

If You Can Make It There, You Can Make It Anywhere **20**

Vickie Killed the Nudie-Cuties **31**

Rent **36**

Doggie Style **47**

Mary Had a Little Lamb **52**

"Do You Mind If I Smoke While You Eat?" **60**

SCREW'ed **67**

Don't Count the Money, Weigh It **74**

PART TWO: PORNO CHIC

To Bowl or Not to Bowl? **81**

Size Matters **87**

Ebony and Ivory Snow **92**

Hair of the Dog   99

Automated Vending   104

Trading Up   111

The Devil in Miss Steinberg   121

Holmes v. Wadd   132

PART THREE: SHOW WORLD

Boxed Lunch   141

The Ballad of Jason and Tina   154

Turnover   161

Plato's Retreat   168

PART FOUR: FAMILY AFFAIRS

This Thing of Ours   175

Memphis Backlash Blues   180

Deep Cover   192

Nobody Does It Better   199

Looks Like We Made It   204

PART FIVE: PORN GOES BETTER WITH COKE

Down the Drain   211

"Blow"   214

Stayin' Alive   219

Seka to the Rescue   227

Johnny on the Pipe   233

Beauty and the Beast   240

Falling Out   244

St. Valentine's Day Massacre   252

"Ordeal"   263

PART SIX: WONDERLAND AVENUE

The Godfather of Hollywood   275

"It's Not Like You Said It Was Gonna Be"   283

Nobody Waved Hello   289

"Think This Will Fuck Up My Fourth of July Weekend?"   294

PART SEVEN: GETTING OUT

Method Acting   309

On the Lam   315

Don't Embarrass the Bureau   326

Grave's End   332

The Trial   336

PART EIGHT: VIDEO VIXENS

Hooray for Hollywood!   345

Mr. Untouchable   354

Shattered Innocence   359

Fast Forward   365

Club 90   371

Kristie Nussman   377

PART NINE: THE PARTY'S OVER

The Porn Marriage   389

To Be or Not to Be?   393

GRID   396

Pimping and Pandering   402

Who Dropped the Dime on Traci?   415

PART TEN: BACKLASH

The Meese Commission   425

Disappearing DiBe   431

Conclusions 435

Christmas Eve with Lori and the Kids 440

The Last Chance 444

Jail 452

Another Mob Hit? 458

Cry-Baby 462

Divorce: Porn Style 469

PART ELEVEN: FAME AND MISFORTUNE

Rock and Roll High School 477

Tired 488

Cain and Abel 491

The Bombing 498

PART TWELVE: KILLER & FILLER

The Girls who Marc Built 511

Severed 517

The Great Escape 522

John Wayne Bobbitt Uncut 524

Ding Dong, the Witch Is Dead 530

Caught 537

Waiting for Wood 543

Going to Extremes 552

Celebrity Porn 567

Outbreak 574

Source Notes 591

Acknowledgments 601

Index 607

Introduction

Of the seven years it took us to complete *The Other Hollywood*, we spent roughly half the time trying to sell the book to a publisher. Surprisingly—or not—pornography was considered an uncommercial venture by the literary publishing industry, who seemed to believe that even people who watched porn would not want to read about it. It wasn't until we produced the three-hour television series *Adults Only: The Secret History of the Other Hollywood* for Court TV—and it became that channel's highest rated original program to date—that the New York publishing world took notice. In the end, it was the maverick publisher Judith Regan who took a chance on us; we can only hope this book will live up to her expectations.

Just before this book was sold to ReganBooks, my girlfriend, Shannon McNamara, died, after injecting herself with black tar heroin that had been infected with flesh-eating bacteria. When the infection spread throughout her body, Shannon was forced to undergo surgery to amputate her leg and did not survive the operation. I didn't know she had been using dope, nor dealing it, and the resulting emotional fallout was crippling for me. For some time I couldn't face the book—or myself, for that matter. It was Gillian McCain, my coauthor on *Please Kill Me*, who reminded me that if I didn't continue my work on *The Other Hollywood*, no one else would tell the story of the porn industry's rise from a marginal criminal enterprise of starving hippie actors and mob-sponsored back-alley loops to the multibillion-dollar juggernaut it is today.

Through me, Gillian had become friends with former porn stars Jane Hamilton (whose stage name was Veronica Hart), Sharon Mitchell, and Tim Connelly, and she realized that their story demanded to be told—without the cheap put-downs and hip moralizing that every magazine reporter who went slumming in the porn ghetto had already exhausted. As Fordham professor Walter Kendrick wrote in *The Secret Museum: Pornography in Modern Culture*, "Pornography turns writers and readers alike into amateur psychologists, who never ask what an object is, only what is meant by it. . . . Pornography names an argument, not a thing."

What I remembered, from my conversations with Gillian, was the goal that had started me down this path in the first place: to try to capture the birth and first few decades of the porn film business in all its hilarity and horror, to tell the story of America's obsessive love/hate relationship with sex through the voices of those who embodied it. It was Gillian's inspiration that sent me back to work, and I'm grateful to her for it, as for so much else.

All these many words and hundreds of pages later, I'm certain we've left out as much as we were able to put in. If we haven't managed to include your favorite porn star or stories from the making of your favorite porn film, I'm sorry. I regret that this isn't the history of gay porn: We tried, but in the end discovered that that's another book unto itself. And to all our born-again Christian friends, I'm sorry that we're not judgmental in our narrative—but to our minds porn's been demonized long enough. What we wanted to do, instead, was to let the people involved speak for themselves: the actors and actresses, cops and mobsters, producers and directors, photographers and writers, hustlers and suitcase pimps, and everyone else in between. Whether my cowriters, Jennifer Osborne and Peter Pavia, and I have succeeded is for you to decide.

—Legs McNeil
October 2004

THE OTHER HOLLYWOOD

Prologue:
the
NUDiE -

Left page: *clockwise from left:* Bettie Page, Tempest Storm, Bunny Yeager.

Right page: *clockwise from top left:* Bunny Yeager and Bettie Page with cheetahs; posters for Irving Klaw's *Teaserama*, Doris Wishman's *Diary of a Nudist*, Russ Meyer's *The Immoral Mr. Teas*, Howard W. "Kroger" Babb's *Mom and Dad*; Dave Friedman.

JOHN WATERS (FILMMAKER): There was a theater in Baltimore, where I grew up, called the Rex Theater, that showed all the nudist camp movies—which was what we had before porno.

Since I was twelve years old I'd read *Variety*, which was the only paper that covered the pornography business at the time. *Variety* reviewed every film—and I saw them all. Not just the exploitation movies, but the nudie movies, which had to be the most ludicrously unsexual films ever made, like a girl on a pogo stick or a nude volleyball game. You just saw their backs—asses and tits, but never dicks.

DAVE FRIEDMAN (EXPLOITATION FILM PRODUCER): The exploitation business was an extension of the circus carnival—girlie shows, freak shows, gambling games, rides, ballyhoo, hullabaloo, all done at a local level. But think about this: If you're in the carnival business, you can be in only one place at one time. And if you get rained out, you're dead.

But what if, all of a sudden, you can put this stuff inside? And be in more than one place at one time? That's when these guys started figuring out: "Hey, we'll put this crap on film!"

JOHN WATERS: Kroger Babb was one of the first great exploitation filmmakers. He went around to bingo halls and firehouses with his movie *Mom and Dad* that played for ten years all over the whole world.

Why? Because *Mom and Dad* showed the birth of a baby. It was the only way to show parental nudity at the time. I guess men liked looking at the vaginas, and ignored the baby—which is really scary—birth as an erotic act. And they would have men see it in the day and women see it at night. They also had fake nurses selling sex education literature.

So Kroger Babb is one of my heroes. I mean, I have the poster for *Mom and Dad* in the hallway of my house.

DAVE FRIEDMAN: The exploitation filmmakers quickly realized they could make a picture about any controversial subject—as long as it was done in bad taste.

They had to do only one thing: They had to "square it up," like you do in the carny. The "square-up" is the pitch at the beginning of the picture where they say, "The producers of this picture show you these scenes not in any terrible attempt to exploit this subject, but to make the public aware that these things exist in our beloved land, and that through education it will be brought to the attention of the proper authorities, so that child marriage can be stamped out, so that dope can be stamped out, so that miscegenation can be stamped out, so that juvenile delinquency can be stamped out . . ."

JOHN WATERS: The exploitation film business was an industry based on slowly and sneakily showing what the studios wouldn't show—like the nudist camp movies.

DAVE FRIEDMAN: These movies were about as erotic as walking through the cold storage room of Swift and Company in Chicago. You got these poor, tired old dames with their breasts hanging below their navels, and these old guys walking around . . .

Nudist camps were the salt mines of sex, so to speak.

ROGER EBERT (FILM CRITIC): The nudist camp movies were one of the most pathetic and least significant of the 1950s subgenres, of interest largely because of the actors' difficulties in manipulating bath towels while standing in shrubbery. Their inevitable strong point was a volleyball game made somewhat awkward by the need for the male actors to keep their backs to the camera.

DAVE FRIEDMAN: Nudist camp movies couldn't show "pickles and beaver"— which was the trade term for genitalia.

ANN PERRY (FILMMAKER): If you accidentally got a shot of a man's penis, the cameraman would yell, "PICKLE!" and have to reshoot the scene.

JOHN WATERS: That took a long, long time—to show pubic hair. So you really had to use your imagination—because naked people hidden by pogo sticks are not exactly erotic.

BUNNY YEAGER (MODEL/PHOTOGRAPHER): Doris Wishman made all her movies down here in Miami. I did a lot of her stills. Doris was a pioneer, of sorts, because nudist camp movies were pretty bold for that time, even though she wasn't showing *total* nudity. I think the first one was called *Nude on the Moon.*

DORIS WISHMAN (FILM DIRECTOR): I don't care what people say. I make my films with love and care, and as I always say, "Not Eastman Color, but Wishman Blood."

BUNNY YEAGER: Doris couldn't afford to shoot her films with sound in them, so when somebody's talking, you only see the reaction shots. After filming was finished, she would hire experienced actors and have them dub in the sound in New York.

DORIS WISHMAN: I think Chesty Morgan was from Poland. So I had to dub all of her lines because you couldn't understand what she was saying. And a lot of the people I worked with couldn't speak properly, so I had to go back and dub in their lines, which was more costly—but at least it was professional, and you could understand what they were saying.

DAVE FRIEDMAN: Bunny Yeager was very important in those early days because she had a stable of chicks in Miami that you couldn't believe. You see, Bunny had something going for her as a woman. She would see a beautiful girl walking down the street, and she could walk up to her and ask her to pose.

BUNNY YEAGER: I was always out looking for girls because at that time I had a rivalry going with Russ Meyer. We were both selling pinups to the same magazines. And Russ always had the big-busted girls—bigger than anybody. And I just thought, *"Where does he find them?"*

DAVE FRIEDMAN: Bunny would say, "Excuse me, dear. I'm Bunny Yeager. Have you ever considered modeling?"

The girl would say, "No."

And Bunny would say, "Well, *would* you consider it? Maybe with underwear or maybe . . . uh, *nude?*"

If that would've been me, the girl would've smacked me in the mouth.

BUNNY YEAGER: I was a high fashion model. I posed in furs and dresses and did runway work. And if you did that, you weren't supposed to do bathing-suit modeling, but I liked bathing-suit modeling—so I went out and got my own work.

I was kind of a maverick at the agency; I did what I wanted to do. They didn't like it, so I said, "As long as you get paid your fee—what do you care?"

BILL KELLY (FBI SPECIAL AGENT): I was in love with Bunny. When she was thirty years old, she was the best-looking thing on two legs you ever saw.

CHUCK TRAYNOR (LINDA LOVELACE'S FORMER HUSBAND AND MANAGER): Was Bunny Yeager good-looking? Well, you know, to a sixteen-year-old, anybody with long blond hair and big boobs is good-looking, ha, ha, ha. That was enough for me.

BUNNY YEAGER: I had been called "The World's Prettiest Photographer" on *U.S. Camera* magazine. Here's how it happened: Roy Pinney, who was a New York photographer, came down to Miami every year to shoot stock photos—a woman pushing a grocery cart, a woman holding a baby—and he used me as a model.

After we finished, Roy said, "Let's shoot some cheesecake—you know, in some bathing suits."

So while he was shooting me, he asked, "What are you doing these days? Anything new?"

I said, "Oh, I'm going to photography school."

He said, "That's a good angle. I'd love to do a human interest story on you."

I said, "Well, that's lying because I'm not really a photographer; I'm just taking this course for the fun of it."

DAVE FRIEDMAN: Back then, there were thousands of young girls and guys that lived up north, and come wintertime, they'd do anything in the world to get out of that weather. They'd come down to Miami and become waiters, waitresses, whatever—anything to make enough money to spend the winter in Florida.

BUNNY YEAGER: That's how I met some of the girls, because I'd modeled with them. Most of them were too shy to pose in bikinis, so I was thought of as a little risqué. But that's how I met Maria Stinger; her husband showed me a picture of his wife and asked me to make a bikini for her. He said she was shy, but she looked like a movie star. I said, "Does she do any modeling?"

Eventually she agreed to let me shoot her at her house. But I preferred shooting in natural light, so I asked her, "Would you like to pose with some wild animals?" She said she loved animals, so I said, "Let's go up to 'Africa U.S.A.' in Boca Raton. I'll make you a little leopard bikini, and we'll take some pictures with live cheetahs."

It was actually for a school assignment—we had to shoot something in color, which was new at the time. My instructor said, "These are pretty good. Maybe you should try to sell them to a magazine or something."

I asked, "Are you kidding?"

He said, "No. I'm serious."

So I did, and it sold for a cover right away.

CHUCK TRAYNOR: One of the first jobs I got after I married my first wife was driving a dump truck for the Three Bays Improvement Company, which was digging the Kendall Canal.

And while I was working there, I found out that along the Kendall Canal lived Maria Stinger, one of the early pinup girls. Well, for some reason I thought—like most guys—that if a chick poses for a pinup magazine, she must run around her yard nude, too.

So I used to climb this fucking crane to look over the top of the trees to see into Maria's yard. I did that every chance I got—but I never saw her.

BILL KELLY: Of course Bunny knew I was an FBI agent, but she used to talk to me anyway—halfway. She would never implicate anybody. She was reluctant, and I don't blame her. Bunny wasn't into it very heavy.

But it is true that Bunny Yeager was America's most prominent female nude photographer at that time.

BUNNY YEAGER: The *American Weekly* used my photos in a big spread; then *U.S. Camera* picked it up, and they're the ones that put me on the cover. And that was great because I started getting phone calls from people all over the place, and one of those people was Bettie Page, the famous pinup model.

The first photos I shot with Bettie were taken in my studio. After that we shot at the beach many times—though we did no nudes.

Bettie had a couple of bikinis that she had made—which I found very interesting because I had never met anyone who made bathing suits like I did. I designed the leopard suit she wears in the Africa U.S.A. pictures that are so popular. I wanted to avoid trouble, so I designed two suits—a one-piece and a bikini—and Bettie said, "Here, give me the material. I'll take it home and sew it." That way she didn't have to come in for the fitting.

CHUCK TRAYNOR: Lo and behold, one day I stopped in front of Maria Stinger's house, and there was this woman outside unpacking some stuff, and I said, "I always wanted to meet . . . uh . . . Maria. . . ."

And this lady looks at me and asks, "Why?"

I said, "Well, because . . . I . . . you know, I'm a fan."

She said, "You ever wanna be in a movie with her?"

I said, "Sure."

She said, "Well, my name's Bunny Yeager, and we're gonna be doing a movie here. If you wanna be in it, I sure could use you."

BUNNY YEAGER: Chuck Traynor said that when he was sixteen he knocked on the door? No, I don't think so. Maybe he would've liked it that way. Maybe he called me up and offered his services—I don't remember that. But I do remember Chuck Traynor.

I always liked Chuck. He was always a good old country boy from Homestead, Florida—very likable, very charismatic, very laid-back, easy to get along with, and quick to laugh.

CHUCK TRAYNOR: I was supposed to screw Maria Stinger in the movie, but at that time they only did simulated sex. So I played with her tits—that's when they used those real hard implants in girls' tits, and I wanted to see if they felt like plastic. But they were real.

BUNNY YEAGER: I just think commercially, you know? If I'm going to shoot a girl, all I'm thinking about is, "Can I sell this?"

So I was lucky to run across this new magazine, *Playboy*. I thought, "They run pictures of pretty girls. Maybe they'd like my photography. I think I'll send it to them."

BILL KELLY: Bunny Yeager was a friend of Hugh Hefner's, and supposedly the word "bunny"—the idea for *Playboy* bunnies—was based on her. Now, whether that's fictitious or not, I don't know.

BUNNY YEAGER: I get a call from Hugh Hefner, but I have no idea who Hugh Hefner is because he isn't anybody yet; he was just this kid out of college who'd started this magazine.

Hefner said, "We're looking at these pictures you sent us, and we'd like to use them." So that's how I got my first *Playboy* centerfold: Bettie Page. And Hefner started telling me all his dreams for his magazine, and I liked him. I thought he was very charismatic.

DAVE FRIEDMAN: I first met Bunny Yeager when Herschell Gordon Lewis and I were down in Miami making a nudist camp picture. A friend of mine, Wally, who worked for *Playboy*, gave me Bunny's phone number. So I called her, and she asked, "How'd you get this number?"

I said, "Wally at *Playboy* gave it to me."

And she said, "Oh? Well, I guess you're okay then. See, I get all these creeps that come down here and say they're going to make a nudist camp movie just to meet girls, and I can't stand them!"

CHUCK TRAYNOR: I was sixteen or seventeen years old when I first got in the movies—a nudist camp movie. On my first shoot they wasted a whole roll of film because when I squatted down with my back to the camera, my balls were showing.

DAVE FRIEDMAN: You had to hire some good-looking models to play nudists. We learned that the hard way.

See, one time Herschell and I went to make a movie at Miss Zelda's Nudist Camp. Miss Zelda was like this Creature from the Black Lagoon. She said, "You boys will have to take off your clothes if you want to come in here . . ."

Now neither of us are exhibitionists—but we needed a place to shoot. So Herschell and I stripped down. We go have lunch with all these nudists, and they're eating Franco-American spaghetti—and Miss Zelda's breasts are *in* the spaghetti.

I said, "Herschell, enough of this." That's why we called Bunny Yeager. When we met her, I said, "We need some girls."
She asked, "How many?"

BUNNY YEAGER: I learned how to make movies by watching people like Doris Wishman, who would hire me to take stills on sets. Then Russ Meyer came along with *The Immoral Mr. Teas*. Like I said, Russ and I were always competing with each other. So when Russ branched out into movies, my husband and I thought, "Maybe we could do that, too."

DAVE FRIEDMAN: Russ Meyer and I were both in the signal corps during World War II. I was just an instructor; I never got overseas. But Russ was a real hero—he filmed Patton's march across Europe.

So I didn't meet Russ until after the war, when Pete DeSinzy, his original partner, introduced us. One day I got a letter from Pete that said, "My friend Russ Meyer and I have made a picture, and we'd like you to play it in a couple of your houses."

So I went up to San Francisco. Pete had a little theater down on Church Street and a burlesque house—the El Rey Theater in Oakland. The first thing he and Russ had ever done was a picture with Tempest Storm called *The French Peep Show*.

ROGER EBERT: After the war, Russ Meyer failed, like most service cinematographers, to find a job inside the Hollywood union system. So he moved to San Francisco, shot some industrial films, gained a reputation during the 1950s as a leading pinup photographer, did about a half dozen of *Playboy*'s earlier Playmates and shot an obscure mid-1950s burlesque film, which starred Tempest Storm.

DAVE FRIEDMAN: The Tempest Storm film wasn't a short, it was a feature because you know, with girls like Tempest Storm, they knew how to sell themselves so beautifully.

And some of those burlesque stars weren't the greatest looking women, but they just *exuded* sex, and they knew how to present it. They could get these guys so excited it wasn't even funny. They had more body movements than a Swiss watch.

TEMPEST STORM: See, I met Elvis Presley in Las Vegas in 1956, when I was working the Dunes, and Elvis was the headliner at the Riviera. The first time he played Vegas he was a big flop. Anyway, he came over to the Dunes to see my show, and I just thought he was adorable. Oh, I fell in love with him—are you kidding? So, I picked up a few of Elvis's movements ha, ha, ha. We did talk about dancing and compared notes. He gave me a few pointers, and I gave him some.

Was Elvis a good lover? Yeah! He was the King. Yes. Definitely. No complaints. It was a wonderful night. But the next night, when I went into the show, the big boss said, "Did you have a good time last night?"

I said, "Yes. I went to sleep."

He said, "But did you go alone?"

Here I was, trying to be very discreet—be a lady about the situation—and the whole hotel knew about it.

RUSS MEYER (FILMMAKER): When I first met Tempest Storm I was so in awe of her great big cans that thoughts like performing badly or ejaculating prematurely ran through my mind—all connected to the dick bone. So when I made my move to hump the buxotic after the last show in her Figueroa Street scatter, I felt inadequate, plain and simple. Fuck, what can I say?

DAVE FRIEDMAN: Russ Meyer made the first nudie-cutie in 1959 called *The Immoral Mr. Teas*. It was without a doubt the first nudie-cutie. Absolutely.

ROGER EBERT: *The Immoral Mr. Teas* [was] shot in 1959 at a cost of $24,000 and largely improvised during a four-day shooting schedule. *Teas* was partly bankrolled by a San Francisco burlesque theater owner and was the first authentic American nudie.

The notion of directing the ultimate nude volleyball game did not much appeal to Russ Meyer. He felt that the success of *Playboy* had prepared the American market for an unabashed, high-quality skin flick. The occupation of his lead character and a great many of his interior locations were suggested when his dentist agreed to let his office be used on a weekend.

As Meyer explained, "The chair was well-lighted."

RUSS MEYER: I invent the plots myself—usually while I'm alone in the car. I have a clipboard and a felt-tip pen, and I jot down things that turn me on. I assemble these situations in my mind. I imagine how they develop. Then I bring in a writer to put it into script form. But it's all right here. It's all right here, and it's me.

DAVE FRIEDMAN: I was trying to sell Rose La Rosa—who owned the Esquire Burlesque Theater in Toledo, Ohio—a film Herschell and I had made called *Living Venus*. And while we're negotiating, Rose said, "Hey, can you guys make some little one-reelers—ten-minute things—with pretty girls in maybe their bras and panties . . . or maybe *just* their panties . . . or maybe even without the panties if you just showed their fannies?"

I said, "Yeah, why?"

Rose said, "Well, there's still fifty or sixty burlesque houses in the country, and they'd pay you a hundred dollars for each."

I did the math and asked, "Oh, *really?*"

So as soon as I got back to Chicago, I said, "Herschell, how much would it cost for us to do some of these one-reelers?"

Herschell said, "We can make 'em for about six hundred a piece."

And it was just at that moment that *The Immoral Mr. Teas* opened, and I happened to go see it.

ROGER EBERT: The premise of the movie is simple: Mr. Teas is a harassed city man, cut off from the solace of nature and burdened by the pressures of modern life. He can find no rest, alas, because he has been cursed by a peculiar ability to undress girls mentally. At the most unsettling times—in a soda fountain or dentist's office—women suddenly appear nude.

What's worse, Mr. Teas cannot even control his strange power; it seems to have been invested naturally in him and doesn't require the magic sunglasses or secret elixirs employed in such *Teas* imitations as *Bachelor Tom Peeping.*

DAVE FRIEDMAN: So after I saw *The Immoral Mr. Teas,* I said to Herschell, "Instead of us making five or six of these little one-reelers, let's make five or six one-reelers with some kind of a continuing thread, and we'll put them together and have a feature film when we're done."

And Herschell said, "That's not a bad idea."

BUNNY YEAGER: After *The Immoral Mr. Teas,* my husband and I took every dollar we had—ten thousand dollars—and made a movie.

Room Eleven had only two locations because my husband said that was the only way to make money. Half the movie took place in the lobby and the other half upstairs in room eleven. There was no dirty language, no complete nudity, and only simulated sex scenes.

And of course you can't make a low-budget picture and have stars because stars mean money. I don't know how many couples we had, but the story was about all these different types of people that came to rent room eleven.

DAVE FRIEDMAN: So Herschell and I wrote five or six vignettes—of course, they always had a dirty story to them—and we called this thing *The Adventures of Lucky Pierre.*

We got a nightclub comic named Billy Fallible from the William Morris Agency who played Lucky Pierre. Then we went up to Minneapolis and found a couple of little blond girls and brought 'em back down. The rest of the girls we picked up were strippers from around Chicago.

Anyway, when I sold the picture to Dan Sonny, he said, "The girls in your picture look like the grandmothers of the girls in my picture."

I said, "But Dan, you're out in Hollywood. I mean, they raise 'em out there for these things. But Chicago—it's a different thing."

BUNNY YEAGER: We shot *Room Eleven* in two days. We knew we could pay these "actors" to do something and then they might not show up the second day, and we'd have no movie. But everybody that wants to act in a movie wants to have lines. They want to be seen with their clothes on. They don't mind taking them off, but wow, if they have lines! So we made them do the nude scenes first, and that's why they all showed up the next day—to do their lines.

DAVE FRIEDMAN: I took the finished *Lucky Pierre* back to Rose La Rosa and said, "Rose, now I took your advice, but we made 'em features."

She said, "That's pretty good."

And I said, "I want you to play it, and I want forty percent."

She said, "Are you outta your mind?"

I said, "Rose, I wanna tell you a little secret. There's a new game in town. It's called film. Every week, I'm gonna send you a couple of cans of film. And the only thing you're gonna have to pay on that is the express charge from Chicago. And you can run those two cans of film fifteen times a day, and nobody's gonna argue back with you. Your girls aren't gonna demand more money. You don't have to worry about any stagehands. Those drunken musicians you got down there, you can tell 'em all to get lost."

I could see Rose's eyes lighting up. And I said, "And you won't have any catfights backstage between the girls, and you won't have to put up with them beefing about doing an extra show on Saturday night because this can of film *doesn't talk back*."

She said, "Dave Friedman, we're in business."

So that's basically how I took a lot of burlesque theaters in this country and turned them into adult theaters overnight.

BUNNY YEAGER: *Room Eleven* played mainly at drive-in theaters.

The sex was all simulated. In other words, you could not show a man's penis. And the "actors" usually kept everything covered up by being real close together. So basically they'd just be rolling around on the bed.

Just fun nudity, you know? And, yeah, a lot of kissing.

DAVE FRIEDMAN: Nudie-cuties were very rigid in their construction—you had the boy/girl scene, the girl/girl scene, the orgy scene, and then the kiss-off. They worked just as long as you had those elements in it.

And in the beginning, of course, you didn't dare show pubic hair. An L.A. vice squad cop told me, "If we see pubic hair, then it's porno-graphic—and that gives us an excuse to pick up the print."

It wasn't until probably 1968 that we began to show pubic hair. And the first nudist camp picture to show "pickles and beaver" was *Raw Ones*.

BUNNY YEAGER: As nudity became more acceptable, nobody wanted to buy my beautiful bikini shots anymore. The men's magazines wouldn't buy from me anymore. They said I was old-fashioned. They wanted explicit nudity, and I didn't want to shoot it.

DAVE FRIEDMAN: The heyday of the nudie-cutie was 1967, 1968, 1969, and 1970. Those were the years I was turning out *Brand of Shame, The Head Mistress, Lustful Turk, Trader Horny, Thar She Blows, Starlet,* and *The Erotic Adventures of Zorro*—some of the greatest films of the genre. Classics that still live today, ha, ha, ha.

BUNNY YEAGER: We stopped making our movies because all the distributors were calling and saying, "Make it more sexy!" Pornography was becoming legal.

We liked making our movies—and I didn't see anything wrong with nudity. But I guess there was a certain morality that we didn't want to cross. Pornography is a whole different bag. There's a reason for it, and there's probably a place for it, and I mean, everybody's got a right to do what they want to do. But I had no reason to get into that world. I didn't need it. I didn't want to be making it: in stills or movies.

So I laid down my camera for about ten years, till the time came again when I could sell sexy glamour photos without being crude. By the time the 1980s were over, my work was well-accepted again.

DAVE FRIEDMAN: Even though they killed off burlesque—and killed off girlie shows at carnivals—the nudie-cutie films were the answer to the showman's prayer. Because he no longer had to worry about live talent, which was always a problem.

Now, of course, instead of the voyeurs staring at some tired old burlesque broad up there, live, onstage—they were suddenly looking at gorgeous, young, blond, tan California girls, in all their pristine glory, with their beautiful little breasts, and their pert little nipples, and their dimpled little behinds—in Technicolor—on screens forty feet wide and twenty-five feet high.

Where would *you* go?

Part 1: THE SWORD SWALLOWER

1968–1973

GERARD DAMIANO'S
DEEP THROAT

HOW FAR DOES A GIRL HAVE TO GO
TO UNTANGLE HER TINGLE?

EASTMANCOLOR

Left page: *clockwise from left:* Linda Lovelace, Chuck Traynor, Gerard Damiano, poster for Gerard Damiano's *Deep Throat*, Louis "Butchie" Peraino.

Right page: *clockwise from top left:* Marilyn Chambers, Eric Edwards, Carol Conners, Marc Stevens, Jamie Gillis, Sharon Mitchell, Lenny Camp, promotional photo for Alex de Renzy and M. C. von Hellen's *Sexual Freedom in Denmark* [aka *Pornography in Denmark*], Georgina Spelvin, Harry Reems.

The Turkey Raffle

MIAMI
1968–1969

CHUCK TRAYNOR: I wanted to own a topless bar because I wanted to be around topless girls, and that's a great way to do it.

I was making good money flying—first crop dusting as a pilot for Minute Maid Orange Juice and then for the Ocean Reef Club. But bars were expensive, so I ended up buying an old raunchy beer bar on North Miami Beach, at 123rd Street. I think I paid maybe $2,000 for it. It was a real wreck.

LINDA LOVELACE (PORN STAR): I was getting on the Taconic State Parkway in New York, coming out of second gear—it was raining. And this big Chrysler came over the hill; I could see he was going into a skid and coming across the highway. This all happened in two seconds, and then it was over.

My forehead and face hit the windshield; part of one eye was hanging down, my jaw was broken, and my lower front teeth were sticking through my chin. The steering wheel broke my ribs and lacerated my spleen and liver. This was followed by a leaking of my intestine and peritonitis.

CHUCK TRAYNOR: We painted up the place, put in colored lights, I hired some girls, and called it the Las Vegas Inn. It was a topless beer bar.

But because I was catering mostly to bikers and construction workers, it soon became a *nude* beer bar. I mean, my girls would be totally nude when they weren't supposed to be, but they'd do it with the door locked, and luckily they never did it with any ATF agents in the place.

LINDA LOVELACE: When they released me from the hospital, I went back down to Florida to live with my parents to recuperate, and my mother was really rough on me. "You have to be in by eleven o'clock. Call me, when you get there—so we'll know where you are and who you're with." And if I came in one minute after 11:00 P.M., she would smack me in the face.

I had just turned twenty-two.

CHUCK TRAYNOR: I had a big, two-story house, with three or four girls living with me downstairs, and upstairs was a room we just used for screwing around.

Then a friend of mine, Warren, broke up with his old lady, and said, "Chuck, I need a place to stay for a few days."

I said, "Okay, come stay with me. Stay upstairs."

LINDA LOVELACE: My mother would even look up my date's driver's license to make sure he had no violations or anything. And most of the guys I'd go out with had to borrow their parents' car, and my mother would ask them if they had a bank account and how much they had in their savings. You know, like, *whoa*, too many rules and regulations.

CHUCK TRAYNOR: I don't think Linda was a prostitute before I met her, and she really wasn't one after I met her, either. But she was not an inexperienced little farm girl from northern New York—like she'd have you believe.

When I met her, she was dating another married guy—a biker who used to come in my bar all the time. He kind of told me about her. She was kind of a hot-to-trot, sleep-around kid.

LINDA LOVELACE: My best friend Patsy is actually the one that introduced me to Chuck Traynor. He told her he was looking for bathing suit models or something. Patsy didn't go out with him, but she had danced in his topless bar. That didn't bother her at all. But I never would've done it.

CHUCK TRAYNOR: Patsy brought Linda into the bar one night. She was kind of a cute, skinny-looking chick, but she had this big scar down the front of her body.

Patsy said, "Oh, she's really depressed because she's got this big scar, and nobody wants to go out with her."

Later, I came up with the idea about the necklace to cover the scar. I showed her how to put the beads in front of her and dance topless. Even when the necklace swings or moves, there was still a shadow. So the necklace always drew enough attention away from the scar.

LINDA LOVELACE: When I met Chuck, he had a Jaguar and a bar, and it seemed like he had his life together.

So my mother didn't do that to Chuck—ask all those questions. I think he got off the bank account rap by telling her he had his own bar. Plus he had an XKE Jaguar. My mother was impressed with that.

CHUCK TRAYNOR: I told Patsy, "Hey, I got a roommate, Warren, and you know, the four of us can go someplace."

It was basically a double date. Warren had one of them fancy-ass Mustang Mach IIs. So Linda started dating Warren and moved into my house with him.

LINDA LOVELACE: Chuck said I could stay at his house, so I wouldn't have my mother constantly telling me what time to be home and stuff like that. I viewed it as a good opportunity for me in a lot of ways.

CHUCK TRAYNOR: One time I was gonna go upstairs and take a shower, and I said, "Hey, Warren, ya wanna take a shower with Linda and me?"

He said, "Yeah." So the three of us took a shower.

You know, Linda was no virgin.

LINDA LOVELACE: Chuck did have lots of money all the time, and he'd take me to dinner. We'd drive around during the day and stop at some shop, and he'd buy me a shirt or something or a piece of custom jewelry. Some hippie kinda thing. But I think his car impressed me more than anything.

CHUCK TRAYNOR: Even though Warren went back to his wife, Linda kept staying at my house, and I was having sex with the three or four other girls living with me. We had a giant double waterbed, and Linda just sort of became one of the girls on the giant waterbed. It was totally open. I mean, the girls ran around the house nude most of the time, probably because they ran around the club nude most of the time.

LINDA LOVELACE: When I was younger, my father and I were really buddies. We were very close, even though I had a half-sister. Then we moved to Florida when I was sixteen, and my mother started to go through this change of life, and she got really strange.

She accused my father and me of having an affair because he wanted to buy me a sports car to go to college with. He was just proud of me; he was just excited he could do something for me. And my mother made all these weird accusations and gradually my father's and my relationship sort of dwindled into nothing.

LENNY CAMP (PHOTOGRAPHER/CONVICTED CHILD PORNOGRAPHER): Linda followed Chuck around like a puppy dog. She had read, "The way to make your lover fall in love with you is to write your name on his shoes, on the toilet, on the milk bottles . . ."

Linda would write, "Linda and Chuck, Chuck and Linda, Linda and Chuck," on all kinds of paper, and leave them all over the house. Pinned up to the wall, taped to the refrigerator . . .

LINDA LOVELACE: Chuck wasn't ugly, so I started dating him. At first he was like a gentleman—a real human being, you know? He would open the car door for me and light my cigarettes.

CHUCK TRAYNOR: Linda was never a steady girlfriend or anything when we lived at the house. I was going out with a doctor's daughter, named Ginger, that was about fifteen or sixteen years old. It was funny, her father hated me because I was in my mid-to-late twenties—and here I was with his "virgin" daughter.

LENNY CAMP: Chuck was a funny guy. These girls did fall in love with him, you know? Like the first girl that he had was eighteen years old, but she was madly in love with him. She was at his beck and call. She would do anything for him. *Anything.*

LINDA LOVELACE: There were a lot of strange things going on at the bar. When we walked in to close out the register—the girls would usually call Chuck to tell him not to come yet. But this one night some of the girls were topless when we got there, and some of them were naked. Let's just say strange perversions were going on.

Chuck said, "I should have called first to make sure things were okay. These girls are getting out of hand! I'm going to have to put a stop to this!"

CHUCK TRAYNOR: We'd do a turkey raffle, but it really wasn't a turkey we were rafflin'. On Friday evening, everybody came in, paid a buck, got a ticket, and drew a number out of a hat. Then we had a drawing, and if you won a number from one through seven—that stood for each one of the seven girls—then you got the girl you drew.

You got her for whatever you wanted her for. I was selling five or six hundred dollars' worth of tickets a week. But if we didn't know you, if we thought you were a cop, then you got the turkey.

You could always tell who the cops were, and we'd bring 'em this old dried-ass-up turkey out of the refrigerator.

And he'd go, "What's this?"

I'd say, "It's the turkey you just won."

He'd say, "Well, I thought . . ."

I'd say, "You thought *what*? What'd you *think*?"

We got away with that for a long, long time. But the cops were always after my ass.

LINDA LOVELACE: The girls were turning tricks there; they were having orgies there after-hours. I was so naive about that kind of stuff, I really was. When Chuck said, "Well, that one's a hooker, and that one's a junkie, and that one's a prostitute . . ."

CHUCK TRAYNOR: Linda didn't like that too much.

LINDA LOVELACE: Chuck told me, "I had this old business where I used to get people together, and you know, they'd spend some time together." Eventually I realized he was talking about prostitution.

BILL KELLY: Chuck Traynor was a nickel-and-dime guy as far as I was concerned. He wasn't big-league or anything. So I don't think I ever did a real extensive investigation on him. I considered Chuck Traynor a pimp. What else would you call him? Miss Linda Lovelace's agent?

CHUCK TRAYNOR: Linda didn't have any problems with anything back then. She now says that orgies and things that went on were actually set up hooker deals, and that she hated that, and I'd beat her up if she didn't do it, but that was bullshit.

I mean, everybody would just get stoned and party, you know?

If You Can Make It There, You Can Make It Anywhere

NEW YORK CITY
1969–1970

HARRY REEMS (PORN STAR): In 1969, everybody in the East Village was going to make it as an actor. Whether you went to an anti–Vietnam War rally or a macrobiotic restaurant, all the talk was about auditions.

MARILYN CHAMBERS (PORN STAR): I grew up in Westport, Connecticut, about fifty miles west of New York City. When I was about sixteen, I learned how to write my mother's name on notes to get out of school— and then I'd take the train into the city to go to auditions.

My whole growing up consisted of me in front of a mirror playing records like *West Side Story* and *Bye Bye Birdie*. I really wanted to be Ann-Margret, to tell you the truth.

ERIC EDWARDS (PORN STAR): While I was in college in Waco, Texas, I got a scholarship from ABC Television to go to New York to study at the American Academy of Dramatic Arts. They auditioned twenty thousand people from all over the country, and I think they picked sixteen people. I mean, this was the big point in my career, it was like a stepping stone—I was getting letters from Lillian Gish, from the president of ABC, from all these top executives saying, "You have received a scholarship to come to New York."

In fact, Lillian Gish handed me my diploma. Henry Fonda was there backstage; I spoke to him in awe. I was, like, melting.

GEORGINA SPELVIN (PORN STAR): One of my first experiences in New York was when the state employment office sent me to see about a modeling job. It was a big, high-class studio, and I had to see someone with one of those hairdresser names: "Mr. Charles" or "Mr. Gary."

After everyone else had left, he brought me into the studio and—through the course of taking many pictures—he eventually got me very drunk and nude and then he balled me. I don't even remember how I got home; I passed out midway through the thing. But I never got the chance to tell him I had the clap, and I wondered how long it took him to find out and connect it to me.

MARILYN CHAMBERS: My dad was in the advertising business, and he really tried to discourage me from modeling. One of his big accounts was Avon—"DING DONG! AVON CALLING!"—so he knew about models. He told me, "It's a cutthroat business. It really stinks. And I don't want you to be involved."

ERIC EDWARDS: When I got to New York I was signed with the William Morris Agency. I had a three-year contract. I was sent out to different auditions and movie companies, and I was getting work—I had Close-Up toothpaste and Gillette TracII commercials running on television.

HARRY REEMS: I enrolled in a no-fee neighborhood acting class. Presto! I was doing *Coriolanus* in some marginal coffeehouse where they passed the hat around at the end of the performance. I hammed it up to high heaven. I was lousy. But those scrapings out of the hat somehow kept me alive until my roommate split for greener pastures. In no time, I went from burgers and beans to eviction notices and welfare.

MARILYN CHAMBERS: I figured the best way to get involved in being an actress was to be a model. So I went to the Eileen Ford Modeling Agency first—and Eileen Ford told me I was too fat. And my face wasn't angular enough. And it was too flat. I was so humiliated.

Then my dad started telling me, "Well, you're too fat." But I wasn't fat. I was *never* fat.

GEORGINA SPELVIN: I wanted to be a dancer. My first love has always been ballet; I still think it is the high church of dance. I still practice the principles on a daily basis. But I had neither the training nor the body to make it as a dancer.

But I was fortunate enough to get a job as a replacement dancer in *The Pajama Game* on Broadway. Then I got into the chorus; then I got the understudy to the lead role. When the lady playing it, who was a gal named Neile Adams, decided she would rather run off and marry Steve McQueen, I got to play the lead role for the last year that the show ran in New York. Then I was invited to recreate the choreography and the role for a touring company that went to South Africa.

SHARON MITCHELL (PORN STAR): My dad was a cop. A drunk, dysfunctional cop. You know, a womanizing kind of guy. My kind of guy, ha, ha, ha! A guy that I've been role modeling after—and looking for others just like that—all my life. I learned a lot of interesting examples from him. You know: lying, cheating, and associating with mobsters. I always had an Uncle Don this, an Uncle Vito that.

Now that I look back on it, I had every toy in the world. And we had dryers and washers and everything. I mean, cops don't make that much money, and we had this huge house.

Then my mom hit him on the head with a frying pan—because he was out fucking someone else—and the marriage was over shortly thereafter.

MARILYN CHAMBERS: So after that I went to the Wilhelmina Modeling Agency—and, God, Wilhelmina was just so nice to me. She accepted me, and she signed me. I was totally thrilled.

Needless to say, though, I didn't get that many modeling jobs. It was tough because at that time Twiggy was in—flat and skinny. Even though I didn't have big boobs or anything, I was very athletic.

I did do a Clairol commercial, and they ruined my hair. It was falling out in the sink. It was horrible.

GEORGINA SPELVIN: When I came back from South Africa, I couldn't get another Broadway show, try as I might. I did shows and stock and touring companies and what have you, but my next appearance on Broadway wasn't until *Cabaret*. And again, I went in as a replacement and did the show for about the last year and a half of its run. By that point, I was getting pretty long in the tooth to be a dancer. And I got tired of not having any money.

ERIC EDWARDS: I had major commercials running on television and had some good residuals coming in. Still, there were times I needed to pay the rent.

But it wasn't just the rent. I was going through a divorce—and I thought the porn business would help me to prove I was a sexual person. My wife wasn't all that interested in sex. She blamed me for all of our problems. And I believed her. I thought I was a lousy fuck.

So when I saw an ad in *Screw* magazine that was looking for actors and actresses who were willing to, you know, take off their clothes and "do it," I submitted my photo.

GEORGINA SPELVIN: I started working for the JCPenney Company in the audiovisual department, creating slide shows, creating soundtracks, doing a lot of tech stuff. And in the course of that, we made a series of short films—what they called point-of-sale (P.O.S.) presentations—around department stores.

I became absolutely entranced with film and film editing. I thought, "This is what I want to do when I grow up! Thank you!"

HARRY REEMS: One day two old veterans of burlesque came to the drama workshop looking for a "third banana," a young guy who would help them through all the wheezes that have been used on the circuit since the beginning of time—the nuthouse bit, the golf bit, the crazy doctor bit.

The old duffers offered me a hundred and seventy-five clams, and I was on my way. First stop: Staten Island. The next stop was Atlantic City. There we got third billing behind the headliner, Damita Jo, and "The Astonishing Assie: Interpreter of Exotica," which translated to "stripper."

SHARON MITCHELL: Where I grew up in Jersey, I was a hick, and I was adopted. My family were farmers. New Jersey was the Garden State—all dairies and farms and woods and lots of snow and animals.

My mom was having trouble getting child support from my dad. So it was me and mom and my grandmother. I was down on a dirt road, you know? The house looked like *Tobacco Road*. I was really embarrassed to walk into my own house. When the school bus would drop me off, I would walk to the neighbors' house.

HARRY REEMS: Assie really lived up to her stage name. She was a beautiful Puerto Rican; woman—and she'd come out onstage and say, "El-lo, my name is Assie; would you like to see my pussy?"

Assie would lift her skirt and underneath she was wearing a G-string with a pussycat appliquéd on. For me, it was love at first sight.

TEMPEST STORM: They called it flashing. They'd flip the G-string up real fast. Right in your face.

Most of the girls were willing to do whatever it took. There was no more art to it anymore; it became just a way for the girls to make fast money, which I don't put down. To each his own.

SHARON MITCHELL: When you're adopted through the Catholic Church, you have to attend parochial school. It's a lease that comes on the child that can't be broken. And the nuns come every month to check up on you. I think if that lease is broken, they take you and resell you to someone else—probably a zoo or a circus, you know?

I had a uniform, but I think I destroyed it because I was dying to get out of Catholic school. I think I got out sometime after grade school—after confirmation. You have to go through so many sacraments, and then you're allowed out. But there was a condition—I had to go to catechism, which was fine.

It was the sixties, and my mom went out and bought me my first colorful outfit to wear to school. It was a little pink and purple flowered miniskirt. I had purple fishnets with a little garter belt thing.

And I had hot pants.

HARRY REEMS: I couldn't take my eyes off Assie those first few nights. About the fourth or fifth night she asked me if I'd like to go out with her after the last show. A friend of hers was a cocktail waitress in a club up the street. The waitress friend loaded us with drinks that really got us bombed.

We left the club at dawn. Assie agreed to have a nightcap—just one—in my fleabag room. Drunk as I was, I was still nervous as hell.

MARILYN CHAMBERS: Fortunately, the Cybill Shepherd look came in—so it was a lot easier for me to start getting some work. They'd call me in once or twice a week.

Then I got a call from Procter & Gamble to audition for the new Ivory Snow box. I was chosen as a finalist. And then I had to go before the clients, and they took me out to lunch—all these men in their three-piece suits. They were very nice. But little did naive Marilyn know that everyone's always trying to get into my pants. I'm thinking like, "Oh, gee, they really like me!"

HARRY REEMS: Assie gave phenomenal head but only up to a point. Then we were into a balling scene. I went into my standard missionary position.

"Harry," said Assie, "I like you. You are a nice boy. But you have much to learn about how to make a woman happy."

SHARON MITCHELL: I had a lot of drunken sex, mostly with much older people in Camaros. I never hung out with my peer group. I just used to go to bars and fuck factory workers. I don't know why. I think they were just there, and I could drink with them.

And then I had sex with my girlfriends.

The first one was about sixth grade. I seduced one of my girlfriends, under some guise of comparing pussies or something. She was definitely down for it.

Then I fucked all her brothers. She had a few brothers, so I had sex with the whole family. It was kind of neat. The whole family was nice.

My favorite wasn't the older brother, the one that deflowered me, although he was very nice. It was the younger brother, who was more tender; he used to hold me afterward. I thought that was really nice. Then there was once when all three of us had sex together—my girlfriend, her brother, and me.

HARRY REEMS: It seemed like we fucked around the clock. Not to mention all around the house. It was idyllic. Assie was thirty-one, and I was twenty-one. I was having sex until it was coming out of my ears.

MARILYN CHAMBERS: I got the job, and I was just ecstatic. I thought, "Wow, this is cool. Here was this box that was totally antiquated, like from the fifties—and they're updating the box cover photo with me!"

HARRY REEMS: When we got back to New York from Atlantic City, it was not the same between Assie and me.

She was doing a two-week gig at a burlesque theater on West Forty-seventh Street and the crime and grime of New York had gotten to her. She wanted to go back to Puerto Rico, to her family, and maybe open a beauty parlor there.

So Assie went back to Puerto Rico, while I poured over the casting notices in *Backstage* and *Show Business*. I landed a twenty-five-dollar-a-week job and an Equity contract playing in a weird thing called *Spirit Orgasmics* at Cafe La Mama in the East Village. It was a bomb.

"Fuck it," I told my roommate. "I'm going to Puerto Rico."

MARILYN CHAMBERS: When I went to shoot the picture for Ivory Snow, one of the photographers was this really old, old ancient man. And they had the baby for me to hold, and when you shoot children, they can only work for a certain amount of time. Then they have to sleep. So when the baby's down sleeping, this old guy was chasing me around the dressing room, trying to get into my pants.

SHARON MITCHELL: I got married at seventeen. Larry Kipp. I met him, and he was a crazy guy. My family threw me an incredible wedding, and I thought, "Well, this really sucks!"

I went to my wedding only because I felt bad about my family spending all this money.

But they said, "Fuck it. If you're not happy, we'll kill him." My dad had done something to a boyfriend who'd hit me once—he threw him in jail forever.

I said, "No, Daddy, don't kill Larry."

HARRY REEMS: When I got to Puerto Rico, Assie said, "Go back home. It won't work. I'm ten years older. We come from two different worlds."

Then we fucked.

Then she said, "Stay."

So I faked my way into a job teaching scuba diving at La Concha Hotel, though I had never scuba dived in my life. I went to the library and read up on it the weekend before I started work. During the first two or three months I taught some two hundred people how to scuba dive, without once putting the tanks on my back.

MARILYN CHAMBERS: That old Ivory Snow photographer was disgusting. It was gross—this seventy-year-old guy right on me!

I mean, I was running around, going, "What are you doing?! Get out of here!"

After we shot the box, they told me it was going to take about two years to get my picture on the new one.

I said, "Whatever."

HARRY REEMS: It was high season in Puerto Rico—and open season. Suddenly a whole Disneyland of vacationing goodies materialized: Hank Aaron; and Mike Seiderhaud, the champion water-skier; and Tom Weiskoff, the winner of the Golf Open came down to shoot some Wheaties commercials.

And one of the local talent agents got me into the act. In the water-skiing commercial, Mike Seiderhaud was supposed to fall. I was the one who stood in for him and took the fall.

But I had a double role in that commercial. After that spill, I could be seen close-up in the stands, yelling, "HEY, SEIDERHAUD, YOU DIDN'T EAT YOUR WHEATIES!"

I made it into the Hank Aaron commercial, too. When Aaron slices the air, I was in the stands booing and yelling, "HEY, AARON, YOU DIDN'T EAT YOUR WHEATIES!"

FRED LINCOLN (PORN STAR/PORN DIRECTOR AND PRODUCER): That's how I got into porn—doing television commercials. See, me and this guy Paul Matthews were doing a Benson & Hedges commercial together. It was the one where I'm sitting on a float in the pool, smoking a Benson & Hedges, and I turn around and look at a girl in a bikini and the cigarette blows up the float, and I fall in the water. It was about, you know, what lengths people went to for these extra long cigarettes.

On the set, Paul and me were talking about girls and stuff—and he asked me if I wanted to do a fuck film.

To be honest with you, for years I used to dream of some guy coming up to me and saying, "Hey kid, you wanna make a fuck film?"

SHARON MITCHELL: Larry hit me—and I remembered, you know, about my mom and dad. My dad hit my mom once, and that's all it took. My mom said, "That's it." Because once that happens—it never fucking gets better. I mean, guaranteed that it never gets better. You've just got to move on with your life—because all of that heal-change crap will never work.

Larry was fucking crazy. I saw him put his head through a plate glass window. He'd terrorize me, like step on the gas when I was in the car, and say, "So, you want me to do this?!!" Sheer abuse and terror.

Eventually, Larry killed himself. Maybe eight years after we got divorced. I take no responsibility for it.

MARILYN CHAMBERS: After I graduated from high school, I was going out with this guy, Patrick, who was an actor and a model. In those days they weren't all gay, ha, ha, ha.

He asked, "Do you want to go to see a real movie being made?"

I said, "Yeah! I'd love to."

Patrick was playing either Robert Klein or George Segal's stand-in for the movie *The Owl and the Pussycat.*

So I get to the set. I've got my little portfolio with me. I'm nervous. I'm standing around watching, totally intrigued, like, "Wow! This is what I want to do!"

HARRY REEMS: Enough money from the Wheaties commercial trickled down to Puerto Rico for me to live it up. I wined and dined Assie and took her to casinos. Then I deserted her for a week and blew a lot of money. And a lot of girls. Assie blew up like a cyclone when I crept back.

Out came the Latin jealousy and the temper tantrums.

"I cook dinner. You be here on time. Do those whores you go with cook dinner for you?"

I was deeply fond of her. And I loved all the creature comforts of home, of being looked after. But finally I had to admit that she was right. We came from different worlds.

MARILYN CHAMBERS: While I was on the set, Barbra Streisand started pulling some shit. She was really childish. Yeah, I really don't want to say that, but I mean she was just horrible! Just a real witch, you know? To *everybody.*

Ray Stark was the producer, and Herbert Ross was directing. So Ray Stark was walking around the set, and he came up to me and asked, "Are you an actress?"

I said, "Oh, yes! Of course."

He said, "Well, you know, we just happen to be casting for the part of Robert Klein's girlfriend. Would you be interested in trying out?"

I said, "I'd love to!"

HARRY REEMS: Back in New York, I floundered. There were a few more commercials—Ballantine Ale, JCPenney, Dickies work clothes, a toilet tissue. . . .

But these were test commercials, and somehow I managed to spend the bread faster than it was coming in.

GEORGINA SPELVIN: I opened my own editing facility down in the West Village. It was called The Pickle Factory, and we were doing a lot of underground films at that point. I was very much into the peace movement. By the end of the sixties, beginning of the seventies, I was interested in making revolutionary films and ending world hunger.

We were scrambling to make the monthly rent on the place to begin with, so I said, "Okay, it's near the first of the month again, and we don't have any money! Somebody's got to make some money!"

So I bought all of the local trade papers—*Showbiz* and *Casting Call*—and I just called everybody who was casting films. At that time, there was a lot of tits and ass films going on. Nudie-cuties.

I'd say, "I know I'm not what you're looking for in the way of casting; but, I can coil cable and make coffee. I'm looking for any kind of a job. Do you need anyone?"

And, indeed I got someone who said, "Well, we need someone to scout some locations for us."

I said, "You got it! What do you need?"

So I began to get a reputation as someone who could get things done. And the next thing I knew, I was getting calls to do casting.

MARILYN CHAMBERS: Ray Stark takes me by the hand; he's about seventy-something—all the old guys like me, ha, ha, ha—and he takes me upstairs to a room, and there's a whole bunch of women in there auditioning.

I'm sitting there thinking, "Yeah, right, there's no way I'm going to get this."

They call me in, there's a whole bunch of people sitting around a table, they asked me some questions, I go back out, and they come out and say, "You got the part."

I went, "What?! You're kidding?!" It was like being discovered in Schwab's Drugstore.

HARRY REEMS: I was broke. I was taking out small loans to pay the rent and telephone bill. So I put the question to a buddy in the National Shakespeare Company. "Do you know how I could get some fast bread?"

He said, "Yeah, I do, if you consider $75 'bread.'"

I said, "I consider $75 'bread.'"

He said, "You can pick up $75 a day doing stag films."

Stag films! Was he kidding? What would that do to my burgeoning career as an actor on the legitimate stage?

So I said, "Thanks, but no thanks."

JAMIE GILLIS (PORN STAR): I was driving a cab a few days a week and doing Shakespeare at the Classic Stage Company in Manhattan at night. Driving a cab part-time is pretty brutal. You know, I'd wake up at dawn, drive a cab twelve hours a day, and then I'm doing Shakespeare all night, you know? Pretty heavy.

MARILYN CHAMBERS: So they take me down to the set of *The Owl and the Pussycat.* They get me undressed and throw me in bed with Robert Klein. And I was supposed to be topless, but Barbra Streisand said, "Absolutely not."

Then we did a thing where I'm walking to the door with him when we're leaving. It took me about two or three days to shoot it; I was so nervous. But that's how I got my Screen Actors Guild card. And that's how I moved into the city, got my first apartment on Thirty-third and Third—and started going to acting classes.

ERIC EDWARDS: About six months after I submitted my photo to the ad in *Screw,* I got a call. A guy said, "Can you do it? Because we're having problems with the guy who's supposed to do it right now."

I said, "Sure, man. I'm a swinger, you know, my wife and I are cool. No problem."

I hung up the phone and the shakes started to settle in. I was thinking, "Oh my God—I'm gonna go over there! Can I really perform?"

JAMIE GILLIS: I was looking at the ads in the *Village Voice* for jobs, you know, to see if there was something else I could do besides drive a cab. I would never have looked for it, but under a part-time job listing I saw something like "modeling" or "nude modeling"—something that sounded easy enough.

So I call up the guy and then went over to this dirty basement on Fourteenth Street, next to a funeral parlor. There was a mattress on the floor and this guy in overalls, with long hair, who looked sort of like a hippie, says, "I'll take your picture."

HARRY REEMS: Then a letter arrived from the bank threatening to put out a warrant for me if I didn't start showing good faith, so I asked my friend if the stag film offer was still open.

JAMIE GILLIS: So the guy shoots a black-and-white Polaroid of me—and sure enough, he calls me to come in and do a loop. And that's how I started working for Bob Wolfe.

FRED LINCOLN: I was still doing legitimate commercials and stage work, but when Paul Matthews asked me to do that first fuck film, I said, "Well, who am I gonna be working with? What's the girl look like?"

I figured it was some beast they were gonna get me.

He said, "Oh, I'm meetin' her tonight. We're gonna have a coupla drinks; come along if you wanna meet her. Her name is Utta. She's from Germany."

I go meet her—and my God, she was beautiful. Aww, she was gorgeous; blond hair, German, big tits. I said, "Holy shit. How much you gonna pay me to do this?"

He said, "A hundred bucks."

I thought, "I'm the luckiest guy in the world!"

Vickie Killed the Nudie-Cuties

MIAMI
1970–1971

BUNNY YEAGER: If Chuck Traynor called me and said, "I have a pretty girl for you to shoot," I knew she would be pretty. But then he brings over this girl, Linda Boreman—and the trouble with Linda was that she was flat chested. Not that there's anything wrong with small bosoms, but what I'm thinking is, "I can't sell her."

Another thing: I didn't want to bring this up, but Linda had a scar all the way down the middle of her chest. But I shot her anyway, more as a favor to Chuck.

CHUCK TRAYNOR: I'd made a big mistake with the Las Vegas Inn because in Florida, if you owned a bar, you had to have a P.I.C. card, which stands for "Person in Charge." And the person with the P.I.C. card—could be one of the girls or a manager—had to be there all the time.

Well, the ATF came in once, and nobody had a card. So they closed me up.

LINDA LOVELACE: At that point, Chuck wanted me to go out in the streets and pick up girls to get them to work for his prostitution business. And I was not very good at that at all. I thought, unconsciously, "Well, he's finally going to get rid of me."

He told me that I was a failure at what I was doing, but he didn't get rid of me. Chuck decided that moviemaking was his next step.

BUNNY YEAGER: It was while we were doing our second film, *Sextet,* when Chuck called and asked, "Can't you use Linda in the film?"

I said, "Well, we've got everybody that we need, but I guess we could throw her in as an extra . . ."

So you have to look fast to catch her. She's just sitting on some guy's lap on a couch during a party scene. And I only used her because of Chuck.

CHUCK TRAYNOR: Linda just hung in and hung in after the ATF closed the Las Vegas Inn, so I said, "You know, we should make porno movies or something."

I had an old Bolex Double-A film camera that shot sixteen-millimeter film. You shot one side, then turned it over, and shot the other side. Then the lab cut it in half, and you had two eight-millimeter films.

LENNY CAMP: One time me and Sam Menning, a guy from New York, were making a nudie-cutie film in some condo in North Miami Beach. It was strictly simulated sex, soft-core, because it was 1971, and nobody was doing hard-core then, except for loops.

We had this biker from Homestead, Florida, doing the film with his girlfriend, some girl named Vickie. Since it was soft-core, the guys weren't allowed to get erections when we were shooting. But while we were taking a break, her boyfriend got an erection, and Vickie says, "Watch this."

She started at the top and went right down to the bottom. And that was the first time I'd ever seen deep throat.

And I was like, "Oh my God; I can't believe this!"

VULTURE (SOUTH FLORIDA MOTORCYCLE GANG MEMBER): Almost all of us bikers were all hanging out with strippers because we were partying all night, getting high all night, and sleeping all day, you know? So the best kind of girlfriend to have, for us, anyway, was a stripper because then she'd be off working, making the money, while we was out whoring around!

Plus, you could throw her on the back of your bike, and if you wanted to go to Atlanta, or New Orleans, or whatever, there was always some strip clubs she could work at. So you could stay on the road as long as you wanted and not have to worry about the money situation.

LENNY CAMP: Vickie was so amazing that Sam Menning made a phone call to some money guy who told him to film her doing it. But Vickie's biker boyfriend didn't want her to do it, so Vickie slipped me her phone number before they left. About an hour later I called the number and I said, "Get on a bus, and come over." You know, I didn't even tell her to take a cab.

So Vickie came over, and she stayed at my house. And she tells me, if she didn't do deep throat, she couldn't be a biker mama in this motorcycle gang in Homestead.

VULTURE: Everything was free love. We weren't passing around our old ladies, but we had plenty of chicks that hung around the club that would fuck whoever wanted to fuck them. You know, if ten guys wanted to fuck 'em in a night, that was fine. They had no problems with it. And chicks with chicks. It didn't matter. I mean, sex was just no big deal.

LENNY CAMP: So the motorcycle gang from Homestead are really the people who invented deep throat, but Vickie is the one who disseminated it.

Yeah, of course she showed me how she did it. I had her staying at my place—are you kidding? Who the hell wouldn't? And it was unbelievable. Just *unbelievable!*

BILL KELLY: I spent half my career on Lenny Camp. I got him in the penitentiary so many times, I lost track. Lenny Camp was the Pied Piper of photographic pornography in South Florida. His real name was Leonard Joseph Campagno—Scumbag-Number-One-of-All-Time.

LENNY CAMP: Vickie ends up staying at my place, and Sam Menning is giving her work doing bondage movies, so she could make some money.

So one night there's a knock at the door, and there's Chuck Traynor and Linda Boreman. So we got to talking, and we went up to my spare bedroom, and Linda and Vickie started making it with each other.

Oh, no, it wasn't at Chuck's prompting. Shit no, he was in the corner reading *Playboy*. Linda just did whatever she wanted. She and Vickie were doing this on their own—and both of them swore they had never done anything with a girl before.

So I told Chuck, "Vickie does this thing—what she calls deep throat. She goes with these bikers in Homestead, and you have to be a deep-throat girl to hang out with these guys."

But Chuck was always very blasé. He was like, "So what? What does that mean?"

CHUCK TRAYNOR: I learned the deep throat technique in Japan when I was over there in the Marines. A buddy of mine and I lived with two hookers who could do deep throat—as well as a lot of other tricks.

One had the ability to expand her ass big enough to put a fist in, and she could do the same thing with her cunt—expand it and tighten it back up to be able to hold your finger. But the deep throat technique, like anything else, can be learned in a couple of days.

LENNY CAMP: Ninety percent of what Chuck says is just total bullshit. The night I told him about Vickie and deep throat, Chuck just stayed in the corner while the girls were teaching each other how to use the double-ended dildo on the bed.

Vickie didn't perform deep throat on Chuck that night. No, Chuck was very, very, very shy as far as having sex in front of people—although he liked watching other people have sex.

LINDA LOVELACE: I think Chuck fucked me once a month or every six weeks—and when we had sex, it was bad. At first, I thought there was something wrong with me. I guess a woman always figures it's her fault at first.

I was so dumb.

LENNY CAMP: Chuck had nothing to do with the girls. He was trying to be like Hugh Hefner. Oh, he would have loved to have been Hefner. He thought he *was* Hefner. But Chuck was a superpimp, that's all he was. He put the talk on everybody. I mean, as far as he was concerned, it was whatever the girls could make, and whatever he could get away with. That's all he wanted.

CHUCK TRAYNOR: I'm shooting porno movies of Linda and other girls, and then Linda moved in to a houseboat with me and some other girl, and that's when Linda became my old lady.

Did I fall in love with her? Love? I think I probably loved her, somewhat. . . . I mean, it probably wasn't like the way John Derek loved Bo Derek. Because, you know, they called me the John Derek of the porno business.

LINDA LOVELACE: My closest companion when I was with Chuck was my vibrator.

LENNY CAMP: In the meantime, behind my back, Chuck gave Vickie his number. Within a matter of a week or so, Chuck, Linda, and Vickie were traveling to Coconut Grove and South Miami, putting on shows for people.

I didn't even know. A guy that worked in a bank down in Miami told me about it. He said, "Remember that guy, Chuck Traynor? He got two girls, and they put on an act. And they don't get that much money, either."

I said, "Yeah, that sounds like them."

CHUCK TRAYNOR: See, in Miami, a $100 trick isn't that easy. Unless you're tied to a hotel or something, you had $20 tricks, maybe, or $25 tricks, but Linda was limited because she wasn't really glamorous. She didn't have any clothes. She couldn't go to the beach and talk with anybody because, you know, she is not really a talker.

In Miami, if a guy's going to pay $100 or $150, he wants a chick he can take out to a club and carry on a conversation with. So we decided to go to Aspen, Colorado, because a friend of mine was opening a club out there, and he really liked the way our bar had been clearing $2,000 a week.

LINDA LOVELACE: I had learned not to press Chuck for details, but this time he volunteered a little information. A friend of his had just started a bar in Aspen, and he needed a go-go dancer and an after-hours hooker.

CHUCK TRAYNOR: We got as far as Biscoe, Arkansas. We were in a Volkswagen, and a drunk rolled into us and totaled the car.

LINDA LOVELACE: All of a sudden, Chuck's little Volkswagen just took off. It had been hit from behind by a station wagon driven by a drunk. We swerved to the right, then to the left, then off into a ditch, and over onto one side. The next thing I knew, truck drivers were crawling all over the car, looking for a way to lift us out.

I heard one of them say, "That little car has had it."

CHUCK TRAYNOR: The accident put Linda back in the hospital, and it put me in the hospital for a couple of days—screwed my teeth up here in front. The ski season was starting in Colorado, and by the time Linda got out of the hospital it was too late to go there. The guy hired another manager, and we were stuck in Little Rock.

LINDA LOVELACE: Little Rock was definitely not Chuck's sort of town. So we got a ride to New York—and that was definitely Chuck's kind of town.

CHUCK TRAYNOR: I didn't know anybody in New York, but I'm a pretty fair cameraman, and I had done loops in the past. So we came here to the cold and rented an apartment in New Jersey.

LINDA LOVELACE: After putting up a month's security and month's rent, Chuck had less than $50 left. He invested it in purchasing every sex tabloid in New York City.

There were hundreds of people who made their livings peddling sex in New York. What's amazing to me was how quickly one got to know them all. They were all links on the same chain; you met one person, and he passed you along to the others. The still photographers knew the club owners who knew the madams who knew the eight-millimeter directors who knew the peep show kingpins who knew the adult bookstore owners and on and on. I swear, before the week was out, Chuck Traynor managed to meet every prominent pervert in New York.

CHUCK TRAYNOR: When we got to New Jersey, Linda went up to see her sister in upstate New York. I stayed in the city and said, "I'm gonna go find something to do."

So I went down to Forty-second Street and met a black guy who wanted to shoot crotch shots of chicks. I said, "I got a chick for ya."

I went back, got Linda, she posed for him, and then I asked, "What's there to do here in New York? A country boy like me? A good honest John . . ."

Rent

NEW YORK CITY
1970–1971

FRED LINCOLN: I did my first loop for Butchie Peraino. I went to this place in Brooklyn, and Butchie was shooting film and Vinnie, his bodyguard, was shooting the stills. Butchie and I got along, and we were friends ever since. We were just the same kind of people. Italian people. And as I said, the girl was just gorgeous!

I guess she was a German hooker. Blond hair, big tits, yeah, a beautiful girl. Oh, it was incredible!

CHUCK TRAYNOR: When we first came to New York, someone said, "Go to the Film Center Building. There's a lotta stuff goin' on over there."

So I go up to the seventeenth floor, and I meet Lou Perry, who was really Lou Peraino. They all called him Butchie. I just walked in and asked if they were hiring anybody, and the girl sitting in front said, "You wanna be in a movie?"

I said, "Uh, yeah, I'll be in a movie."

She said, "Well, go in the back; talk to Butchie."

So I go back there. He was sitting in his office. I said, "I make movies. I've made a lotta movies." I had made two or three, you know.

Butchie said, "Well, tell you what. Why don't you make me a few movies, and bring 'em in, and I'll see if we can do it. How 'bout that?"

So I said, "Okay."

FRED LINCOLN: I don't think Butchie made any more loops after that. I think that first one was for fun; he was horny or something. But as soon as he figured out how to make a loop, he had other people make them. He bought eight-millimeters from other people.

CHUCK TRAYNOR: I went and got Linda and rounded up some more people on Forty-second Street, just anybody that I talked to for more than two minutes. I'd ask, "Do you wanna do a porno film?"

Most of the girls I knew back then were girls who were either dancing or turning tricks—but I mean, I'd ask waitresses, anybody. And usually I'd do it in a joking way, so if they screamed I'd say it was a joke.

If they said, "Well, yeah, I dunno, maybe. How much money can I make?" then I'd take them up to the apartment and start making porno movies on the Bolex.

ERIC EDWARDS: The place we shot my first loop was some loft on Forty-second Street. It kind of looked like a bedroom/studio set, with one cameraman with an eight millimeter windup camera.

I was scared shitless, shaking up a storm, because I had no idea what I was in for. The cameraman was Teddy Snyder, and the girl was Linda Lovelace, only she wasn't Linda Lovelace yet—she was just Linda Traynor, Chuck's wife.

CHUCK TRAYNOR: We had gotten married before we left Miami. Mainly it was for her parents. Her mother was the kind that was always sending out private detectives and threatening this and that. She said, "You're taking my daughter across state lines. I'm gonna getcha."

And I said, "Fuck her. We'll get married, and then she can't do nothing," and that's what we did.

ERIC EDWARDS: So it was Linda and Chuck and another girl, some redhead. Chuck couldn't perform, so I was brought in to perform with these two girls. And I started feeling fine, you know? I mean, I had two women that were kind of cute, and I was gonna make forty bucks, so I thought, "Wow!"

GEORGINA SPELVIN: I had done some casting for a film on a boat, and one day a guy who was working the lights came over and asked me if I would play this madam. The older woman they had gotten to play the madam for all of the white slave traffic that was coming and going on this boat had gotten a better job.

So I said, "Sure." But I foolishly asked for a script—and they just stared at me, of course. They said, "Oh, just make up anything you want. But it does require a hard-core scene."

The movie was called *High Priestess of Sexual Witchcraft.*

ERIC EDWARDS: Even though I was nervous, I did fine—probably because Linda did perform deep throat on me that very first time. And I was amazed.

She swallowed my member all the way. I had never had that, no, no. There wasn't even a *name* for it because *Deep Throat* hadn't come out yet.

The girls got fifty dollars, and I got forty, which was all right, you know, fine, fine, fine. We were there for about two hours. And from my first loop on, Linda kept calling me, saying, "Hey, you did good. Do you wanna work again? I got another job for you."

GEORGINA SPELVIN: I had helped cast the large black mass scene for the film. And while this scene was being shot, I was sitting on the throne next to the high priest of sexual witchcraft—who turned out to be Marc Stevens, who naturally asked, "What's a nice girl like you doing in a place like this?"

And we got to chatting. Very funny guy. And we just had a good time, you know?

Marc Stevens was called Mr. Ten-and-a-Half because he reportedly had a ten-and-a-half-inch member when it was fully erect.

HARRY REEMS: The address I had been given to go to shoot my first loop was in the East Seventies. The address turned out to be a tenement, a fourth-floor rear walk-up.

I buzzed the buzzer of one Caprice Buzzard. Behind the door, there was lots of shuffling and shushing.

"Who's there?" a man whispered.

"It's me. The new boy," I said.

GEORGINA SPELVIN: I was having sex with the high priest and with the dude that was playing my son.

Was I nervous? No. He was a very attractive young man, and I had always felt that having sex was the friendliest thing two people could do. I only realized in retrospect that I'd been the school tramp. I was the girl all the guys would take out to fuck—but never took to the dances.

HARRY REEMS: "The new guy's here," Caprice Buzzard yelled. I assumed I'd be working with her, and I wasn't turned on by the idea.

Then I heard footsteps in the back room. Someone came down the hall toward me. It was a beautiful girl with a magnificent body. She looked like a young Gene Tierney. She wasn't wearing a bra.

I knew I'd have no problem getting an erection. Or getting rid of it. In fact, it was starting already.

The girl was Tina Russell.

TINA RUSSELL (PORN STAR): I did not have any idea what was involved in a pornographic film. In the beginning, I had no type of contact with any part of the business. My husband, Jason, had seen only a couple of eight-millimeter loops years before while in the army.

Anyway, my friend Suzanne, who had done some films, suggested the idea of us making loops because she really liked Bob Wolfe, the director. "He's a real character!" she said.

So as relaxed about nudity as we had always been, by ourselves and with our friends, we decided sure, why not? I assumed that we would make love—only it would be for a camera.

Well, Bob Wolfe shot a ten-minute loop, during which he would leave the camera unattended several times while it was still running, and disappear for two minutes. Each time he returned with a fresh beer and yelled, "All right, sweetie, I'm comin' in for a close-up."

So that was it! A few kisses, a lot of tongue action, some fondling, and a lot of spread shots. All I had to remember was to be sure not to look at the camera and to be sure to keep my legs spread directly to the camera.

GEORGINA SPELVIN: We made quite a few films. I called them one-day wonders. Marc Stevens and I had sex together on-screen many times, but he was like my kid brother. I didn't have "affairs" with anybody; I just had sex with a lot of people—there was a group of about six players. I referred to us as "The Rep Company." It included Marc Stevens, Harry Reems, Eric Edwards, Sean Costello, and of course Tina and Jason Russell.

TINA RUSSELL: There was an incredible contrast between the types of jobs we did in those days. One night it was working in a dirty studio in the Forty-second Street district doing a soft-core, S and M job. The next day, it was a short job requiring a half-hour to an hour of making love for a hard-core fill-in, to spice up a film shot years before. Or maybe a job requiring only straight acting, not even nudity, in a higher-budget production.

HARRY REEMS: When I arrived to shoot my first loop, Tina Russell was dressed like a hooker—in a short, short ribbed maroon miniskirt and a black pullover jersey and high heels. And no bra. Then a handsome, thin, bearded young man joined us.

"Hi," he said. "I'm Jason. Tina's husband."

My erection dropped like an express elevator.

"Are you going to be in the film, too?" I asked Jason.

"Nope. Not today."

"Why me instead of you?"

"Because Tina and I have done too many together. Caprice thinks a new face and bod are needed. I agree."

I was confused and embarrassed. All the blood in my system rushed to my face. "But . . . but," I stammered, "they told me I'd have to have . . . relations . . . with . . ."

Jason laughed. "Relax, man. You're trying to ask me if it's okay to fuck my wife. Of course you can fuck my wife."

TINA RUSSELL: Jason had to convince Harry that it was all right for him to fuck me.

FRED LINCOLN: Tina never cared about who Jason fucked, and Jason never cared about who Tina fucked—they were genuine swingers. I mean, I went over to their house once and fucked Tina while Jason was eating dinner.

I think Tina and Jason Russell were two people from Amish country, and they were childhood sweethearts. Tina adored Jason. She did everything for him. And she was a natural sex person. So the business didn't bother her when they both got into it.

HARRY REEMS: To relax me that day, Jason gave me a joint. He passed another to Tina and lit one for himself. I felt anything but relaxed.

The first scene we shot on the street. As soon as we were done with that, Caprice was ready with our next instructions.

"Now the two of you go upstairs to the bedroom. Tina, you get Harry to the bed and undress him. When you get him undressed, you'll give him head."

I had never really heard the expression "give head" before. I had to ask what it meant.

GEORGINA SPELVIN: The boys would trade off holding the camera, and there was usually a sound person and perhaps one person handling lights. Sometimes there would be another cameraperson, other than the actual players. The film was basically cut in the camera—and the idea was to make up a story and work through the story in one day. One day of shooting and one location. And we would do all kinds of crazy and silly things to work in the six obligatory fuck scenes.

HARRY REEMS: It started out with Tina kissing me. It was such a tender kiss that I fell in love with her all over again. She was trying to tell me, "Don't be scared. I'm going to help you all I can."

Then the scene went from the sublime to the ridiculous. "And then," Caprice cut in, "I'll walk out of the closet, and it'll be a happy surprise for you, Harry. You'll have two girls going down on you. You'll really get your money's worth!"

GEORGINA SPELVIN: I was using all kinds of different screen names for every film—Ona Turale, Connie Lingus, ha, ha, ha! Though, strangely enough, once I started doing hard-core films, I wasn't promiscuous in my personal life.

For one thing, I had this crazy idea that you didn't fuck outside the industry. You kept it within this group of people because otherwise you might "pick up a nail, and bring it home." This was like a family.

HARRY REEMS: This had to be one definition of heaven: getting sucked by two women simultaneously and getting paid for it.

"Okay, Tina, get on top of him," said Caprice, "and start to fuck, and I'll back off."

Loops—or stags—were silent, so it was okay to say anything as long as you weren't facing the camera. If you were facing the camera, you should be saying something appropriate to the action so that good lip-readers in the audience wouldn't be put off.

Tina mounted me. I came instantly.

TINA RUSSELL: It is not difficult for me to let myself go and to be my character in a film. I do not want to be a great, well-known actress—it's too much of a hassle. Besides, I love what I am doing.

I am a porn star.

HARRY REEMS: "Open your legs, Harry," said Sam the cameraman.

"Yes," said Caprice, "take it out, and come on Tina's thigh."

"I already came," I panted.

There was a moment of dead silence.

"WHAT!" screamed Caprice. *"What the hell do you mean you already came?"*

"I came," I repeated limply.

"Cut the camera!" Caprice yelled, *"This dumb jerk came!* You schmuck, don't you know you're supposed to come outside her? That's the money shot, the wet shot. The camera has to see your cum. Don't you know that much, you nebbish?"

"I'm sorry," I said sheepishly. "Maybe tomorrow I can—"

"Tomorrow! You're damn well going to do it over again *today.* You're not leaving this house until I get a cum shot out of you. Now how long do you think it's going to take before you can get it up again?"

"I don't know," I said honestly.

"All right, we'll clear out and leave you alone. You can start beating your meat or whatever. When you get it up and ready, yell."

Tina, bless her, stayed in the room with me.

TINA RUSSELL: Harry had been uptight that day, and I made him feel good.

HARRY REEMS: Tina did a deliriously good job on me, and I erupted right on schedule. But there wasn't a second to savor the post-ejaculatory glow.

"Okay, get your clothes on, Harry," Caprice was saying in her smart executive voice, "get your money, and get out."

Tina Russell said, "You're good. Would you like some more work?"

"Sure," I said.

With that one word, my new career was launched.

GEORGINA SPELVIN: I'm not a very good cocksucker, but I am a good actress. Every role I've ever gotten has dealt with things that have been foreign to me, so I simply try to make them a part of my experience in order to portray them convincingly. If I have to learn how to twirl the baton, I'll do the best I can to learn it in the time I have available. If I haven't got enough time, I'll learn how to fake it.

You see, in my personal life, I didn't achieve a real orgasm until I was twenty-six, and it was a great mystery to me at what point the body takes over—is no longer controlled. That's why when women talk about orgasms, they say if you're not sure, you haven't had one.

HARRY REEMS: The guys were getting $75 for a day's work and the girls $100. I protested, and it worked. We all got the same pay, except for the girls who did anal scenes, who got an extra $25.

GEORGINA SPELVIN: The girls went on strike and said the boys should be paid as much as the girls. So everybody got $100. And then it went up to $115.

HARRY REEMS: I never knew what I was being hired for. I just went and came. Some nights I'd literally limp home, I'd be so sore.

GEORGINA SPELVIN: There are so many films out there that have been made of cutting-room trash, with different names—and since I never received a royalty, not one penny, from any film I ever made, I cannot tell you what I did or did not do.

If my picture is there, and you're absolutely sure it's me, then chances are I did it, ha, ha, ha. If the name alone is there, and you're only seeing scattered body parts, it could or could not be me. I can't guarantee it.

HARRY REEMS: I stayed out of acting from April to June, except for an occasional loop. Then an enormous, nine-foot beanpole Jamaican by the name of Smitty entered my life. Smitty said, "Hey, Harry, you want to make some films?"

FRED LINCOLN: Smitty basically did loops. He was a one-man band. He'd set the lights, set the camera, and then we'd just do whatever we wanted to do.

HARRY REEMS: God knows where Smitty got the money to become a producer. Maybe selling coke to Caprice or pulling heists in the garment center. Nobody ever dared to ask. Big, black, skinny—Smitty was the "open sesame" to the "summer of my content" and to the most fun I've ever had in the profession.

JAMIE GILLIS: That summer was a terrific time because there were a lot of film companies in Times Square. Harry Reems was there and a guy named Sean Costello, who was a wonderful character. I met Harry at Sean's office, when we started doing loops together.

HARRY REEMS: Jamie Gillis was very much with us in the making of those loops. Jamie's into everything sexually. There's almost nothing that doesn't turn him on. Guys, gals, S and M. You name it, and he'd love to do it. When none of the rest of us wanted to work with a woman, we'd call Jamie in. Even if a woman stank to high heaven, Jamie would eat her right up.

JAMIE GILLIS: Those guys who had seniority, Harry, Sean, and Fred—who had been around a little while—got the prettier girls. Sean, of course, would get the top one. Then Harry got some, too. It took a while before you could lay claim to the really hot ones.

But one time there was one girl, Lucy, who was so, so cute, that I just kept fucking her.

I pretended that I couldn't come. So I just kept fucking her and fucking her—for I don't know how long. I just wanted to keep her, you know? I figured, well, she wasn't going to come home with me, so this might be the only chance I had. So I just kept everyone waiting on the set—while I kept fucking Lucy.

FRED LINCOLN: Jamie used to get next to 'em and he would be fuckin' 'em and he would whisper in their ears, "You fuckin' hate me now, but I don't give a shit, cause I'm gonna fuck you for two hours and then I ain't gonna come for another hour and then when I come, I ain't even stoppin', you cunt!"

JAMIE GILLIS: I did think about sex a lot. I did enjoy sex a lot, probably more than the average guy.

And no, I wasn't molested as a kid. When I was eleven, some old guy did try to molest me. He took me home and said, "I'll give you a quarter to watch me play with myself," and he showed me a dirty magazine—a sunbathing magazine, one of those nudist magazines.

The old guy said, "Let me see your thing. I bet you've got a big one."

And that was the only reason I didn't take my pants down. I was eleven years old, and I knew I didn't have a big one. If he'd said, "Oh, I like little boys," I'd have said, "Oh yeah, sure, buddy." But I thought, "If I didn't think I'd disappoint ya, I'd do it." That was as close as I ever got to being molested.

HARRY REEMS: Smitty paid Sean Costello a sum of money to produce five loops a day. The first thing Sean did was to hire me and Fred Lincoln to help him produce, direct, and act in these films.

Sean, Fred, and I must have made 150 loops that summer. We earned our nickname of "The Dirty Three." We created a whole new atmosphere. The Dirty Three were about as reliable as anybody in the industry for getting it off on cue—perhaps the most reliable. That's why we had all the work we could get and why we kept hiring one another when we were commissioned to make loops.

FRED LINCOLN: It was me, a guy by the name of Sean Costello, Harry Reems, Paul Matthews, Jamie Gillis, and Jason Russell. Of course, there was Tina Russell, Jason's wife, who was magnificent and that was it. We were like the core of guys that did the films. But it was the hippie days, so a lot of people would drift in and drift out—but we were the core group of porn actors.

HARRY REEMS: The Dirty Three were so horny that sometimes we'd get into the bathtub with our partners and fuck between loops. But we wouldn't come—because we knew we had to save it for our "art." In another half hour we'd be doing another loop.

FRED LINCOLN: Smitty is the only casualty I know of in this business. He fell out of a hotel room window. Yeah, poor guy. Nobody knows who he was working for. We didn't know anything in those days.

GEORGINA SPELVIN: There were rumors that the mob was financing these films. I never knew it for a fact; I never met anybody that had Mafia on their shirt: "Members Only," ha, ha, ha. I wouldn't know a Mafia if I saw one! And I wasn't paid by check, so I didn't have any name on the check to refer to. I was usually paid in cash.

FRED LINCOLN: Why did Smitty get thrown out the window? I dunno. Smitty did a lot of stuff; he must have stole money. But I don't think it was the mob because Smitty was into some shit. It's too bad he went out the window, though, because he always got the best-looking girls. Smitty had good taste.

GEORGINA SPELVIN: People would ask, "Aren't you afraid of the mob coming in and interfering in your life?"

I'd say, "What mob? C'mon, you've got to be kidding!"

I mean, it was a wonderful atmosphere! For all of my dealings with people in the porn business—any porn film I made—if I went in to talk with anyone about doing a film, I didn't have to audition. People called and begged me to work for them, begged to give me money. And money was what I really needed at that point. Money is still what I need. I haven't outgrown that.

If I wasn't comfortable with the people or with the circumstances, I'd just say no. It was that easy. I was never forced to do anything.

HARRY REEMS: Late 1971 was the high noon of the business. Everybody was getting into the act. You could stand on a street corner in Times Square waiting for traffic lights to change and ask a stranger, "How's the new film going?"

Almost never would anyone ask, "What film?"

Anyone who wanted work could find it. You had the luxury of turning down three, four, or five jobs a day.

ERIC EDWARDS: I was still signed with the William Morris Agency, when the Leiber Brothers—the advertising agency—wrote me a letter. Obviously, one of their executives found a loop or something that I did and canceled my Close-Up toothpaste commercial. The words of the letter were something about how it was discovered that I had "done nudity."

Heaven forbid! I had taken off my pants!

JAMIE GILLIS: The first time I saw my picture on a poster I was furious and even thinking of suing somebody—because there were pictures of our faces.

I thought, *"My God, I'm a serious actor. People are gonna see this poster, and it's gonna ruin my career!"*

You see, I was still working with the Classic Stage Company, and we were having a limited audience doing some *Pericles* or some far-out Shakespeare thing, so I said to them, "You know what we should do to attract noise? We should do this nude! You know, just do *Pericles* nude, and people will come. It's never been done!"

The director said to me, "You know, Jamie, I think you're in the wrong company." Ha, ha, ha—in a way he was right.

ERIC EDWARDS: What was funny about the Close-Up ad being pulled—it was this commercial that involved a girl and a guy on a beach, and it was called "Smiles and Whispers," and my line was, "And because we smile and whisper a lot, we carry Close-Up with us wherever we go."

"Because we smile and whisper a lot?" It was a very sexual commercial. I could have redefined the whole meaning of Close-Up!

In any case, it was pulled off the air. And after they pulled that, my Gillette TracII and Coleco Toys commercials were pulled off, too.

FRED LINCOLN: Harry Reems and I were walking down Eighth Avenue one day. We went past a theater called the Cameo, and there's Harry's picture with one of these girls on the poster. And Harry just went fucking ape shit. *"What are they doing? This is gonna kill my career!"*

I said, "Harry, you ain't got no career. This is what we do. We make an occasional commercial, but this is it—we get laid, and they give us a hundred bucks."

Doggie Style
NEW YORK CITY
1971

FRED LINCOLN: I used to have to chase Linda Boreman, or Linda Traynor, whatever she was calling herself, away from me on the set. She was a pain in the ass. She would just get down between my legs and try to open my fly. And I'd say, "I gotta work."

I mean, everybody fucked while they were waiting to fuck. We'd fuck before—we'd fuck after—we'd fuck during. But I didn't like Linda; there was just something about her . . .

So did I do any scenes with Linda? No. I just did pretty girls.

ERIC EDWARDS: I think it was Linda who called me and said "Hey, I got a new guy, Bob Wolfe, that's doing stuff. Let's do another scene."

Linda liked working with me. Or fucking me, I should say. She liked the idea of me being able to perform. I would get called by Linda, so I also did several scenes for Bob Wolfe, not just the famous one.

CHUCK TRAYNOR: Bob Wolfe made a million loops. He was a nice, black-haired guy. I think Linda and I made probably between ten to fifteen loops at that time for him. It's really hard to say because with someone like Bob Wolfe who shoots with two cameras you never know how many you've made.

FRED LINCOLN: They would call us—I think it was Vinnie, Butchie Peraino's bodyguard—and say, "Come at nine o'clock in the morning."

We'd show up, and they'd figure out who's gonna work with who and who's gonna do what. That's the way we worked, cause, you know, we were stoned, ha, ha, ha! This was the hippie days: We'd smoke a joint, we'd do acid, and we'd fuck.

CHUCK TRAYNOR: Bob Wolfe was, of course, doing the freakiest films. He had a place down on Fourteenth Street. Linda and I were sitting there, and he just asked her.

He asked, "Lady, would you ball a dog?"

And she said, "Sure."

LINDA LOVELACE: Bob Wolfe asked me, "We've been thinking of making a dog movie. Would that interest you?"

I said no before I even considered the question. A dog movie? A *dog* movie? I knew they weren't thinking about *Rin Tin Tin* or *Lassie Come Home.* They were undoubtedly considering a girl-meets-dog movie.

CHUCK TRAYNOR: I was sitting there, and Bob Wolfe said, "Jesus, we could do three or four films, and I could pay you some extra money." So I figured, what the hell?

LINDA LOVELACE: "There'd be a lot of money in it," Bob said. "A lot more than usual."

"I'm not interested," I said. "I'm afraid of dogs."

ERIC EDWARDS: I've known Chuck Traynor for a long time, and I have never, ever seen anything other than a businessman in him. I've never seen any kind of malevolence in him. He was more involved in the business and getting his wife to do certain things. But I never, *ever* saw any kind of abuse.

LINDA LOVELACE: The following morning, Chuck informed me that I would be making a movie with a dog. I didn't say anything to Chuck. I knew the only time to tell him was when the other people were around. Witnesses.

There would be a beating, I knew that much, but it would be easier on me if other people were nearby. For once, the prospect of a beating was not the worst alternative. Any beating, no matter how severe, would be better than being raped by a dog.

Our destination that morning was a studio down in the East Village. A large room . . . the usual clutter . . . the double bed . . . the movie lights . . . the cameras . . . the director, Bob Wolfe—fat and greasy and black-haired.

ERIC EDWARDS: I always felt that Linda was enjoying everything that she did in front of the camera. I never had a feeling that she was *not* enjoying herself.

Even with the dog—and I was *in* that loop.

LINDA LOVELACE: Chuck led me back into the main room. Wolfe and his assistant were sitting behind a small table. Chuck joined them on their side of the table.

"Okay, Linda," Wolfe said. "Why don't you get undressed, and we'll get on with this."

"No."

"I'd advise you to think that over pretty carefully," Wolfe said.

I looked at the three men. And then I noticed that on the small table directly in front of them there was a gun, a revolver.

"Now, are you sure you don't want to make this movie?" Wolfe asked.

"Take off your clothes, cunt," Chuck said.

ERIC EDWARDS: There was no gun pointed to her head; there were no people around, other than Bob Wolfe and me. There was no forcing her to do anything. Chuck wasn't even there, not on that particular set. He was more of a manager that came in to make sure everything was okay and then would leave.

CHUCK TRAYNOR: It wasn't my film. So I wasn't even on the set. Bob Wolfe came up with the idea. It was just these guys trying to think of new things to come up with so they could make another movie.

ERIC EDWARDS: The dog wasn't on the set already, no, I don't believe so. I think I just went in front of the camera with Bob, shooting, doing a scene with Linda. We finished the scene, and the plot was advanced: "Oh, okay, the boyfriend now leaves to go to work, and the doggie comes in to satisfy Linda."

LINDA LOVELACE: As I reached up to unbutton my blouse, I knew I was surrendering. If I could have foreseen how bad it was going to be, I wouldn't have surrendered. I would have chosen the possibility of death.

I am able to handle almost everything that has happened to me in my life—but I'm still not able to handle that day. I've been raped by men who were no better than animals, but this was an *actual* animal—and that represented a huge dividing line.

ERIC EDWARDS: After my scene with Linda, I sat on the set, and I saw this guy bring in—I'll call him "Fido"—a greyhound, I believe. Maybe an Afghan, shaved, but it was a short-haired dog.

Thin tail.

LINDA LOVELACE: When the film began I was to be in bed with Eric Edwards, who would stay with me for just a few minutes, just long enough to seem to get me aroused, and then leave me. At that point, I was supposed to look frustrated, unsatisfied.

As Wolfe directed the action, he said, "Now look around the room . . . slowly . . . slowly. . . . Now you see your dog, and you go, 'Oooooh!' And now you look excited. . . . Make it look like all of a sudden you're coming up with a brilliant idea. . . . That's right, now snap your fingers."

ERIC EDWARDS: When I saw what was happening in front of my eyes, my jaw dropped to the floor. Because Linda did something that totally blew my brains out. She immediately went down on the dog.

LINDA LOVELACE: They had the dog lick me. All that time they were telling me to smile and to laugh. I was supposed to look very excited. I was feeling nothing but acute revulsion. Even as this was happening to me, I had trouble believing it. How much time was I actually with the dog? Maybe an hour or two, but there seemed no end to it. I felt sure he would bite me.

"Okay, Linda, get down on your hands and knees. No, down on all fours. That's right . . ."

ERIC EDWARDS: She just went down on the dog, got him excited, and as soon as Linda got on all fours, the dog mounted her because the dog knows that when somebody's on all fours, bang—we know what that's all about.

LINDA LOVELACE: It went on, without end, until Bob Wolfe's voice came through the fog.

"Okay, we got enough," he said. "Wow—far-out!"

"I never thought we'd get this," his assistant said.

ERIC EDWARDS: After it was over, I could see that the dog had actually ejaculated inside of her. I could see the expression on the dog's face. Dog pulls out, asks for her phone number, smokes a cigarette, and everything was over.

LINDA LOVELACE: When they pulled the dog away from me, I was in the deepest valley I'd ever been in, devastated, wanting only to die. I looked up and saw Chuck.

CHUCK TRAYNOR: I wasn't there. I had come down around noontime and went out to get some apple pie at this little dumpy joint around the corner. I cut the slice of pie and I happened to see something and I turned it over—it was all moldy on the bottom, all green.

ERIC EDWARDS: Linda didn't seem upset. No, not at all. Linda just seemed to me like a hippie, free-love chick, you know? She had the headband, beads, the whole thing. Free love was all around.

LINDA LOVELACE: Chuck was staring at me, studying me, measuring my reaction. He had to realize this was the worst moment of my life.

ERIC EDWARDS: At that particular time, everybody was trying to do dog movies. But the dogs had to be able to perform. There were several times when we would have a production scheduled, and the girl would sit back—and the dog didn't want to have anything to do with her whatsoever.

We'd try mayonnaise, we'd try hot dogs, we'd smear stuff on her pussy, and it wouldn't work. The dog would whimper and whine and back off.

But this particular dog that worked with Linda was a pro.

SHARON MITCHELL: They were shooting up in Carter Stevens's studio, and I walked in and saw Linda having sex with these dogs. It didn't look like they were forcing her to do anything. It looked like they were forcing the dogs!

I was really young and new and going up there to shoot a scene with Chuck Vincent. When I walked in there and saw that, I was like, "Okay, I'm out of here."

They were like, "No, no, no. We're shooting another scene in another part of the studio later in the day. You're just here for makeup."

But I was like, "No way, man."

So I ran down the stairs. It scared me. It was just too weird because nobody was holding anybody anywhere. Nobody was forcing her to do anything.

BILL KELLY: Linda was making bestiality movies, and Chuck was involved in that with her. Linda even admitted it before the Attorney General's Commission. Supposedly she made them under duress. I don't know whether I believe her or not. Because there was more than one bestiality film. And I even knew who one of the dogs was. I think it was Bruno or something—a great, big, damn dog.

I can't even remember the breed.

Mary Had a Little Lamb

NEW YORK CITY
1971–1972

JOHN WATERS: To me, the day porn films became legal was in 1969 when they showed *Pornography in Denmark* in a commercial movie theater in New York City, and it didn't get busted. *Variety* will back me up on this.

I hitchhiked from Provincetown, Massachusetts, all the way to New York to see it because I knew it was historic. *Pornography in Denmark* got around the law because it was "a serious documentary," right? It was supposedly "socially redeeming," but it showed penetration. That opened the doors to other movies, like *SEX U.S.A.* and eventually *Deep Throat.*

It was a big deal because after that there was no turning back.

That's the day exploitation films ended—the way Andy Warhol ended Abstract Expressionism in one night by that soup can, the way the Beatles ended rhythm and blues in one night on the *Ed Sullivan Show.*

BUTCHIE PERAINO: I invested money in a company that went bankrupt. We then made two pictures. One was a documentary called *SEX U.S.A.* and the other was called *This Film Is All About.* . . . That's right—blank.

New York papers won't even use the word "sex" on movies like this. To give you a for instance, *SEX U.S.A.* in the *Daily News* was printed *XEX U.S.A.*

FRED LINCOLN: I went to work for Gerry Damiano and Butchie on a film called *SEX U.S.A.* Linda Boreman was in it before she was Linda Lovelace. Paul Matthews was in it, Tina Russell was in it, and Harry Reems was there—everybody that was around. Again, we just did it and walked away. It wasn't a loop; it was a feature. Gerard Damiano did features. This was before *Throat.*

HARRY REEMS: *SEX U.S.A.* was the first interview-type thirty-five-millimeter film. It was shot in a West Side studio. We all watched one another take our clothes off. Then we went—two by two—into six or seven cubicles and there we stayed with our sexual partners while the narrator explained very pedagogically what we were doing.

FRED LINCOLN: You see, what Butchie really wanted was to make features. That's what he always wanted—to make motion pictures. It's kind of a sad story—here's this mobster's son who wants to be an auteur, you know?

That's why Butchie picked Gerry Damiano—because I don't think Gerry ever did loops. Butchie put up the money because he knew Gerry could make a feature.

HARRY REEMS: Gerard Damiano was a grown-up Wizard of Oz, a short, jolly, jelly bean. He had a gray goatee and a funny little toupee. He was sort of the stereotype of the second-string Hollywood director. But Gerard Damiano has been called the Mike Nichols and Ingmar Bergman of porno films.

FRED LINCOLN: Gerry was a decent guy, but he did try to rip me off for twenty-five dollars on *SEX U.S.A.* The budget was really tight; there wasn't any money, so he tried to pay me seventy-five bucks a day. I said, "No way."

I said, "Listen. Don't fuck with me. I'll break your fuckin' legs."

Then Butchie asked, "What's goin' on'?"

I said, "Gerry told me he was bringin' me a hundred bucks a day. Now he wants to give me seventy-five."

Butchie just said, "Pay him."

BUTCHIE PERAINO: *SEX U.S.A.* cost about twelve to fifteen thousand dollars to make. So far it's grossed six hundred thousand.

So we decided to do another film, but we didn't want to do a documentary. There was this film, *Mona,* that we had seen. It was different. It had a story. It was what you would call "improvisational." We thought of doing the same exact thing.

LINDA LOVELACE: Andrea True was the one that mentioned to Chuck Traynor that she knew this guy, Gerard Damiano, who was going to make a thirty-five-millimeter, big-screen pornographic movie.

CHUCK TRAYNOR: I would see Gerard Damiano coming in and outta the Perainos' office. Yeah, I was friendly with him, but it's like two guys that are pushin' wheelbarrows. If one guy has been there a long time, he thinks he's a superior wheelbarrow-pusher to the other guy. Plus he was making sixteen-millimeter films, so he's big-time. I'm a little guy because I'm making eight-millimeter loops. Plus I swept the office, fixed the lights, went on locations, drove cars, stuff like that.

RAY PISTOL (PORN PRODUCER): Chuck and Linda came in to see Butch, and Chuck had loops underneath his arm. Chuck put one on—and it was Linda's doggie flick. And Butch said, "We don't do that shit here."

Butchie threw them out of the office. This is from Butch directly. And in the anteroom, outside, Gerard Damiano was coming up the elevator as Chuck and Linda were leaving, and they started a conversation.

GERARD DAMIANO: I'd like to say something poetic, like *Linda came in beauty like the night,* but it's not true. She came in wearing army boots, an old army jacket, and a wool hat pulled over her head.

LINDA LOVELACE: Yeah, that army jacket. Chuck made me look like a hippie chick. It's not something I ever would have been caught dead in.

But compared to men like Bob Wolfe, Gerard Damiano was like Cecil B. DeMille.

CHUCK TRAYNOR: Gerard Damiano was a pretty easygoing guy. I mean, he had a little bit of an air, like I say, because he was the director of feature films. And back in the early porno days, a feature film was a "FEATURE FILM." Gerry was working with the Perainos—he was their director. And he was a good director; he knew about shooting sixteen-millimeter, you know, reversals and two shots and one shots and all that shit.

RAY PISTOL: Chuck and Linda and Damiano hit it off and decided to go to a swingers' club that night. And that was the night that Damiano saw Linda's talent. He came back the next day and hit Butchie up to completely change everything around.

BUTCHIE PERAINO: To be honest about it, we couldn't come up with anything too good. We were just going to do another *Mona.* Then somehow Gerry Damiano seen this girl at a party. I assume he got fixed up with her.

GERARD DAMIANO: Fortunately for Linda—and for me—I was casting for a sex insert, a short segment for a full-length movie. So I asked her if she would do it, and she said yes.

HARRY REEMS: I was doing some loops for Gerry that summer and working behind the camera with him a little. One morning he called me and asked me if I'd be able to show up that day to do some shorts.

When I got there, he said, "You're going to do an anal scene with Linda."

This was my introduction to Linda Lovelace.

But that morning she was very nervous. She acted like a complete beginner. Gerry soon guessed that her nervousness had more to do with the presence of her husband/manager, than any feelings of inadequacy about her assignment. When he made that discovery, he sent the husband on errands. With Chuck temporarily out of the picture, Linda relaxed and turned in a performance, to say the least.

GERARD DAMIANO: I met Linda on Wednesday and did the insert on Thursday. And it was when she did the insert that I realized the talent that she had.

HARRY REEMS: Gerry convinced Linda that she should do her best because this would be a cut or two above the run-of-the-mill loop. In the loop, Linda played a nurse, and I was the patient. I'm shown in bed wearing some crazy underwear with hearts and flowers. My cock is wrapped up in bandages with a bow at the tip. My nurse pats my bandaged member, which is in an enlarged and inflamed state.

"No," I protest. "It hurts."

My nurse won't be dissuaded. Off comes the bandage, and nursie is soon applying oral therapy to the ailing organ.

LINDA LOVELACE: It's impossible to perform the act unless there's a straight line from mouth to throat—like a sword swallower. So how could we arrange it? We tried every conceivable way until we at last found the proper position for the camera to catch it all. It amounted to a kind of 69 position, with my body kind of flat against Harry's chest. I struggled at first—but it began to work and work well. When I felt him straining, I had to put his throbbing cock all the way down.

HARRY REEMS: I knew the anal scene was coming up so I asked Linda, "Would you like some K-Y Jelly or something?"

"No, no," Linda panted, "Just let me give you some more head."

Giving more head she became frantic—her tongue and lips were everywhere. Then I felt the muscles in the back of her throat opening up. Her head lowered over me. Suddenly I could feel my cock go right into her throat. *I couldn't believe she ate the whole thing!* My cock and balls and half my pubic bush were all engulfed in that cavernous, deep throat.

GERARD DAMIANO: Linda knocked me out the minute she started going down on Harry, doing her *Deep Throat* thing. Harry was very heavily endowed. I had never seen anybody take a cock that deep before.

HARRY REEMS: It was a frightening sensation. My first thought was, "Will she bring me back alive?"

But she kept going up and down all the way. The muscle in her throat was relaxed. Her breathing got noisier and noisier. She started to drip from her nose and over her chin. She let out animal shrieks.

"Okay, I'm ready," she finally gasped.

Her cunt and anal passage were both sopping wet. Gerry's eyes nearly popped out of their sockets and the cameraman's jaw brushed his shoes. I think all of us there knew we were present at a significant moment in sexual history.

I fell instantly—though briefly—in love with Linda. We balled our brains out and fucked every which way.

That loop was eventually inserted in *Deep Throat.*

CHUCK TRAYNOR: Gerry Damiano wasn't the first person to see Linda give deep throat, no. She did deep throat people in the early loops. But obviously nobody realized that this was a really unusual talent. Gerry was the first one to take it seriously. I mean, I didn't realize the power of it because I had lived with it all my life.

GERARD DAMIANO: In selling her attributes, Chuck probably mentioned she could take a large amount of cock. But, again, it was very hard then to describe it. I'm sure he wasn't aware of what he had there; if he was, Chuck has proven himself to be enough of a businessman over the years that he would have handled things a lot differently.

BUTCHIE PERAINO: Gerry came in the next day and said that as he was driving over the Fifty-ninth Street Bridge, he was thinking of Linda. What she had done was fantastic. He'd never seen anybody do like she did. So he thought, let's make a picture about this girl.

GERARD DAMIANO: I was so knocked out over what Linda did that I went home and wrote *Deep Throat* over the weekend. Linda was doing something that defied description. You have to understand, at the time there was no such expression as "deep throat." I invented it. Now it's sort of a byword; you think, "Wow, I wonder if that girl can give deep throat?"

And Linda looked like the girl next door—though she actually wasn't—so I wanted to develop for her a caricature of what every man wanted the girl next door to be. And the name "Linda Lovelace" I created for her—after I wrote the script.

LINDA LOVELACE: Butchie Peraino did not like me. He didn't want that sweet, innocent look that Mr. Damiano was going for. He wanted a bubble-gum chewing, bleach blond with large breasts. He thought his twenty-five thousand was just gonna go to waste.

GERARD DAMIANO: One of the most difficult things was to convince my partners that Linda was worth starring in the film because of the way she looked. Outwardly, she wasn't particularly sexy or exciting. All they could see was her army boots and stocking hat.

LINDA LOVELACE: I will say this about Butchie Peraino, he never talked behind my back. Anything he had to say about me, he said right to my face and generally at the top of his voice. Butchie and Damiano were in nearby offices, and they constantly shouted their opinions from one room to the next.

Butchie would point out that this was their first feature film and that their entire futures were riding on it.

Damiano would say that he understood that perfectly and that's why they should use me. Butchie would shout back that he had never heard of a female star of a pornographic movie without big tits.

"BIG TITS SELL TICKETS!" Butchie yelled.

"LINDA STAYS!" Damiano shouted back.

And I did. Chuck was to be paid a flat hundred a day for my role in the movie, a total of twelve hundred dollars.

GERARD DAMIANO: I said I would make Linda a star if she would volunteer to work and rehearse. I'm not talking about giving blow jobs. I'm talking about delivering lines and getting her to act.

LINDA LOVELACE: Butchie Peraino said, "We've never even seen this broad talk!"

"So we'll give her a little test," Damiano said. "We'll see if she can talk."

My test for the role struck me as a strange one. Damiano asked me to recite, "Mary Had a Little Lamb."

That was my screen test for *Deep Throat.*

I stood there and recited "Mary Had a Little Lamb" two different ways—first a straight dramatic reading, then laughing all the way through, as though it was hilarious. I guess they were testing my dramatic range.

GERARD DAMIANO: I would walk Linda around crowded rooms, asking her to yell, so she would get over her shyness—to get her to project.

LINDA LOVELACE: When Butchie Peraino kept criticizing me, Chuck began to panic that all that money would fall through. One day Chuck came up with a brainstorm. "We could get Butchie to change his mind, if you'd just go in there and give him a blow job."

I walked into his office. He was seated at his desk, going through piles of paper. He glanced up at me for just a second and then returned to his paperwork. "Lock the door," he said, not looking at me.

"C'mon," he said, "Let's get this over with."

I went over beside him and got down on my knees and started to work on him. As I was doing what I had to do, he went on fussing with the papers on his desk. Then he suddenly stopped, leaned back on his chair and looked up at the ceiling. His whole body stiffened, relaxed, then stiffened again. "All right," he said, "Get out of here now."

CHUCK TRAYNOR: Butchie used to eat pizza while Linda was givin' him head. He used to say, "Well, you're doin' a good job." Yeah, there was no love lost between 'em.

LINDA LOVELACE: I didn't really like Butchie because all he was interested in was "experiencing the product." He wanted to see what it was like to have deep throat done to him. I had to become a "satisfier" for him, I guess you could say.

HARRY REEMS: I couldn't wait to work with Linda again. When Gerard told me he had a script for *Deep Throat*, I read it with great eagerness. In the script, I saw a part I was dying to play—and my part was dying to play it, too.

"No, I can't use you," Damiano said. "We're going to Florida to shoot, and it would be too expensive to take you."

I was crushed.

CHUCK TRAYNOR: I don't know how I got to meet Butchie's father, Anthony Peraino, Sr., but I always called him "Mr. Peraino." I told him about locations in Florida because you gotta remember I was tryin' to get back to Miami. So I bust ass and made some phone calls and got some places lined up.

LENNY CAMP: Chuck Traynor was nuthin'. He was less than nuthin'. He couldn't get anybody, couldn't get any locations. So they called me.

BUNNY YEAGER: Somebody called me wanting me to get them some girls for *Deep Throat*, but when they told me they had to do hard-core sex, I said, "Absolutely not. I can't—I don't know anyone like that, and I wouldn't ask anyone to do that anyway."

HARRY REEMS: I wanted to be a part of that production. It didn't matter if I acted or not. In fact, I preferred *not* to act.

"Tell you what," I said to Gerry. "If you put me on as crew, I'll work for twenty bucks a day."

Gerry's eyes opened wide.

"Maybe we can work something out," he said. "Maybe we can put you on as gaffer and grip."

CHUCK TRAYNOR: So Mr. Peraino, Anthony Sr., was driving down to Miami and, I asked, "Hey, can Linda and I ride with you?"

He said, "Sure."

This came up later in the *Deep Throat* trial, that he transported us across state lines for illegal bullshit, but it wasn't any illegal bullshit. I just asked him for a ride.

LINDA LOVELACE: When we were driving to Florida, Chuck was desperately trying to push me to do something sexual with Tony—Mr. Anthony Peraino, Sr. But he wasn't the least bit into it, and of course I wasn't either. He was too nice to embarrass me like that.

So I'd get yelled at every night for not doing it, you know—"Why don't you grab his dick while he's driving and give him a blow job?"

CHUCK TRAYNOR: You remember them old leather sheepskin coats from the hippie days? Well, Linda had one of those, and it got rained on someplace in New Jersey, and it smelled terrible. When those coats got wet, they smelled real bad. So old Mr. Peraino stopped the car and said, "Chuck, if you do me a favor, I'll do you a favor."

I asked, "What's that?"

"If you'll throw that thing out, I'll stop and buy her a good coat."

HARRY REEMS: On January 11, 1972, I left for Florida. And *Deep Throat*. And I did indeed drive Gerard Damiano's blue and white Cadillac to Florida—that flashy Caddy you see in the movie. I'll always think of it as the pimpmobile.

FRED LINCOLN: The reason I wasn't in *Throat* was that, as I said, Gerry Damiano tried to rip me off for twenty-five bucks on *SEX U.S.A.*

ERIC EDWARDS: The only reason I wasn't in *Deep Throat* was that I was doing summer stock at the time. I probably could have had Harry Reems's role if I had been in New York because there was only like a handful of people doing porn. But I was still a so-called "legit" actor, so I was doing summer stock shows around Florida, South Carolina, and Virginia, performing in *Man of La Mancha*, stuff like that.

"Do You Mind If I Smoke While You Eat?"

MIAMI
1972

LENNY CAMP: Originally, the *Deep Throat* script was on three-by-five cards. Then all of a sudden it was mimeographed, and somehow I got a copy. To me it was just another piece of shit.

GERARD DAMIANO: In Miami, Chuck made Linda wear these cutoff jeans that were so short and so tight that the lips of her pussy would hang out the sides. She did have nice long legs, and anyone passing by would have to notice.

But in Chuck's mind, anybody who did look at her was grounds for taking Linda back to the hotel and beating the shit out of her.

Obviously she was supposed to do it but not *enjoy* it.

LINDA LOVELACE: After the first night of shooting, we were in a hotel room. And the whole crew was in an adjoining room. Music was blasting, everybody was laughing having a grand old time.

And then Chuck started in about how I smiled too much on the set that day and that I didn't do anything freaky to anyone, and I didn't expose myself to anyone, and all these different things. And then all of a sudden he started punching me and kicking me and threw me against the wall. And then he picked me up and threw me on the bed. And I started screaming. Everyone became very quiet. The music was shut down. The laughing stopped.

"I'm thinking, wow, what soulless people. No one's going to help me." And not one person came.

CHUCK TRAYNOR: Did I beat her up? Well, yeah, I wouldn't bullshit anybody. You know, I'm not Goody Two-shoes or "Joe Innocent." I've always tried to deal with people two ways: I talk to them as long as I think I can talk to them and then I hit them. With Linda, if she and I got into a hassle, it wouldn't be beneath me to backhand her or bend her over my knee and beat her ass. She dug it, you know?

GERARD DAMIANO: I've often tried to pinpoint the psychology of Linda. She seemed to have a distinct sadomasochistic relationship with Chuck, to the point where he constantly dominated her. They were never anywhere where she wasn't holding him or touching him. There was always a physical closeness or contact. There was this strange need all the time. And she was never out of Chuck's sight. They were always a little apart from the group.

But as close as they were in the daytime, I knew Chuck would bang Linda off the wall all night. The next day she'd appear on the set black-and-blue.

CHUCK TRAYNOR: When Gerry used to have trouble with Linda, I'd say, "You tell her you'll beat her ass or something if she don't do so-and-so."

GERARD DAMIANO: I had brought Harry Reems down with me to Florida as production assistant. I thought Harry had already been overexposed in X-rated films. But he was looking to break out of performing and learn the technical end of the business.

I really dug Harry. He's a professional, he's a romantic, and he's an exhibitionist. You have to be one if you're going to look good in an X-rated film. Harry knew where his own particular head was, and he could get it up anytime you wanted. Even so, I hadn't written a part for him in *Deep Throat.* But I couldn't find anybody in Florida to play the doctor, so I finally asked Harry.

He loved it! He was completely turned on by Linda. He couldn't wait to ball her. I wrote the part pretty close to his own personality—he's zany, he's crazy, he gets excited, and he jumps up and down. Harry's always turned on, *and* he's got talent.

LINDA LOVELACE: One reason Harry Reems became a porn superstar—I suppose *the* male superstar of pornographic movies—is that he appears to be fairly intelligent, and he has a good sense of humor.

Harry's strongest appeal to me, however, was the fact that Chuck constantly referred to him as "that asshole," and Harry pretended that Chuck did not exist.

Every time Harry had a chance to speak with me alone, he'd tell me he could make me a star, that I should join him in making bigger and better porno movies. The implication was always there: Harry would take care of everything—once I got myself away from you-know-who.

HARRY REEMS: Linda had nice legs, small tits, but then, you know . . . I can get turned on by a picture of Minnie Mouse. So I got into a sexual thing with her, but Linda and I never had a chance to have sex off the set. But I kept eyeing her, and she kept eyeing me.

LINDA LOVELACE: Chuck didn't like Harry Reems at all. I assumed this was because Harry was young and good-looking. When I saw how upset Chuck was, I decided I would pretend to enjoy it with Harry. When Damiano was through filming, Chuck could hardly wait to get me alone.

"What the fuck do you call that?" he snapped.

"What do you mean?"

"Don't try and tell me you weren't really into that," he said. "You were *too* fucking into it, if you ask me."

"I don't know what you're talking about, Chuck." All innocence. "You're always going around telling me I'm not freaky enough, that I should get into it more. What do you want from me?"

CHUCK TRAYNOR: Linda enjoyed the sex in *Deep Throat*. Oh, yeah, sure—she said she did. She told Harry she did—and everybody else. Linda was not a prude, and I didn't change her. And Harry Reems was an okay guy. I never had any real problems with him.

BILL KELLY: Harry Reems was a very likable sort of a guy for being completely amoral or immoral. He'd joke with you. And I think he was a pretty good comedic actor. He was the only redeeming thing in the entire movie, as opposed to Linda Lovelace, who's got as much acting ability as a lamp.

LINDA LOVELACE: The big scene in the movie is when Harry playing a doctor, discovers that my clitoris has been misplaced and is located in my throat. Although we tried this scene several times, we could never get it quite right. We never had any trouble with the action, only with the lines. We'd do the sex scenes just once, and then we'd hear Damiano say, "That's a take!" But when we so-called actors had a simple line or two to deliver, we'd be there for hours trying to get it right. Harry and I took turns messing up our lines in one big scene until Damiano finally lost his patience. Then the director took the unprecedented step of calling for a rehearsal. Harry and I were told to keep going over the lines until we got them right.

"It's not so bad," Harry was supposed to say, "You should be thankful you have a clitoris at all."

"That's easy for you to say," I replied through teardrops. "How would you feel if your balls were in your ear?"

"Why, then I could hear myself coming!" Harry said.

Well, it was hard not to laugh.

GERARD DAMIANO: When Linda would start to relax and enjoy her work, Chuck was a nuisance. If she enjoyed it *too* much, she knew she was in for a bad time later on. She constantly kept looking over her shoulder, worrying.

So the way I overcame that was to employ Chuck as a production assistant. When we came to a crucial scene, the production manager would send him on an errand of some sort, and Linda could relax.

LINDA LOVELACE: Chuck became Damiano's gofer—he'd go for coffee, beer, lunch, cigarettes, anything that would keep him out of the way. Then Damiano would close the set so that he couldn't return until we completed shooting the scene.

CHUCK TRAYNOR: I was the production manager on a legitimate film with directors and grips, so I took my job real serious. I was a marine and a pilot—you do things by the numbers, you know?

Of course, Linda didn't understand my position. I was in an odd situation because I'm the production manager—but I'm also representing the star.

GERARD DAMIANO: Chuck mystifies me. He's innocuous, he's not a continental lover, and he couldn't get it up on the *Deep Throat* set, but you have to admit the man must have something. It mystified me then, and it still does.

There are very few relationships that I have seen in the porn industry that rival Linda and Chuck's. Most of the girls work on their own. They are their own bosses. They do what they want—because they want to do it. It's very seldom that I see relationships like Linda's.

CHUCK TRAYNOR: My business was creating a superstar. And you don't create a superstar by namby-pambyin', kiss-assin' around, and givin' her roses—it just don't work, you know? You're fightin' a real strong, uphill battle.

So did Linda and I have fights on the set? Yeah, we did have a disagreement, a pretty strong disagreement. She was telling me she didn't wanna do scenes that day, that she had a headache or a backache or ass-ache or somethin'.

HARRY REEMS: When the old mafioso who was putting up the money, Anthony Peraino, Sr., dropped down to Miami to see how things were going, he asked, "Where's da broads?"

Mr. Peraino was accustomed to going first class. He required a change of broads every night. Along with the sheets.

LINDA LOVELACE: Anthony Peraino, Sr. had given his son Butchie the twenty-five thousand dollar bankroll for the movie. That's why it was so important to Butchie that the movie be a success. And it also explains why Butchie was so critical of me. It wasn't just that I might ruin his first film or cost him his twenty-five thousand. I might make him look bad in front of Daddy.

HARRY REEMS: I contacted a local filmmaker who had hookers working for him. They "sunlighted" in loops and stills and cheesecake photography. So we had all the women we needed.

LENNY CAMP: This guy that I used to do stills for called me for *Deep Throat*, and said, "Lenny, you gotta help them."

So I met with the director, Gerry Damiano, and we started badly, right off. I said, "You know, I want five hundred bucks for what you want me to do, and I want two hundred and fifty bucks now."

He said, "Fat chance."

I said, "Yeah, okay. I'll see ya round."

So I get home and there's this phone call, and the guy says, "Hey, come back here; we've got the money for ya."

So I go back and he hands me the money right off the bat. Most of these guys were liars and creeps and tried to get away without paying anybody.

BILL KELLY: Lenny Camp was the still photographer on *Deep Throat*. His name's in the credits. He was a sex maniac. Never met a nastier guy. He used to go around conning people left and right. He rented a big mansion over in Golden Beach. And he had no intention of ever paying any rent—rented it under the name Leonard Shut-eye or something like that. I mean, this guy is notorious. Never been anybody like Lenny.

LENNY CAMP: Carol Conners's muscleman boyfriend called me up and said he had a model for me. They came to my house, and I was gonna shoot Carol in the nude, and she's posing, and she said, "I hate this shit."

She said, "I'd rather fuck ya than take these pictures."

I said, "Well, lock the door."

Was she a good fuck? The greatest.

Within days I got her the role in *Deep Throat*.

CAROL CONNERS (PORN STAR/*GONG SHOW* HOSTESS): It was basically a fluke getting the part playing the nurse in *Deep Throat*. I met a guy in Miami Beach, and he more or less talked me into meeting this director, Gerry Damiano, who asked me to read some lines from the movie. Then somebody asked me to recite "Mary Had a Little Lamb" in the funniest way I could.

GERARD DAMIANO: Was I nervous about using Linda, a girl with small tits? Well, in writing the script I dealt with it by never showing her completely nude. Remember, I had to hide her abdominal scar as well. Sometimes she wore a white slip. I tried to maintain a mystery about her by keeping some part of her anatomy clothed during the film.

LENNY CAMP: Carol Conners was in my car, and we drove over to the Voyager Hotel where they were shooting, and I said, "You got a girl with tits? Linda Lovelace has got no tits!"

CAROL CONNERS: The girl who had been originally cast as the nurse had a run-in with the director, and it just so happened I was the same size and the uniform fit me. They were ready to shoot, and there I was.

CHUCK TRAYNOR: Carol Conners—great boobs. But I don't think they were gonna find a blond with big tits that could do deep throat.

CAROL CONNERS: I didn't even know I was going to be fucking in the film until they had already started filming. I really didn't know what I was supposed to do. At first, I was led to believe I would be an extra, lying in a bikini by the poolside as Linda and one of her girlfriends were talking.

At that time in Miami, not that many people were trying to break into porn films. It was more or less hard to get people to be in an X-rated film.

BUNNY YEAGER: Carol Conners—Chuck Traynor told me about her. I think she was in one of our nudie-cutie movies. I can visualize her sitting on this guy's lap.

She had a bodybuilder boyfriend. He used to come into my studio with her, and he had full control of her. I could never really get to work with Carol because he was always hanging on her, always trying to get the best deal for her.

The girls' boyfriends, I usually found, were only interested in one thing—the money angle. If there was enough money, they'd let them do anything.

I don't know whether I'd go so far as to say that they were pimping them off, but I knew that if the boyfriends didn't think they could make *Playboy,* they weren't interested in posing just for me. But if they could get in *Playboy* and make all that money, then the boyfriend was pushing them.

LENNY CAMP: Chuck Traynor was a pimp. Always. Most of the girls that Chuck had were not models. They were just girls, that's all.

SHARON MITCHELL: Chuck Traynor was really the first of the "suitcase pimps"—you know, boyfriends that become their girlfriends' managers. Now the porn business is filled with them, but when I met Chuck, this was new, and I just knew he had some sort of weird power and control thing—and wanted control over someone's life for the money.

I could just see him taking advantage of a person that really had the same issues that I had—about having to have attention and being a star and all that. No one gets into this business unless you got a real need for attention. I don't think a lot of healthy people are attracted to this industry, ha, ha, ha.

BILL KELLY: I had good informants in the local film processing plants, so I knew every dirty movie that was being made in South Florida.

But I didn't know *Deep Throat* was being made here because they didn't process it down here. They took the raw film and sent it back to New York.

LINDA LOVELACE: Every evening, after we finished shooting for the day, Chuck and I drove the film out to the airport. It was shipped up to Butchie Peraino in New York, where it was processed and studied. And every day Butchie would call Damiano to complain. We could hear only Damiano's side of the conversation—so I would hear Damiano yell that I was *not* too skinny, and I was *not* too flat chested, and I was *not* too amateurish.

GERARD DAMIANO: Linda was pretty naive in the early days. One night, after shooting, we went out for dinner, and Chuck ordered a shrimp cocktail for her, and when it came she was amazed. She didn't know what it was. It intrigued me to think that one of the best cocksuckers in the world could be so impressed over a shrimp cocktail.

LINDA LOVELACE: *Deep Throat* itself took up only twelve days of my life—six before the cameras, another six waiting around for the sun to come out. Probably the most important thing to happen to me was a rechristening.

Gerard Damiano came up with the name Linda Lovelace for the character in his movie. There had been a BB, for Brigitte Bardot, and an MM, for Marilyn Monroe, and now he wanted an LL. In time, I came to dislike the name because of what it stood for. But the truth is this: Linda Boreman and Linda Traynor never managed to get away from Chuck. It took a Linda Lovelace to escape.

CHUCK TRAYNOR: There never was a Linda Lovelace. *I'm* Linda Lovelace. Linda Lovelace got where she got because of my brain, not because of her throat.

SCREW-ed

NEW YORK CITY
1972–1973

BILL KELLY: I turned out to be the dummy in the *Deep Throat* case because I didn't know it was going on originally. I'll take the hit on that one.

I didn't get criticized by the FBI, but after *Deep Throat* became a cause célèbre, some of the bad guys—the other pornographers—kept trying to embarrass me. "Yeah, if you're such a great FBI agent, Kelly, how come you didn't even know the biggest porn film in history was being made within walking distance of your house?"

DAVE FRIEDMAN: *Deep Throat* was like *The Blair Witch Project* of its time.

BILL KELLY: In 1971, an element of the Colombo family of the Mafia named the Perainos came down here to South Florida to make—for less than twenty-five thousand dollars—the first "porno chic" movie, *Deep Throat*. Their eventual gross exceeded 100 million dollars, of which they got to keep at least half.

CHUCK TRAYNOR: I never paid any attention to what the Perainos were working on around the office. So I never knew what else they were involved in. I mean, I just did what I was supposed to do, and that was it. Was I a good soldier? Yeah, ha, ha, ha. I guess so. But I don't ever recall them going, "Shhhhhhh!"

LINDA LOVELACE: Chuck never told me that the Peraino family were members of organized crime. I don't really think Chuck was too aware of it in the beginning. You know, they were just somebody who wanted to do a movie, and he had the product.

I was aware that they were a tightly knit family, ha, ha, ha. I kind of liked the fact that they took care of each other. And I thought Mr. Anthony Peraino, Sr.—Butchie's father—was a wonderful person.

LOS ANGELES TIMES, JUNE 13, 1982: FAMILY BUSINESS: "Anthony Peraino, Sr., a reputed 'made man' (officially initiated) in the Mafia, allegedly a member of the Joseph Colombo crime family. A record of six arrests in New York—including gambling, tax evasion and homicide by auto—but no convictions. In the late 1960s, Anthony Peraino became involved in the burgeoning pornography business. He got in on the ground floor of what turned out to be organized crime's most profitable new business venture since it got into narcotics in the 1950s."

CHUCK TRAYNOR: See, I'm Italian, and my grandfather is Sicilian. He came from Mount Vernon, New York. He used to sell artichokes, and he was sort of involved with the boys. So, to me, the Perainos weren't anything out of the ordinary. I mean, in Vegas, probably half the people you talk to are involved, you know? So I never thought of it as organized crime.

BUTCHIE PERAINO: By the time we finished *Deep Throat* we spent $40,000. I was very worried. How would it be accepted? Before we released it we had a screening. Personal friends, exhibitors, sub-distributors.

Well, I've been to many X-rated movie screenings, but this picture, when she first gives throat, four or five of the men in the audience said, "HURRAY!" and by the end of the sequence there were fifteen guys standing, and they went into a very big applause.

AL GOLDSTEIN (PUBLISHER OF *SCREW* MAGAZINE): The people who owned the World Theater in New York City told me they had a great fuck film they wanted me to see. At first, they thought the title might be *The Sword Swallower,* but they were afraid newspaper advertising departments would refuse to run that title. The alternative, *Deep Throat,* seemed innocuous enough.

GERARD DAMIANO: When we finished that film, the Perainos objected to the title. "No one will understand it! It's not catchy enough!"

"Don't worry," I told them, "*Deep Throat* will become a household word."

AL GOLDSTEIN: I went to review the film, and I was suddenly confronted with Linda Lovelace on-screen. She was lovely, thin, young, and fresh. Most of the women in fuck films have pimples on their asses or are uncommonly fat. Because I have a weight problem, I like very thin women. I mean, I like them emaciated.

Deep Throat was cute; it moved along. It had music. It had wit. But mostly it had Linda in it as a brilliant cocksucker.

NORA EPHRON (WRITER): I have seen a lot of stag films in my life—well, that's not true; I've seen about five or six—and although most of them were raunchy, a few were sweet and innocent and actually erotic. *Deep Throat*, on the other hand, is one of the most unpleasant, disturbing films I have ever seen—its not just antifemale, but antisexual as well.

AL GOLDSTEIN: While I was writing my review, I couldn't forget the cum pouring out of the corner of Linda's mouth as she sucked Harry Reems's cock. I got so hung on that film I got eleven hard-ons. I gave *Deep Throat* a hundred—the maximum score on the Peter-Meter, our yardstick service to readers on the erotic content of movies.

BUTCHIE PERAINO: *Screw* magazine reviewed it a week before it opened and said it was the best porn film ever made. At that point we knew we had a hit on our hands.

AL GOLDSTEIN: Before my review, the film opened and closed in California in four days. After my review, it quickly became a huge hit in New York, breaking house records.

DAVE FRIEDMAN: Look, I'm not putting Al Goldstein down. I like Al very much. But I don't think it was his review of *Deep Throat* that made the movie so successful.

When the picture first came out, it was just another porno. I was one of the early people to play it—in Portland—and it was just another week. Wasn't anything to write home about. Vince Miranda opened the picture in Los Angles at one of the Pussycat Theaters, and it did very ordinary business, nothing spectacular.

Okay, so it opens in New York City, and it was doing so-so business. And then Mayor Lindsay decides to crack down on pornography, and he confiscates the print. And of course the bust became big front-page news in all of the New York dailies: "MAYOR CRACKS DOWN ON DEEP THROAT."

Well, right away, the national media gets on to it.

BILL KELLY: *Deep Throat* opened simultaneously in three hundred theaters around the United States in 1972. I went to the first showing on Miami Beach at the Sheraton Theater with Jack Roberts from the *Miami News*. The line went all the way around the side of the theater and halfway down the next block.

Roberts wrote it up as a piece of garbage in the *News,* but the *Miami Herald* gave that piece of 59 minutes of filmed oral copulation about five million dollars' worth of free advertising. So did almost every other liberal newspaper in the country.

DAVE FRIEDMAN: Finally, Sam Lake, who was running the World Theater at the time, got an injunction, and he reopened the picture, and they were lined up around the block. Because people who had never dreamed of going to see a porno movie before suddenly came out in droves. People were coming to the theater in limousines. It became de rigueur, you know—you had to see *Deep Throat.*

And out of that picture came a new phrase in the American lexicon: "porno chic."

Naturally, Al Goldstein would take the credit for it, but if Mayor Lindsay had just let the picture alone, it would've been just another porno picture that came and went.

JOHN WATERS: *Deep Throat* had this great advertising campaign—you could never get away with this now, but even the *New York Times* ran the ad: "IF YOU LIKE HEAD, YOU'LL LOVE THROAT."

GERARD DAMIANO: For the first time, people weren't embarrassed to be seen by their friends leaving a theater showing a pornographic film. In fact, in certain circles and in certain cities, it became almost a necessity to see the film in order to keep up your social status.

Businessmen were taking their clients, husbands were taking their wives, girls were taking their boyfriends. It was a film whose time had come.

HARRY REEMS: They all came. Mike Nichols and Truman Capote. Ed McMahon, Johnny Carson's sidekick, came with six guys and a case of beer and stood out front afterward—trying to get passersby to come in.

CHUCK TRAYNOR: When Johnny Carson went to see *Deep Throat,* then it became chic.

BUNNY YEAGER: Movie stars would never admit to seeing pornography before *Deep Throat.*

SAMMY DAVIS JR.: *Deep Throat* had just been released and was playing at the Pussycat Theater in Santa Monica. People were talking about it; they wanted to see it, but the Pussycat was not a place you went to. And a porn film like *Deep Throat* was not something you could order from the studios.

I told my wife, Altovise, "Let's rent the Pussycat for a few hours one night, have it cleaned up, keep the popcorn stand open, and invite all these straight people here to go see *Deep Throat.* It would be marvelously decadent to have them sitting there seeing the big thing on the screen and then take them to the Bistro for a foie gras and Chateau Margaux kind of supper."

We invited Suzanne Pleshette and Tommy Gallagher, the Berles, Dick and Dolly Martin, Steve and Edie, Shirley MacLaine—people who would never go to the Pussycat. I took them over in limos, which was safer than leaving your expensive paint job parked in that neighborhood.

HARRY REEMS: Even former vice president Spiro Agnew had a private screening at Frank Sinatra's place in Palm Springs.

CHUCK TRAYNOR: After we got the movie finished, they all went back to New York, and we didn't hear anything about it for a while. And then all of a sudden a phone call came from the Perainos, saying they were gonna fly us up—first class—to New York. Well, you know, being a pilot and all, I said, "They don't fly you first class unless something's going on here."

LINDA LOVELACE: Butchie Peraino said he would pay all travel expenses if we would come up to New York and be interviewed.

When we saw Butchie, suddenly it was, "You're looking well, Linda," and "How's life been treating you, Linda?" This was the same man who wanted me fired off the set because I was "ruining" his movie.

BUTCHIE PERAINO: *Deep Throat* opened up against *Cabaret* and the sequel to *Shaft*—and we outgrossed them both.

CHUCK TRAYNOR: When we got to New York, the Perainos were trying to downplay it. The movie had opened, and suddenly Linda was a big star. She just hadn't appeared anyplace yet, you know? And they didn't wanna tell her that, or tell me, because they figured it's gonna cost 'em more money—which it did.

LINDA LOVELACE: Neither Chuck nor I could imagine why any newspaper would want to interview someone who had been in a hard-core porno movie. But neither of us knew that *Deep Throat* was being treated as something more than a routine dirty movie.

Our first official interview was with *Screw*.

AL GOLDSTEIN: We met in a small, cold, seventeen-dollar-a-night hotel room, and it was the most difficult interview I ever conducted because Linda is really inarticulate. Chuck Traynor did most of the talking. After the interview, I said, "Listen, I'd like you to suck my cock."

I figured Linda was just a hooker anyway, so I wasn't embarrassed. She said fine, Chuck said, "Okay," and she blew me.

LINDA LOVELACE: We had been told that since *Screw* was largely responsible for *Deep Throat*'s success, we were to be very cooperative. Whatever *Screw* wanted, *Screw* was to get.

AL GOLDSTEIN: Here I was with the world's greatest cocksucker, and yet it was a lonely experience. I had never fucked a woman in the mouth like that before. It seemed so hostile. I felt very alienated.

I was sweating. She was hot. But it was false because it was not spontaneous. I have an average-sized cock of about seven inches, and the fact that it disappeared down her throat interfered with my concentration.

I kept thinking: "Am I *that* small? Is she *that* good? Should I come now?"

My attention kept wandering. She was sitting on my face in a 69 position, and as I was eating her, I knew I wasn't bringing her any pleasure. I was feeling very selfish, so I asked, "You don't really come this way, do you?"

She said, "Yeah, I come."

LINDA LOVELACE: Goldstein was a pig, but I could numb myself to that experience. It was harder to numb myself to this new phenomenon—being interviewed.

AL GOLDSTEIN: When it finally dawned on me that this was a nonmonetary gift from the distributors for my review, I was able to come in a detached sort of way. But it was like working. I felt like a hooker faking orgasm with a john. I left there feeling sad.

But my partner, Jim Buckley, photographed this summit meeting. I ran the photos of her sucking my cock and my description of it. It was a paradigm of personal journalism.

FRED BIERSDORF (PERAINO FILM DISTRIBUTOR): You wouldn't believe the calls Butchie Peraino was getting from people who wanted a print of the movie. You know, prominent people, like government officials. And whenever somebody's secretary would call for them, Butchie would get on the phone and say, "Hey, if he wants a print, he can damn well call me himself."

CHUCK TRAYNOR: The first time I realized *Deep Throat* was a success was when one of the secretaries in the Perainos' office said to me, "Jesus Christ, the fuckin' phone's ringing off the hook with people trying to get in touch with you."

All I could say was, "Huh?"

She said, "Yeah, *Playboy*'s trying to get in touch with you; *Esquire*'s trying to get you. California's been calling all day."

Later I found out that these people were telling everybody that Linda's unavailable, she's got a husband that's a fanatic, and you can't talk to her. They wanted to keep her under wraps, you know?

LINDA LOVELACE: My father went to see the movie—because he wanted to see if it was really me. And he came back and said, "Yup, it's her, but it's some kind of trick." Then he went and sat down on the couch with his peanuts and beer and watched *Wild Kingdom.*

AL GOLDSTEIN: After the Lovelace story appeared, I began running anything I could find about Linda. She was my Marilyn Monroe. If I were a faggot, she would have been my Judy Garland.

LINDA LOVELACE: The key to it was that it was a comedy—that's what made *Deep Throat* a success.

FRED LINCOLN: Linda thought they liked her *acting*! Jesus Christ, instead of being a masochist, she was a fucking idiot!

Don't Count the Money, Weigh It

NEW YORK CITY/MIAMI
1972–1973

BILL KELLY: After *Deep Throat* was released, I had an informant in the Perainos' office in Wilton Manors, Florida—in their lawyer's office—and he calls me and says, "You are not gonna believe this, Kelly. We got so much damn money in the main office up here, we can't move around. The money is getting in the way. We got it in garbage bags stacked up in here. We don't even count it anymore."

CHUCK TRAYNOR: All my life, people asked me about the Perainos: "How'd you get along with those people?"

I said, "It was very simple. We shook hands. I never signed any contracts. I kept my word. They kept their word."

They said, "Well, why didn't Linda make a fortune on *Deep Throat*?"

I said, "Very simple: because we were walking up and down Forty-second Street making eight-millimeter movies, and they brought us in, they paid her $500, and a couple hundred dollars a day and all that, and they had no idea *Deep Throat* was gonna be <u>Deep</u> <u>Throat</u>.

If you're gonna pay me ten dollars to dig a hole in the backyard, and I take the ten dollars and dig the hole and hit gold, then am I supposed to get the gold mine?

I mean, you told me to dig the hole, and you gave me the ten dollars. So good luck, you know? That's the way I felt about the movie. But Linda was pissed.

BILL KELLY: I said to my informant, "What do you mean, you don't count it? What do you do with it?"

He said, "We weigh it."

CHUCK BERNSTENE (ACCOUNTANT) [FBI WIRETAP]: "The money was coming in like, you have no idea—we used to walk out with stacks, you know, from the theaters. Maybe some weeks it was a hundred and fifty thousand—but we'd have to take fifteen G's off the top to pay the checkers—but I was getting like a G-note a week."

BILL KELLY: The checker would go up to the owner of the theater and say, "Five grand now, or else."

The owners of the theater would say, "What do you mean, or else?"

The checker would say, "You don't pay me, you'll find out what else."

I remember about maybe four "or else's." A couple of them only had to do with the Perainos sending somebody out to take the film off the projector and giving it to a competitor across town—or burning down the theater.

FRED BIERSDORF: I was like a kid in Disneyland. Everything was strictly cash. I mean, if somebody wanted a mink coat they'd just walk into Bonwit Teller and plop down twenty thousand dollars. In a meeting one day, I asked Uncle Joe [Joseph Peraino, Sr.], "How much money has *Deep Throat* brought in?"

He didn't say a word, and damn, ten minutes later they asked me to come out of the room, and they asked, "Hey, what do you want to know for?"

I said I was sorry I brought it up.

BILL KELLY: I said to my informant, "Well, why the hell don't you take the money to the bank?"

He said, "Well, da boys," meaning the Perainos, "saw you sitting out in the church parking lot across the street, and they're not afraid of you 'cause they know the FBI can't do anything to them—except put them in jail. But you had another guy with you, and they think the other guy is an IRS agent. And they're afraid of the IRS because they'll take the damn money away from 'em. And they don't wanna lose that money, so they're not gonna move it. They're gonna keep it here under guard."

NEW YORK TIMES, OCTOBER 12, 1975: ORGANIZED CRIME REAPS HUGE PROFITS FROM DEALING IN PORNOGRAPHIC FILMS: "*Deep Throat* was made by an organization called Gerard Damiano Productions, owned originally by Louis Peraino, son of Anthony Peraino, and Gerard Damiano, who directed the film.

"When the film was released and began to make money, Louis (Butchie) Peraino bought out the interests of Gerard Damiano for $25,000.

"When a reporter remarked to Mr. Damiano that he seemed to have received unfavorable terms in the deal, Mr. Damiano replied, 'I can't talk about it.' When the reporter persisted, Mr. Damiano said, 'You want me to get both my legs broken?'"

BILL KELLY: Gerard Damiano went to one of the Perainos and asked for more money—and they told him, "Gerry, the only thing you're gonna get in addition to what you already got is two broken kneecaps." So Damiano backed off in a hurry.

FRED LINCOLN: You have to understand the way I feel about things, all right? When I was in Wes Craven's *The Last House on the Left,* I made nine hundred bucks. I was the bad guy; the guy who gets his dick bit off in the end.

Okay, so the movie made $55 million. They didn't owe me a penny of that money because we made a deal. They said to me, "It's gonna take a week to do this. We can pay you nine hundred dollars, all right?"

Now, I could've said, "I want nine hundred bucks and forty percent of the gross." Okay? But I didn't say that. I said, "Okay, it's a deal," and I signed a contract.

So Gerry Damiano also felt bad because *Deep Throat* made $55 million, and he didn't get $20 million. But the Perainos paid Gerry Damiano. I mean, that's what Hollywood people do—they go and do an independent movie and pay everyone nine hundred bucks a week, and when the movie makes a hundred million, they don't turn around and say, "Hey, let's give you ten percent."

FRED BIERSDORF: Later Uncle Joe took me to lunch and ordered me a whole lobster. I was so nervous there was no way I could eat. You know, Uncle Joe is about as big as that door over there. And he put his arm around me and said, "Fred, you asked that question this morning. Well, Butchie's got eight kids, and Joe [Butchie's brother, "Joe the Whale"] has kids, and their kids and their grandkids have nothing to worry about the rest of their lives. Does that tell you how much the movie brought in?"

PHIL SMITH (MIAMI FBI ORGANIZED CRIME SQUAD SUPERVISOR): Bill Kelly was running around, licking his chops, saying, "We're finally going to get legitimate! We're finally gonna show once and for all that pornography is controlled by organized crime!"

Because nobody in the bureau was really excited about pornography. The O.C. connection—the organized crime connection—was what they were looking for . . . and Kelly finally found it.

BILL KELLY: I'll tell you something that you've never heard before: One reason that *Deep Throat* had the success that it did and launched the whole porno chic movement, was that J. Edgar Hoover died in 1972, the same year the movie came out.

Had he lived and been in full possession of his faculties, I think Hoover would've gone berserk with the success of *Deep Throat*. I mean he would've had us out kickin' tail in every jurisdiction where it was presented. J. Edgar Hoover would not have permitted *Deep Throat* to have gotten the jump on law enforcement that it did.

And I believe, had Hoover lived, we would not be in the same terrible condition nationally that we are—as far as obscenity is concerned.

Part 2:
porno-chic
1973–1976

The Mitchell Brothers Present

the all-American girl

MARILYN CHAMBERS

Behind the Green Door

adults only

...thers film group/san francisco

Left page: *clockwise from top left:* Marilyn Chambers, Reuben "Nebeur" Sturman, Robert "DiBe" DiBernardo, Marilyn Chambers on Ivory Snow box.

Right page: *clockwise from top left:* Jim and Artie Mitchell, poster for the Mitchell brothers' *Behind the Green Door*, John Holmes, Annette Haven, Al Goldstein.

To Bowl or Not to Bowl?

SAN FRANCISCO
1973

MARILYN CHAMBERS (PORN STAR): When *The Owl and the Pussycat* was finished, Ray Stark asked me if I wanted to go out to California and go to some of the premieres. I said, "Yeah!"

So here I was—this little hippie chick who had always wanted to go to California—staying in a suite at the Beverly Wilshire. I had no clothes to wear, but it didn't matter because I never made it to the premiere.

JIM MITCHELL (PORN PRODUCER/DIRECTOR): I was studying political science at San Francisco State. I was thinking of going to law school, but I started taking a couple of classes in television and filmmaking. That's when I got the idea—why not make a couple of eight-millimeter porn films and make some money on the side?

That's how I got into sixteen-millimeter. My roommate bought a used movie camera, and we got together with a couple of guys who were into TV, and then it was just a question of how to get our sixteen-millimeter loops reduced to eight-millimeter, making copies, finding out about the market, and things like that.

Actually, there was no market—or, I should say, there was only an under-the-counter market. To get a better feel of what was going on in the business, I took a job at the Roxie Theater, which was running black-and-white beaver films.

MARILYN CHAMBERS: Why didn't I go to the premiere in Los Angeles? Well, I met Jim Brown, the ex-football player, at this club the Candy Store, and he asked me if he could take me to the premiere.

I said, "I guess so."

Well, he's totally against drugs and all that stuff. So, I'm waiting for him to come pick me up in my hotel room—and I'm smoking a joint.

When he came to get me, he said, "You've been smoking pot!"

I said "What? I am *not!*"

JIM MITCHELL: Around the time I was working at the Roxie my brother Art got out of the army, and he had some money saved up. All my money was tied up in the eight-millimeter things; I wouldn't have been able to expand without some additional finance. So we formed a partnership and decided to make some beaver films.

MARILYN CHAMBERS: We were late to the premiere, so we couldn't get in. We went to his house instead. I was, like, there for three days. It was scary because he's a big tough guy. I liked him—of course I did. That was the exciting part of it. But after three days, I was glad to get out of there, you know, in one piece.

ARTIE MITCHELL (PORN PRODUCER/DIRECTOR): We borrowed an eight-millimeter camera, went to the beach, and found this girl there running up and down the beach.

I asked, "How about taking your blouse off?"

And she did it. This was in the late 1960s—everybody wanted to do that. It was like the "Age of Aquarius" here. And it was an easy way to make twenty-five bucks—take your clothes off, and do a beaver movie.

C. J. LAING (PORN STAR): I was from New York, so I was confused in San Francisco. When you're twenty and you're hungry and the rent's due, you're really just an idealistic youth; you're not a whore.

Even though you are.

So I started working North Beach, started hustling, rolling drunks. They'd come into the Nude Encounter, a massage parlor where I was working. There was "nude wrestling" and "nude encounter," you know, in different rooms. I don't know if there could be actual physical contact, but they could look at you naked. Maybe there were hand jobs—you know, look at my titties, and get a hand job.

While they were doing that, I was lifting money out of their wallets. Oh yeah, I don't know how much I could make because I was just so sloppy. I guess I didn't have a sense of pride in my work.

JIM MITCHELL: Art and I would make a beaver film for, say, a hundred bucks. You'd pay a girl twenty-five dollars, buy forty worth of film, and still have thirty-five for processing and incidentals. When you had it done, and if it was any good at all, you could easily get two hundred bucks, so that was pretty nice.

We didn't really know much about filmmaking, but there wasn't a lot of product around.

C. J. LAING: But whatever I was making was never enough because I needed money to go to Texas to fuck Sam Cutler, the road manager of the Grateful Dead. He was the English guy responsible for hiring the Hell's Angels at Altamont.

I was Sam's little slut. I wanted the glamour; I wanted to be somebody. I wanted to belong to a rock group.

But I needed Quaaludes and Clark bars to give head.

JIM MITCHELL: We started off shooting single beavers. Then it went to two girls. Then it went to three girls.

C. J. LAING: One night I was in my communal sleeping room, at a house owned by the "Angels of Light" cult, and this gorgeous girl Tina came home with a hundred dollars.

I said, "Where'd you get it?"

She said, "The Mitchell brothers."

So I did one film for the Mitchell brothers. Period. One little loop, part of this series of films called *Juke Joint*. I do recall giving head and everybody going, "*Oh!*"

That's how I got the money to go to Texas to fuck Sam Cutler.

ARTIE MITCHELL: Our movies have always been dirty hard-core. That was the idea: always to come up with a better fuck film.

MARILYN CHAMBERS: After Los Angeles, I went to the premiere in San Francisco. I was staying in this suite at the Fairmont Hotel—I mean God, Columbia Pictures didn't spare any expense. And I fell madly in love with San Francisco, and I wanted to stay.

In New York I had met this guy from the band It's a Beautiful Day, and they had this ranch up in Northern California wine country. So I went up there for a couple days and messed around with them, went to some of their concerts, and took acid. It was really fun.

Then I went back to New York, and I was really depressed because I couldn't get any jobs. The new Ivory Snow box hadn't come out yet. So I packed all my stuff and drove out to San Francisco in a U-Haul with some guys from Connecticut.

JIM MITCHELL: We made a couple of movies for another guy, and he didn't even get us passes to the movie or something. So we said, "If we're gonna do this, we might as well get a theater."

We found this building and built it up: the O'Farrell Theater. Then we *really* started making movies.

JACK BOULWARE (WRITER): When they were making those eight-millimeter loops, there was pornography being advertised in all the newspapers and in some cases being *written up* in them. The police were going nuts trying to figure out a way to regulate this.

Every week they would send police officers to the Mitchell brothers' theater to watch the films in the dark and scribble notes on the plot lines—what little plot lines there were. It got to the point where they would just call the theater and say, "Can you come down? We have to arrest you again."

JIM MITCHELL: We had more or less always known what was coming. We also had, you know, a layman's interest in pornography as students, as everyone else had at the time. So we decided if we were getting arrested for simulated beaver, why not go ahead and run hard-core? That's what people wanted to see. So soon we realized we needed to make a big, huge feature film to really sort of take it to another level.

MARILYN CHAMBERS: When I moved to San Francisco, I met this guy playing bagpipes in the street. I gave him some money, ha, ha, ha. And I kept giving him money. That turned out to be my first husband, ha, ha, ha. Boy, I know how to pick 'em, don't I? Jesus.

We wound up living together in this big, huge Victorian house, which was like a commune. He played bagpipes for money on the street. I was doing a whole bunch of odd jobs: hostess in a health food restaurant, topless, bottomless dancer—you name it, I was doing it, just to get by.

JIM MITCHELL: We had a want ad in the *San Francisco Chronicle* that said, "Mitchell brothers casting for feature length film." We didn't get too many responses—just five or six hundred. And believe it or not, Marilyn Chambers is one that came through the door.

MARILYN CHAMBERS: One day I read an ad in the newspaper that said, "Now casting for a major motion picture."

So I called up, and they said, "Oh, we finished casting."

I said, "Oh, no, you have to wait! I'm coming down there right now! Please . . ."

They said, "All right, come down."

So I went to Stage A, on Tennessee Street, in the warehouse district.

ARTIE MITCHELL: When I first read the story of *Behind the Green Door*, it was a short story that was being handed around underground, about twenty typed pages. People read it in fraternity houses and troop ships, those kinds of places. I read it in a college cafeteria seven or eight years before, not knowing then I'd even be making erotic movies.

But it stuck in my mind, and Jim and I thought of it, and we said this would make a good script. So we got it, and we adapted it.

MARILYN CHAMBERS: I walked in, and there are all these people filling out these green forms. On the questionnaire it got to the point where they asked me if I wanted a "balling or non-balling role."

I didn't understand what they meant. I thought it was a misspelling for "bowling." I wasn't a very good bowler.

Then I'm thinking, "Wait a minute—they mean *fucking*? Oh, no. Absolutely not. I may be naughty, but I'm not *that* naughty."

I got up and started to leave—the building was this big warehouse-stage kind of thing, with a long stairway going up to some offices on top, and that's where Art and Jim Mitchell were standing. I had no idea who they were, but they were looking down at me.

ARTIE MITCHELL: I called to her, "Hey! You! By the door! Come on up here. . . . Where the hell are you going? What's the matter? At least come up, and talk to us? You don't have to take off your clothes to *talk* to us . . ."

MARILYN CHAMBERS: Art had on this sweater vest and button-down shirt, and nobody in California wore those clothes. But I'm from the East Coast, so I was used to that preppy shit. It was totally Antioch! I felt comfortable with them. They were very friendly, very cool, very San Francisco, and very hip.

JIM MITCHELL: I told her, "You just happen to be who we're looking for. Marilyn, you're the girl next door. You're the face every guy dreams of shoving his cock into. But he never does because he can't find you! You're fresh air and apple pie."

ARTIE MITCHELL: I said, "Listen, you're classy, and this is going to be one classy film. We're putting everything we have into it. Let us just explain the concept, tell you the story. The whole thing is a fantasy."

MARILYN CHAMBERS: I had done a film called *Together* with Sean Cunningham—it was supposed to be a documentary—and I was topless in that, and it didn't bother me.

But actual *sex*? The only kind of sex I'd seen in movies were "smokers"—what they used to call stag films—the kind with the guys wearing black socks and sunglasses. *Not* very sexy.

JIM MITCHELL: I said, "We've been pretty successful making hard-core films. This film here is our shot at breaking through to a mainstream audience. So it's not like we're asking you to star in a fuck film. This is going to be a *real* movie about *real* sex."

MARILYN CHAMBERS: I didn't think I'd be able to fuck on camera; I'd thought I'd break out into a rash or go crazy. But I liked their approach. They didn't say, "Well, honey, you gotta screw me first." It was, "Here, smoke a joint," you know?

ARTIE MITCHELL: That just isn't part of the test. That's more like what goes down in Hollywood. Making fuck movies is different somehow; there's no casting couch—it's almost too obvious a thing to do.

MARILYN CHAMBERS: There was no script. There was a story, about a woman who's kidnapped and taken to this club. They showed me these pieces of yellowed paper that were worn from being passed around during the war. I guess one guy wrote his fantasy down, then passed it on to the next guy. That's how *Behind the Green Door* came to be.

And I thought, "God, this might be cool. Maybe I can use it as a stepping stone to legitimate movies."

ARTIE MITCHELL: *Behind the Green Door* was the first film we'd put real money into and took more time with to get up to the point where it was even in a different class.

We'd taken one month to make one previous feature, but we were learning about cinematography at that point, not thinking we were immediately going to make a masterpiece. We had to learn the skills.

See, there was no precedent to go by, except the old black-and-white stag films. That's probably why so many of the early porn films looked like that. People didn't know what to do, you know? "Okay, we're going to make an erotic movie—uh, what do we do?"

MARILYN CHAMBERS: Nobody was doing full-length features. So I said to the Mitchell brothers, "You know, if I do this, I want this amount of money, and I want a percentage of the film."

They said, "Don't call us; we'll call you."

I said, "Okay, fine." *Phew!* So I went home—and then I got a call, like, an hour later. The Mitchell brothers said, "Okay, we've got the contracts ready. We'll be right over."

They called my bluff, so I had to do it, ha, ha, ha.

Size Matters

LOS ANGELES
1969–1973

AL GOLDSTEIN: John Holmes was the biggest cock in the business. He always had mythic stature to me. He was almost in the world of Greek Gods. He walked among us with that massive tool, banging on the floor like some huge dinosaur.

So when I met him, I figured I'd meet a guy who had paradise regained, who had everything. Instead I met a sociopath and a liar. In effect, every manifestation of this man's life was a lie, a distortion, duplicity, a quagmire of deceit.

The one truth was he had a big dick.

SHARON HOLMES (JOHN HOLMES'S FIRST WIFE): I came home from work one evening and found John measuring himself in the bathroom. This was about three or four years after we'd been married.

I thought this was a little strange but okay. So I started dinner, and John came in and said, "I think I've found what I want to do."

That's when he said, "I want to do porno."

I said, "Movies?"

He said, "Wherever it will take me."

I was appalled. I'm sorry; I was appalled. It didn't sound like something one would want to make one's life's work. But what do you say?

BILL AMERSON (PORN PRODUCER/JOHN HOLMES'S BUSINESS PARTNER): I first met John in 1969 while casting for some still-photo porn magazine stuff at the Crossroads of the World on Sunset Boulevard.

We had an open casting call. It was toward the end of the day and in walked this really skinny kid with an Afro haircut. He didn't look like the type we could use.

My partner said, "Have him go in the back room, take off his clothes, take a Poloroid, and then say, 'Thank you very much'—and that's the end of that."

So we went into the back room.

John undressed.

He turned around. I looked at it and said, *"You're going to be a star!"*

SHARON HOLMES: John out and out told me, "This is probably my only shot at being famous for something. I really want to do this."

I said, "Are you asking for permission?"

John said, "No, I'm going to do this."

It took me a while to react because I didn't believe I was hearing this. I told him I wasn't particularly happy about it because it was one step up from, or one step below, prostitution. So I thought, "Maybe this is a passing fantasy—who knows . . ."

BOB CHINN (PORN DIRECTOR): I'd just come out of UCLA film school and started making porn films for a budget of about seven hundred and fifty dollars. One day this scruffy, bushy-haired guy came up to the office looking for a job as a grip or a gaffer. He had this big Afro-looking hairdo.

I told him, "We don't have any openings for grips or gaffers."

Then he said, "Well, I'm really an actor. My name is John Holmes."

That sort of rang a bell because one of the actresses I knew had mentioned this guy—told me about his attributes. So I said, "Okay, so you're John Holmes. What have you done? Show me your credentials."

And then he showed me his credentials.

BILL AMERSON: It was thirteen-and-a-half inches long. I know because John measured it many times for many people who didn't believe him. And they'd ask him how thick it was, and he'd say, "Grab my wrist."

But I didn't think he would stay in the porn business very long because he was very nervous. He was an awkward kid. He was like a fish out of water. He just didn't seem to fit.

SHARON HOLMES: When we were first married, John was very quiet and not very sophisticated—he was a country boy. And believe it or not, he wasn't comfortable in large groups. It was hard to get him to agree to go to a Christmas party. I think he was very aware of the fact that he was not as educated as he wished he could be. And I think that made him self-conscious around my nursing school friends.

So even though I was only a year older than he was, as far as education went, I was ten years older because John never really went beyond the ninth grade. He was very, very possessive of me and pretty dependent on me to pay the bills and that sort of thing. I mean, I didn't realize until after we had been married a year that he had never filed a tax return.

BOB CHINN: After he showed us his credentials, my partner and I sat down and said, "We can make a film with this guy."

My partner said, "God, what a wad that guy has."

I said, "Let's call him 'Johnny Wadd,' make it a private detective thing."

We wrote the first script on the back of an envelope and shot it two days later. I hired John Holmes to play Johnny Wadd at the unheard of price of seventy-five dollars a day; at the time we were paying actors only fifty.

SHARON HOLMES: John had always told me, "Somehow in my life, I'm going to be a millionaire. I am not going to be the failure my father was and my mother is." He really felt they had nothing to show for all the years they had lived on the planet. That's why he decided to go into porno—he thought it was his instant ticket to fame and fortune. I was speechless.

John was very immature when we got married. I first met him in 1964 when he was involved with a fellow nursing student friend of mine, and they came over to have dinner. When he broke up with her about two months later, John started bringing me flowers and asking me to go out with him.

John was very, very sweet. He always had an arm around me, we were always holding hands, and things just gradually evolved into a real tight relationship. And we were married five months later.

BOB CHINN: New York was our biggest market, and within two weeks of us sending the film out, our distributor in New York called and said they wanted more films with Johnny Wadd.

Then I called John, hired him, and we shot *Flesh of the Lotus*. It took one day to shoot the film, we developed it the same night, and then we cut the original negative. It was out on the market within a few days. Within a week after it was shot, it was playing the theaters.

BILL AMERSON: At first John didn't really like the name Johnny Wadd, but it went over big, and John became a star behind that name. We'd run into people, and they'd call out, "Hey, Johnny Wadd!"

I'm not sure why people were so fascinated by the size of his penis. I just know they were. And it was a great marketing tool, if you will.

SHARON HOLMES: It wasn't until our wedding night that I found out about his large appendage. Mmm-hmm. He hadn't warned me about it. And I was probably thinking, "Oh dear," because I think I was the last virgin left—certainly in California.

But it was no big deal for me because John was a great lover. Very, very thoughtful and very, very gentle. He wasn't a maniac. Not at all.

BILL AMERSON: The Johnny Wadd series was the start of the star system in the adult film industry. It became famous throughout the world.

SHARON HOLMES: At first, I think John was probably a bit embarrassed by his size because he knew he was different, but I don't think he knew just *how* different. I can't imagine why not because he was in the service, he was familiar with whorehouses in Europe, and had sex with married women. He had a lot of sexual experience. But I don't think John realized how terribly unique he was until he got into porno.

AL GOLDSTEIN: I was always fascinated with John Holmes because he had everything I didn't have. He was hung like a horse; I'm hung like a squirrel. He had what all the guys dream about. We're all size queens. We want to have that big cock.

I'm not gay, but I thought one day I'd love to suck that cock. Feel that power. Transcend my limit in size and swallow his virility in the same way some African tribes cannibalize their enemy. I could see blowing him and swallowing his sperm—and being better for it.

BOB VOSSE (PORN PRODUCER): I'll give John credit; he was the easiest to work with from the girl's point of view because he was extremely gentle. He was nice to the girl, he gave her presents—that he probably stole the day before—but she would love him for it. I never had one girl complain or refuse to work with him again.

In fact most of them asked, "Can I work with John Holmes again?"

ANNETTE HAVEN (PORN STAR): I ended up doing my first film with John Holmes, but he wasn't a name to me. He was just the star of the film or really his dick was. That's basically what sold John.

But I was impressed with him because he had the wit and the extremely good mind to set up the arrangements so that Lesllie Bovee and I were sharing a bedroom that adjoined his suite.

So I ended up exploring John's little suite area, and it was really interesting. His entire bathroom was one big line of vitamin bottles—about forty-five bottles—because he was into health food. And then he showed Lesllie and I our room, and then gave me some really excellent head. Got me off, too.

I'm a jawbreaker, a serious jawbreaker, particularly at that time. You give me head for three or four hours, so what? But John got me off in fifteen or twenty minutes.

BOB VOSSE: Some of the girls John would work with would fall in love with him.

I'd tell John, "Do you remember that cute little girl you worked with on that film?"

He'd say, "I didn't like her."

I'd say, "But she keeps calling; she wants to see you."

He'd say, "No, I don't want to see her."

He really had no interest in them. After one time, that was it. Except if he was fresh, and he'd slept the night before, then he would do a good job. Sometimes he would do two groups in a day.

ANNETTE HAVEN: After John got me off, he didn't want to fuck me, which was even better. He went and fucked Lesllie Bovee, which was perfect. So John made a very big hit with me.

And when he got on the set, he did his thing, didn't try to make a romance out of it. He was a professional. Got it up, got it off, and got the hell out of your hair.

BOB VOSSE: John wouldn't go to sleep and wake up fresh and ready to work. Instead he'd pick up one of the little girls he hadn't worked with yet—or maybe it was the girl he was going to work with the next day or some girl who was scheduled to work with some other guy—and talk them into coming up to his room that night. Of course he'd sleep with them, then they'd go to the set to shoot, and he'd have no interest in them, didn't want to work with them.

So that was part of my job—find enough girls to feed the monster.

BUNNY BLEU (PORN STAR): John and I went on a promotional tour in Texas signing autographs in adult bookstores, and it was really wild—because women would line up around the block. They would actually piss their pants they were so excited to meet him.

One lady actually went home, changed, cleaned up, came back, and said, "I want another autograph." That takes a lot of balls. I don't think after peeing in my pants from meeting somebody, I would come back and see them again.

Ebony and Ivory Snow

SAN FRANCISCO
1973

JOHNNY KEYES (PORN STAR): I was in San Francisco, and a bunch of kids said, "Hey, listen, they have an audition for this movie, right? Let's go check it out."

So we go down—and it was for *Behind the Green Door*. I mean, I was in a nude scene in *Hair,* but the Mitchell brothers asked, like, "Would you do X-rated?"

I said, "Ah, man. Fuck this. I don't do no X-rated movie shit. I'm in theater. I'm a thespian, you know?"

But the Mitchell brothers had seen me in *Hair*. They called me back and said, "Listen, man, you should come play this part. There's gonna be a lot of money, and you're gonna be on a trapeze, and this chick's gonna suck your dick . . ."

MARILYN CHAMBERS: I was still pretty nervous. The black-and-white sex thing—I knew this was a very big taboo, as it still is in our country. And I thought, "Now my father's really going to kill me!" Ha, ha, ha!

JOHNNY KEYES: I couldn't do the part of the guy on the trapeze—I think I missed the date—so Jim and Artie said, "Well, you're gonna be the guy behind the green door, and you're gonna make love to this girl, Marilyn Chambers."

And then they were like, "Listen here. You take her out, and get to know her."

So I took her to a restaurant called the Triton right on the water in Sausalito. Then I took her home, and we fucked for a couple of days. She was, just—well, she was impressed.

MARILYN CHAMBERS: When I saw Johnny Keyes's thing, I went, "Oh, shit! Oh my God! I'm not sure if I can get this inside of me."

JOHNNY KEYES: In those days it was taboo for black men to fuck white women, but I had been fucking white women for years. When I was playing in a band in Waikiki, they would come in from all over the world. . . . I was young. I was a real handsome dude, too. That didn't hurt.

MARILYN CHAMBERS: The first day, we had a couple beers and a joint or something to loosen up. I really didn't want to know too much about what was going to happen. Because in the movie I am supposedly kidnapped, and I wanted it to happen like the real thing.

It was really fun—they blindfolded me, put a gag in my mouth, and threw me in this car. We did it at night, and when we got somewhere, they shoved me through this door. And I didn't know where I was going. For real.

It was really cool. It was interesting to be able to just go with it because it was safe, but it was still scary. It was a great fantasy.

JOHNNY KEYES: I was fucking the hell out of this chick—I was acting like I was ten thousand Africans making up for that slavery shit. Here's this white woman that the African is fucking to get revenge on all those white motherfuckers that used to rape our mothers and aunts all those years ago, right? That's what I used as an incentive to fuck Marilyn Chambers.

MARILYN CHAMBERS: That scene broke out of the old porno mold of handheld cameras and lousy color and showed people that there's a great deal of beauty in the mystery and majesty of an orgasm.

I call it artsy-fartsy now because I've seen it so many times, but the first time a person views it, they're kind of stunned. And they get all horny inside. Of course, that sequence is the ultimate in the fantasy of man conquering woman.

JOHNNY KEYES: I made love to Marilyn for about an hour and forty-three minutes without stopping. She came about seven, eight, nine times, and then she fainted on me.

MARILYN CHAMBERS: When Johnny put it in, it hurt—I had tears in my eyes. And then it just clicked. It was like going from being scared to *"Yeah!"* You can see that in my eyes. It was a primitive, animalistic type of thing. And then we were on our way, ha, ha, ha.

JIM MITCHELL: We were scheduled with the six nuns for two days, and Johnny Keyes for two days, and the trapeze people had two days. Then the audience orgy was to be a master cover scene with fifty people for one day, then each group for two days. Seven or eight days in total.

But then, after stalling for a year and a half, we finally had to go to trial. See, we got busted three weeks after we opened the O'Farrell Theater in 1969. We've been in a lot of court battles since then—local, muni, superior, state, appellate, State Supreme Court, federal, federal district, Federal Ninth Circuit of Appeals, U.S. Supreme Court.

We've won all the way to the Supreme Court.

JACK BOULWARE: San Francisco Mayor Dianne Feinstein acted as a schoolmarm to the Mitchell brothers. She would attempt to regulate them, and they would gleefully thumb their noses at her.

They were harassed by her so many times—via the police department—that they actually put her home phone number on their theater marquee that said, "For a good time, call Dianne."

She had to change her number—and then they got her new number, and they put it on the marquee again!

JIM MITCHELL: So on the day of the big orgy—we had costumes, people, makeup, a set—we had to go to trial. So we started our trial, and we had to shoot the big scene in one day!

JOHNNY KEYES: My fuck scene with Marilyn was so intense that the sixty or seventy people who were hired to be the audience, just started taking off their clothes and fucking!

It was like a nightclub setting: Me and Marilyn were onstage, and these actors and actresses were sitting there watching the scene. But everybody got carried away watching us—and they just started fucking. They must have had three cameras, and they just let them roll.

JIM MITCHELL: We shot five thousand feet in one day—until we just couldn't shoot anymore. After we ran out of film and turned all the cameras off, it got pretty weird, man. It got a lot funnier than what was on film.

JOHNNY KEYES: You know, if you're in a room where everyone is making love, man, it's going to get pretty freaky. And, oh yeah, it was!

MARILYN CHAMBERS: What's a better turn-on than five different guys jerking off all over a pretty girl's face and letting her lick their sperm from her lips and chin?

C. J. LAING: I was totally jealous that I wasn't in *Behind the Green Door.* Completely. I wasn't pissed at the Mitchell brothers, more dejected. But I didn't complain to Jim and Artie—and what, risk them saying they turned me down because I'm a little scrawny kid from nowhere?

JOHNNY KEYES: At the premiere of *Behind the Green Door,* there were all kinds of women trying to fuck me. I mean, one chick was like half owner of some big hotel. And I was having a blast! I was young and full of cum, baby! And people at the premiere were sitting in the audience playing with each other. Shit, you'd see people getting turned on because the movie was like, really psychedelic!

ARTIE MITCHELL: About the time *Behind the Green Door* opened, Marilyn came over and said, "The new Ivory Snow box came out—and here it is." And Marilyn was on it, right?

MARILYN CHAMBERS: I had failed to mention to the Mitchell brothers that, "Oh, by the way, I posed for the Ivory Snow box a couple of years ago. And I think it's about ready to come on the shelves."
Jim and Artie just went, "What!!? Oh my God!!!"

JOHNNY KEYES: One day we were having a big barbecue out at the Mitchell brothers', and me and Marilyn went to the store to pick up some turkey wings. I walk down the soap aisle and see this picture of Marilyn on the Ivory Snow box, holding this baby. I grab it and go back to Marilyn and say, "Hey, look at this box!"

MARILYN CHAMBERS: So we all went to the grocery store, and there it was. It was like "Cha-ching, cha-ching"—the sound of a cash register, you know?

JOHNNY KEYES: Dollar signs just rolled in Art Mitchell's head.
Then they went back and started all this publicity—but I was the one who found the box! In the store! It was an accident!

ARTIE MITCHELL: We knew it was big. But we didn't want Procter & Gamble to pull out of it immediately—at all. So we all decided to wait at least six months, to make sure they had the box out *everywhere.*

JIM MITCHELL: We went to New York and opened the movie. The first week we did thirty thousand dollars total between two theaters, which wasn't very good. We had fifteen thousand dollars in advertising, we had houses to pay for, and we'd been advanced fifteen thousand. And we didn't get a check, right? We needed the money.
It had only been three or four months after the Ivory Snow box had been out, but we decided, "What the hell? We have to go with it."
Russ Fradkin was doing the publicity for the theater in New York. We went to him and the theater owner, and we said, "Here's the story. . . . here's the boxes."

They didn't get it, really. They didn't know how big it was. So we told them, "Call Earl Wilson, the columnist; give it to him first."

Wilson sat on it for a week, called back, and said, "It's not an item."

ARTIE MITCHELL: The *New York Post* sat on it for three or four days, so I just took the Ivory Snow box, told Russ that Procter & Gamble were the largest television advertiser in the world, and went to Tony Mancini, a reporter for the *New York Post*.

You see, *Playboy* had already done a story on Marilyn and porno, and we dropped the Ivory Snow story on the writer. He was going to get a break on it. But this was three months before publication. A long wait.

So I told Tony Mancini what the story was, he called Marilyn out in California, and it made the second page.

JIM MITCHELL: The box office the next week went to $60,000. It was unnatural, no doubt about that. We weren't trying to say how smart we were.

ARTIE MITCHELL: Straight fluke! What an avalanche of free publicity! We were just standing in the wings. It came up, and we just had to play the cards that were dealt out.

You can't break the chariot of Procter & Gamble's Ivory Snow—which is sixty percent of their action—that often, you know? The girl who was on the Ivory Snow box before Marilyn was on it for twelve years. They don't fuck with that box! That box is their baby. They went through two years of backroom bullshit to finally agree that that was the look they were going for—the young, blond mother image. Only this young blond turned out to be a porn star.

And then we went to Cannes right as the story was breaking.

MARILYN CHAMBERS: Never before had an adult film been reviewed at the Cannes Film Festival. It was quite something.

JOHNNY KEYES: Jim and Artie called me and said, "You just got nominated for an award at Cannes for the best fuck scene ever shot!"

ARTIE MITCHELL: At Cannes, we were up at the top of the theater. After the movie was over, they turned up the house lights. But the people wouldn't leave. We couldn't tell if they liked us or hated us. It seemed as we looked down there, there were all these faces from all over the world just looking up at us. A cold, weird kinda thing. Like they didn't know where we were coming from at all. I was getting a bit nervous. Then six police officers came in and started working their way up to us.

Finally, one drunk Frenchman stood up and started shouting, "FUCK! FUCK! FUCK! SHIT! SHIT! SHIT!!"

The cops dragged him out, and that kind of broke the ice. Then everyone left. They'd been sitting there, for about five minutes, in sweltering 85-degree heat. They were stunned. Really stunned.

MARILYN CHAMBERS: The press was just phenomenal. I mean, I was just inundated. I was famous overnight because of the Ivory Snow box and *Behind the Green Door*. Kind of a paradox, but the press ran with it. *Show* magazine was saying, "This is the new Marilyn Monroe!"

I got a ten-page spread in *Playboy*—a celebrity layout. I was signing thousands of pictures. *And* I started getting calls for straight movies.

ARTIE MITCHELL: At 2:00 P.M. the next day, they showed the movie again. We stayed down on the beach this time. We got reports that there were crowds of people outside. They couldn't all get in. The police asked us to cancel our third show to avoid a riot. The word had gotten around pretty fast.

JIM MITCHELL: We came back from Cannes and had another Ivory Snow box press conference. That's what was so funny. It was a good story. It hit everywhere. So now hundreds of reporters showed up. They had nothing, but they rehashed the same thing. And the story went out again.

MARILYN CHAMBERS: We were treated like movie stars. We had limos, and suites at the Plaza Hotel, and Cristal champagne, and openings, and premieres and it was just so glamorous—really, really glamorous. Johnny Carson lined up to see the film. I mean, you had to go to the theater and stand in line, so you weren't anonymous. You were there for all the world to see.

JOHNNY KEYES: I got fifteen hundred bucks for a day's work. That's pretty good. But then, after it became a hit, we renegotiated. And I got part of the movie. They gave us residuals. Yeah, the Mitchell brothers were all right with me and Marilyn. Not with nobody else. They paid people good, but me and Marilyn's the only ones who got residuals.

JIM MITCHELL: *Behind the Green Door* brought Marilyn about twenty-five thousand dollars, plus residuals, and there were no sour grapes about it. She made more money on *Behind the Green Door* than anyone in the history of this business has ever made as an actor or actress in a movie.

JOHNNY KEYES: I did about three more movies for the Mitchell brothers. But none of the other women I worked with were big stars; they were just regular nude people. Was I turned on? *Yeah*! They was bringing all these little chicks for me to fuck, and of course, I would have my pick of the girls. And they were paying me!

MARILYN CHAMBERS: The next film I did for the Mitchell brothers was *The Resurrection of Eve,* which didn't have as much success as *Green Door.* But that was okay because I really wanted to do legit films.

I was still just this little hippie chick in San Francisco, married to this hippie bagpipe player who did nothing.

Hair of the Dog

NEW YORK CITY/CHICAGO/LOS ANGELES
1973

LINDA LOVELACE: The one good thing about Butchie Peraino was that he introduced me to Sammy Davis Jr., who was doing a telethon for seat belt safety, and I was going to be on with him. I was gonna do a skit or something on the show because if I had my seat belt on, none of this stuff would have happened to me.

But they wouldn't allow me on. They wouldn't even open the door to let me in. Sammy came out and was all apologetic. He tried his best, but they didn't want me. Sammy said, "We'll have dinner or something later."

I think probably deep down inside, I was hurt. But Sammy and I went out for dinner later that night, and then we went back to his hotel.

CHUCK TRAYNOR: Sammy used to tell me he was more interested in meeting and knowing me than he was in fucking Linda. He would fuck her, but that was secondary. He said, "I gotta know how you control women. I gotta know what makes them follow you like they do. What motivates you? Why do you do it?"

I said, "Well, beats shovelin' shit for a living."

AL GOLDSTEIN: I ran the stuff in *Screw* about the eight-millimeter films Linda had made before *Deep Throat,* where she gets fucked by a dog and gets pissed on—and Linda and Chuck got terribly angry. I tried to explain to them that anything she did was news. Apparently, they felt being a cocksucker was news, but to be fucked by animals—that was too kinky to be published.

So I became the enemy. Two of her friends—managers or whatever you want to label them—called me up and said they were going to break my legs.

CHUCK TRAYNOR: When I found out Al Goldstein was doing some stuff about bestiality on Linda in *Screw,* I was up there with the Peraino people in their office, and I told them I didn't like it.

I told them I was gonna go show Al Goldstein which way to think. They said, "Well, if you wanna do it, go ahead, but anything he writes about us is okay because it's just more publicity."

AL GOLDSTEIN: Linda's book, *Inside Linda Lovelace,* came out almost twelve months to the day after I met her in that hotel room. She had a fancy press party in New York to launch the book. I've never seen the press more awestruck. They were fighting to get her autographed photo.

During the party, Chuck Traynor called me over and said there were grand juries that were trying to nail her on the dog photos, that they had these big movie contracts and that I should lay off.

LINDA LOVELACE: Al Goldstein was trying to sign me for his movie, but I wasn't interested. Let's just say the script left me cold. That marked the day that *Screw* started screwing me. I wanted to sue them for their untrue allegations, but my lawyer advised against it.

AL GOLDSTEIN: In *Dog Fucker,* Linda was still not the cocksucker or charmer that she becomes in her later work. In any film retrospective on Linda Lovelace, I'm sure that this short will merely be a historical footnote in her thrilling show business career.

LINDA LOVELACE: My lawyer said the magazine meant nothing in the straight world, and to the *Screw* readers—who are very important to me—it wouldn't matter either. His contention was that those readers are much too sophisticated to believe ridiculous claims and too sharp to believe it was really me in that bestial photo.

NICK TOSCHES (WRITER): Linda claimed that Goldstein was a liar, that she was not the lady receiving the dog in the film, and that Big Al was just pissed off because she refused to act in his movie, *It Happened in Hollywood.*

Goldstein in turn slapped a $250,000 slander suit on Linda, saying that, yes, it is she in the film, and she shouldn't deny it—she should be proud of it.

CHUCK TRAYNOR: Why did Linda deny the dog-fucking pictures? Well, Linda never realized that people were interested in her as a freak. She figured, "If the dog-fucking pictures come out, I'm dead."

LINDA LOVELACE: We were living back in Florida when Hugh Hefner contacted Butchie Peraino, who said that Hefner wanted to meet me and

Traynor—but Traynor was into the D-O-G thing. I think that was Hefner's motivation. I mean, that's what he was looking forward to seeing, you know?

AL GOLDSTEIN: Only in America could a cocksucker go so far.

CHUCK TRAYNOR: Hefner sent his personal plane down to pick us up to bring us to California. Well, I had a great, big, old dog named Rufus, and he flew to California with us. Hefner had these sheep dogs, and Rufus was put in the kennel with them—and that night Rufus killed one of Hefner's sheep dogs and seriously chewed the other one almost to death.

So Rufus wasn't real welcome around the Hefner mansion after that.

LINDA LOVELACE: Hefner was a terrific guy. A wonderful guy. He did something that Chuck could never do. He treated me like a human being.

Chuck got his kicks from weird things—like imagining how many guys could manage to stick their fingers up my behind when I wore a short skirt. When we first met Hefner, Chuck would make me go around the Playboy mansion in Chicago to see how many butlers and servants could stick their fingers in me or whatever. He used to say that if Hefner heard about me doing that, he would think I was really great. But when I finally met Hefner and got to know him, I found out how totally wrong Chuck was.

CHUCK TRAYNOR: Linda never realized that the doggie movie was probably one of the only reasons Hefner was interested in her in the first place. Hefner's probably got the second or third biggest porn collection in the world.

And I think Hefner's interest in me was that he would show me old eight-millimeter porn films, and he'd ask, "Do you recognize any of these people?"

I'd say, "Yeah."

He'd ask, "What are they doing now? Where's this girl now?"

It was a big fascination with him. I'd find out by calling people I knew and asking this and asking that. I did that for quite a while for him.

Hefner wanted to have a file on all the people that had ever done porn and their whole life history. "Did they graduate from school? Did they go to work? They go to college? Are they working now? Did they get married? Did they have kids?"

LINDA LOVELACE: Hefner would have "orgy night" in the pool—inside the cave. He would come down to the Jacuzzi, and as soon as he took off his bathrobe and stepped into the water, Chuck started pushing me toward him.

Chuck's primary goal was to bring me and Hugh Hefner together sexually. He saw this as the beginning of a great palship. Chuck had this picture of Hefner and himself as arm in arm buddies, dividing up Playmates and Bunnies equally. Of course that never came down.

Hefner was into frolicking around, going from one girl to another. He carried a huge bottle of Johnson & Johnson's baby oil with him, and he was rubbing everyone down with the oil. There were about twelve people in the Jacuzzi, and before long they were all coated with oil.

CHUCK TRAYNOR: Was Hefner into bestiality? No, I don't think any more than anything else. I think it was just a fascination. Hefner put up with Linda, but I think he wanted to see her screw the dog. The idea was to at least see it once. He was more of a collector and a researcher about it. Hefner was like an expert in "Porno Trivial Pursuit."

I liked Hefner, but I liked Sammy Davis Jr. more. Sammy was a knockdown guy. We partied, we orgied, we drank, smoked, and fucked from one end of the country to the other. Sammy was a real hell-raiser.

LINDA LOVELACE: Chuck wouldn't take part in an orgy himself, not as a rule. He had sexual problems he didn't want revealed. He was naked in the water, but if a girl came up to him and tried to get something started, there'd be no reaction.

But then this girl—who loved being the center of attention—and I got together, and the rest of the orgy goers stopped and formed a circle around us so that they could get a closer look at what was happening. It was like an old Fred Astaire movie where all the dancers suddenly stop and form a circle around Fred and Ginger.

CHUCK TRAYNOR: Were Hefner and Linda sexually involved? At parties probably, yeah. But not romantically sexually involved. I know Hefner separates sex and emotion like I do. Sure they balled, but as far as any more involvement than that, I doubt it. It was just an ego trip for Hef to have Linda Lovelace around.

LINDA LOVELACE: Then Chuck decided to demonstrate a new trick he had been practicing—putting his entire fist into me. One of the other men held my body out of the water, and then the girl took over for Chuck, doing the same thing with her fist. At this point everyone applauded, again, just like in an old Fred Astaire movie.

CHUCK TRAYNOR: As Linda became more of a commodity, I became more possessive of her. I can't really say I was overly possessive because around Hefner's house she did what she wanted to do—pretty much.

LINDA LOVELACE: The next time I went into the Jacuzzi, Hef was there. He was soft, gentle, and shy. But he was basically honest and happy. I decided I wanted to fuck him and give him some good head.

I was standing there in the Jacuzzi next to a girl, and Hef said, "Why don't you two start?" The chick was great looking, so I didn't have much of a problem getting into it. It was a good time. I went down on the chick, circling my tongue around her clit. The king began getting excited, just watching. The next thing I knew, I felt a tongue flicking away at my clit.

CHUCK TRAYNOR: Is Hef great in bed? I wouldn't want to have to live up to the standards that are set, not by him, but for him. I think he's probably like anybody else. Probably a little more introverted than anyone would believe. But his whole organization is totally opposite, so Hefner has to stand for his organization. He makes a big to-do about it. He always has a good-looking girl hanging on his arm—or two or three of them. But I think he'd just as soon be upstairs in the bedroom, watching television or something, than balling those three girls.

LINDA LOVELACE: Man, Hef really knew what he was doing. Just when I was beginning to go wild, I felt a hot cock forcing its way into my ass. My ass just happened to be up toward him, and I hope he dug it because I was having a delicious time. He gave me the best ass-fuck I've ever had. A good, steady humping that kept getting more and more frantic.

I could have sworn he giggled when he turned me over. Then he began to fuck me. A nice, deep, slow fuck, which had me gasping after fifteen minutes. The average guy gives you about twenty-five thrusts with his cock before he comes. But Hef was a master. We both came together, and it was tremendous.

But that was the only time we ever made it together.

MARILYN CHAMBERS: I'd gone to the Playboy mansion only once, and that's when Linda Lovelace was around Hefner. She was putting on a revue for Las Vegas. She was going to be onstage at Caesar's Palace—and that's what I wanted! I was like, "Oh, why couldn't that be me?!"

But I never did meet Linda. Never face-to-face.

Automated Vending

CLEVELAND
1973

BILL KELLY: Reuben Sturman was by far the most important pornographer in the history of the world. He started out in Cleveland, his hometown, selling comic books—a real nickel-and-dime operation. Then he found out girlie magazines were a hot item, so he went from them to soft-core porn, then to hard-core porn—movies and then videotapes.

In the early 1970s, Sturman was the richest and most famous, most powerful man in the entire world in porno.

Everybody kowtowed to Reuben Sturman.

LARRY FLYNT: I've known Reuben Sturman for over twenty-five years. I consider him one of my few friends. He was a gentleman, a very bright guy. You know, in the 1960s, Reuben had twelve hundred adult bookstores nationwide.

Yeah, he was on par with many of your typical franchise operations. Just like McDonald's.

ROGER YOUNG (FBI SPECIAL AGENT): Reuben Sturman developed the idea of the peep show booths. And he developed another idea: say you and I are running a store—we're independent. Well, he sells us his product, okay? And then he goes, "Every time you show that, every time you sell that, I get a piece. In the peep show booths or over the counter."

So he starts making money that way—let's say you have to put in enough quarters to pay five dollars to see the whole show, well, he wants a buck or two. Even if we bought them; even if we think we own them.

STEVE RUDNICK: When I was sixteen or seventeen, in 1973, I needed a job. The construction industry was in a deep recession. There were daytime bowling leagues springing up all over town, filled with electricians and carpenters. So my friend Stewart Liebowitz's mother was a bookkeeper for a company, Automated Vending, that had an opening.

But you had to be eighteen. But I don't think they were too big on checking my bonafides, so I got the job.

ROGER YOUNG: Reuben would sell the actual peep show booth through Automated Vending, but he still maintained a percentage of showing the film in the booth. He had another company, called Diversified, that did the distribution of the videotapes for the people who bought the booths.

And the collection of the quarters was done by another company.

STEVE RUDNICK: I asked Stewart what they needed help doing there, and he said, "Uh, we make peep show booths."

I looked at him and asked, "You make *what?*"

He said, "You know, you put a token into the slot, and you watch a porn movie. We build them, load up trucks, and drive 'em all over the country and up to Canada, too."

BILL KELLY: Reuben Sturman had at least six lieutenants whose principal jobs were to go around to his bookstores and make sure the money count was okay and to empty out the peep show machines.

I've seen these guys go into these dirty bookstores, which a lot of folks call "adult bookstores"—I call them porno garbage dumps—and they'd fill up two five-gallon buckets full of quarters on a regular basis.

Now I guarantee you, I can't pick up a five-gallon bucket of quarters, and neither can you or anybody—short of somebody from the Miami Dolphins. And these guys would pick up two of them and walk out of the place after giving half the proceeds to the owner or manager of the store.

Big money.

STEVE RUDNICK: You'd put a token in a coin box, push a button, and then the circuit board would tell one of two or four projectors which one to turn on. They were eight-millimeter or Super Eight film projectors. They would get them by the carload from someplace in Taiwan or Japan. Very cheap, crappy projectors.

My job was to take the brand new projectors, open up the case, take out a capacitor, and put in a resistor, then take out one dry chain and put in another. It was very, very mundane.

REUBEN STURMAN: With the peep booths, that's when my thing took off. Money was coming in so fast I didn't know what to do with it. Guys come in with bags of $50,000, $100,000. They would throw it on the desk. I say, "Thanks, Bill." Away they go.

STEVE RUDNICK: I was working there after school until eight o'clock at night, and I'd say there were fifteen laborers. There were other people during the day that I didn't know about. They had a couple people that went out on the road, setting up the stores, which were all prefab. They built the booths from scratch. They'd bring in truckloads of plywood and cheap wood-grain paneling, staple them together with a pneumatic stapler, and then cut them down. One would be a wall, and another one would be a door or something like that. Incredibly sloppy. It always killed me: In order to "dress it up," they would buy mile after mile of cheap wooden corner molding, and I'd have to sit there and stain each piece.

They could take a clean shelf and make a store in three or four days, tops—forty-eight hours, if they worked around the clock.

ROGER YOUNG: Jimmy "The Weasel" Frattiano told me flat out that Reuben Sturman was owned by the Gambino family. That Robert DiBernardo, a Gambino associate, was the one controlling him. And Sturman became the wealthiest man in the world in pornography. I mean, the skim just from his peep show booths was probably two million a day.

LARRY FLYNT: Even if you go back to the 1960s, when Reuben Sturman and Mike Thevis and Robert "DiBe" DiBernardo and those guys pretty much carved up the country, it still was not a Mafia organization. Now, they have always attempted, at every opportunity that the government or the prosecutor gets, to insinuate that most pornography is produced by organized crime. I know all of the major players in this industry and absolutely none of them is connected to the Mafia.

ROGER YOUNG: In 1971, there was a meeting in Las Vegas of the Big Three. At that time it was Milton Luros, DiBe—Robert DiBernardo from Star Distributors in New York—and Mike Thevis from Peachtree in Atlanta. Those were the big pornographers in the United States—bigger than anybody else.

They met with their attorneys and divided up the United States—organized their distribution rights and who would sell what to who where, and what attorneys would defend what sections of the United States. Mike Thevis had the South/Southeast, DiBernardo had the Northeast, and Milton Luros had west of the Mississippi.

BILL KELLY: I got this from the case agent on Mike Thevis. He had an informant, and the informant and his wife had to be put into a secret location because Thevis was gonna murder him.

The case agent said that the informant told him, "Thevis personally murdered various people in the porn business and one innocent bystander. His associate, Roger Dean Underhill, and a nonassociated real estate agent, a salesman named Golanti, who was a friend of Underhill's, were murdered by Thevis in the 1970s in Atlanta."

Thevis got life for those murders on a federal civil rights violation. He was convicted in 1978.

The informant also said, "Thevis murdered a guy from Miami, one of our informants: Kenneth "Jap" Hanna, who was a porn dealer in Atlanta. Thevis shot him in the lungs and right between the eyes while Hanna was sitting across the desk from Thevis in his office."

I remember that one—he took him out to the Atlanta airport and left him in the trunk of his car.

Thevis had been one of the top three pornographers in the United States until he went away. And then along came Reuben Sturman.

ROGER YOUNG: Robert DiBernardo had to take Sturman for a sit-down in front of Ettore Zappi, who was the national coordinator for the Gambino family for pornography nationwide. So, at one point, Sturman didn't pay a bill; a guy complained to the Gambinos—a soldier—and Zappi says, "Bring Sturman in here."

So DiBe brought him down to Fort Lauderdale. Sturman, I think, realized what was going on. And a day or two before the sit-down, Sturman pays the debt off—sends a check or makes a phone call.

And Zappi thanked him for paying off this debt—thanked him very much for helping him to pay that off. And that's what it boiled down to: Sturman paying the debt.

But Ettore Zappi never really got out of porn. He was an old guy then, in his eighties. He died.

STEVE RUDNICK: In the work area, there were a couple of overhead garage doors, always locked, and the door to the rest of the building was also locked. Everybody came in through the outside overhead door, and before they would raise it you had to ring the buzzer three times—in a special way because they were afraid of getting raided. I don't know if it was the cops or the FBI they were worried about.

ROGER YOUNG: Teddy Rothstein was there at Star Distributors. Teddy wasn't making money until they brought DiBe into the Gambino family and Star Distributors. That's my understanding.

Reuben really wasn't brought in. Reuben grew up on his own and then was just taken over or, rather, "approached" by DiBe, who said, "I'm your man, and you will work with me."

STEVE RUDNICK: There was one guy that worked in a hidden room. You could see a doorway going into a room that was hidden behind a huge wall with boxes, which I think were all empty. But if you got into that room, there was a hidden door, and then you'd go into another room—where he would edit the films.

And this guy would come out of there, like, once an hour for a cup of coffee, with red, puffy eyes and say, "I can't look at another movie. They're drivin' me crazy!"

BILL KELLY: Reuben Sturman's estimated income was over a million dollars a day. Whether that's what he actually grossed or not, I don't know. But he had over seven hundred stores around the country. I ran him outta Miami in the early 1970s. He had some operations down here, and I got them all indicted, and I guess they thought they better get outta here. So they left Miami, but his product was still widely available.

LARRY FLYNT: Reuben Sturman beat about forty pornography raps in a row. He was literally giving the government fits because they couldn't get a conviction.

ROGER YOUNG: Reuben Sturman really never let his district managers, at his two hundred plus companies throughout the United States, know how close he was involved with the mob. I mean, they were all in fear that if they screwed up, the mob would come get them—because of Sturman's contacts. But they didn't really know how involved he really was. He never talked about that in front of anybody.

In fact, even when the whole state of Nevada was controlled for Reuben by Ralph Levine, every time something came up about organized crime, Ralph said to me, "Reuben would not let me get on the phone. He would not let me write letters. He would not let me do any of the paperwork that involved those people. Reuben said he'd take care of it. Reuben just said, 'That's none of your business, Ralph, I'll handle this.' With the Perainos, or the Gambinos, or the Columbos, or anybody."

STEVE RUDNICK: The films weren't on a continuous loop, which is what everyone thought. There was this electrical device; it would know when to stop and rewind and when to advance again.

So I'd have to test every projector. It was very, very easy to do—just had to make sure that the motor was running, that the thing advanced, that it ran, and that the lamp went on. Then they were ready to go. And they'd ship extra projectors in case one got broken in transit.

ROGER YOUNG: You see, Milton Luros and Reuben Sturman are relatives, and they became very, very good friends. Milton Luros was in the Los Angeles area and branching out—he was the first one that had divisions and branches in his pornography businesses.

Milton would have one business with a totally different name for the distribution, another business with a totally different name for publication, and another business with a totally separate name on the licenses and the paperwork. All of them were separate corporations. Reuben Sturman learned from him.

STEVE RUDNICK: My parents knew who Reuben Sturman was. "Oh, he's in the comic book business." You know, "Nice Jewish boys don't go into the porn business," you know?

Unless of course they wanna make a zillion dollars. Then, of course, they *jump* into it.

Reuben's reputation was that he was the largest porn magnate that wasn't affiliated with the mob. That was his big selling point: "I'm not connected. This is my own thing."

ROGER YOUNG: That's one thing Reuben Sturman learned from DiBe and from the mob—to be the nicest guy in the world. DiBe was always giving Reuben's secretary flowers. That's where Sturman learned a lot of his tactics because he was probably the most diabolically evil person I think I've ever investigated. Up front, he's one way, but behind the scenes, he was absolutely ruthless.

STEVE RUDNICK: I heard that a couple of film producers would show up from time to time with a limousine full of voluptuous young women—the stars of their recent productions—and they would service the foreman or the boss. But I never saw that; I just heard about it.

For the rest of us, I can't remember if it was Tuesday night or Thursday, but nobody could work overtime because everybody had to go home and watch *Kung Fu* on television. Everything stopped for Kwi Chang Caine. Lights went off. "Everybody outta here, *Kung Fu* is on!"

It was so weird because here's this little Zen light in the middle of all these hillbillies and bikers—the last people you'd think would be interested in that. They'd say, "Oh, I just like it when he beats these guys up," you know?

Maybe there's some connection between the porn industry and the martial arts film business that persists to this day.

ROGER YOUNG: Reuben would have different companies for different functions, and of course his name never, ever appeared on any of the papers. It was only search warrants, good footwork, and a massive amount of interviews and investigation that developed Sturman as being the owner of all these things.

STEVE RUDNICK: The place was run by a guy named Ray. I might've introduced myself once and waved to him a couple of times. He was definitely in a different league. He was well dressed—casually, but expensively. There was an extremely large Cadillac involved with him.

Ray would rarely come onto the floor, and then to talk only to the foreman. But the peep show booths were produced on time and according to his budget. So he must have known what he was doing.

ROGER YOUNG: There is no such thing as *just* a pornography case. It doesn't exist. In my whole career, in Homer Young—my dad's—whole career, in Bill Kelly's whole career, there is no such thing as *just* a pornography case because of all the other crimes being committed—including interstate transportation of obscene matter, skimming and public corruption, under-the-table money, off-the-top money, money laundering, kickbacks to public officials for changing zoning to get a porno store or a sex club where you want it.

LARRY FLYNT: Reuben understood that litigation was very much a part of this industry and that you needed the best and the brightest attorneys to win these cases.

ROGER YOUNG: Times Square had all kinds of sexually oriented businesses. As the value of the land goes down, the other crimes—murder, rape, drug trafficking—go up. And so when Times Square was at its peak in the sex industry—about 1974 or 1975—New York had to borrow money from the U.S. government to operate the city.

STEVE RUDNICK: I remember tripping one day. At that time acid wasn't a recreational drug; it was an educational experience. And it just came to me—these guys are thieves, you know? They're killing people for money.

I mean, maybe you gotta kill people to protect your home or your family—maybe kill for an idea, democracy, or anti-Nazism or something like that.

But for money? It's just not right, you know? As glossy and appealing as these guys were, there was always this realization that "this is blood."

That these fancy clothes are made out of blood, and the jewelry is just bones.

Trading Up

LOS ANGELES/MIAMI/SAN FRANCISCO
1974

CHUCK TRAYNOR: The trouble with Linda started when we went to California. I was trying to line up a show in Vegas for her. We knew Linda had no talent, but Raquel Welch doesn't either. So I gave a guy named David Winters $10,000 to put together a show, and I gave another guy, Mel Mandel, $3,000 to start writing the music, and everything started like it was supposed to.

LINDA LOVELACE: When I became a big name, Chuck saw that a lot of money could be made, and he was more determined than ever that I wouldn't get away from him. But it was very hard not to expose me to other people. Everybody wanted to meet me. He was afraid of that, but he dug it, too.

CHUCK TRAYNOR: I was just doing my job, which was calling Miami and Puerto Rico, trying to get Linda bookings for her show. I finally booked Linda in Miami. A guy down there who owns the Paramount Theater, Leroy Griffith, was going to pay Linda $15,000 a week to go in there with a Las Vegas type–show, comedians, a band, the whole bit. We had gotten a contract for four weeks, with an additional four-week extension, and he had placed the money in escrow.

LINDA LOVELACE: I was supposed to sing and dance. I wasn't really ready for that. But Sammy Davis Jr. had suggested that—for five hundred dollars—one of his friends could help me put the whole thing together.

VARIETY, AUGUST 29, 1973: LINDA LOVELACE TRIES TO SHED "DEEP THROAT" IMAGE FOR MIAMI CAFE BREAK-IN: "Linda Lovelace will shed the *Deep*

Throat image as she heads into the nightclub and stage arena, opening in Miami November 1 and following with the Tropicana Hotel in Las Vegas for a reported $50,000 per week. In Miami to consult with Leroy Griffith, for whom she'll open at the Paramount Theater, and with Sammy Davis Jr., who is supervising the act, Lovelace and her manager, Charles Traynor, said more porno films are not out, but that her career will take new directions."

LINDA LOVELACE: The guy that Sammy Davis Jr. recommended started working with me, and I was awful. He put a lot of effort into working with me, but I think he was just doing Sammy Davis Jr. a favor. So we began to look for someone else. I was desperate. The time was getting closer and closer, and I didn't even know what songs I would sing.

CHUCK TRAYNOR: What happened was David Winters, Mel Mandel, and a fellow named Lee Winkler decided to move in on Linda to get her for themselves, and they fucked everything up. David Winters is a choreographer who had been bankrupt for about a year and was at the end of his rope when I gave him $10,000.

Well, first he started bringing Linda flowers. I learned all this later. He told her, "Hey, that fucking Chuck is getting a big percent of the action. That's stupid. You're Linda Lovelace; he's nothing."

LINDA LOVELACE: When I first met David Winters, he was wearing a ruffled shirt of green velvet that looked as though it belonged in the sixteenth century but somehow looked right on him. Everything about him seemed to say, "I don't give a shit what anybody thinks—this is me!"

He didn't say a word. He just looked straight at me. And then he very shyly gave me a rose.

I found out later that he gave everyone a rose. It was his way of looking at life and dealing with it.

CHUCK TRAYNOR: I don't think any of them realized that *I* was Linda Lovelace. I mean, that body, the throat, and silicone tits walking around out there was bullshit, you know? She was nothing. But they thought she was a gold mine, and I'm sure they figured that they'd get her away from me—so that they could control her—and all the money would come pouring in. But while I'm paying David Winters to put together Linda's Vegas show, the guy's romancing her with these flowers and bullshitting her. And Linda's buying it, you know? She's stupid as shit anyway, so she's listening and believing it.

LINDA LOVELACE: Ann-Margret and Tina Louise were talking to David Winters about doing a Las Vegas act at the same time, and I was hoping he'd do my act and not theirs. I think that the crazy idea of doing an act for Linda Lovelace is what appealed to him. He said it would give him great pleasure if he could pull it off.

MOVIE WORLD, MAY 1974: ROGER HORRIFIED AS PORN STAR TRIES TO TAKE OVER ANN-MARGRET'S ACT! "In her greatest moment, her hour of triumph, Ann-Margret was asked to share the spotlight with yet another queen of her own special brand of art. Linda Lovelace, curly-haired siren and queen of the pornography circuit, was in the audience that opening night at the Las Vegas Tropicana Superstar Theater, intent on furthering her own career and breaking into legitimate theater. Linda merely wanted to share a photo session with Ann-Margret, and she brought along her own photographer just in case Ann agreed. But Ann and especially Roger Smith, who makes all the professional decisions for his wife, were appalled."

LINDA LOVELACE: As the days went on, I got into the singing and dancing lessons more and more. I hadn't heard any music or danced at all with Chuck. But I liked to move. I liked to dance. And now I began to gain confidence.

But Chuck was getting angrier with me every day. And what should have been ten hours became three and four. He would sit in the room and watch the writers and me work, with David at the piano. I could see how he resented it every time I smiled.

CHUCK TRAYNOR: Shit had been going back and forth for a couple of weeks. Linda kept coming on like I was the enemy. I was going to give her a check for $5,000 and started to make it out to Linda Traynor, and she said, "My name's Linda *Lovelace.*"

I said, "Hey, you're my wife; your name's Linda Traynor."

She said, "You just want to make it out to Traynor so you can get half of it."

I said, "Hey, this is California, you get half and I get half of everything. There's no hustle going on here."

She insisted the check be made out to Linda Lovelace.

I said, "Fuck you. It's going to be Linda Traynor or no check."

LINDA LOVELACE: Chuck said he had done a lot for me. But all he had ever done was frighten me. I became a star because people wanted to see me, even if Chuck said he was the mastermind behind me. Bullshit. If that was the case, he could make anybody a household name.

CHUCK TRAYNOR: David Winters told her, "I'm gonna make you another Audrey Hepburn." Those were the exact words he used; he said that to her in front of me one time. That's what David Winters thought in his own pea-brained head, that he could make Linda a legitimate actress.

Then one day I left Linda at rehearsal and went to the office. I called her up at three o'clock to see what time she wanted me to get her.

Linda said, "I'm not coming back to the house. I'm going to go away and think about things."

LINDA LOVELACE: For the first time I told him I wanted to be left alone; I wanted to be free. So I took a deep breath, grabbed a cab, and checked into a hotel.

CHUCK TRAYNOR: I had been getting more and more lenient with Linda, and that's why she wandered off with David Winters. If I had sat on her, like I used to with other girls, Linda never would've had a chance to leave.

LINDA LOVELACE: When I got to the hotel, the first person I called was Chuck. I tried to make him understand that it was over for us, but it was no use. He screamed for two hours and ten minutes that if I didn't tell him where I was, he would find me. I listened to him because I felt sorry for him.

CHUCK TRAYNOR: Linda said, "I'll go sit someplace for a couple of days and think things over."

LINDA LOVELACE: Then I called Sammy Davis Jr., and I think if he had said, "Come over here; you belong with me," I would have gone. Instead, his voice sounded distant to me. He was very sensible: "You have to do whatever you have to do."

When I hung up, I felt terrible. Because I really dug Sammy. And I was really scared that if Chuck found out where I was, he would beat the shit out of me. That moment was one of the lowest in my life. I didn't know where I was going or what was ahead of me.

CHUCK TRAYNOR: I never saw Linda again. The first thing I heard was from a couple of attorneys who were representing her, saying she was filing for divorce and that she would not honor any of the contracts—because she considered them illegal, that she'd been forced to sign them. Linda said she'd done *Deep Throat* under threat that I'd beat her up and that I beat her up once a week. That was her stand.

LINDA LOVELACE: I called David Winters. I told him where I was and asked him to come over. He was there in fifteen minutes. When he came over, I asked him why he had come.

"I'm your friend," he said.

For a few minutes we talked about continuing the act, and then he left. But I knew I would see him again.

CHUCK TRAYNOR: I was left in a real bad position by Linda because we were doing pretty good. We had made about $100,000 in a little less than a year. So, yeah, I was flabbergasted because not only was I stuck, but I was president of a corporation that had committed itself to present Linda Lovelace in Miami.

Not only that, but somebody had stolen my old lady. So I reacted the only way I knew how to react: violently. I was going to find out who the hell was behind this and nail him against the wall.

LINDA LOVELACE: I called a lawyer and finally filed for divorce. I felt so relieved, as if a big cloud had been lifted from my head, and I was excited and anxious about the future.

Even though he wasn't there, David made the day happy. I was happy just thinking about him. It's nice to like someone. I decided that even if I had to run after him and throw myself at him, I was going to get David. I really wanted him.

CHUCK TRAYNOR: I went to David Winters's house, and he insisted he knew nothing about it. I said, "If you're a man at all, don't bullshit me. If you want to take a shot at her, take a shot. Don't sit here and lie because if I go looking for somebody else, and I find out you're lying to me, I'm going to come back, and I'm going to be very mad."

"No, no, I got nothing to do with her," he said.

Meanwhile, the phone is ringing and people are asking, "Is Linda going to be in Miami? Is Linda going to be in Vegas?

So I'm thinking, "Who could I get? Who could I bring up to—or go past—Linda Lovelace's fame?"

MARILYN CHAMBERS: I had had it with San Francisco and the weather—and I knew that I had to go to Los Angeles—which I really couldn't stand, to tell you the truth. It's too phony, and I didn't like the people. But I knew it was the entertainment capital of the world.

Regardless, one day I got this idea, and I found out how to get in touch with Chuck Traynor. I said, "I'd really like to meet you and Linda. Let's get together and have a beer at the beach or something."

He was probably thinking, "Yeah, I'd like to get together and have an orgy." That's where his head was at.

CHUCK TRAYNOR: I told Marilyn, "You know, I got a buncha gigs for Linda Lovelace, but we're not gonna be able to make them because Linda and I have gone our separate ways. Would you be interested?"

Marilyn said, "Yes."

I said, "Can you sing and dance and take your clothes off?"

She said, "Yes."

I said, "All right, I'll put you on a plane."

She said, "You don't need to. I'll be on a plane. Pick me up at the airport."

I had just bought an XKE Jaguar—a brand new one, maroon.

So I drove it out to the airport.

MARILYN CHAMBERS: Chuck told me Linda had spent a lot of his money and that she had fallen in love with the choreographer and left him. Linda said that Chuck had hypnotized her and totally brainwashed her.

Chuck said, "She's got absolutely no talent. She can't sing. She can't dance. She can't even talk, ha, ha, ha. The only thing she can do is do deep throat. And we all know that that's easy if you're shown how to do it."

CHUCK TRAYNOR: Marilyn had reached a plateau with the Mitchell brothers. She'd made two films with them, but they didn't know how to promote an individual—they only knew how to promote films. They're not really managers or agents.

So when Marilyn said, "I'll fly right down there," I called them because they were friends, and being the honest guy I am, I said, "Hey, your star wants me to handle her."

And the Mitchell brothers said, "Couldn't be a better person to handle her than you. Take her."

MARILYN CHAMBERS: Chuck and I got along really well. And I'm thinking, "Why are these people saying all these horrible things about him? He's a really nice guy."

So we stayed up all night talking. And he didn't try to put the moves on me at all, which was like, "Thank you, Jesus!" God, I was so tired of that, you know? He was very much a gentleman.

Were Linda and I rivals? Yes because I felt that I had more talent than she did. I was prettier. She had a big scar all the way down her middle. And I knew Chuck Traynor was behind her success.

LINDA LOVELACE: Elvis Presley was performing in Vegas, and I was out in the audience, and I'm singing the words to myself, and—and Elvis couldn't remember the words. He was fat. It wasn't the guy that was hanging on my wall when I was a kid. I just felt sad for him. Elvis was a really lonely guy.

After the show David and I went back to his suite. We were sitting with him in his bedroom—I don't remember if Liza Minnelli was there or not—and Elvis was doing this karate move, telling one of his cousins, "Hey, come 'ere, make like you're comin' after me with a gun."

And he would do his movements and then say, "Okay, make it like you're comin' after me with a knife . . ."

That was the night before I got busted for cocaine.

MARILYN CHAMBERS: I told Chuck I didn't want to do erotic films my whole life. I wanted to do a couple of them—and then get out of it.

I wanted to be onstage in Las Vegas. I wanted to be Ann-Margret. That's who I really wanted to be. And he was excited because he felt that I possibly could have some talent. So that's the premise we met on.

LINDA LOVELACE: I was in the bathroom of our suite getting ready to go out. My hair was in rollers, I'm putting makeup on, I had underwear and a bra on—and all of a sudden I turn and see these two or three guys with .357 Magnums pointed at me.

I'm like, "Whoa, God, you scared the shit outta me. Tell Marty Feldman he did a good job."

Then I realized that they're not laughing. They said, "Come out of the room."

As I stepped out of the bathroom, I looked to the right, and here is this cop, and he took it right out of his coat, threw it on the dresser, and put my hat over it. You know, then picked up the hat. "Oh, look what I found."

Supposedly, it was an ounce of cocaine. They put it out in the media that I had barbiturates, amphetamines, and cocaine.

***PEOPLE*, MARCH 4, 1974: VEGAS DRUG BUST:** "Linda (*Deep Throat*) Lovelace, accustomed to harassment by film censors, is now facing a more serious charge in Las Vegas: drug possession. Arrested last month, she won a temporary reprieve when the D.A. told the police to provide more evidence. When they did, Lovelace was arraigned on one count of possession of cocaine and released on $7,000 bond. If convicted she faces up to six years in prison."

LINDA LOVELACE: The police take me out to where the living room area was, and there's David on the floor, and there's thirteen undercover cops with .357 Magnums pointed at him.

I'm like, "Oh, shit. What's going on here?"

So we get booked. I don't remember being fingerprinted. I had this sable coat with a fox collar, you know? And this black chick in the holding cell was going, "Oh, baby, wait till I get to you! Oh, look at that coat. What's underneath it?"

I had been through a lot with Chuck, but I'm like, "Oh shit, I ain't ready for this," you know?

MARILYN CHAMBERS: Chuck was getting divorced. I was still married, but that was going down the tubes because my husband was very jealous. And I said to my husband, "Well, why don't you come down to Los Angeles and meet Chuck?" Naive Marilyn, not realizing what Chuck was doing—he was trying to procure me so I could be the next sex symbol.

LINDA LOVELACE: Thank God the cops kept me outta the holding cell. Eventually Elvis Presley sent his man, Joe, down to bail me out.

Then we went over to Liza Minnelli's suite, and Marvin Hamlisch was playing on the piano, doing songs like, "I just got outta *jail!*"

Liza and Marvin were just trying to cheer us up.

I wanted to ask Liza so many things about Judy Garland, her mother, but I was like, "I can't do that."

CHUCK TRAYNOR: Marilyn was married at the time, but that didn't last too long because I told her, "I appreciate the fact that you're married, but there really ain't no room in your life for a husband."

I asked, "What are we gonna do with this guy?"

Marilyn said, "You're right. I don't even know why I married him."

He was a hippie guy that walked up and down the pier in San Francisco playing his bagpipes—that's how he made his money. I thought he really was just gonna be a hassle. So I said, "The best thing we can do is fix him up."

I was dating Jayne Mansfield's daughter then—Jayne Marie—and I think that's who I fixed him up with.

MARILYN CHAMBERS: When my husband came down to Los Angeles, I told him it was over. I tried to fix him up with this friend of Chuck's, but he didn't really go for it. So the last time I saw my husband he was driving away—in my car—with my dog looking out the back window.

Then he called me up and broke every piece of china that I had over the phone, screaming, *"I fucking hate you!"*

He was really pissed. He was really upset. I never heard from him or the dog again.

CHUCK TRAYNOR: Did I want to take David Winters out? Oh, yeah, I would've, in a hot second. I would never have gone behind anybody's back and tried to steal Linda away.

I hate thieves. I'd much rather have you come in with a gun and beat the shit out of me, than sneak in my room when I ain't there and rob me. That makes me violently mad. I don't like to get violently mad, but I do, and when I do, I'm gonna do somethin' about it.

So Butchie Peraino sent Vinnie out to Vegas. I figured Linda was very deeply indebted to me. I didn't really need Vinnie for muscle or anything; I needed him because I wanted somebody from New York that was good.

So Vinnie went up to David Winters's house and talked to him. Vinnie went in with a black rose, and he came out without it, so I'm assuming he gave it to David Winters. But David was too stupid to understand what was goin' on.

LINDA LOVELACE: In the beginning David would read poetry, and if he was leaving early in the morning, there'd be a rose on my pillow. I was supposed to do another film with him. *Linda Lovelace for President,* which didn't have any hard-core sex in it. So I did it.

Then, at one point, I was renting a Bentley, and David went out and bought another car. My accountant just gave him, like, eleven grand without even asking me or saying anything to me, you know?

Then I came across some paperwork where David was paid like $120,000, and he didn't do shit. I was supporting David on my credit cards.

CHUCK TRAYNOR: At the same time I was hooking up with Marilyn, Linda marched into divorce court smoking a cigarette because I always hated girls that smoked. Pow, pow, pow, pow, pow, and the judge said, "Well, that's the end of that."

TIME, MARCH 4, 1974: MILESTONES: DIVORCED: "Linda Lovelace, 22, exuberant blue-movie star of *Deep Throat* whose name quickly became a courtroom, if not a household word; and Charles Traynor, 35, her former business manager who now handles Lovelace's No. 1 competitor, Ivory Snow girl Marilyn Chambers (*Behind the Green Door*); after three years of marriage, no children; in Santa Monica, Calif. Lovelace, who earned $175 a day for her *Throat* role, has recently been negotiating contracts on the order of about $35,000 a week as a nightclub performer. Her most recent appearance in Las Vegas may lead to a six-year command performance: She was arraigned there on a drug possession charge."

MARILYN CHAMBERS: My play ran for fifty-two weeks, the longest-running play in Las Vegas. I got the key to the city. Two shows a night, six nights a week. It was very hard work. I was exhausted.

But when Sammy Davis Jr. would be in town, Chuck and I would go over to his suite and party all night. I had always wanted to do something with Sammy Davis Jr., and when he hosted the *Tonight Show* he was going to have me on as a guest. But the *Tonight Show* wasn't ready for me.

The pornography thing had a bad connotation, and now I was seeing the consequences. I thought it was going to be a stepping stone to bigger and better things. I thought it was going to get me in the public eye, and then I'd be taken seriously as an actress.

That never happened. Instead it was: "You're nothing but a slut, basically, who has sex on screen."

I was crushed because that's not how I saw myself, and that's not how I saw the films. But it was also kind of hypocritical because everybody wanted to know me and meet me.

CHUCK TRAYNOR: On Marilyn's twenty-first birthday I got her twenty-one guys to screw. I knew a lady that owned an answering service, and her son—he was about, shit, eighteen or nineteen years old—was a big fan of Marilyn's.

So he organized it, and that's how Marilyn spent her twenty-first birthday—getting screwed by twenty-one guys. The year before, on her twentieth birthday, Sammy Davis Jr. took us out to dinner. Sinatra was there, too.

When we got married in 1974, Sammy Davis Jr. was our best man. It was a fun wedding, a fun time for everybody involved. And how many people have Sammy Davis Jr.'s name on their marriage license?

Marilyn and I loved each other, and I was always very protective of her.

LINDA LOVELACE: I told David I didn't want to see him anymore after that. He flew to Los Angeles, and then he flew back and beat me up. He beat me up in Kansas City—and it was in front of witnesses, too. I was being dragged by my hair down a hallway in this hotel room. People were standing there, and I was screaming for help and nobody did anything.

It really bothered me—you know, like when they were making *Deep Throat* and I was being beaten in the other room? So that kind of ended our relationship. He was the last person in the world I expected to do that to me. But I said, "That's it."

David Winters may be living off the royalties from *Linda Lovelace for President*—which I never received.

The Devil in Miss Steinberg

LOS ANGELES/ARIZONA
1973–1974

FRED LINCOLN: Gerry Damiano was a funny guy. I don't think he even liked doing porn. But I'll say this for Gerry, he came up with some incredible scripts. He was really talented. I mean, he did *The Devil in Miss Jones* right after *Deep Throat*. And I still think *The Devil in Miss Jones* is probably one of the top three pictures our business ever made.

HARRY REEMS: After Gerry dashed off something over a weekend, he asked me to read the completed manuscript.

"It reads great, Gerry. The only thing is," I said, "is that I seem to have seen this script before. Or something damn close to it."

"What do you mean you've seen the script before?"

"Gerry, it's a steal. I've read Jean-Paul Sartre. This is *No Exit* in its thinnest disguise."

"Well, what do you expect? I wrote it in a weekend."

So that's how *The Devil in Miss Jones* was born.

GEORGINA SPELVIN: Marc Stevens, Mr. Ten-and-a-Half, said to me, "Would you be interested in working on a film for Gerry Damiano?"

I asked, "Who's Gerry Damiano?"

HARRY REEMS: In addition to having a part for me in *The Devil in Miss Jones,* Gerry wanted me to be production manager and to cast for him—all except for the female lead. He had the lead—or so he thought.

Her name was Ronnie. "I can fuck and suck better than any women doing this shit," she was telling everyone. I had seen Ronnie's dumpy body on film and knew she wouldn't do.

GEORGINA SPELVIN: I had no idea that *Deep Throat* was this big break-through film. So when Marc Stevens said, "Gerry Damiano's the director of *Deep Throat!*" I had never heard of him or the movie.

But then Marc said, "He's doing a new film, and he needs a caterer." I said, "Great!"

FRED LINCOLN: After *Deep Throat,* Gerry had a falling out with Butchie Peraino. Because Gerry made *The Devil in Miss Jones* with Jimmy Bogis and Herb Nitke; up to that point, I'm pretty sure Butchie was Gerry's sole banker.

GERARD DAMIANO: I originally owned thirty percent of the profits from *Deep Throat.* It netted more than $100 million. I really don't want to go into it. Let's just say I ultimately got $15,000, which I felt at that point was probably the best I could have done. Because I didn't want anyone telling me the kind of films I had to make. So I made a bad deal. But I've never regretted it.

FRED LINCOLN: Gerry claims he only got $15,000? He may have. He may have told them to stick the $150,000 up their ass. Gerry worked for the same guy I worked for—the front guy for Mickey Zaffarano.

Mickey Zaffarano *was* porn. Mickey was one of the straightest shooters in the business. He looked at the movie, he liked it, he handed you $150,000.

With these other guys, I had to put them against the wall because their checks bounced. I said, "Whoa! I don't know about you, but I don't do this to wear out my old clothes. I do this to eat! You give me a check, I put it in the bank, and I write checks to other people. This check bouncing doesn't work. You can't do that with me 'cause I'll break your fucking legs!"

GEORGINA SPELVIN: A couple of days later I went over to Gerry's office to talk to him about doing the catering for the film.

Damiano told me the budget—and while I was getting over laughing, one of his partners came in and said, "So-and-so is here to read the part for Mr. Abaca."

Gerry turned around to me and said, "As long as you're here, would you mind reading the part of Miss Jones opposite this guy?"

So I sat down and read the Miss Jones part, and everybody just sort of stood around with their chins on their chests. I guess they'd never heard anyone read for hard-core parts who had done any kind of actual drama before.

FRED LINCOLN: Georgina wasn't one of the girls. She was hired to be the caterer on Miss Jones. She was older—she was thirty-seven. Georgina was very talented. Linda Lovelace was never that attractive. Georgina was not stunning, either, but she was a very sexual and charismatic person.

GEORGINA SPELVIN: Harry said, "You have to do this role. You're wonderful."

But the producers and Gerry said, "But she's flat-chested, and she's nearly forty! What are you doing to us!?"

Needless to say, I was kind of intrigued by the idea of doing a lead role. My ego just came in and absolutely gobbled me up in one bite.

HARRY REEMS: One late October day I was carving pumpkins in my apartment. I invited over Georgina Spelvin, who I had met a couple of days earlier at one of the casting sessions for *The Devil.* She'd been in Broadway and Off-Broadway plays and thought of herself as legitimate.

GEORGINA SPELVIN: Marc Stevens introduced me to Harry Reems. A couple of days later, I went over to his apartment and sat and carved Halloween pumpkins with him. It turned out that he and I had several mutual friends in the theater world.

HARRY REEMS: While we were carving pumpkins, I asked Georgina casually, "What are you into sexually?"

"I'm gay," she said.

"Have you ever made it with a man?"

"I've made it with plenty of men. I've been married. I have children. Right now I'm into women."

"Could you do it on camera with a man?"

"It would depend on the man."

"If you dug the guy, what would you be willing to do?"

"If I dug the guy, I'd be willing to try anything. Sex can be very beautiful. With either sex. Even if it's somebody you don't know."

I liked her. She was honest, her body was good, and whatever way she swung, she was sexually "together."

GEORGINA SPELVIN: I was involved with one of the other women in *The Devil in Miss Jones.* She was a lesbian, at least when I met her. Basically, she was a schoolgirl who didn't know what she was. I kind of adopted her. To me, she was a daughter figure. I did not realize that I was a romantic figure to her until it was too late—until she was terribly dependent upon me, and clinging to me, and I didn't realize how unstable she was. I was really terribly worried about her.

HARRY REEMS: "Gerry," I said the next day, "I've found Miss Jones."

Gerry was not impressed with my candidate—until Georgina took off her clothes, and he saw her marvelous body.

Fortuitously, Ronnie called in with an impacted wisdom tooth a day or so before filming was to start.

"How's Ronnie going to do blow jobs with an impacted wisdom tooth?" I asked Gerry. Good question. Gerry threw in the dental floss. Ronnie was out, and Georgina Spelvin was in.

GEORGINA SPELVIN: I took the role very seriously and studied the character. I had all kinds of backstory on who she was, where she came from, everything that had happened to her. I was doing *Hedda Gabler* here, ha, ha, ha!

The fact that there was hard-core sex involved was incidental as far as I was concerned. I was totally deluded. I had made myself believe that I was an actress. I was showing true life as it really was—including actual sex as it really happened—instead of the phony stuff that you got from Hollywood. That was my raison d'être throughout the whole thing. It was okay; I was okay; I wasn't a slut.

GERARD DAMIANO: Viewing sex in a humorous way through *Deep Throat* gave the American public the impetus that they needed to be adult enough to take their sexuality seriously.

So I used my real name—*Throat* was made under the pseudonym Jerry Gerard—and I treated *The Devil in Miss Jones* as though it was a very serious film, and I felt that that's what it was.

FRED LINCOLN: It's a movie with emotion; it's just magnificent. You're looking at a woman who, because of her upbringing, has done what we tell all women they should do: "Don't do this until you find the right person." Well, what happens if you *don't* find the right person? You end up like this lady—a spinster.

ANNIE SPRINKLE (PORN STAR): God was a penis to me. I worshiped penises for years. Worshiped them. Really.

You see, as a girl—Ellen Steinberg, my given name—I was very shy and afraid of sex. I mean, I was a very uptight kid. And my parents were quite open, while I was freaked out. I was terrified about everything—menstruation, giving birth, sex, *everything*.

FRED LINCOLN: Miss Jones is a lonely person who has never felt the joy of touching someone she really cares for. Even if you just care for someone for one night! There's nothing in the world like this. And she was so miserable that she killed herself.

ANNIE SPRINKLE: I wasn't aware of my body developing, until the first day we moved from the San Fernando Valley to Panama—and the guys in Panama City would go, "Hey, baby! Hey, baby! Hey, baby!"

The boys in the San Fernando Valley hadn't done that. The Valley was like this white bread, uptight, suburban thing. Panama was more open, freer—just this tropical paradise.

Except in Panama, the street harassment was constant, which really freaked me out. I was thirteen. I was still a child, thinking, "Why are these guys making these noises?"

It was creepy, very creepy. And it was very cruel. I think it was all about: If they couldn't have you, they had to torture you.

FRED LINCOLN: You see this middle-aged woman sitting in a bathtub, and she takes a razor blade and slits her wrist. You see her just sit there and the blood going into the water.

Fuck, man.

ANNIE SPRINKLE: Homer was my first boyfriend. He held my hand at a movie, and it was just torture. I was just so uncomfortable. Slowly moving his hand over, then he held my hand, and I couldn't enjoy the movie, you know? I was just scared to death.

Afterward, he held my hand again as I was sitting next to my dad in the car. I was sweating. There was no erotic connection.

GERARD DAMIANO: There was no doubt about the depressing and horrible things that were happening to Miss Jones. When she killed herself, you felt it. You knew she was dying because of a lonely existence.

ANNIE SPRINKLE: I was walking down the street in Panama and this classic kind of hippie biker—a big, hunky, hefty guy with a beard—stopped his bike and asked if I wanted to go for a ride.

His name was Van, and I just trusted him. Van and I were together about four or five months, but we didn't have sex. My family was getting ready to leave Panama, so Van set it up so we could go up to his parent's beach house and take mescaline.

It was all psychedelics—all sparkly, sparkly sand, phosphorescent, beautiful moon, stars. We're all alone on this tropical island beach—just gorgeous. It was really a high. And then we went back to his parents' beach house and had our first naked hug and kiss—and he went down on me and licked my pussy.

Oh, it was really nice. It was all new. I thought it was *very* cool.

FRED LINCOLN: But because Miss Jones killed herself, she had to go to hell. And the Devil doesn't know what to do with her. How do you punish this person who has never done anything wrong? Who has no sin and no wants! Because she's never done anything, she doesn't miss it.

How do you punish this person, you know? It's like taking a kid who's never been outside and saying you're grounded.

ANNIE SPRINKLE: I didn't play around with Van's penis until he rode his motorcycle up from Panama to Los Angeles to see me. Penetration came when he finally got his house in the Valley. I was, like, totally awestruck by his penis. The day after I lost my virginity, I was so happy. It wasn't a loss; it was a gain, you know? It was totally an improvement. A *big* improvement. I was so happy; I couldn't stop smiling the whole day.

Van was an artist. He was a carpenter; he made furniture. And we ended up going to an art commune in Arizona together. He was a very talented, creative person. We were in love. But then I wanted to have sex with other people.

FRED LINCOLN: So Miss Jones says, "If I had known this, I would have lived my life differently."

The Devil asks, "What do you mean?"

And she says, "I would've done all those things they told me not to do."

He says, "How about I let you go back to do that?"

And she agrees to it. So first she meets Harry Reems, and he's her instructor.

ANNIE SPRINKLE: Things were going well until this guy at the commune starts flirting with me. He was cute, you know: skinny, lanky, young. He was probably nineteen. So I ended up having sex with him.

It was in his van, and it was very hot. And of course I knew Van was going to be upset—and that I would feel somewhat guilty—but there was no stopping me.

That was really the beginning of the end for Van.

FRED LINCOLN: The sex is so real because Georgina is not a young girl who can go get laid whenever she wants. She's like a little, chubby spinster. All of a sudden she's got guys giving her head for a fucking hour, man. So she's really getting off on this thing.

ANNIE SPRINKLE: It wasn't a big, bad breakup. I just said to Van, "I think I need to get my own place."

So I go and rent a one-room hippie pad for seventy-five bucks a month. And I worked as a hotel maid for two days and cleaned an oven. Then I got a job as a wallpaper hanger and for several months worked on construction projects—and had sex with all the guys on the sites: laid by the carpet layers, nailed by the construction workers . . .

FRED LINCOLN: Georgina's really the only person in *The Devil in Miss Jones.* The other characters come and go. At least there's the Devil to teach her things, but his character is flat, has nothing to it. But Georgina, you see her go from a spinster to a sex fiend. I mean, you really see it happen.

ANNIE SPRINKLE: They were cheating me out of money at the wallpaper job, so I answered an ad for a job at a movie theater and got hired as the popcorn girl. It was called the Cine Plaza Theater, this big, beautiful, old cinema in the heart of Tucson. It must have held five hundred seats. It could have been one of those old vaudeville theaters; it had that feel to it. Of course, I worked the late shift. But I didn't know it was an X-rated theater.

As fate would have it, the first movie they showed after I was hired was *Deep Throat.* I'd never heard of the movie. Nobody had.

HARRY REEMS: A lot went wrong in the making of *The Devil in Miss Jones.* Locations were lost. We went way over schedule. The picture was almost dropped midstream. Two guys had each put up $15,000 to make *The Devil.* When it was made, one of them was convinced it was a bomb and asked to be bought out.

But for those of us who hung in there, it was one of the loveliest shoots ever. It was Georgina's first big movie, and she did a damn fine job acting in it.

ANNIE SPRINKLE: When I went in to watch the movie, I had no idea that they actually filmed people having sex. I'd seen *Playboy* and *Penthouse,* read *The Happy Hooker* and *The Sensuous Woman,* but that was it.

So I was just in awe that they were showing *Deep Throat* out in the open—where anyone could see it. And I just fell in love with Linda Lovelace.

GERARD DAMIANO: Up until *Miss Jones,* I never had anything I wanted to say to the public. If people wanted to interview me because I was a porno filmmaker, I just was not interested in talking to them. But if anybody wanted to speak to me because I made *films,* then I was happy to talk with anyone. I just didn't want to be bothered with speaking to a lot of superficial idiots.

ANNIE SPRINKLE: Did I get turned on watching *Deep Throat?* Fuck, yes! I thought it was the best thing I had ever seen in my life! I watched it probably ten times. I thought Linda Lovelace was so cool. I loved her attitude and her look—and the way she could deep throat was just amazing.

GERARD DAMIANO: The only reason most of my films dealt with pornography was because at that time that was the only media an independent filmmaker could work in. I was gearing my films to sell to a specific market because there was not enough money involved to gear it to any other market.

Working within a limited budget—under $25,000—you could not do the great American love story. For that kind of money you had to stick to the bedroom and then every once in a while you'd get an opportunity to express an emotion other than sex.

ANNIE SPRINKLE: When people ask, "How'd you get into the sex industry?" I say, "Luck, just pure luck."

Two or three months after I started working at the Plaza Cinema, they busted it for obscenity and closed it down. I ended up working in a massage parlor.

At that time, all the massage parlors were in little trailers. This guy named Zeke ran it. He was a big, tall, gorgeous hippie guy—and very charismatic. I had the hots for him. But I don't remember if I fucked him— I can't remember all the people I fucked, you know?

Did I go from hand job to blow job to fucking them? No, I just went right into fucking, the first day. Oh, totally—I wanted to fuck them.

GERARD DAMIANO: *The Devil in Miss Jones* came about for basically the same reason *Throat* came about, but adversely. With the success of *Throat,* everybody and his brother was running around trying to make a sexy, funny, camp picture. I felt that if this is what everyone else was doing, it was time to do something different.

ANNIE SPRINKLE: I was not into romance. I was into pure sex. You know: one guy, two guys, five guys. No women at that time, just guys. Because my mother was so intense, I didn't want to be around women because I felt judged by them. My dad was the sweet one, so I was more attracted to men. Men felt safe. I was very threatened by women—unless they were prostitutes.

So all the girls at the massage parlor were great. There were hippie girls, as well as some seasoned prostitutes that had worked in Vegas—and biker women, and some drug addicts. It was kind of homey, you know?

So I had a great time. I worshipped and adored all the girls. And I was fascinated by prostitution, as I still am.

FRED LINCOLN: At the end of *The Devil in Miss Jones,* Miss Jones is back in hell. And she's with this guy—Gerry played the part—and he won't fuck her; he won't touch her; he won't do anything.

She's going crazy! She just wants sex.

ANNIE SPRINKLE: My pornography connection came about when the State of Arizona tried to find *Deep Throat* obscene. They busted the film in

1973 and everyone involved in it. But it took six months until I got a sub-poena. I have no idea how they found me, but somebody actually showed up at my door and handed me one.

It was totally ridiculous that they called me to testify—the popcorn girl at the theater—because I didn't know anything. But that's how I met Ger-ard Damiano.

FRED LINCOLN: You want to talk about a woman who liked sex? Annie Sprinkle really liked sex, man. But I didn't even know that Gerry had an affair with Annie. Even when Annie was eighteen, the S and M came from her, not from Gerry. Annie—boy, she was a freaky little girl, man, let me tell you. I don't know where all that came from.

ANNIE SPRINKLE: There was a witness room where we all sat around while we waited to testify, and I'd never seen Gerard Damiano, but someone introduced him to me as the director of *Deep Throat*.

I was starstruck. I was like all hot for him. He was forty-six years old, and I was eighteen. And he was just charming—Italian, with a great sense of humor. I just adored him.

The first thing I said to him was, "Will you teach me how to deep throat?"

GERARD DAMIANO: The only people that's worth knowing are people who take what they're doing seriously, more than the average person. Maybe it was my own defense of what I was doing. If I didn't take myself seriously, why should anybody else?

ANNIE SPRINKLE: We went out to dinner that first night. And then I had sex with Gerard Damiano. I had sex with him three or four times during the trial. We had great sex, really great sex. And I think he was taken by me in a way—probably our artistic sensibility just gelled and our interest in porn.

ERIC EDWARDS: I didn't know Annie at the time, but I did know Paula, Ger-ard Damiano's girlfriend. I worked with her. I love that term, "Worked with her."

You know, everybody says that in this business. "Well, I worked with so-and-so, and I worked with so-and-so."

"Oh, you mean you fucked them?"

"Well, yeah, that's what it boils down to."

Yeah, so I "worked" with her in the early days. In fact, she was one of the loop people. And she was a sweetheart, very easy to "work with."

So that's why I didn't know Gerry was having an affair with Annie. But I've never been that close with Gerry.

GLORIA LEONARD: Gerard Damiano was the Fellini, or you know, the Scorsese of porn. A lot of these guys use a lot of Catholic symbols—undertones and overtones of pain and pleasure in their films. I didn't know Annie Sprinkle at this point, but Damiano sort of lets this out—when he had that big S and M relationship with her.

GEORGINA SPELVIN: Do I think that *Miss Jones* has a lot to do with the Catholic-guilt thing? Absolutely. You know, pain and pleasure—there's a thin line, you know? George Carlin said it best: "You know, Catholics, they're always pushing for pain, and I'm always pulling for pleasure."

GERARD DAMIANO: Do I think I'm personally responsible for some of the movement toward sexual liberation in this country? Of course I'm responsible!

Is Linda Lovelace responsible? Is Jamie Gillis responsible? Is Harry Reems responsible? We're *all* responsible—every fucking one of us. We went out there and did things that were never done before. And we weren't ashamed of it; we did it, and we had fun.

ANNIE SPRINKLE: Linda Lovelace and Gerard Damiano were staying at the same fancy hotel in Tucson. Linda was always hanging out by the pool in a bikini. Chuck Traynor wasn't around. But I met Linda briefly and I said, "Oh God, you're my hero!"

She was kind of aloof—friendly—but aloof. She didn't really want to talk; she just wanted to get a tan and be left alone. Linda didn't look like she was too worried about the trial.

LINDA LOVELACE: Why have me go all the way to Tucson, Arizona, to be a witness for the government? It was the publicity. The publicity for the government was terrific in places like Kentucky and Arizona. I made the front pages of newspapers in those towns, just because I was there.

ANNIE SPRINKLE: Of course there was a lot of news about the trial. It was kind of exciting, and I think I was happy to be a part of it. You see, the massage parlor where I worked got busted quite a few times—but I was never there. Yeah, I was just always lucky—but I kind of wished I had been busted, too. I felt like I missed out on some rite of passage.

So now I finally got my chance to be busted, with Gerard Damiano—but he wasn't in Tucson that long, maybe a week. Then he went back to New York, and we stayed in touch. Was I in love? I would say, "smitten."

But yeah, we had started a hot affair. About a month later, when Gerard had to go to San Francisco, he sent me a ticket to go meet him. That's when *The Devil in Miss Jones* came out.

GERARD DAMIANO: MGM called me after I did *The Devil in Miss Jones,* after they'd read some of the reviews—and the film's grosses I might add—and made me a fat contract offer. Jim Aubrey sent his limo over for me—the whole impressive bit. But in addition to giving me an offer to make films under their auspices, they also gave me a formula. I had to make a film for them that had at least one hippie scene and one lesbian scene, among other things.

I don't make films to formula. I write my own films and direct them depending on what subject matter I choose to do at the time and how I choose to relate it.

MGM couldn't understand that, so the offer is still on my desk—and MGM is out of business.

FRED LINCOLN: I know that Hollywood came to Gerry and offered him to do some movies, and he was afraid. Why? I honestly don't know. *Deep Throat* made fifty-five million dollars. If that don't ring Hollywood's bells, man, I don't know what does! That's all they're interested in—the bottom line.

GEORGINA SPELVIN: *The Devil in Miss Jones* is pretty existential, especially for a porn film. I think that's the reason that it got the kind of critical notice that it did. But it was not really a very successful porn film. I mean, guys came out of that film shaking their heads, saying, "I came here to jerk off; I didn't come here to think!"

ANNIE SPRINKLE: When I got into the sex show biz, I wanted a new name. Ellen Steinberg just didn't sound sexy enough to me. I was lying on my bed, and I heard a voice whisper, clear as a bell, in my ear, "Annie Sprinkle."

I had been using the name for several years when my Uncle Sylvan sent me this photo he took of a tombstone he found in Baltimore. I got an eerie feeling. Annie M. Sprinkle was born in 1864 and died when she was only seventeen in 1881. In my travels, I later met one of the Sprinkle family descendants who confirmed my suspicion that Annie M. had grown up in a strict religious community and had never married.

It's likely that she died a virgin with unexpressed passion and desire. I believe that it was her spirit that whispered her name in my ear and that she now lives vicariously through me. She guides me and keeps me safe from harm. I have taken flowers to her grave.

It's a nice story, isn't it?

Holmes v. Wadd

LOS ANGELES
1973–1976

SHARON HOLMES: There was a period of time when John was gone for almost five months working in Hawaii doing nude dancing. He may have been doing photo layouts—I have no idea what he was doing. I'm pretty naive about this stuff. But that was as much as he was willing to tell me. I think that made it a little more palatable. If he was away, it wasn't affecting us.

BOB CHINN: It was a strange period to be shooting porn in Los Angeles, because Los Angeles County Vice were busting shoots. That's when I thought, "Why don't we all take a vacation? Go to Hawaii?"

I took my crew, and we went to Hawaii and made a film called *Tropic of Passion,* which was really a lot of fun. There was no pressure. John enjoyed it. I enjoyed it. Everybody enjoyed it.

SHARON HOLMES: It wasn't until 1973 that I found out how really deep John was into pornography. He had been lying quite a bit, saying, "No, I'm not doing a film; I'm doing the lights or the sound."

I found out because he left a still photograph out for a promo of one of the films he'd starred in. It was hard-core, showing penetration, with women. Up until then I hadn't seen any of that.

I just looked at it, and I thought, "Oh! Oh! Oh!" And it chewed at me, and it chewed at me, and it chewed at me . . .

BILL AMERSON: The 1970s, for me, was a continual hiding, peeping, and running from whatever authority wanted to stop the flow of adult businesses. There was a lot of police harassment. At that time, I was not only in the adult film business but also owned bookstores and theaters around Southern California and some in Arizona.

SHARON HOLMES: I talked to John about it. I said, "I want to know exactly what you are doing and how often."

John had never lied to me. If I confronted him, he could not lie to me. He'd try to gloss it over, and I'd know he was doing it, and it ate at me for about two months.

And then I thought, "I'm married to a whore."

I mean, that's the only thing I could equate it to. I felt it was a betrayal.

BILL AMERSON: The LAPD formed a very special vice squad for pornography. We nicknamed them the "Pussy Posse."

We had "Pussy Posse" T-shirts made up and mailed fifteen of them to the Los Angeles Vice Squad, which, looking back on it, wasn't the prudent thing to do. It really pissed them off. I don't think they ever wore the shirts.

BOB VOSSE: What's weird is no one in the industry knew John Holmes socially. John had no social life; he'd never stick around for parties, and he had very few friends. I tried to be John's friend. We worked together in many places, many times; I shot more than half of the films that John made in his life. But he never trusted me. He never trusted anyone.

So if you want to talk about John Holmes's social life, you're going to have to talk to someone else.

DAWN SCHILLER (JOHN HOLMES'S GIRLFRIEND): When I was fifteen, my father divorced my mother in Florida, and I chose to move with him to California.

But we had nowhere to live. Then a hitchhiker we picked up on the way to California told us we could stay with his girlfriend. But when we got there, she said she would have to ask the manager first. So in walked John Holmes. He was the manager of the apartment complex.

John looked me up and down and then asked me how old I was.

I said, "Fifteen."

And he went, "Mmmmmmm, too bad."

SHARON HOLMES: By 1973, I was literally eating my own guts alive because of the emotional upheaval of trying to deal with John's porn career and maintain a physical relationship with him. I couldn't handle it anymore; I was hospitalized with pancreatitis.

The doctor sat me down and said, "You know, if this keeps up, you're going to lose your pancreas. You have to do something about this. Do you know what is bothering you?"

Surely, you jest. Of course I knew.

So when I got home, I told John, "I have no problem with your living with me, but I don't want anything to do with you physically. I don't want to hear about what you're doing. I'll do your laundry. I'll be your mother, I'll be your confessor, I'll be your sister, I'll be your friend, but I don't want to be physical anymore."

He begged and pleaded, saying, "This porn stuff means absolutely nothing to me."

I said, "John, it doesn't mean anything to you, but it means a lot to me. I'm married to a hooker. I'm not comfortable with that. I can't handle it anymore."

So by 1975 we no longer had a physical relationship. We slept in the same bed, we hugged, we kissed, we felt intimate with each other—but not sexually intimate.

So John found Dawn, a skinny fifteen-year-old whose dad was one of those expatriates who settled in Thailand after Vietnam because of the drug connection. On his first trip home after the Vietnam War, Dawn's father told his wife he wanted a divorce and that he wanted to take the kids to California—to Disneyland.

When they got here, they moved into our apartment complex—five people in a one-bedroom apartment.

DAWN SCHILLER: John knew that me and my sister liked to smoke pot, and he always came home with the best stuff. He'd say, "Here, try this," flick it on the couch, and leave. He always had a dramatic air. And I thought, "God, he's cool!"

My sister thought he was weird because he was too old to be hanging around us. She figured that out. But I liked him.

SHARON HOLMES: Dawn was a very nice-looking girl: big-boned but skinny. And John hired Dawn and her sister, Terry, to do the gardening around the apartment complex, so they could make their own money. Their father had money, but he didn't spend it on his kids. He was always off doing some business deal with his friends from Thailand.

DAWN SCHILLER: John Holmes courted me for about a good six months— and always with my sister, like a chaperone. He had to pay her in armloads of frozen Snickers bars, so she wouldn't bitch about having her apartment used or having to share her pot.

TOM BLAKE (LAPD VICE DETECTIVE): In 1973, we had an informant that advised us that John Holmes was going to be involved in a film with some other people, and we were told that they would be meeting at a certain location in Hollywood.

They would tell the actors and actresses to go to a restaurant at a certain time and wait. They'd never tell them where the film was actually being shot.

We were able to find out what restaurant they were at, and we observed that several women—plus some males, including John Holmes—were at this location. We ran license numbers of the vehicles and found out the names of these people. Then we followed them from Hollywood out to Moorpark, in the Valley, and observed them going to a residence.

DAWN SCHILLER: John and I were getting closer and then he started getting camping trips together—to the beach—in his van. He had a Chevrolet van with a WADD license plate. I guess that was a porn series that he did. The camping turned into overnight camping, always with my sister, and John always made it fun. He'd build a big bonfire on the beach, and we'd eat peanut butter brown sugar chocolate chip cookies, which is the ultimate when you're stoned.

He was quite a romantic.

TOM BLAKE: John was very famous. He was probably the biggest male porno star in the United States through the seventies and eighties. He was very well known for his tool, if you want to call it that.

We'd seen him at several locations but had never been able to make a case on him. And John, most of the time, did not procure people to be involved in films.

John was basically working through an agent—but on this particular film, he was actually the one that procured these two girls who lived in Calabassas.

I believe they were only sixteen or seventeen years old. We found this out because we made the search warrants on the house where they shot the film. Then we obtained the film from the laboratory and viewed it and ran the licenses through the DMV and found out who the two girls were. Then we interviewed them.

DAWN SCHILLER: One time John set it up at the beach so that my sister couldn't be there and asked me to go camping by myself. And, like, we both knew this was the night.

TOM BLAKE: We obtained the arrest warrant through the Ventura County district attorney's office. Then myself and Detective Joe Gandley and a couple of other people went to John Holmes's house in Glendale.

We knocked on the door. John answered it and let us in. We met his wife, Sharon. Very nice lady. We sat down and talked a little bit. We advised him that we were arresting him for pimping and pandering for that film shot in Moorpark.

He said, "Oh no, those girls?"

I said, "Yeah, those girls."

I think he knew they were young, and I think he probably knew that they were the ones that talked about him.

I mean, he was really nice. He says, "I'm an athlete. I don't smoke. I don't drink. I run every day." He had a cupboard in his kitchen that probably had twenty-five or thirty vitamins he took every day. He was a health fanatic.

Anyway, we ended up arresting him and booking him. And I did not see him until we went to court up in Ventura.

DAWN SCHILLER: So we went to Malibu, walked on the beach, and it was a full moon. It was low in the sky. It was perfect, and John was very quiet. We just sat on the rocks and watched the moon. The atmosphere was magical.

TOM BLAKE: I think that this was John's first real encounter with the LAPD—as far as being arrested. We went to court, and after being convicted of pimping and pandering, John was going to be sentenced to three years in jail.

He had an option through his attorney to either cooperate with me and be on probation for three years—or do three years in jail.

So John decided he'd talk to me. He and I worked together for three years, until the terms of his probation ended in 1976.

DAWN SCHILLER: Without saying anything, John got down from that rock and just took my hand, and we walked to the van and that was the night.

Yeah, I was completely shocked by how large he was. But it was like being a virgin again. He was very attentive. He knew how to get you to relax, you know?

And he was extremely gentle and extremely awesome. Just *awesome . . .*

TOM BLAKE: John would tell us who would be shooting the films—the producers, the directors, and sometimes the money people backing the films. And when the films were being shot, he would tell us where the actors were being picked up.

All this made our work much easier.

DAWN SCHILLER: When Tom Blake—Big Tom, we called him—called on the phone at Sharon's, that meant something, like some mysterious signal. It was a code word, and I was absolutely supposed to put the call through, no problems. He was the only person that had the home phone number, so that was a big deal.

TOM BLAKE: Through John Holmes, we already knew the shoot location, so we could set up police officers for surveillance with our vans and our cameras. We'd shoot people coming in and out of the location. It was perfect identification.

DAWN SCHILLER: Big Tom was always immediately directed to either Sharon or John. I handed it to Sharon if John wasn't there or straight to John if he was. If not, it was, "Just tell him Big Tom called."

SHARON HOLMES: After Dawn and John became intimate—though I didn't know it at the time—Dawn became like a daughter to me, and I tried to show her that John wasn't God almighty. But I guess to a fifteen-year-old who's getting showered with gifts—and John telling her how wonderful she was—she would have done anything he wanted.

And eventually she *did* do anything he wanted.

DAWN SCHILLER: I felt as if I was his newborn child. I mean, that's how precious he treated me.

But then John would have to go away to do a film. I knew what kind of movies he was making, but we never really talked about it. I just knew he was going to work. It was called "going to work," and he never brought it home.

Part 3:

SHOW

1975–1977

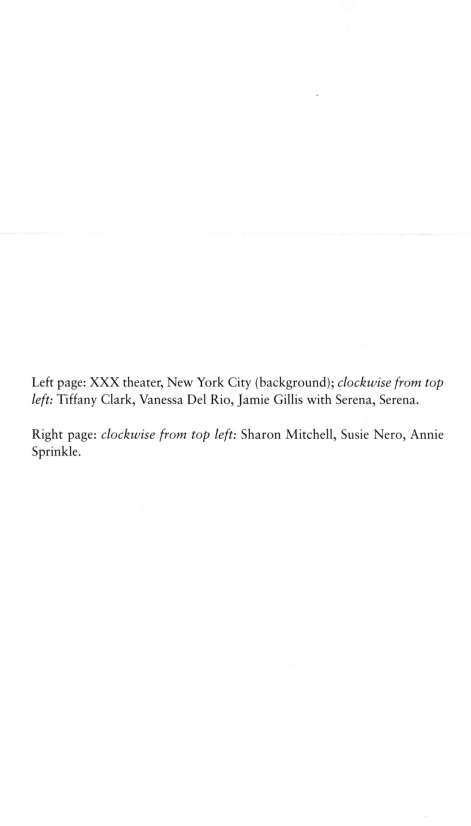

Left page: XXX theater, New York City (background); *clockwise from top left:* Tiffany Clark, Vanessa Del Rio, Jamie Gillis with Serena, Serena.

Right page: *clockwise from top left:* Sharon Mitchell, Susie Nero, Annie Sprinkle.

Boxed Lunch

NEW YORK CITY
1975–1977

VANESSA DEL RIO: I started go-go dancing at Billy's on Sixth Avenue.

One day this guy walked in with a dollar in his hand, and there was a girl dancing on the stage. He threw the dollar on the stage, stuck his finger in her pussy, and then just kept walking. It was like, "Stick your finger in a slut for a buck." I don't even think he looked at her.

ANNIE SPRINKLE: It was the Harmony Burlesque—that was changed to the Melody Burlesque—that started the trend of porn stars doing live burlesque. Tina Russell was the first porn star I remember appearing in person at the Melody. It was a big deal for a porn star to be so out in public, and it was successful.

SHARON MITCHELL: I was one of the first porn stars that was billed as a "porn star" who started stripping at the Melody Burlesque on Forty-eighth Street. None of the old strippers liked me. Except Tempest Storm—who I actually started as a cofeature underneath. Oh, I loved Tempest! She was so great to me. But all those old strippers were like, "What do you think you're going to do?"

I said, "Bump and grind."

They said, "Ha! Not with that body, kid!" Because I was this skinny girl, I went out there and tried to imitate what they were doing, and it wasn't quite working. The old strippers were like, "Kid, isn't there some other kind of dance you can do?"

So the first thing I stripteased to was the entire "Rhapsody in Blue"— from beginning to end. All in lace, jumping around the stage and doing leaps and bounds and high kicks and spread shots everywhere! It was fabulous!

FRED LINCOLN: The Melody was owned by my friend Freddie Cincadi, who was also the assistant district attorney of New York City. How he got away with that for twenty years, I don't know. But Freddie was my best, best buddy.

We hung out. I brought girls to him. I brought Serena to the Melody. I brought Annette Haven to New York. I brought Lesllie Bovee, Sharon Mitchell, and Ming Toy. Anybody that was in the business, I put them in the theaters, and they made a ton of money.

VANESSA DEL RIO: The Melody started the famous "boxed lunch"—which was when the girls sat on the stage or on the bar in front of a guy—and the guy would eat her out. It cost a dollar! Then she'd wipe herself with a baby wipe and move to the next guy, until she made her way around the bar. And in the middle of the stage was a little mountain of baby wipes.

ANNIE SPRINKLE: All those baby wipes! There would be twenty dancers on the stage with their legs spread in a line, and each dancer had her own box of baby wipes mixed with dollars bills! And that's where lap dancing started.

FRED LINCOLN: The girls used to make so much money. My God! Those guys were just lined up. All I could think of was, "Wow, men are really pathetic."

ANNIE SPRINKLE: The Melody was way ahead of Show World on everything.

VANESSA DEL RIO: At that time, we didn't really have much to do with Show World. The Melody was true burlesque.

FRED LINCOLN: The Melody used to call it "Mardi Gras," when the customers could lick the girl for a dollar a lick. The girls used to take the dollar and throw it over their shoulder; the guy would get down, lick once, then this leg would push him away, and the other leg would reach out and grab the next one; the girl would take his dollar and throw him out.

It was like this leg assembly line.

What was funny was we went out in the lobby and the guys would talk about how they got to the girl! They'd say, "Wow! I could feel it trembling. If they gave me just one more minute . . ."

SHARON MITCHELL: I was doing a movie and two guys were going to stick their cocks in me, at the same time, both in my pussy. And my pussy's not really big. I certainly wasn't going to let them fuck me in the ass. Because I knew damn well my asshole's about the size of a fucking dime, a pea. I thought, "No, that will never work."

But I really didn't know how to say no.

I had befriended these guys I had done a couple movies with on and off, and a couple of girls that were really nice to me, like Vanessa Del Rio—who protected me and really helped me.

Vanessa said, "You look like a kid from Jersey!"

I said, "I *am* a kid from Jersey!"

So she took me shopping, and spent like two thousand dollars on me in one day. She took me to the Late Show and Trash and Vaudeville—all those little hip places. They cut my hair and whipped me into shape.

ANNIE SPRINKLE: When Show World started to have porn stars appear live, that's what put me through college.

TIM CONNELLY (FORMER PORN STAR): First Rod Swenson booked Show World—he's the guy who married Wendy O. Williams and managed the Plasmatics. Wendy used to do live sex shows at Show World long before I got there. Then Rod Swenson gave way to Freddie Lincoln, who was a great guy—and then Freddie Lincoln gave way to Ron Martin.

But there was a short time when Ron Martin booked the show downstairs, and Freddie booked the show upstairs.

FRED LINCOLN: I used to do a thing in New York City's Greenwich Village called the Party, which came about because I took an ad out in *Penthouse* asking if anybody had any bizarre fantasy that they were afraid to share. And we got thousands of letters—some of the most pathetic creatures on earth, ha, ha, ha. And we would reenact them in this loft in the Village—every Friday and Saturday night. It was a big success; it was packed every weekend.

Before we closed, Ron Martin came down and said to me, "I wanna take you uptown to Show World. And you can have the lower theater."

I said, "And I can do anything I want?"

He said, "Yeah. Anything you want."

TIM CONNELLY: Fred started this thing at Show World called the Ultra Burlesque—which could be anything; S and M shows or burlesque skits, live sex or strippers.

The concept was "what you gave them is what they expect they should get"—it could be Serena coming from San Francisco and stripping; if she wanted to fuck, they'd bring a guy to fuck her. And depending on how she wanted to fuck, they'd bring in a dominant guy or a submissive guy. At that time, Joey Silvera was working there. Jamie Gillis would blow in every now and then. Helen Madigan and Marc Stevens—it really was anything goes.

SHARON MITCHELL: Vanessa Del Rio lived in Independence Plaza, and I was doing a movie with her. But I really wasn't up on my cocksucking technique.

She said, "Well, you know, I can help you with that."

So one day she takes me over to see her boyfriend, Johnny. She sets up a three-way mirror around Johnny's dick. She gives me a bunch of coke, right? And teaches me how to suck dick. "Now be aware of your nose and your angles. . . . It has to feel good as well as look good . . . and watch the camera now . . ."

It was really helpful. Because when I was sucking Johnny's cock in front of the three-way mirror, I could see how I looked from every side.

Then I got into pussy hair coiffing. So I would exchange these cocksucking lessons in exchange for coiffing Vanessa's pussy hair.

FRED LINCOLN: The Mitchell brothers and I used to exchange people for our clubs. I would call them up, and we would discuss different girls and different acts. See, I was the first person to ever put porno girls in theaters and nightclubs in New York.

I did it by convincing this guy, Bernie, to hire Bambi Woods. He paid her three thousand dollars and told me, "If she don't make this money back, you gotta pay us."

I said, "Don't worry. I'll get your money back."

She packed the club.

TIM CONNELLY: When I came to New York, I was married to an English girl, a girl I'd met in Chicago. Our marriage had pretty much failed, but she wanted to come with me to New York.

We were walking through Times Square, and we decided to go to Show World. I couldn't believe there was this giant multilevel emporium of pornography, you know?

We went into one of those dollar peep-show booths. The screen came up, and there was this pretty good-looking Puerto Rican girl. And my wife, who was pretty normal in terms of sexuality, gets wildly turned on by this naked girl writhing and masturbating and talking dirty to us. I had never had that experience with her before. So on the way home I just pulled her in to some building and took her on the stairwell and fucked her because we were just so turned on.

I felt weird about it afterward. You know, like what the fuck happened to me? I knew I was entering a new area. It was exciting—and confusing.

SHARON MITCHELL: The years 1975, 1976, 1977 were the beginning of the great era of smut on Forty-second Street because that's when it changed over from those old burlesque strippers to porn stars and rock and roll girls.

TIM CONNELLY: That night, my band and soon-to-be ex-wife went to Max's Kansas City to see Sirius Trixon get married onstage. My band sits down—and Sharon Mitchell's right across the table from us.

I thought, "This is unbelievable." Sharon Mitchell was being regarded with as much celebrity as Allen Ginsberg and Andy Warhol and Brian Eno, who were all hanging out. The band and I just wanted to meet Brian Eno and John Cale and give them our tapes. Hopefully they'd want to produce us or something. So it was new to me—this connection between strippers, porn stars, and rock and roll.

SHARON MITCHELL: New York—it was just all new. It was wild—amazing, you know? I'm having experimental sex—sex with young girls, kinky sex. Because all these young girls had crushes on me, you know? Young girls loved me. I was slick; I was very masculine. I was very rock and roll and pushy and wiry and people loved me. Because I was "Sharon Mitchell," and people loved that.

TIM CONNELLY: One of the guys in my band was dating Lolly Holly, the guitar player in Krayola, a New York all-girl punk band. Lolly was a stripper, and they wanted to bring in a drummer—this porn star/stripper named Helen Madigan—and they asked me to teach her to play drums.

I needed the money, so I agreed to do it. For Helen's first drum lesson, I had to meet her at the Melody Burlesque, where she was working at the time.

When I got there, I walked in the middle of a Mardi Gras, which is when they send the girls to circulate in the audience. It's the equivalent of lap dancing now, but then it was this dollar-a-lick thing.

C. J. LAING: I went back to New York from Texas after visiting my rock and roll boyfriend—and the Mitchell brothers had just come to New York. And we got together and partied, and they introduced me to the Buckleys, who had done *Screw* with Al Goldstein and were making their first movie. So that's how I did my first movie with Jamie Gillis.

TIM CONNELLY: I was just fascinated by what the girls were doing at the Melody—and that the guys were paying for it. Coming from a good-looking rock and roll band, I never had a problem getting pussy. So I was just blown away that guys would pay money to have these girls bounce in and out of their lap for ten seconds.

SHARON MITCHELL: One night I got a call from Jamie Gillis, who had a horribly filthy apartment on Forty-sixth Street and Ninth Avenue, in Hell's

Kitchen. Hadn't cleaned it in years—and Jamie has weird eating habits. I mean, you open up his refrigerator, and there's like bull's balls and fucking pickled eyes and pigs' ears. It looks like a vivisectionist's fucking refrigerator, you know? Goats' heads—weird fucking shit he'd buy in Chinatown.

So anyway, I get this call from Jamie and he says, "Uh, Mitch, can you come up? I need some help."

I said, "Sure," because Jamie was one of the big brother guys that watched over me. Him and John Leslie and Eric Edwards—all those guys really flanked me and took care of me. So I would never ask, "Why?" even though it was two in the morning. I just said, "Okay." I mean, I was up anyway. So I got in a cab and went up to Jamie's filthy apartment, and he and C. J. Laing were having some kind of a weird sexual session. He had her head in the toilet—and he needed both hands to, like, keep her breathing and the toilet flushing.

He needed another hand to help get her head out of the toilet—so she wouldn't drown.

TIM CONNELLY: Helen and I went back to my loft, and I tried to give her a drum lesson, but she was so fucking uncoordinated. I mean, she couldn't even hold the sticks in her hands. But she just had this infectious laugh; she was really cute and sexy.

So after about half an hour I said, "You know what? Let's not push it the first time. Maybe I'll get you a Mel Bay book—the basic textbook of drumming—and then I'll teach you how to read music."

I gave her a pair of my sticks to take home, and she was so excited. She started running the sticks between her legs, right?

It had started snowing really heavily out so I said, "Maybe you should get going."

She said, "Well, you know, I can hang out . . . if you want . . ."

SHARON MITCHELL: It was something with the pull chain and the drain—and we needed four hands to get the girl's head un-flushed and save her. It was a weird incident. But a nice one. I mean, it wasn't like everyone didn't know Jamie had a penchant for weird S and M scenes.

I was just glad I could be there for my friends, ha, ha, ha.

C. J. LAING: There was some little talent agency in Times Square that represented me. This old woman ran it, and she was a cunt. Oh, she was horrible!

So I started doing a lot of porn—and I started becoming like a circus-act girl. I was the girl that did farm boys that were coming in with eighteen-inch cocks. These guys that couldn't speak but had . . . anomalies, right?

I'm the girl that deep-throated John Holmes, and I'm the girl that double fisted with this one and that one—and did all of these very intense sex scenes.

I purposely would not act. I despised the people in these films that said they were actors.

I was like, "You've got to be kidding me! This is about fucking and sucking!"

SHARON MITCHELL: The two big places to dance were the Melody Burlesque and Show World. But Show World was really happening: It had four floors with different types of sex—you know, transsexuals, porn stars, unisexuals, S and M shows. Everybody was there, and we were all featuring at different times.

One night, Vanessa Del Rio was downstairs at Show World—and Ming Toy and I were cofeaturing upstairs. That's when the vice detectives walked in.

ERIC EDWARDS: I met Arcadia Lake at Show World. Marc Stevens introduced us. Then I did a couple of live sex shows with her. It was not professional. It was like, "Oh, wow, I like her! I'll go do it onstage! Why not?"

I was doing penetration right there onstage with her. And then I invited her to go with me to Jamaica because I liked her.

SHARON MITCHELL: I was doing this well-choreographed act—a Western show with Roy Rogers chaps and a little bra. I had six guns, little snappies, a whip, and lollipops to hand out to the audience. By the third song I was down to bra, panties, garter belt, fishnets, and boots, right?

And that's when one of the DJs spots the vice detectives in the house. This DJ was an ex-con, a junkie of course, and he could smell a cop. So he turns the music down and says, "Ladies and gentlemen, thank you very much. Let's hear it for Sharon Mitchell!"

The audience got all uptight because I hadn't taken anything off yet. So the officer says to me, "You better put your clothes on because we're going to go for a little ride downtown."

I said, "I don't want to go for a little ride. I have another show at midnight."

TIM CONNELLY: After the attempted drum lesson, we just sat there talking. And Helen told me all about herself, how she grew up in California and started doing porno movies up in San Francisco. I think she told me the first movie she did was *Teenage Peanut Butter Freaks*.

Then she started making porno movies and stripping in New York and became friends with Marc Stevens. That intimidated me a little bit because he was known as Mr. Ten-and-a-Half.

I was like, "Oh, fuck! I got no shot here!"

I didn't even want to pull my pants down around her. For a moment I thought, "What am I getting into? I'm throwing myself up against all these guys that have giant cocks!"

Then I thought, "Well, just ride it out. Let's see what happens."

SHARON MITCHELL: The cops followed me upstairs and kept trying to put an officer in the room to look at me while I changed. They hadn't seen me naked so they didn't know what sex I was. They couldn't tell, so finally they told me I was under arrest. They busted me on obscenity—even though they knew I hadn't taken off my clothes. They just fucked up.

So I get dressed, and they take me downtown to the Tombs for the grilling, and the first question they asked me was, "What sex are you?"

I said, "Aha! So, you don't know, do you?"

Now, I have the gift of being able to piss standing up if I want. So I said, "You'll have to guess."

They said, "You'll have to take a piss sometime."

I said, "Yeah, you're right. I probably will."

TIM CONNELLY: Helen and I talked until about four in the morning, and then we had sex for like four or five hours. I had a nine-to-five job at the time, but I bailed on that.

And I thought, "What am I doing?" This is the road to ruin, you know? The sleigh ride to hell—and it was great!

Around noon, Helen wanted to go back to her apartment on the Upper East Side, which had a couch and a mattress and a bunch of really cool records. And G-strings hanging all over the place because her roommate was Nikki Knights, who was also a stripper.

I was like, "This is fucking *great,* man!"

ERIC EDWARDS: Then I found out Arcadia's problem: heroin. I said, "Well, let's fix this. I'll help you."

SHARON MITCHELL: So they put me in the tank with all the transsexuals, and I learned a very valuable trick that evening. I learned how to make blue eye shadow out of matches. So all was not lost in the Tombs that night.

ERIC EDWARDS: I could have fallen in love with Veronica Hart—who was just coming on the scene—but I was in love with Arcadia when I met Veronica. I'm a monogamist, and I had said to Arcadia, "You and I can fix this heroin problem."

So I played doctor for a year. I was decreasing her dosage little by little and taking her on vacations and stuff like that. I was totally in love with her.

FRED LINCOLN: I wrote around eight skits for the performances at Show World, and then after the show, we would invite people up to get beat. And I'm tellin' you it was so good. I played Pink Floyd music. I had lighting cues. I had strobe lights. I had a bouncer—a huge black guy who was six-foot-six. His girlfriend was a little, teeny thing—five foot.

He would tie her up to this pole and take this bullwhip and whip her with it. You'd hear, "WHHHHAAACK!" The Pink Floyd is going, "Bbummmmbadummmmbadummm!" And the strobe lights are going, and you see this big, black, oiled guy and this little girl go, "Aaaaaaaahhhhh!"

You'd hear the whip cracking and see her getting whipped, but she had a leather vest on, and it would hit the vest. It never hurt her—but nobody knew that.

Fucking people went crazy. *Variety* reviewed it and said that if all pornography were like this, it would be reason enough to legalize it. Of course the cops came the next week and busted us anyway.

SHARON MITCHELL: The cop asked me, "Which bathroom do you want?"

I said, "The men's room."

So I went in, stood up, and peed in the urinal. The cop was looking. When I came back from the bathroom, they checked off "male" on the booking sheet.

The lawyers were going crazy because everybody else wanted to sign off on some lesser plea for prostitution. I said, "No way! I didn't do anything obscene, and I'm not a fucking prostitute! Why the fuck would I do that?"

Show World really liked that and provided me with some hotshot lawyer. God, it must have cost them thousands. We continued on with the case—and I won it.

TIM CONNELLY: Even after we started fucking, Helen still couldn't play drums. So I told her, "Look, I really think you're great—I want to hang out with you—but you can't fucking play."

Helen was fine with it—relieved, actually. So Krayola found another drummer, and I ended up moving in with Helen into that apartment—which was actually a duplex she shared with some of the girls from Krayola.

Helen and I lived downstairs. The band I had moved to New York with—the Boo Hoo Band—had broken up, and I'd played some gigs with Richard Hell and had gotten ripped off. So I was broke, with no gigs, and the rent due.

That's when Helen said, "Look, if you want, I can get you into a movie."

ERIC EDWARDS: I got Arcadia down to zero. In fact I've got a picture of her going "thumbs up!" Wonderful. Beautiful. I loved her then. That was great.

And then she met somebody else and got back into it.

FRED LINCOLN: I went out to San Francisco to do a movie, and while I was gone Ron Martin changed everything I'd done at Show World. He was so jealous of my success. He tied this one girl up and let this other girl beat the shit outta her onstage.

I said, "What the hell's the matter with you? That's not what we're doing—hurting people. This isn't what she signed on for! We're puttin' a show on. This girl is full of fucking welts, you idiot. What if she gets a lawyer?"

Ron said, "Oh, they loved it."

TIM CONNELLY: At that time, the downstairs theater at Show World was like a really old fashioned burlesque theater. It was about a hundred seats and a stage with curtains that opened and closed and a dressing room behind it. And upstairs was the S and M show. That was more of a "T" stage with chairs around it. Eventually it was known as the "Triple Threat Theater."

FRED LINCOLN: So Ron and I split up, and every week the police would come. Sometimes they would spot me in the back and say, "Hey! What do you do? You look like a producer to me!"

I said, "How the fuck do I look like a producer, you idiot? I look like a hipster!"

KELLY NICHOLS (PORN STAR): Fred Lincoln was great. He was always fun to work for, very enthusiastic and weird. He'd say, "Just go for it. Do something different." He had this long, white hair. He was almost a psychic touchstone because he was older than all of us.

FRED LINCOLN: I was doing film, *An Adult Fairy Tale,* in San Francisco with Serena at the same time I was booking Show World, so when we finished the film I brought her back to New York with me.

JAMIE GILLIS: I met Serena in Los Angeles in about 1973—but she was living with a guy, so I let it go. About a year later she was independent, and she came to New York to dance at Show World.

FRED LINCOLN: So I was with Serena, and Jamie Gillis wanted her. We both liked her, although I had already done her in San Francisco. But it was pretty funny—the three of us went out one night, and Jamie wanted Serena so bad. You know, we were having some drinks, and we went here and there, and then we went to a hotel room. And when Serena went to take a leak, Jamie ran into the bathroom to be her toilet.

So I said, "Okay, Jamie. You win."

I just left. That's when Jamie and Serena became an item.

KELLY NICHOLS: Serena was a nude model with me in Los Angeles. I knew she was a dominatrix, and I knew she was gorgeous. I used to love to look at her because she looked like a drawing—like Jessica Rabbit. She would wear these short miniskirts and thigh-high wool stockings and these shoes—and she had these big, full lips. Just gorgeous.

I thought, "That's what I wanna be when I grow up!"

SERENA: My ex-husband, John Gault, got me into porn. We were just a couple of kids living on the streets of Berkeley and hitchhiking around California. John helped me from the beginning. Neither one of us knew anything about the porn scene, but John kept people in line who would have taken advantage of me.

But he didn't relate to me fucking other men. There was this really bad film called *Love, Lust and Violence* where I gave someone head. It was the first hard thing I'd ever done without John, and he was very pissed. I had to turn down lots of films because I would only work with John. And that caused a lot of tension between us. I probably never should have gotten him involved in the business at all. That's why I was very glad to meet Jamie Gillis.

JAMIE GILLIS: I went to see the show—just to see Serena—and I went back to her hotel with her right after. We had sex, and I thought that was going to be it. But then we started hanging out, and I'd go to the shows. It was fun because she'd be working in these little hot pants, and I'd watch her, and she was just having a good time being a really sexy young girl. That was a great moment in New York. She was so free.

FRED LINCOLN: So I hooked Jamie and Serena up, and they were together for years. And when they became an item, I put them in my live sex show at Show World. Oh, they were wonderful onstage! It would start with Serena dancing through the audience for tips, and then Jamie would catch her sitting in somebody's lap, and he'd snap, "What are you doing?"

Serena would say "I . . . I . . . I was making extra money, baby—for us."

Jamie would say, "Well, how much did you make?"

She'd say, "Two dollars!"

Then Jamie would just grab it from her.

JAMIE GILLIS: Serena and I would have sex onstage for the hell of it. We lived in the neighborhood, so it was just something to do. I was really having a lot of fun with it.

I like sex. The idea that there's something weird, far-out, or freaky about that is strange. I think of myself the same way Marc Stevens's mother described him—as "an actor with a specialty."

SERENA: I come best, generally, when I'm onstage dancing. When I say "dancing" I mean working on and off at Show World doing their "Bizarre Burlesque." But I don't do a burlesque strip. The only instrument I play is my body, and I'm very good at it.

I'm first and foremost an exhibitionist—and if I ever make contact with someone, they've been fucked, and they know it. I see a lot of wet spots in their pants, those daddies out there. They feed my energy. So with all those people's energies supporting me, their mouths hanging open, sitting on the edge of their chairs while I do my number, I explode. That's my biggest come—like my fluids are gushing down my leg.

JAMIE GILLIS: What gets me off most of all is to find something that somebody likes. I like pleasing women. It's partially a submissive thing and partially a power thing.

People used to joke that Serena and I were sort of like I'd met my match or she'd met her match. Both of us could be dominant or submissive. One time she left a rose and a whip on the pillow—a little of each, you know?

FRED LINCOLN: Jamie would get pissed off with Serena and start doing things to her, then another girl would come out and take care of Jamie, then he would tie 'em up and hoist 'em upside down, then they would—I mean, we'd do anything we want. It was so wonderful.

BILL MARGOLD (FORMER PORNOGRAPHER): Jamie and Serena were perfectly matched. They were in love—but they were also in mutual awe and mutual idolization of each other. So they played the S and M game very, very well.

SERENA: Would I say that I loved Jamie? Madly. I gave Jamie everything. If Jamie had come to me and said, "Hey, bitch, I want to piss on you. I want to shit on your face," would I like it? Sure I would—not from every man, but because he's Jamie and because that's part of it. This all stems back to, "Daddy didn't give me enough love." I hope I will always have that need, that drive to create.

JAMIE GILLIS: Once I wiped Serena's makeup off on the toilet just for a hot scene. It was like, "You filthy little whore. Dirty girl . . ."

She said, "Well, you know, my father would have done something like that. . . ."

SERENA: When I was fourteen my mother fell in love with this man who had just gotten back from Vietnam. She wanted him as a son, if she couldn't have him as a lover.

My mother was going through menopause, I was going through puberty, and the guy was middle-aged. He lived around the corner, and we just fucked and fucked. I spent most of my time there; it was all right with mom, as long as I brought him over once in a while.

Once, during our lovemaking, he talked me into letting go and letting it happen. Once I stopped thinking about it, I could have orgasms.

FRED LINCOLN: Jamie and Serena's shows were just Friday and Saturday nights at midnight—so we wouldn't get busted.

SERENA: Jamie and I also sometimes switch roles three or four times during lovemaking. We'll tease each other over our cappuccino, with our looks, with our bedroom eyes. Maybe I'll stroke my tit in the restaurant. Then we go home and we completely try to ignore it. Then I put on whatever I find sexy—it may be my fuck-me, high-heel sandals and my hot pants, or a negligee—and dance around the room or get out the whip or whatever.

Then I usually totally ignore Jamie. Like last night, I just was looking out the window—while he was fucking me. I was talking to everybody that went by, waving and half crawling out the window, trying to get away from him. Walking around the room, and he's still in me.

He was calling me a bitch, a cunt, a lot of verbal exchange. There's a lot of that with Jamie. And I'm just ignoring him with my body, like, "Get away from me, fuck head. You *worm*!"

He loves that, but the next step may be that he tears himself out of me, slaps me across the face, throws me across the bed and rapes the shit out of me. And if we break out of that, we probably look each other in the eye and give each other a real sweet kiss and become lovers.

The Ballad of Jason and Tina

NEW YORK CITY/MIAMI
1976–1977

TIM CONNELLY: I shot my first loop for Jason Russell—Tina Russell's husband—at Adventure Studios, Gerard Damiano's film studio in Astoria, Queens. Helen Madigan warned me that Jason was kind of crazy—and he was an asshole on the set, you know, barking at me. And then in the first scene—the first loop I shot—I came on Helen's face.

I came right in her eye. Blam! My first scene, and Jason starts yelling at me while I'm coming, "Fuck! What are you doing? Not in her fucking eye!"

I'm like, "Oh, fuck."

Helen was laughing, you know? I mean, where was I *supposed* to come? It wasn't like it was something I'd ever done before, you know? I mean, if a girl's giving me head and I'm gonna come, I'm gonna come in her mouth—not on her *face*.

FRED LINCOLN: Once Jason Russell started making money and directing, he was not so nice to Tina. And she adored him. She did everything for Jason. Tina never cared who he fucked, but Jason abandoned Tina when he fell in love with Jean Jennings.

This is hard for me because I introduced Jean to Jason. I met Jean Jennings in Florida when Sean Cunningham did some movie down there. We had gotten this director named Brad Talbot, who used to do spaghetti Westerns, and he wrote this supposed spectacular hard-core movie called *Full Moon Murders.*

TIM CONNELLY: Jason was furious with me. He didn't want me to do another loop. But someone—it wasn't Gerard Damiano; I think it was one of the guys on the crew—talked Jason into letting Helen and me do another loop.

I said, "Look, I know you said on her face, but I'll get the next one right. . . ."

And the next one was fine—I came about four inches lower.

Jason was like, "Okay. . . ."

FRED LINCOLN: So Sean brought me down to Miami to work on *Full Moon Murders,* and they brought Harry Reems down there, too. When we got there, nobody could fuck but me and Harry. All the other guys couldn't get it up. So Sean was like, "My God, I've got a really nice script here. I've got yachts and airplanes. I've got houses with pools and shit. What am I going to do?"

I said, "Just make it arty. You know, we're here, and you've already spent all the money. Let's just do it."

Now, Jean Jennings came to us through Lenny Camp. He's the guy who gave us the girls. He knew all the girls; he was probably giving them all Quaaludes and fucking them all. And he liked them young—they were all underage.

SHARON MITCHELL: People were surprised that girls started in porn when they were underage, but I wasn't surprised because I started underage, you know? I starred in my first feature, *Joy,* when I was seventeen, but I had to wait two years for it to come out. So in the meantime I did loops and stripped.

FRED LINCOLN: I was nice to Jean Jennings during the filming. I mean, she was sweet: a beautiful, blond kid. And I guess Lenny Camp got jealous and told Sean, "This guy Freddie Lincoln better stop talkin' to this girl, or I'm pullin' all my girls off your movie!"

So Sean came to me and said, "I don't know what to say. . . ."

I said, "Hey, don't worry about it. I won't go near her."

But what Lenny did was the worst thing you could possibly do—because now Jean wanted to know, "Why was I ignoring her? Why aren't we flirting anymore? What happened? Am I losing it?"

You know, you're talking about a kid who's just discovering her sexuality. And all of a sudden, someone's not fallin' for it; holy shit! That destroyed her.

BILL KELLY: Lenny Camp used to photograph probably thousands of girls between the ages of fifteen and eighteen or nineteen, and he sampled the merchandise on frequent occasions—even with the young ones.

FRED LINCOLN: When Sean told me what Lenny told him, I said, "Okay, fine. I'm not saying another fucking word. But when I leave Florida, that little girl is coming with me."

Sean said, "Ha, ha, ha."

I said, "You want to know something, Sean? When it comes to women, there isn't anything I can't do, and I don't give a shit who they are."

SHARON MITCHELL: I was very impatient as a young porno star. When *Joy* finally came out, I got a taste of what it was like to watch myself on the silver screen and see my pussy sixteen feet high—like it should be.

There was a theater in my neighborhood called the Variety Photoplays on Third Avenue and Thirteenth Street that attracted the raincoat crowd—like the Fourty-second Street theaters where the drunk black guys talk back to the movie. You know, this wasn't a "couples theater"—they used to run second- or third-run porn movies along with rock and roll features. It probably had something to do with "community standards"—so the theater wouldn't get busted.

So there was actually a bill that read, "Sharon Mitchell/Jimi Hendrix."

FRED LINCOLN: Where did Lenny Camp find them in Miami? Are you kidding me? Thousands and thousands of kids go to Lauderdale and Miami every year. Jean was different—I mean, she lived there, but she was running away from home. And then she, you know, bumped into Lenny Camp.

She was a pretty cool little girl. God, she was so sexy. So beautiful.

SHARON MITCHELL: When I was in theaters and watching my movies, I liked the way I looked; I liked everything about it. So I went over to the Variety, and there I was—on-screen—giving John Leslie a blow job.

I was watching myself and looking over at the front or second row, and there was an older gentleman masturbating to me giving John Leslie head on-screen. And in the movie, John was playing an older man.

So as I was watching this older guy jerking off to me, the idea occurred to me, "What if I actually crawled up and started sucking this guy's dick? That would really be a turn-on!"

He looked like a clean guy—a nice guy. So I was scooting over one seat to the next, jumping across the aisle, watching him masturbate to me. Finally, I crawled up to him and started sucking his dick.

FRED LINCOLN: When we finished the movie, I took Jean Jennings and another of Lenny Camp's girls back to New York with me. He didn't like losing this girl—the only one who had a brain in his whole fucking stable.

So back in New York, we're having a birthday party for Jean at Bernard's, and she asked, "Could you buy me a drink?"

I said, "A *drink*? What are you talking about? Are you *underage*? You're underage! *Shit!*"

SHARON MITCHELL: I was trying to duplicate the pace of the blow job on-screen with the actual blow job I was giving this old guy. He didn't look down for a while; he probably thought I was a guy because hustlers would give blow jobs in there for five dollars. And he probably wasn't gay; he was just there to get off.

So he didn't look down for a while, but when he did, he looked up at the screen, then looked down again, then up again—and then he went "Ugghhh!" and grabbed his fucking chest!

I went, "Oh, *fuck*!"

He was gasping, and he fell over. He was having a heart attack! So I ran and got one of the gay ushers, and they called 911, and the paramedics came and took him out. As they were carrying him out, he gasped to me in this tiny whisper, "Thank you."

FRED LINCOLN: With Jean, you know, this was child pornography, and I wasn't into that. We thought these were legitimate girls. I had no idea how old she was. I guess it would all have come back to Lenny Camp, though, because he was the guy that would furnish their fake IDs.

SHARON MITCHELL: I don't know whether the guy lived or died, ha, ha, ha. But I think I certainly gave him a great exit—if he did die.

FRED LINCOLN: Do you know what the fuck could've happened if they knew Jean Jennings was underage? She could've destroyed us all: Sean, everybody.

Lemme tell you something. If ever anybody fucking deserved to get nailed for kiddie porn, it was Lenny Camp. He was a real scumbag.

BILL KELLY: I think I first got on to Lenny Camp in 1969. He was taking sexually oriented pictures of juveniles then. I got him with Donald Birdy the first time for income tax evasion about twenty years ago. He went away for it, for just a period of months.

Lenny had two angels—guys that financed him. One was Ben Tobin, one of the richest men in South Florida—there's a foundation named after him. He was a real big real estate owner. The other was Harold Chaskin, another multimillionaire.

FRED LINCOLN: Jason Russell fell in love with Jean Jennings, and you know what? He became a jerk, not a prick. Everybody fell in love with her. I fell in love with her when I first met her.

Vinnie Rossi just went absolutely ape-shit. He followed me around like a puppy and said, "I'll give you money! Anything!"

I said, "She's not like that. She only does it with people she likes."

Vinnie was a dog. You know, he loved her so much. And Jean used to just laugh at him.

BILL KELLY: Ben Tobin and Harold Chaskin used to like young girls, and Lenny Camp used to supply them with the merchandise—some of whom I've interviewed. But not one of them was ever cooperative, until I finally got one that was working as a secretary—a good-looking chick, Zaris Soltan. She was seventeen going on forty—and she talked about getting in a hot tub with them.

LENNY CAMP: Why do I think Zaris Soltan agreed to cooperate with Bill Kelly? Come on, get serious. Get *serious*! Those guys, once they—this was all bullshit; it's all Bill Kelly bullshit! They threaten them! They do the good guy/bad guy deal, you know? They do all kinds of stuff. Every lawyer I've ever talked with has told me, "You are no match for the FBI. That's all there is to it. You can't win."

BILL KELLY: Zaris Soltan got in a hot tub with three eighteen-year-old girls and was photographed by Lenny Camp in the apartment of Harold Chaskin in a condo in Hollywood Beach named the Quadromain.

LENNY CAMP: I had all these IDs of Zaris's and tons of pictures of her. But the thing was that so many things disappeared, so many things that—I didn't know that Kelly had a key to my place, and he walked in and out, you know, just like I did. Negatives and pictures disappeared—I used to have people fill out long application forms, to find out what they did, and what they wanted to do, and what their background was, and stuff like that. But little did I know that it would just be fodder for Kelly—to harass these people for days and weeks and months.

Bill Kelly called me the Pied Piper of porn? Well, he was the Pied Piper of shit!

BILL KELLY: We got the pictures, we got the statement, we got an indictment against Lenny Camp, and he got fifteen years for taking pictures of a seventeen-year-old girl in a sexual situation, which constitutes child pornography.

He served five-and-a-half.

FRED LINCOLN: When I met Jean she was high on Quaaludes. That was what that prick Lenny used to do—get all them girls strung out. That way they'd do what he told them.

How old was Jean when I met her? I don't know. Jean was almost six feet tall, and she was the most beautiful creature! Who the hell ever knew she was a little kid?

When I brought Jean up to New York, she said, "I don't want to make any movies."

I said, "Fine. I don't care."

TIM CONNELLY: Jean Jennings was total white fucking trash from Florida. She was underage; *hot*. Cute. Sexy. Young. Blond. Tight body. Unbelievably perfect—except that once you heard her talk it was all over. She was just dumb and ignorant—like a sixty-five-year-old woman living in a trailer in Gainesville, Florida. It was a big turnoff—except for a guy like Jason Russell.

FRED LINCOLN: This other girl I brought up from Florida and I made a home movie together when we got back to New York. Just for fun because this guy did this incredible script. There were supposed to be other people in the movie, but then the guy who was making it changed the script—and then it was the two of us. I'm like, "Come on, you expect us to carry a fuckin' big ass movie with just the two of us?"

And he did, and he made money on it.

And then Jean Jennings went to Italy. That was cool with me. Did it break my heart? No, it was fine. I mean, I never get jealous. I probably just went to Bernard's.

SHARON MITCHELL: Bernard's was a theater district bar where we would all hang out. One of the owners of the Melody owned Bernard's, so all the porn stars flocked there. And there were always these neat, new kind of stripper girls coming in, plus the Times Square theater crowd, and all these porn people, and agents, and directors. Freddie Lincoln was there, Annie Sprinkle, Tiffany Clark, myself, Jamie Gillis, Marc Stevens, Tim Connelly, Helen Madigan, C. J. Laing. It became *the* hangout for the porn scene.

TIM CONNELLY: Helen told me to meet her at Bernard's, across the street from the Melody Burlesque. She told me to get whatever I wanted to eat or drink, and when she came over, she'd take care of the bill. So I was getting into that whole musician/stripper thing—she's paying all the bills, and I'm the trophy stud.

ERIC EDWARDS: I never really hung out with "the" crowd, but I went to Bernard's. You'd walk in, go down a couple of steps, and pick a table on your left-hand side.

The bar is on the right—and there you would see all the faces that you probably just "worked with" for the day: Kelly Nichols, Vanessa Del Rio, Tim Connelly, Marlene Willoughby, Susie Nero—and all the girls coming off their shifts at the Melody.

RHONDA JO PETTY: I went to New York, and the only time you'd see me out was on a set or at Bernard's—that is, in the bathroom at Bernard's doing cocaine. You could always get cocaine at Bernard's.

TIM CONNELLY: Tina Russell had been a pretty hot looking chick, right? You know, having seen her face in pictures and on billboards in Times Square, I was thinking I was going to meet this beautiful little wood nymph.

But when I walked into Bernard's with Marc Stevens and Helen Madigan, Marc said, "Oh my God. Tina's here."

Helen said, "Oh, shit."

I asked, "What's the matter?"

Helen told me, "Tina's in bad shape."

FRED LINCOLN: Maybe a year before Jason hooked up with Jean, Toby Ross did this film starring Tina Russell called *Not Just Another Woman*. Toby had billboards on Broadway and on Sunset Boulevard with Tina's picture on them. Tina—she was gorgeous. Oh, she was beautiful.

TIM CONNELLY: Tina was estranged from Jason at that point because he was with Jean Jennings. And she was just a mess. She smelled, and she was fat and bloated from booze and dope—it was like Anita Pallenberg, you know? Just horrible. I mean, you could feel the negativity coming off her. I thought I was going to meet this beautiful girl. Instead, I met this troll.

FRED LINCOLN: I used to say to Jason, "You know, how come Tina's not working?"

He'd say, "Oh, she doesn't want to." But that wasn't true at all. Jason just didn't want her around. Jason just abandoned her for Jean. It was pretty sad. That's what broke Tina's heart, and she just started drinking.

TIM CONNELLY: Whenever I saw Tina in Bernard's after that—which was like three or four times—she was on dope and drunk every time. You know, just fucked up. It was scary because she was completely bloated. I think she was trying to kill herself. Slowly.

FRED LINCOLN: Yeah, Jason really upset Tina because when he fell in love with Jean, he made Tina work as Jean's makeup person. What the fuck was that? Tina could still work; Tina could still make movies. She was incredible.

TIM CONNELLY: Jason Russell was a little intimidating, and I could see how he could be controlling. I mean, I never worked for him again after I came in Helen's eye.

I can still hear him barking at me: "Come on her mouth! *Come on her mouth!*"

FRED LINCOLN: When Jason left Tina, she just fell apart. She just couldn't deal with it. It broke her heart; it really did. And she just hit the bottle. And drank herself to death.

I think she was in her twenties.

Turnover

NEW YORK CITY
1976–1977

FRED LINCOLN: I was working as a production manager for Gerry Damiano and his partner, Vince, another hairdresser from Queens. They were making a movie called *Satisfiers of Alpha Blue,* and Tiffany Clark was one of the people Gerry had brought in to star in it.

TIFFANY CLARK: When I got off the plane, and Fred Lincoln picked me up, it was love at first sight. Well, to be honest, *lust* at first sight. Fred dropped me off at my hotel, and it was the usual boring things: "Do I know my lines? What will I wear tomorrow? And how the hell am I going to get this man to fuck me?"

There had to be a way. I mean, he was only human, right?

FRED LINCOLN: I picked Tiffany up at the airport, and she was wonderful. So full of life, so . . .

TIFFANY CLARK: The next morning Fred came to the hotel to pick up some of the other girls who had to be on the set early. When he got there I was downstairs waiting for him—casually sitting in the lobby smoking a cigarette. When he approached me, I told him I just wanted to make sure I knew what time my call was.

FRED LINCOLN: Tiffany was wearing her sexiest outfit. The connection was instant.

TIFFANY CLARK: Fred is not a stupid man. By the way I was dressed it was obvious I wasn't concerned with work; I was interested in getting laid. Fred played my game. He told me he'd be back at noon to pick me up. I smiled and returned to my room. I knew by the look in his eyes that until noon I would be close in his thoughts.

FRED LINCOLN: When I came back to the hotel, Tiffany was really flirting with me.

TIFFANY CLARK: When we got to the set we were both too busy to pay much attention to each other, but Fred found a moment to ask me out later that evening. I, of course, accepted, seeing that he made it sound so innocent— I mean, he asked if I'd like to see some of New York before I went back to L.A.

FRED LINCOLN: We went to Bernard's—and we couldn't keep our hands off each other, so eventually that was the end of the tour.

TIM CONNELLY: I was hanging out at the Melody, watching Helen Madigan strip, and I went into the bathroom to take a piss, and I hear this porn actress I know in the next stall selling a vial of urine to a guy.

He's going to pay a hundred dollars for this vial, but only if she can pee in it while he watches.

I just thought, "I love my life! *I love my fucking life!*"

KELLY NICHOLS: I started as a makeup artist in L.A., but then I did a girl/girl scene to get money to go see my boyfriend, Barry, in New York City. So I did not see this as being a career move. This was just something to make money, like nude modeling.

But when I got to New York, Barry didn't look like Barry. He'd completely cut his hair, and bleached it bright yellow. Real punk. He lived in one of those godawful apartments on Seventy-first and Columbus—you know, you walk in and there's the bunk bed and a bathroom over here and a window to jump out of—except it's facing bricks, ha, ha, ha. And if you don't get along with the person you're with, oh God help you!

This is what I walk into: Barry needed money for rent. He's two months behind. So already I'm right back in the pattern. We go to his work. Well, the theater he's working at is Show World. And he's not a projectionist; he's an actor on stage. And he's been fucking Serena, who I knew when she was a nude model and was with Jamie Gillis.

I'd given up everything I had in L.A. to come out to New York. I wasn't prepared for this.

TIM CONNELLY: Helen would be the feature dancer once a month at Show World and then she'd dance periodically at Mardi Gras on Saturday. And I learned early on—don't ask. Because I'd go meet her on a Saturday afternoon, and she'd smell like cigars and have, you know, a purse full of one-dollar bills and some coke, and all I really cared about was, "She's got coke! She's going to buy me lunch!"

But Helen always seemed to want to take a shower right away, before we jumped into bed, which was fine with me. So I looked the other way. I didn't really know what she was doing, and I didn't want to.

KELLY NICHOLS: When I get to New York, I'm just with Barry. So whatever he says goes. I will follow his lead. If he snorts it, I'll snort it. Well, we meet some people, and they decide to take me to an after-hours place, the Nursery, where we meet up with some old girlfriend. They lay out some lines, and I don't like coke, but I do it 'cause everybody else is doing it.

I snorted what I thought was coke—and that was the end of me. Barry says I walked away with somebody. I don't know; I was so angry with him later on, but I realized he was also under the influence. But he should've protected me. I don't know what I expected, but I ended up with my clothes off, in a room apparently under the club. Some poor guy was handing me my clothes and trying to get me outta there. I don't remember any of it.

I just felt really sick and violated and—and just awful. It was the first time I got raped. My pants and panties were torn; I had to use my shirt to cover myself. I had no money. I didn't know how to get to where I lived from the Nursery. The guy took pity on me and gave me some money, and I think I must have given good enough instructions to get me to Columbus and Seventy-first.

TIM CONNELLY: I'm sure there were probably some guys, some good-looking guys, and after a couple of vodkas during Mardi Gras, Helen probably grabbed some cock and went a little bit further than I would have been comfortable with.

But I just felt like I had to look the other way because who the fuck am I to judge? I'm dating a stripper. How can I say, *"You can't spread your pussy that wide?"*

At the same time, if I'm in Bernard's waiting for her and a stripper walks in and takes me in the bathroom and wants to fuck me, I'm gonna nail her, you know?

KELLY NICHOLS: Some time in the morning, I stumbled home and sat outside the door. Barry finally came home three hours later. And again, there were no apologies.

He was angry with me for some reason—I don't know why. I was the one that got abandoned. So Barry talks me into going to work at Show World.

TIFFANY CLARK: The next day I was supposed to leave. Fred drove me to the airport, and when I got out of the car—then came the tears. He was a wonderful man—what could I do?

Fred held me in his arms and told me not to worry; if we were meant to be together we would. Well, as it happened, when I got to the ticket counter they told me there was no plane until the next day. I called Fred, and he came back to the airport. Fred and I seem to spend a lot of time in airports.

When he came back, he told me he could get me to another airport in time to catch another flight if I wanted to. I asked what he meant by "if I wanted to," and he just smiled. Well, I never answered until the last minute, when Fred had to make a decision—either go straight or turn to go home.

We both looked at each other at the same time and said, "No airport!"

KELLY NICHOLS: It was kinda fun working at Show World; it was like I was in theater. Barry was a good actor. It was funny. He put on some little shorts and put a collar on my neck with chains. I wore some little Danskin spandex thing, which would later be torn off of me. And some whips and stuff. But it was not sex. It was just goofy stuff.

They were paying us sixty dollars a show or so, but Barry had a friend there named Tim Connelly and his girlfriend Helen Madigan. Helen and Tim were doing the sex shows, and they were cool as cucumbers. Tim was in a rock band. Helen was gonna sing, and she was a stripper on the side. I started to feel okay after I'd met them; seeing another couple that acted like all this was normal *made it* more normal. Tim was just really pragmatic: "Okay, I gotta do another show."

TIM CONNELLY: Helen and I were on-again, off-again. She was living with her sister sometimes and staying with me part of the time. That's when I met Kelly Nichols, who I really liked and we really hit it off. Unfortunately for Kelly, her marriage to Barry was crumbling.

KELLY NICHOLS: Basically, Barry got us thrown out of the apartment on Seventy-first and Columbus, so basically we were on the street. I was paying the rent; we'd go to nice restaurants, and I'd pick up the tab. I wanted it to be okay between us.

At some point, though, I ran outta money. Then Barry heard that somebody was gonna do a porn film. It turned out to be this sweet little gay guy named Chuck Vincent. Chuck took a look at me and said, "Oh, this is great. You're a Penthouse Pet," which I had been when I was nude modeling. I started off working with Hal Guthu, who also did nudes of Demi Moore. And Chuck Vincent loved the fact that I could do dialogue.

Chuck said, "We're gonna shoot all around Europe. We're gonna do Florida. We're gonna do San Francisco. We're gonna shoot all over."

But Barry and I, who are married at this point, are literally on the streets, living in a hotel off of Forty-second Street. A real divey Times Square place that smelled horrible. One day I got on the elevator and an old lady jumped on my back and started hitting me on the head. Just insane.

The Chuck Vincent film had a real complicated plot, so Barry insisted that we get four thousand up front. Chuck was very cool; he gave us the four grand. He was going to pay me sixteen thousand, so we could get a fresh start. This was a good thing.

Well, Barry flips out. All of a sudden he gets righteous: "Now we have the money; let's split." He wants to leave. It was really weird; I still had a moral code—these people had paid us money. They deal with banks. They could lose more than their asses. And we made a promise. You make a promise; you stick with it.

We ended up having a huge fight, with him crying on the floor screaming at me, begging me not to be in porn. So Barry's outta my life. He just goes away.

Then I was alone. Just on my own.

TIM CONNELLY: One day Helen and I were doing shows at Show World, and Kelly Nichols came to see us—and ended up on stage with us. Kelly was high, really high—speed or coke or PCP or something. I was really high, too; it was one of those moments where I just thought, *I'm going to be in trouble later,* you know, because I'm letting this whole thing happen around me.

Here's Kelly, this available woman who wants to fuck. And here's my girlfriend, who's really high and is throwing herself into the moment because she can feel this energy exchange between us and she just wants to be in the middle of it because otherwise she's going to get left out. I fucked Kelly onstage. It was weird; I didn't like it. It wasn't what I wanted. But then Helen had to go on the road for a couple of weeks . . .

KELLY NICHOLS: I'd met Tim through Helen, who I became friends with while I was with Barry. Tim used to ask me to come see him play; the two of them would call me when they were out at the clubs. So I went out and hung out with them as a couple. What I didn't know was that things were blowing up between them. Tim was working hard as hell to play drums, and he was a great drummer. Helen was partying a lot. And their scene was quickly deteriorating.

TIM CONNELLY: Did I fall in love with Kelly Nichols? Absolutely, immediately. She was the love of my life at that point.

KELLY NICHOLS: Tim was working at a restaurant by day and being a rock and roller at night. He invited me out once to hear him play, and I found it fascinating. I really liked the rock and roll scene. I had been involved with this goofy disco shit in L.A., largely because I could get away with it. You know, cute girls and gay discos go together.

But with a rock club, you needed a reason to go inside, unless you're a groupie—and that wasn't really my gig. I'm too shy to be a groupie. But when I went to see Tim, I had a reason to be there. So we quickly kind of fell together. We were two lonely souls who hadn't found ourselves yet, and our view of life was that it was just the two of us against the world.

So Helen moved out, and I moved in.

FRED LINCOLN: Tiffany and I had the most idealistic relationship any couple could have. She was with me for two weeks. We never fought. We were never jealous.

We went to the Hellfire Club, and these Swedish twins were hitting on her. I mean, these guys looked like models—you know, ripped abs, big muscles—and she was like, "Wow! They want me to fuck both of them!"

I said, "You know what? If there were girl twins here, and they wanted me to go home with them, and you didn't let me, I would never forgive you. So go! Enjoy! Have fun! This doesn't happen every day."

Tiffany was back by 5:30 in the morning. She said they weren't as much fun as me. What can I tell you? That's the kind of relationship we had.

KELLY NICHOLS: Angel dust was my drug of choice. I turned Tim onto it 'cause I found out he wants to run and be real rock-and-roll skinny, too. So he smokes it and goes running. Half the time you go running. And half the time you're stumbling around in the dirt. Then we both find out we like to fuck on it.

But I'm going through this kind of weird moral quandary because I have a girlfriend who's hooking, and she wants to know if I want to try it. So I try it a couple of times but don't like it. Tim was just like, "Whatever brings the money in."

FRED LINCOLN: For my birthday, you know what Tiffany brought me? An eighteen-year-old Amber Lynn. You've got to be pretty secure with your relationship to bring somebody an eighteen-year-old Amber Lynn. Because let me tell you, when Amber Lynn was eighteen, she was a fucking album cover, man.

If you didn't do music, you would do it purposely just to put her on your cover.

KELLY NICHOLS: I was friends with this beautiful black model named Ingrid, who really was one of the Hollywood players. She was an actress, she was on the cover of the Ohio Players album, and she dated all these different successful guys, including Warren Beatty. Ingrid always had some rich guy she was bopping. She did the guy who directed George Hamilton in some movie. She was bopping him. Some of them were real dates—Warren Beatty was one of those. She just loved to fuck him.

TIM CONNELLY: Kelly Nichols and I met Bud Lee with Hyapatia Lee at Bernard's. Bud was just a porn star husband. He was trying to push us into swinging with him. At that point Kelly and I had done some swinging and weren't really interested. I don't know why because boy, in retrospect, the whole concept of me fucking Hyapatia Lee and Kelly Nichols sounds pretty good.

But at the time I think I was turned off by Bud's suitcase-pimp attitude. Kelly obviously didn't want to sleep with him. And that's always a big part of it, you know? No matter how much you want to get involved, if your partner doesn't want to fuck the guy, then . . .

But I mean, once we told him, "Forget it—it's not gonna happen," then it didn't fuckin' matter, you know?

KELLY NICHOLS: Tim told me I could be the next Seka, if I wanted to be. We were all amazed with Seka, this new girl who was starting to make loops. She was the first woman who had an inkling of what a women's career could be in pornography. The rest of us were little round pegs not fitting into square holes because we never looked at what we were doing as a job; it was just a passage to something else. We were just doing this until we figured out what we were gonna do next.

Plato's Retreat

NEW YORK CITY
1976–1977

FRED LINCOLN: Larry Levenson was kind of a mutt. You know, he wasn't exactly what you'd call a handsome man. He was a fat, Jewish guy who was going to school to become a manager at McDonald's. He met this girl who happened to be a swinger, and she took him to parties. But Larry noticed that when he went to parties he didn't get laid 'cause he was a mutt. But he also noticed that no matter how old the guy who owned the apartment was or what he looked like, he *always* got laid.

LARRY LEVENSON (OWNER OF PLATO'S RETREAT): I guess I had to be with every woman who walked into my place. I was accused of that. I denied it. But sitting here and looking back, any good-looking girl that came in, I wanted to be with her.

FRED LINCOLN: Larry was an annoying fucking guy that was always trying to get laid, you know? Pushy and obnoxious. And the only reason I had anything to do with him at all was because of Tiffany. She had got us talking because Larry was like a groupie to porno people.

JAMIE GILLIS: Larry basically came from a square life. You know, a square, sex-once-a-month-with-his-wife type. And then he fell into Plato's and started fucking like a bunny. He was already forty-five or something.

He told me he asked his doctor, "Is this okay?"

And the doctor said, "As long as you're enjoying it, no problem."

FRED LINCOLN: Anyway, Larry got some people to give him money. He rented a health club on Fifty-third Street and handed out fliers for everybody to go there. There'd be plenty of booze. And they'd get twenty bucks per couple. It was pretty successful, but it just wasn't comfortable—fucking on tile.

And then Larry found some other guys, and they gave him the money for Plato's Retreat, which he opened on Fifth Avenue. Plato's and Studio 54 were the most popular clubs in New York. And Larry's got all kinds of celebrities, and everybody's going, "Hi, Larry!"

So he became a celebrity.

JAMIE GILLIS: I was the only guy that was allowed in Plato's without a date. I would go because Larry was a friend and a fan. He would tell me what girl I could say I was with so I'd look good, like I brought a date. He would just pick somebody out and say, "You're with her." And it was fine. I could practically live there.

ANNIE SPRINKLE: I started going to Plato's Retreat with Peter Wolf, the publisher of *Chic*, because Peter was kind of the guy about town. I mean, we covered all the new sex clubs and all the events. I worked for him for a year-and-a-half as a sex journalist, and of course we would be having sex with everybody. We'd photograph it and write about it. And Plato's was a hell of a place!

C. J. LAING: While everyone was going to Bernard's and Show World, I was going to swing clubs. And I'm amazed—I was eighteen years old—that everybody wants to fuck me, ha, ha, ha.

But there was also a club on Seventh Avenue in the Twenties, where people met and then went to people's houses. Someone had this amazing town house in Gramercy Park with a swimming pool on the ground floor. On the basement floor, there was this amazing play space. And I used to go party there all the time. It was a bunch of fucking suburban schnooks in some fancy town house fucking around. But—I don't know; they liked me. For some reason it made me feel good.

I wasn't doing stuff for drugs, and I wasn't doing it for money; I was doing it for the attention and the sex. Yeah, definitely—them wanting me.

JOSH ALAN FRIEDMAN (WRITER): I met Butchie Peraino through Candy Samples at wherever she was headlining one night on Forty-second Street, near Eighth Avenue. Butch owned the whole operation, but I didn't realize he was the guy who made *Deep Throat.*

Butchie was really a throwback, like a street mobster—a down-and-out Lou Costello kind of a guy. You know, he looked like a guy who hung out at the racetracks all his life, big bags under his eyes. I wouldn't say he was happy, but he was a very fun guy.

So Butchie comes up to me and introduces himself and his partner, some other mobster. At that time I was a little bit known through *Screw* and *Midnight Blue,* and I was there to do a dressing room thing with Candy Samples. And I guess Butch wanted to meet Larry Levenson—because Al Goldstein was betting that Larry couldn't come fifteen times in a day. Larry said he could do it easy. Fifteen times.

BUTCHIE PERAINO: No man can come fifteen times. I'm a gambler; I bet horse races, football games. I can't resist a good bet. My partner and I would like to bet ten thousand dollars cash that Larry can't do it. And if he does, I'd be honored to lose.

LARRY LEVENSON: Tell those fuckin' greaseballs they're on! Get the cash, bring it here for proof, and I'll start coming on the spot—right in their fuckin' face. I need the money bad.

Now I gotta go; I'm busy fuckin'.

JOSH ALAN FRIEDMAN: Somehow I became the intermediary in this contest. So I'm in the back room with Larry Levenson, Butchie, some of Butchie's partners, and Al Goldstein. They were all putting money down. Butchie was joining in on a bet. And thank God, I didn't hold the money because it got up close to ten grand.

LARRY LEVENSON: Tell those assholes to come down at four o'clock and watch me start fucking. Baseball players need batting practice, right? Well, I'll be warming up all day, hours before the event. Oughta come six times before nine o'clock, and I want those assholes to come and watch me spurt. I'll even shoot some in their face for 'em.

BUTCHIE PERAINO: What is he, nuts? He's gonna fuck all day before the contest? I know a good bet when I see one!

JOSH ALAN FRIEDMAN: I was just sort of the insignificant guy in the back—the intermediary between everybody from my desk at *Screw.* The arguments about Larry Levenson coming fifteen times in a twenty-four-hour period went back and forth for weeks: "Well, how do we know if he came? He's got to pull out."

"Well, that's a good point. Let's make that a condition. And then how are we going to see it?"

"Well, you've got to have a flashlight. . . ."

Butchie didn't trust this guy. And Larry didn't trust another guy. So I had to find referees that were not connected to either, to be there the moment Larry pulled out—from a mouth or a cunt.

BUTCHIE PERAINO: Larry may utilize fluffers, watermelons, stroke books, or harems of women to summon forth the gop. If no women show, however, his palm must suffice. I crossed out everything but women, I told him no masturbation, no tricks—just women, that's all I care about.

And I don't care how many broads he uses at once, or how he fucks 'em, as long as he pulls outta their mouths or cunts before he shoots, so we can see it.

JOSH ALAN FRIEDMAN: Then a night was designated at Plato's Retreat—a big Friday night or Saturday night, whatever—when the clock would start. Everyone met in Larry's lair, with a bare lightbulb hanging down off the desk and guys counting grubby money. And low-level mobsters who were making bets over the phone, at the same time—horse bets and stuff.

It felt very much like the 1940s—nobody finding any semblance of humor in this, not even amused by it. Larry's got a whole lineup of girls outside. And there's like over a thousand people at Plato's that night—which was typical for a weekend.

PATRICE TRUDEAU (SWINGER): I could teach any woman how to be a great whore. I'm a born whore. Not a slut—you know? The other girls are sluts. They're doing it because he's the King of Swing, and they'll fuck anything with a dick, some money, and a name.

I'll make Larry come seven or eight times tonight, and I'm the only one getting paid for it. A whore does it for money, for power. A slut does it free. So don't you dare think of me as a slut.

My sixteen-year-old brother had me blowing him when I was four. He taught me how to suck cock by practicing on his. And my mother was a French prostitute. So it runs in the family.

LARRY LEVENSON: I need a looser pussy now. Patrice is too tight. My hard-on isn't hard enough when I penetrate, and she's too tight for me to pull out fast. So I'll use Vickie next.

JOSH ALAN FRIEDMAN: That night was unlike any other in my life. I stayed there the whole twenty-four hours, and I came out of there thinking, "Jesus Christ, did I imagine this? Did this really happen?"

JAMIE GILLIS: Larry did it! You try to come fifteen times—that's a *lot* of come! I could never in my wildest dreams come fifteen times, but Larry did—and that's great, don't you think?

Ah, Plato's. Hot times! For a while, it was fabulous. Just hundreds of women floating around. Men would come over and ask me to fuck their wives, you know what I'm saying?

Part 4: FAMILY

Know your... **FBI**

FEDERAL BUREAU
OF
INVESTIGATION
UNITED STATES
DEPARTMENT
OF JUSTICE

AFFAIRS

1976–1977

1979 INTERNATIONAL SUMMER
CONSUMER ELECTRONICS SHOW

June 3-4-5-6, Chicago,
McCormick Place/McCormick Inn/Pick Congress Hotel

PATRICK SALAMONE
GOLDE COASTE
          SPECIALITIES
GRAND CAYMAN BWI

DISTRIBUTOR

BROKERS
LIQUIDATORS
CONSULTANTS

PAT SALAMONE
BRUCE WAKERLY

Golde Coaste Specialties, Inc.
MIAMI, FLORIDA — CAYMAN ISLANDS

7470 N.W. 8TH STREET
MIAMI, FLA. 33126

(305) 261-6309

Left page: *Top row:* Bill Kelly, Robert "DiBe" DiBernardo, Michael "Mickey" Zaffarano, Anthony "The Old Man" Peraino. *Second row:* Larry Parrish, Theodore "Teddy" Gaswirth, Joseph "Joe the Whale" Peraino, Norman "Norm" Arno. *Third row:* Rhonda Jo Petty, Robert "Bobby" DeSalvo, Theodore "Teddy" Rothstein. Bottom: Pat Livingston and Bruce Ellavsky.

Right page, *clockwise from top left:* Seka; Bill Brown; Pat Livingston's Golde Coaste Specialties business card as Pat Salamone; Pat Livingston (right) with guns and unidentified agents, Pat Livingston's Golde Coaste Specialties pass for C.E.S. convention.

This Thing of Ours
NEW YORK CITY/LOS ANGELES
1976–1977

LAPD DETECTIVE GLEN SOUZA (ORGANIZED CRIME INTELLIGENCE DIVISION): The eight-millimeter X-rated film was a multimillion-dollar business, and Norm Arno was the front man. He was a big, dumb, dirty slob. Everybody hated Norman Arno. But he had control of the eight-millimeter films, probably because he was Mickey Zaffarano's representative out here in Los Angeles.

OPERATION "AMORE" REPORT: MICHAEL ZAFFARANO: Subject is an old capo in the Bonanno crime family. Information has been received that Zaffarano has been working very closely with Gambino interests in New York City, Los Angeles, and Miami. Los Angeles Police Department states that the Bonanno family through Zaffarano is the controlling porno power in California.

GLEN SOUZA: You couldn't produce or manufacture or distribute porno without these people. And a lot of these guys had positions, just because of their upbringings and their families and their childhood friends. There was tremendous loyalty to the old neighborhood and the family. It was unbelievable.

RUBY GOTTESMAN (PORNOGRAPHER): See, Norm Arno lived across the street from me in Coney Island. My sister would babysit for him. No, wait a minute, I think his sister babysat for me. Anyway, his mother and my mother were very good friends. They walked the Coney Island boardwalk together in the wintertime.

Norm Arno's real name was Bobby Kraw. He changed his name to Norman Arno when he moved to Los Angeles. But Norm was my best friend in Coney Island. I was working for him, collecting bets for him.

CHUCK BERNSTENE: Norm Arno was partners with Ann Perry and Noel Bloom. They had a little mail-order place on La Cienega Boulevard and

Pico. And they were into eight-millimeter loops—that "Swedish Erotica" series. This was before videotape, when there were only eight-millimeter loops.

ORGANIZED CRIME CONTROL COMMISSION REPORT, STATE OF CALIFORNIA, DEPART-MENT OF JUSTICE: ARNO, NORM: From 1970 to 1974 Arno was involved in many organized crime–connected pornography operations in Southern California. In late 1974, he opened a film duplicating operation to duplicate hard-core pornography as well as legitimate motion pictures. Arno was the business partner of New York Mafia member Michael Zaffarano.

RUBY GOTTESMAN: *Deep Throat* came in at the end of 1972, and Norm Arno got friendly with the guys who made it, the Perainos. And the Perainos' guy on the West Coast was Joseph "Junior" Torchio, who was nuts. Completely out of his mind. They sent him out here because he was too crazy. It was either send him out here or kill him.

So Norman got to be partners with Junior for the West Coast's distri-bution of *Deep Throat*. They were collecting the money, and my job was to bring the money from California to Tony and Butchie Peraino in New York.

DAVE FRIEDMAN: I met Norm Arno about the time *Deep Throat* surfaced. When Kurt Richter and I started our video company, TVX, Norm started his company, VCX, about two months later. And he had one thing: He seemed to have the rights to *Deep Throat* from the Perainos.

CHUCK BERNSTENE: Because they grew up with him, the Perainos gave Joseph "Junior" Torchio the right to distribute the picture on the West Coast. And that's how Norm Arno got to distribute *Deep Throat*— because he was partners with Junior.

RUBY GOTTESMAN: I got $500 a week to deliver the money in a bag to the Perainos. I was gettin' the money from Junior Torchio. I never looked in the bag. If I had to take a piss, I'd take the money with me. Anywhere I went. I didn't look inside because it was like two or three hundred thousand dollars.

CHUCK BERNSTENE: I never practiced accounting until Norman said, "Chuck, I want you to take care of a couple of pictures that are coming out—*Deep Throat* and *The Devil in Miss Jones*. I want you to check the theaters."

So I became Norm Arno's accountant, and I hired some theater check-ers with clickers, so we could count everyone that came through the door to see *Deep Throat*.

DAVE FRIEDMAN: The Perainos would have these stand over guys—checkers—go out with the picture. Worst mistake in the world. Because he's standing there, checking everybody in, and settling with the exhibitor every night—like we used to do back in the road show days. All the exhibitor has got to do is ask, "How much do you make?"

God knows how much money they lost because these people could be bribed easier than anybody in the world.

CHUCK BERNSTENE: Since the theaters were open twenty-four hours a day, I had three eight-hour shifts of guys count the people that walked in. And people were lined up for blocks and blocks to watch *Throat* and *The Devil in Miss Jones*.

I had seventeen theaters in Los Angeles that I would have to check. And after we counted how many people went in, the theater owners would pay me in cash, and I would meet with Norman Arno at Barney's Beanery and turn the money over to him.

BILL KELLY: The checker would go up to the owner of the theater and say, "Five grand now, or else."

The owners of the theater would ask, "What do you mean, or else?"

The checker would say, "You don't pay me, you'll find out what else."

There were maybe four "or elses." A couple of them had to do with the Perainos sending somebody out to take the film off the projector and giving it to the competitor across town—or burning the theater down.

DAVE FRIEDMAN: That's what Bobby DeSalvo taught the Perainos—that there was nothing easier to reach than the stand over guys. Because Bobby DeSalvo was a film pirate. He was pirating *Deep Throat*, and the Perainos asked, "What are you doing?"

DeSalvo says, "I'm Italian. I'll handle your pirates," and they hired him. If *Deep Throat* had been handled by a somewhat legitimate distributor, without the stand over guys—the checkers—it probably would've doubled whatever they made.

CHUCK BERNSTENE: One time I delivered the cash from *Throat* to Butchie Peraino, and he says, "You're about eighty thousand short."

I says, "Go fuck yourself, Butchie. I'm never short. Take it up with Norman and Junior."

It was always like that between the Perainos and Junior Torchio and Norman Arno. It would go on every week. Hearing about one of them shorting the other, or one didn't pay the other. These guys don't pay anybody. They were always cutting each other up instead of working together.

Everyone was always stealing, lying, and cheating from Mickey Zaffarano. I was the only one outta that bunch that didn't. Mickey even said to me once, "You're the only guy I can trust."

BILL KELLY: Robert DiBernardo and Mickey Zaffarano were the most important people in the whole business. I was told that Robert DiBernardo was such a good moneymaker that he was given at least some measure of control over the porno industry for all the five New York Mafia families.

And Mickey Zaffarano was like DiBernardo. Everybody was afraid of him because he was a capo in the Bonanno family.

FRED LINCOLN: Mickey Zaffarano was The Man because he owned the Pussycat theaters. The only other theaters were jerk-off theaters, and the Pussycat was a big, beautiful theater.

Were the Gambinos and the Columbos friendly? Sure. Everybody's friendly—unless they're at war. I'm telling you the truth. Everything was done at sit-down meetings. Everything was above board.

RUBY GOTTESMAN: When Mickey was about to open the Pussycat, the owners found out it was him, so they doubled the down payment or somethin'.

Mickey wound up on the short end of it and had to give 'em two or three million dollars, so he didn't have enough money to put up the signs. He went to Robert DiBernardo, and DiBe gave him the money for the sign. So he had a big neon sign on the Times Square building, you know?

FRED LINCOLN: DiBe was the boss behind the screen that you never really got to see, this secret guy that everybody talked about and everybody liked. Very smooth. Very gentle. He was the peacemaker who kept everything in place. But I avoided all of that. The only contact I wanted with anybody was, you know, "Give me a cute girl, and give me my hundred bucks!"

BILL KELLY: I would mention Robert DiBernardo's name to various pornographers around the country, and they'd freeze because he had a reputation for getting you killed. It was like if you said, "Al Capone" sixty years ago.

GLEN SOUZA: Robert DiBernardo was a very powerful and feared man. He had no fear. My understanding is that he had killed a lot of people.

DiBernardo was not a punk; he was an enforcer who came out here for the mob guys back east. DiBernardo would beat the shit out of people. Jack Molinas told us that DiBe beat up Norm Arno in his shop because Norm was probably stealing or skimming—not giving a full account.

We tried to talk to Norm Arno after he got beat up, but he wouldn't say anything. He was scared to death.

CHUCK BERNSTENE: I don't know if Norman Arno couldn't count or maybe he was illiterate—I'm not going to say anything—but there was always something missing, and the Perainos were always blaming me for Norman's missing money.

GLEN SOUZA: The rules were if Norm Arno was Mickey Zaffarano's guy, then DiBe couldn't beat him up—except if Arno was stealing for himself. In other words, Mickey Zaffarano's supposed to get all his money, and if Norm Arno is diverting some of it, DiBe was very capable of going to Mickey and saying, "Hey, we want all of our money!"

And Mickey would say, "Fine. Gotta keep these guys honest."

CHUCK BERNSTENE: Norm got better when Mickey Zaffarano came out to California in 1975—during the *Deep Throat* and *The Devil in Miss Jones* days. Thank God for Mickey: He was a collector; he knew how to handle all these slime bags. He just had that aura about him—you'd pay him.

Norman never said a word of disrespect to Mickey Zaffarano. Norman was like a child to Mickey.

GLEN SOUZA: We could never figure it out—Arno was such a fool, such a slob, so dumb. Why did he have such power?

In 1975, Junior Torchio got killed in Vegas. What a tragic accident, ha, ha, ha. The way I heard it, two guys chased him out into the street and threw him in front of a car.

It was written up as a traffic accident.

CORONER'S REPORT, CLARK COUNTY, NEVADA: Victim had no shoes or shirt on and was unable to locate any at the scene, but NHP (Nevada Highway Patrol) stated that they were there and that his shirt was torn off and he was knocked out of his shoes. NHP stated that no charges will be filed against striking vehicle.

BOBBY ELKINS (PORNOGRAPHER): I knew Junior Torchio. They ran him down. There were a couple of reasons. Torchio was creating a lot of police problems. He was always in the limelight—and they told him to stay away from all the bullshit. But he won't listen. He was getting into fights, getting into trouble, and everybody was talking about him.

Somebody told me that they killed him—they waited for him and ran him down.

RUBY GOTTESMAN: I was relieved when Junior Torchio got killed. It was like, you know, "Whoa, they finally got ridda him," cause I think one way or the other, he woulda killed me, or I woulda killed him. 'Cause he was crazy. He was just not in control of himself.

Memphis Backlash Blues

LOS ANGELES/NEW YORK CITY/MEMPHIS
1976–1977

BILL KELLY: The Perainos made so much money on *Deep Throat* that they went out to Hollywood and developed their own legitimate motion picture film studio—Bryanston Films. They bought up something like nine scripts and hired a lot of technical people, cameramen, directors, and technicians. They spent all this money out there, but they never really made a movie. However, they did go into the national distribution of a number of very violent—but not obscene—motion pictures.

AL RUDDY (PRODUCER OF *THE GODFATHER*): Bryanston Films was a company a lot of people were aware of in Hollywood. Bryanston were, in effect, picking up films—and I throw myself in this same category, unfortunately— that a lot of the majors didn't want to distribute. They were too sensational, or the studios thought they didn't have big potential.

I think it was fairly common knowledge that Bryanston was a company that was controlled by the boys—the mob, organized crime.

BILL KELLY: *The Texas Chain Saw Massacre* was distributed nationally by the Peraino family. I don't know how much money they made off of that, but I'm sure it was a lot. But eventually they went belly up, so to speak.

AL RUDDY: Bryanston never had the chance to really function because you can't have a distribution company if you can't get films to distribute. If you come around to a producer or a director and say, "I'd like to distribute your film," he'll say, "Well, what other films have you distributed?"

And if you say, *Deep Throat*, they'll say, "Well, I'm not sure that's quite what we had in mind."

LARRY PARRISH (U.S. ATTORNEY): In 1976, a United States Marshal had gone to a theater in Memphis to pick up a film called *School Girls,* which we later prosecuted. And when he was there, he saw previews to a film nobody had ever heard of called *Deep Throat,* and when he came back he told us about it. He didn't even know the name of it. But we knew it was a film that deserved to be prosecuted—and we proceeded from there.

BILL KELLY: What Bryanston did was they bought a lotta people—directors, scriptwriters, cameramen, and so forth—and overpaid them, like a thousand percent more than what they were worth. For example, if you could buy a script for ten grand, they'd pay a hundred grand. They were throwing money around. *The Hollywood Reporter* thought they were great. I was reading it, you know, and it said, "The Perainos are here. Isn't that wonderful?"

AL RUDDY: My only recollection of the meeting with Joe "The Whale" Peraino was that he was very affable, you know? You never walked in and said, "Oh my God, am I gonna get outta this office alive?"

The Perainos were very excited about what they thought they could do with my movie *Coonskin.* It was an absolutely straightforward meeting with a man who wanted to be a distributor. Look, I've dealt with plenty of people in my life who came from varied backgrounds—including people who've been in organized crime—and I found Joe the Whale a guy you could do business with, no question about it.

LARRY PARRISH: *Deep Throat* was a dirty sixteen-millimeter film, and the FBI agents up in Chicago found it—and determined that it was going to be shipped back to Memphis and distributed out of there.

So FBI agent Joe Hester came to me and asked if I was interested in prosecuting it. I told him I would be more than happy to—but that he needed to talk to my boss, Mr. Turley.

BILL KELLY: Bryanston Films didn't make any films that I'm aware of, but they bought the distribution rights to a group of violent movies—*The Texas Chain Saw Massacre, Andy Warhol's Frankenstein,* and *Return of the Dragon* by Bruce Lee.

So they made a lot of money distributing those films. *The Texas Chain Saw Massacre* has been seen by innumerably more people than *Deep Throat.* About twenty million people saw *Deep Throat,* roughly, if there's a hundred million-dollar take. Probably fifty million people saw *Texas Chain Saw Massacre.* I mean, I was teaching police recruits, and I'd ask, "How many of you saw *Texas Chain Saw Massacre?*"

About 75 percent of them raised their hands. I said, "Congratulations.

You sent two and a half dollars of your money to the Columbo family in Fort Lauderdale. . . ."

AL RUDDY: I'll tell you one thing you cannot do: You can't come in as a Bryanston into Hollywood and say, "Give me the film, or I'll kill you," you know?

The Perainos came into town with a big bankroll. And you can't walk around with that visibility and ever try to muscle anybody. I mean, that's out of the question.

Quite often, you go to the other extreme. You know, you wanna show that you're more honest than most of the other thieves around Hollywood. I think that's what the Perainos did.

BILL KELLY: Even though the Perainos made tons of money distributing *Texas Chain Saw,* the traditional Hollywood people really stung them bad because the Perainos had absolutely no experience in motion picture film production. They started spending money like water to make some films, and even then they never got one in the can. The producers just ran wild with the budget and frankly wiped them out—and then came Larry Parrish in Memphis.

LARRY PARRISH: After Joe Hester talked to him, Mr. Turley came walking back into my office and said, "Okay, you're going to be my lawyer on this. Do what you need to do. I don't want any popcorn sellers, ticket takers, or things of that nature. If you can't get the people who manufactured it— who are profiteering off of it—don't do it. But use your best skill, and call me if you need me."

With that, Joe Hester and I became a team. Joe was with the FBI, and I was with the United States Attorney's office, so we began to prosecute Interstate Transportation of Obscene Material cases—ITOM for short.

BILL KELLY: Larry Parrish happened to be a Knoxville guy—he went to the University of Tennessee Law School. He was a stand-up guy and a very dedicated Christian. He was really after these pornographers, and as an assistant United States attorney he had the authority. Larry is one of the real heroes in the Justice Department in the last twenty-five or thirty years.

Larry also had a young FBI agent out there in Memphis named James Donlan, who was in the bureau maybe six months. A first-office agent. And he was assigned as the primary agent in the *Deep Throat* case—which I thought was a mistake because he didn't have any experience, you know? But he did a magnificent job. He was the coordinator of the whole operation for the entire United States.

LARRY PARRISH: Interstate Transportation of Obscene Material is a crime that is prosecutable anywhere that the material lands or passes through. And in our earlier cases, we had established a use of a conspiracy theory.

But *Deep Throat* was distributed in a different way from *School Girls*—because it was distributed "out of the trunk of a car." They had runners who would physically carry the cans from city to city—and sit in the booth with the ticket seller and take the cash. They would stay for a while in a city while the film was playing, then they would leave town with the film and with the cash that had been collected in its sale.

So it was a process of locating the people who were distributing it—and it turned out to be the Perainos, who were in New York. They were using Fort Lauderdale as the place from which they distributed it—and they would send their runners all over the United States. Well, we flipped some of those people who gave us information.

NEW YORK TIMES SUNDAY MAGAZINE, MARCH 6, 1977: PORNOGRAPHY ON TRIAL: "The government had an informer named Phil Mainer working with the producers of *Deep Throat* in Florida. Mainer disappeared. His car was found with two fingers in it. Later, the rest of him was found in a shallow grave in Ohio."

LARRY PARRISH: We just went where the investigation led us. Now, with Harry Reems—whose real name is Herbert Streicher—that was a matter of prosecuting the actors and actresses.

We just felt that the actors and actresses should be prosecuted. And Harry was the actor in *Deep Throat* and *The Devil in Miss Jones*—two cases where we decided to prosecute.

HARRY REEMS: I was brought before the grand jury. It was embarrassing—not because of what I am or what I do, but because I was considered a criminal.

"Now, who's that with you in that scene?" I'd be asked.

"That's Juicy Lucy."

"What's Juicy Lucy's real name?"

"I only know her as Juicy Lucy."

"Who hires you?"

"Usually it's the director."

"Who pays you?"

"Usually the producer."

"Now we're getting somewhere. Can you give us some of their names?"

"I don't know their names. Everything's on a first-name basis. Everybody's John or Dick or Pete."

"Do they make checks out to you signed just 'John' or 'Dick' or 'Pete'?"

"We usually get paid in cash."

"That might be of interest to the Internal Revenue Service. . . ."

FRED LINCOLN: Harry Reems was just a nice, decent guy. He had no malice. I mean, he worked two days a week; he made maybe two hundred dollars. Gerry Damiano probably tried to get him for seventy-five a day because that's the way Gerry was.

So they went after Harry Reems, thinking this kid wouldn't be able to defend himself.

And even Harry didn't know Hollywood was gonna get behind him. And all those guys—Jack Nicholson and Warren Beatty—headed up his legal defense fund.

TONY BILL (PRODUCER OF *THE STING*): I didn't pay much attention to *Deep Throat*. I don't know any of my friends that particularly had anything to say about it, but one day I got a call from a lawyer in Los Angeles who was the head of the ACLU, and he said there was a trial about to go on "that is going to be a landmark trial." He explained to me the conditions of the trial, and then he said, "We would very much appreciate it if you would appear at the trial as an expert witness."

I asked, "What am I supposed to be an expert in?"

He said, "Well, you've been an actor, and you're a producer and a director, so you can speak with authority on the roles of all those parts in the production of a movie, and because of the quality of the work that you've done, you're a great spokesman for our side."

So I said, "Sure, I'd be happy to."

FRED LINCOLN: Larry Parrish said, "I could get Ann-Margret and Jack Nicholson, too, for that movie *Carnal Knowledge* because if we get the actors, then they can't produce more films."

I watched this guy and I said, "Holy shit! This man is *scary!*"

He was gonna arrest Jack Nicholson! And Art Garfunkel! Because the state of Georgia had found *Carnal Knowledge* obscene! Larry Parrish wanted to put them in jail for twenty years, the fucking creep. The guy was a maniac.

BILL KELLY: There were a number of Hollywood luminaries that came to Memphis to lobby against the government prosecuting an actor. They were very upset. They said, "You can't prosecute an actor for making an allegedly obscene movie!"

My response to that was, "Just watch us."

HARRY REEMS: They didn't get anything out of me. The moment I got sprung from the grand jury, I tore ass to Gerard Damiano and told him the fuzz was hot on the trail of the eight-millimeter filmmakers. He called the Perainos, and overnight they cleaned out their offices of thousands of loops.

"Thanks, kid," said Butchie Peraino. "You're a great kid."

I had perjured myself, but it wasn't to save the skins of a couple of mobsters like the Perainos. It was in defiance of the stupidity and rigidity of the whole principle of censorship—that elected or appointed "judges" that can decide what is fit for adults to see or read in a free society.

TONY BILL: I had won an Academy Award for producing *The Sting*. My company had produced *Taxi Driver*. I produced a movie called *Hearts of the West*. I had acted in a bunch of movies. I was getting ready to direct my first film. So I was part of the Hollywood establishment in many ways.

And Larry Parrish, who was the federal prosecutor, was trying to get the makers of *Deep Throat* by trying the actor as an accomplice to the crime—because if he could get his hands on the actor he could find the rest of them, I guess. So the punitive crime was transportation of pornographic material across state lines.

So rather than go after the people that made the movie, he decided to go after the performers—in this case the male lead, Harry Reems—as an accomplice to the crime, as if he had driven the getaway car at a bank robbery.

C. J. LAING: I went to a Harry Reems legal defense fund-raiser at Elaine's. I donated money, and Harry was shocked that I did that. We had this conversation about our comings and goings and attractions—you know, what was going on. And I guess I had matured a little bit, become a little bit more of a woman.

So I went home with Harry that night. An uncle of his had an apartment on East Thirty-fourth Street that we could party in. It was Jamie Gillis, Harry, and myself. You know, we just always sort of had these sexual romps. I wasn't into threesomes, but with Jamie and Harry it was just us.

This was before Serena.

LARRY PARRISH: Linda Lovelace had been granted immunity by a grand jury in New York, so we didn't have an option of prosecuting her. She was subpoenaed by the grand jury in the Eastern District of New York, and she appeared, was granted testimonial immunity, and testified at length to everything there was to know about *Deep Throat*.

So that immunity kept her from being indicted by us, but it also made her a witness. She could never refuse to testify, and she was subpoenaed fifteen or sixteen times around the country.

CHUCK TRAYNOR: I was a witness. They threatened me with prosecution, and then they called me in and asked a buncha questions. I just always thought, "What are they gonna do? Put me in jail? For what?"

I never had any big fear of Larry Parrish. I didn't tell 'em anything. But I could never figure out why—when they would bring me to Memphis—they didn't bring Linda. I mean, they knew who she was. She had testified before a grand jury before. But I don't think she ever really had anything intelligent to say to them. Parrish probably talked to her once and thought, "Man, this chick's a dingbat; no sense gettin' her in court."

LARRY PARRISH: I had subpoenaed Linda Lovelace to testify for us but decided at the last minute not to use her because she was very, very flaky. She had recently testified in Albuquerque—and she was late to court. The marshals had to go get her. Then she came to court with her hair in rollers. She had just become a spectacle, and we didn't need her, so I didn't use her.

BILL KELLY: I spent three years working on *Deep Throat* before we ever got it to trial in Memphis. That was probably the most complicated obscenity investigation I ever worked on. *Deep Throat* required a lot of work because there were hundreds of people involved. You know, you had three hundred theaters showing the film. You had at least three hundred employees out there, one or two in every theater, working for the Peraino family.

So you don't meet a lot of high-class people in the porno business. All these people were either immoral or amoral. And a lot of them had mid-Mediterranean backgrounds, ha, ha, ha. As a *Miami Herald* article put it, "Organized Crime Muscle Dominates Porno Distribution."

LARRY PARRISH: I never saw *The Godfather*. When you live in the midst of this real mob world stuff, why go see a movie about it? When you spend time with real people and see them shedding real blood and see the horror of it all from the inside rather than the outside, then why go see it portrayed as fiction? To me, it just loses something.

AL RUDDY: I met with Joe Columbo—head of the Columbo family—before we made *The Godfather*. They wanted us to remove the word "Mafia" from the script, which was actually easy to do because it was used only once.

Remember when Bobby Duvall comes to Hollywood, to meet the producer to give Johnny Fontane the job, and the producer flips out? And he says, "No guinea, gumba, greaseball, wop. Mafias are coming out of the woodwork . . ."

Now it was, "No guinea, gumba, wops are coming . . ."

So that was the whole thing. That's all they wanted, and that's all they got. I never had another problem with them. And they helped us shoot *The Godfather*.

BILL KELLY: This is a very large courtroom in a new Federal District Court in Memphis, and it sits right smack on the Mississippi River, okay?

So over on the side of the courtroom closest to the river are twelve defendants—all the Peraino gang and a couple of other guys and Harry Reems and eight lawyers. And one of these defendants was Joe the Whale, who weighed at least 350, if not 400, pounds. He took up two chairs.

On the other side of the courtroom was Larry Parrish and an FBI agent named James Donland, the case agent in Memphis, who did the best job I've ever seen done by a new FBI agent. There must have been four tons of meat on the defendants' side—and 350 pounds on the government's side. The courtroom was so weighted that I could almost see it starting to tilt and flip over, right into the river.

LARRY PARRISH: Even Harry Reems, who was subpoenaed, did not want to sit with those people. There would be the gang around the defendants' table, and over there in the corner would be Harry Reems sitting on a bench. And the judge would say, "Mr. Streicher, you gotta get over here with the defendants! You can't sit over there!"

TONY BILL: I did answer a lot of factual questions: "What does a producer do? What does a director do?" Then, at a certain point in the trial, Larry Parrish asked, "Who paid for you to be here today?"

I said, "I'm not being paid to be here today."

He said, "Well, who paid your travel expenses?"

I said, "I did," which he was kind of flummoxed by.

It was a curveball for him to discover that an expert witness he'd intended to portray as a mercenary had in fact not taken a dime. It was the first chink in his armor.

BILL KELLY: I talked to Harry Reems at that trial. He was as nervous as a cat on a hot tin roof. He didn't want to be associated with these people of mid-Mediterranean origin, him not being one of them, see?

I think he was looking at me to sort of shelter him from these people—and here I am trying to help put him in jail along with the rest of them.

TONY BILL: The next tack Larry Parrish took was a line of questioning about pornography—"What did I consider pornographic?"

I allowed as how I didn't think there was probably any subject that couldn't be treated with taste, with artistic expression, and that there was probably no subject that was off base when it came to artistic expression, in a movie or a painting or a poem or a novel or whatever. I couldn't think of anything that was inherently pornographic.

BRUCE KRAMER (DEFENSE ATTORNEY): At the beginning of the trial the jury was fairly friendly to us. They would look at Harry, make eye contact with us—until the day we all got on the bus and went to a Memphis midtown theater to see a screening of *Deep Throat*.

After that, their demeanor changed. I mean, it's one thing talking in the abstract about explicit motion pictures and another thing for these people to actually see it.

TONY BILL: Larry Parrish continued that line of questioning by asking, "What about bestiality?"

I said, "Well, one of the most famous images in the history of art is 'The Rape of Leda by the Swan,'" and that stopped him.

To my great pleasure, when it was all finished, and I got down from the stand, the head of the ACLU turned to me and said, "You've turned the tide of this trial. That was brilliant. He should never have asked you that question."

LARRY PARRISH: After the jury saw Harry Reems in all his glory on a huge screen—everybody just stared at him once they got back in the court room.

Harry Reems was an embarrassed bird. He was humiliated by that experience, you could tell. He never told me, "I was humiliated," but he had this air of guilt about him, as if he knew he had done something wrong.

BRUCE KRAMER: Joa Fernandez, the cameraman on *Deep Throat*, took the stand, and Larry Parrish was very animated, very intense, as he led him through his direct examination.

Joa Fernandez was a very hip character. A dude, ha, ha, ha. So when Larry asked Mr. Fernandez to describe a group sex scene in the movie, Fernandez said, "Hey, man, there ain't no group sex in *Deep Throat*."

Larry was taken aback, and asked, "Mr. Fernandez, weren't you the cameraman on this film?"

"Yes, sir."

"And you filmed all of the scenes?"

"Yes, sir."

Then Larry starts describing the scenes in detail—almost frame by frame—and asking Joa if he remembers them. "Do you recall the scene where Mr. Reems is engaged in cunnilingus with so and so and at the same time so and so is engaged in fellatio with Mr. Reems?"

"Yeah, yeah. I remember that."

Larry asks, "Well?"

And Joa Fernandez says, "Hey, man, that's only three—that ain't no group."

LARRY PARRISH: I am probably an overly modest person, personally. But if you're going to prosecute this stuff you have just got to steel yourself to it and just do it. And probably, sometimes, in trying to overcome that part of me, I would overdo it.

So now we're at the end of the trial, and we have just seen the film, ha, ha, ha, and it's time for me to make my final argument.

I said, "Now, I'm really not trying to personally offend you, and I'm not trying to offend myself, but let's just take a five-minute segment of this film, and let me describe it to you, as you saw it from the screen. . . ."

BRUCE KRAMER: When Larry Parrish was describing that scene, he was, in my opinion, absorbed in a morbid, pathological, salacious, lascivious, lustful description—because he got to the point where he was describing cum dripping off the woman's lip.

I thought that was unnecessary.

LARRY PARRISH: I went through it—"Did you see him take his penis out and ejaculate all over Miss Lovelace? And did you see the semen run down out of her eyes into her mouth, and she licked it with her lips?"

After about three minutes of that, the jurors were filled with hatred, thinking, "You pervert, shut up."

And then I just stopped and said, "Did you feel all those feelings running through your veins? Did you feel the feelings you were having toward me? That's called prurient interest—what you were reacting to is that you were hearing me describe what any normal human being would say is an appeal to prurient interest. Now when the judge asks you to find whether or not this film appealed to prurient interest, think of how you felt when I just described that scene.

"There's no way—there's no way on earth that any of this material can be found nonobscene."

BILL KELLY: Larry Parrish took every one of those twelve defendants to trial, with their eight high-powered lawyers, and he just beat them down and whacked them good—and every one of them got convicted.

LARRY PARRISH: The Perainos convicted themselves on the organized crime front just by their demeanor, their attitude, the way they talked to each other, and the way their lawyers spoke.

They were just obnoxious.

They were Yankees—bad Yankees. They were everything you see on TV. They'd get up and strut and preen and try to be smart alecks and irritate the judge and jury. I just gave them some rope and watched them hang themselves.

BILL KELLY: They didn't get much in the way of sentences, though. The head of the operation, Anthony Peraino Sr., got convicted, but he decided he wasn't going to jail—so he took off for Italy and stayed gone for about five years.

NEW YORK TIMES, MAY 1, 1977: EIGHT MEN SENTENCED IN *DEEP THROAT* CASE: "Fed. Dist. Judge Harry W. Wellford has sentenced eight men convicted in the *Deep Throat* obscenity trial to prison terms ranging from three months to one year and has imposed fines of up to $10,000. Harry Reems had his conviction overturned. Those sentenced are Michael Cherubino, Anthony Novello, Joseph and Louis Peraino, Carl Carter and Mario DeSalvo. Plymouth Distributors is fined $10,000."

BILL KELLY: Bobby DeSalvo was the international distributor for *Deep Throat.* He thought he was getting shortchanged because all this money was coming in. But the Mafia is not a good place to go to collect money.

Bobby DeSalvo's body was never found because he went to Italy to try to collect additional money from the Peraino family. We traced him as far as London and haven't seen him since.

I imagine he's fish food.

RUBY GOTTESMAN: It was my job to pick up Bobby DeSalvo when he came to Los Angeles and drive him around in the Mercedes. He came out every week from Florida. Nice guy. He gave me two-hundred-dollar tips and took me to lunch and dinner.

Then a week or two goes by, and there's no Bobby.

So I go to Butchie, "Where's Bobby?"

He says, "Forget about it."

I says, "What do you mean, forget about it?"

He says, "He ain't comin' no more."

I says, "Oh, yeah? What happened to him?"

He says, "I ain't tellin' ya. None of your business."

I find out Bobby's with the fish.

FRED LINCOLN: Butchie Peraino did nothing but make movies; that's all he ever fucking wanted to do. He didn't extort from people, he didn't hit people, he didn't hurt people—he made movies. That's what he did, that's what he always wanted to do, and that was his love.

BILL KELLY: On the second trial the government decided, "Well, we got our shots in," and they dropped the charges against Harry Reems. That was Larry Parrish's decision, originally, I think. But the government deliberately drew a lot of attention to that trial because they prosecuted an actor.

If they hadn't prosecuted Harry Reems, I don't think it would have been an important case—and it certainly wouldn't have drawn all that heat from the directors and the actors and producers in Hollywood.

NEW YORK TIMES SUNDAY MAGAZINE, MARCH 6, 1977: PORNOGRAPHY ON TRIAL: "On December 8, Harry Reems and Alan Dershowitz were addressing the prestigious Harvard Law Forum, a law-school-sponsored series of lectures. They would be followed a week later by William Colby of the C.I.A. and had been preceded, some years back, by Fidel Castro. This was the kind of company that Harry Reems now kept."

FRED LINCOLN: Harry Reems started to believe his own press. He was better than this, better than that. He was drinking, he was doing coke—I mean, he was drinking *a lot.*

C. J. LAING: Harry got another big film and was given a lot money by some producer to do promos and was staying in big hotels and going to Cannes. This was when I hooked up with him. You know, he's in New York, staying at the Pierre.

Then Harry got an invitation to the Playboy mansion. When we went there, it was right after Dorothy Stratten was murdered. But Harry's a little savvier now, so he's working the angles of the distributors, and he's hanging with Hef—and that I didn't like. I didn't like hanging at the Playboy mansion.

It was very intimidating for me. I felt sort of thrown to the wolves. I didn't feel very protected as his girl. I felt like prey. And not very attractive prey, with all these blond androids around—all these rubbery, fantastic women. I just felt awkward.

FRED LINCOLN: Harry was living at that Malibu house, hanging out with Steve McQueen. I never went over there. I wouldn't hang out with a guy, but if it was Ali MacGraw, I'd go for sure. But I wasn't hanging out with guys; I never have. I mean, Butchie was an exception, but even Butchie and I didn't hang out that much.

C. J. LAING: In Malibu, Harry was drinking vodka, and one day he put a gun to my head. We were on the deck of his house, and he said to me, "Suck my cock. Where's the cunt? Suck my cock. *Where's the cunt?*"

See, I always had a bottle of his sperm with me at all times, you know, so that I could reproduce our children at a moment's notice. I wish I still had these little things. The Christmas gift he gave me—sperm.

FRED LINCOLN: Harry wasn't a good actor. If he was, they would've given him a piece of the pornos. But he couldn't carry them.

Harry wasn't a great actor—but he was a great fucker.

Deep Cover

MIAMI/CAYMAN ISLANDS
1976–1977

WAYNE CLARK (METRO-DADE COUNTY POLICE DETECTIVE): We were investigating pornography in Florida for years at the Dade County Organized Crime Bureau, but we were only getting the guys that worked in the bookstores. We were arresting clerks and seizing some merchandise, but it was a lot of wasted time because we weren't getting any of the distributors.

See, we wanted to prove that organized crime controlled the production and the distribution of pornography in the United States, and particularly in Dade County.

So we applied for a federal grant, and we were given federal monies to do an undercover operation. So that's how we started this "MIPORN" thing. But it wasn't called MIPORN yet; we called ours "Operation Amore."

BILL KELLY: Wayne Clark and Al Bonanni made a lot of inroads. They were telling me how successful they had been, but they said, "This thing is just too big for Metro-Dade. We don't have the money; we don't have the man power. This is a federal case that should be worked nationally. Will you take it over?"

I said, "I'd love to, but I gotta get permission from headquarters."

PHIL SMITH (FBI SPECIAL AGENT): Nobody was doing anything in pornography, except Bill Kelly, who was always running around trying to make obscenity cases. He's good-hearted, but he did only local stuff.

One day I get a call from a sergeant at the Metro-Dade Police Department—Wayne Clark, who said, "I got this source, and he's too big for me—you know, he's talking about nationwide distribution and everything."

So I brought Wayne Clark over to the office with his source. I talked to the informant, and he told me all the things he could do in Detroit, Cleveland, Dallas, New York, and Los Angeles. He was willing to cooperate because he had a problem; he was hung up. We had something good on him—some felonies.

I said, "Okay, let's see what we can do."

EDDIE FITZGERALD (MIAMI PORNOGRAPHER/INFORMANT; NAME CHANGED): Bonnani and Clark said what they wanted to do—go undercover and use my partner, Joey [name changed], and me to vouch for them, but I says to 'em, "Well, that's great, but count me out."

But to Joey, it was excitement—all expenses paid, you know? Joey had a bookstore. He was just a good-hearted slob, never made any money. And when I opened up the warehouse, he came to work for me.

So I said, "Joey, do whatever you want, all right? But count me out."

And the cops said to me, "Look, the only thing we want from you is to keep your mouth shut."

I said, "I'll just say, 'If you're with Joey, you gotta be okay.'"

PHIL SMITH: So I proposed to set up an undercover operation using Wayne Clark's sources because these guys had entrée all over the country. I wrote it up and sent it to the bureau and they approved it because that was a big deal then—everybody was looking for undercover cases.

EDDIE FITZGERALD: Teddy Gaswirth was a big pornographer for the Zappis in Los Angeles. Unfortunately, Teddy was cheatin' on his wife, and during the relationship he had stolen some money and tried to put the blame on me. According to Teddy, I purchased this stuff from him and never paid him.

Willy Bittner contacted me and said, "Eddie, we know you didn't do it. We know who did. But we need you out there to confront this individual because he is saying you did it."

So I had to go to Vegas for a sit-down.

PHIL SMITH: Now, since I put the operation together, I gotta find someone to be our undercover guy. I had a guy on my squad by the name of Pat Livingston who had done a little undercover stuff in Detroit—and he was a pretty good bullshitter. Plus, he was the only guy I had with any experience. Like I said, I had limited resources. So I said, "Okay, we'll use him."

But I wasn't sold on Pat Livingston.

EDDIE FITZGERALD: I jumped on a plane and went out to Vegas. Willy Bittner, Teddy, Nat "the Arab" Gamma, and a guy from Rhode Island, Kenny

Guarino, were there—and those are just the guys I recognized. Ten people were there, having a meeting at a hotel.

Then, they call Teddy Gaswirth up. Well, when Teddy walks into the room and sees I'm there, his whole facial expression just changed, and he started crying.

Teddy finally admitted he was involved in gambling and involved with a woman, and he was just squandering the money. You know, living high off the hog.

I guess everybody figured they were gonna put a hit on him or something like that, but all they wanted was their money back. I guess Teddy was a good earner for them.

PAT LIVINGSTON (FBI UNDERCOVER AGENT): I first met Bruce Ellavsky when I was working undercover in Detroit. I just felt comfortable with Bruce from the get-go. We just really connected. We were both real staunch supporters of J. Edgar Hoover. Bruce was more conservative than I was, but he was an excellent agent, very good at what he did, and a great guy. So when I went to Miami and started working on MIPORN, I knew I wanted Bruce to come down and be the other agent. I knew him, and I'd worked with him; I could trust him. When you're out there undercover, you got to protect each other. You have to know exactly what the other guy is thinking. I was comfortable that Bruce could do that.

So I called him and talked to him. He was having trouble with his wife, Pam, at the time. He was anxious to leave New York and come down to Miami—but he didn't know if Pam was coming or not.

BILL KELLY: Pat Livingston and Bruce Ellavsky came here in August 1977, and my job was to train them both to be pornographers.

Well, I'd never done that before. I knew how to be a pornographer, but I'd never trained anybody. And these guys knew nothing about obscenity when they came down here. So, initially, I thought these guys couldn't break into the porn industry. I just didn't think they had enough experience.

PAT LIVINGSTON: Bill Kelly brought out a double-dong dildo. I mean, I didn't know what a double-dong dildo was. Do *you* know what a double-dong dildo is?

It's about two feet long, and two girls use the same dildo at the same time. And Kelly's explaining this to us, and I mean, you know, I didn't know up from down.

BILL KELLY: I'd been fooling with these porno guys for fifteen years before MIPORN started, and I didn't know an awful lot about the inner workings of the day-to-day business operations. I had never gone out and made a large-scale buy. I could never go undercover because everybody takes me for a c-o-p as soon as I stick my nose in the door—especially if I got a cigar, which I always do.

BRUCE ELLAVSKY (FBI UNDERCOVER AGENT/PAT LIVINGSTON'S MIPORN PARTNER): We were not like Bill Kelly. We were learning as we were going. And I think early on Kelly didn't think we would be successful.

BILL KELLY: I had Pat and Bruce for, probably, two weeks. I gave them a minimum amount of training. I told them who their targets should be and what mistakes not to make. I said, "Don't ask for kiddie porn because they'll know you're a cop. And don't pay sixty dollars for a tape you can get wholesale for forty."

PAT LIVINGSTON: Bill Kelly was just a hard-nosed agent. Straight by the book and as strict and gritty as you can be. He's a tough guy. And he took pornography pretty seriously.

BILL KELLY: After a couple of weeks with me, Pat and Bruce went out and set themselves up in a warehouse near the airport as blue jeans salesmen. We bought a lot of blue jeans and stocked that place with them, but that was just the cover for them being pornographers.

PAT LIVINGSTON: We'd make a splash by walking into an organized crime hangout—a bar or restaurant—and rather than giving the waitress a hundred-dollar tip, we'd give her a pair of Jordache jeans. They'd go into the ladies' room, try them on, and come back out in the jeans. It was fun, but it also it made the waitresses remember us because designer blue jeans were a real commodity then.

BRUCE ELLAVSKY: I became Bruce Wakerly and Pat became Pat Salamone. We wanted to call our company "Gold Coast Specialities," but that was already taken. So we put an "e" on gold and an "e" on coast and became "Golde Coaste Specialties." And every once in a while we even had to sell some blue jeans to people—at discount—so we lost a little money on that.

PAT LIVINGSTON: We tried to look like minor mob guys. You know, silk shirts with an open collar. Silk suits. Sharkskin shoes. I even had a sharkskin suit.

BRUCE ELLAVSKY: We also had an undercover apartment where Pat and I supposedly lived together—to save money, you know? We had it furnished, and we had clothes in there, and we tried to make it look lived-in.

PAT LIVINGSTON: Oh God, we had our first undercover car—I never had a new car in my life, much less a Cadillac, you know? We had a pink Cadillac for our undercover car—"the pimpmobile."

BRUCE ELLAVSKY: After we set up the warehouse and the undercover apartment, we realized we had a problem: The porn people we were buying X-rated films from were eventually going to start wondering, "Who are these guys selling this merchandise to?"

BILL BROWN (ATTORNEY/FRIEND OF PAT LIVINGSTON AND BRUCE ELLAVSKY): When Pat called me during the summer of 1977, I hadn't seen him for two-and-a-half or three years. His career in the FBI was skyrocketing as my career as a lawyer was plummeting.

I'd built a successful Miami law practice for six years, made a lot of money, had a Mercedes, had a house in Coral Gables, and everything was going well—until everything fell apart.

I went through a very difficult divorce—and ended up living on a houseboat in the Dinner Key Marina. I didn't have a piece of clothing that wasn't mildewed. I'm paying a mortgage on the house, rent on the boat— so my life was in real turmoil.

PAT LIVINGSTON: We couldn't resell the porn we were buying to other people, so we decided to set up a business operation for laundering our product—a mail-order business in the Cayman Islands.

I'd tell them, "That way the Feds can't get me. I'm outta the country. See, I take all my orders through the Cayman Islands—then I fill them stateside."

BILL BROWN: I was hired to set up the corporation. So Pat, Bruce, and I fly down to the Cayman Islands, hail a cab—and on the way to the hotel Pat says to the driver, "Where are the girls? Take us to the girls!"

Pat gets the cabdriver's name, gives him forty or fifty dollars, and says, "You're our man while we're here. Drop all your other work—you work for us now; we'll pay you. And where are the girls?"

So the driver says, "All right, I'll take you to the Cayman House, a grand old house, for the finest dinner."

I was just dumbfounded. Because I'd have trouble saying to a cabdriver, "Where are the girls?" I mean, I have trouble giving a maître d' twenty bucks to get a nice table.

But Pat knew how to do it.

I mean, maybe Pat would be remembered as an asshole, but he would be *remembered*—and that's what it was all about.

BRUCE ELLAVSKY: Pat was the best at undercover. That was his forte. He was fantastic.

BILL BROWN: Our first night there, Pat and Bruce struck up a conversation with a fellow at the bar who smuggled stamps out of Sweden. Immediately, Pat and Bruce were passing themselves off as smugglers. Pat and Bruce talked to this Swedish guy at the bar, and then they set up a meeting the next morning to develop a new smuggling operation.

And I was dumbfounded, just dumbfounded, that people would fall for this. Pat and Bruce were selling themselves. I saw them do it in front of my eyes. Pat much more so than Bruce, but together they made a pretty good team.

BRUCE ELLAVSKY: Pat and I were able to communicate mentally and play off each other. He knew what I was thinking, and I knew what he was thinking.

BILL BROWN: I mean, we met girls at the hotel. The women were just dates; they weren't hookers or anything. One of them worked at one of the hotels, giving snorkels to the tourists. Another worked at the airport restaurant. Just ordinary girls—nineteen-, twenty-, twenty-one-year-olds—gorgeous, chocolate-skinned beauties.

At two or three in the morning everybody went their separate ways. I ended up sleeping with mine; they ended up sleeping with theirs.

BETTY JO (AN EX-GIRLFRIEND OF PAT LIVINGSTON, NAME CHANGED): I wanted to get intimate with Pat sexually because he intrigued me so much. He seemed to have a certain amount of class. It wasn't, "Hey, baby, let's get high." We just liked each other. I was used to European men, to a lot of flash and fun and men with money, and Pat had a taste for nice things. He seemed to be the kind of guy I could relate to.

BILL BROWN: That's why Pat was able to pull off the operation. Nobody else I know in these undercover operations ever came as close as Pat. Frankly, Bruce would never have come as close because Bruce is just not that type.

BETTY JO: Bruce was as different from Pat as night and day. Bruce is a very realistic, down-to-earth person.

BRUCE ELLAVSKY: Pat used to aggravate me because he beat me in almost everything. You know, I always thought I was in pretty good shape, and I'd go running with him, but Pat always ran a little faster. When we'd play tennis, he was always a little bit better.

So in the beginning, I think I was a little apprehensive about going undercover—but, yeah, I was excited. It seemed like something you read about somebody else doing.

PAT LIVINGSTON: Just don't ask me whether I was a better dancer than Bruce. Most people say he's a better dancer, but unquestionably I was.

BETTY JO: Pat was very confident, very proud of himself. He was sort of a loud person, cocky, swaggery. Pat always seemed in control. And Pat's much better looking in person because his personality comes out. He's charming, and he can seduce you into doing anything he wants. . . .

BILL BROWN: For me, the trip to the Cayman Islands was a watershed. It changed my life. Because while watching Pat and Bruce, I understood salesmanship for the first time—and the implications of this to me were just tremendous.

I was in a flux in my life, trying to decide what to do. I always believed that ability was everything and that the show—the clothes one wore, the office one had, the car one drove—really didn't make much difference.

Then I realized that being a lawyer—winning in court, winning trials, winning clients—*is* salesmanship. My wardrobe changed, my office—parquet floors, oriental rugs. It was the beginning of me building a really good, successful law practice.

Pat taught me that I can change the hand I was dealt—that it isn't written in stone that I have to be the way I am. He showed me how to choose.

BETTY JO: I felt like Pat was in control of the act, totally in control. But I never felt it was the real person. Even in bed he seemed to be odd. I even remarked to my friends, "I don't know this man."

BRUCE ELLAVSKY: You have to have a certain personality to be able to do undercover, but you really should be acting, rather than *becoming*. And during the operation Pat started to *become* his undercover persona.

Actually, *becoming* is much easier because if you become that person, you won't screw up.

Nobody Does It Better

MIAMI/LOS ANGELES
1977

GORDON MCNEIL (FBI SPECIAL AGENT): The real emphasis of MIPORN was getting to organized crime—pornography was just the vehicle we used to do it. So we had a seminar in Quantico, Virginia, at the FBI Academy in 1977 where I selected the national targets in the MIPORN investigation.

BRUCE ELLAVSKY: We had the benefit of the briefing in Virginia, so we knew pretty much who the major players in the industry were. Then we set out to see if there was a logical way to deal with them. I mean, you don't just roll into town without somebody introducing you. So our plan was to do it step by step, to play off one to get to another.

GORDON MCNEIL: We knew that MIPORN wouldn't be considered a success unless we ended up indicting Mickey Zaffarano and Robert DiBernardo. If we didn't get them, the operation would be a failure.

BRUCE ELLAVSKY: We had intelligence that Robert DiBernardo was a made member of the Gambino family, and Mickey Zaffarano was a made member of the Bonanno family.

RUBY GOTTESMAN: CPLC was a big distributor in California—I was buyin' stuff there—and their guy comes over to me and says, "Hey, we got some guys from Florida; they wanna buy some sixteens."

I was the guy for sixteens. So I says, "Who are these guys?" He says, "Ah, they've been in Florida. I know them. I dealt with 'em. . . ." Because you always had to be careful.

Pat Salamone and Bruce Wakerly—sure enough, those are the guys.

DICK PHINNEY (LOS ANGELES FBI AGENT/WEST COAST OBSCENITY EXPERT): I had information from an informant in Los Angeles that there's two guys in Los Angeles from Miami, and they're involved in porno—supposedly big guys, yet I don't know who they are. It turns out to be Pat Salamone and Bruce Wakerly.

So I made some calls back to Bill Kelly and asked, "Who are these guys from Golde Coaste Specialties?"

Well, Kelly knew, of course. But he couldn't tell me because he wasn't authorized to.

BILL KELLY: I had to lie to Phinney. I said, "I don't know anything about them."

Phinney said, "Gee, you oughta know about these guys. They're right outta Miami—your town."

I said, "All right, all right. I know, but I never heard of them. . . ."

DICK PHINNEY: I can understand the secrecy; they had to keep as few people knowing about it as possible. I was brought into it later—because it was obvious I was going to know anyway.

In fact, so much of the work was going to take place in Los Angeles, they needed my help for guidance and background.

BILL KELLY: Phinney was really upset with me. He was my best friend in the bureau at that time; we worked very closely together for fifteen, twenty years. So he was mad as hell.

But I told him, "Look, I didn't have a choice. I was told not to tell ya until it became absolutely necessary."

RHONDA JO PETTY (PORN STAR): When *Little Orphan Dusty* came out, my dad called me. See, it was a very big hit. I didn't expect that. I walked out the door after the shoot, and they said, "What name do you want to use?"

I said, "Just use my real name." I didn't think it was going to go anywhere.

Then my dad called me and goes, "I'm going to break your legs and arms!" Because I used our family name. That same day I'm driving down the freeway in my little VW, and this Jewish guy—who was kind of balding—pulls up alongside me in a Mercedes. He's going, "Pull over! Pull over!"

BRUCE ELLAVSKY: Let me put it this way: You don't walk into the porn industry off the street, okay? We needed somebody to vouch for us. Fortunately, we had a guy in Los Angeles—Ruby Gottesman—that we'd dealt with early on. If anybody got us an entrée into the porn industry, it was him.

RHONDA JO PETTY: We got off the freeway, and this guy says, "Come on," and he's got all this coke, and I'm going, "Oh, I don't know about this. . . ."

We go to my apartment and he's got all this cocaine and we snort cocaine and we're talking and his name was Ruby Gottesman. And he says, "Oh my God! You're Rhonda Jo Petty. I sell your films!"

PAT LIVINGSTON: Ruby Gottesman was a funny guy. I liked him. You had two kinds of people in the pornography business: businessmen who just happened to be pornographers and used it as a vehicle to make money, and the ones who enjoyed it—sleazy idiots who relished using the women.

Ruby used women like the others did, but he was above the average street-level porn guy. He was like a go-between between the distributors and the mob people who would finance the movies.

RUBY GOTTESMAN: Pat was like five-foot-five, a little, skinny guy. He looked like a gay guy. I never thought he was FBI.

DICK PHINNEY: I got feedback from my informants that Pat and Bruce were probably gay. Typically, people in the porn industry would be provided with a woman—if they wanted—and Pat and Bruce went out of their way to not have women. So that made them suspicious.

RHONDA JO PETTY: I'm still freaking out because of my dad, so I go, "Well, I don't know what I'm going to do. My dad's gonna kill me. I need to go hide."

Ruby went and got me a place in Manhattan Beach. He became my sugar daddy and hid me out there for almost two years.

RUBY GOTTESMAN: I never dreamed they were FBI, you know? They were wastin' money and travellin' too much. So after a while I sold them a lot of X-rated tapes.

RHONDA JO PETTY: Ruby was one of the top ten video pirates. I'd be flying all over the United States—to Hawaii—with him and all these films. Finally, I realized what he was doing—was illegal.

I didn't know anything in the beginning, but as time went on, I started realizing that he was black-marketeering. But I was too fucked-up on coke. I didn't really care—the coke was just flowing, and I was away from everything.

And Ruby was making so much money it was fucking ridiculous.

RUBY GOTTESMAN: Rhonda Jo Petty was the Farrah Fawcett look-alike porn star. She looked a little bit like Farrah Fawcett—if you were drunk. She was busty, and she had that Farrah Fawcett hair.

One time I picked up Rhonda and took her over to where Pat and Bruce stayed, this hotel by the airport, the Marriott in Marina Del Rey. I took Rhonda there and says to her, "I never asked you a favor before. Do me a favor—I have an idea that these guys are cops. See if you can find out?"

RHONDA JO PETTY: Ruby was paranoid—I figured he was on too much cocaine. So I went up to a hotel room to meet these two men. Ruby wanted me to do something to make sure they were who they said they were.

PAT LIVINGSTON: We spent a lot of time with Ruby, hanging out, learning about the porn industry, how it worked, who some of the players were, getting the right names.

Ruby was just a real likable character—you know, kinda balding, cowboy boots. He was married, but he had his women on the side, and he was very proud of that.

You know how some people are funny, and you just like to hang out with them? Ruby was like that—and he introduced us to a lot of people. He even had one of the stars from one of his movies come to see us.

RUBY GOTTESMAN: When we got to their hotel, Rhonda took each one of them into the room—separately. Bruce stayed maybe five minutes and Pat maybe three minutes.

She told me she blew them both. She said they came fast. I don't know; I wasn't in the room, but I know she was great on head. She gave great blow jobs, and she looked nice.

RHONDA JO PETTY: I just kinda asked them questions. Ruby wanted me to do something to make sure they were who they said they were. It had nothing to do with me having sex with them.

PAT LIVINGSTON: Rhonda Jo Petty was hot. Oh yeah, it was, just, *nice.* . . .

RUBY GOTTESMAN: Rhonda came back with nuthin'. She said she don't know if they were cops or not. She couldn't find out anything.

So I says, "Did you see any guns?"

She says, "No."

RHONDA JO PETTY: As far as I could tell, they were who they said they were. I don't even know what they looked like. You know the only reason I remember it at all? Because I didn't have to fuck 'em, ha, ha, ha!

RUBY GOTTESMAN: Rhonda was flighty. She didn't give a shit. She was always chasing young boys. I'd come home, and she'd be doing a sixteen-year-old.

I says, "You do that again, and you're out of here. I don't want no sixteen-year-olds here—get me in trouble. They gotta be eighteen!"

RHONDA JO PETTY: My relationship with Ruby was—I kind of lived my own life, you know? I was totally hidden, and we had very little sex because he had a little dick and couldn't get it up. Sorry, but he did!

And when you're doing that much cocaine, you can't have sex! He was too fucking coked out all the time. But it really wasn't about sex. I think it was about having somebody to do his cocaine with because his wife drove him nuts. She was a real bitch—very demanding. She wanted this, and this, and that, and that—and he was killing himself to give it to her.

I think I was his getaway. He'd come by, do his coke, and relax.

BRUCE ELLAVSKY: Ruby took a liking to us, and the next thing we knew he was vouching for us in New York and other places—and arranging for us to go to these clandestine porn conventions.

They were secret meetings where the major players in the porn industry would meet in a particular hotel in a particular city once or twice a year.

Everyone in one place.

Looks Like We Made It

NEW ORLEANS/NEW YORK CITY
1977

PAT LIVINGSTON: Ruby Gottesman really helped us get to the next level. The New Orleans porn convention was the first big one Bruce and I went to, and we got in there through Ruby.

The porn people would follow on the heels of a legitimate publishing convention—they would come in for three or four days at the tail end. Of course, the hotel people never knew.

BILL KELLY: I would follow Pat and Bruce to the porno conventions and harass them, to give them additional credibility with the underworld. If I had the opportunity in a hallway or on a stairway—with other pornographers watching—I would deliberately bump 'em with a shoulder and try to knock them down.

I'd say, "You guys are from my hometown. I don't like pornographers from Miami."

PAT LIVINGSTON: We had talked to the bureau about needing girls for cover because we knew we would be offered some at the New Orleans convention if we didn't have women with us.

The bureau just ignored it. Their suggestion was, "Well, why don't you be homosexuals?"

So I posed the question, "What happens when they send a guy up to the room?"

Dead silence on the other end of the phone.

BRUCE ELLAVSKY: Pat and I were in the lobby when Ruby told us he wanted to introduce us to someone in the restaurant around the corner. That's when we met Teddy Rothstein.

Teddy told us that he could supply Golde Coaste Specialties with hard-core eight-millimeter films, magazines, and videotape cassettes—and that he would like to introduce us to Andre D'Apice, a producer of eight-millimeter films.

PAT LIVINGSTON: It was the first real inroad the bureau had ever made into organized crime control of the porn industry—our first real confirmation that organized crime players carved up the country for their porno business.

So immediately after the convention we flew to New York, where we had set up a meeting at Star Distributors on Lafayette Street. The elevator opened up into a huge area—a maze of offices and people milling around. It looked like a shipping warehouse. A lot of boxes and film.

Ruby Gottesman gave us a guided tour. He knew everybody, so we floated around with him, making conversation. Then we sat down with Teddy Rothstein, and he introduced us to Robert DiBernardo—DiBe—who looked more like a Wall Street broker than a mobster.

He wore dapper Italian designer suits and a Rolex watch. He looked dashing and debonair and had the air of being in charge.

BRUCE MOUW (FBI AGENT/GOTTI STRIKE FORCE): Robert DiBernardo was a soldier in the Gambino family who was very active in labor racketeering and the construction trades—and a prolific moneymaker. Everybody knew he had Star Distributors—which was a multimillion-dollar porn company—and a big house on Long Island. He was one of the first wiseguys to drive a little Mercedes Benz convertible.

But the mob old-timers, for whatever reasons—out of their own sense of perverted morality—found pornography to be distasteful. They had no use for pornography or prostitution.

ROBERT DIBERNARDO (FBI WIRETAP): Castellano uses me. He makes me look bad. He says, "Look at DiBe; he makes his money in pornography!"

Mr. Fucking Clean. Does it stop him from taking his cut? "Sorry, Paul, you don't wanna touch those dollars—there's pussy on them." Ha! He'll take 'em anyway.

He wants it both ways. Get paid; act clean. My ass.

BRUCE ELLAVSKY: DiBernardo was definitely the boss. When he was telling stories about his childhood you could hear a pin drop. Nobody was gonna cut him off—regardless of how they felt about the story—because everybody respected him or feared him.

Then DiBernardo asked me and Pat, "What type of pornography business do you have there?"

Pat and I told him it was a mail-order operation—basically eight-millimeter films—but that we were thinking about getting into the video-tape market.

PAT LIVINGSTON: I was talking big numbers—said we'd buy ten thousand magazines that we could turn over in a day. Plus, I told him we operated out of the Cayman Islands, which enhanced our mail-order business. It showed how we could be moving such large quantities, that we weren't just selling to a lot of little people in Miami—which also gave us credibility.

BRUCE ELLAVSKY: DiBernardo and Teddy Rothstein went into an office and had a closed-door meeting. Then Ruby Gottesman went into the office and had a meeting.

While I was waiting for DiBe, Andre D'Apice came up to me and told me that during the New Orleans convention, there was a lot of apprehension about our porn operation. He told me that Teddy Rothstein had done some checking into the background of Golde Coaste.

PAT LIVINGSTON: We were told Teddy Rothstein flew from New Orleans to Tampa to talk to Paul Howard about us. And Paul Howard verified our story to Rothstein. I guess he did it to help me out because I was a good customer of his when we started MIPORN.

OPERATION AMORE REPORT: "PAUL HOWARD, aka Dilbert Eugene Craver. Subject worked for TED ROTHSTEIN and STAR DISTRIBUTORS for twenty years in New York City and Cleveland. Subject became ill in 1974 and was semiretired by ROBERT DIBERNARDO. DIBERNARDO and ROTHSTEIN ship subject pornographic films so Howard can earn an income in Florida by distributing to retail stores."

PAT LIVINGSTON: I was concerned when I heard Teddy Rothstein checked us out with Paul Howard. All this was coming back to me through Ruby Gottesman, who was now my confidant. He had a lot of information about people being killed—bombings in Chicago, etc. Gottesman told us about a guy who got hit in the head because he hadn't played ball with Mickey Zaffarano on some movies.

So we had all this hanging over our heads—if we said the wrong thing, if our cover was blown. We were in for some real problems. And we didn't have any cover from the FBI, we didn't have weapons; the only protection was being the pornographers we said we were.

So I was thankful that I had gone the long way in setting the undercover operation up, step-by-step-by-step.

BRUCE ELLAVSKY: I wasn't in fear. I wasn't paranoid. But sometimes, because of the people we were dealing with, I'd think, "Jeez, how the hell did we pull this off?" When we went to a city, we couldn't have the local FBI office surveilling us because they might blow our cover. If you're worried about the danger on this kind of operation, then you really shouldn't be doing it. I mean, we were pretty much out there on our own—but it's a voluntary thing. Nobody was forcing us to do it. So you assume the risk and don't really dwell on it.

PAT LIVINGSTON: Finally, DiBernardo says to me, "Rothstein and Andre D'Apice speak for me."

So we were given the okay to deal with Star Distributors. Then, Andre D'Apice comes in, and we talk price. We talk about doing a large deal with large numbers, and Andre agrees to bring the product and the film over to our hotel later that afternoon.

On the way back to the hotel, Ruby says, "Look, you've got to be careful dealing with Rothstein and D'Apice. DiBernardo will have you hit in the head if you don't deal with them right."

So we meet with Andre D'Apice at the New York Hilton and put our deal together. And Andre says the same thing, "The deal's good—you're dealing with good people—but if you fuck us, there are people who'll kill for DiBe." That put everything in perspective.

Then he says, "So, are we going to Plato's Retreat tonight? I can get us three whores. . . ."

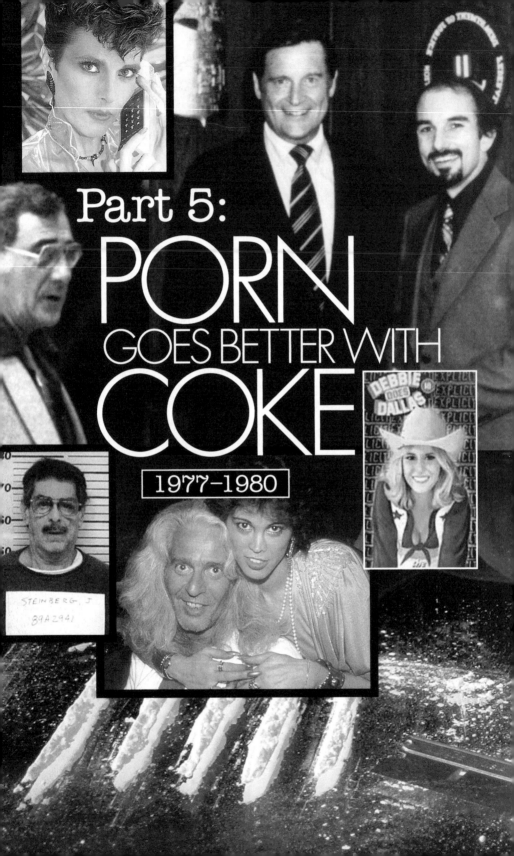

Part 5:
PORN
GOES BETTER WITH
COKE

1977–1980

STEINBERG, J
89A2941

DEBBIE
DOES
DALLAS

EXPLICIT

Left page, *clockwise from top left:* Gloria Leonard, Gordon McNeil and Pat Livingston, box cover for Jim Clark's *Debbie Does Dallas*, Fred Lincoln and Tiffany Clark, Joel Steinberg, Andre D'Apice.

Right page: John Holmes and friends.

Down the Drain

NEW YORK CITY
1977–1978

FRED LINCOLN: The idiots that kept the books for Plato's kept both sets in the same place. I don't quite understand that. Larry Levenson told me that the mob broke his legs with bats and shit a couple of times. So now the IRS gets the real books—not the cooked books—and Larry's going away for tax evasion. Of course they wanted the guys behind Larry, not Larry, but you get your legs broken with bats twice—you know, you kinda think twice about talking.

AL GOLDSTEIN: I'm the publisher of *Screw*, right, and when I come to Plato's all I get is a massage. Never have I gotten laid there, just massages. Maybe when Larry goes to prison, I'll take over as manager, and then I'll finally get laid. I'm forty-five years old and still inept. Josh Alan Friedman, look at him. "How old are you? Twenty-five?"

Just a kid, but he thrives on sleaze, lives in Times Square. It's okay for him to be inept, but there's no excuse for it at my age.

PATRICE TRUDEAU: Al Goldstein wants me. I'll charge him five hundred dollars. He's a little Jew, so I'll settle for four hundred. I know he's an asshole. I can talk to you one way, but I have to talk to him because he's a rich asshole. Besides, I want his digital watch. It's a beautiful watch, like a Piaget. That's what I would really like—a Piaget watch.

AL GOLDSTEIN: I usually don't get laid unless I pay for it. If I were a real swinger like Bernie Cornfield or Hugh Hefner, I would be getting laid every night by lots of new people. That doesn't happen. But I'm obsessed with it. I feel I'm much more typical of the normal American male than affluent people who have their choice of harems.

FRED LINCOLN: Why'd Larry get his legs broken twice? I guess because he fucked the wrong people twice.

So Larry's telling me his story. So I said to him, "Wow. This is incredible. You know, this would make a good movie."

And Larry said to me, "Well, okay, if you wanna do the movie why don't you come here?"

I go and I take the recorder and Larry tells me his story and I was transcribing it into a script.

Now Larry's getting ready to go away to prison for three to five, and he said, "How about you and Tiffany run Plato's for me while I'm gone?" Because I was married to Tiffany Clark at the time.

So I said, "Yeah, sure."

TIM CONNELLY: Helen Madigan and I went to Plato's when Larry was still running it. It was just really gross. The place was disgusting. I once went into a big room where they had a big hot tub—and Goldstein's in the hot tub and he's fat. The reality about swingers is that, for the most part, they're not very good-looking.

FRED LINCOLN: While Tiffany and I were in Plato's, I didn't pay attention to what Tiffany was doing. We always had that kind of a relationship. And they'd pass the freebase pipe around, and I'd take a couple of hits, and I'd get up and go fuck.

I was in Plato's! I wasn't there to get high.

So I never even realized that Tiffany was standing there with Larry and those other people and staying with the pipe. I never realized how much it affected her.

TIM CONNELLY: Plato's was really about Larry and Fred running the show and doing their thing. And the guys that were getting close to them were guys that had money or had access. I was always under the radar. I would come to Plato's, fuck their old ladies, fuck a couple of chicks, and then leave. I didn't really want to be a part of their world because I wasn't an equal, on their level.

FRED LINCOLN: Larry would always let celebrities into Plato's. He let Sammy Davis Jr. in—anybody who was a celebrity could come in, with or without a girl. Richard Dreyfuss used to come in every night—and he was on the balls of his ass—a stone coke freak.

While Larry's in jail for tax evasion, I'm talking to Richard Dreyfuss, and I said, "You're a great actor. How'd you like to play Larry if I do his movie?"

I'm thinking, motherfuckin' *score*—because this guy's got an Academy

Award, you know? And he was perfect to play Larry. He's a mutt, too—but a very talented mutt. What a fucking score and a half!

So I go visit Larry in prison, and I tell him, "Wow, Larry, man, I think Richard Dreyfuss'll do this *movie!*"

"Fuck him! I don't want him to play me. *I* want to play me!"

I said, "Larry, you gotta be kidding me. You can't even do a talk show. You can't play you!"

"Why not?!" he asks.

I said, "You know what, Larry? Let's just forget the whole thing. Because if you're turning down Richard Dreyfuss . . . lemme tell you something, you grab him now. He's gonna sober up, and he ain't never gonna talk to you again."

That's when I realized, "Oh my God, I'm dealing with an idiot."

That's when I said to Tiffany, "Let's just get out."

"Blow"

NEW YORK CITY
1977–1978

FRED LINCOLN: Cocaine swept New York like a fucking raging fire. I used to love driving at night—you'd stop at a light, look in the other car, and see all these torches blazing. It was amazing to me anyone would do that outside. How stupid. But they did it anyway.

Everybody was doing cocaine.

SHARON MITCHELL: I had been working steadily. Gloria Leonard was editing *High Society,* and I was working there during the day and babysitting for her at night. I was doing a couple of Off-Broadway plays, and I was in a rock and roll band. You know, we'd do these a cappella versions of "Peter Gunn"and we'd all dye our hair flaming pink and drive motorcycles around the Mudd Club and then scale the side of the building. Just some fun shit. It was great to be young and alive and creative. It was a great life. That's when I started getting into drugs.

GLORIA LEONARD: They had started *High Society* with a different girl. What the fuck was her name? Jesus. Brie? She used a couple of names. She was a cutie. She looked a little like Courteney Cox. Brie something or other.

Well, anyway, as it turned out, she was purely a figurehead. And, uh, with drugs being so prevalent on the scene in those days, not the most reliable spokesperson.

I had been a stylist for Peter Hurd, who was a photographer for a lot of the girlie magazines. And we shot a lot of stuff for *Cheri*—and even *High Society*—before I became publisher. I would do the makeup and wardrobe, set up the whole scenario. He just came in with the camera and shot the girls with whatever I put there.

So I had a magazine background and brought to the table a certain wisdom that a lot of the younger girls didn't have. Because by that time I was thirty-six or thirty-seven years old.

RHONDA JO PETTY: I did a lot of shoots for *High Society* and *Cheri*. That's how I met Gloria Leonard—on a shoot for *High Society*. We became very good friends. We partied together—everything then was cocaine and Quaaludes. We all loved Gloria because she was smart. She was like an older sister or aunt to a lot of us.

GLORIA LEONARD: I was not publisher of *High Society* in name only. I came in every day. I wrote cover lines, I wrote captions, and I went out and supervised shoots. I'd go on the road and meet with wholesalers and do six or seven interviews a day. We had a public relations firm that represented us. I used to travel probably an average of a hundred thousand air miles a year for them.

RHONDA JO PETTY: I'd go see Gloria a lot. . . . And then—Oh God!—she'd be out of town shooting, and her boyfriend, Bobby Hollander, would call me, and I'd end up at his place because of the drugs.

And that wasn't a real good thing—but it didn't end up being a problem because she knew that Bobby screwed around on her a lot.

GLORIA LEONARD: *High Society* decided to use my voice on a recording giving a little preview of what was coming up in the next issue. But the day the magazine hit the stand, we blew out the circuits for, like, a four-block radius.

So then we bought twenty answering machines. And I figured, "Okay, this should handle it." Then the twenty grew to a hundred. There was no way we were making money; it was costing us money to buy all these machines! We couldn't figure out how to make money with this system—until the 976 thing.

SHARON MITCHELL: I could go anywhere I wanted; I could do anything I wanted. I didn't wear fucking clothes—I wore maybe a G-string and a mink coat. I had a lot of money. It was great then—just great! Coke really helped because I was afraid I was going to miss something. I was really enjoying life so much. Coke really helped me stay up for quite a few years.

Then I started shooting it. And that was fabulous!

GLORIA LEONARD: The genesis of that whole 976 phone sex thing was that AT&T and Ma Bell were told by the federal government that they had to break themselves up. And a part of the breakup was that they had to make some of the 976 numbers available to other sectors of the market.

It used to be that the 976 numbers were the weather, the horoscope, dial-a-joke—you know, that kind of thing. And they had no method for distributing these numbers. They just picked names out of a hat.

And, as luck would have it, we came away with one of them—they picked our publisher's name. Drake or Crescent. I don't know which name they were using in those days.

SHARON MITCHELL: All I had to do was hide a little briefcase of coke in my apartment and let some guy come pick it up in two weeks, and somebody would give me an ounce of coke. I didn't have to fuck them. They just told me not to get into it.

They were heavy-duty Colombian guys, you know? And I just felt completely complete whenever I did that stuff.

And then I lost that connection, probably because I did something inappropriate. I really don't remember—but I'm sure it was something inappropriate.

GLORIA LEONARD: Phone sex was a huge success. There was one cartoon done by Rigby in the *New York Post* after it turned out that the Pentagon had made seven thousand dollars' worth of calls in one day.

And so they started putting blocks, you know, on outgoing calls. ABC was one company that ran up a huge bill.

FRED LINCOLN: Tiffany bought, like, three grams once. She cooked it up. She was lucky she got two hits outta that. I said, "What the hell is that?"

Nobody knew what the hell they were getting. No, it just swept—not only New York—but also the whole country. California had a lot. Jesus, directors, producers, everybody.

GLORIA LEONARD: After phone sex became so successful, there were attempts to stop it by lots of religious right and political right-wing groups that said this was inappropriate. I mean, I was on every talk show you could think of. Oprah, Maury, Larry, and Geraldo. There's hardly a talk show I haven't done. I was basically saying that this is a matter of choice, if you want to call the number or not.

"Well, what if kids listen to it?" So, what are they going to hear? A girl moaning and groaning and enjoying herself? I mean, better they should hear that than some of the other horrors that are going on. I was just trying to shoot holes in the stupid hypocrisy of it all.

SHARON MITCHELL: Then I was doing other forms of coke—but I couldn't deal it because I was doing too much of it.

GLORIA LEONARD: We fought for a lot of years. Laurence Tribe was *High Society*'s counsel of record. He's a professor of law at Harvard with Alan Dershowitz. He made the case for us in the Supreme Court—and won!

FRED LINCOLN: After we left Plato's, Tiffany stopped doing coke. Tiffany and I never had a freebase problem until then. Never had a cocaine problem before that. I used to buy a gram of cocaine, and it would last us two weeks. I could leave it on the table, and she would never even touch it.

SHARON MITCHELL: I had a lot of bad episodes. I mean with guys with guns. I used to get high with this lonely guy, an eccentric crazy guy named Joey. He dealt Uzis. He was Greek.

FRED LINCOLN: So Tiffany stopped freebasing. Six months went by; she was dancing, she was doing movies, and I thought, "Well, if she stopped, I guess she didn't really have a problem."

I made a mistake and bought her some coke one night. It was the beginning of the end because we had stopped. So I blame myself for that.

GLORIA LEONARD: *High Society* is the pioneer of phone sex. It was my idea. And I never realized a single dime off it.

SHARON MITCHELL: Joey used to build these incredible pipes and smoke from them. We'd sit around and smoke and talk. Every once in a while he'd just take out an Uzi and shoot holes in the walls—probably shot some of the neighbors.

He was crazy. I used to, like, take another shot of coke and pretend it didn't happen, you know?

FRED LINCOLN: I had said to Tiffany, "We can't do this. I can't do this shit. You're ruining my life. We don't eat. We don't go out. The only people we hang out with are people who do this shit."

I said, "I want nothing more to do with this coke thing."

SHARON MITCHELL: I moved to Thirteenth Street, and I was hanging out with some well-known rock and roll people. They were getting really high downstairs in this town house, and I was upstairs. So I said, "I want some of that."

The dealer was like, "No. No, no."

So I went downstairs, whining, "Give me some, man!" And they said no because they liked me. Everybody liked me. They thought they would protect me as long as possible. And they didn't want to give me any of their dope, you know. So they gave me this cotton shot.

And I was like, "Oh, wow!"

FRED LINCOLN: There was this guy from New York who owned some escort services, and he was really after Tiffany. He used to give her all the shit she wanted. He used to make Tiffany's mouth water—for smoke.

He got all the girls that worked for him strung out. He had this girl Harley, who used to go and get girls for him. I've got to admit, he was a pretty shrewd businessman. He even sent his girlfriend after me!

SHARON MITCHELL: I went, "Oh! Oh, man!" That was just, like, such *peace.* It was just peace and solace. And I had control. I had control. I felt like I'd been waiting my whole fucking life for this shot.

FRED LINCOLN: Why didn't I have the guy who was giving Tiffany shit whacked? 'Cause I'm not like that. I'm a nice man. Bad karma.

I figured it was my fault. I thought about it for days, and I figured out I'd have to get every drug dealer—anybody who ever gave the stuff to her—and that would include me.

SHARON MITCHELL: I probably instantly got a habit. I did good stuff—I had a lot of money. I didn't even know I had a habit, not really. I always had stuff. I made sure I was always in the right place to be around people that had stuff. I had huge tracks. I would go to work, and everybody in the business knew I had a habit.

But I performed really well. I did what I needed to do. I believe heroin made me function. Heroin and coke together made me function really well for decades. I was able to get things done. I was able to come—make myself come on camera—so it helped me.

FRED LINCOLN: Tiffany knew I was in town; she called me. I knew the people she got stuff from. It was pretty sad. She was goin' out to cop as soon as I gave her the money.

She didn't wanna go to a detox. She liked her life. She was runnin' from the cops. She had broken parole. The federal marshals were coming for her.

SHARON MITCHELL: Did I shoot up on the set? Yeah. Oh, sure. Everybody knew. I didn't hide it. If you hired me, I had to know where the nearest methadone clinic was ahead of time, so I could transfer my dose.

I never hid the fact that I was a drug user. And nobody seemed to mind. They were like, "Okay, that's Mitch, and that's what comes along with her."

FRED LINCOLN: I realized it was my fault—bringing people to the house, buyin' the stuff and doin' it. It wasn't even Tiffany's. If I had never said that one day, "Let's do this," I don't even know if it would've happened because she would never go and do anything without me.

Stayin' Alive

MIAMI
1978

BILL BROWN: It was June 21, 1978. I'd just come back to my office, and there's a message, "Call Bruce. Emergency."

I called Bruce, and he said, "Pat's been arrested."

PAT LIVINGSTON: I meet Andre D'Apice at the Pancake House in North Miami Beach. I pick him up in the pink Cadillac—the pimpmobile—and we're gonna do one of our porn deals.

So Andre's got a box of, maybe, twenty-four movies he brought down as samples, and he throws the box into the trunk of my car, and we jump in and start driving down One Hundred Sixty-third Street. That's when we get pulled over by the police.

Fine. No problem. I get outta the car and, you know, give them my license. Fine. But then the cop says, "Come on back here. You have to open the trunk of your car."

I said, "I don't think I'm gonna do that."

AL BONNANI (METRO-DADE POLICE DETECTIVE): Our surveillance unit in the OCB [Organized Crime Bureau] was following Frank Cochiaro—Big Frank from the DeCavalcante crime family in New Jersey—and Livingston showed up with Andre D'Apice. They sat down, talking deal, and then they went to the trunk of the car. Our surveillance men made a determination—and they moved in.

BRUCE ELLAVSKY [FBI WIRETAP]: "Did you hear what happened to Pat? He got busted for possession of pornography. Yeah, it was a screwed up thing, man. They were following somebody—Frank Cochiaro—who was with Andre. . . ."

PAT LIVINGSTON: Little did I know that Andre was being followed by the Metro-Dade Police. It turned out that, besides doing our porn deal, Andre was in Fort Lauderdale to do an alleged drug deal with Frank Cochiaro—prior to meeting with me. That's why the Metro-Dade cops were following him.

AL BONANNI: I knew Pat Livingston was undercover as Pat Salomone and so did my bosses, but that was it. Only three or four people knew that we flipped the informant and had given him to Livingston—and no one knew we had turned our investigation over to Livingston and the FBI. So, of course, no one in OCB surveillance knew.

BRUCE ELLAVSKY [FBI WIRETAP]: "So the cop starts asking Pat all kinds of questions, you know, let me see your registration; this and that. But Pat hadn't done anything wrong—nothing. Then another cop shows up and says, "This car might be stolen." Pat says, 'It's not a stolen car; it's a leased car. Here's the lease papers—call the guy.'

"So the cops go back to their car for a while; then they go back over to Pat and say, 'Get your hands on the roof.' "

"They put the cuffs on him. And the other cop goes into Pat's car, takes the keys out of the ignition, and opens the trunk. There's a box in there, all sealed up. The cop cuts it open and grabs the stuff. But it was soft-core stuff—you know, bondage, eight-millimeter films.

"Still, they threw Pat and Andre in jail for about six hours."

BILL BROWN: This was really a disaster. Pat and Bruce had put a year into establishing their credibility—and now it's all going down the tubes because Pat's been arrested on a traffic violation.

AL BONANNI: Our guys thought it was a coke deal going down, but then the trunk was opened and they saw obscenity. So they took them to Station Six and called me. I went down, and there was Livingston with his little goatee. I told the cops, "You've got a problem here. You just arrested somebody you shouldn't have."

BILL BROWN: When Bruce called to tell me Pat had been arrested, he was jumpy and nervous—and if you know Bruce, he doesn't get jumpy and nervous. Then he told me Andre had been arrested with Pat.

Andre D'Apice is bad news—New York, Star Distributors, Robert DiBernardo. Andre is the number three man in this organization.

Andre D'Apice made my blood run cold. I was afraid of him.

So I said, "Okay, I'll get them out. What's the bond?"

Bruce said, "A thousand dollars."

Andre and Pat were being held in the North Miami Substation, so I called the bondman—and we drove up there to bail them out.

PAT LIVINGSTON: When they took us to jail, they started asking us questions, you know, "What's your occupation?"

I said, "Well, I'm self-employed. . . ."

I was talking bullshit, but I carried a little notebook in my back pocket—and in it was a list of names and numbers of organized crime guys, names of porn contacts, names of informants. So they got that and thought they really had something.

BILL BROWN: Pat and Andre were arrested around noon. I got the call at three and drove up there at about three-thirty to bail them out.

Pat came out, snapping fingers—you know, real cool, "Hey, what's happening?" Pat's just rolling with it. He's feeling good.

I'm nervous.

Then Andre walks out. Andre is a mean motherfucker.

So we start talking, and Andre's real grim because—I found this out later—he'd been told not to deal with Pat and Bruce because they were on the watch list. They were suspected of being FBI.

So Andre thinks that this is *the* bust—and that Pat and Bruce have set him up.

BILL KELLY: Andre was the muscle; he was the scare guy. If Robert DiBernardo ever wanted to intimidate anybody, he'd send Andre. And, of course, DiBernardo had Don Carlo Gambino and Paul Castellano behind him. So Andre was dangerous.

PAT LIVINGSTON: Andre thought I might be an informant. It was like, "Why did we get stopped? Why were they following us?"

Andre knew it wasn't Frank Cochiaro. So if it wasn't him, he had to think, "Maybe it's this other guy, Pat Salamone."

So, oh God, yeah—I had to go through a dance to convince Andre that I wasn't an informant. I was saying, "What the hell is goin' on here? Why'd they arrest us? They're not lookin' at me! Are they lookin' at you? Have you done any drug deals? I haven't done any drug deals!"

We both didn't know until afterward. We had no clue.

BILL BROWN: Andre kept saying to me, "All the stuff we had in the car was soft-core—none of it was hard-core. . . ."

And I'm talking like a lawyer, "Well, Andre, the basis for obscenity is community standards, so you never know what might be considered obscene and against the law."

But Andre keeps saying, "But it was all *soft*. . . ."

And I was uncomfortable because I'm representing Pat, and I don't like being in a quasi-legal capacity for Andre.

Then Andre's lawyer from New York calls me, an attorney by the name of Joel Steinberg, and now I've got to lie to him—give him a line of bullshit, which I didn't like at all.

JOEL STEINBERG (CONVICTED OF MANSLAUGHTER IN DEATH OF HIS SIX-YEAR-OLD DAUGHTER, LISA; EX-HUSBAND OF BATTERED WIFE HEDDA NUSSBAUM): Bill Brown didn't disclose that he was FBI. But Brown became friendly with me, and when I went down to Florida I hung out with him. He was appreciative of my legal knowledge because, you know, I was the "New York lawyer."

BILL BROWN: I knew if Andre D'Apice got convicted, I could envision Joel Steinberg standing up before a bar association trial for malpractice—saying, "This lawyer, Bill Brown, was telling me things about the case that were simply not true, and I represented my client based on those misrepresentations. Andre was convicted and went to jail based on those lies."

PAT LIVINGSTON: Joel Steinberg was just your typical sleazy lawyer. And he's telling Bill Brown, "Lemme get up and say something. I gotta look good for Mr. D'Apice here. Lemme get up there. . . ." He didn't do anything.

JOEL STEINBERG: Basically, I came into the case immediately after Andre D'Apice was arrested. What happened was that they drove up in their pink Cadillac convertible to the airport, took delivery of this brown paper-wrapped package—which I think had four canisters of video in it—thinking it was drugs.

But they reviewed the film—and you can't do that. It's a first amendment violation, search and seizure. A first amendment claim, all of which was over Bill Brown's head because I realized in a minute he wasn't a criminal lawyer.

BILL BROWN: Joel Steinberg suffered the problems of any lawyer coming from out of town—or coming in on a case late. He's lost control; he's got to justify his existence, so he's saying, "Let's ask for a jury trial. . . ."

But my game plan was to get the prosecutor to drop the case. Because once they swore in witnesses it was all over for Pat because he had already received orders from high up in the FBI: "Do not lie under oath."

They said, "If you have to take the oath, that's the end of it—we're throwing in the towel—because the first question is: 'State your name.'"

PAT LIVINGSTON: After the arrest I went to the Bridge Restaurant to meet Andre. The Bridge Restaurant was one of three or four places that were hangouts for wiseguys. So whenever we went to those places, we made a big splash as Salamone and Wakerly.

We threw a lot of money around at the Bridge in particular and got to know the owner and the chef well. When we'd come in for dinner, the owner would take us back in the kitchen, you know, "Hey, what's the special tonight?"

So that night I go to meet Andre—I was there by myself—I go into the kitchen, and there's two guys with guns waiting to take me off into a car. I didn't know them, okay?

We drive out on Western to Fort Lauderdale, then further west out onto a sandy road. Then we get out of the car. They open the trunk, hand me a shovel, and say, "Start digging."

BILL BROWN: Fortunately, the arrest didn't make any sense. They got Pat on an expired tag. Pat didn't own the car. So it was a bad arrest.

PAT LIVINGSTON: I started digging a hole. The two guys are saying, "Look, we know you're a snitch. We know that *you* know that there's a problem here. So you might as well tell us right now. . . ." They were claiming I was an informant.

BILL BROWN: So my argument was that the officer had made an illegal arrest, and I could prove it. And once the initial arrest is improper, then anything that flows from that is fruit from the poisoned tree. In this case it was those two cartons of porn films in the trunk of the car. If you can't introduce the films at trial, you have no evidence—you might as well drop the case.

PAT LIVINGSTON: They were saying, "Who are you working with? The FBI? Broward County? Dade County?"

I'm getting down to about my ankles, and I can't say, "I'm a cop." I'd be dead then. My only chance was to say, "Look, you can kill me, but you're going to die because you've made a big mistake here."

And I kept digging.

BILL BROWN: I made an appointment with the prosecutor and went up to his office—I wore my brown clothes, no flashy clothes, because I was trying to come off as someone who did not present a challenge.

I said to him, "Look, you've got a bad arrest here. They arrested him initially for an expired sticker, and it wasn't expired, and I'll show you why. . . ."

I'd been to the Bureau of Motor Vehicles, and gotten a copy of the law and the lease agreement. He said, "You're right. We'll drop it. What do you want to do?"

I said, "I'd like you to make an announcement that you're dropping the case—either now or at the hearing next week."

And he said, "Why don't we wait and make the announcement at the hearing?"

I said, "Okay." But now I'm worried. Is he going to remember? Or is there going to be another prosecutor transferred in? Or is the supervisor going to say, "You've been dismissing too many goddamn cases. I want you to go in there and fight and win."

You never know.

PAT LIVINGSTON: I didn't have a gun on me. I didn't have identification. The only way out was to be who I was. I was Salamone.

I had to convince them that they're wrong—and if they did kill me, that they're going to die, too.

After a while, they said, "All right, let's go." They threw the shovel back in the trunk, and we drove back to the Bridge Restaurant and had dinner with Andre.

And I tried to eat the Italian meal that was in front of me.

BILL BROWN: When we finally went to court, I walked up to the prosecutor and said, "Do you remember me? I'm Bill Brown. I came to your office?"

He looks at me. He's seen a thousand lawyers in that three weeks.

I said, "You told me that you were going to dismiss this case? I think you made a note on the outside of your file right there. . . ."

He looks at it and says, "Your Honor, we're dropping the prosecution. Thank you very much."

JOEL STEINBERG: I ended up standing up and representing all these people because Brown said, "You handle it." We went to court—one case; I appeared, and it was suppressed.

BILL BROWN: This was a significant event: probably thirty people in the audience and another thirty up around the bench.

Like all winning clients, Pat wants to stay and chat. It's the winning lawyer's job to grab the client and drag him out of the courtroom before the judge changes his mind.

I said, "C'mon, Pat. *C'mon!*"

The room was full—the FBI people on one side and representatives of the New York mob on the other. All the mafiosos there to see if their guy was gonna get caught, and all the FBI brass waiting to see if their operation is going to get blown. It was really something to see.

BRUCE ELLAVSKY: As it turned out, Pat and Andre's arrest may have helped us because it looked as if Bill Brown had been instrumental in getting the case thrown out. Plus, the camaraderie of Pat and Andre having been arrested together.

BILL BROWN: It was celebration time. I mean, everybody's slapping each other on the back and generally acting like we had just done something very important.

So we decided we were going to have a big celebration that night. We went to the Grove for one of those hideously expensive dinners. Pat and Bruce had called the FBI, and they flew two undercover female agents down from Detroit that day. They had to go to the airport and pick them up. I didn't know the girls were agents, but I found out later.

JOEL STEINBERG: We were real bosom buddies because I won the case for them, and they were genuinely appreciative.

BILL BROWN: I had met a girl in the bar of the Omni Hotel and asked her to come to dinner with us. So Andre starts going after this girl, and she loves Andre: She thinks Andre is just the nicest thing going. Andre is her type of guy—the real macho, tough, bragging type. Like, "I'd fuck you all night." But from Andre, you wouldn't characterize it as dirty and gross, just supermacho tough bragging—and Andre could carry it off.

Andre didn't say a lot—but he said enough.

PAT LIVINGSTON: After dinner, we went to the Mutiny, a bar in Coconut Grove.

BILL BROWN: It was well past midnight when we get to the Mutiny, and we are all approaching the limit of our alcoholic intake. And it's rolling now—girls, music—but Joel Steinberg is now going downhill rapidly, just really obnoxious. He's abusing the women, and he's screaming for cocaine, saying, "LET'S GET COCAINE! LET'S GET COCAINE!"

Just generally acting like a pig. Joel was very aggressive, very rude, and very drunk. I mean, just a bad guy. There was just something wrong with the guy. We all talked about it later.

You know, "This guy is sick. He's a sick puppy."

BRUCE ELLAVSKY: Joel Steinberg was kind of a sleazy guy. He thought he was smooth with the ladies, but he didn't pay for anything. I just didn't want to deal with him, you know?

PAT LIVINGSTON: Joel Steinberg—what a scumbag.

BILL BROWN: Even Andre was saying what an asshole this guy was. Joel had all these grandiose plans, and Andre picked up very quickly that it was all a bunch of horseshit. Joel was trying to figure out how he could justify a five-thousand-dollar fee when all he did was introduce himself at court. And that was it—he didn't do anything else.

And at the party, I think Andre's thoughts were very similar to mine, "This guy doesn't get out much, you know?"

JOEL STEINBERG: They brought in this absolutely beautiful woman—who I didn't know at the time was an FBI agent—and she was trying to hit on Andre D'Apice.

BILL BROWN: The woman I brought from the Omni bar eventually lost favor with Andre—she was putting on airs or something, like she probably wouldn't fuck him. So Andre started making a heavy move for the blond FBI agent.

In the meantime, I invited some girls I knew vaguely—one was a realtor—to come back to my house with us.

PAT LIVINGSTON: Andre was all over the female FBI agent, and he's trying to drag her off. But she was supposed to be my date, so she grabbed my crotch and said to Andre, "I've got all I want right here, thank you very much." It was absolutely the right thing to do at the right time—and that's why she was there.

BILL BROWN: Then Joel got out of hand. He tried to bite the realtor's breast—you know, leaning over, mouth open, drinks falling all over the place. She got up and said, "You pig!"

Then she left.

I had invited her back to my house, and she was game—but when Joel grabbed her and bit her on the tit, that was a little much. I said, "Let's go. It's time to go; let's get out of here."

So we went to my house. Some of the girls were there; Joel drove with one of the girls to the house, and he wouldn't get out of the car. It was one of those drunken scenes—I'm dragging Joel out of the car, and he's screaming, "WHERE'S THE FUCKING COKE? WHERE'S THE COKE? WHAT THE HELL'S GOING ON? WHAT KIND OF GROUP IS THIS, NO COKE? COME ON, LET'S GET SOME COKE!"

And the girls were just disgusted. You know, "What a pair of assholes! Let's get out of here!" So the girls left, and Pat must have taken Andre and the female FBI agent home.

So that ended that night.

Seka to the Rescue

NEW YORK CITY
1978–1979

SHARON MITCHELL: I went to Reuben Sturman to get the money for a couple of movies I directed. I'm not really an experienced filmmaker; it was just something I wanted to do. But I really didn't get a sense of Reuben at all because by the time I really knew him I was at the height of my drug use.

FRED LINCOLN: Sharon Mitchell is my buddy, since she was eighteen—since she started. So Mitch called me up and told me she met this guy, and they were gonna do a movie. And she said, "But I don't know enough about it, and I'd like you to work maybe as the production manager."

SHARON MITCHELL: I worked with two partners in Brooklyn; we set up a corporation to sell shares of the film, so the money comes directly into the bank.

I spent some of the money—but I didn't want to fuck with these people too much—because I knew where the money was coming from.

FRED LINCOLN: I go to the set, and I'm watching Vanessa Del Rio looking at the lighting and the cameras. And I say, "You know what? You ain't got shit." We'd been shooting for two days, and these guys ain't got the faintest idea what they're doing.

I said, "We've shot two thousand feet of film, and we've only done three scenes. That's insane. You're getting ripped off. I'll tell you what—stop the shooting until we see the rushes."

So we did that. Did they suck? Yes. Camera's flying all over the place.

This guy, Ernie, did the movie only because of me and Mitch; now he's thinking we ripped him off. But we never touched no money.

SHARON MITCHELL: Actually, I brought Fred in because I hadn't spent *all* the money—but I had spent about half of it. So I relied on him to help me a lot.

FRED LINCOLN: So I said, "You know what, Ernie? Why don't you let me get you a realistic budget, under fifty grand. Mitch and I will do it free until we sell it. We'll go back to San Francisco and shoot it."

Ernie's hemmin' and hawin', "How do I know you're not gonna rip me off?"

I said, "I'm trying to make this right. I can't do anything else. I didn't take no money."

He said, "How do I know she didn't give you some?"

I said, "Because I would've let us finish the movie. We woulda split it, and you woulda been fucked. Whatsa matter with you? I wouldn't have stopped the movie if I had a part of it."

"Okay," he said. "Let's do it."

SHARON MITCHELL: Fred had no idea where the money originally came from. We had to get other backers; it was a pretty intense situation.

So Fred and I coordinated to raise more money together.

BILL KELLY: Everybody kowtowed to Reuben Sturman. He used to come to these porn conventions and be treated like royalty. He would have an entourage following him around. Reuben actually looked like he was somebody important. And he was—if you don't mind dealing in pornography.

ROY KARCH (PORNOGRAPHER): I was standing at the CES [Consumer Electronics Show] in Vegas with my boss at Gourmet Video—Howie Wasserman—when a guy comes over with another guy—a mobster. The other guy's got an attaché case handcuffed to his hand.

I'm facing front, and they're talking behind me, and I hear, "Come on, I want to handle your stuff."

Howie says, "I can't do it. I want the stores myself."

He says, "Let's go up to my suite. You can have this briefcase."

Howie says, "Why do I want that briefcase?"

The guy says, "Because there's a million in cash in this briefcase."

Now, at that point I had to stop myself from turning around. You know, this is none of my business—but when I heard a million in cash, I wanted to see who the fuck is talking. But I didn't turn around; I watched them walk away. Then I asked, "Who was that?"

Howie says, "That was Reuben Sturman."

I said, "Well, why don't you want to do business?"

Howie says, "Don't want to."

I don't think Reuben ever got Gourmet Video's line. Howie really wanted to hold his product and distribute it himself. Howie's very smart. He made a lot of money from direct distribution to stores—at forty dollars apiece, not twelve dollars like it is today.

FRED LINCOLN: We couldn't get a man, and we couldn't get Vanessa Del Rio back to do the film, and Mitch is totally freaking out.

So I said, "You know what? There's this new girl everybody's talking about. Her name's Seka."

That was the first time I met her—when I booked Seka for our film.

ROY KARCH: When we were doing *Dracula Sucks* out in Los Angeles with Annette Haven, John Holmes, Kay Parker, John Leslie, Paul Thomas—all the big names—we put an ad in *Variety* looking for other talent.

We got a letter back—with pictures—from this woman, Dorothy Yontz, who wrote, "I have a bookstore in Virginia with my husband, and we saw your ad in *Variety*, and I'd like to get into porn."

Ken and Dotty were their names. We saw the photos, flew her out, and Bill Margold gave her the name Seka.

She was gorgeous.

SHARON MITCHELL: Seka's real name was Dotty. She had little poodles; and I had to coach her on how to get rid of that horrible Southern accent. She was very sweet, but I didn't have a crush on her. I thought she was a marketable commodity for my movie. She was very nice, very cool, and I just liked the way she liked to fuck. It was genuine.

GLORIA LEONARD: The first time I met Seka, I think she was shooting loops for *Swedish Erotica* with my husband, Bobby Hollander, somewhere in New York.

She was sort of a cheesy, cheap looking blond from the South with too much turquoise eye makeup and too many silver rings on.

But she was hot, you know?

FRED LINCOLN: So we shot the movie, *A Place Beyond Shame*. Ernie made his money back—including the original $60,000 that had been blown. He ended up making about forty or fifty thousand.

SHARON MITCHELL: *A Place Beyond Shame* was Seka's first movie. I probably made about $35,000 off of it. And then I sold some more shares when my heroin addiction really hit. I wish I still had those shares now because that film made a lot of money.

FRED LINCOLN: Before our movie, all Seka had done were a bunch of loops for Caballero. And she had this pimp husband, Ken—who thought he was Elvis—who had no idea what he was doing with her. And she was *sooo* good, this girl. So I called Freddie over at the Melody and said, "Boy, you gotta hire this girl. She's gonna be really on top in our business."

ROY KARCH: Dotty and Ken would call me up from the Sahara Hotel—three blocks from my house on La Brea—and say, "We're in town—bring someone over."

Because Ken was horny, and Seka liked the way I eat pussy. So I would always find a girl and say, "You wanna fuck Seka?"

"Yeeeaaah," said the chick. But the real gig was that she had to fuck Ken.

SHARON MITCHELL: I think Seka's husband wanted to be Chuck Traynor—the star maker, you know? He was cool and harmless but just sort of a suitcase pimp.

TIM CONNELLY: A suitcase pimp is a guy who is the boyfriend/manager/husband/sometimes-sex-partner-on-camera, and who ultimately holds the wallet. He's a pimp—but he's a suitcase pimp, which is a little more high-toned than just a pimp. He's got one girl, and he's working at promoting/managing her. And he always speaks in "we" rather than "I."

"If *we're* going to do this double penetration movie, *we* need to make a little more money if you're going to put that dick up *her* ass. . . ."

They always break at that point.

VERONICA HART (PORN STAR): Chuck Vincent, who I loved, told me never to work for this Lenny Kurtman guy. But I saw some of his stuff at the World Theater and it was good—people were actually acting.

So I go to work for Kurtman, and Seka's in the movie, too. I'm working with this guy, Cole, who's predominantly gay. The way they were shooting is when I got the guy hard, they'd be shooting the soft shots—you know, facial reactions. Then when we'd go to shoot the hard shots he'd be soft again, so I'd have to work him up again. This went on for a while.

FRED LINCOLN: Seka finally saw what an asshole her husband really was. He was fucking every girl at the Melody.

I mean, she'd work, and he'd take the money—and then get her more work. Ken got her to work for Lenny Kurtman; she did ten movies in a week. That's what this fucking moron was doing to her—instead of making her a high-end girl.

VERONICA HART: So Lenny Kurtman takes me to the side and says, "Honey, aren't you a little tired? Don't you want this to be over?"

I'm going, "Well, okay," because I just want everyone to be happy, right?

And he goes, "We'll get this over with right away."

So I assume the doggy style position, and Lenny whips his dick out, pumps three or four strokes in my ass, then comes all over my butt. I didn't know much about the business, but I knew that wasn't right.

I felt like a piece of shit. I cried on the way home.

GLORIA LEONARD: Leonard Kurtman was the kind of guy that, if another male was having a problem, he would jump in and just get shot from the waist down. You could always tell it was his little fat, stupid dick when you saw it on the screen—and I hated that.

FRED LINCOLN: Ken sold Seka too cheap. If you get overexposed in theaters, it fucks you up terrible. Seka knew it. So she finally broke up with Ken. And he was brokenhearted. That's when Seka decided to stay in New York.

VERONICA HART: I came back to the shoot the next day and told Seka that Lenny Kurtman made me feel cheap. He had no idea he had done anything wrong. He asked me to go to the Bahamas with him. He was completely clueless that the way he acted was out of line.

I told Seka, and she was just really great. She said, "Oh, that's bullshit. You didn't have to do that, darling. You don't have to do anything you don't want to. These people are lucky to have you here." Seka was just great.

JAMIE GILLIS: I loved Seka. She was my little boy fantasy, like, "Wow! I'd like to fuck her." She was porn, but a little bit above it—sort of a white-trash queen in a way that I found really erotic.

So I said to her, "It's nice for me to have someone in the business I can look up to." I didn't think of her as one of the girls I was going to fuck no matter how much I wanted to. She was *desirable*.

FRED LINCOLN: The girls used to tell me that Ken's whole apartment was a shrine to Seka. All the walls had posters of Seka—pictures of her every place—and he'd be looking at them when girls were giving him head.

He managed some more girls and tried to get over her, but—yeah, he was brokenhearted.

JAMIE GILLIS: Seka and I went to Show World. I still had the run of the place at that time, so I just took her back where the girls were dancing behind the peep show machines and said, "Come inside." Then I started fucking her in the peep-show booth.

FRED LINCOLN: Seka didn't care who she worked with. You know how some girls have a list? She and Ken had been swingers in Virginia, so Seka didn't give a fuck—"Just bring 'em in, and I'll fuck 'em!"

Did I fuck her? Oh, yeah. We were good friends.

JAMIE GILLIS: The peep-show girls are usually upstairs dancing; the guys looking through the windows sorta go up to the theater to watch the show. But while I'm fucking Seka, I'm hearing people go, "HEY! HE'S FUCKING SEKA IN THE BOOTH!" And she was like a major celebrity in the business, so everybody in the place knew it was happening.

It was funny because all these windows started flying up—these guys couldn't put the quarters in fast enough. It was *fun!*

GLORIA LEONARD: Seka was the platinum princess, and she was there at the right place at the right time. Seka's very smart when it comes to how to manipulate men. You know, I'm a Jewish girl from the Bronx, and unfortunately when I was born you had to get in line for different things. There was a line for "cash," but I thought they said "hash," so I got on the wrong line. So I never had any of that "buy me-get me-take me-bring me" thing going—which is unusual for my cultural background.

But Seka was good at it. Still is.

VERONICA HART: Seka was the first woman I ever did on screen. I felt kind of a sisterhood with her. I just loved her—as long as I have a face, Seka will always have a place to sit.

Johnny on the Pipe

LOS ANGELES
1978–1979

BILL MARGOLD: John Holmes became the single most recognizable name in the history of the adult film industry and proof that all men are not created equal.

There is an orgy scene in *Disco Dolls* where I'm being blown by Lesllie Bovee, and John's being worked on by four people next to me. All of a sudden his dick popped out over my head, and I looked up at it—and it was like the opening shot of *Star Wars*.

I had the feeling that if I got hit in the head by that thing, I'd get a concussion. So my dick, which was happily ensconced in Lesllie Bovee's mouth, was no longer interested in working. And she laughed, and he laughed, and I had to laugh at myself.

Such was the legacy of The King.

ANNETTE HAVEN: What was interesting was that John Holmes really only worked on camera. His cock was impressive visually, but, let's face it—as the joke goes, if John ever got fully erect, he'd lose consciousness due to lack of blood to his brain. Because his dick really was *that* big.

And it's true that his cock was never hard. It was like doing it with a big, soft loofah sponge. You had to kind of stuff it in. I don't know about other women, but I prefer something in a smaller size that's actually rigid, and functions really well. Being stuffed full of loofah is kind of interesting, I guess, but not exactly a turn-on.

DON FERNANDO (PORN STAR): The first movie I did with John Holmes was *California Gigolo*. He played an eccentric rich guy who couldn't keep it in his pants, and I was his man Friday—a butler kind of guy. It was a take off on *Fantasy Island*. We wore the white suits, and it was quite fun.

It was on that movie that I saw his cock for the first time. We did a scene where we were right next to each other; we had two lovely young ladies in the doggie position, and we were plugging away and high-fiving each other. And I remember looking down—it was incredible—and thinking, "That guy's got a big cock." It was *scary*.

But I didn't envy him. Actually, I felt a little bit of pity for him because I never saw him penetrate anybody fully. I remember thinking, "Gee, I feel sorry for that guy. I don't think he knows what it feels like to put it in all the way to the hilt."

RICHARD PACHECO (PORN STAR): Every woman who made a name for herself in this business, sooner or later, was ritually enlarged by Mr. Holmes. Some women just found God and were gone. They had reached the promised land, and their scenes were magnificent.

Then there was the other crowd whose faces looked like somebody at a medical exam, wondering when the pain was going to start.

And then there were those who went, "Get this out of me, *now!*"

GLORIA LEONARD: I had never met John Holmes until we were cast together in three films that were going to be shot in France.

They brought me and John and a couple of other American actors and actresses over, and one or two tech people—but largely, the cast and crew were French. The first film we did was in Paris. Then we did two more at a marvelous sixteenth-century chateau a couple hundred miles from Paris on the coast of Brittany in a little town called Quimper—which John insisted on pronouncing "kimper."

John's a man of culture. He's got a lot of class. Too bad it was all low!

SHARON MITCHELL: When I first worked with John I was petrified because I'd heard the guy had this huge dick. And I was really quite scared because I really wasn't that experienced sexually.

John came in and the first thing he asked me was, "Do you do drugs?"

I said, "Yeah, I do drugs."

Then he opens up this briefcase and in it there's little sections—you know, like a pillbox that says *Monday, Tuesday, Wednesday,* but this was, like, for a whole month. It was like a fishing tackle box, and in each section there's various powders and colored pills.

And he says, "What do you like? Downers? Uppers? Speed?"

I said, "I like downers. I'll take a little bit of that and one of those and a couple of these. . . ." So in this loop we did, John is fucking away, and I look like I'm completely dead. It was a really strange thing because I don't remember having sex with him.

GLORIA LEONARD: John was great! I mean, I had all of my girlfriends tell me, "Oh, he's so big," and you know, "Sometimes he doesn't get really hard," so I was getting all this advice from this one and that one; you know, from Lesllie Bovee and other girls who had worked with him.

Well, I don't know if it was the French air, honey, or because I was new meat or something—but he was like a rock the whole time! And he could be very charming. We're shooting this sex scene, and they go, "Okay, that's enough." And we were just getting into it, you know? So John grabs me by the hand and drags me down the corridor of the chateau to an empty room—where there's a bed—and we finished the scene ourselves.

We bought a set of matching Dupont cigarette lighters while we were there—I still have mine. And many months later he sent me a huge box of photographs of our time together in France—with a lovely note and a sterling silver straw from Tiffany & Co.

BOB VOSSE: By the mid-seventies, John Holmes was getting a thousand dollars a loop, which was quite a bit more than anyone else in the industry. And in all fairness he deserved more; his loops and his films were outselling the competition by at least ten to one.

His worst loops, even when they were terrible—and it didn't matter who the girl was—if John Holmes was in it, would outsell everything.

So his prices kept going up, and he deserved it.

JOEL SUSSMAN (PHOTOGRAPHER): John got real spoiled. He became bigger than himself and made lots of money doing it.

I think that was what propelled him into insanity more than anything else. It was that too-much-too-soon thing. You know, where you start with cigarettes and go to smack. And what do you do after smack? You start doing weirder things to yourself.

He was like a rock star. He did the same thing rock stars did—go up high and burn out. And then you can't get back in the atmosphere. His life was like a cartoon, and then it became real. When it was a cartoon it was fun, but when it was real it was ugly and scary.

GLORIA LEONARD: John could also be something of a prima donna. I told him in France, "This set is only big enough for one prima donna, and I'm it." He laughed.

BILL AMERSON: The myth that created John Holmes was my doing. I was John's manager and his agent his entire career, and together we came up with the myth that was John Holmes—things like him being a gigolo, about him flying to Europe and turning tricks with wealthy women.

It all added to his box office. And that's what it was all about.

SHERI ST. CLAIR (PORN STAR): The way he was built, John couldn't help but be put on a pedestal. People couldn't quite believe that he was so endowed; they were rather amazed about the whole thing. And it was reinforced over and over again.

Suddenly you're a celebrity. You go to the awards ceremonies, and you're constantly being bombarded by people asking for autographs.

One day you're the girl working at the coffee shop, and then suddenly you're bigger than anybody else.

And John fell into that; he became a celebrity and lived and breathed that twenty-four hours a day.

BILL MARGOLD: John had no understanding of what fame was—that fame is omnipresent, and that when you're famous you have to answer to the bell every day. And sometimes you just don't want to get up. So in order to get up, you use things to get you up to avoid the reality of being up.

BILL AMERSON: One time John and I were up in Yosemite, fishing, and we ran out of gas. It was during the seventies gas crisis, when you could fill your tank only on alternate days if you had an odd or even license plate. And this wasn't our day.

So the attendant comes over, and all of a sudden John goes into his Johnny Wadd character—the deeper voice, the attitude, this stance of power—like a detective, like a Damon Runyon character.

And the guy filled up the van with eighty gallons of gas, just because John had turned into the Johnny Wadd persona.

People would do that. We would be flying someplace and John would go talk to the ticket taker, and he would say, "I'm Johnny Wadd!"

And they'd say, "Oh yeah, we know who you are," and we would always be put on the plane first.

He used that character a lot, and he actually believed at times that that was who he was. He became Johnny Wadd in his own mind; he thought he could do no wrong—that he could solve all these cases. He was just crazy at times. I don't know about delusional—but yeah, a little loony. It was embarrassing.

REB (FIRST PORN AGENT): I'm not a psychiatrist, but my feeling is that John had multiple personalities. We were on the set once, and it was John's turn to work, and we looked all through the house and couldn't find him.

I looked everywhere; his vehicle was still out in front. Finally, I looked in this small closet—and there was John, rolled up in a little ball, and he was afraid. He wouldn't tell me what he was afraid of; he was just afraid.

BOB VOSSE: When John was shooting *Prisoner of Paradise* the producer had arranged to have a CBS news team come in and interview him. Their angle was that we had a female director, Gail Palmer. So our producer was briefing him on what to say during the interview.

John was sitting in the makeup chair. Gail came up and tried to get him to go over the script, since they had a little extra time. But John didn't want to have any part of it.

The producer and I walked away, and a minute later we heard, "SMASH! BAM! BOOM!"

We looked over at the makeup table, and there were John and Gail fist fighting as hard as they could—and the makeup girl is screaming, "They're killing each other!"

So our producer pulled them apart—just as there was a knock on the door.

It was the CBS crew.

They come in, set up, and they're ready to go. And the first question they ask is: "John, how is it working with a female director? What are your feelings about Gail Palmer?"

John says, "Oh, she's the greatest director, the most sensitive I've ever worked with."

And this is less than two minutes after he had his fist right in her eye.

BILL AMERSON: When I first met him, John wouldn't do any drug but marijuana. He was afraid of everything else. Then around 1975 or 1976, he got turned onto cocaine by a producer.

There was always cocaine around. It was a commodity in the adult film business. People were *paid* in cocaine.

Anyway, John lived with me at the time, and two hours after he had finished on the set he was still buzzing. He was running around doing things, like waxing his car, washing the dishes, and cleaning the floor. And this was like two in the morning. John thought this was the greatest discovery of his life. That was the first time that John snorted cocaine—and then he snorted it on almost a daily basis for the next few years.

SHARON MITCHELL: Everyone had cocaine. Everyone had some heroin. Everyone had whatever they did—PCP, speed, pot. People carried it around with them.

I'm not necessarily saying we needed it to perform in the movies. I'm just saying we preferred it. We carried it one step further than the sixties. It was free sex and a lot of drugs. It was a sign of the times, and everyone was packing whatever their preference was.

But we would all share. We were good that way.

BOB CHINN: At that time, just shooting an X-rated film was subject to a bust for pimping and pandering. And if you had drugs on the set, that would definitely mean jail. So I wouldn't tolerate drugs on my shoots.

One day I caught John with cocaine on the set. I flushed it down the toilet and said, "John, you can't do this!"

He became petulant and wouldn't work. It cost us a lot of time. I said, "John, I haven't paid you yet. Finish the film, get your money, and then do whatever you want."

From that point on I couldn't work with him. It was just too difficult.

SHARON MITCHELL: One time I was shooting a film with John in Laurel Canyon, and he just disappeared. Everyone on the set thought he went out for lunch; we were waiting and waiting—and it was getting dark. No one knew where he was. And then all of the sudden we heard a little scream from one of the bedrooms. Some woman had opened up a closet, and John was in there with a base pipe, getting high.

He'd been on the set all day. He just looked up and said, "Where were you guys? Nobody came to get me!"

BILL AMERSON: John still tried to work, but he got a reputation for not showing up or for spending most of the time in the bathroom. And people didn't want to hire him anymore—because John always got paid up front. So producers got to the point where they didn't want to do that anymore because he wasn't reliable.

So that kind of slowed his career down.

GLORIA LEONARD: I hadn't seen John Holmes for years. I'd just moved into this house in Los Angeles, and he shows up at my doorstep. I don't know how he found out where I lived. I was with Bobby Hollander at the time. And I had a girlfriend visiting me from New York, staying in our guest room.

And he comes in and starts cooking coke—and I'd never seen cocaine based before because all I'd ever done was snorted, you know?

And then Bobby comes home.

BOBBY HOLLANDER: I came home from work early one day, opened up the front door, and the house smelled like somebody was frying grapes. I asked, "What the hell is this?"

I didn't notice any other cars or anything strange. So I walked into the living room, and the first person I see is John Holmes. He's standing in front of the coffee table, and I notice he has a plaid suitcase, like a little kid runs away from home with. It's on the coffee table with the lid up. John's holding something in his hand; the smell is coming from him.

Gloria's sitting on the couch with another girl, and she says, "Oh, Bobby, I want you to meet John Holmes."

GLORIA LEONARD: Bobby was a big cokehead in those days, too, so he and John started rapping.

I mean, in Paris, John wasn't that into drugs. And I had only snorted before; freebase was all new to me. I didn't know that people did these things. I didn't know about basing. I mean, really. I was that naive.

BOBBY HOLLANDER: I take a look in the suitcase, and there's six freebase pipes in it, a blowtorch, and a bottle of 151 Bacardi rum to make the torch. And John is taking a blast off the pipe.

John asks, "Do you want to get a little buzz?"

So we got high that day, and Gloria and I were showing everyone around the house. We went out to the pool, and I was bragging about getting new cars the next day.

GLORIA LEONARD: John tells Bobby he can get him some coke, so they agree to meet back at our house the next day. I tell John that we're gonna be gone in the morning because we had to go see an agent about car insurance or something, that we wouldn't be home until noon.

BOBBY HOLLANDER: We had an eleven o'clock appointment to pick up the cars the next day—they're beautiful; I loved them. We drove home.

GLORIA LEONARD: We come home at noon, and our house is empty. Everything and anything of value is gone. I mean, forget the good jewelry—they've taken the costume jewelry, alarm clocks, toasters, hair dryers—anything they could get more than a dollar or two for. And I had no insurance—that was the heartbreaker.

BOBBY HOLLANDER: The television is gone, the VCR is gone, cameras are gone, jewelry is gone—the bedroom is completely ransacked—the guns were gone.

And the only person that knew we were going to be gone at that particular time, that day, was John Holmes.

Later, the neighbors said they saw a van being driven away by a description of a man who fit John. That's who I believe burglarized the house.

GLORIA LEONARD: John seemed like such a happy-go-lucky dudeski the day before, you know? Supposed to meet him the next day at noon, and, when we come back at noon our house is empty.

And of course he never showed up. So what would *you* make of that?

Beauty and the Beast

LOS ANGELES/HAWAII
1978–1979

RUBY GOTTESMAN: Norm Arno had all the money in the world, but he just didn't wanna take care of himself. That's the way he was. Didn't think he deserved it or something.

He had that stuff on his legs—what do you call that? It peels—the skin peels off the legs? Psoriasis. And he'd wear the same pants for a week, you know? So the pants can stand up by themselves? That's the kinda guy he was.

And his mouth was terrible. He had bad teeth, but he wouldn't go to a dentist. I finally sent him to one, and he got new teeth.

TOMMY SINOPOLI (PORNOGRAPHER): Norm wasn't too attractive. He had a balding head and a terrible skin rash. What do they call it? Eczema? You know when the skin peels, and you constantly scratch it? He had it on his face and all over his body.

BILL KELLY: Norman Arno was the ugliest guy you'd ever wanna see. He looked like an American Yasir Arafat.

CHUCK BERNSTENE: So Norman didn't score with chicks. No, he didn't. Never.

TOMMY SINOPOLI: The first time Norm met Lorene Smith, she was dancing in a topless club in Hawaii. When a woman like that pays attention to a man like that, the guy goes gaga.

So I guess Norm was enamored of her. And I thought it was great that he would finally have somebody. I mean, had you ever seen Norm, you would say to yourself, "Thank God I look like me."

RUBY GOTTESMAN: Lori was a hooker. She was bad news. She fucked every-body in Hawaii—she was fucking four guys when Norman met her—and he fell in love with her. Two-dollar hooker. Piece of shit. Big girl. Ugly, not even nice lookin'. I mean, *I* didn't think she was anything nice.

LORENE SMITH'S SANITY EVALUATION: "While living in Hawaii, working as a prostitute in a massage parlor situated over an adult bookstore, Ms. Smith met her husband, Norman."

DAVE FRIEDMAN: Norm was out in Hawaii, Lori was a hooker, and she spent a couple of nights with him. Then, Norm got very sick, and no one ever paid any attention to Norm. When most people saw him coming they'd cross the street. But while he's in the hospital—out there in Hawaii—Lori came to see him.

Why? I don't know. I don't believe anything about hookers with hearts of gold. But Norm was so impressed that she came to see him in the hospital—that he married her.

LORENE SMITH'S SANITY EVALUATION: "Norman was twenty-seven years her senior and was reported to be involved in the distribution of pornographic materials. At the time that Ms. Smith met Norman, he was reportedly dying of cirrhosis of the liver. She indicated that she married him in August of 1977 but did not love him, but 'felt sorry for him.'"

TOMMY SINOPOLI: I stood up for them at their wedding; I think I was the best man. If I'm not mistaken, Lori later ripped up the marriage certificate—because my signature was on it.

I guess you could say she disliked me.

Probably because I was as powerful as she was, and she felt threatened. I was threatening her control over Norman. But Norman just thought it was funny—because she was crazy. But I was just happy he'd finally found someone for his own, you know? That's always nice.

CHUCK BERNSTENE: I was in Norman's apartment on Fountain when Lori arrived from Hawaii. She flew in by herself. Norm had somebody pick her up, if I'm not mistaken. A big girl, tall. Pretty stocky. Long brown hair. I think she was oversexed or something. I noticed it right away.

Well, Norm left; he went somewhere. I walked over and got a drink, and she came toward me. She got very close to me, and I felt that she wanted to play. She wanted to fuck. I really mean that. She was coming on to me.

I walked away from her. I don't mess with people in the industry, and I'd never mess with people that I'm partners with or associated with. So she hid in one of the bedrooms of his condo until he got back about an hour later. I was watching TV.

And then she told Norman that she wanted to make it with me. Seriously, I got no ego trips, you know? Norman said to stay away from her.

Weird chick, totally weird. Just everything about her was weird.

GLEN SOUZA: Norm Arno was a laughingstock because he married a whore.

CHUCK BERNSTENE: They called her "Norm's whore." Everybody hated Lori Smith.

RUBY GOTTESMAN: Lori didn't like me. She didn't like any of Norm's friends. I came there one day, and he says, "She got me a picture of her on the wall."

I says, "Okay."

He says, "That's what I got for my birthday present."

I says, "Oh, that's very nice."

He says, "Yeah, it cost her five thousand retail."

She bought this painting of herself from some guy for five thousand dollars; it looked terrible. I figured it's worth, maybe, two hundred bucks.

LORENE SMITH'S SANITY EVALUATION: "Ms. Smith stated that as her husband's business grew and became profitable, much of the X-rated business was placed in her name for 'tax reasons.' Ms. Smith claims that her husband was once offered 'eleven million dollars for the business.' She stated that her husband became increasingly psychologically abusive to her, described him as being critical and non-involved to the extent that she lost 'sympathy' for him."

CHUCK BERNSTENE: I don't even think Lori really liked Norman. You know, Norman—in his own way—was a good human being, but he was sick. I mean, sick with trying to find love that was never there. I used to tell him, "Norman, let the woman like you for you. Not because of what you do for a living or because you have money."

RUBY GOTTESMAN: One time Norm tells me, "There's so much money my fingers hurt. I can't even count it. There's shopping bags full of hundreds."

It was unbelievable the money they had. Unbelievable money. So all Lori did was shop. One day, I come there, Norm says, "She's just cleaned out a box: two hundred and fifty thousand dollars."

Norm had a safe deposit box with two hundred and fifty thousand in it, and she cleaned it out. She opened a bar for her father in Columbus, Ohio. Norm told me she used to go back home all the time and take the money there.

And then he gave her some more money. Norman kept on telling me how much money she was taking from him.

CHUCK BERNSTENE: Lori was on drugs. Coke. A lot of coke. I guess a thousand a week. And she was sending money back to her father for his failing restaurant.

LORENE SMITH'S SANITY EVALUATION: "Ms. Smith indicated after her marriage, she began to lead an extremely affluent lifestyle with an inconsistent involvement with her children, specifically relying on nannies for much of the day to take care of her children. As the marriage failed, she became involved in extramarital affairs and relates that one child was born from this involvement."

CHUCK BERNSTENE: Norman was a sick human being. Just to be that whipped by a pussy, you know? When there are so many other girls around? But, I don't know; he just loved her.

And they had so much money. They threw a party at the CES show in Chicago that musta cost a hundred thousand dollars. There were maybe two thousand people there. I just remember the ice sculpture—"VCX"—melting.

BILL KELLY: At one of the porno conventions, one pornographer hired a photographer to take a picture of me being embraced and kissed by Norm Arno's wife, Lori Smith, and Harry Mohney's girlfriend, Gail Palmer, who used to be his front in Wonderful World of Video.

So I'm standing there, and suddenly Lori Smith jumps me on the right side and Gail Palmer on the left.

They throw their arms around me, and they start to try to kiss me, and the photographer stands up with his Speed Graphic–type camera to take a picture.

Well, I figured, "I don't think the FBI director would be too happy with this picture, so I better do something."

So I gave 'em both a shot in the ribs with my elbows and knocked 'em off, and then I took on the photographer.

I don't think that camera worked too well after that.

Falling Out

MIAMI/SEATTLE/LAS VEGAS/HAWAII/NEW JERSEY
1979

GORDON MCNEIL: My wife had been talking to Pam Ellavsky, so I knew Bruce's wife was absolutely ripped that MIPORN had gone on this long. My own wife was telling me, "She wants him outta this thing, and he wants out, too."

BRUCE ELLAVSKY: When I had to go to Seattle on my wife's birthday with Lisa, a female FBI agent, it didn't make my home life real happy, you know?

Pat was separated from his wife, Vickie, early on in the case, so he didn't have the same issues I had. Because I still tried to go home whenever I could, whereas Pat was available twenty-four hours a day. You know, "Come on, let's go, let's go."

PAT LIVINGSTON: Bruce, the family man—*right*. He slept with more girls than me—before, after, and probably now.

I don't know if Lucie and Bruce ever got together or not. All I know is that Lucie didn't like me.

LUCIE VONDER HAAR (FBI SPECIAL AGENT): I adored Bruce. I enjoyed him very much. I liked every guy I worked with undercover—except Pat Livingston.

Pat, in my opinion, was very insecure and tried to overcompensate for it. For example, one night in Seattle it was just us—Pat, Bruce, Lisa, and me—having dinner, and I saw no reason for Pat to order an expensive bottle of wine. I mean, there were no "bad guys" around. There was no necessity for it; we weren't playing our roles.

PAT LIVINGSTON: Lucie was kind of a load.

LUCIE VONDER HAAR: Pat and I had words over the wine. I've never been accused of being shy, and Pat decided that he was going to leave the dinner table and go upstairs. So when Pat left the table, Bruce said, "Aren't you gonna go get him?"

I said, "No. He's an adult. Let's just enjoy our dinner."

PAT LIVINGSTON: Lucie was harsh.

LUCIE VONDER HAAR: When we left Seattle, Pat was adamant that he needed more legroom on the plane. Based on his stature, I can't imagine he would have to wait for a DC-10 airplane for legroom—especially since I was probably five inches taller, and *I* didn't need to wait for a DC-10.

So I said to him, "You wait for your DC-10. I'm getting back to Miami as soon as possible."

If you don't have a good self-image, you probably shouldn't be working undercover.

PAT LIVINGSTON: It seemed perfectly logical and normal at the time, you know? See, I would not give up being Pat Salamone. I loved that character because I could do things as Pat Salamone that Pat Livingston could not do. And that was a great vehicle for me. It was a lot more fun to be Salamone. At the time, of course, I didn't see the downside.

BILL BROWN: On a typical day Pat would make thirty phone calls to the West Coast, make a half dozen deals, set up a half dozen appointments, con a half dozen people, and Jesus, you know, that's praiseworthy. So I didn't notice Pat was a little neurotic.

PAT LIVINGSTON: Before we went to Seattle for the convention, Norm Arno—Marty Bernback's boss—had screwed us by not providing us with pirated videotapes of some straight movies that we ordered and paid for. Norm had substituted X-rated movies for the pirated ones. So to get back at him, we ordered twelve thousand dollars worth of tapes—and then bounced the check on Marty. On purpose.

MARTY BERNBACK (FBI WIRETAP): "Pat, when I saw ya in Seattle, I says to whoever was standin' there, 'Nice guys; we do business with 'em.'

"So I'm askin' you as a gentleman to pay this bill. Pat, it's my money. You understand? If you can't pay it all at one time, fine, send me some payments. But you're tellin' me to kiss your ass—and you don't wanna pay me? You're tellin' me you're gonna fuck me for twelve thousand dollars?"

BRUCE ELLAVSKY: We paid Marty Bernback with three or four checks dated a week apart. Then we went back to Miami and stopped payment on all the checks. We thought that would probably get his attention.

MARTY BERNBACK (FBI WIRETAP): Well, I'm gonna tell you something, pal—I ain't gonna take this layin' down. I'll be in Florida this coming week, okay? And I'm gonna tell you something right now—I'm gonna get my money!

PAT LIVINGSTON (FBI WIRETAP): All we do is try to make a dollar. And I'll tell ya, it goes right back to Norm—he fucked me on the straight film deal we've tried to put together, and that was like five or six months ago. I paid him money up front for it. He made me sit for two or three months, and then he gave me some X-rated films—which was GOOD, you know, and I'm moving that. But we made the deal for the straight films, and then he held my money for, like, two or three months. Norm put it to me—that's the way I see it.

MARTY BERNBACK (FBI WIRETAP): Norm put it to you? So you're gonna *fuck me* for twelve thousand dollars, huh? You paid us, and then you stopped payment on the checks? We didn't think you'd pull any kinda shit like this, not in my wildest dreams. And now you're tellin' me you don't wanna pay me? Okay, I'll be down there with three fucking goons, and we'll do this the hard way.

You don't know what I'm gonna do? I'm gonna be down in Florida, Pat, with a coupla people to see ya, and I'll get it outta ya one way or another, okay? If I gotta take your fucking leg off, I'm gonna take your leg off. You're not gonna fuck me outta twelve thousand dollars!

BILL BROWN: Pat played the tape back for me, and his reaction was, "I think we got the son of a bitch. Sounds like extortion to me. That's a threat. We got him."

Pat was thinking like a law enforcement person. He won; he succeeded in doing what he was trying to do. But as Pat and Bruce's ability to manipulate and fool the bad guys increased geometrically—their personal relationship deteriorated incrementally.

PAT LIVINGSTON: Bruce met Kathy early on in the operation. She had just the right look—blond and beautiful. That's what we were looking for. Then Bruce could say to the porn guys, "Why would I wanna go with somebody else when I can be with her?" And she was working for an airline, so she could fly anywhere and meet us free.

But I'd get pissed at Bruce because he would want to stay and screw around with Kathy instead of going out with me. One time Teddy Gaswirth needed me—he'd had a falling out with Eddie and Joey; so I was going to be his South Florida distributor, moving fifty thousand dollars at a time through Eddie.

So Teddy Gaswirth wants to meet us in Vegas to talk about the deal, and Bruce gets pissed because he's with Kathy, and he doesn't want to go to Vegas.

BRUCE ELLAVSKY: When you're living the role of an FBI agent, a father, a husband, and an undercover guy, you have a lot of things to juggle. So you start thinking less about your real identity and more about your undercover identity. But the danger is that you get too deep into it. And a lot of bad things can happen when you get too deep into an undercover role.

PAT LIVINGSTON: Bruce and I just looked at things differently. I'm all jacked up to go to Vegas and meet Teddy Gaswirth, and Bruce has made a date to see Kathy and wasn't going to break it. Bruce's priorities were different from mine.

We hollered back and forth. I go to the airport about eleven o'clock— Gaswirth's there—and Bruce shows up with Kathy, who didn't mind going to Vegas. She was great, so it worked out perfect.

PAM ELLAVSKY: I think the scariest time came when Bruce crawled out of bed at nine o'clock one morning and poured himself a Bloody Mary.

A Bloody Mary in the morning scared me to death. I wondered, "Is this how it's going to be? Is this the new Bruce Wakerly, who needs a drink in the morning to calm his nerves? Or is he so strung out that he just has to have something?"

BRUCE ELLAVSKY: Pam was thinking, "Will I get my husband back a little different from what he was when he started?"

PAM ELLAVSKY: We just went on not communicating, and then I was sitting in the kitchen, and Bruce came in and said to me, "I don't think I love you anymore."

PAT LIVINGSTON: Pam found out about Bruce's girlfriend—she found a picture of her. That was kinda stupid of him.

Do I think Bruce fell in love with Kathy? Oh, absolutely. I mean, he wanted to tell Kathy that we were agents. And that drove me fucking nuts. I threatened to go to Gordy McNeil and get Bruce off the case if he did that. I think that was around the time he told Pam, "I don't think I love you anymore."

PAM ELLAVSKY: I gagged on my food. I couldn't swallow it. I just took off and went back to my parents in New Jersey.

BILL BROWN: Bruce and I talked very freely and openly about Pat. At first he was concerned about my relationship with Pat because I was friends with Pat first. But he came to see that I cared about both of them.

So Bruce trusted me, and I would confirm for him that he wasn't being unreasonable or disloyal because he was disappointed in some of the things Pat was saying and doing—things like Pat lying in his personal life when it was totally unnecessary—and lying to Bruce.

PAT LIVINGSTON: Bruce would use me as cover to go to bed with girls he wanted to. I didn't really care.

But Bruce would pass information about me to Pam, to keep the emphasis off of what *he* was doing—to divert her from asking, "Where were *you?*"

So Bruce would feed Pam stuff on me, which was like throwing gasoline on a fire. Because he'd tell her about girls I was with—and Pam would pass it along to my wife, Vickie.

PAM ELLAVSKY: When I was home at my parents, I began to realize that there was no future for Bruce and me beyond MIPORN. We had been into this undercover operation for a year-and-a-half, and as far as I was concerned, Bruce never saw beyond the operation.

Bruce was off on some trip, and I was crying. I'd convinced myself that it was over. Then the front door opened—and there was Bruce.

PAT LIVINGSTON: Bruce would never take a chance. The prime example was when we were in Los Angeles meeting with Chuck Bernstene, who had cut us in to Al Nunes in Honolulu.

Al Nunes was a big supplier of pirated videotape cassettes. Supposedly, he was an organized crime figure in Hawaii. I didn't know that for a fact, but I talked to Dick Phinney in the Los Angeles FBI office, and he said, "Yeah, Al Nunes is a major target for the Honolulu FBI."

So I said to Bruce, "Shit, I'm going to Honolulu because I've got the perfect cut in to Al Nunes from Chuck Bernstene."

So Chuck Bernstene called Al Nunes on my behalf and said that we were coming out.

BRUCE ELLAVSKY: Al Nunes wasn't one of the original targets we had talked about—but he was definitely what you'd call a target of opportunity. Anybody that's doing child pornography is worth going after. And my philosophy was always that you seize the opportunity.

But in this case, we probably could have gone next week, or two weeks later, or even a month later—it probably still would have been there. As a matter of fact, in some ways I think that going there immediately raises some suspicion. I'm surprised that Chuck Bernstene didn't say, "Hey, they're dropping everything and going to Honolulu? What's the story on that?"

CHUCK BERNSTENE: That was the worst introduction of my life. But everybody was just out for themselves. Anybody that had money—cash, green—can just come in and do anything they want in this business. If you walked in with fifty thousand dollars, I'd pat you on the back and say, "My friend, my friend, come on, let's have a drink. . . ."

Money is money. And I thought Pat was just a guy with money. Pretty well off. I liked the guy. I liked his ease. So when Pat wanted more films, I sent him to Al Nunes.

RUBY GOTTESMAN: Yeah, Al Nunes, nice guy. I went to see him once in Hawaii. He had, like, a general store near the army base over there. Nice, like a small-town setup—like a general store for the soldiers. The kiddie porn, I don't know anything about that. I don't know. Was he dealin' kiddie porn to the Japanese?

No, to the soldiers, mostly.

PAT LIVINGSTON: Dick Phinney said that they'd been trying to get Al Nunes for a long time. So I said to Bruce, "Let's go see him, make some buys, and satisfy Honolulu's needs for securing a number one target."

And Bruce said, "Look, the bureau's not gonna like this. They're gonna ask why we're going. If we go out there, and we don't make a case, it's gonna look bad."

Then he went back to Miami. Left me high and dry in Los Angeles and that pissed me off.

BRUCE ELLAVSKY: I wanted to get away from Pat. I don't think there was one event that turned our relationship—there were a lot of events. Just a lot of things that led me to believe it was time to throttle back a little bit.

BILL BROWN: I think Bruce was fearful that he could not speak his mind about things that pissed him off about Pat because Pat would tell Pam about the other women, and of course, this built an enormous resentment in Bruce. It's why relationships break up.

PAM ELLAVSKY: The day after Bruce showed up, we were sitting in my parents' living room. We were both practically in tears because we both had decided that it was over.

Then all of a sudden, we started talking about what was beyond MIPORN. What was there?

And we realized there was us, there were the kids, there was a future. We just talked and talked and talked. From that point on, it got better.

BRUCE ELLAVSKY: There's a certain amount of glamour to working undercover. But after a while, once you've been to the same places and done the same thing repetitively and you're with the same people that you really don't wanna be with, it gets old, you know? I wanted to go home to my wife and family.

PAT LIVINGSTON: I would never have let Bruce go off to Hawaii by himself. You just don't do that. So yeah, I felt betrayed when he did that to me. My partner was deserting me in the middle of the mission.

So I went to Hawaii by myself and called Al Nunes. He sent a chauffeur to pick me up and drove me out to his grocery store. Nunes had his offices upstairs.

I meet him there, make a purchase of a pirated videotape cassette, make a purchase of some pornography—and then we talk about doing a deal on some child pornography.

CHUCK BERNSTENE: I put Pat in touch with Al because he sold X-rated material. Al was one of Norm Arno's biggest accounts. Very nice person. Paid his bills like clockwork. I never knew he dealt in child pornography. What people do is their business.

PAT LIVINGSTON: It was pretty well-known within the porn industry that you had to be crazy to deal in child pornography. There were a couple of people that made these films—but not many.

BILL KELLY: Pornographers were scared to death to deal in kiddie porn because the penalties are horrendous. I mean, you can get a quarter million dollar fine and up to fifteen years in prison. So child pornography was never a big part of the porn industry.

It was bad business because you're going to get all kinds of heat.

PAT LIVINGSTON: Al Nunes showed me the films, and some of the kids were really little, and they were performing adult sex acts. I mean, these weren't eighteen-year-old girls pretending to be little girls. Most of the films featured an adult and a child—either a young girl with a adult male or an adult female with a young boy.

I had two boys around the same age as some of the kids in the films, so I wanted to take this fucker out and just strangle him, you know?

Instead, I had to talk to Nunes about how great the cum shot was.

Nunes was purporting to have a Chinese buyer for the films, and he was holding that up to me, saying, "If you don't want this I've got another buyer."

So I made the deal.

But it was difficult. I had to get drunk after that one. I mean, I would've gotten drunk anyway, but now I just had a better reason.

BILL KELLY: Pat went to Hawaii and caught a child pornographer, which was the most substantial conviction we had in MIPORN. But yeah, I heard that he and Bruce had a falling out, but I don't know what the details were.

BRUCE ELLAVSKY: I think if Pat was aggravated about me staying behind, he should have talked to me about it. But Pat wasn't great about saying what he was thinking, you know? You were supposed to figure it out.

It's certainly something that we could have talked about. I don't know what Pat did or didn't do—I don't think that he called back and talked to Gordy about it and said, "Do we need to go today?" I think Pat just went.

PAT LIVINGSTON: Bruce didn't go to Hawaii because he was afraid the bureau might think badly of him. He was waiting for me to fall on my face—but instead I brought back the goods. I should've been pissed; Bruce hung me out to dry. But fuck, I made the kiddie porn deal.

I made the case.

BRUCE ELLAVSKY: After that, Pat and I could still work together professionally, but I don't think we really liked each other anymore. I mean, I wanted MIPORN to be successful, but I also knew it was just a part of my life. But Pat was really obsessed with the case. He was consumed by it.

GORDON MCNEIL: I knew Pat and Bruce had grown to dislike each other. I don't know why—maybe it was spending so much time together.

So Bruce told me he wanted to get out. And I knew, without Bruce ever telling me specifically, that it was because of Pat.

BRUCE ELLAVSKY: Any time you're working undercover for a few years, you're pushing the envelope. I mean, we didn't go to the office; we had no real association with other FBI agents. Our only contact with reality was through our supervisor, Gordy McNeil, who was fantastic throughout the whole thing.

So I was ready to do something else. I would say to Gordy, "Hey, you know, I've had enough. I'm ready to pull the plug. I gotta get out."

GORDON MCNEIL: I knew Bruce wanted out very badly, but we hadn't gotten Mickey Zaffarano—and as far as I was concerned, a case without that guy wouldn't prove the organized crime connection. Without Zaffarano, everybody else was small potatoes. We had to get the principal players. So I pushed Bruce to continue on.

BILL BROWN: By the time their personal relationship had deteriorated to the point where it wasn't worth much, their ability to manipulate the bad guys was so great that they didn't need any great trust in each other.

I mean, they did trust each other in their undercover roles but not in their real ones.

St. Valentine's Day Massacre

NEW YORK CITY/LAS VEGAS/
LOS ANGELES/MIAMI/LOUISVILLE
1980

PAT LIVINGSTON: The New York Police Department had full-time surveillance on Mickey Zaffarano, and they located him at one of his offices in New York.

I was in Baltimore when I got a call from Bill Kelly saying Zaffarano was definitely in. I immediately flew to New York and took a cab to his office.

I got off the elevator and walked right into Zaffarano. I practically had a heart attack.

FRED SCHWARTZ (U.S. ATTORNEY): We had not been able to get to Mickey Zaffarano. Finally, in the last month of the investigation, we developed a strategy. Pat was buying *Debbie Does Dallas* from a fellow in California—Joe Ariano, aka Joe Black—who claimed he had the right to sell it even though it was generally recognized in the industry that it was a Norman Arno movie; Zaffarano had given Arno the right to sell it.

So the strategy we developed was that Pat would go and talk to Zaffarano and say, "Hey, I want to do the right thing. Does Joe have the right to sell *Debbie Does Dallas*?" and then tie into the conspiracy that way.

GORDON MCNEIL: I specifically split Pat and Bruce up at that particular point, so Pat ended up going to New York by himself—and he just walked right into Zaffarano's office.

PAT LIVINGSTON: I said, "Mickey, I'm Pat Salamone from Golde Coaste in Miami. We've done some deals with Joe Black, and we got a lot of tapes of

Debbie Does Dallas, but we don't want any problems moving it in South Florida.

"Joe says you gave him permission to distribute *Debbie Does Dallas,* and I want to know that Joe's okay, that we're not going to have any problems with you."

Zaffarano's looking me over, and he's a menacing looking guy. My stomach was in knots. I was unarmed. I knew I could get hurt in a situation like this.

CHUCK BERNSTENE: Mickey was about five foot ten, five foot eleven, close to two hundred pounds, strong as an ox. He looked like a fighter. He told me he did eighteen years in prison for murder. I don't know how true that was, but, uh, I mean, you don't ask somebody that says he was in jail for murder if he did it, you know?

PAT LIVINGSTON: Finally, we walked from the hallway into Mickey's back office with the tapes and film reels, and Mickey says, "Joe's okay."

Now I've got it.

This tied the whole fucking two-and-a-half-year investigation together because Mickey Zaffarano was acknowledging that he had control over *Debbie Does Dallas.*

CHUCK BERNSTENE: Everybody knew Mickey was the boss. Matter of fact, one day Mickey had all those guys up in Stewie Siegel's office, and he got 'em all down on their hands and knees. Then Mickey said, "Now look, scumbags, Chuck Bernstene wants his money, and you're gonna pay him."

Mickey was probably one of the finest guys I've ever met in my life.

PAT LIVINGSTON: I knew all I had to do was get Mickey to corroborate a few things, and that would tie him into everything. So I asked him, "Joe Black said he went to jail for you—is that true? Joe Black did time for you?"

It was like a light went off in Zaffarano's head. You could see it in his eyes. His whole demeanor changed. His body tensed. His eyes got big.

CHUCK BERNSTENE: I told Mickey that I thought Pat Salamone and Bruce Wakerly were cops. He said, "You're probably right."

PAT LIVINGSTON: If he had a gun, Mickey would've shot me—because if I was really Pat Salamone I would not have asked that type of question. Because Mickey Zaffarano was the boss. But it was the absolute end of the investigation so you go for it. You play all your cards.

So Mickey said, "Get the fuck out of here, and don't ever come around again."

254 The Other Hollywood

I got out the door real quick. I think I hit the stairs because I didn't want to wait for the elevator. All that emotion going through me—it was a rush. Because we got Zaffarano.

That was it. The investigative phase of the undercover operation was over. Now it was just a matter of mopping up the search warrants.

RUBY GOTTESMAN: A funny thing happened when they indicted us all. It was Valentine's Day, 1980. I went to Vegas early in the morning to sell a guy some films, and on the way to the hotel my limo got into an accident. It was raining, and we got hit. The next thing I know I'm on the floor, and I'm feeling around to see if everything's all right, and a paramedic opens the door.

He goes, "Are you okay?"

Now, I know I'm gonna make a claim here because I know this is a good, *good* accident.

So I say, "Oh no, my back is bad; I can't move. I gotta go to the hospital."

But then I says, "I got a box in the trunk. I can't go nowhere without that box!"

So the paramedic takes the box out of the trunk—filled with porn films—and he says, "Look, I got them. They're in the van, okay? Now you can go."

So they take me to this county hospital, and I'm layin' there, and the doctor says he don't find no broken bones—there's nothin' wrong. I says, "What, are you crazy? I can't move my back!"

As soon as the doctor leaves, I sneak out to make a phone call to my wife—to tell her to come to Vegas for the weekend—and sure enough, I get my son, who tells me that mommy's in jail, and the FBI ripped up the house.

My son says, "They locked up Mommy!"

So I says, "I gotta get outta here."

NEW YORK TIMES, FEBRUARY 15, 1980: 55 PERSONS INDICTED IN PIRACY OF FILMS AND IN PORNOGRAPHY—FBI INVESTIGATION CALLED BIGGEST ATTACK AGAINST ACTIVITIES: "A federal undercover investigation has resulted in the indictment of 55 persons in 10 states in the largest effort ever against the distribution of pornography and film piracy."

MARCELLA COHEN (U.S. ATTORNEY): On February 14, 1980, there were simultaneous search warrants conducted at thirty locations in sixteen cities throughout the United States. Four hundred FBI agents made the arrests, as well as conducted searches throughout the country, and fifty-five individuals were indicted.

TOMMY SINOPOLI: It was like the St. Valentine's Day Massacre or some shit.

CHUCK BERNSTENE: I was at our office on Cherokee with Dave Hedley, a couple of salespeople, and a couple of girls—when twenty LAPD cops and a half dozen federal agents came in and busted me.

They made a big production out of it.

They took me to jail in downtown Los Angeles, and when I saw the forty guys in a holding cell—Norman Arno, Teddy Gaswirth, Tommy Sinopoli—we all looked at each other and started laughing. They had arrested everybody in the business.

I looked at Norman, and he just shook his head. I said, "Norman, I told you they were cops, didn't I?"

He just grunted.

RUBY GOTTESMAN: When I got back from Vegas, I stopped off at some liquor store on Ventura Boulevard, and there's a big headline in the *Los Angeles Times* afternoon edition, "BIG MOB RAID: FIFTY-FIVE PEOPLE INDICTED," and they got my name as one of the people missin'.

I called a friend, and he says, "Don't go home—the FBI is lookin' for you."

So I hide out in the Holiday Inn like two blocks away; I call my lawyer up, and he makes a deal. So I give myself up, and I'm in jail, and I hear all kinds of stories about how Mickey Zaffarano—who was my good friend—had died that day.

BRUCE ELLAVSKY: Unfortunately, Mickey Zaffarano had a heart attack at the time we arrested him. Mickey heard that FBI agents were en route to his office, and he was scurrying through some kind of tunnel under his office complex when he had the big one.

***NEW YORK TIMES*, FEBRUARY 15, 1980: 55 PERSONS INDICTED IN PIRACY OF FILMS AND IN PORNOGRAPHY—FBI INVESTIGATION CALLED BIGGEST ATTACK IN THESE ACTIVITIES:** "Mr. Zaffarano, who was 56 years old and a resident of Wantagh, Long Island, died, apparently of a heart attack, after learning that FBI agents had visited his business, the Pussycat Theater, and tried to serve him with an arrest warrant."

***MIAMI HERALD*, FEBRUARY 15, 1980: MIAMI BASED FBI INVESTIGATION BREAKS UP PORN FILM NETWORK:** "Zaffarano, once bodyguard for Mafia chieftain Joe Bonnano, owned theaters in New York, Boston, San Francisco and one in Washington, two blocks from the White House. The Justice Department identified Zaffarano as a capo, or underboss, in the Bonnano crime family. He previously had been convicted of assault and robbery but was acquitted on obscenity charges in 1977. Zaffarano was considered the major distributor of adult movies in the United States."

RUBY GOTTESMAN: Mickey was one of the smartest guys I ever met. He knew everything.

When my wife found out Mickey died, she was cryin', and Norman was cryin'. They were all in the same paddy wagon when they got arrested, and everybody was cryin' about Mickey. Norman was cryin' 'cause Mickey was his meal ticket—because Mickey was a made man.

ARTIE MITCHELL: Mickey was funny as hell. Everything was just business to him. He wanted to be involved in porn, sure, but he didn't have a big sex thing. All's he wanted was a girl down on her knees in the back of the limo blowing him.

Mickey was a real gentleman.

PAT LIVINGSTON: I found out that day that Mickey Zaffarano croaked. Yeah, it was great. But if you put that in I'm gonna be in big trouble. Law enforcement officers are a little sick. You gotta be a little sick to do this stuff.

ARTIE MITCHELL: We'd flown in from California for Mickey's funeral. Our hair was long and blond, and the mob bodyguards assumed we were FBI.

I said, "No way! We're the Mitchell brothers, you know?"

They didn't know.

I said, "Like, *Behind the Green Door?*"

"Oh, yeah." So they let us in, and we got to pay our respects. But I thought, we can affect wise guy personas, but what's the point? The wise-guys and the FBI were both bad for business.

FRED SCHWARTZ: There was a media splurge a day or two after the arrests. FBI agents around the country were calling the Miami office to ask things. I was calling. Marcella Cohen, the other prosecutor, was calling. Everyone was calling—and Pat wouldn't put anybody on.

"Bruce isn't here," he'd lie. "Gary isn't here. I'm the case agent. I'll handle this."

BILL KELLY: The phone would ring and some agent not connected to MIPORN would answer it. Pat would physically grab the phone away from the guy and say, "Listen, Mister, you don't talk about MIPORN. That's *my* case. *I* talk about it."

If you knew Pat before he went into MIPORN and then after he came out—they were like two different guys.

BILL BROWN: It was my first brush with real big publicity. *Newsweek* wanted to talk with me. Everyone was calling. And Pat was just loving all the publicity, but Bruce didn't want any of it.

And then the *Miami Herald* article came out with a front page headline that basically said MIPORN was conducted by Pat Livingston and "his inexperienced rookie sidekick, Bruce Ellavsky." It went on to say, "Pat did this, and Pat did that . . ."

My heart and my stomach just did flip-flops. I mean, it was terrible. It was awful. This was the worst thing that could have happened.

BRUCE ELLAVSKY: Yeah, I was offended over the article because I thought I carried my share of the load, you know? In fact, with the paperwork, I thought that I did the bulk of it. So I was angry and the way I deal with things like that is—I go to the person and say, "What's the story?"

BILL BROWN: Pat went all over the place to deny he said it. But any small shred of hope that their relationship could be patched up was gone. Bruce was deeply hurt by that inaccurate, distorted, unfair, and terrible article.

BRUCE ELLAVSKY: Pat said, "I don't know anything about it. I feel terrible about it. It's not true—blah, blah, blah."

GORDON MCNEIL: I was astounded by Pat's behavior. I thought his conduct was just bizarre. I mean, Pat told me, "I want to be a grade fifteen agent, and I want to be set up in West Palm Beach, Florida. And the way I see my future in the FBI is this: I'll be the rabbi of all undercover operations. Everyone will come to me and bounce their ideas for operations off of me, and I will give it my blessing or thumbs down."

FRED SCHWARTZ: Pat was living the life, not of a jet-setter, but of a high-rolling businessman. Gordy McNeil had given both Bruce and Pat pretty much free rein, so Pat could make his own schedule. If he wanted to sleep late, he'd sleep late. If he wanted to stay out late and not get up the next day, he wouldn't get up. He could make his own rules—the way he dressed, what he did, where he went.

But the day after the indictments came down, suddenly Pat was a nine-to-five agent again. He had to wear a jacket and tie, and go into the office, and listen to me tell him what was going to happen next.

BILL BROWN: Pat would just let these absurd situations develop. Like some woman would show up at my house and ask, "Is Pat here?"

I'd say, "No, Pat's not here."

She'd say, "Who are you?"

"I'm Bill Brown."

She'd say, "But this is Pat Salamone's house, isn't it?"

I'd say, "No, this is my house. Pat doesn't live here, but he's here a lot. Is there anything I can do?"

She'd say, "We're supposed to have a party here at nine o'clock." I mean, I would try to be as polite to the person as I could. Then Pat would show up, and I'd just let it go.

But afterward I'd tell Pat, "You tell people that my house is your home, and I'm your guest, and it's for no reason. If it was part of the operation, that would be wonderful. But it's over—and this is just some cocktail waitress you met in Hialeah. I mean, come on?!?!"

It was insanity.

GORDON MCNEIL: Pat thought he was going to sit there in West Palm Beach, and everyone from the FBI would come to him with their undercover proposals, and he'd say, "Yes, that sounds good" or, "No, that sounds bad."

And Pat would make all the decisions. This is really what he was saying to me. This is really the way he saw himself. He felt the bureau owed him.

So I said, "Pat, I feel relatively sure that the bureau will say, 'You gotta be kidding. You're not going to sit up there in West Palm Beach and have all these undercover agents kiss your ring all day.'"

PAT LIVINGSTON: I wanted it my way, and I tried to get it. And I pissed everybody off. I don't know why Gordy hung in there. I don't know why he didn't punch me out a couple times. He should've just fucking decked me, you know? I guess it was because that was the other Livingston—that was Pat Salamone.

FRED SCHWARTZ: Once there were indictments, I asserted a lot more control. You see, it was Pat and Bruce's case when they were investigating it, but I had to win it in court.

I might have gone too far in asserting control, and I think Pat resented that. But I have as big an ego as Pat does—and this had now become my case.

PAT LIVINGSTON: When do things go bad with Fred Schwartz? When he won't let me run the case, ha, ha, ha.

I went from total control to having to defer to prosecuting attorneys. I was thinking, "How can they do it better than me?"

It was gonna be my way or no way.

GORDON MCNEIL: Pat almost got into a fistfight with Fred Schwartz. Pat was saying, "I'm the one who's calling the priorities on this!"

Of course, Fred told him, "Well, you may be calling the investigative priorities, but we're calling the prosecuting priorities."

And Pat felt he should be controlling the prosecution side, too. It was not a good situation.

FRED SCHWARTZ: I thought Pat was overreacting in resenting my coming into the case. But I didn't think there was a psychological problem until a meeting I had with him in March 1980.

I was trying to push Pat to do something, and I said to Kelly, "Bill, I'd like you to sit in on this meeting." I wasn't physically afraid of Pat. I just felt that if there was going to be a showdown, I wanted witnesses. I wanted to have somebody there to make sure it wasn't my ego that was causing the problem—and to verify if there really was a problem with Pat.

BILL KELLY: Fred Schwartz called me and said, "You better get down here. Pat and I've got a problem."

FRED SCHWARTZ: Bill and I sat there for over an hour listening to Pat lecture me—rambling, disjointed—about how he was the case agent; how this was his responsibility; how he saved Bruce's marriage by bringing Bruce down here; how Bruce resents him now . . .

BILL KELLY: It got to the point where Pat was physically threatening Fred Schwartz—the lead federal prosecutor in the case. Pat was about two seconds from throwing a punch at him. And Pat would've cleaned up on Fred because Pat was a tough little guy. So I had to get up and intervene.

Later, I said to my wife, Virginia, "This guy, we'll never make a regular 8:15-to-5:00 agent out of him again. He's too far gone."

PAT LIVINGSTON: I never got a sense that my emotions were out of control. The way I looked at it, it was the other people having problems. They weren't aware of the total picture, so if anybody had a problem, it was them. I didn't want to hear it.

I had kept everything inside me for so long and hadn't gotten any outside help. Because outside help was a threat to my existence.

PHIL SMITH: Undercover guys gotta live the role. You can't be thinking about ten other things. And that's the problem—the better guys get into the role, and they can't get back out.

I mean, how are they gonna be normal again? They're out there knockin' around, throwin' money around, shmoozin' with the broads— now all of a sudden you're gonna come back and sign in every morning? It don't happen.

So how many of these guys do you recover? How many of them ever go back to being a regular agent? Nah. You lose 'em. It's a fact of life.

FRED SCHWARTZ: After the meeting with Pat, I looked at Kelly and said, "Bill, I think Pat really has significant problems. I'd like to talk to you and Bruce and see what we can do."

I think the bottom line was that it would be best for me to be the one to talk to Gordy McNeil and Art Nehrbass. It's not something you do lightly—you don't go to a SAC [Special Agent in Charge] and say you think an agent you've been working with for two-and-a-half-years has psychological problems. But I went to them and said, "Let's at least have Pat evaluated."

GORDON MCNEIL: I wrote a communication to Washington saying that Pat Livingston did not appear to be functioning normally after the MIPORN operation came to an end. I wrote that he had delusions of grandeur—he thought he was going to be elevated to some lofty position in the bureau—and that he was just acting strange. I was basically asking for the authority to get a psychiatric evaluation of Pat Livingston.

But because I didn't want Pat to get suspicious, I had Bruce Ellavsky evaluated, too. And Bruce was mad as hell at me.

So I said, "Bruce, I know you appear to be absolutely, totally normal at this point. But just do me a favor and get an evaluation too, so Livingston doesn't think we're singling him out."

PAT LIVINGSTON: Art Nehrbass and Gordon McNeil sent me to a psychiatrist named Dr. Balasini in Miami. It was presented to me as just a normal thing to do after an undercover operation. I wasn't advised by either one of them that they saw a problem on my part. As a matter of fact, it was set up that Bruce went along to make it look like a normal practice.

I was very reluctant to go to the psychiatrist because I thought that would be a threat to my career. The bureau—more so than the banking industry or the other professions—just doesn't accept mistakes. You can't have a flaw.

But I did see Dr. Balasini and basically told him what he wanted to hear.

FRED SCHWARTZ: The psychiatrist said that Pat was fine. I know Pat fooled him, but Pat's behavior changed after he went to the psychiatrist. There wasn't overt antagonism. There wasn't resistance. There wasn't that fight for control. It was almost as if he was saying, "I see you have the weapons to hurt me. Therefore, to hell with it; I'll do what I have to do."

PAM ELLAVSKY: Pat wanted to keep going out every night, and Bruce would say, "There's nothing to go out for."

Pat would say, "Oh, yes there is. We're going to do this, and we're going to do that. . . ."

And Bruce would say, "No, Pat, it's over. I'm not going."

BRUCE ELLAVSKY: I went to the SAC and told him I didn't think Pat should ever work undercover again. I mean, even after the case ended Pat continued to use his undercover name.

BILL BROWN: We were driving up to Mr. Laff's restaurant—where Pat was still introducing himself as Salamone—and Pat was telling me, "I want to get divorced from Vickie. I want custody of my kids. I want to be an undercover agent. I want to go to Las Vegas and gamble."

I said, "Pat, do you realize how preposterous what you just said is? I know you love your children, but you're not home long enough to take care of a cat, let alone a child."

VICKIE LIVINGSTON (PAT LIVINGSTON'S WIFE): About a month after the indictments came down, Pat was real nice to me all of a sudden. I couldn't understand why he was being so cooperative.

BILL BROWN: I said it in a nice way, but I said, "Pat, you are exhibiting the classic symptoms of a person who is neurotic. You think, act, and behave in a dissimilar manner. You probably don't realize what you're doing, but you need professional help, and I wish you'd go see a psychiatrist."

VICKIE LIVINGSTON: What led me to let Pat come back? I don't know. He came over on Derby Day—the first weekend in May—and said he'd made a big mistake and that he wanted to come back. It was a couple of days before we were going for our final divorce. I just didn't know what to do. I was really torn. I said, "You've got to be crazy. I can't believe how you've thrown me these curves."

I was just really confused. Pat was calling me at work and begging me—calling me all hours of the night.

PAM ELLAVSKY: They were about three days away from their divorce when Pat crawled back to Vickie on his hands and knees. I mean, you just never knew what Pat was going to do next—there was just so much conniving that went on. Pat seemed not to want to intentionally hurt Vickie, but he was constantly hurting her anyway. He never told the truth. And I saw her suffer.

PAT LIVINGSTON: I knew it was a loveless marriage, but hey, that's okay. I tried to keep the marriage together for the kids. I was going back to Vickie because I had the two best boys in the world. I could have transferred anywhere in the country, but Vickie wanted Louisville because her family was there. So I let her pick Louisville.

VICKIE LIVINGSTON: Pat was using moving to Louisville as a way to lure me back.

I didn't get back together with him because that's what I wanted. I told him flat out that I didn't love him, but I felt I owed it to the kids to see what would happen.

I thought, "What do I have to lose? I'm planning to move to Louisville anyway. If it works out, fine, and if it doesn't, I'm where I want to be."

PAM ELLAVSKY: Vickie told Pat, "Okay, you transfer us to Louisville, and you can come home." And that was it. We never spoke again.

BILL KELLY: Pat and Bruce were praised as the heroes of the whole operation, and they were. They lived in constant danger for a long time. They were both given transfers out of Miami, where naturally they were still in danger. Livingston was transferred to Louisville at the request of his wife. Ellavsky went to Boston.

PAM ELLAVSKY: We were all on the same bowling team together, and we just couldn't talk anymore. Vickie just couldn't face me. She couldn't look me in the eye.

VICKIE LIVINGSTON: The weekend we moved to Louisville I was standing outside a church in tears. Bill Brown had said, "He'll never make the transition back to the real world."

I knew he was never again going be the man that I married; I knew in my heart that he would never make it back.

Then, that night, Pat said he was going back undercover. I was furious. I said, "We're not even here two days, and you're going back undercover? My God, what have I gotten myself into?"

"Ordeal"

MIAMI/LONDON/LONG ISLAND
1980

LINDA LOVELACE: Larry Marchiano was going out with my sister, and I went to Florida for a deposition, and I just started talking to Larry. So then Larry came out to California. And it was a bad choice I made there. When I was getting married to him, I'm like, "Wait a second, can I have my baby and be without you?"

CHUCK TRAYNOR: Linda moved out to Long Island and re-associated herself with Larry Marchiano, who is the father of her first kid.

Linda had been with him before me, that's how I knew about it. I had a Polaroid picture of 'em. Linda must've been fifteen, sixteen, when she met him. I don't know how they met. I don't know if he went to high school with her. I just remember the name, and when I was doin' the E! Channel thing, the guy said, "Yeah, she just broke up with Marchiano, her husband."

I asked, "Marchiano? *Larry* Marchiano?"

He said, "Yeah."

I said, "The guy she fucked before she fucked me, you know?"

He said, "Really?"

I said, "Yeah."

He couldn't understand how she bullshitted about that because she said the son was really the sister's, I guess.

LINDA LOVELACE: When I first got pregnant, I was sixteen. I was in New York, but I went to Florida because my oldest sister, Barbara, said I couldn't stay with her because she didn't want her daughters to see me in that condition.

So I went to a Children's Home Society in Florida. I was going to give him up to a foster home until I could produce on my own. I went to school to become a keypunch operator. In the hospital, five hours after the baby was born, they brought me papers to sign. I was in such a fog—they doped me up so much—I could hardly talk and could hardly see. My mother said, "These are circumcision papers."

I asked, "Are you sure?"

She goes, "Yes."

I asked, "Not adoption papers?"

She said, "No, circumcision papers." So I proceeded to sign and let them take my son. I thought he was going to a foster home for three weeks, then I called this woman up, and I said, "Well, I got my keypunch operator's certificate; I can get a job. I'm ready to take my son," and she started laughing hysterical on the phone. "You'll never see him again," she said. "Those were adoption papers, you fool, not circumcision papers."

CHUCK TRAYNOR: Was Linda ashamed about giving up her son for adoption? No, it sorta came and went. It was somethin' that came up; she mentioned it. I didn't even think about it as an adoption. I thought she just gave her son to her sister. It was just somethin' she did because she wasn't able to take care of a child.

LINDA LOVELACE: That's what I wanted—a baby. Then Larry could go away. I was supporting him for a long time. A very, very long time. I think the first five years we were together, he didn't work.

Was I pissed? I think I was more pissed that I was married to him—but I wanted kids.

CHUCK TRAYNOR: Linda came into Vegas with this play. She was gonna do her acting, and Larry Marchiano was her manager. The play was so bad—the second night, this guy comes over and says, "Jeez, I went in to see Linda Lovelace in a play."

I said, "Oh, yeah? How was it?"

He said, "Well, about halfway through the play, this lady sittin' beside me asked, 'I wonder when Linda Lovelace is gonna come on?' And she'd been onstage since the very opening scene."

I said, "She must be makin' a big impression."

LINDA LOVELACE: Larry and I went to Vegas because I was in a play there: *My Daughter's Rated X.* The play closed after two weeks, but we stayed in Nevada a little bit—up in the mountains.

CHUCK TRAYNOR: Linda's play folded—and Larry Marchiano got taken to the padded cell ward there for goin' berserk one night. I don't know if it was pills and booze or what, but the fireman that took him down there was a friend of mine, and he said, "Oh yeah, we were rollin' him out in a straitjacket. He was tellin' Linda, 'REMEMBER, THE SHOW MUST GO ON! REMEMBER, THE SHOW MUST GO ON!'"

LINDA LOVELACE: We went to New York and lived in his parents' basement for a while. Then we moved to Long Island—Santa Merchas, which means "the center of more riches for the fishermen." I think the first two years we were there we were on public assistance. One time, Larry took the rent money and flew to Ohio to see his brother. That's when he thought people were following him.

MIKE MCGRADY (COAUTHOR OF *ORDEAL*): I was writing a column for *Newsday*; and I heard from a lawyer in Bayshore—Victor Yanicone—that Linda Lovelace was living on welfare on Long Island. Victor—who became a mutual friend—described this tale of terrible poverty. He said that Linda was eating dog food.

I said, "Well, there's gotta be a story here."

I arranged to meet Linda in Victor's office the first time. And she started telling me the story that she'd been brutalized and forced into everything.

Oh yeah, I had a lot of trouble believing it at first. See, I was one of the many local columnists who had interviewed her when *Deep Throat* came out, and from all I could see she was a willing participant—and I had met Chuck Traynor at that time as well.

LINDA LOVELACE: I was kinda hesitant about writing my story. But one afternoon I was sitting there watching Phil Donahue, and Susan Brownmiller made the comment, "Oh, a lot of people do pornography to get into Hollywood and become a star—just like Linda Lovelace."

It made me so mad that I called up Mike McGrady, and he called up Lyle Stuart, the publisher, and said, "We're going to do a book."

I'd been thinking that maybe I could slip away and live a normal life, you know? But after that *Donahue* show, I said, "No. This isn't right." That's when I made the final decision to go for it.

MIKE MCGRADY: Linda told me that if I saw *Deep Throat*—which I hadn't seen at that point—I would notice huge bruise marks over her body. I'd never heard that before, and it seemed strange to me that that would've escaped people's attention. But when I saw *Deep Throat* I saw that her thighs were indeed black-and-blue.

But before being totally convinced, we put Linda through two days of lie detector tests with a guy in New York, who was considered the best in the business.

PEOPLE, JANUARY 28, 1980: MRS. MARCHIANO CALLS HERSELF 'A TYPICAL HOUSEWIFE': THE WORLD KNEW HER AS LINDA LOVELACE: "What happened is told in her just published autobiography, *Ordeal,* a nightmarish portrayal of sexual perversion and enslavement. Between 1971 and 1973, she says she was transformed from the relatively innocent manager of a clothing boutique into a numb and brutalized sex machine who graduated from cheap street-corner tricks to celebrity bedrooms, among them Sammy Davis Jr. (Davis responds: 'The whole thing is ludicrous.')"

GLORIA LEONARD: *Cosmopolitan,* back in the day when Gloria Steinem was still a part of it, once did a cover story of a headless woman. She was just nude from the neck down, holding flowers over her breasts—and the cover line was something like: "Erotica vs. Pornography: Do you know the difference?"

I thought, "Here they are pooh-poohing it and making hay out of it, but they have it as their cover story. They're selling it and exploiting it themselves! Well, I'm just doing the same thing. And who are you or any other female to consider my choice of what I want to do any less valid than your choice?" It only causes more dissension. It's not going to unify women.

MIKE MCGRADY: I was there when the polygraph test was being administered. We asked her questions for two days. By this time I had gathered the information from her, so we asked questions about every part of the story—every part that might be considered libelous.

Linda passed with flying colors. Linda cannot lie—as near as I can tell—and get away with it. She's very transparent, and during her first interviews as "Miss Deep Throat," no one took what she was saying seriously, that she was having a wonderful time.

So I don't think she fooled anyone—but I didn't see any signs at that time that she'd been beaten or tortured or anything. The story itself was horrifying, and you might've thought, as I did, that when you have one of the leading celebrities tell a tale of great sex and violence, it'd be easy to sell. But the truth is I was turned down by thirty-three publishers before I went back to Lyle Stuart and said, "Please publish this book."

GLORIA LEONARD: Marlene Willoughby, Annie Sprinkle, and I went up and protested at the *Cosmo* offices. Yeah, it made all the news that night—and the next day, too—in New York City.

We had gotten the proper permit and all that. Somebody from *Cosmo* came down to talk to us; but we said, "No, we want an audience upstairs." And they wouldn't let us up. But we made our point.

LINDA LOVELACE: When *Ordeal* came out, I did the *Phil Donahue Show.* He does that little brief interview with you before he opens it up to the audience, and the first question from the audience was from a woman who asked, "What in your childhood led you to be so promiscuous?"

I was like, "Hello—did you hear anything that I said?"

I was twenty years old, heading in one direction, and all of a sudden, my life's taken away from me. Even though I got free of Traynor, here I am, a middle-aged woman, and I'm still dealing with *Deep Throat.*

NEW YORK *DAILY NEWS*, MAY 30, 1980: NOW HERE'S A SWITCH DEPT.: "Porn star Linda Lovelace will join Women Against Pornography for a demonstration here tomorrow at Seventh Avenue and Forty-eighth Street at 11:00 A.M. to protest a dirty movie. The movie? *Deep Throat.*"

GLORIA LEONARD: Women Against Pornography first came about in the early eighties. They had a little storefront office in Times Square. What was their purpose then? Beats the shit out of me!

They just thought porn degraded, defiled, and debased women—the same old stupid argument. You know, it causes crime, teaches men not to respect women, yadda, yadda, yadda.

LINDA LOVELACE: Some people from Women Against Pornography watched the *Donahue* show. And then Gloria Steinem contacted me, and she tried very hard—everybody tried real hard—to find some way that I could seek legal action. But there's just no laws for victims in our society. Only for criminals. So we weren't able to do too much.

So I did a press conference with Women Against Pornography when I was eight months pregnant with my son, Lindsay. It was a rainy morning at the end of May 1980, and they had a big demonstration outside the Frisco theater where they were showing *Deep Throat.*

There was a press conference afterward at the "Women Against Pornography" offices. That's where I met Gloria Steinem and Catherine MacKinnon. And Valerie Harper—"Rhoda"—she was really fun and great. Yeah, she said she was gonna come out and have hamburgers and hot dogs, but she never did.

GLORIA LEONARD: Nobody really paid a whole lot of attention to *Ordeal* when it came out, you know, it terms of its credibility. I mean, this was a woman who never took responsibility for her own shitty choices—but instead blamed everything that happened to her in her life on porn. You know, "The devil made me do it."

NEW YORK *DAILY NEWS*, JUNE 8, 1980: A STRANGE BEDFELLOW FOR THE WAR ON PORNOGRAPHY: "Linda Lovelace has been born again. She is now Linda Marchiano, a Long Island housewife, mother of a four-year-old son and due to give birth again this month. She is also the author of a book called

Ordeal (Citadel Press, $10), which chronicles the two-and-a-half years she claims she spent as the virtual prisoner of her former husband, pimp-pornographer, Chuck Traynor."

GLORIA LEONARD: In *Ordeal,* Linda describes being beaten up on the set of *Deep Throat.* But the truth of the matter is that nobody that had anything to do with the film touched her—she was beaten up at night by Chuck Traynor in the privacy of their hotel room. It was her own poor, shitty choice of a companion that got her beat up. Nobody in the porn business—that had anything to do with the film—laid a hand on her, other than in a loving way.

LINDA LOVELACE: The book tour was hard. It was one of those twelve cities in ten days kinda deals, you know? Fly in and get to your hotel at like 1:00 A.M., then be up at five to do a morning show and then back on the plane. You know, you're doing like, God—I don't know how many. I would do like eight or nine interviews in one city—and then be off again.

Larry was with me the whole time. He wasn't real supportive of me; he had me convinced that if I went out and got a job someone was gonna recognize me and that I was gonna get raped.

But he was the one to get me up and going, you know? I'm a slow starter, so yeah, he would kinda get me going. But there was too much drinking.

I mean, goddamn—I ended up having to pay for the whole alcohol bill. I think one night we drank ten bottles of Mumm Cordon Rouge. Ten bottles! Thank God it doesn't give you a headache.

So yeah, there were times when I drank with him because he would get mad at me if I didn't drink, and then he'd be verbally abusive to the kids.

GLORIA LEONARD: I thought Linda was just a wacko. I was in a green room once for a TV show in New York, and Linda was going to be on the show. She comes in looking like hell, squints her eyes, looks at me—and goes, "You're in porn—I can tell from your eyes!"

I'm telling you the truth, ha, ha, ha. That's a direct quote!

CHUCK TRAYNOR: I was in England, and Sammy Davis Jr. sent me a manuscript for *Ordeal.* I read it, and then Hefner's secretary called and said Hefner was kinda upset about it, 'cause Linda was talkin' about this and that and the parties at his house.

Did Hefner wanna sue? I mean, Hefner surely had the means and attorneys to sue. But I think he just agreed, you know; it would just be more publicity for them.

LINDA LOVELACE: The three of us—Chuck, Sammy, myself—were in the screening room watching a porno movie. Or rather, the two men were watching the movie. I was on my knees in front of Sammy, deep-throating him while he watched the movie.

"I really dig that," Sammy was whispering, "I'd like to know how you do it. When are you going to teach me? When you going to show me how you do that? Hey, you think Chuck would mind?"

"Mind?" I whispered back. "No, that's the kind of thing he'd go for in a big way. But let me set it up for you."

Of course, this was definitely not the kind of thing Chuck would go for in a big way.

"Hey, you can't just sit there and watch," I said to Chuck. "You just can't sit there."

As I talked to Chuck, I signaled for Sammy to come over. Chuck grunted at me and shifted his weight, making it easier for me to do the job. I was the one who unzipped his trousers, but I wasn't the one knelt in front of him.

A minute or two went by before Chuck realized that something was different. Then, although Chuck didn't utter a sound, his eyes were screaming for help. I just shrugged my shoulders and laughed.

Each time that Sammy showed signs of slowing down, I kept him going with instructional encouragement. It was, ironically enough, the same instruction that Chuck had once give me.

"No, no, Sammy," I said, "push down a little more—he'll like that. Yeah, that's right. Keep going. You're doing fine."

CHUCK TRAYNOR: I called Sammy back and said, "Sam, this is a fuckin' joke. Other than the fact that she's talkin' about you and I havin' sex or somethin'—well, I guess we'll have to get married now—but just forget about it."

Sammy and I never had sex.

Sammy said, "I don't know where any of this shit came from. You think we should sue 'em?"

I said, "No because if we sue 'em, it's gonna go into litigation—that's publicity. Think about that. That book could be in litigation for years—and sell millions and millions of copies. And we ain't gettin' a penny."

I said, "If they wanna make a deal with us, fine, you know. But if they're gonna play this game, let 'em play it. I don't give a shit."

PEOPLE, **JANUARY 28, 1980: MRS. MARCHIANO CALLS HERSELF 'A TYPICAL HOUSEWIFE': THE WORLD KNEW HER AS LINDA LOVELACE:** "'Little by little I found out what pornography meant,' recalls Larry [Marchiano], 32. A construction worker, he was shown a still photo from one of Linda's gamiest eight-millimeter films by a coworker one day on the job.

'I turned around,' he says, 'and walked I don't know how many miles that day.' For a time he was plagued by the predictable taunts, but he says he has learned 'to care only about Linda and not so much other people.'

For her, that support has been crucial."

LINDA LOVELACE: Larry would go, "Oh, I'm gonna go look for a job." You know, "Yeah, *right*." He would leave first thing in the morning and not come home until after midnight. So my world was my children.

You know, all the kids in the neighborhood were always in my yard. I got pieces of wood, and they would make street names after themselves—and we built huts and dug holes in like hidden shacks, you know? I was always doing stuff like that with the kids, and I was happy.

PEOPLE, **JANUARY 28, 1980: MRS. MARCHIANO CALLS HERSELF 'A TYPICAL HOUSEWIFE': THE WORLD KNEW HER AS LINDA LOVELACE:** " 'I thank God I can be with my husband and trust him,' Linda says. 'He is the only human being I had met who wasn't strange or didn't get into some sexual problem.' "

LINDA LOVELACE: Larry took our son out one time and instead of changing his diaper, he went to three friends' houses; the mothers weren't around. So he took Dominick to the emergency room and said to them, "There's a problem down here."

The nurse took the diaper off, said, "Oh, great" and took care of it.

I mean, what's so hard about changing a diaper?

In some ways, yeah, Larry was a bit like Chuck. But then again, no. Larry wasn't into pushing me into that kind of thing and making me go for that kind of a lifestyle. But he was very jealous. I really didn't have any friends.

PEOPLE, **JANUARY 28, 1980: MRS. MARCHIANO CALLS HERSELF 'A TYPICAL HOUSEWIFE': THE WORLD KNEW HER AS LINDA LOVELACE:** "Linda still fears retribution from Chuck Traynor—especially in the predawn hours after Larry has gone to work—and she complains of chronic insomnia. Her financial situation is precarious; she and Larry rely partially on welfare."

LINDA LOVELACE: One night we came home, and Lindsay had some friends over, and one of the kid's cars was like a little bit on our next door neighbor's driveway. Larry had told the kids, "Don't block anybody's driveway."

Larry was drunk, of course. So he totally flipped out and tried to beat this sixteen-year-old kid up, trying to yank him out. The kid was like, "Mr. Marchiano, I'm sorry. Let me just go move my car."

NEW YORK *DAILY NEWS,* **JUNE 8, 1981: LIZ SMITH,** *PEOPLE ARE TALKING:* "The party at London's Cafe Royal for Linda Lovelace and her book *Ordeal* ended in a ruckus. When reporter Paul Pickering asked Linda a very nasty question about her past, the *Deep Throat* star's husband, Larry Marchiano, punched him out. (Maybe Larry should change his name to Rocky.)"

LINDA LOVELACE: The kid was scared. Larry ripped the chain that he had around his neck, you know, ripped the buttons on his shirt. And I'm like, "Hey, you know, chill here."

So we're back in the house, and I'm telling Larry to chill out, and he shoved me. I fell back on the stairs and did something to my thumb—bruised it severely, but it didn't break. So the cops take him away for domestic violence, and then the state picks it up.

"Wow," I thought. "Now I don't have to worry."

NEW YORK *DAILY NEWS*, JUNE 25, 1981: LIZ SMITH, *OTHER VOICES OTHER RUMORS*: "Linda Lovelace and her husband Larry Marchiano insist he did not hit Paul Pickering, but rather tried to reason with the British reporter in spite of rude remarks about Linda. When this proved futile, Larry claims, he walked away. Linda is disillusioned by her appearance before the London Literary Press Club. Members laughed when she tried to speak about pornography involving infants and children. She says, 'They could just as easily laughed about Hitler and the concentration camps!' "

LINDA LOVELACE: I'd be sleeping and all of a sudden I'd wake up, and Larry would be there staring at me. He'd break into the house, and he'd just be staring at me, you know? It was kind of freaky.

And then, within thirty days, he was engaged. He got married. But it didn't last a year.

Now he's engaged again, you know? And when he's not engaged, he's like, "Uhhh, you think we could get back together?"

I just say, "NOOOO!"

Part 6:

WONDERLAND

LOS ANGELES POLICE DEPARTMENT
PRELIMINARY INVESTIGATION of
MURDER

| OCCURRED IN/ON (St. Bar, Bank, Veh. Resid, Vac Lot) | | |
| residence | Combined Evid. Rpt. | PCD 5 | DR ATTACHMENT 81 520 902 | MULTIPLE DRS ON THIS P |

PREMISES IF RESIDENCE GIVE TYPE Yard, Single Family, Hotel
single family

LAST NAME, FIRST, MIDDLE (Firm Name if Business)
MILLER, Joy Audrey   SEX F   Descent W   AGE 46   DOB 5-14

RESIDENCE, BUSINESS ADDRESS   ZIP CODE   PHONE
R. 8753 Wonderland Ave. 90046   650 4447

VICTIM'S OCCUPATION

R.D. 621   Prints by Prelim Attempted   Obtained

DATE & TIME REPORTED 7-1-81 1600

STOLEN/LOST $ RECOVERED $ Ext. Dal Arson/)

CONNECTED REPORTS—Type & Dr. No.
See below

Type of Window or door (Wood Slider, Glass, Wood Sash, Etc.)

M.O. UNIQUE OR UNUSUAL ACTIONS THAT MAY T
entered residence case.

killing her

...victim with blunt instrument

BORIS YARO / Los Angeles Times

AVENUE

1980–1981

CASE REPORT

Page 1 of 2   CONTINUATION SHEET

3   Informant: Detective Tom Lange
LAPD Robbery Homicide
Ph# 485

RICH...
LAUNIUS, ...37
MILLER, J. ...38
DEVERELL, W.   81-8539
Date Found 7-1-81
Homicides

The decedent's are 2 males and 2 females, all Caucasions, found dead July 1, 1981, in a residence located at 8763 Wonderland Avenue in the Hollywood Hills.

Case #81-8536 is a female (Victim 1) approximately 25 years of age and as yet unidentified. Decedent is lying on livingroom floor, face down. Decedent is dressed in a t-shirt type nightgown, a pi... and white sleeping bag (probably a "snug sac") is wrapped around between decedent's legs. Decedent has multiple lacerations to head. No defense type wounds noted, no broken fingernails. Rigor of a 2 to 3 noted throughout body. Lividity is likewise a 3+, consistent with body position and permanent. Evidence collected at scene on this decedent consists of hair, nail scrapings and 1 miscellaneous packet, containing what appears to be hair taken from left hand and forearm.

Case #81-8537 is a male (Victim 2) ...ed as LAUNIUS, Ronald Lee age 37. Decedent is lying supine bedroom, upstairs and to the right as you enter the residence. Decedent is dressed in under-

Left page: *clockwise from top left:* Small photos: Wonderland Avenue murder victims Ron Launius, Bill Deverell, Joy Audrey Miller, and Barbara Richardson. Large photos: Wonderland Avenue murder victims' bodies at crime scene.

Right page: *top to bottom:* copies of the Los Angeles County police report on Wonderland murders; newspaper clipping of article on Wonderland Avenue murder investigation showing Adel Nasarallah (aka Eddie Nash); newspaper clipping of article on Wonderland Avenue murder arraignment showing John Holmes.

The Godfather of Hollywood
LOS ANGELES/OKLAHOMA
1980–1981

CHRIS COX (NIGHTCLUB OWNER): In the early seventies, Eddie Nash was known in Hollywood as the "Godfather." It was well-known that he pretty much ran everything; if you wanted to get something done, you had to see Eddie Nash.

When I first met Eddie in 1970, he had six or seven nightclubs in Hollywood—a gay club, a Polynesian restaurant, a couple of strip joints, and a Middle Eastern place. All these clubs were doing well, and none of them competing with each other.

TOM LANGE (LAPD DETECTIVE, ROBBERY/HOMICIDE DIVISION): I wasn't really familiar with Eddie Nash, but my partner, Bob Souza, had heard of him from being in Hollywood Dicks [Hollywood Detectives] in 1969 or 1970. Of course, there was a big scandal in Hollywood Dicks in 1970. The cops were all dirty, and they were on the take; they were selling what we call "5-10s"—padding confidential information on real bad guys and getting paid off—or getting free women, free meals.

Eddie Nash loved the cops. He'd say, "Come on in; we'll set you up!" It's not a direct payoff—but when Eddie's name comes up, you remember he's the guy who bought you dinner and bought you drinks all night. So that kind of nonsense went on, and of course all those guys went to prison—but one of the players behind that was Eddie Nash.

CHRIS COX: So I come along and open a gay after-hours club right across the street from one of Eddie's clubs. And this creates some problems. Club owners weren't that congenial with each other back then. There were a lot of bomb threats—fire captains arriving at midnight on a Saturday night, things like that.

Then Eddie offered to buy into my club a few times, and I didn't go along with it. After ten months, my club burned down.

So in the beginning Eddie Nash and I were competitors. But after a while we became close friends. Eddie became like a mentor to me.

DAWN SCHILLER: John Holmes referred to Eddie Nash as "brother." Eddie was portrayed to me as an extremely dangerous person that we didn't talk about. We were barely able to breathe around him because it could be taken wrong. I didn't really understand the social structure—other than it was based on fear.

I finally got to meet Eddie Nash after sitting outside of his house more days than he knows because John started taking me with him when he went on drug runs.

I never went into anybody's home. John would always make me wait in cars, hiding there, with nothing but a Coke can to pee in and a freebase pipe. And John would come by every twelve hours or so and drop off a freebase rock.

CHRIS COX: I first met John Holmes at my nightclub, the Odyssey. He was brought into my office by a mutual friend. This was in late 1980, and it was kind of unique to meet him because he was so well-known. I remember seeing his movies as a kid. *Everybody* had seen his movies as a kid.

But when I met him he was pretty heavy into coke. I think his career had gone down the tubes, and he was basically homeless, living in the back of an old milk truck—pretty much living day-to-day. He carried around a big aluminum briefcase loaded up with freebasing paraphernalia—butane, propane, pipes, and nozzles, all the equipment we were using in those days.

DAWN SCHILLER: John did bring me into Eddie's house a couple of times. He basically sold me for dope. He needed to get high, and he gave me—the teenager—in trade.

One time it was my birthday, and I was drilled with this story that I was supposed to be John's niece from Oregon, in town, looking into nursing schools.

CHRIS COX: John kind of befriended me because the drugs were flowing pretty heavily. He knew a good thing when he saw it. Those were the days when everybody was carrying around a two-gram bottle of coke, know what I mean? It was just the right thing to have.

And there was an elite group that was doing the freebasing—because it was so expensive. It was like $2,800 an ounce, so it was just affluent people who could afford to do it back then. There were small cliques around town with little freebasing empires.

DAWN SCHILLER: John warned me about how Eddie Nash would treat me. He told me that Nash would leave me alone in the living room for hours with the drugs, money, and jewelry in front of me. And the whole time I was being watched through a two-way mirror. I was left in the living room for hours with all these things in front of me. Nash did it to see if I was on dope. And at that time I was so addicted to coke, you know? So I just broke into cold sweats waiting to be called into the bedroom.

Finally I got traded off.

Nash paid me in coke. When John picked me up I turned all the coke over to him, and then told him—word for word—everything that happened. He backhanded me so hard my tooth went through my cheek.

Why? I guess because there wasn't as much cocaine as they originally bargained on. I think it had to do with the fact that Eddie Nash could tell I wasn't John's innocent niece from Oregon. I mean, he could tell that I had smoked freebase before.

CHRIS COX: There was me and my group, and then there was Eddie Nash and his group, centered around Nash's house in the Hollywood Hills on Dona Lola Drive. His place was a split-level house with a big living room area that was like the waiting room. And people would come by to see Eddie, who was usually in the bedroom. It was like getting an audience with the Pope—you know, you had to wait your turn. The living room was like Siberia; everybody looked very dejected out there. But a chosen few got to go in right away, no waiting. And I was one of them.

But then in 1980 I kind of got put out to pasture, after I introduced John to Eddie Nash. When I first brought John over to Nash's, it was like bringing over a celebrity. There were lots of girls there, and they were pretty much bumping into each other to get to John. He was well liked up there. He was a conversation piece. John and Ed hit it off very well, and John started spending all his time over at Eddie's.

My feelings weren't really hurt. I understood what was going on: John was doing what he had to do to get his own supply.

DAWN SCHILLER: The only other house John took me into belonged to this lady that he'd worked with on a porn movie. She lived in one of these massive apartment complexes alongside the freeway in the Valley and turned tricks in her home.

One day John walked me into her condo and announced that I was going to be working for her. She had a list of clients I was supposed to see. They came at certain times during the day, and I, you know, had to take care of them.

What it boiled down to was that John sold me to her, too. And he got whatever money was my cut.

CHRIS COX: I watched Eddie Nash's empire grow and grow—and then I watched it decline. Finally, I saw him locked in his room, his hands all burned from the freebase pipe, and down to a hundred and forty pounds, and you know, never going to the office anymore. They had to bring the paychecks up to him to get them signed. I just watched Eddie deteriorating.

I tried to stop it—tried to help him when it was happening, tried to keep him from losing his wife and kids.

JEANNA NASH (EDDIE NASH'S EX-WIFE): After our separation, when my parents and I took the children to Oklahoma to my aunt and uncle's farm, my husband hired a girl to follow us.

She came to the farm in order to find out if a certain man was with me. After she left, my husband called me and said to come home immediately.

When I refused, he said, "Don't come back to California, or I will have two men waiting at the airport to kill you, and I will have your parents killed."

CHRIS COX: Eddie's house was on a pedestal; he kept his house and his family away from all of the dirtier parts of his life. He was a good father, too. I'd watch him with the kids and how he dealt with them and stuff.

When the freebasing started to get heavy, he was doing it in hotels and apartments and stuff. But then he gradually started to bring it home.

Jeanna was threatening to leave, and all of his other people were saying, "Fuck her. You don't take orders from *anybody*. Why should you take orders from her?"

JEANNA NASH: My husband tried to convince my father that I had been with other men. When my father disagreed, my husband became very angry and said, "I am going to kill all of you, and I'm going to kill her. She is a hooker."

CHRIS COX: When I talked to Eddie alone, I'd say, "You know, Nash, you're wrong here. Jeanna's stayed with you all these years. She lays at home in bed at night with no one else to talk to—it's four or five in the morning—and she knows that you're with somebody.

"She's willing to accept it; she loves you that much. She knows she didn't marry an insurance man who works nine-to-five. She must have married you because she liked you. But now you're starting to bring it home."

I told him that it was wrong to bring it into the house.

JEANNA NASH: My husband called me later that evening and said, "Send your father out, and I will kill him and leave the rest of you alone."

I, of course, refused, and he then asked that I send my parents home so we could talk alone. I told him I was too afraid to do that. He then repeated that if I did not do as he told me, he would shoot all of us, including the children.

CHRIS COX: I tried to patch it up with Jeanna and Eddie. Then Eddie started getting suspicious of me talking to her. He thought that there might be something going on there. And he'd ask, had I ever seen her with any other guys?

Jeanna couldn't take it anymore. She moved out—she was staying at her mother's house in the Valley—and Eddie said he heard my voice in the background on the phone with her. All this madness. And somebody said he saw my car outside of her house. This was during Eddie's paranoia stages.

JEANNA NASH: My husband later returned to the house, and we went into the kitchen, where I tried to calm him down. He told me to pack up the children and come home with him at once and that if I would confess to all the men I had been with, he would forgive me.

I told him I had been faithful to him throughout our marriage and that I wasn't having a relationship with anyone. He said he did not believe me and then threatened that he would return later to slit my throat. There was some food and water on the table that my husband picked up and threw at me. He grabbed me by the hair and said, "Go ahead and call the police. I may be in jail, but I can still have all of you killed."

CHRIS COX: After Jeanna left, the house started deteriorating. It became the party house; it was always loaded with people, and traffic, and cabs, and everything.

Eddie turned the family home into a whorehouse.

The girls showed up at the house, like, seven in the morning—as soon as Jeanna was gone, you know?

But the main thing was the pipe. The pipe was more important than anything else.

JOHN HOLMES: I bought cocaine from the people on Wonderland Avenue. They were heroin addicts who lived in an armed camp. They had two stolen antique guns worth $25,000—which I took to Eddie Nash in exchange for $1,000 worth of heroin. All they had to do to get the guns back was come up with the $1,000—but whenever they got enough money, they'd always call another connection and spend it.

So the guns were with Eddie Nash for a week, then two weeks, then six weeks. Eddie wanted his money—the people on Wonderland wanted their guns back—and I was right there in the middle.

That was when the people on Wonderland Avenue got the idea to rob Eddie Nash.

BOB SOUZA (LAPD DETECTIVE, ROBBERY/HOMICIDE DIVISION, PARTNER OF TOM LANGE): John Holmes was shooting off his mouth about Eddie Nash at the Wonderland Avenue house—and Ron Launius heard him talking about it and started asking a lot of questions: "Has Nash got any dope? Has he got any guns? Any jewelry?" Ron Launius was a fucking thief from way back, so he's thinking, "Hey, this looks like a pretty good score."

The Wonderland Avenue gang were doing residential robberies at that time. That was their big thing—going out and ripping off other drug dealers. You know you got some tough bastards when they're robbing other dope dealers. Because they know they're gonna face some guns.

DAWN SCHILLER: When I was turning tricks for the lady John set me up with, it was like the old Little Orphan Annie story—you live in the orphanage, and you have porridge and that's it. And you do your chores, and you don't complain. And if you complain you get a severe beating.

I complained while we were out driving one day, and John, that fucker, just pulled off the freeway and threw me in the trunk—and wouldn't let me out until I agreed to go back to turning tricks.

DAVID LIND (MEMBER OF THE WONDERLAND AVENUE GANG): It was John Holmes's idea to rob Eddie Nash—because he knew Billy Deverell and Ronnie Launius had done it before—robbed large drug connections. The plan was that John was to go in the house and leave a door open for us.

DAWN SCHILLER: One night, when the madam was out, John came in and asked me to draw his bath and get him a cup of coffee. Up until this time, he hadn't taken his eyes off of me. I was watched instantly because they knew I'd run any second. So when he asked me to go get him a cup of coffee—while he was in the bathtub—it was my chance to make my break.

I went out, and I mixed the coffee, and there was a sliding glass door behind me—and I ran.

I ran to the nearest place—a Denny's restaurant—and called my mother collect in Oregon. She said she would send a bus ticket to the bus station in Glendale. But I didn't really know where that was because I didn't have a driver's license. John didn't allow me to drive. And the freeway system was a mystery to me, you know? One minute we were in Studio City and the next in Hollywood. I also knew that John would follow me to the bus station.

So I was standing in the Denny's, and there was a little old man watching me, and he saw that I was crying. He thought I was hungry, so he bought me a bowl of chili and started talking to me.

TRACY MCCOURT (MEMBER OF THE WONDERLAND AVENUE GANG): One day I walked into the Wonderland Avenue house, and John was talking about robbing Eddie Nash. But, you know, lots of people talk that way. I just thought it was one of *those* conversations.

DAWN SCHILLER: I told the old man what was happening and that I didn't know what to do. It turned out that he lived in a semiretirement home. He said he'd let me sleep on his floor if he could touch my butt.

I asked, "Is that all?"

So it was kind of cute. I had to be smuggled into the retirement home because if the people who ran the place found out, I'd be thrown out of there. But all the other old people were in on it. So I slept on his floor and the next day—they had a community dining room—it was a "toast under the table" kind of thing.

Then I called the guy at the Glendale Bus Station and asked him if anyone had been there looking for me. I described John to him, and he told me that somebody like that had just left. I guess he realized I was desperate, so he picked me up in the San Fernando Valley and brought me to the bus station at the exact time when I could get right on the bus. Then he loaned me five dollars to have sandwiches on the way.

And so I made it. I got away.

DAVID LIND: John would take weapons and jewelry from the house on Wonderland Avenue over to Eddie Nash's and then come back with heroin.

DAWN SCHILLER: I was at my mother's in Oregon for a couple of months, and John called every day, begging me to come back, telling me how much he loved me. That he was sorry, that he'd never hit me again. Saying it was the drugs. Telling me if we just got away from the drugs, everything would be all right.

I cringed. I believed that to be true—but then I didn't because there were too many days where he'd smash the freebase pipe, telling me, "That was the last one that I'll ever do!"

Again and again and again.

But he wheedled his way back in, and I started to believe him. You know, telling me he just wanted to be with Sharon and me and just live our lives. Just get away from the porn industry and everything else that messed up his head, messed with his emotions. And get away from the drugs.

Of course, I didn't know that his plan was to rob Eddie Nash, that that was going to be the big bank we were going to get away on.

Anyway, John talked me into going back. I would fly down from Oregon, and he would meet me at the Burbank airport.

JOHN HOLMES: The Wonderland Avenue gang were going to break into Eddie Nash's house, rob the place, and kill everyone there. I knew if I told Eddie about it he would send over his people, and it would be the Wonderland gang who would be killed. So I agreed to leave a sliding glass door open at Nash's house if Billy and Ronnie would guarantee that nobody would be hurt.

I was between a rock and a hard place.

"It's Not Like You Said It's Gonna Be"

LOS ANGELES
1981

DAWN SCHILLER: A week before the murders, John picked me up at the Burbank airport. Just as we were about to walk out the door he turned around, went over to the conveyor belt, picked up a bag that wasn't mine, came back, grabbed my hand, and we walked out the door.

That was my first clue. Inside, my gut froze. I was thinking, "Oh shit, nothing's changed." But I had finally given in and come back.

John said he was off the stuff. And then we checked into this dive hotel on Ventura Boulevard and immediately got high.

DAVID LIND: I didn't know who Eddie Nash was, but John suggested that Ronnie Launius, Billy Deverell, and I should rob him because Nash was in possession of a considerable amount of narcotics, cash, and jewelry.

DAWN SCHILLER: John didn't have much coke, so he said, "Okay, I'm going to go take care of that, and then we'll be out of here." He promised he'd be back in the morning.

But he didn't come back—and since I didn't have any money, I got kicked out of the hotel.

I was literally standing on the street crying—with my dog in my suitcase—going, "Fuck, now what?"

A bunch of pimps and johns wanted me, and I contemplated turning a trick, but then, I was like, "I don't want to have to do that again!"

DAVID LIND: John was in debt to Ronnie and Billy Deverell. He was also complaining that he didn't have enough money to pay his film editors for his latest film—a documentary on him called *Exhausted*.

So John drew an entire diagram on a piece of paper of the inside layout of Eddie Nash's house.

DAWN SCHILLER: I'm still crying when this lady pulls up in a white van, with a couple other people—young adults. She told me her name was Ivy, and asked me, "What's the matter?" So I told her. Ivy said, "I'm a member of this Christian group, and we're all going to paint this house. If you want to make some money and make some phone calls, I can help you out."

I guess she wasn't too threatened by a girl with a suitcase and a chihuahua. So I went with her. I left messages on John's machine, then helped them paint this place, and spent the night at Ivy's apartment.

TRACY MCCOURT: John and Ronnie were drawing up plans—you know, to find out where the bodyguard slept, where the guns were, how many windows were in the back of the house—the whole thing.

We made a couple of dry runs. But we had to call it off a couple of times. One time everybody was going to forget it, so me and Billy were going to do it. But John kept going over to Nash's house and doing so much cocaine that he wouldn't come out for three or four hours.

DAVID LIND: On Monday, June 29, 1981, Ron Launius provided John Holmes with money to purchase some narcotics from Eddie Nash.

TRACY MCCOURT: When we left Wonderland Avenue, we passed John on our way to Nash's. He was driving down the hill, and we were going up. We stopped, and he told us, "GET HIM!"

So we went to the house, and—and got him.

DAVID LIND: At Nash's there was a chain-link gate that we just pushed open. We went to the sliding glass doors, which were left open by Holmes, and entered the guest bedroom.

There was a doorway leading into the hallway, and I saw the bodyguard, Gregory Diles—a 300-pound black man—coming out of the kitchen with a serving tray in his hands.

I shouted, "FREEZE! POLICE! YOU ARE UNDER ARREST!"

Then Ronnie and Billy threw down on Eddie Nash. I had a leather case containing a San Francisco police officer badge; we all identified ourselves as police officers, and we were all armed. So we lay Gregory Diles on his stomach to handcuff him. But while I was cuffing Diles, Ronnie bumped my arm, and the gun went off.

Eddie Nash immediately fell to his knees and asked Ronnie to say a prayer.

TRACY MCCOURT: I was sitting in the car waiting—when I heard a real loud noise and knew it had to be a gunshot. It sounded like a Magnum shot, but I calmed down by telling myself that any of the neighbors would have thought it was a load of lumber falling off a truck.

DAVID LIND: Diles suffered some powder burns, which caused him to bleed. Then I finished handcuffing him, laid him on the floor, and put a throw rug over his head—so he couldn't observe what we were doing.

Eddie Nash was on his knees, with his hands behind his head. Ron and Billy proceeded to take Nash into his bedroom, and I followed. Eddie was asked to lay facedown on the carpet. Ron proceeded to a wardrobe closet, where there was a floor safe—as we had been informed by John Holmes.

Bobby asked Nash for the key or combination—I don't really recall which—and Nash told us the correct answer. Ronnie proceeded to open the safe and withdraw a half-pound storage ziplock bag that was approximately three quarters full of cocaine.

John told us earlier that there was also a laboratory vial, approximately eight to ten inches in length and half an inch in diameter, full of heroin—which he called "China White"—in the area of Eddie Nash's dresser. We picked that up. There was also an attaché case full of money and jewelry. Holmes told us about that, too. We found everything.

Inside the attaché case was a considerable sum of money in twenties, fifties, and one hundred dollar bills, and a considerable amount of gold jewelry and diamonds.

Then, I taped up Gregory Diles and removed the handcuffs—because the handcuffs could have been identified by what was engraved on them—and went to the bedroom and taped up Eddie Nash and threw a sheet over him.

After that, as we were getting ready to leave, Ronnie pulled out a knife and started to cut Gregory Diles. I interfered and told him, "We've got everything we need here. Let's go."

Then, I opened the front door and signaled to Tracy McCourt. He started to back the vehicle up. Then, Ronnie and Billy and I went out the front door. Ronnie carried the attaché case, which had the bag of cocaine in it and the gray-green metal box, and I think he had the heroin vial in his pocket. I came out last carrying the two antique rifles, which were wrapped in white plastic like a shower curtain.

Then we all got in the car. Billy got in the front passenger side. Tracy McCourt was driving, and Ron and I were in the back. Then, we drove to the Wonderland Avenue house.

JOHN HOLMES: They robbed Eddie Nash and brought back heroin, cocaine, jewelry, ten thousand dollars in cash, and the antique guns.

DAVID LIND: John was waiting inside the door when we arrived. The first thing he wanted to know was exactly what happened. He seemed very excited about it. He was happy that we were able to accomplish what we had set out to do.

I told Ron not to tell him anything.

BOB SOUZA: Holmes was afraid of Ron Launius, the leader of the Wonderland Avenue gang. Launius called Holmes "donkey dick," which would be a compliment to most guys, but the way Launius said it, it was an insult.

Launius used to say to Holmes, "Hey, show 'em your dick. Pull it out."

Launius treated Holmes like a butt boy, and he was a tough son of a bitch.

DAVID LIND: Then, we went to Ronnie's bedroom and put everything on the bed and of course there was quite a bit of excitement. I said, "Well, let's get this thing over with." We then proceeded to weigh out the drugs and to count the money.

There were five of us involved in the robbery. Ronnie Launius, Billy Deverell, and I were to receive 25 percent of what we took. And John and Tracy McCourt were to split the remaining 25 percent of the drugs and the money.

TRACY MCCOURT: When we got back to the house, I just started getting very nervous. I looked out over the balcony and saw a car that looked like the Lincoln Continental that was parked at Eddie Nash's house. I told everybody about it, but they were so high and screwed up on drugs that they paid no attention. That's when I got really nervous and decided to leave on my own.

DAVID LIND: Immediately after everything was divided up Tracy left the house. Ronnie and John and I were in the living room—and John said that it still wasn't enough money. He still didn't have enough to pay his film editors and as there was a considerable amount of jewelry—still to be peddled to a fence—John was going to wait around for that money.

So Billy took the jewelry to the fence and came back a few hours later, in the early evening, with the money. Everybody was in a pretty good mood after the success of the incident, and we proceeded to just have a good time.

Then we used narcotics. Everybody did.

I don't remember when John left. I do remember when I left. I left approximately nine or ten o'clock the next morning. That was the last time I saw any of them alive.

DAWN SCHILLER: The next day I painted the house again, and when I got back to Ivy's apartment, John called and came over.

Ivy lived with her sister—who was not a Christian. Well, when John walked in, he asked if anybody wanted to do a line. Ivy didn't say anything, but her sister said, "SURE!"

So John pulled out his briefcase, and there was the largest pile of cocaine I've ever seen in my life. It was the pile they ripped off from Eddie Nash. But I didn't question it.

We spent the whole night, pretty much, in the bathroom. And John said, "This is how we're getting out of here—this is our bank." He said we needed to sell it—that's what we'd use to get away. And Ivy's sister was knocking on the bathroom door asking for more, you know? It happens to everyone who says "yes" the first time, ha, ha, ha.

John had a couple of Tarot cards in his briefcase; he used them for drawing out lines. After we all got high, John and I went to the store. When we got back we tried to buzz ourselves in, but Ivy wouldn't let us back in.

She stood on her balcony, waving a Christian flag and swearing that John was the devil—because he had used a Tarot card to cut his cocaine with.

JOHN HOLMES: The only time I've been out of control was when I was free-basing cocaine. In less than two years I smoked away a couple of apartment buildings I owned, my house, my antique store, my hardware store, and my career.

I stayed up for as long as ten days at a time. If I ate at all, it was half a taco from the Taco Bell drive-through every four days. When I looked in a full-length mirror, what I saw could have been liberated the day before from a Nazi concentration camp. I went from 170 pounds to 142 pounds. I was so emaciated that I couldn't shoot movies anymore. I hadn't had sex in six months, and all my wealthy female tricks were gone.

DAWN SCHILLER: I don't think Ivy knew who John was; she just thought he was the devil. Here she had done this Christian thing for me and opened the door to her house—and the devil came walking in.

Ivy kept waving the huge flag on the balcony, cleansing herself or something. I didn't even know they made flags that big. John had wanted to use her apartment as a cover. Nobody knew we were there. It was perfect. But she wouldn't let us back in.

Ivy was yelling from the balcony, "I KNOW WHAT YOU ARE! I KNOW WHAT YOU DID TO MY SISTER! GET BACK, SATAN!" And I'm like, "Can I have my dog and my clothes?"

Ivy brought them down in the elevator, handed them off, and then went back up without even looking at us.

JOHN HOLMES: Not only had I smoked away more than three-quarters of a million dollars, but also I had degenerated into a gofer—running around selling drugs to people that were so sleazy I would have crossed the street to avoid them in the past.

I sold five ounces of cocaine a day to rock stars, murderers, dentists, restaurant owners, burglars, Mafia hitmen, attorneys, producers, directors—anybody who was buying. I was paid each day with a marble-sized rock of freebase, which was worth a thousand dollars. That adds up to $365,000 a year. I smoked it all.

I even had to borrow money for gas.

DAWN SCHILLER: After we left Ivy's, we checked into this motel down the road and just got high. We got way high for about a week. It was another sleazy motel—but I was glad that there was a fast-food joint that sold hush puppies next door.

I think we slept for a little bit, you know, because we ate that chicken and those hush puppies, and we watched some TV. I'm not even sure if we had sex or not, but John left pretty quick because I know we didn't have that pile of coke with us for very long. He packed it all up—I think he left me a little rock and a pipe and went out.

But this time the place was paid for, so I don't know how long he was gone.

Nobody Waved Hello
LOS ANGELES
1981

CHRIS COX: I just got back in town on July 1, 1981. I was in Europe, and I had heard that something had happened over at Eddie Nash's because I had called just to say hello.

Eddie was enraged; I could tell just by his tone on the phone that something had happened. And then I started hearing rumors that somebody had robbed his house.

At that time, it wasn't known that John Holmes was involved in setting it up.

DAWN SCHILLER: Gregory Diles picked John up at his answering service office on Santa Monica Boulevard in Hollywood. It had some catchy name like, "Just Listening," or something like that. It was just this cell-block-looking building.

So John was picking up a stack of messages when Gregory Diles grabbed him. John said he got in the car, and "they" put a gun to his head. John said "They."

CHRIS COX: So I went to Eddie's house, and, well, it was very tense up there. There was a lot of movement around in and out of the bedroom. I don't recall if I saw Eddie or not—possibly, very briefly. But the mood—the feeling in the house—was like ice. You could cut the tension in there with a knife.

And John Holmes was standing over toward the dining room by the bar, looking very, very nervous.

Eddie was just not in a welcoming mood, so I didn't stay there long.

JOHN HOLMES: The day after the robbery, I was tortured for fourteen hours by Eddie Nash and eight of his bodyguards, as sixty or seventy people walked through his house making their regular drug buys. I sat in a room off the entry hall, my hands bound with black electrical tape. Blood was pouring from my mouth where Eddie had hit me with a gun. Nobody waved hello.

CHRIS COX: Before I left Eddie's house, I had a small conversation with John—but I don't recall what it was. It just wasn't an atmosphere where anybody was doing much talking. I know there was a rumor that John had been roughed up, but I didn't see any bruises or anything like that; I didn't see any evidence of that.

FRANK TOMLINSON (LAPD DETECTIVE, ROBBERY/HOMICIDE DIVISION): Right after the robbery, John Holmes said Eddie Nash held him at Nash's house, took his address book and—right in front of him—wrote down the names of John's family. John said that Nash told him that if he ever talked to the police, he would kill a member of John's family.

John then said that Nash took him—at gunpoint—to the house on Wonderland Avenue and that John knew what was going to happen, but he had no choice—that he had to set things up and let them in.

John said that he was there when the murders occurred but that he himself did not hurt anyone, that he was just there.

SHARON HOLMES: It was the early morning—nothing was moving in the streets—when John came knocking at the door. I see very well in the dark, so I realized it was John. I just left the latch on the door, and asked, "Why are you here?"

This was the first time I had seen him, literally, since March. He asked if he could come in. That's when I realized—from the night-light in the entryway—that he was covered in blood. It was in his hair, on his head, around his ears, all over his clothes—he wasn't dripping, but you could tell something had happened. He mumbled about how he'd had a car accident. "Could you help clean me up?"

Dope that I am, I let him in the house.

He said, "I have to get into the shower."

I figured he had a cut on his head, that that was where all the blood was coming from. But when we got into the bathroom, I realized he wasn't bleeding, that the blood had come from somewhere else.

He said, "I need to get in the tub."

This was classic John, from 1973 on—whenever anything unpalatable or difficult for him happened, he got into the bathtub. It was like Lady Macbeth washing her hands of the responsibility.

So he got into the shower—ran the water as hot as he could stand it— and kept dunking himself. Then I attended to the cuts on his face. He looked worse than I had ever seen him.

The bath water was pink. I mean, it was obvious there was a lot of blood there, but when he slid up the back of the tub, I'm not seeing anything that's accounting for it. No wounds that would explain that amount of blood.

I said, "There wasn't any accident. What happened?"

He looked me straight in the eye and said, "I was at a murder. Four people got killed, and somebody is after me."

Of course, nothing was in the news by then—so I had no idea what he was talking about.

DAWN SCHILLER: I was watching the news in the motel room—John wasn't back yet—and they were pulling the bodies out of the Wonderland Avenue house.

I knew that house. I'd sat in the car in front of that house many times. I'd seen those people go in and out. And my heart just went into my gut because I just *knew*.

I mean, it was all bad. John wasn't there, and the big pile—it was adding up.

SHARON HOLMES: John said, "Four people were killed in front of me."

He was almost incoherent.

Then he proceeded to tell me about the robbery the day before—that he had set up—and how it was carried out in a manner demeaning to Eddie Nash.

Then he told me that these people—who had cut him in for drugs and money—had been killed.

I said, "What do you mean they were *killed*?"

John said, "Well, Greg Diles picked me up on Santa Monica Boulevard in the late morning/early afternoon and took me to Eddie's house."

When they got there, Eddie started flipping through the pages of John's black address book and telling him that he was going to hunt his family down if John didn't tell him who had done it and where they were.

Eddie said, "We need to know how to get to them."

So John explained to Eddie Nash that they had dogs at the Wonderland Avenue house. They also had a gated stairway and that they had to know you or they wouldn't let you in.

John also told Nash that they had a hidden part by the garage, leading to the gate. So if someone looked out the door and saw it was John, they would open the gate—it had a buzzer—and go back into the house.

So that's what they did—they went to the house on Wonderland

Avenue and buzzed John in. The three men went in, and Gregory Diles went with John—he had his arm in a grip—and took John through the doorway and slammed him up against the wall and held a gun to him and said, "Keep your mouth shut, and don't you dare close your eyes."

Gregory Diles held him in the doorway with a big grin on his face. John said something that always stuck in my mind—he said, "Diles would look at me, and he'd roll his eyes, and it was like looking at the shark in *Jaws* when it was ready to eat someone. You know, those cold dead eyes?"

SUSAN LAUNIUS (SURVIVOR OF THE WONDERLAND AVENUE GANG MURDERS): I was laying down on the bed beside Ronnie Launius, watching TV. And it seemed like there was a bunch of people coming in and out.

Then it seemed like people were moving faster.

I don't remember nothing after that.

SHARON HOLMES: John told me that the men had beaten these people to death and ransacked the place—and I'd heard enough. I don't think there's anything anyone can tell you more appalling than that they participated in a murder or were responsible for it.

I asked, "You stood there and watched this?"

John said, "Yes."

I said, "These people were your friends."

And he said, "They were dirt. They were filth. It was them or me."

I didn't really want to know a whole lot more at that point because I felt if he were told that he had to hit someone or beat someone—under threat—he would do it.

It's my understanding that there was blood everywhere and that everybody must have been splattered with it. So I said, "And they let you go because you did this?"

John said, "Yes, but they drove me there and left me there. I had to find my way back to my car looking like I looked."

He ran, and he walked. He said he would've tried to hitchhike—he'd done it before—but not the way he looked, all bloody. He walked back to Santa Monica Boulevard to pick up his car and then drove over to my house.

I don't think I said a whole lot after that.

Then, John went back to the Valley, where Dawn was.

DAWN SCHILLER: When John finally got back—he was gone overnight and came back about midday—I didn't say anything about the murders, of course.

John just looked exhausted. I never saw his eyes so red. They were bloodshot red, as if he'd been crying. I mean, we had been up for days, but his eyes were just brilliant red. And he was in the weirdest mood—just very low. It was different from being mad. I mean, this was something he wouldn't even take out on me, you know?

So he took a couple of Valium and laid down and went to sleep. I was still up. And I watched him toss and turn and then he screamed, "BLOOD! BLOOD! THERE IS SO MUCH BLOOD!"

That was the final gut stabber for me.

The day before, things had been hopeful—we had money and a big pile of coke—there was hope. And then he comes back a day later, and the money's gone, the big pile of coke is gone, and he's screaming about blood.

No, this wasn't good.

CHRIS COX: I don't know why Eddie Nash didn't whack John Holmes; I have no idea. Holmes was the Judas that set Eddie up to be robbed for twelve hundred dollars or whatever it was—and two-and-a-half ounces of dope. I mean, Holmes did it, red-handed, acknowledged and admitted, you know? So, I don't know.

I guess Eddie liked celebrity.

"Think This Will Fuck Up My Fourth of July Weekend?"

LOS ANGELES
1981

BOB SOUZA: It was the start of the Fourth of July weekend and I was in the Robbery/Homicide office until about noon. I wanted to get a jump on the holiday weekend, so I left early. And as I was walking out, somebody said, "Hey Souza, you guys are up for Hollywood this weekend." Meaning me and my partner—Tom Lange—were on call if anyone got murdered in Hollywood.

So I said, "Yeah, there'll probably be a triple ax murder in the Hollywood Hills just to fuck up my Fourth of July weekend."

LINDA MITCHELL: I'm a paramedic with the Los Angeles City Fire Department. On July 1, 1981, just shortly before 4:00 P.M., our dispatcher called and said we had a possible dead body at 8763 Wonderland Avenue.

When we arrived, in bedroom number one, I saw a female. Susan Launius was lying on the floor. She had an obvious head injury. And she had an amputated finger.

It was a fresh amputation.

And there was blood. It was mainly on the wall right behind her head. We couldn't determine what the damage was caused by—but she had a lot of deep wounds on the top of her head.

The patient was semiconscious. Her vital signs were within stable limits. But she was completely incoherent. She was moaning more than anything, and she was mumbling a word occasionally, but it didn't make any sense to me.

We couldn't even get her name out of her. We just had her as Jane Doe.

We examined all the other four victims at the residence and pronounced all of them deceased. I pronounced two of the people; my partner pronounced the other two. We are not the coroner. We couldn't determine the time of death. They were, very obviously, dead, though.

I then transported the victim, Susan Launius, to Cedars-Sinai Hospital.

TOM LANGE: I was out at a friend's home in Agua Dulce, out in Antelope Valley. He had a few acres out there, and several horses, right on the edge of the Angeles Crest Forest. So I was just relaxing, fooling around, when I got called to the phone. It was Lieutenant Ron Lewis from Detective Headquarters who said that we had what appeared to be four victims down in the Laurel Canyon area. Lewis did not give a lot of information on the phone, but he did tell me roughly how to get there.

I knew where Bob was—out by his pool, napping. So I called him and told him to meet me there.

BOB SOUZA: I went home and got in my flotation device—was cruising around the pool and having a couple beers—when the phone started ringing off the hook. It just rang and rang. So I finally got up to answer it, and it was Detective Headquarters, and the voice said, "Where the fuck have you been? We've been trying to get ahold of you since four o'clock!"

I said, "Well, I've been here. I didn't hear the phone."

I forget who it was, but he said, "Well, goddamn, man, we got a big one up in Laurel Canyon. Looks like it could be a quadruple murder."

I figured they were screwing with me, so I said, "Yeah, right," and hung up. But he called right back and said, "Bob, I'm not shittin' you. Lewis is upset, and he wants your ass out there." Ron Lewis was our lieutenant.

I said, "Are you kidding me?"

He says, "Shit no, we got four down in the house and another one in the hospital. It might turn out to be five."

I said, "Oh, shit," got the address, and headed out.

TOM LANGE: Oh boy, it was a madhouse. I'd never been to this area before—it was kinda secluded, up narrow winding mountain roads, right off of Laurel Canyon.

The first thing I saw when I arrived was just a mass of media—trucks and antennas. It was difficult getting into the location, and once I did it was later in the afternoon.

I was met by several of our people—various lab people, print people, photo people, criminalists—a lot of people, mostly milling around.

BOB SOUZA: I mean, this was absolutely incredible. From the bottom of the hill all the way up to this house, all you could see was a string of red lights. I had to get somebody to move their black-and-white so I could get in. I drove on the sidewalk half the way up and parked in a driveway behind somebody's car.

I mean, it was just incredible. The press were already there, and there was a helicopter circling.

Just the typical mess.

TOM LANGE: I was given an initial walk-through by the Robbery-Homicide detectives before Bob Souza got there. They showed me what they had— four victims throughout the house, and blood everywhere. Someone described it as "walking in with a bucket of blood and just throwing it against the walls and over the carpets."

BOB SOUZA: I got out of the car, and Tom Lange's standing there with his sleeves rolled up—it's hot out—and he's walking around out front with his clipboard. I go up to him and ask, "Think this will fuck up my Fourth of July weekend?"

He's trying not to laugh because he's got all these cameras around him.

TOM LANGE [TESTIMONY]: I am a police detective for the City of Los Angeles assigned to the Robbery/Homicide Division. On July 1, 1981 at 6:20 P.M., I arrived at 8763 Wonderland Avenue in Los Angeles. The purpose was to investigate a reported quadruple homicide.

I entered the two-story residence on Wonderland Avenue, went up the stairs—into the front—and observed the first victim, Barbara Richardson, lying facedown in the living room, just off the balcony.

I proceeded to the rear of the house and went up one level—three stairs— to a rear bedroom where I saw the second victim, Ronald Launius, lying in bed. There were extensive wounds on him as well as on Richardson.

They were both apparently dead.

I then went through the kitchen—upstairs to the second level— and entered a bedroom. I observed the third victim, Joy Miller, with severe head trauma. She was apparently dead and on the floor, again near the second-story balcony. I observed the fourth victim, William Deverell, with extensive head injuries, also apparently dead.

Then I was informed that a fifth victim, Susan Launius, had been transported to the hospital and was in surgery.

DAWN SCHILLER: I got this horrible feeling. The bodies are being pulled out of the house on TV, and John's screaming this stuff behind me, and I know we've been there before, you know?

It's bad, bad, bad, bad, bad, bad, bad, bad. It's so bad that you don't want to make the air move because you'll find out more, you know? You know that feeling? If you don't move, nothing else will happen?

SHARON HOLMES: My thought was always that if John could stand there and watch it, if they'd said "hit them," he'd do it—because John was going to try to save number one. John could always manipulate his way out of any situation and turn it to his advantage.

I was devastated. I just couldn't believe—no matter what John had become—that he could be involved in this. I just had to learn to find a way to live with it.

DAWN SCHILLER: At the end of every show—or in the middle—they'd say, "Four killed on Wonderland Avenue. Film at eleven," or "Police find fifth victim alive. Watch the news at eleven o'clock." Teasers, right?

So when John woke up, I said, "Did you see this?"

He didn't say anything; he just sat up. I was still sitting on the edge of the bed. I said, "You were dreaming. . . ."

John asked, "What?"

I said, "You were screaming about blood. . . ."

He said, "Oh, I opened the trunk and hit myself on the nose, and I got a nosebleed." Which was total bullshit; even I didn't believe it—and I believed a lot of his bullshit—because it was not what I had asked. It wasn't what I had meant. I just thought he'd had a nightmare—you know, "Was, like, a monster after you or something?"

But he gave me some lie—which made me feel even worse.

TOM BLAKE: I knew that John Holmes was running around with Eddie Nash and those people even before the murders went down. I heard that John was using dope because the people who were working the porno section of Administrative Vice kept telling me, "Hey, we got word from other snitches that John is really strung out."

I said, "You've got to be kidding me. When I worked with John, he didn't use that stuff."

And they said, "Nope. The guy is strung out. He's trafficking for a guy named Eddie Nash up there in North Hollywood. He's a mule."

I said, "Boy, he really changed since I knew him."

DAWN SCHILLER: There was just a quietness about John. He got real introverted. There was a definite change in him. Dope wasn't on his mind—it had shifted.

We were still at the motel for a couple of days. John was at the window a lot—and he put the dresser in front of the door. He was very paranoid, but he was *always* paranoid—he was always, always, always making sure he wasn't being followed. But when he put the dresser in front of the door, that was a little bit extra.

TOM LANGE: We needed to find Holmes—and Detective Tom Blake was being cagey because ultimately we find out that Blake had Holmes on the string as an informant for many years. Blake is not being obstreperous or anything else; this is his job—he's doing what he's supposed to.

So we say, "Look, you got your porn stuff here, and we got four murders—maybe soon to be five—and we think maybe there's some organized crime involved. This is nasty stuff, and you're gonna have to come around and give him up."

Blake said, "Well, I haven't seen him for a long time, but maybe I can find him."

Well, maybe? Hell, *do it.*

Ultimately Blake makes attempts to find Holmes, and of course, in the end, cooperates with us.

DAWN SCHILLER: I was doing John's fingernails and they kicked the door straight flat down. They did a like 1–2–3 silent—I don't know how many of them—but it went, "BOOM!"

It sounded like a bomb. I had my back to it. I just saw John's eyes go like this, and I jumped into his lap and turned around, and there were guns—three or four at least—and they said, "FREEZE!"

I didn't think it was the police. I thought it was thugs—you know, other dealers or something—because guns were pointed at our heads.

I thought, "This is it. This is the end."

The room was just full of people—plainclothes detectives and uniformed cops—and everybody had weapons, and they were all drawn. I just looked at the guns, and I thought we were dead. Our number's up.

It wasn't until they took us that I realized they were the police. So I thought, "Oh, good. We're not going to die."

SHARON HOLMES: I think, in all honesty, John's soul was no longer his own at that point. He realized that himself—that he had no control of his life—because he had allowed this to happen.

I said to him, "These were your friends." He said, "These people were dirt." The look on my face must have implied what I wanted to say to him—that you can't live with yourself or be normal when you're involved with something like this.

I think John understood what I meant.

DAWN SCHILLER: They got us out of the motel pretty quickly, and immediately separated us. I mean, we didn't speak to each other. John looked over, and all I said was, "I have my dog."

So they brought a little kennel carrier out for Thor, my Chihuahua, and brought him to the station with us. I was put into a room with no windows—just a door—and the window of the door was covered. I sat there for a long time by myself without my dog, and then they came in, asked me what I knew, where I'd been, and I told them I was in a motel.

"Where was John?"

"I don't know. He was out."

"Do you know these people?"

"No, I don't know any names."

SHARON HOLMES: For me, John died that night. All of the good—what little remained—was gone from him. His life had no meaning to him after that; he just did what he had to, to survive.

John had given up his soul.

DAWN SCHILLER: When the cops released me, I told them, "I don't have anywhere to go."

They said, "Well, we'll take you wherever."

I was still in my pajamas. They gave me my dog back. They liked him because Thor had pissed on somebody's locker that they didn't like.

So I said, "Sharon is the only person I know." I was really scared. I didn't want to go to Sharon's; I was ashamed and afraid of her disappointment in me. But I had nobody else to turn to.

SHARON HOLMES: Dawn came to my house because she had nowhere else to go. She said, "John's been taken in for questioning."

DAWN SCHILLER: When Sharon opened the door, I said, "John's been arrested."

She said, "I know."

Then she just looked at me and said, "There's food in the fridge, and the couch is ready."

But Sharon didn't want to talk about it. I think she went back to bed, then got up and went to work. But she came home early, and we got a phone call from John, and he was freaking out. He said there was a threat in jail, and if he stayed any longer, he would be dead. We had to get him out; we had to scrape up money somehow, or he was going to be killed.

So Sharon tells me this, and I'm thinking, "Oh my gosh, what do we do?"

Sharon says, "Well, I don't have any money."

A couple of hours later, we get a call from Big Tom, who says they have John in protective custody. Big Tom said they have John in a position where he's going to give them some information, but that he won't do it until he sees us first.

SHARON HOLMES: Big Tom wanted to know if Dawn and I would meet John somewhere—that he was trying to cut a deal. That's when we ended up at the Bonaventure Hotel.

DAWN SCHILLER: There were cops all over the place at the hotel—they had them at checkpoints. When we arrived, there was someone talking into a walkie-talkie; they'd radio ahead, "They're here."

Then we had an extra escort at the door—and then we went up in the elevator. There were two rooms with an adjoining door; they took us in one room and searched us.

I'd smuggled a favorite bud of pot in to John—that he had saved in Sharon's bathroom. They patted us down, then brought us into the other room. John was there, and he just gave us this big hug—each of us—and was so glad to have us there.

TOM LANGE: At first, it was decided to stroke John Holmes. Well, it's a little late for that—now it's time to clamp down. Holmes is not thinking straight. He's probably terrified; he may've been involved in the murders.

You don't stroke somebody like that—you hard-ass 'em. You don't put them up in the VIP suite of the Bonaventure and Biltmore hotels and have Sharon and Dawn up there with him—ordering Johnny Walker Red and filet mignon day after day, giving him everything he wants.

What are you gonna get outta somebody like that? Nothing. And not only that, but Lieutenant Ron Lewis told us we couldn't interrogate Holmes. He was obviously getting it from somewhere, and we were livid—absolutely *livid*.

DAWN SCHILLER: That first night we didn't really talk about what was going on. We ordered food. John said, "You can order whatever you want." So we ate and watched TV and relaxed. It felt safe, like being at home. It was a real comforting feeling after all that stress. It was healing.

Then we all just went to bed and slept. There was only one California king-size bed. John lay in the middle and Sharon and I laid on either side, which was the first time that we ever did that. I knew he had his arm around me, and I'm pretty sure with Sharon as well. It was something that we all needed.

Then the next morning he told us he needed to talk to us both. He went into the bathroom with Sharon first. They were in there for a while.

SHARON HOLMES: I told John, "Even if this works out, I won't go with you. I've lived with enough upheaval, and there'll never be a life for us— because you can't change."

He cried and begged and pleaded, but for him to be able to stand there and watch these people be slaughtered—I couldn't live with that.

I didn't want to put up with screaming and nightmares—I didn't want to have to relive that kind of experience. It was just the complete opposite to what my life was about.

My life was about *life*—not about death and drugs and porno.

DAWN SCHILLER: John told me he had information that the police wanted, but he said, "I'm not going to do it unless you and Sharon go with me into protective custody."

John said that Sharon had agreed to go into protective custody with him. He said, "This means we're going to have to change our names; we're not going to be able to contact our families. It'll just be you and me and Sharon—and we'll have the dogs, and there won't be any drugs, and things will be like they were."

I said, "Yeah, I'll do it."

There were tears. He was crying, and I was crying because this was definitely serious.

This was a big life change.

SHARON HOLMES: We were at the Bonaventure Hotel Friday, Saturday, and Sunday, and then they moved us to the Biltmore. We were only at the Biltmore for twenty-four hours because they weren't going to give John what he wanted in exchange for rolling over on Eddie Nash—witness protection. I guess they didn't believe he had information.

DAWN SCHILLER: John was going to give them this whole criminal organization, not just the murders—but he wasn't going to go into it with me. John didn't want me to know that kind of stuff. Even though he was abusive—at a fucking drug-crazed, dysfunctional level—I was also his precious little girl he had to protect, you know? Twisted, but that was our relationship.

SHARON HOLMES: John was going to lay out the whole Mafia connection to the pornography industry for them. The money laundering in New York, Miami, and Chicago—he would bring back huge sums of cash. He was acting as a courier—as well as other things.

John specifically talked to the district attorneys about arson. I know he talked about the Israeli/Lebanese Mafia connection with Eddie Nash, and I know he also had a connection to a Chicago family—a hitman who'd graduated to overseeing the porno connections here in Los Angeles. God knows what else he did.

But I guess they didn't believe John had anything.

DAWN SCHILLER: John asked me what the police had asked me, and I said, "They wanted to know about the people that were murdered."

John said, "I went to go get my messages, and when I got back in the car, they put a gun to my head. I was forced to open the door for them," meaning the door at the Wonderland Avenue house. Then he said, "And I had to watch"—and there was such horror on his face—that horrible scene flashed in his face—that I realized this was real.

SHARON HOLMES: I guess the gist of the matter was, they would see about making the arrangements—as long as John testified against Eddie Nash. Whether John was just completely terrified for himself and his family, or just for his family, I don't know.

DAWN SCHILLER: After about three days of this—between the Bonaventure and the Biltmore—John comes in and says, "Well, that's it."

I said, "What do you mean?"

He said that they were letting us go.

I said, "What happened to the protective custody?"

And he said, "They don't want that anymore."

It didn't make sense to me, but the police were packing up and everybody was leaving. So they drove us back to Glendale. And they let us go.

I mean, they weren't holding us, so I thought, "Well, good. He's out of jail, and we don't have to disappear from our families and change our identities."

Then John said, "We've still got to worry about the people that want to kill me. . . ." He said, "We've got to run. We have to run!"

I assumed Sharon was going with us, but John told me that she was going to stay in Glendale and make sure that the animals were okay—and that she would meet us later.

SHARON HOLMES: They drove Dawn and I home. John was with Detective Lange.

TOM LANGE: John and I are in North Hollywood—over here off of Lankersham—and I was gonna drop him off. He had to pick up his car, which had been impounded. I looked at him, and I said, "Listen, there's no tape recorders here. There's nobody else here, John—there's only you and me. Tell me, this son of a bitch Nash, did he do it?"

Holmes says, "Yeah, Nash did it."

He said it with sincerity, and he looked me in the eye when he said it. At that point I knew everything that we thought was true. But it's one thing to get him to say it to me—and it's another to get him to testify.

Then he said, "But you're not gonna hear it from me."

DAWN SCHILLER: They let us go late in the afternoon but by the time we got back to Sharon's it was evening. I dyed John's hair black. Then he and I went out and spray-painted his Chevy Malibu—primer gray with a red top. It was really crappy. It was like so fucking bad. It had big spray-paint drips all over it.

Later that night, we met Sharon at the grocery store parking lot. I don't know if she had to go and get whatever little money she had out of the bank, but she gave it to us.

SHARON HOLMES: When John asked if he could borrow money from me, I said, "I know you're not borrowing it; you need it. I have twelve hundred dollars, and you can have it. Meet me at the Safeway."

When he met me, John asked if they could stay at my house, and I said, "No, but I have the keys to another place where I'll be moving, and you can stay there." So he and Dawn stayed there that night—in the attic. John said he had some things he had to do the next day—which, I found out later from Dawn, meant going directly to Eddie Nash's.

DAWN SCHILLER: John went to get money from Eddie Nash to leave town. He dropped me off at Dupars—the coffee shop down the road from Eddie's on Ventura Boulevard—where I had waited plenty of times before. Word was that there were all these contracts out on us, and the police were probably going to come back after us.

It's "us" because I was hooked back up as his girlfriend—again.

But before John went, he said, "I'm going to tell Eddie that I've got all this information written down and addressed to a bunch of different officials, and if I'm not back in an hour, then it'll be mailed. So if he doesn't let me leave, you know, everything I know will be out."

That's when I realized that all the information John was going to tell the cops about Eddie was real.

TOM LANGE: We definitely felt John Holmes was gonna get whacked because it was evident that he knew too much. But right after we released him, Holmes went straight back to Eddie Nash's—so now, of course, you can't trust him.

DAWN SCHILLER: It was over an hour before John came back. I said, "What happened?"

John said, "Let's get out of here," and he paid my tab, and we went outside. He said, "What time is it?"

I told him it was evening; it was already night.

John said, "I went up there, and Diles put a gun to the back of my head, and he made me get on my knees and beg for my life. And Eddie asked, 'Why the fuck shouldn't I blow your brains out right here? Why should I believe you? How do I know you didn't already tell them everything?' "

So John had to convince them that he hadn't told the cops anything.

TOM LANGE: John probably felt that he'd go up to Nash and say, "Hey, I didn't tell 'em anything. They had me for days, and they have no idea what the hell they're doing, and I didn't tell 'em a damn thing, Eddie."

That's probably why he went up there.

DAWN SCHILLER: John played the bluff—he swore that he had someone waiting for him, that if he wasn't back—and he was already late—he had a bunch of letters addressed to a bunch of different people, ready to go.

I think a thousand dollars is what John was going to ask Eddie for.

So Eddie ended up letting him go after begging for his life, and we were supposed to come back in an hour and check the mailbox. Immediately I said, "Fuck it. There's a bomb. It's a fucking booby trap! We're going to go up, and they're going to get us both! Let's not go!"

TOM LANGE: John Holmes tells me on the one hand that Eddie Nash was the killer, and then he goes up there for dope. This is the type of person you can't trust—once they start talking out of both sides of their mouth.

DAWN SCHILLER: So we went up to Eddie Nash's. John pulled the car up—I got down underneath the blankets in the back—and John jumped out.

I didn't see him walking, but I heard his footsteps. I heard a mailbox open and close, and he came right back into the car, then we took off as fast as hell.

I opened the envelope, and there was five hundred dollars. It was only half of what we asked for.

SHARON HOLMES: John called and said, "We're going to be leaving tonight. Meet me at the Safeway again."

So I met him there. He asked me again if I would go with him, and I said, "No, I won't." Then I went over to Dawn—because I thought he was going to beg and plead again—and said, "I'm sorry I turned my back on him." I hugged her and said, "Take care of yourself, and take care of him the best you can." Then I walked over to my car, watched them leave, and went home.

That was the last I saw of John—for a while.

DAWN SCHILLER: Then we took off. It was really bizarre because once we started getting out of the area we got in a better mood. We just played some music and drove through the desert.

The sun was coming up the next morning—you know that dusky light?

Well, a hawk flew in front of us, and we hit it and killed it. John flipped out. He said that from a hunter's point of view—and John was a hunter—that this was a very bad omen. He got really pale about that; it was like a really bad sign.

There was a long silence after that.

Part 7:
Getting

...he was John Holmes, porno mov...
...es police, he was part of a 1981 multiple murder,
...at remains officially unsolved. Now Holmes'
...says that he came to her and confessed: 'The
...ers... I was involved... I know who did it.'

Defendant John C. Holmes was escorted from courtroom during 1981 legal
proceedings leading to his trial on murder charges. He was acquitted.

Associated Press

Holmes' Confession in Bathtub:
Told Wife of Role in 4 Murders

...ERT W. STEWART, *Times Staff Writer*

the crimes, never told his wife the names
...assailants

Out

FBI agent's arrest
may hurt porn cases

Left page: *left to right:* John Holmes in clipping on Wonderland Avenue murders; Joseph Peraino Jr.'s body at crime scene.

Right page: Veronica Zuraw's body at crime scene; Bruce Ellavsky and Pat Livingston in article on MIPORN.

Method Acting

LOUISVILLE/ST. MATTHEWS/MIAMI
1981

PAT LIVINGSTON: I was ready to strap on my Pat Salamone identity and roll anytime. I had my goatee and my Salamone look. And I was fairly famous then. Or at least well-known, no question about it. So I went in and talked with Joe Griffin and Mike Griffin—they were on the Louisville FBI organized crime squad, and they were aware of MIPORN. So we talked about me doing undercover work.

GORDON MCNEIL: I got a call from the FBI supervisor in Louisville, asking me about using Pat Livingston in an undercover operation up there. I told him, "No way. Don't use this guy in an undercover op. Absolutely, positively, do not use Pat in any undercover capacity."

PAT LIVINGSTON: They had a police chief down in that area—a bad guy that they'd been trying to get for a long time. He had some New York connects, and they thought I would be a good guy for that. So we talked about the possibility of an undercover operation. They had information that people had to pay this guy to open up a lot of businesses. I was told to go to this hick town in Kentucky, get to know him, and see what I could dig up.

So that's what I was assigned to; for the first three weeks I was off on this cop getting pictures and doing surveillance.

VICKIE LIVINGSTON: On November 8, 1981 a local station telecast the MIPORN story on a fictional TV show called *The New FBI*. And Pat was riding this great high from it—just as he was going back undercover.

PAT LIVINGSTON: There was no question that the show was based on the MIPORN story. The names weren't the same, but the situations were. They even had Dick Phinney on the set advising them.

Phinney told me they were specific about it—he told them about funny instances that happened along the way, and you could see them in the story.

I was trying to figure out who was supposed to be Bruce and who was supposed to be me.

VICKIE LIVINGSTON: Nobody ever mentions that TV show, but I think it's important—to understand what happened next.

PAT LIVINGSTON: On November 10, 1981, I pick up my youngest son, Greg, at day care. I got the bureau car, and I drive us down to the Bacon's Department Store. Greg was sleeping, so I left him in the car. I was just knocking around Bacon's, and I'm looking for lamps for the house. So I'm looking around; I got some clothes—picked up some jeans, I forget what else—and put the clothes in a bag. Then I went from that department to the lamp section and was stopped by a security guard.

The security guard came up to me and said, "I need to talk to you."

HOPE JOHNSON (BACON'S SECURITY GUARD): He was dressed really nice. He had a three-piece suit on. He looked kind of foreign to me—I don't know if it was the beard or the mustache—and I thought, "He's gonna steal."

And then he went through the men's department with this big old bag. He picked up a Christian Dior sweater and looked around at the salespeople, but he didn't bother to look at me, probably because I looked like some schoolkid. Then he went to the back of the department, got over to where some jackets were, lowered the bag to the floor, shoved the sweater in there, picked the bag up—and when he picked that bag up, he looked up at me.

Then he walked around an iron railing and put his hand on the door, getting ready to go out.

PAT LIVINGSTON: I was in the back part of the men's shop, near where the coats were. I couldn't have got to the door. There was a metal railing between me and where the door was. You had to walk out by the cash register and out of the building. I wasn't going away from the store. I was still in the store, shopping.

HOPE JOHNSON: He just argued with me all the way up the escalator. I don't like to make a scene, and he kept saying to me over and over, "I don't understand! What is this all about?" He kept after me, over and over.

I said, "We'll talk about it when we get to the office."

But he kept at me so much—all the way up the escalator—that I went ahead and said, "It's about the sweater you put in the bag."

We got to the top of the escalator on the third floor, and I said, "I want the bag." Because I thought he would dump it on me. So I took the bag from him.

PAT LIVINGSTON: When did I give her the bag? Probably somewhere between going up the escalator and going into the office.

HOPE JOHNSON: When we got to the office, both of my bosses were present—Mr. Imhoff and Mr. Nally. They asked him, "Where did this bag come from?" He said he didn't know. He was very excited, very jumpy, nervous.

PAT LIVINGSTON: They asked, "Are these yours?"
I said, "Yeah."
They asked, "Did you pay for them?"
I said, "No."
They asked, "Why haven't you?"
I said, "Well, I haven't paid for them yet. I've got the money here."
They said, "We're gonna have to call the St. Matthews police."
I said, "Fine. Call them."

LARRY POWELL (ST. MATTHEWS POLICE SERGEANT): When I arrived at Bacon's and got to the third floor, I could hear someone saying, "There's been a big mistake here," outside the office door.

When I walked into the office, he stopped arguing, and Hope Johnson told me what happened. I asked him for his driver's license, and he handed me a Kentucky operator's license with the name Patrick Salamone and his picture on it. He had a South American type of look to him—Ecuadorean or something, with that Fu Manchu goatee.

ED HORNING (ST. MATTHEWS ATTORNEY): That's where Pat screwed up big-time, by not having his Pat Livingston, FBI agent credentials on him. Instead he showed them his Pat Salamone, Florida scumbag license.

PAT LIVINGSTON: When they asked, "Who are you?" I pulled out my wallet and gave them my Salamone license. I knew I had the Livingston license on me, but I went through all the actions of being Salamone. I think I just reacted.

Livingston came in, but I didn't have any way of bringing him to the forefront. I had a license to show I was Livingston, but I chose to identify myself as Salamone.

I guess I *was* Salamone.

ED HORNING: That major stumble by Pat started the whole roll of dominoes tumbling. I think if the St. Matthews Police realized he was an FBI agent from the start, they would've said, "No, we're not gonna do this. We're not arresting an FBI agent."

LARRY POWELL: I filled out the offense report first. Then I walked over to him and told him he was under arrest for "theft by unlawful taking" and read him his rights. I had him stand up, turn around, searched him, and then I put the handcuffs on him.

PAT LIVINGSTON: I said, "Look, I've got my son in the car."

LARRY POWELL: I saw a little boy sleeping on the front seat of a red Mercury. Salamone was still handcuffed when I asked him, "Why did you leave this little boy out here?"

He says, "He was asleep, and I didn't want to wake him up."

I says, "What if he woke up, and there's nobody here? He could try to get out of the car, scared to death."

He says, "I don't know."

PAT LIVINGSTON: I had never left Gregory in the car before. That is bizarre in and of itself. It was irrational, illogical. I had a myriad of questions going on in my head about what I was doing and why I was doing it: Why did I leave Gregory in the car? Why did I find myself in that position? Why did I identify myself as Salamone? Why didn't I have my FBI credentials on me? Why did I leave the house with Gregory in the first place? It was a bureau car. I shouldn't have had Gregory there to begin with.

LARRY POWELL: He didn't mention anything about his other son until we got to the station. He was looking at his watch and says, "I got another son who's gonna be home in a little while." He said his wife was at school, and he didn't know if he could get ahold of her. I asked about neighbors; and he said there was someone who could go over and intercept the boy when he got off the school bus.

VICKIE LIVINGSTON: The door was open, and there were cars in the driveway. I was a wreck because I didn't know where the kids were. The first thing that came to my mind was that one of those mob guys had come and hit Pat and taken the kids. I called my sister, and she didn't know where they were. Then Michael called from across the street and said, "Mom, we're over here." He said a policeman brought Gregory home.

MICHAEL GRIFFIN (FBI SPECIAL AGENT): It was approximately 5:00 P.M., and we were preparing to go to a going-away party for an agent being transferred—when I was notified that I had a phone call.

It was Pat Livingston. He wanted to know if I was sitting down. I said no. He said, *"Sit down,"* and I sat down. Then he said that he had been arrested for shoplifting and was currently being held at the St. Matthews Police Department.

I was waiting for the punchline. I asked, "Are you *joking?"*

He said, "No, I'm not."

I asked him, "Did you tell the policeman who you work for?"

He said, "No, I haven't."

I said, "Well, who do they think you are?"

He said, "I told them my name was Pat Salamone."

After that I spoke to the arresting police officer.

LARRY POWELL: Salamone handed me the phone and said, "Here, he wants to talk to you."

So I take the phone and say, "Yes?"

The guy on the other end says, "Can you tell me—just briefly—what happened?"

I says, "A Bacon's security guard caught him leaving the store without paying for merchandise. It was a hundred-and-fifty-seven dollars, and they caught him trying to go out the door with it. So we placed him under arrest, and we're taking him down to be booked at the Hall of Justice."

The guy on the other end of the phone says, "My name is Agent Michael Griffin with the FBI, and the man you have is an FBI agent, and he'd like to give you some more information."

He said, "Follow your normal procedures." They wanted it by the book.

MICHAEL GRIFFIN: I asked the officer what his procedures would be after the booking at the St. Matthews Police Department. He said he would take him downtown to the county lockup.

PAT LIVINGSTON: I guess I expected it to end there, but they sent me to Johnson County Jail. The cop took me downtown, didn't handcuff me. Told me about other agents he knew. Kind of bizarre. Almost like we were going down to the jail to interview a prisoner or something.

FBI Agents Michael Griffin and Tom McQuade were already at the jail when I came in. I went through the booking process, and they said, "Look, we'll get you out of here as quick as we can. Meet us at over at—Jolly's or Lolly's, a cop bar about a block or two away—when you get out."

VICKIE LIVINGSTON: I got the kids back. They didn't know what in the world was going on. I kept saying, "Are you sure a policeman brought Gregory home?" But Gregory didn't have any clue about what was going on. I hung in there, in limbo, until Pat called at about 9:30 P.M. He said he had a problem. I don't think he told me what it was until he got home.

He was just a basket case. He did admit he'd been arrested, but kept saying, "It's a big mistake. It's a big mistake."

I said to him, "I hope to God that this isn't true."

He said, "You know it's not true. You know I wouldn't do something like that."

When I saw in the papers the next day what the items were—designer jeans, and that type of thing—I knew he did it.

ED HORNING: I didn't know Pat. The first I heard about him was when I picked up the local paper, and it said that an FBI agent had been arrested at Bacon's for shoplifting. I thought, "What a buffoon."

BILL BROWN: Frankly, it did not surprise me that Pat had been caught shoplifting because I knew something weird was going to happen to him. I mean, I could see the excitement—the rush of being undercover again in Louisville—was just consuming him.

BRUCE ELLAVSKY: I was working out when I heard that Pat had been arrested.

I wasn't totally shocked, to tell you the truth. Did I want to go up there and ask, "What the hell is going on?" Not really. There was nothing I could add. And Pat didn't go out of his way looking for my help. I don't think there was anything I really could have done for him.

FRED SCHWARTZ: I said, "Oh shit, Salamone got us again." Pat's arrest didn't shock me as much as trouble me. I certainly didn't anticipate the effect it would have on the case. I thought that Pat would get out of it because I thought Pat could get out of virtually anything he wanted. I thought he'd talk his way out of it somehow.

MARCELLA COHEN: There is no way we could ever have anticipated what happened with Special Agent Patrick Livingston in Kentucky with regards to the shoplifting. It was extraordinary. And of course we had to notify the court, and we did.

ED HORNING: If I was a defense attorney in the MIPORN case, and I heard about Pat's shoplifting charges, I would have thought I'd just won the lottery.

PAT LIVINGSTON: I didn't want to admit that I did it. I was embarrassed because I screwed up good cases that the bureau had made in MIPORN. The fact that I was arrested for shoplifting made it more difficult to prosecute them. As an agent, you can't embarrass the bureau—that's the cardinal rule. The cardinal sin is to embarrass the bureau. It shouldn't be that way, but the bureau is the bureau.

On the Lam

LAS VEGAS/MONTANA/ARIZONA/MISSISSIPPI/MIAMI
1981

DAWN SCHILLER: It was my understanding that Sharon was going to meet up with us later. I had no idea that she said no or that she was not going into protective custody with us, either. John had told me she said, "Yeah." So I thought, "Oh, we're working toward getting better. There's no drugs; we're leaving the area that caused us all this shit." And John was holding my hand again; he was being romantic.

Then we hit the hawk.

SHARON HOLMES: John was the youngest of four children. He grew up in rural farm country in Ohio. His father was an alcoholic, and whenever John talked about him it was about arguments and yelling, and his father falling across beds and vomiting all over the kids.

His parents separated when John was three or four. John had two older brothers and an older sister.

Mary, the mother, had not worked—she was a housewife—so John, his mother, sister, and two brothers moved into a project in Columbus, Ohio, and became a welfare family. They moved in with another woman who had two children—both boys—that was in the same predicament.

They lived there until John was about seven.

DAWN SCHILLER: The first place we stopped was Las Vegas. John went into the casino while I waited in the car because I wasn't old enough to gamble yet, and we didn't want to take any chances.

So John went in—I don't remember if it was the Aladdin or the Stardust—and he came back really quick and was scared to death, and I'm like, "What's the matter?"

He told me a very scary person had sat down next to him at the roulette table, and I was led to believe that it was one of the people who had a contract out on him.

SHARON HOLMES: Dawn said that John got in the car—he was white as a sheet and trembling—and they got the hell out of there.

I have no idea who this man was, but John always called him "H the P" after "Harry the Pick."

John came home one day and said, "This is a poker buddy of mine—I want you to hear his voice." I have never heard a more chilling voice on an answering machine in my life.

I mean, talk about the "Godfather"—it was that type of thing. An ice pick, that was his choice of weapon.

John said, "Harry came from the Chicago mob, and he's out here supervising the legitimate laundering of money from various interests of theirs."

I mean, the voice on the telephone was enough to scare the shit out of you.

DAWN SCHILLER: "H the P"? I'm not going to say that. I'm not saying it. What did Sharon say?

SHARON HOLMES: John had an early introduction to pornography at about the age of between four and a half and five. He was home with the chicken pox, and when his mom came home from working a night shift she noticed this little collection of boys and girls underneath their first-floor living room window.

When Mary finally got closer, she realized that John had a nudie magazine, and he was in the window, showing the centerfolds to the four- and five-year-olds. They were all laughing and hamming it up, until mama got into the house, grabbed the magazine, and paddled his fanny with it.

DAWN SCHILLER: We decided to go stay with John's sister in Montana because it was safe there. It was in the woods, and it was with family. Maybe we could get a fresh start. So we went to Montana via Utah; we had money for motels then. John wasn't thieving yet—he had become the person that I knew in the beginning.

It seemed like we were trying to heal a bunch of bad stuff that had happened between us, that was all supposedly because of dope.

SHARON HOLMES: John was eight or nine when his mom remarried Harold—who worked for the phone company as a lineman—and they moved from Columbus to a rural area in Ohio called Pataskala.

Harold had bought Mary her own house. I think it was probably about two years later that David—John's half brother—was born. Harold must have been in his late thirties or early forties. He was about twenty years older than Mary and he was really good to the kids until David came along.

David was his, and these other four children weren't. So it became, "I don't have to be nice anymore."

DAWN SCHILLER: Was John's sister happy to see him? Not really. She probably just wondered how long we were going to freeload off her. She had a small apartment, a job, hadn't seen her brother in years, and hadn't heard good things about him.

SHARON HOLMES: John was the youngest and probably the most insecure of the four of them. He was still wetting the bed when he was seven. In the projects, the three boys had slept together in the same bed. Then suddenly everybody had a room of their own, and they thought it was wonderful. John discovered the woods and the stream and the fishing and frogging, and he was really happy there—until David came along. Then his stepfather turned on all four of the kids. You know, "These are your kids, and I'll tolerate them—but David is mine."

DAWN SCHILLER: We stayed with John's sister for about a week—just kind of laid around on the couch and fattened up, ate, and slept. Then we got a call from his mother in Ohio saying that the FBI had been there looking for us and that we were listed as armed and drug-crazed.

We didn't have a weapon, and we hadn't been on dope since we left, you know?

So I said, "Let's go to Florida and try to make a new life. It's like, you know, far enough away, and it used to be my old stomping ground. It's a good place."

John thought, "Why not?"

SHARON HOLMES: Because John was the youngest, he took the brunt of Harold's anger. He was the one that was always getting beat up because he wasn't smart enough to get out of the house when he saw Harold coming. The other boys were older, so they were in junior high school and high school when John was still in elementary school.

DAWN SCHILLER: After we left Montana, John got pulled over for speeding. I swear to God, I thought we were busted. We didn't want to swallow, waiting for the cop to come back from checking the license. But it turned out it was okay—I guess we weren't on the computer yet—and the cop just gave us a warning. He didn't even give us a ticket, just sent us on our way.

SHARON HOLMES: When David was born he became the center of Mom and Dad's attention. Mom was good to all of their children, but an infant requires a lot more of her attention. And of course Harold, being older, thought the baby was great—you know, "This is mine, but I'm not going to change those diapers or feed him."

As David got older and began to walk and talk, John—being the closest in age to him—got tattled on. The others were smart enough to stay away from home as much as they could. It wasn't a tremendously happy household.

DAWN SCHILLER: We drove through Arizona and Wyoming. We stopped at Custer's Last Stand, and we saw the Grand Canyon and Scottsdale or Flagstaff where there's that Giant-Meteor-Crater-thing. We, like, got a magnet and picked up pieces of the meteorite. Then we went to the Petrified Forest and stole a bunch of petrified trees in our socks.

We were having fun—doing tourist stuff—but when we hit Oklahoma we started to get low on cash, so we slept in the car as much as we could. Then, right around Mississippi, John started creeping around and breaking into cars again.

He came back one night with a gun. So we did have a gun—I think it was a .38—and we got some cash that way. I'm not sure about any jewelry, but I remember camera equipment and pawning it in the next town or maybe the next state.

SHARON HOLMES: When Mary and the kids were on their own, mealtime had always been a big event—everybody talked about what their day had been like. But at Harold's table you kept your mouth shut. Mom and Dad could talk, but nobody else could put in their two cents' worth. Things escalated when John reached his teenage years, and Harold was backhanding him—off a chair or across the room.

DAWN SCHILLER: We finally got to Florida—Hollover Beach and Collins Avenue is where I grew up for awhile—and we stopped at a place called the Fountainhead Hotel. We had enough money to pay for a couple of nights, but then we started to run out. John is a great one to befriend people and shoot the shit with them, so we got to be friends with Big Rosie, the manager, and she hired me as a maid. Her boyfriend, the handyman, put John to work on a couple of things, but they didn't really need him. So Big Rosie's boyfriend got John a job working construction on another hotel down the road.

SHARON HOLMES: When John was sixteen, his half brother, David, snitched on him. Daddy comes home and David says, "John did this!" Guess who got beat?

Harold threw John down the stairs and came after him.

Even though John only weighed 110 pounds, he was six feet tall, so when he got up off the floor he decked Harold. And John told Harold straight out—as his mom was coming through the door—"You touch me again, and I'll kill you." John went into the army soon after that.

DAWN SCHILLER: We changed our names. I was still Dawn, but John was now "John Curtis." And he was really nice at first. John was a really good artist, and he would sit and draw pictures of me or my dog. And he would buy me a strand of garnets—which is my birthstone. It was really nice.

But then his paranoia and possessiveness started coming back. He started saying, "We're never going to get out of here unless we get more money!"

I guess he noticed that there were girls on the beach working as hookers, and I was oblivious to that. Don't ask me why—there was just a coping blindness that I had. Then he started telling me I needed to go out there.

I said, "No, please, I don't want to!"

John got really pushy, and I started to get scared. He would withhold his affection and act hurt, you know? He would manipulate me in that way—I'm not doing it, so I'm hurting him.

He'd say, "I'll keep an eye on you at all times—it will be real easy."

There was a couple of X-rated motels across the street. I was just freaked out because I didn't want anybody at the hotel to know that I did that. I was totally embarrassed, you know?

So here I am carrying tons of shame and humiliation—and John dresses me up in a bikini top and some shorts and tells me to go out.

I just did it, you know, because we were at that eggshell stage again—where I didn't want to do anything to make him hit me. Of course, he was going to hit me whether I did it or not.

SHARON HOLMES: After the fight with Harold, John escaped out the back door—with his mom running after him—and spent two days roaming the woods. Harold always went to his mother's on Sundays, while Mary and the kids all went to church. So John waited until Harold had left, and then he went to his mother and said, "I'm going into the army. I need you to sign me in. I'm not going to stay in this house, or I will kill him."

Mary felt that was the lesser of two evils and signed him into the army. Two weeks later John was in boot camp, and from there he was sent right to Germany. He was in the Signal Corps. Most of the time he was in Nuremberg—almost the full three years.

DAWN SCHILLER: I would just walk on the beach and get approached by men—it was no problem. I think it was fifty bucks for sex, and anything below that was, like, twenty bucks. The clients were nice—they weren't scary—they weren't going to kill me. I could handle them, and sometimes it was just more pleasant to be with them than it was to be with John.

SHARON HOLMES: When John came back from the service he spent about ten days in Ohio, and that was enough. Harold was civil to him because when John came back, he was bigger, and it was like, "We can't harass this young man now because maybe he will kill us."

That was all John needed, to see his mom and say, "I'm going to California." And he did. He'd been in California for probably a year when we met.

DAWN SCHILLER: My turning tricks probably lasted a good two weeks. When I would come back, that's when the bad times would start—because John was extremely possessive and jealous. He'd say, "Was that all the money? Why did you take extra long? I was watching you—I saw you with two men!" Which was total bullshit, but I would freeze up in panic, knowing where this line of questioning was going—to me getting hit.

He would drag me into the bathroom and fill up the tub with hot water and scrub me down, all the while telling me I was a filthy whore. *I* was the whore. *I* was the slut. *I* was the dirty whore that just wanted it and asked for it. While I'm being scrubbed in the bathtub, you know?

He had a deep, deep, deep illness. Very twisted. A very twisted man.

SHARON HOLMES: John had the drive for fame. But he also had an extremely low sense of self-esteem. That never changed. He loved the adulation because it didn't matter what he was famous for—it built up his ego, what little there was of it. He really felt he had nothing else to give besides his unique attribute, which is kind of a sad reflection.

DAWN SCHILLER: When I finally refused to go out on the beach—and John didn't have enough patience to manipulate me in any other way—he hit me.

That was the first time he hit me since we'd left Los Angeles. The door of our room was ajar, and I grabbed the opportunity and ran. I ran down the stairs into the back by the pool, in front of the snack bar, "Joe's," which was run by an Italian guy who always had the best sausages and spaghetti sauces. We ate breakfast with the people from the snack bar every day.

But John caught ahold of me by my hair and yanked me down in front of the snack bar, jumped on me, and pummeled the hell out of me.

He just exploded. Everybody just watched, and they couldn't believe that this was the same mild-mannered, really nice, courteous person they knew.

Then John just yanked me back up and dragged me back to the room, where he gave me another couple of blows. Then he flung me onto the bed and told me to shut up.

SHARON HOLMES: I don't think John ever felt comfortable with who he was and what his background was. I think fame gave him a false sense of security, like, "Well, I must be good if all these people think I am."

And yet he knew it wasn't really what he wanted to do—it was what he felt he *had* to do. He felt there was nothing else he *could* do. It would involve too much time to educate himself or really get into something else. Pornography was fast fame and fortune, as far as John was concerned.

DAWN SCHILLER: John went to work the next morning, as usual, and there was a knock at the door right after he left. It was Big Rosie and a couple of other people who lived there. They said, "Pack your bags. Grab your dog; you're out of here."

I said, "Where am I going to go?"

This one chick, Louise, was a stripper, and she'd just got her house from a divorce settlement. She also had a little girl, Heather, about five years old. Big Rosie says, "You're going to go with Louise and Heather, and you're going to watch Heather while Louise is at work."

SHARON HOLMES: I was John's safe house—and the only person he could be himself with, could show his vulnerability and his low self-esteem. I don't think anyone else was aware of it because John had developed a different persona. He was like, "This is JOHN HOLMES, who I have created." That is the side people saw, but they didn't know about his capabilities, you know, as far as what he could do artistically—other than what was artistically pornographic.

TOM LANGE: Frank Tomlinson, who's another outstanding investigator, had a thought. Dawn is from the Portland, Oregon, area, and she'd disappeared with John. So Frank gets in touch with Dawn's brother in Oregon to see if he's heard anything—and uses the tactic that Dawn's life is in jeopardy—she's with John Holmes, and the cops are gonna kill him, or Nash is gonna kill him, or a hired killer is gonna kill him—so help your sister, that type of a thing. The brother ends up telling Frank that she's down in Florida, and Frank and I go down there and hook up with Florida Metro-Dade cops.

322 The Other Hollywood

DAWN SCHILLER: I stayed at Louise's maybe a week. When I got there, I called my mother, and I said, "I'm finally away." I told her I had the gun, and I gave her the number where I was at. It was such a relief finally being able to contact my family again; it was something I needed to do.

She said, "Are you okay? Don't go back to him. Don't go back to him no more!"

I said, "No, I won't, and I love you, too. I'm just going to work here for a while. I don't think John knows where I'm at."

TOM LANGE: Dawn's brother told us that her roommate, Louise, was dancing at an all-night strip club. I don't drink anymore, but I used to. Frank never did; he's a born-again Christian.

So we were staked out on a bar on Eighth Street and Le June where Louise worked as a stripper. The plan was to identify her, go outside where Metro-Dade was waiting, and follow her home—so we could find out where Dawn was staying. It sounded great.

We go in the bar—and we look like cops to begin with—so I told Frank, "You gotta order a beer or something or they're gonna look at you funny." So he does, and he just sat there and glared at it. Frank never took a sip. I ended up getting a 7-Up or something.

DAWN SCHILLER: A few days after that, I got a call, and it was John. I don't know how he got that number, but he did. He was crying, and he said he was so sorry—you know, the same thing. He's so sorry, he knows what he did was wrong, and he doesn't blame me if I never forgive him.

He was giving me this ploy, which he had really never done before. He understands if I don't want to be with him, but could he just see my face one more time?

I was crying, too. I said, "But you promised you would never hit me again. You broke your promise!"

He said, "Please, please just let me see your face one more time. That's all I ask of you. I won't ask you anything ever again."

I just said, "No." A really strong, very powerful "No." I had never said no to him before—and I meant it, you know? I wasn't going to give him that. I wasn't going to give him any more parts of me. I think he said something like, "Well, please think about it. I'll call you later."

I said, "No, John. I won't."

TOM LANGE: We identify Louise, the stripper, but it's now 2:05 A.M. I realize, "This is an after-hours place—wait until the cops find out about this." Then we find out bars in Miami don't close; they're open all night long. Finally, around 5:00 in the morning, Louise leaves, and we follow her, pat her down, one thing leads to another—and she gives us Dawn.

The brother met us down there.

DAWN SCHILLER: About a week after I talk to John, Louise let me know my brother was on the phone.

I got on the phone, and he goes, "Hey, what's up?"

I said, "Hey, not much." I was really happy to hear his voice. I go, "Where are you? Did Mom tell you that I left John, that I'm in Florida?"

He says, "Yeah. I'm in Florida, too." We grew up in Florida, so this was not unusual. My brother was always running away. So he says, "Yeah, I've got a rental car."

I said, "How did you get a rental car?"

He goes, "Oh, one of my friends had a credit card. Let's have a beer, you know, and like, talk. I haven't seen you in a couple of years. What's been going on with John and stuff? I'm just around the corner from you. Tell me your address."

I said, "Well, I'm not with John anymore, and I hope everybody leaves me alone. I took his gun, and I'm not with him, so there's no reason for anybody to want to be after me anymore."

I gave him the address, and he says, "I'll be there to pick you up in a few minutes."

So very quickly—he pulls up in this white rental car. He says, "Oh, I've got a six-pack. Come on, let's go talk. I know this park over here." Which is not suspicious to me because it used to be his stomping ground. So we go to pull into this park, and just as we're pulling in, he says, "I've got something to tell you."

I said, "What?"

He says, "Well, the cops are waiting for you here."

I just about blew. I started screaming and crying and going, "WHAT THE FUCK! I'M NOT TALKING TO NO FUCKING COPS!" Because here I was still under the impression that they took away our protection, that they did us a dirty deed. I said, "But John gave them all the information, and they stabbed us in the back!"

TOM LANGE: The brother approaches Dawn on our behalf and says, "Listen, Tomlinson and Lange are here, and they need to talk to you."

DAWN SCHILLER: My brother said, "No, no, no, you don't understand, they just want to know where John is."

I said, "Well, you know, that's the last thing that I want to do—I'm not going to rat on him. Let it be whatever—but I don't want no hand in it. I won't fucking do it. Do you know I have a gun in my purse?"

He said, "What the fuck?"

I said, "I don't want to go to jail. I didn't do anything. I've got this for my protection."

While all this is being said, the car is stopped, and Detectives Tom Lange and Frank Tomlinson are standing there. There was even a local cop with them.

TOM LANGE: So we meet Dawn in the park and tell her she's in jeopardy.

DAWN SCHILLER: We got out, and I was still crying, and I'm like, "I can't believe you did this to me! I can't believe you did this to me!"

My brother told them, "Just a minute," and he came over, and he put his arm around me and walked me down to the water. He said, "Look, there's a lot of bad people out there who still want you."

I said, "But I'm not with John anymore!"

He said, "Yeah, but they're real close to getting him, and the best thing you can do is turn him in because that will get the heat off."

He said, "These people are here to protect you. They don't want you; they just want to know where John is, and he'll be safer in jail."

And so I conceded to that because it made sense, you know?

TOM LANGE: Dawn was even younger than I thought.

DAWN SCHILLER: I said, "Yeah, I'll tell them where he is. I've got the address in my purse." I had the card for the Fountainhead Hotel in my purse, so I flopped down on the parking lot floor, and I was crying and stuff. The gun is, like, right on top of this hippie purse, and I go, "Oh yeah, by the way, I've got his gun."

I just plopped it out and put it on the pavement, and they kind of took steps back, and reached their hands over their weapons—they didn't know what the fuck.

But I'm oblivious to that shit. I was just unloading my purse. That was, like, one of my happiest memories: "Scared you—ha-ha!"

TOM LANGE: Dawn gives John up, and he's at a flophouse—right over on the Ocean and Collins Avenue, in the North Beach area.

DAWN SCHILLER: I found the card, and I said, "He's here. He's not armed; I have his gun. He's working at this place, and these are his hours. He's pretty calm right now, from when I talked to him last. You know, he'll probably offer you a cup of coffee. But you've got to promise me one thing. . . ."

They asked, "What?"

I said, "After you have him, call me, and let me know if he's all right, if you got him all right." Because they were telling me that there were people that were really close to getting him, and I was nervous that he was going to be killed any second. So they promised me they would do that.

TOM LANGE: We went in there, and I grabbed Holmes and laid him out and cuffed him. He had dyed his hair and tried to alter his appearance. He didn't fight us. He was cooperative; he kinda knew we were coming and said something to the effect of, "I'm glad it's you—this is finally over."

FRANK TOMLINSON (LAPD DETECTIVE): Detective Lange and myself were present when Mr. Holmes was arrested. He was transported to a facility to await booking at the county jail in Miami, so at that facility we caught up with him and had a brief conversation.

After that, Mr. Holmes made the statement that he knew what had happened at the house on Wonderland Avenue. He then stated that he would have to think about what he wanted to do and that he would let us know whether or not he was going to tell us what happened.

TOM LANGE: We brought him back to Los Angeles to be prosecuted.

Don't Embarrass the Bureau

LOUISVILLE/MIAMI
1982

VICKIE LIVINGSTON: Pat had told me he didn't want his parents to know he'd been arrested. He thought it would all be resolved, and they would never have to know.

He couldn't even believe it himself. Pat was in shock. He was just out of it.

MIAMI HERALD, FEBRUARY 20, 1982: FBI AGENT'S ARREST MAY HURT PORN CASES: "In a move that may jeopardize its case against several accused pornographers, the U.S. Justice Department has acknowledged that one of the FBI undercover agents who ran Operation MIPORN has been arrested for shoplifting."

PAT LIVINGSTON: I'd spent the night at my girlfriend's house. I was in North Miami, coming down the I-95, when I first heard it on the news. Did they mention my name? Damn right they did. So I got off at 103rd and picked up a newspaper at a 7-Eleven. I was hoping my dad wouldn't read it.

MIAMI HERALD, FEBRUARY 20, 1982: FBI AGENT'S ARREST MAY HURT PORN CASES: "The arrest of Agent Pat Livingston, after the investigation concluded, but before all the cases were tried, was disclosed in a letter sent to U.S. District Judge Eugene Spellman by Fred Schwartz, an attorney with the Justice Department's Organized Crime Task Force."

NANCY LIVINGSTON (PAT'S SISTER): My father read it in the paper. He was just crushed. He said, "Nancy, sit down. I have something to tell you. It's about your brother."

I said, "I already know."

MIAMI HERALD, FEBRUARY 20, 1982: FBI AGENT'S ARREST MAY HURT PORN CASES: "According to the letter, Livingston was arrested on a felony shoplifting charge in November after he allegedly tried to remove more than a hundred dollars' worth of clothing from a department store."

NANCY LIVINGSTON: I told my father that Vickie had told me, but I also told him, "Pat was gonna kill Vickie if she told you." I said, "Pat wanted to tell you himself, but he kept putting it off. It wasn't that he wanted you to find out this way. He wanted to tell you himself—in person—but he couldn't."

VICKIE LIVINGSTON: Pat's parents had no idea he was in Miami, and he didn't want them to know.

PAT LIVINGSTON: After I read the newspaper, I went to Bill Kelly's house. Kelly and Dick Phinney were there. There was a hearing going on. I didn't know where I was going. God, I was scared. Scared and anxious, wondering should I call my father now, before he reads the article? Or should I take a chance that he hasn't read the article?

NANCY LIVINGSTON: That night my father went to the hospital. He was perfectly awake and coherent; he was in pain, but he was talking as we were driving. But when they did their EKGs, we discovered that he had had a mild heart attack.

PAT LIVINGSTON: From Bill Kelly's, I went to Bill Brown's house in Coconut Grove. I jogged and ran down Old Cutler Road—ten miles, maybe—to Bill Brown's house. Then I drove back to Louisville.

Nancy called me the next day. She said it was serious with Dad. I didn't get back down to Miami until Monday.

VICKIE LIVINGSTON: Pat's parents read the paper on a Saturday morning and on Sunday night his dad was already having chest pains. They took him to the hospital Sunday night, and he had a massive heart attack.

I came home from school at about nine o'clock—the kids were already in bed—and Pat was sitting on the side of the bed like he was in a trance or something.

I said, "What in the world is the matter with you?"

He said, "I just got a phone call." I thought he said it was about *my* dad, and I started to get really upset. But then he said, "No, it's not your dad, its mine."

NANCY LIVINGSTON: Pat went alone to see my father. He told him exactly what was going on, but I don't know what was said.

PAT LIVINGSTON: My dad couldn't talk. God, that was devastating. I had so much I wanted to say. He had eye movement, his lips moved, he understood, but he couldn't talk.

So I tried to say the things that would bring him back. I tried to assure him that everything was okay with me—that there was no problem, that things were going to work out fine.

NANCY LIVINGSTON: All Pat said when he came out is that Dad understood everything. From that time on, Dad got progressively worse.

VICKIE LIVINGSTON: He died about ten days later.

PAT LIVINGSTON: I was at the hospital when he died. He was on strictly life support, pacemaker, tubes. We could see he was dead already. It was a decision of shutting down or keeping him alive.

BILL BROWN: I went to the funeral. It was unbelievably sad. I mean, Pat was pretending; there was not one ounce of genuine emotion at that funeral. That was such a personal tragedy for Pat. I mean, there was just no way anything was going to get through to his insides at that point. He was acting like a host at a cocktail party.

PAT LIVINGSTON: I really tried to avoid thinking about whether I had caused my father's death or not—but the reality was there. He had read about it in the paper on Saturday, had the brief heart attack Sunday and the serious heart attack Monday.

I kind of blocked it out. I just wasn't ready for it.

BILL BROWN: Pat was like a piece of cast iron now. I mean, he didn't tell the girl, who he was making love to, that his father died. When she found out, she said to Pat, "You mean your father died, and you didn't tell me?"

Pat was like, "Yeah, he died last month."

It was striking to me how a person could be so emotionless. Of course, the reality was he was dying inside.

ED HORNING: I read Pat had been caught shoplifting, but I didn't give it a second thought until I got the phone call. Pat was already out of jail—the FBI had already provided a good lawyer to represent him. But then an FBI agent I had gone to college with called and said, "This phone call did not take place. Do you know about Pat Livingston? The agent that was arrested for shoplifting?"

I said, "Yeah."

He said, "He needs a lawyer—a *real* lawyer—somebody who can take care of him, who can defend him on this, because the bureau's gonna push him in front of the bus."

I said, "He's got a lawyer."

My friend said, "No, he's gonna get fucked by the bureau. He's gonna get *fucked*. Will you talk to him? Can you help him?"

ED SHARP (FBI SPECIAL AGENT): I was the first one who decided to fire Pat from the bureau. Did I have any qualms? No. The deciding factors were his attitude at the time and the fact that he didn't use good common sense; he had his son locked in the car while he was shoplifting. His judgment was poor; he got arrested for a crime. As an agent—not a support employee—he'd had better training than that.

That he lied initially—that didn't help him.

ED HORNING: I scheduled an appointment to meet Pat. This guy pulls up in this Datsun 280Z in front of my office, and he looks like a pimp. He had on a sport coat and one of those gold chains with a medallion. He had a goatee. My impression of the FBI was the kind of agents you'd see on TV. So I thought, "This can't be Pat."

But it was.

Even after I got the charges dropped, Pat was still really stressed out, so I recommended he go see a doctor to get some help.

FRED SCHWARTZ: Yelvington and Blasingame in Louisville were both old-line J. Edgar Hoover types—who were only concerned that Pat lied to them—and didn't want to look at the underlying reasons.

I think that philosophy eventually carried away the bureau. It got to the point, I was told, that there were two letters on the director's desk—one that recommended keeping Pat—and helping him—and one that recommended firing him. And the director went with the old-line guy and fired him.

PAT LIVINGSTON: On May 12, 1982, Michael Griffin said, "Let's go up and see Blasingame."

Blasingame was sitting there like a little Cheshire cat stuffed into his three-piece suit. And Griffin says, "Sit down on the couch."

Blasingame just handed me a letter. Being the bright agent I am, I read it and figured out I was fucking fired.

***MIAMI HERALD*, MAY 15, 1982: FBI BOOTS OUT MIPORN UNDERCOVER AGENT:** "Celebrated FBI agent Patrick Livingston, who says he was torn apart emotionally by his dual life as a high-rolling undercover pornographer, has been fired by the FBI."

ED HORNING: Here's a clean-cut, all-American guy who's on a golf scholarship to the University of Florida and ends up in the FBI—and they turn his whole world upside down.

They put him in a pink Cadillac with a bunch of pimps, take him away from his wife and two kids, and make him hang around with sleazeballs who make porno movies.

And then when he gets jammed up in Louisville they fire him. It's amazing. I've never seen anything like it.

BILL BROWN: When Pat was suspended by the FBI, I went to them and accused them of shooting their wounded. Pat was wounded, and they were terminating him—because he embarrassed them.

I mean, Pat was the lead person that was going to testify in the MIPORN cases. Now his credibility was on the line—and the FBI's credibility was on the line.

ED SHARP: "Don't Embarrass the Bureau" was a term that was talked about at the time. You'll never see that in writing—no official documents—but you heard it all the time.

BILL BROWN: I mean, the FBI had acknowledged that there was a problem because they sent Pat to see a psychiatrist before anything happened. Even during the MIPORN investigation there were all kinds of problems.

So when Pat was arrested for shoplifting and terminated by the FBI, I felt it was unfair to Pat because he was wounded in the line of duty. Psychologically wounded, but no less wounded. And my accusation, frankly, resonated in the bureau, and they understood that at a certain level, it was true. But the bureau just wanted to get rid of him.

FRED SCHWARTZ: James Yelvington and James Blasingame were people to whom Pat had been a great pain in the ass. He was an agent on their books that they really couldn't use very much. He hurt their travel budget. He was a smart-ass; a wise guy. They were just appalled that this could happen.

PAT LIVINGSTON: It had been a full six months since the shoplifting—that's an inordinate amount of time for the bureau to let something like this hang. The criminal charges had been dropped, so I didn't have to go through a trial. So the firing was unexpected; I didn't know it was going to come.

ED HORNING: The FBI kind of set themselves up because they had suggested, in order to justify their position, that Pat was unstable—mentally, emotionally, whatever.

So I thought, "Fine. If you want to dismiss him, I'm gonna help get this guy on some kind of federal disability. I want a worker's compensation claim."

FRED SCHWARTZ: Had Pat still been in Miami with the people who he had worked with—who he had brought glory to and who understood the situation—I think it would have been different. I think the coming together of Louisville and his personality is what caused the bureau to react the way they did.

MARCELLA COHEN (U.S. ATTORNEY): The arrest—combined with other information we received—led us to the conclusion that we could no longer use Pat Livingston as a witness. His credibility had become a source of great concern. So Judge Spellman, who was the trial judge, set up hearings to determine what should be done under the circumstances.

BILL KELLY: We had a four-day hearing before Judge Spellman about Livingston's credibility—and Pat just couldn't give that judge a straight answer. The judge would say, "When you went into that department store and were arrested—were you Pat Livingston or Pat Salamone?"

Pat says, "Gee, I don't know, your Honor. I might've been this; I might've been that. . . ."

I listened to this for four days. The judge finally gave up and said, "All of your credibility is gone."

So we had to reindict all the MIPORN defendants based on the testimony of Bruce Ellavsky alone.

BRUCE ELLAVSKY: I was not real happy being the only witness in all these trials.

BILL KELLY: Out of fifty-five defendants we had to drop six—because only Pat had evidence on those ones—and one of those six was Reuben Sturman, the most important pornographer in the world. So it was a tragedy.

It is the all-time horror story of FBI undercover operations.

DAVE FRIEDMAN: I told Dick Phinney, "Boy, I'd hate to be in your outfit. In my outfit in the army, if some guy screwed up, we stood behind him. But you guys evidently don't."

Phinney just turned red and said, "Beat it."

RUBY GOTTESMAN: Do I think Pat was crazy? Yeah. I think the undercover work got to him. I think what happened was, in some way, he wasn't an FBI guy no more. Now he was a mob guy, a gangster. He thought he was a wiseguy, and he liked that better.

PAT LIVINGSTON: I killed my father.

Grave's End

BROOKLYN
1982

MIAMI HERALD, FEBRUARY 27, 1980: DEATH OF MOB'S PORNO KING TAKES WRAPS OFF GUNMEN: "The death of organized crime's pornography czar, Michael (Mickey) Zaffarano, will touch off a gangland war among Mafia chiefs seeking control of the multibillion-dollar porno industry, according to knowledgeable law-enforcement sources."

BOB HANSON (NYPD DETECTIVE): Back in the early eighties was the beginning of the big Columbo war, where there was a couple of factions of the Columbos splitting up. They were starting to have a little strife amongst themselves—but greed is usually the overwhelming reason why people kill people.

MIAMI HERALD, FEBRUARY 27, 1980: DEATH OF MOB'S PORNO KING TAKES WRAP OFF GUNMEN: "Zaffarano's key role as the arbitrator among the various Mafia families lusting after profits from the porno business makes Zaffarano's unexpected demise a serious concern. His death 'brings violence back' to the smut business, according to one law enforcement source."

CHUCK BERNSTENE: Mickey kept the peace a lot. That's what he was, a peacemaker. When he died, who filled that role?

BILL KELLY: Joe "the Whale" Peraino and his son—whose name was also Joe—were in the Gravesend section of Brooklyn when these two gunmen came after them. One of the gunmen had a pistol, and I think the other one had a shotgun; they were being chased down the street in a residential area.

The two Perainos ran up on somebody's porch and started beating on the door trying to get in. The woman who lived there, Veronica Zuraw, was hanging up clothes in the house. So when she gets to the door—here comes a blast of a shotgun. Hit her right in the head and killed her, dead. A completely innocent victim.

NEW YORK *DAILY NEWS*, **JANUARY 5, 1982: 2 DIE, 1 HURT BY SHOTGUN:** "As the two reached the porch and began to bang on the door, the gunmen jumped from the car and fired at least five shotgun blasts in what police called an apparent gangland hit.

"Joseph Jr. was struck in the chest and killed instantly. His father was hit in the buttocks.

"Veronica Zuraw, 52, was killed by a stray shotgun blast that tore through the window of her kitchen on the second floor.

"'She was hanging up a shirt in the closet and the blast blew her head off,' said a police officer."

BILL KELLY: The young Joe Peraino got hit and killed. I don't know how many times he got hit. Some police officer or FBI agent told me that Joe "the Whale" got hit nine times—but because he was so fat, the bullets never hit a vital organ. So he survived.

Can you imagine getting shot nine times and surviving?

NEW YORK TIMES, JANUARY 5, 1982: TWO SLAIN AND ONE HURT IN MOB-STYLE SHOOTING: "Joseph Peraino, Sr., who was convicted in Miami on December 6, 1981 of six counts of interstate shipments of pornography, was the target of the gunmen, according to other law enforcement officials familiar with the case."

JAY DOLTON (NYPD DETECTIVE): Mr. Zuraw states that he had come up from the basement with six pairs of trousers. He said, "Ronnie was in the kitchen. She was going to the guest closet in the hallway to get hangers. I heard what sounded like machine-gun fire. I turned and saw Ronnie on the kitchen floor. I went to Ronnie to try to help. I ran up to the bedroom and called 911. When the police arrived, I had to unlock the door to let them in."

NEW YORK CITY MEDICAL EXAMINER'S REPORT: "On January 6, 1982, the M.E.'s office received a call from Detective Morrison, and he stated to the assigned, that deceased Joseph Peraino, Jr., the cause of death was shotgun wounds to the face, neck, head, and brain.

"He also stated the cause of death of Veronica Zuraw was shotgun wounds to the face, neck, head, and brain."

JAY DOLTON: Joseph Sr. has been shot by seven bullets in the right buttock. He's in stable condition but not critical. No major vessels or bones or other organs are involved in the injury. However, his condition is perceived to be "serious."

MICHAEL CROISSANT (NYPD DETECTIVE): Mr. Peraino is at this time a patient at the Helen Hayes Hospital for injuries he received from the shooting. Mr. Peraino was asked by the assigned if he could state what happened the night of January 4, 1982.

At this time, he stated that all he could remember is that he and his son, Joseph Jr., went for a walk, and while they were walking, men with guns started to chase them, and they ran down a street and up a stoop seeking shelter. When they were at the top of the stoop, they were shot, and that is all he can recall. Mr. Peraino was then shown photos and asked if he could identify any of the photos as the perps of this shooting. He stated that he could not identify the perps even if he was shown life-size photos, due to the quickness of said event, and it was dark.

BOB HANSON: Henry Pastori, one of the alleged shooters, was killed six weeks later. I think Henry Pastori was assigned to do this, and he didn't do it right, because the old man, Joe the Whale, lived. So that's one problem that he had. The other problem was that he killed an innocent bystander.

MICHAEL CROISSANT: Mr. Peraino was shown a photo and asked if he knew Mr. Henry Pastori. . . . Mr. Peraino stated that he did not know Pastori, nor does he remember ever seeing him. It has been established that Peraino and Pastori were acquaintances.

BOB HANSON: It's the second problem that he has to be concerned with— because a lot of government agencies are not as concerned when one bad guy kills another bad guy, even though we investigate it like any other case. Society itself doesn't get that upset about it.

But society *is* very upset when innocent bystanders get killed. That brings heat on everybody. So odds are that Henry Pastori screwed up— botched the hit—and ended up getting killed for it.

MICHAEL CROISSANT: According to an FBI informant, Henry Pastori pointed out the Perainos to two Columbo soldiers, who killed Joseph Peraino, Jr., and Veronica Zuraw.

On February 12, 1982, Henry Pastori was shot and killed in the Six-one Precinct and was our complaint number 2169. After viewing the foregoing fact that the perpetrator is deceased and cannot be prosecuted, this reports that the case be now closed: EXCEPTIONAL CLEARANCE.

BOB HANSON: It was the Columbos who were behind the hit. Rarely do we find out the exact reason it happened, but usually it has something to do with money. Money or disrespect—those are usually the two reasons we end up with.

NEW YORK TIMES, JANUARY 6, 1982: BYSTANDER KILLED IN MOB SHOOTING WAS A SOCIAL WORKER AND EX-NUN: "Mrs. Zuraw was born in Brazil as Veronica Vestena. She had become a nun, and as Sister Mary Adelaide received an undergraduate degree from Fordham University's School of Education in 1964.

"Her 1974 wedding to Mr. Zuraw was attended by Anthony J. Bevilacquia, now Auxiliary Bishop of Brooklyn.

"Father Failla said Mrs. Zuraw had actually run the Italian Board of Guardians office, an affiliate of Catholic Charities of Brooklyn at 1781 Seventy-third Street, Brooklyn.

"A funeral mass is to be offered Friday at 9:30 A.M. at St. Mary Mother of Jesus Church, Twenty-third Avenue and Eighty-fourth Street, Brooklyn."

The Trial

FLORIDA/LOS ANGELES/BELIZE/THAILAND/JAPAN
1982–1984

DAWN SCHILLER: After they arrested John, they drove me back to Louise's house—the stripper—and I stayed there until I heard from my father. He called after he opened the paper and read, "John Holmes was arrested in Miami Beach."

He called and asked, "Where are you?"

I told him where I was, and he came and picked me up and took me back to his place—he had a nice house in Pompano with a pool.

My dad just cracked open a beer, and we sat down, and I told him my long, emotional story. He would just sit there and nod, and every once in a while he'd reach into his pocket and break a Quaalude in half, and just hand me one, and open me another beer.

When I was done with the story, I got the spins, and I'm like, "Dad, I have to puke."

He says, "It's all right, babe." He walked me down the hall to the bathroom, and he held my hair while I just heaved my guts up.

It was like the nicest thing my dad ever did for me—holding my hair when I puked.

REUTERS INTERNATIONAL NEWS, DECEMBER 7, 1981: ACTOR ARRESTED: "John Holmes, 37, was arrested in Miami on Saturday and brought to Los Angeles, where he is being held on a charge of suspicion of murder, police said."

FRANK TOMLINSON: On Monday, December 7, in jail at the Parker Center, in an interview room, Mr. Holmes said that he—indicating Eddie Nash—had him taken at gunpoint to the house on Wonderland Avenue and that

Holmes knew what was going to happen but that he had no choice, that he had to set things up and let them in.

SHARON HOLMES: One morning I went into work and this girl I work with says, "Did you know John is back in California? He's down at county jail."

It's almost prophetic that I learn about it that morning because that very evening John calls and tells me he really wants to see me. I said, "Why, John?"

He said, "You're the only person who doesn't want a piece of me."

And I thought, yeah, I can tolerate seeing him once a week, and yes, if he wants me to write him, I'll write him, and I'll send him pictures of the dog. All this just to keep him sane, you know?

DAWN SCHILLER: After I puked, my dad said, "I'm going to Belize."

My dad was trying to get some money from this chick—she came from a wealthy family—to start a hotel in a resort area. So we went to Belize for six weeks to check it out. And he paid for it.

UNITED PRESS INTERNATIONAL, FEBRUARY 2, 1982: HOLMES ORDERED TO STAND TRIAL: "Porno star John Holmes was ordered Tuesday to stand trial for the murders of four people bludgeoned to death in a Laurel Canyon home last July, although a detective said he was forced to set up the slayings.

"Holmes, 37, charged with four counts of murder and one count of attempted murder, could face the death penalty if convicted."

FRANK TOMLINSON: John said that he was there when the murders occurred but that he himself did not hurt anyone. At that point I told him that one of his palm prints had been found in a location and a position above one of the victims.

I suggested to him that perhaps Nash made him strike one of the victims—thinking that if he himself were involved in the murders, he would be afraid to talk.

I assured John that he was just as guilty of first-degree murder for what he had told me in regard to going to the house to allow the killers inside as he would be if he had struck one of the victims.

John stated that he had not hit anyone and that he did not know how his palm print could have been near one of the victims.

DAWN SCHILLER: When my dad and I got back to the States, I started to have to think about money.

My dad says, "Well, we decided not to buy in Belize—we're going to go to Thailand. But if you want to go, you've got to come up with your own ticket."

I wanted to go. But I don't have any skills—I mean I'd been a nurse's aide, but that didn't make you much money. And I needed money pretty fast.

So my dad opens up the paper and goes, "What does it say under 'dancers'?"

I go, "Wanted: Dancers. Top money. Great tips."

He said, "Dawn, strip clubs."

I go, "That sounds too scary."

He goes, "I'll go with you. It should be safe if I go with you."

I figured that Dad was big and bad enough, so I get dressed, and we go into this place—the Pink Pussycat on Seventeenth Street Causeway in Fort Lauderdale. The owner says, "Have you ever done this before?"

I said, "No."

He said, "Well, we'll need to see you dance."

SHARON HOLMES: I went down to the jail once a week. I had Wednesday afternoons off, so I would leave the office at 12:30 and go down. Sometimes I would wait two or three hours before they let me see him. I took a book with me—I think I was the only literate person there.

I'd get to spend about an hour with him. John was always paranoid that they recorded everything, so we'd just talk about my family. He'd want to know how Grandma was and how my mom and my dad were. You know, "What have you been doing in the office?"

Just light stuff. Everybody else wanted something from him, and he knew I didn't because what I wanted he couldn't give me . . . or didn't want to.

DAWN SCHILLER: My father's at the bar of the Pink Pussycat with his friend Mick—this English dude he traveled the world with—and I come out and go, "I've got to audition."

My dad's like, "Okay."

I was scared to death. I did three straight shots of whiskey and just bit the bullet. I had this purple dress on—and that comes off—and I think a G-string.

So I go up there and dance to "Start Me Up" and "Another One Bites the Dust."

FRANK TOMLINSON: Holmes said that Eddie Nash held him at Nash's house, took his address book, and wrote down the names of his family, and that Eddie Nash told him that if he ever talked to the police, he would kill someone in Holmes's family. And Holmes said that that was why he was afraid to tell me what happened.

DAWN SCHILLER: When I finished dancing, I put my clothes on and went and talked to the owner. He goes, "You can start tomorrow. . . ."

I wanted to leave but my dad says, "Come here a minute. I've got to shake your hand. There's no fucking way in hell I would ever take my clothes off in front of a bunch of people. You've got balls."

This is an immensely proud moment in my life, you know? I go, "Did you watch?"

My dad goes, "No, I couldn't watch. I had to cover my eyes and shit. But I'd look over at Mick, and his eyes were glued to the stage. All I could ask was, 'How's she doing, Mick?'"

"And Mick was saying, 'She's doing real good, Bill. Real good!'"

My dad was, like, way proud of me, you know?

UNITED PRESS INTERNATIONAL, JUNE 25, 1982: HOLMES FOUND INNOCENT: "Porn star John Holmes was found innocent Friday of murdering four people found bludgeoned to death in a Laurel Canyon bloodbath last summer."

AL GOLDSTEIN: Despite his acquittal, Holmes was kept in jail, first on a stolen-property conviction, then on contempt-of-court charges for refusing to answer the grand jury's questions about the Wonderland Avenue killings.

DAWN SCHILLER: I raised about fifteen hundred dollars for a round-trip ticket to Thailand. My dad and I went together. He prepped me about traveling. He said, "Once you fly someplace, it'll never get out of your blood."

He would set me up for these things, and I would get so excited. We flew into Bangkok and I was like, "WE'RE ABOUT TO LAND! WE'RE ABOUT TO LAND!"

REUTERS INTERNATIONAL NEWS, NOVEMBER 22, 1982: JUDGE ORDERED HOLMES RELEASED: "A judge today ordered pornographic film star John Holmes released from prison after he had apparently told what he knew about one of Hollywood's most grisly murders, the bludgeoning death of four people.

"Holmes, 38, was acquitted in June of the murders after his lawyers said he had been taken to the scene at gunpoint, but did not take part in the killings.

"Holmes had been held in prison for 111 days for contempt of court for refusing to give details of the murder.

"But today Holmes appeared before a grand jury behind closed doors.

"'Holmes answered each question put to him,' Deputy District Attorney Robert Jorgensen told reporters. After the hearing, Superior Judge Julius Leetham ordered the release of Holmes."

SHARON HOLMES: When John got out of jail, he called me and said, "I want to go away and start a new life."

I could hear a party in the background—and he's going, "SNNNNIFF"—and I said to myself, "Geez, he just got out of jail, and he's already snorting coke."

I had never used the word "fuck" in my life, but I said to John, "Get the *fuck* out of my life," and slammed the phone down. I just couldn't believe he had the audacity.

DAWN SCHILLER: It wasn't a big deal when I told my father I was going to become an escort. It was something I knew how to do, and he knew my story, you know? I had given him that seven-hour debriefing of what I had been through with John.

I had my freedom. I had control. I was doing it for a purpose—for money to spend like I wanted.

I took pride in the fact that I wasn't just doing twenty-dollar blow jobs and stuff like that, that I was making good money. I felt like I was getting paid for what I was worth. I was getting a lot of self-esteem.

John was very open about talking about how sex was a good thing—that there was nothing bad about it. And that we were all whores. That was his theory of life.

SHARON HOLMES: John was let out of jail in November 1982. I waited a year; then on Christmas Eve 1983, I built a fire and opened up the Pandora's box—John's trunk. When I found out what was in there I said to myself, "Uh-uh. I'm not going to be party to this anymore."

John was planning on using the trunk as blackmail against the famous people in the photographs. It was like his retirement fund. But I wouldn't be a party to blackmail.

DAWN SCHILLER: I'd have to fly to Japan to see my sugar daddy like once a week—that was it—and he'd pay my rent and give me a bunch of money. But I also worked in a hostess club where you offer fruit and things like that, and you have to look pretty, and be polite, and listen to them talk while they drink. And you try to get them to drink more.

It was very prestigious, too.

Wives would commit suicide because their husbands didn't go out to a hostess club with their bosses after work because, you know, "Oh my gosh, you're not good enough"—it was a loss of face.

But then my sugar daddy paid for me to go to school in Bangkok, so I would be gone for three months and then come back for a couple of weeks. And he visited me in Bangkok a couple of times, and I had to take him out to the live sex shows and show him around. You know, get his name written by someone's pussy. He was all happy.

SHARON HOLMES: Was what was in John's trunk incriminating? Oh, yes. I think it would have been very embarrassing to people if their spouses knew. Did I recognize a lot of the people as famous people? Oh, yeah. People who are in the paper, on television, on a regular basis. Probably 50-50, movie stars and politicians. Celebrities. It could have brought down the California state government.

I burned everything—every piece of paper, every photo, every loop.

DAWN SCHILLER: My friend Donald got me this job through a friend—who turned out to be part of the Yakuza—at this hostess club down in the Goya, and I ended up getting trapped down there.

They wouldn't let me leave. I begged them. Then they sold me to this other Yakuza guy who would take me around with all his bodyguards and shit—and he had tattoos, and permed hair, and you know, no little finger and shit.

They kept me in this room; I wasn't allowed to go anywhere. I was pretty much property. Were they forcing me to be a prostitute? Yeah, a couple of times. And, you know, I wasn't given any money.

I was just made to stay in his place while they had their big scary meetings with little cutting-off-little-finger ceremonies.

So I told them, "I know a place to get bulletproof vests in the United States, and if you let me go over there, I can hook you up."

So I went and never came back.

SHARON HOLMES: I guess John was afraid to call me after that last phone call. But his brother called me about a year and a half later and said, "John's back in Ohio."

I said, "That's nice."

David said, "Um, I'm out here visiting friends, but I'm going back, and John asked me if I could pick up his trunk?"

I said, "I don't have it, David. I don't have any of his things."

And that was true because I'd burned them.

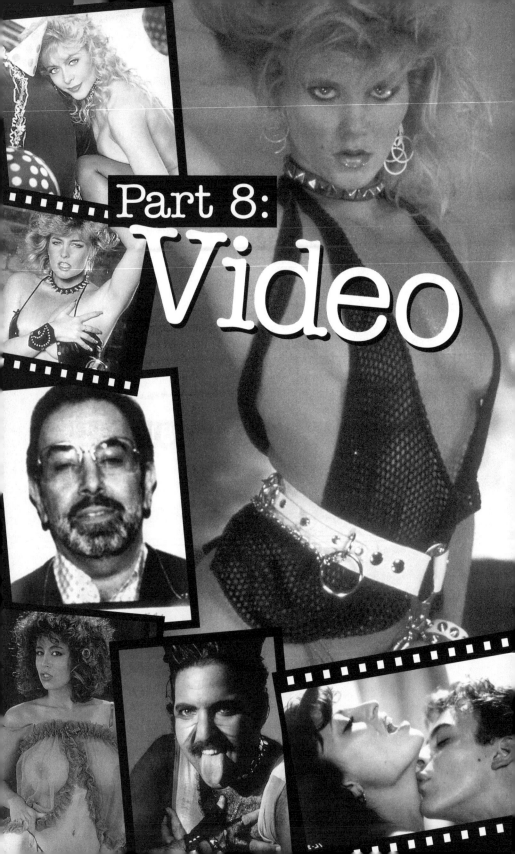

Part 8: Video

Vixens

1981–1984

Left page: *clockwise from top left:* Nina Hartley, Ginger Lynn, Kelly Nichols and Jerry Butler, Ron Jeremy, Christy Canyon, Reuben Sturman, Rhonda Jo Petty.

Right page: *clockwise from top left:* Bobby Hollander, Gloria Leonard and Henri Pachard; Shauna Grant, Traci Lords in *Traci, I Love You,* Jim South, Candida Royalle Traci Lords in 1992.

Hooray for Hollywood!

LOS ANGELES
1981–1982

MICHAEL LONDON (WRITER): A lot of what happened to Colleen Applegate wasn't very different from what happened—years ago—with girls who had some dream of stardom in the legitimate film business.

I don't think wanting to be in sex films was what was driving her; it was that I think that she wanted be the center of attention, to be successful. She had these huge, vague dreams of stardom.

And what Colleen Applegate of Farmington, Minnesota, had to offer was something in precious short supply in Hollywood: innocence. For a business devoted to spinning fantasies about the archetypical midwestern girl-next-door, Colleen Applegate was the real thing.

KAREN APPLEGATE (COLLEEN'S MOTHER): You see movies about young girls wanting to be movie stars who get out to Los Angeles and get mixed up with the wrong people—but you never think of it happening to you. Colleen just wanted to be somebody. It wasn't enough for her to stay in a small town and work in a bank.

GINGER LYNN (PORN STAR): I left my hometown when I was nineteen. I came to California from Rockford, Illinois, to visit my grandfather, who was very sick. I had one suitcase packed with my things.

I thought that when you lived in California, everything was free and beautiful and you lived on the beach, you know. It was the eighties. I had this delusion that everything was like it was in the movies.

KELLY NICHOLS (FORMER PORN STAR): I was the girl who gets murdered in the bathtub in *Toolbox Murders*. That's how I got my SAG card. Yeah, I'm the girl on the poster. I was getting paid for it—but I wasn't that excited about it because I don't want to be a straight actress. Bob Veze, my mentor, was always very frustrated with me because he thought I could be Demi Moore—who came out of his studio.

But I didn't want it that bad, and you have to want it bad to exist in Hollywood. You've got to be willing to go to all the auditions. I went to auditions, and I hated them. I didn't want to stab anybody in the back. I didn't want to fuck to get a part. I just didn't care that much.

Instead I'd say, "I don't need the part. Just invite me to one of your parties—then I'll fuck you!"

MICHAEL LONDON: Colleen Applegate was accompanied to a Steve Hicks photo session by Mike Marcell—her longtime Minnesota boyfriend who drove her west. The pair had scouted a variety of jobs in the month since they arrived in Los Angeles, but nothing had come through. Then one of them spotted an ad for World Modeling, an agency in the Valley that aggressively seeks out new recruits for "figure modeling."

JIM SOUTH (PORN AGENT): To me, Colleen had a real look. When I first saw her she was very classy, with an almost girl-next-door look. I thought she was very nice and would do very well.

TIM CONNELLY: Jim South is the ultimate porn broker. He runs an ad in every goddamn local newspaper in Los Angeles, and 90 percent of the girls who come into the business get in by answering that ad.

He's really the same guy that'd be selling you an encyclopedia or a Bible or a hooker on a street corner. He's really just selling a commodity. And he never wavers from that.

MICHAEL LONDON: Steve Hicks's photo session immediately led to others, so ultimately Colleen's relationship with her boyfriend soured. The pair broke up less than two months after they reached Los Angeles. Marcell joined the army, but before signing up he called up his family and friends in Farmington with a hot piece of gossip—Colleen Applegate had become a nude model.

PHILLIP APPLEGATE (COLLEEN'S FATHER): I don't think it would have been such a big deal if Mike Marcell hadn't talked about it.

MICHAEL LONDON: Mike Marcell was angry. He was hurt and he felt rejected. Colleen was clearly moving on to more worldly men, and that was his way of striking back.

GINGER LYNN: I was living in my grandparents' fifth-wheel trailer in Revins, California. Then I moved up to an apartment building with a beautiful pool—unfortunately it had a crack in it and no water and rats lived in it. I lived in a one-room studio, and I was paying triple what I had paid for a two-bedroom, split-level apartment in Illinois.

GLORIA LEONARD: My husband, Bobby Hollander, was Colleen Applegate's manager. She was that homespun little midwestern kind of girl that guys *love*. That shiksa-blond-thing, you know?

MICHAEL LONDON: Bobby Hollander began managing Colleen in the fall of 1982, casting her in several feature-length productions for his Gourmet Video line. Hollander even coined what he felt was an appropriately "classy" screen name: Shauna Grant.

BOBBY HOLLANDER: When I first met Colleen, she was making a hundred dollars a day, which was more than her father made. Remember, this was a girl who came from Minnesota in a polyester dress and a pair of wedgies. Under me, her pay rate rose to nearly fifteen hundred a day for hardcore—and seven hundred a day for nonsexual roles. Offscreen, she received star treatment—limousines, first-class hotels, and her own makeup artist, Laurie Smith.

LAURIE SMITH: She always played the one who stays a virgin for the whole movie and then gets laid in the final scene.

KELLY NICHOLS: Shauna was best friends with Laurie Smith, who was Bob Veze's girlfriend after me. So we were just a tight little circle.

MICHAEL LONDON: At that time—this was pre-video—they were still making actual movies. They were shot over multiple days, the budgets were larger, and there were more of the trappings of a real film—so it was easier to delude yourself that you could use this as access to the legitimate film business.

GINGER LYNN: I had a boyfriend in Illinois who decided—since I now lived in California—that he loved me. So he moved in, and I found myself paying all of the bills.

Was he an asshole? No, more an opportunist than an asshole. We began to have problems.

KELLY NICHOLS: I worked as Jessica Lange's stunt double for *King Kong*. They wanted to use the gorilla hands on me—they were like these robot hands with fur.

But after the first day of shooting the hands broke. So I got the run of the MGM lot for two weeks. I just walked around in my little costume, and onto the set of *New York, New York*, and *Logan's Run*.

GINGER LYNN: I always had high expectations of myself, but they weren't really about being in the entertainment industry. I didn't come to California to become an actress or a star. I never saw myself like that.

When I was growing up, I wasn't a cheerleader, I wasn't a jock, I wasn't one of the popular people. I was what we used to call a "head." You know, I hung out in the alley and smoked pot.

EDDIE HOLZMAN (PHOTOGRAPHER/COLLEEN APPLEGATE'S BOYFRIEND): Someone told Colleen Applegate that I made a comment about her weight, so she starved herself. It made me feel awfully powerful. She was very vulnerable at the time. On our third date, she told me she loved me. I told her to slow down and get ahold of herself.

MICHAEL LONDON: Eddie Holzman was a photographer for *Playboy*, *Penthouse*, and *Hustler*, but he had his dividing line. He wasn't happy when he found out that Colleen was doing movies behind his back. You know, everyone in that world has their line: "This is acceptable, and this isn't."

EDDIE HOLZMAN: I got tired of being the father figure. She was so young and innocent; she could be an instant star in porn—and instant gratification was what she wanted. Like cocaine.

RHONDA JO PETTY: In 1979 or 1980, I was going out with a big shot at MGM. He'd call me up and say, "Meet me in front of the Beverly Hills Hotel." Then he'd pick me up and take me to his house; his wife would be out of town. His house was just absolutely outrageous. He used to even send for me at his fucking office. I don't even know how I met him. It was purely sex and money, ha, ha, ha. He paid me a thousand bucks a night.

KELLY NICHOLS: They were going to use my boobs because Jessica Lange didn't want hers showing when King Kong's finger came down her chest. But then at the last minute, Jessica decided she *did* want her boobs in the movie.

I really didn't belong in the Hollywood system.

GINGER LYNN: I went to the Colorado River with thirty people from my gym, and along the banks they had all these little bars with signs saying "Hot Legs Contest" or "Wet T-Shirt Contest."

KELLY NICHOLS: I mean, the whole casting-couch thing—there was more crap like that going on in straight Hollywood than in porn. There were more people that wanted parts so bad—and people would hold that over their heads.

GINGER LYNN: We had run completely out of money by the first day, so me and this other girl started entering these contests. I won the first one—it was a "Hot Legs" contest. I made a hundred bucks and I thought, "Oh my God, this is so cool!"

VERONICA HART: The difference between the porn business and the straight business is that in porn you don't have to fuck anybody to get a job. I pretty much fucked everybody in Hollywood, and it doesn't get you anywhere, ha, ha, ha.

Hollywood is all about dangling promises and hopes. That's the most refreshing thing about dealing with most of the people in porn—we're pretty down-to-earth and not full of too much bullshit.

GINGER LYNN: There were all these girls that were extremely well-endowed, and I'm average. And the other girls were taking their tops off and pinching their nipples. I was too shy to do that, but I was willing to show my butt and my legs and you could see my wet nipples through my T-shirt.

I think I won three or four different contests. Between my girlfriend and I, we probably brought in four or five hundred bucks a day.

KELLY NICHOLS: I had one experience with a very famous producer. He really liked me, and it was one of those times when I didn't know what I wanted to do with my life, so I was fucking him. He was trying to promise me things, but I told him, "I'm just here because I want to be."

VERONICA HART: I really believed that there would be a merging of Hollywood and us—although when I went into the porn business, I gave up my aspirations to be a straight actress. I realized when I went into porn that this was not going to further a straight career.

"Fuck the straight business," I thought. "I don't need the hypocrisy."

That was the lovely thing about being in the porn business. I didn't have to fuck anybody or blow anybody to get a job.

KELLY NICHOLS: The producer was trying to tell me, "This town sucks!"

I was like, "No, life is still good. . . ."

He goes, "I'll show you. Just stay in the other room."

He makes a phone call and this little girl comes over. She stands outside his office and starts unzipping her top. She goes in. Brings her portfolio. He talks to her then has me come in and meet her—and then he kicks her out.

He says, "That girl is fifteen and a half. Her mom dropped her off and parked down the block. She was upset when she left because her mom wanted her to stay longer. You know why? Because she wanted her daughter to fuck me. *That's* the town you're living in."

GINGER LYNN: When I got back, my boyfriend and I discussed what had happened on the trip. We thought it would be a good idea if I started stripping at bachelor parties. So I found this quote-unquote agent, and I went to the first bachelor party, and I brought my little tape deck, and my boyfriend came along as a bodyguard.

RHONDA JO PETTY: A lot of these movie star people were very fascinated with pornography, and they'd show up on the sets. Max Baer (Jethro Bodine from *The Beverly Hillbillies*) was one of my best friends. Nick Nolte and Max Baer would hang out together. And they wanted me to come over and party with them a few times, but I never really ended up doing it.

GINGER LYNN: I hadn't really thought it through, so when I walked into this room and there were twenty drunk bachelors waiting for the stripper, I freaked. I ran out and left the tape deck—and my boyfriend—and they beat him up. It was horrible.

So I called the agent and said, "You know what? I don't think I'm really cut out for this."

GLORIA LEONARD: Robin Leach was a gossip columnist for the *Star*, the tabloid that we all know and love. Robin is really one of the few gossip people who enjoys relationships with people like Liz Taylor, Suzanne Somers, and Cher. He's English, and he's terribly charming, and whatever the protocol for gossip columnists is, he's followed it.

So our publicist set up an interview because I was getting a lot of attention as a result of all the celebrity nudes we were running in *High Society*, and of course that was right up the *Star*'s alley.

GINGER LYNN: I found another ad in the paper that said, "Figure models wanted: five hundred dollars to five thousand per day." It was for Jim South's World Modeling in Van Nuys. When I went in, there were two photographers there, and they took Polaroids of me.

RHONDA JO PETTY: Max Baer would call me and just want to know what I was doing and what film I was working on. Then one time I was really sick, and you know what Max did? He sent somebody to the pharmacy to pick up my prescription and bring it to my house.

I really liked him because he didn't really expect anything from me. He'd just call me and say, "How you doing? Me and Nick Nolte are here together. You going to come party with us?"

And I never met him in person, ha, ha, ha, because I would never go! But we continued that phone relationship for about a year.

GINGER LYNN: One of the photographers I met through World Modeling was Steven Hicks. We did test shots for *Penthouse,* and while we were waiting for the answer, Steven was going to Mexico for two weeks. He said to me, "Don't shoot for anybody while I'm gone." But I was brand-new, and I didn't believe him. You know, "Wait *two* weeks"?

Then Suze Randall came in and said, "I'll shoot you now."

GLORIA LEONARD: Robin took me to lunch at a restaurant, which was a romantic, dimly lit grotto. They showed us to a private room to conduct the interview.

We were sitting next to each other in a banquette, and in his clipped English accent, he asked, "Do you wear black panties?"

I was intrigued that somebody would have such naughty nerve. And I said, "I think I have a pair on right now."

He said, "Would you think I was terribly brash if I asked you for the pair you're wearing?"

I said, "Yes, I would, but if you'd like them . . ."

I thought it might enhance his article. So, very discreetly, I wiggled out of my panties under the lunch table, and Robin put them in his pocket.

Robin Leach was a wonderful lover. He was sensitive—he wasn't in a rush—and he was very big on foreplay.

GINGER LYNN: Suze shot me for *Penthouse.* Steven was very upset, but the layout was held for several months, which is very common. At that point *Penthouse* wasn't using women who'd done adult films as centerfolds.

RHONDA JO PETTY: There was this one party in the Hollywood Hills—I don't know how I ended up there, but I did—and Tony Curtis was there. I knew Tony; he would come to the porn sets sometimes. Anyway, he was smoking cocaine, and he's got himself locked in the bathroom, and he's threatening to commit suicide. It took them like two hours to talk him out of the bathroom.

GINGER LYNN: Between the time that Suze shot me and my first layout came out, enough months had gone by that I had begun to do adult films.

KELLY NICHOLS: I met Warren Beatty through my friend Ingrid, who was a model. But I was still shy, and everybody comes up to celebrities and bugs them. If you just walk up, celebrities just see a set of tits. They want to fuck you. Then you're saying platitudes out of your mouth that they're not even listening to. I liked to be listened to, and I like to make a difference.

KRISTIN STEEN (FORMER ACTRESS): I had been called by Shirley MacLaine's brother—what's his name? Warren Beatty.

It was fun getting called by Warren Beatty while my boyfriend was there. He was calling to invite me to his hotel room for a party.

So I went, but he wanted to have a party with these two other girls who were there, and I was very insulted by that. I wouldn't have minded having a party just with him, but not with these two other girls. I mean, come on. So I just got up and left.

KELLY NICHOLS: I just said hi to Warren Beatty—nothing else. But Ingrid had dated him in New York, and she just loved to fuck Warren Beatty. But she never dragged me into it—she was a really good friend.

See, there was a point where the whole idea of star-fucking just seemed like a really cool thing. But I always felt I was kind of excluded because I'm very shy.

SHARON MITCHELL: I hooked up with Warren Beatty through Tracey Adams—who he kept for a while—while Tracey had a gay relationship with the same woman for years. It was pretty much a secret because nobody talked about sex with movie stars. It's just an unspoken code that you don't, you know? You could be shooting dope with the Rolling Stones—but you'd never hear me say that.

KRISTIN STEEN: The two girls with Warren Beatty were beautiful—models or something. I thought it was so weird because I was this skinny, flat-chested chick, and I didn't think I was pretty or beautiful or glamorous. I think he was just calling random women.

I wasn't insulted to find out that that was all he wanted, but it was disappointing. You know, like, "This is the world?"

SHARON MITCHELL: I met Warren a couple of times, and we chatted and became friends. Did he come on to me? I can't answer that, but Warren seemed to know a lot about the porn business. He asked a lot of questions—but not in that fancy, asinine way that most people would bug the living shit out of you. And he knew a lot about sexually transmitted diseases, ha, ha, ha.

VERONICA HART: We're all just real people. I think we're all pretty up-front about what we do. Maybe it's because we're already exposed. You see us without our clothes on. You see us in our most intimate moments, doing stuff everybody else tries to keep secret.

SHARON MITCHELL: It always struck me that you can't make friends with the people in Hollywood because you can't get close to them. I mean, I thought *I* had barriers; these motherfuckers built the wall. You really couldn't get close to these people—they gave new meaning to the word superficial—*and* they had money.

JIM SOUTH: There's a lot of regular movie stars that are really, really, really into the porn business.

TIM CONNELLY: We call them "porn marks."

Mr. Untouchable

CLEVELAND/LOS ANGELES
1982

"A jury in Federal District Court, Cleveland, that acquitted seven persons of obscenity charges, wrote to Judge William K. Thomas a message saying that they do not believe the average person is capable of having a shameful interest in sex.

"Reuben Sturman and six of his employees were acquitted. They had been charged with shipping obscene materials across state lines."

RICHARD ROSFELDER (IRS SPECIAL AGENT): I remember reading in the *Cleveland Plain Dealer* that Reuben Sturman was found not guilty of obscenity—it may even have been front-page news.

I mean, everybody figured Reuben would be found guilty of obscenity. No one expected the acquittal—the agent or the prosecutors or the Strike Force or the public or the media.

NINA HARTLEY (PORN STAR): I met Reuben Sturman a couple of times, and he was very nice to me. I knew the importance of who he was; I knew the significance of him wanting to shake my hand and give me a compliment.

But he thought I was a silly hippie girl because to me sex is utopian, not just a business. And he took it to the whole next level—in terms of sex being a vital business.

RICHARD ROSFELDER: They had interviewed jurors; they were talking about the confusion in determining what obscenity is. And there had been some problems during the trial, where one of Sturman's associates was found in contempt for saying something to a juror.

NINA HARTLEY: I was more fired up with my youthful enthusiasm for my chosen field than Reuben was. I just talked to him about what I hoped to do with adult material—that I liked making this for couples—and Reuben was looking at me like, "I don't understand who she thinks watches this. I mean, it's lonely, single guys."

RICHARD ROSFELDER: How the Reuben Sturman obscenity prosecution in Cleveland ended up with a Strike Force, I'm not sure. But it was the United States Department of Justice Organized Crime and Racketeering Section, which had eighteen Strike Forces in the United States: New York, Chicago, Cleveland, Miami, Kansas City, Buffalo, et cetera, and all of them answered directly to Washington—and to the attorney general.

NINA HARTLEY: But one does not argue with Reuben Sturman; one listens respectfully to his opinion. It was earlier in my career, and since I was living my dream, I was happy.

Reuben was at the end of his career: "Done that, been there, seen it, got the T-shirt," you know? Age and jadedness versus youth.

RICHARD ROSFELDER: I felt pretty bad for the prosecutors and the FBI agent, who had worked really hard to put together a case. But I also appreciated that the acquittal created an opportunity for me to do my thing.

BOBBY ELKINS: Was I competing with Reuben? Well, I was with Danny Apple, and what made Danny Apple was the bookstore on Hollywood and Western—that bookstore made so much money.

This old Jewish guy had wanted to sell it to me—because it was in between a pool hall and a bar that I owned—and he wanted $18,000 for the place. I was negotiating with him when Danny came in and bought it. From that moment on, Danny Apple became a millionaire.

CALIFORNIA ORGANIZED CRIME CONTROL COMMISSION: APPLE, DANIEL JAMES: "Apple was sentenced to state prison in 1954 for burglary and robbery. In 1967, he became active in the Los Angeles pornography industry and is now considered to be a major pornography dealer in Southern California. As of May 3, 1977, Apple had recorded with the Los Angeles county clerk seventeen book or magazine stores. He has business connections with the New York Carlo Gambino Mafia organization."

BOBBY ELKINS: They want to own you, but I wouldn't let them buy in. I said, "Look, I got partners," and I mentioned a few people.

Vince DiStephano and I were really close friends. They whacked Bobby DeSalvo, and they were gonna whack Vinny. They said that he took money; I really have no idea if he did or not.

UNITED STATES PROSECUTIVE MEMORANDUM, JANUARY 1980: VINCENT JAMES DiSTEPHANO, aka "Vince": "Born 12/7/31 in New York City. Last known address: 17248 Barnestown St., Granada Hills, California. DiSTEPHANO works as a manager for LOUIS and JOSEPH PERAINO at Arrow Films and Video, Los Angeles, California."

BOBBY ELKINS: They put a contract out on Vinny. It was the old man, Anthony Peraino, Sr., and the son, Butchie, and the other son, Joe the Whale.

RICHARD ROSFELDER: My partner and I went to the Sovereign News Company to inform Reuben Sturman that he was under investigation. When we got there, we walked up to this guy who was cleaning the snow off his windshield, and he asked, "Can I help you?"

It was really nasty out—the snow was blowing and stuff—and I said, "Yeah. We're looking for Reuben Sturman."

He said, "Go ring the buzzer on the building over there."

So we rang the buzzer and said, "We want to talk to Reuben Sturman," and this guy said, "Well, he just left."

That had been Reuben, cleaning his windshield. This would've been sometime after the acquittal because during the whole trial, Reuben had a goatee, which was uncommon at the time. So Reuben had shaved everything off, and he was waving and smiling as he drove away down the street.

We never did hook up with him.

BOBBY ELKINS: The Perainos all went back to New York, and they let Vince run Arrow Films. They closed Bryanston Films down, and then they said, "Vince, we found this place in the Valley."

It was when I was out of the business. In fact, when I went back over there, Vince was called back to New York, and they had a guy at the airport waiting for him, and we thought they were going to kill him, so we stopped him from going to the airport. We caught him in time and told him not to go there. Vinny's still alive.

ROGER YOUNG (FBI SPECIAL AGENT): Rosfelder started Sturman around 1978, and I started the Sturman case around 1982. Once we knew about each other, Rosfelder and I coordinated our efforts nationally. Rosfelder went overseas and worked the financial part, and I worked the "Interstate Transportation of Obscene Matter" part.

HAROLD LIME (PORN PRODUCER): Reuben Sturman gave me my start. Did he give me permission to exist in this business? Yeah, he was the Godfather.

GLORIA LEONARD: Reuben was like the granddaddy of the porn business. He threw some fabulous New Year's Eve parties.

RICHARD ROSFELDER: Reuben had a three-day event; the tradespeople from all over the world would come to Cleveland for his infamous Christmas parties. It was a real big-time affair. And then when Reuben bought his big mansion out in Shaker Heights, he had the big party out there. Robert DiBernardo was among the guests.

BOBBY ELKINS: Yeah, some kid told me that Reuben was connected to DiBe. Steve loved DiBe. He used to go to New York to see him, and evidently DiBe loved him, too. Everybody liked DiBe; he was a pretty good guy. And DiBe was a real good earner. He was big—one of the biggest.

RICHARD ROSFELDER: Was Reuben Sturman the McDonald's of pornography? Yeah, I would have to say so. He took a hamburger and marketed it in a way that was fairly successful. But his choosing to be involved in the production and distribution of pornography had as little to do with pornography as it did in my investigating him. He did it because he was looking to make a buck.

HAROLD LIME: Reuben financed a lot of my movies—*The Ecstasy Girls*, *Abandon by Night*, and *Society Affairs*. That's why I did *Society Affairs* with Harry Reems—because Reuben wanted to get a "name guy." And I guess nobody wanted Harry, so he was flattered.

RICHARD ROSFELDER: Before Reuben's 1978 trial and acquittal for obscenity, the Strike Force had asked the Internal Revenue Service to investigate Sturman's tax evasion, which included allegations of Swiss bank accounts, phony names, and stolen passports.

ROGER YOUNG: Reuben Sturman's goal was to have a piece of every single hard-core video sold—so that any time anyone sold a video, he would get a dollar or two out of every single one.

RICHARD ROSFELDER: Reuben Sturman's ego required that he fall victim to some vast government conspiracy to bring him down. It's almost laughable.

I was in the office of the attorney in charge of the Strike Force, who appreciated that probably within a few short months, Sturman would be in prison for God knows how many years. But the attorney basically agreed to allow the tax investigation to go forward, as a courtesy to me—a young, naive agent.

Nobody got up after the acquittal and screamed, "LET'S GET THE TAX GUYS TO GET HIM IF WE CAN'T GET HIM!"

ROGER YOUNG: Did Rosfelder go to the Swiss government and get them to open Sturman's bank accounts? Yes.

RICHARD ROSFELDER: The Sturman tax case was the first time in history that the Swiss government produced bank records under the "Organized Crime Exception" to the treaty. And that would support the conclusion that the United States—as required under the provisions of the treaty—presented information to the Swiss government that proved Reuben Sturman was involved in organized crime.

REUBEN STURMAN: I paid a million in taxes every year, but there was a couple of million I didn't tell them about.

RICHARD ROSFELDER: He had about fifty Swiss bank accounts. I don't know how much money he had—millions, anyway. He estimated his net worth at $250 million.

REUBEN STURMAN: I should have paid my taxes.

ROGER YOUNG: Reuben was kind of a straight Jewish guy from a nice neighborhood in Cleveland. He taught aerobics at the YMCA, bowled a lot, and had season box tickets to the Cleveland baseball stadium.

Then he fell madly in love with Naomi Delgado. Reuben said the reason he put money in Switzerland was so that he wouldn't have to give any to his first wife.

BILL KELLY: Pornographers used to come around Reuben's office and throw bags of money at him. Fifty thousand, a hundred thousand—it would stack up like it did in the *Deep Throat* case.

ROGER YOUNG: After Reuben got divorced and moved his headquarters to North Hollywood, he was out jogging all the time. We think he was trying to keep up with Naomi, ha, ha, ha. Naomi is very good-looking, and Sturman was basically infatuated with her. He even had a face-lift to look younger for her.

We knew that Naomi had family in Mexico and that Reuben was trying to promote her singing career.

NAOMI DELGADO: How long did I know Reuben prior to our marriage? Ten years. He had two homes, one in Cleveland, Ohio, and one in Van Nuys, California. In Sherman Oaks, on Waddington Street. I never lived in Cleveland with Reuben.

ROGER YOUNG: Naomi had ulterior motives that Reuben didn't know about—like bringing her whole family up from Mexico as soon as they were married. Aunts, uncles, mom, dad, and all their kids—and all their kids' kids.

As one person explained it to me, "Roger, just be thankful that you've never met her because she is your worst nightmare."

Shattered Innocence

LOS ANGELES/FARMINGTON, MINNESOTA
1983–1984

GLORIA LEONARD: Shauna Grant got in over her head. I think what happens to a lot of girls in this business is that they feel that they have to live out what they perceive to be a stereotypical porn star lifestyle twenty-four/seven.

And *everybody* was doing drugs. I went into a Bank of America and the teller asked me if I could get her some blow, ha, ha, ha!

KELLY NICHOLS: After a while the movies got on Shauna's nerves because she never felt like she was an actress. And she was about as wooden as you could ever get—but she was gorgeous. But she thought I was a great actress, and I'm like, "Oh, come on! It's *porno*!"

JIM SOUTH: Shauna got mixed up with Jake Ehrlich, a drug dealer in Palm Springs.

BUD LEE: Shauna moved in with this guy. As their cover—to explain how they made their money—they owned a leather store.

KELLY NICHOLS: Shauna's boyfriend was always in jail.

TIM CONNELLY: Jake got busted for dealing, but he arranged for Shauna to take care of the leather store and his house while he was inside. They were still "seeing" each other.

JIM SOUTH: Shauna was selling drugs on the side, and Jake knew it. Shauna knew there was no way she could talk her way out of that—and people said she could talk her way out of anything.

And of course, when you're really into coke—which I've never done and will never do—I'm told that you get extremely paranoid.

KELLY NICHOLS: At any given time, Shauna and Jake were either having a lot of fun, or they were in a lot of trauma. They were either partying with John Milius, or they were worried about losing the farm. And in between all of that, she and I were deciding what we were gonna wear, ha, ha, ha.

TIM CONNELLY: I was friends with this porn actor, Joey Silvera, and he would see Shauna whenever she'd come to New York. So one night Joey brought Shauna over, and she was just so totally coked out that she couldn't talk. So I had no interest in her.

You know, after I got high and fucked and had a good time, I'd be that way by three in the morning, frozen in a bathroom somewhere. But Shauna was like that from one in the afternoon, you know?

PEOPLE, MARCH 14, 1988: A PORN STAR'S SUICIDE AT 20 LEAVES A LEGACY OF SHATTERED INNOCENCE: "Shauna's final disintegration began on Feb. 21, 1984, when Jake Ehrlich was arrested for violating probation on a previous drug charge. Left to her own devices, Colleen became depressed and disoriented, squandering Ehrlich's money on drugs."

MICHAEL LONDON: Colleen told friends that she was visiting Ehrlich regularly at the Los Angeles County Jail—but she seems to have avoided all contact.

PEOPLE, MARCH 14, 1988: A PORN STAR'S SUICIDE AT 20 LEAVES A LEGACY OF SHATTERED INNOCENCE: "On March 14 she went to Los Angeles's Ambassador Hotel for the Erotic Film Awards, the porn industry's version of the Oscars. It was her last taste of glamour—Francis Ford Coppola was among the guests at her table. During the night, she received a porn-movie offer, and, with her cash dwindling, she accepted."

HENRI PACHARD: Shauna and Laurie Smith came to visit me at the Hyatt Hotel looking for coke. I didn't have any; I was trying to get some. I was getting scheduled to shoot a movie in the Bay area in a few days. There had been talk about putting Shauna in the movie, so I told her, "I think you're going to be in a movie I'm directing."

Shauna goes, "Oh, wow. Cool."

So they hung out for about an hour, and then Laurie mentioned that she was going to the awards show that night with Francis Ford Coppola and Gray Frederickson, and maybe they'd see me there.

KELLY NICHOLS: I had come out to Los Angeles with Tim Connelly because Shauna and I were both nominated for Best Actress in 1983. Shauna was nominated for Best Actress twice in that category; I was nominated once, and Veronica Hart was nominated once. Even Shauna thought it was weird that she was nominated—she's a bad actress, and she gets nominated twice?

LAURIE HOLMES: Shauna Grant was the only porno girl I ever knew that needed cue cards, ha, ha, ha.

BUD LEE: We were sitting with Francis Ford Coppola, Gray Frederickson, and this guy in this flashy leather coat that looked like it had been simonized—who turned out to be Jake Ehrlich, Shauna Grant's boyfriend. The guy was the cocaine dealer to the stars—that's how he knew all these people.

Shauna got involved in the right circle.

HENRI PACHARD: I was seated down front, and at the next table was Francis Ford Coppola and Gray Frederickson—the guy that did *The Godfather*—sitting with Shauna Grant and Laurie Smith.

So when they called my name out for Best Director, I turned around to get up and Francis Ford Coppola nodded his head and smiled at me because he knew the feeling, you know?

KELLY NICHOLS: When they announced that I won Best Actress, it was such an amazing moment. It was just wild. After the show, Shauna came up to me and said, "I'm really happy you won. You totally deserved it. And I just love you for it."

That was really sweet because Shauna didn't talk a whole lot.

HENRI PACHARD: In my acceptance speech, I talked about how the kind of movies we made required a certain amount of courage, and I referred to the movie *Apocalypse Now*, which I was very much taken with.

Then I said, "And he's here with us tonight, Francis Ford Coppola," and I gestured toward him, they took a shot, and he waved. I said, "This is courage."

He got a big applause and everything.

After the show was over I went off with some girl to get fucked up and get some sex, and apparently Francis Ford Coppola was looking for me.

TOM BYRON (PORN STAR): That was the night Shauna was with Francis Ford Coppola. Was Coppola banging Shauna? Maybe, I don't know.

But do you remember Raven? Okay, Raven had a friend, Laurie Smith, and they used to love to do coke together. They used to hang out at Gray Frederickson's house—he was one of the producers of *The Godfather*, okay? So Gray Frederickson liked to do coke, and he liked porn chicks—you do the fucking math.

SHARON MITCHELL: Laurie Smith and Shauna really had that ticket into *the* Hollywood crowd.

KAREN APPLEGATE: They brainwash these girls and make them believe they're going to do something for them, but their only intention is using them for dirt.

MICHAEL LONDON: Colleen's prospects at the time were uncertain. She told friends that a Hollywood producer had offered her a role in an upcoming film entitled *Sci-Fi High*, but the producer denies it, and the story may have been created out of Colleen's frustration for a career in straight films.

BOBBY HOLLANDER: They were playing with her head.

HENRI PACHARD: I had heard that Shauna was a little bit of trouble—that she was flaky and did too many drugs—so when we were getting ready to go to San Francisco for the shoot, we decided to give her good friend Laurie Smith a job, too, to make sure Laurie delivered Shauna to the set.

MICHAEL LONDON: Laurie Smith was a really tough girl, and she had a definite point of view about how the people in the straight Hollywood world promised jobs to these young girls and did not deliver—but kept sleeping with them in the process.

TIM CONNELLY: The day after the awards show, Kelly and I went to Laurie's hotel room because we were going to buy some coke.

It's the middle of the afternoon, and we end up waiting around for three hours because Shauna went out to do something and got lost—and Shauna *lived* in Los Angeles.

So we got high with Laurie for a few hours. She was just crazy, flitting all around the room.

When Shauna finally showed up, she was just totally coked out. She could barely talk.

KELLY NICHOLS: Shauna was like, "I don't know what I'm gonna do. I'm supposed to work for Henri Pachard in San Francisco, and I don't think I want to."

I go, "Well, don't."

She goes, "I'm just really upset. My boyfriend is in jail again, and I've got this shop."

There were some thugs coming by the shop and hustling for money. I don't know how much of the truth I was getting, but Shauna said their checks were bouncing and she didn't know what to do. It definitely didn't sound fun.

TIM CONNELLY: Kelly and I decided to leave because we had to fly to San Francisco the next morning—Kelly was going to work for Alex DiRenzy—but Laurie and Shauna were trying to get Kelly to take Shauna's part in Henri's movie because Shauna didn't want to go.

KELLY NICHOLS: Shauna knew that if they could get another star of equal value, then they wouldn't be as hard on her. Like if Shauna could promise that I would be there, then they wouldn't slam her as bad. You know, all would be forgiven.

I was like, "Okay, fine. I can do it. No big deal."

She said, "But you've got to tell me for sure if you're gonna do it."

I said, "Okay, I'll tell you for sure."

MICHAEL LONDON: On Tuesday, March 21, Jake Ehrlich reached Shauna by phone at MGM/UA, where Frederickson and Beckerman had offices. A long, loud, hysterical call ensued. When it ended, Shauna left for the airport to fly to Palm Springs without a word to Laurie Smith.

HENRI PACHARD: The night before she was supposed to come to San Francisco, Shauna called and said, "I guess if I don't show up a lot of people are gonna be disappointed, huh?"

I said, "Well, we're all counting on you being here."

You know, I told her, "I've never had a chance to direct you, and I hear you're really good, blah, blah, blah."

She said, "Okay, I'll see you tomorrow."

"Great, honey. Thanks. See you tomorrow."

KELLY NICHOLS: I called Shauna at her house in Palm Springs, and she sounded in really good spirits.

She said, "Thank you for working. I just don't feel like going up there."

I said, "You sure? Everything's fine?"

She said, "Yeah, I think I'm just gonna hang out here for a while. But I really, really appreciate it."

In retrospect, without reading too much into it, she just didn't want the wrath of one more person against her.

HENRI PACHARD: Laurie calls me up on the morning of March 21, 1984, and tells me that Shauna "sort of had an accident."

I asked, "What happened?"

"Well, she kinda shot herself in the head, sort of."

I asked, "Is she dead?"

Laurie said, "Uh, sort of." Really. Denial. This is 5:00 or 5:30 in the morning, and Laurie said that Shauna took a rifle and shot herself.

Laurie said, "Can I please come do the movie anyway? I need to get out of here. I'm really scared."

I said, "Absolutely."

KELLY NICHOLS: I got a call from Laurie. She was freaked. They wouldn't let her in the hospital room because she wasn't family. Because Shauna was still alive when they got to the body. She was a vegetable, but she was still alive. They had her on a respirator, and a whole side of her face was gone. Laurie was just . . . you know, this was her friend.

HENRI PACHARD: As I understand it, Laurie was in one room—fighting with one of her boyfriends—and Shauna was in another room with some coke dealer, who was sound asleep. And Shauna took the guy's rifle, put a bullet in it, and shot herself in the head.

FILM WORLD REPORTS, **MONDAY, APRIL 16, 1984: SHAUNA GRANT DEAD:** "One of the top X-rated film actresses, Shauna Grant passed away last March 23rd at approximately 9:00 P.M. in Palm Springs, California. She was twenty years old, but had already established an impressive career as both a top-rated nude model as well as being an extremely popular erotic actress."

KELLY NICHOLS: I was very freaked out. I was still caught up in that "I just talked to her!" mode. And some people were coming out with the theory that Shauna had killed herself because she hadn't won best actress—which was just not the case at all.

HENRI PACHARD: Laurie comes up to San Francisco, broken rib and all. I put her in the movie, she did her thing, and we kept on going.

TIM CONNELLY: Laurie Smith didn't want to stay with the rest of the cast, so she ends up staying with Kelly and I in our suite at the Miako Hotel.

So there we are, smoking PCP—Laurie wouldn't smoke any of that—sitting in the bathtub, doing coke—and we're all naked. We weren't fucking; we were coke buddies.

We're all talking and crying and ruminating about what Shauna's death is all about. You know, why does this happen? And what does it mean?

HENRI PACHARD: Shauna wasn't having any fun out of life. To Shauna, everything was like, "I had to do, should be, gotta do this, gotta do that"—a lot of people were pulling her in every different direction.

I don't think she offed herself because she had to do another porn movie. I think she offed herself because she couldn't find any drugs and then depression set in.

KELLY NICHOLS: Shauna was the first publicized porn death. There were a couple of earlier ones, but this was the biggie because porn was starting to get more accessible through the VCR. It just had tabloid written all over it. And Shauna was beautiful. She made great print.

Any time a girl dies, it's like a little piece of us dies. It feels a little like, *If we're not careful, that could be us.*

TIM CONNELLY: Shauna's was the first death by suicide in the industry, and it really had an impact. I mean, it was like there was a huge cloud hanging in the air. Things got kind of weird.

Fast Forward

LOS ANGELES
1983

JIM SOUTH: I started Ginger Lynn. I loved Ginger, okay, but I didn't light up with Ginger initially.

GINGER LYNN: When Jim South first asked me to make a film, he said, "Well, we want you to do commercial," and I'm thinking toothpaste—Pearl Drops, okay? Remember the commercial where she licks her lips? Then I found out "commercial" means "sex"—commercial scenes are sex scenes.

I said, "There's no way."

JIM SOUTH: If the girls are reliable and dependable and, God willing, not into drugs—and if they at least study the script, and they give good "ohhs and ahhs," and they're sexy, then they'll probably go far.

By the same token, if they're two hours late, or stoned, then they're probably not going to last long.

GINGER LYNN: I had the same stereotype image that many people did—that everyone in the industry was a hooker, a slut, and a drug addict. So I said, "I'm not that kind of a girl. I would never do that."

Then I met this girl in Jim South's office, and she was beautiful, intelligent, and articulate. She was wearing this long, white dress, and she was holding one of those long cigarette holders, and she was just so cool.

I said to her, "You don't do porno, do you?"

She said, "Yeah."

And I thought, "Well, you don't *look* like that kind of a girl."

So I took her to lunch, and I basically just asked her every question I could think of.

TIM CONNELLY: Jim South is brokering flesh. Pure and simple. From what I've seen, if he sees somebody who's not interested, he tries to get them out of there as fast as humanly possible, and if they're interested, he tries to get them as much work as possible.

GINGER LYNN: I went back into Jim South's office and said, "I'll do it, but I want script and cast approval, and I want a thousand dollars per scene."

Jim South was on the floor rolling in laughter, thinking I'm a complete idiot, and he says, "You'll never work!"

I said, "Well, these are the things that I need in order for me to feel good about what I'm doing."

HENRI PACHARD: Women didn't discover their power until video came along. Until then the power belonged to the director.

How much would I get paid to direct a film? Fifteen thousand dollars and up.

KELLY NICHOLS: Ginger fascinated me. She and Joanna Storm had that blond thing down. I mean, I felt sorry for the guys that even came near them. Ginger and Joanna could talk the talk—and walk the walk—and get anybody to believe anything. And they'd have no guilt about getting guys to buy them things. It was almost some kind of inborn thing—you know, "It's my right."

And some people can get coked and be like assholes, but Ginger was a sweetheart, always cheerful.

GINGER LYNN: I made all of these demands, and David and Svetlana—the people making the movie—agreed to all of them. I have a contract, I'm working with people that I find attractive, and then it hits me: *I've never fucked on film.* What if I'm horrible at it?

So I go back to Jim South and say, "I need to do a practice movie."

TIM CONNELLY: I didn't get Ginger at first. Ginger looked like she was right out of a Huey Lewis video. She's the cute blond—the accessible, engaging girl that always wanted you. Except that I didn't think that's what you wanted in a porn star. Maybe I was wrong.

GINGER LYNN: I walk into this little apartment in Santa Monica, and Ron Jeremy is there. Now Ron is not the most attractive man I've ever seen, ha, ha, ha. I looked at him, and I almost left. Then I thought, "You know what? If I can do it with this guy, I can do it with *anybody.*"

So we did the loop—Ron was sweating and smelly and hairy and fat—and Mike Carpenter is telling me, "Lick your lips," and when I saw the loop, I really was so exaggerated in my movements that it was hysterical.

The second loop that afternoon was with Tom Byron, and Tommy became my favorite man in adult films. He was sweet, kind, funny, sexy, hot; he had a big dick. He was just great.

TOM BYRON: Ginger Lynnnnnnn; she's *fine*. I was one of the first guys to fuck her on camera. Yeaahhhh. It was *goooood*. Man, she was great! It was for a fucking Mike Carpenter's *The Golden Girls* loop, man.

She was so perfect, man. She was like a doll. Her fuckin' body was just flawless, and she was nasty, man. She'd fucking tongue your ass—and nobody that looked like that was nasty like that back then—you know what I mean?

GINGER LYNN: Tommy Byron was somebody I always loved to be around— sexually, socially, in any situation. We had this chemistry; we just clicked.

TOM BYRON: Ginger and I were great in the sack, and we were very friendly with each other. I mean, Ginger's just a wonderful person, you know? And a great sexual performer. I have nothing but respect and love for her.

BILL MARGOLD: Ginger is the definition of a star. She has it. And Ginger elevates sex to a whole other level of heat because she likes what she's doing, and she's good at it. I have great respect for her.

GINGER LYNN: My first photo shoot was in September 1983. In December, I went to Hawaii with David and Svetlana to do *Surrender in Paradise* and *A Little Bit of Hanky Panky*.

TIM CONNELLY: Obviously I was wrong because Ginger became one of the biggest porn stars of all time.

HUMPHRY KNIPE (PHOTOGRAPHER, DIRECTOR, HUSBAND OF SUZE RANDALL): Some gals are extraordinary sexual animals. You can tell because they don't get dry, and they don't get sore.

I mean, these are sordid details—but there's the gals who are putting K-Y Jelly on all the time, and then there's the gals who fool around *between* the scenes, like Ginger Lynn—an animal, absolute animal. Ginger was a remarkable sexual athlete.

BILL MARGOLD: The three most important women in this business are Marilyn Chambers, Seka, and Ginger Lynn. They're the most famous landmark women. They came along at exactly the right time. Chambers kicked it open with *Green Door*, and then Seka transformed film into first-grade video—she was really the performer who carried the seventies into the eighties. Then Ginger picked up the ball and ran with it.

KELLY NICHOLS: There's just always some key people that stick out. Ginger packaged herself. Before, you'd go see Kelly Nichols and the rest. Now you'd buy a Ginger Lynn tape just to see Ginger Lynn.

VERONICA HART: If I'd been smart, I would have hung in through video. Because Ginger Lynn—oh man, she cleaned up. Made a bunch of money.

SHARON MITCHELL: Everybody who had a VCR had a Ginger Lynn movie. And I was in every Ginger Lynn movie—or at least all the popular ones.

TIM CONNELLY: We—the generation of adult performers who shot on film—all felt we did what we did for more than just the money or the fame. We *liked* what we did. We felt there was craft to it, a certain element of art to it. And talent and inspiration. We didn't think it was just that we were beautiful, and we can fuck for a lot of money.

HENRI PACHARD: I didn't like video. But the industry just kept moving toward video and speed and box covers, and more and more directors were getting into the business.

Well, they'd always been around, but now they were finding work. Like, "What I'd really rather do is direct" would be the thing you'd hear in the 1980s.

GLORIA LEONARD: Anybody can shoot video. *Anybody.* Shooting film requires great skill. You need to know how to light a set and where to put the camera. You have to know direction. I mean, at the risk of sounding like a big snob—which is perfectly fine with me—I was no longer interested when I saw what was happening to the industry. It just wasn't the same anymore. And frankly, had it started out like that, there's no way I would ever have participated.

TIM CONNELLY: My feeling was that if you're going to do something really low-budget and not very professional, then I'm not the person for that job. Because at the time there were quality actors and performers in adult films—people who could carry a thirty-five-millimeter film in a theater. They could act well enough and fuck memorably enough to glue some guy to his seat. There was a certain amount of talent that would compel a consumer to want to sit there and watch something because there was no fast-forward back then.

Now you can't even think about porno without thinking about fast-forward, which is really a testimonial for why people didn't want to do videos.

HENRI PACHARD: When I first started shooting movies, I'd be so excited that I wouldn't be able to sleep the night before. I'd wake up at five o'clock in the morning, and my girlfriend would say. "Honey, you can sleep another hour and a half."

I'd say, "No, I gotta get up. I gotta study my script."

I was so excited. Then I'd be on the set ready to just shoot my brains out, great.

Then I remember getting out of bed and thinking, "Oh God, I have to shoot a movie today? And I've got one day to do it in?"

And that very same morning, there'd be some kid half my age hopping out of bed, saying, "I'm shooting a video today, and I've got *all day* to do it."

And his perception made him the better director that day. I was beat before I even got out of bed. That's when I started to realize: Times change.

VERONICA HART: People made so much money in the beginning of video. They were selling those tapes for $79.95, you know? I mean, it was BIG MONEY!

ED DEROO (PORNOGRAPHER): The turning point came in 1982, when it finally went all video. I missed film tremendously. Film had soul; video has nothing. Video's just a way of making money. It flows like water, but film had a texture, a feeling, something you could grab onto and feel.

But when we started selling video we went from making just under a million to around ten million dollars in two years. It was scary—particularly because I had a goddamn FBI agent telling me, "If you buy a Mercedes or a Rolls Royce, we're gonna come after you."

Once I saw the money rolling in, it scared the hell out of me—because now I was a target. I wasn't just some small person trying to make a living anymore—I actually became a big company.

So in that period I had a lot of paranoia.

TIM CONNELLY: At the dawn of video, people started shooting adult movies on tape and then selling them as films. The production costs became a tenth of making a film, and they pushed out the same number of copies, raking in huge profits. Instant millionaires.

GLORIA LEONARD: After the advent of video, the types of girls that got into the business changed. I started calling them "The Stepford Sluts." They talked alike, their hair, their tits—there was a so-called line drawn in the sand. I won't say it lowered the bar in terms of talent because there were still some pretty decent girls around. But for the most part, it attracted a different kind of performer.

KELLY NICHOLS: Ginger had really good PR. Some performers have a really healthy interaction with their fans—I'm a combination of shy and embarrassed for them—but Ginger expects adoration and gives back blessings. Which is GREAT! The fans love that. They're basically a lot of submissives out there, okay?

GLORIA LEONARD: I don't know that Ginger was so much the jumping-off point for the change in porn, as much as video was. Because Ginger was, and is, in my opinion, a good little actress. She was a hot number on the screen, and she was something, you know? As opposed to some of these girls today who get these contracts, who, as far as I'm concerned, are *less* than mediocre.

TIM CONNELLY: One of the things that was really talked about at the time was the concept of the "Video Vixen"—a girl who appears in videos and has got sort of a style comes across as incredibly telegenic. And Ginger Lynn is the quintessential "Me Generation" porn star, you know?

It was all about ME—"I'm beautiful and I fuck and I'm great and I'm hot and I love it and I want it and it's not about the money—but I'm rich and successful."

And that's appealing. Who would not want that? Who would not want somebody like that?

Club 90

NEW YORK CITY
1983–1984

CANDIDA ROYALLE (PORN STAR): I was a feminist before I was a porn star. It happened after high school. I had moved in with my older sister in the Bronx, and I had to get a job to support myself. I had been forced to take typing in high school, so I went and interviewed for this job as a private secretary for one of those young, up-and-coming executives—who was all of twenty-four at the time—and I got the job.

VERONICA VERA (PORN STAR): I had always wanted to write, and I had come to New York and interviewed at various publishing houses. But I couldn't type, and you had to know how to type.

So I wound up on Wall Street. And after working on Wall Street for a bunch of years, I decided that I was either going to write or forget my fantasy to be a writer.

But the only person that I knew who was making a living as a writer was editing *Penthouse Variations*.

CANDIDA ROYALLE: It was such a learning experience because I was the least qualified of all the women who'd applied. I really learned what sexual harassment was, only we didn't have a name for it back then.

VERONICA VERA: Through writing an article for *Variations*, I met Marco Vassi, a fabulous erotic writer, and he and I became lovers for a short while. I said I wanted to learn about S and M, so he took me to Wood-stock with him to visit Charles Gatewood. That's where I met Annie Sprinkle.

Annie had just come back from Europe with a whole bunch of

European pornography, and she said, "Look what I brought!" And it was just this shower of full-color, glossy, very expensively printed magazines.

Annie and I hit it off immediately.

ANNIE SPRINKLE: Veronica Hart and I were in this movie, *Pandora's Mirror*, that was shot at the Hellfire Club. I wasn't very good, but Veronica was very good—*and* she was pregnant.

GLORIA LEONARD: When we found out Veronica Hart was pregnant, Annie and I both decided we'd, you know, do the baby shower thing.

CANDIDA ROYALLE: Club 90 really came out of a baby shower that we threw for Veronica Hart. All kinds of women came, but by the end of it all Veronica's straight friends had left, and the ones who stayed were all porn girls. Porn stars. And we had the best time.

ANNIE SPRINKLE: It wasn't really until the baby shower that I ever really hung out with these big stars. See, a lot of times I'd be in a movie with someone, but I'd never meet them because our scenes were shot at different times.

It was kind of like that with Veronica. She was the big star. Yeah, big, big, *big* star. She was very loved.

VERONICA VERA: It was just like a regular shower, except we had this body builder in a bikini. But then as the shower was just winding down, somebody put on the soundtrack to *West Side Story,* and everybody—all these frustrated ballerinas and girls who'd gone to tap-dancing school—started dancing around, and that's when we realized, "Oh, we have a lot in common here!"

CANDIDA ROYALLE: It was like we were fourteen. We were singing songs from *West Side Story* and having such a wonderful time together. And then we thought, "We should do this more often." So we decided to start meeting regularly.

GLORIA LEONARD: It occurred to me—having already been a veteran of some therapy—that women in this business have problems that are truly unique unto this occupation. It's not like being a hooker; it's not like anything else. Keep in mind that this was the era of filmmaking; video wasn't even a blip on the radar yet. And none of us ever dreamed that our films would be ultimately preserved for posterity.

ANNIE SPRINKLE: I was having a problem being a prostitute. At a certain point I would be with a client and just burst out crying, you know? So I stopped. I felt like I needed to do something else with my life—and yet I was still kind of addicted to the money and the sex and the people and the attention.

It was a really hard transition. It was also about not being the young party girl anymore. I was starting to get more serious. All my friends from Panama were all doing amazing things, and I thought, "Well, I can't be a prostitute forever."

GLORIA LEONARD: We met at least once a month. We had meetings at other people's houses, sometimes mine, sometimes Veronica's. But the meetings seemed to be most comfortable at Annie's—at her old address at 90 Lexington Avenue. Hence, Club 90.

I mean, I still maintained a circle of friends who were not in the adult business. I still went to the theater. I still listened to jazz. I had a life. I had a daughter to raise.

ANNIE SPRINKLE: I really needed a support group, and Veronica was pregnant, and she was going through changes. We were all going through changes.

VERONICA HART: Show business is not kind to aging women. If you've been a sexpot all of your life—or known for that—it's very difficult when you start getting into your forties and fifties. It kills you. If they haven't cultivated anything else, boy, it's easy to get bitter. Mean *and* bitter.

CANDIDA ROYALLE: I had joined the Women's Liberation Movement before porn because after experiences with men in the workplace, I started to get really angry about things.

But I left the women's movement because it was getting split up—and that whole lesbian-feminism was coming in—what eventually turned into the Dworkinites and the MacKinnonites. Antisexuality—I mean, that's just not for me.

KELLY NICHOLS: I mean, when you first meet a guy, how do you tell him you're a porn star? But you have to—eventually. And it has to be before it's gone too far, or they feel bamboozled. There has to be a fine timing, between where they just look at your tits and look at you as a slut—and where they think of you as a person. And if you really like them, it changes the dynamics, and it's really strange. You're just marked for life.

GLORIA LEONARD: I always had to make my own way. I never got any financial help. I mean, I raised my daughter alone. I never got a dime in child support. If I didn't work, we didn't eat.

VERONICA HART: When I went on *Phil Donahue,* we were supposed to talk about life after porn—but of course we didn't talk about life after porn; we talked about porn. The media only wants to portray us as victims. They want sensationalism and ratings, period.

CANDIDA ROYALLE: At the time, there was a woman named E. Jean Caroll, who was doing a big piece for *Playgirl*—when *Playgirl* was still a decent magazine out on the West Coast.

This was going to be the chance to finally tell the world what we were really like—not just this simple bimbette-victim piece. So she interviewed Veronica Hart, myself, Tiffany Clark, Annie Sprinkle, and Kelly Nichols.

We devoted a lot of time to E. Jean Caroll. We devoted an entire day to this beautiful photo shoot, with us all dressed up in Gibson Girl outfits, and we all gave her very long interviews.

Then, when the issue came out, the one she focused on the most was Tiffany Clark—because Tiffany most fit what people expected the porn star image to be. I mean, bless her heart, Tiffany's a very sweet girl, but she was probably the least clever and the most fucked-up. Definitely the most troubled.

Before the article came out, E. Jean Caroll would call me up for advice on men. She was really perplexed about how to give a good blow job.

So I really gave it to her in a letter. I was like, "You wasted our time. You lied to us. You did the same old crap—just feed the public what they want to hear about the typical porn star."

I said, "The next time you want to learn how to give a blow job, watch one of our movies!"

That's when I got a letter from something called Franklin Furnace. They were going to put on this big two-day show—with an installation called "Could There Be a Feminist Porn?"

So I went to the group and said, "This is our opportunity. No one can take this away from us now. Let's tell the world who we really are and what we're really about."

So we all decided that what we would do was a reenactment of one of our support group meetings.

VERONICA VERA: So we did this show called *Deep Inside Porn Stars* in early 1984—it was a dramatization of Club 90. We did it at a festival called "Carnival Knowledge." The festival invited all these women to answer the question "Is there a feminist pornography?" It was held at the Franklin Furnace, which at the time was like one of the cradles for performance art in New York.

KELLY NICHOLS: For an hour, we gave the public one of our Club 90 meetings. It was so much fun. We came in dressed in grungy clothes, and underneath we had all the porn gear. And we'd talk.

Like Veronica Hart rolled in a stroller, acting like she was feeding the kids. We said, "What's up, Veronica?" And we got coffee for each other and made it like a coffee klatsch kind of thing. And then the lights would go down, and one by one we'd get up and do some little something that described ourselves.

I had a slide show where I started off with one of the pieces you see in *Cosmo*—where they have the person with the blank face—and then the next slide is like dots of makeup, and then it just goes on.

So by the end of my little spiel, I'm in full makeup. I basically just described what I felt: "Porn has been veddy, veddy good to me. I enjoy it. I love hiding behind it. It's been a place for me to wait and figure out what I want to do when I grow up."

Veronica Vera gave a slide show of all of her travels around the world—you know, she was in Egypt on a camel, and she'd talk about it. And every time the lights went back on, we'd go back to our talk about day-to-day.

Then we had Susie Nero—who looked like an R. Crumb drawing—big legs, big girl—and she just got up, turned to the audience, and goes, "I don't have a lot to say. All I know is that someday I'm going to marry an Italian and have a lot of babies. And what I do is dance, and I'm gonna show you."

Then she hit the music, and she did a great striptease for everybody. She was pure, simple, to the point. That was her moment—it was great.

Annie broke your heart—she had so much inside her—this little suburbanized girl from the Valley growing up as "Ellen." She did this whole number about "Ellen versus Annie."

She'd say, "Ellen likes cards with puppies. Annie likes the Hellfire Club. Ellen likes to make money. Annie likes to spend it. Ellen likes to take pictures. Annie likes pictures taken of her."

Annie's splits start getting weirder and weirder. At the very end of her whole diatribe, tears are rolling down her face, and she's saying what Annie wants and what Ellen wants, and they're just so diametrically opposed—and you hear sniffling from the audience.

It was so powerful.

We all had glasses on, we had sweats on, and we just had all this clothing underneath, and every time the lights went down, a piece would come off. You'd have Annie sitting there with a sweatshirt and a tiara. Our tennis shoes would come off and heels would go on. So we became what people expected us to become—by the end we were porn stars.

GLORIA LEONARD: We were actually recruited by a Broadway producer to "kick it up a notch," as they say.

VERONICA HART: Joe Cates came to us and basically wanted to buy the idea of *Deep Inside Porn Stars*, but we didn't want to give up creative control of it.

GLORIA LEONARD: It came down to where the producers thought we were stupid porn bimbos, and they could rob us blind for the rights—and the writing of it—and the talent of it. We figured, split five ways, it was not a worthwhile venture. So we never moved forward.

VERONICA VERA: As Club 90 got more serious and began to meet on a regular basis, Kelly Nichols, Sue Nero, and Sharon Mitchell dropped out. Those three were still making movies.

VERONICA HART: Susie Nero and Kelly Nichols stopped coming to the meetings. At that time in their lives, I think it was too much of a commitment—and people were really trying to get down and deal with their shit, and I don't think they were in for that.

KELLY NICHOLS: I was working. So sometimes I would be on the East Coast or the West Coast and not be able to make meetings—and there would be harsh feelings because I didn't attend the meeting. It's like, "Sorry! I'm doing what we're talking about," you know?

VERONICA VERA: That was kind of the big difference between us. The rest of us weren't really making movies. And so they were still kind of living "the porn star lifestyle" and partying hard. I guess that was a little different from where we were coming from. Maybe we seemed like old fogies to them, ha, ha, ha. We weren't so much the party animals, but they were.

So they dropped out of Club 90 during that first year, and the rest of us continued—and have continued it for almost twenty years. We're still meeting online.

Kristie Nussman

LOS ANGELES
1983–1984

JIM SOUTH: There was a little bitty photo studio in World Modeling, where my desk is now. I was in the office next door. Kristie Nussman came in with a guy, his name was something like Rogers. She actually had a state ID with her picture on it, and a matching birth certificate.

TRACI LORDS (JANUARY 14, 1985): How do I spell my first name? It's K-R-I-S-T-I-E. But yeah, everyone calls me Krissy. And the last name is N-U-S-S-M-A-N. Yeah, this is for your own. You're not going to write any of this?

JIM SOUTH: So I sent Kristie into the little photo studio and told her—like we do with everyone—"Please strip your clothes. I'm going to take a couple Polaroids"—we get them started with that.

TRACI LORDS (JANUARY 14, 1985): I was twenty-one when I was a model, originally. It got a little slow—then I started nude modeling.

JIM SOUTH: I went back into my office. This Rogers guy, who claimed to be Kristie's stepfather, was going on and on about how Kristie knew who Ron Jeremy was. He was sure, in almost no time, that Kristie would be doing X-rated movies. This conversation happened while Kristie was still in the studio getting dressed.

So I confirmed her age and bing-dadda-bong we were off to the races.

TOM BYRON: Traci was hot. She was on the cover of all the magazines—very much in demand as a print model.

TRACI LORDS (JANUARY 14, 1985): Oh yeah, I get a lot of public recognition. I mean, everywhere I go, I'm a cover girl. Even if I don't even have a layout—they just put me on the cover to sell their magazines.

TOM BYRON: She was actually the centerfold of the Vanessa Williams issue of *Penthouse*. Kristie had done that before she'd done her first movie.

GINGER LYNN: I remember meeting Traci in the parking lot of the grocery store across from Jim South's office. I thought she was a hooker. I never for a moment thought anything as to her age or if she was legal. She was definitely hard. Definitely—even then.

JIM SOUTH: Traci was very professional as a businesswoman, and to coin a Texas phrase, she was "slicker than owl shit in an okra dish."

You ever eat boiled okra?

TRACI LORDS (JANUARY 14, 1985): I always liked the name Traci. Then I went, like, looking up in the sky, and I went like, "Ha-ha!" and said to myself, "Ha-ha—Traci Lords."

TOM BYRON: I met Traci on the set of *What Gets Me Hot*. Traci had a nonsex role—just a masturbation thing. In those days, you went from figure model to soft-core still model to movies. It was a gradual progression—they didn't unload everything on you all at once—because it was still in the era of quasi-legality.

HUMPHRY KNIPE: I was working on my old, red Cadillac when I noticed this gorgeous brunette with this older guy—must have been in his fifties, gray hair, hobbling up our driveway. Her shoes were too small or something—real high heels; she could hardly walk. She was not very elegant.

TOM BYRON: I was the new kid on the block—kind of an up-and-comer—and I looked at her and said, "Oh my God! This girl is *gorgeous!*"

HUMPHRY KNIPE: After I finished with the car, I went in the house, and Suze Randall was talking to them. Except for that initial impact she had on me in those particular heels, Traci was gorgeous—baby-faced, sulky expression, *very* sulky—and she was nervous, ha, ha, ha.

Was she gonna pull this off or not?

TRACI LORDS (JANUARY 14, 1985): I'm twenty-two. I'm five foot seven. A hundred and fifteen. The color of my hair? Chestnut brown, I guess. Measurements? Thirty-six on top. D. Waist? Twenty-four. Hips would probably be about thirty-five or thirty-six.

TOM BYRON: Traci comes up to me and says, "Oh, hi. Who are you?" And before I know it she's sitting in my lap, and we're fucking kissing, and it just blew my mind because I got this beautiful goddess all over me.

We just fucked all the time. I was in my twenties, and she had a California driver's license that said she was Kristie Nussman and eighteen. I had no reason to doubt her.

HUMPHRY KNIPE: Suze and I did the initial shoot of Traci at our studio in Venice. It was policy at the time to take a picture of the girl holding her ID—so it was unmistakable that the model was connected with that ID. "Kristie Nussman" was on her birth certificate. She had California ID. So Suze took that Polaroid—and after that it was business as usual.

TRACI LORDS (JANUARY 14, 1985): What lured me into films? The money, and the fun—both. It was for a piece of ass. I didn't have a boyfriend. I've had about five or six boyfriends, so I wouldn't say one. How long do they last? Not long. About as long as instant breakfast.

HUMPHRY KNIPE: Traci actively promoted herself. I was not aware of anyone else—besides this shadowy stepfather figure—and he disappeared very quickly off the scene. She was just a regular girl being booked through a regular agency like everybody else.

TOM BYRON: Traci was one of those girls who in high school would always be going off with the football jock. I couldn't believe a girl this gorgeous was attracted to a dork like me. Because I looked real young, and I thought of myself as incredibly lucky to be in this business, you know? It was mystifying. And, I was completely infatuated with her.

TRACI LORDS (JANUARY 14, 1985): How old was I when I first started having sex? Nineteen—because I was brought up that way. Are my parents separated? They've been divorced since I was about four. My mom had custody. I decided to go see my dad. I lived with my dad for a while. He's an electrician. He lives in West Virginia, and he's real old-fashioned.

My mom had me when she was about sixteen, so she's in her forties. She's an airline stewardess, and she flies all over the country. I see her a lot. She comes into Los Angeles probably a couple of months out of the year. She answers my fan mail, ha, ha, ha.

TOM BYRON: I was too shy to ask her home that night, and I was still befuddled why this gorgeous woman was like paying attention to me. But I got her number, and we talked. We had sex the first time offscreen.

HUMPHRY KNIPE: Suze took Traci down to Mexico for a shoot, and, oh boy, she fucked her way around. It was, you know, anyone and everybody in the house—all night—and she'd be fresh as a daisy the next day.

Phenomenal sexual appetite. A very passionate girl. And fun—a load of fun.

GREG DARK (PORN DIRECTOR): Traci comes over to me on the shoot with this new guy, Dick Rambone—who has fifteen and a half inches—who was having trouble getting it up.

Traci asks, "You think I'm going to help him get it up, don't you?"

I said, "No. I didn't ask you to."

And she said, "I'm not going to."

About five minutes later she comes back and asks, "It's really fascinating, isn't it?"

I ask, "What?"

Traci says, "His dick. I wonder how big it can get?"

TRACI LORDS (JANUARY 14, 1985): I've been wild about sex from day one. And I *do* scream. I've always been a screamer. That's not an act. On my first video I tried to be quiet, but I couldn't muffle myself. Then everyone started going, "Yeah . . . yeah . . . *yeah!*" And I thought, "Oh good, I'm allowed to do this!"

I didn't know they liked noise. I'd never seen a porn flick—how was I supposed to know?

GREG DARK: I said to Traci, "I don't know how big his dick gets. I guess it's not going to get big at all on this shoot."

Traci said, "I bet you I can make it get up!"

So I said, "Well, I don't know, I can't ask you to try."

She said, "I just want to because it's so *fascinating.*" She said it like his dick was this disembodied thing.

JIM SOUTH: I got Traci *a lot* of work. The first or second shoot she did was for a guy named Lance Kincaid. And according to Lance—who only shot single-girl or simulation, where you're just touching—Traci ended up getting on top of someone and having sex, so he had to stop the shoot.

TOM BYRON: The first time I had sex with Traci on-screen was during a still shoot, which turned into a hard-core scene because we were so hot for each other. It just kind of slipped in: "I'm sorry," you know?

GREG DARK: Then Traci jumped on this guy and started sucking his weenie for, like, the next three hours. Meanwhile her pussy's getting sopping wet—we didn't even have to spray water on it for realism. It was all I could do not to dive in between her legs and do her. It was rough. I got a headache from the whole thing.

HUMPHRY KNIPE: Did Traci enjoy sex? Undoubtedly. Not just having sex on-screen because there's a certain amount of fakery that goes with that, but offscreen—you know, assistants, realtors, just about everybody.

One of our assistants told me what a great fuck she was. He said she had an amazing muscle. I was too embarrassed to ask, ha, ha, ha, "Ah, what exactly do mean?" I just thought, "Uh-huh."

TRACI LORDS (JANUARY 14, 1985): All my boyfriend has to do is stick it in— if I haven't had it in a while, I'm already getting off. Ten seconds, two strokes. I like to come about three or four times. The first time is okay; the second is something. The third and the fourth are just like, "EEEEEAAAAAAHHHH!"

GREG DARK: Here's Traci sucking wildly on this guy's dick—with her pussy dripping—and the other girl there is going, "How can she do that? It's completely gross and look—look! She's *turned on!*" She thought it was the sleaziest thing she'd ever seen.

CHRISTY CANYON (PORN STAR): Traci Lords knew more about sex than the whole porn industry put together.

TRACI LORDS (JANUARY 14, 1985): I like to see the dick in my face when it's coming. On the face first. Oh, yeah, I like the way it pulsates before it comes. I like the big dicks.

CHRISTY CANYON: I didn't have a car at the time—or it was broken, or something like that—so I was waiting for a girlfriend to pick me up at this bus stop in Hollywood when this guy pulls up in a brand-new, white Trans Am. He gets out and says, "God, you're so pretty; you've got such a great body. How would you like to make a lot of money?"

I said, "I don't even know your name!"

He said, "I'm Greg Rome," like I should know who he is. He gave me a card from World Modeling, with Jim South's name on it. And he goes on to say, "It's figure modeling. There's some nudity, but nothing else. No sex or that kind of thing."

So I took the card and threw it somewhere in my apartment, thinking, "I'll never call." But I never threw the card out because I was working three different menial jobs just to get by.

TRACI LORDS (JANUARY 14, 1985): I will not be with girls that are underdeveloped. That's one of my strong rules. I like boobs and asses and nice figures. I don't like fat at all. I like long hair. And I favor blonds.

Why the boobs? I like the way they feel. I like to play with them.

RON JEREMY: Traci had the most nicest, natural tits of anybody I've ever seen—other than Christy Canyon. Traci's would slope straight out. Silicone can't do this. And then there were the nipples—big, thick, red nipples. I mean, aureolas—oh my God!

CHRISTY CANYON: One day I was down to five dollars in the bank. My rent, car insurance—everything was overdue—and my phone was going to be turned off. So I found the card and called the number. I worked for nine months straight after that.

TRACI LORDS (JANUARY 14, 1985): I like Ronnie Jeremy. He can fuck good. And Tommy Byron's pretty good.

TOM BYRON: Traci lived in Redondo Beach, and she didn't have a car—which, you know, was because she wasn't old enough to fucking drive a car, I guess. I don't know.

I would pick her up, and she would stay at my apartment in Sherman Oaks because she was booked all the time. She worked *all* the time.

HUMPHRY KNIPE: Traci was Suze's good model. Suze shot twenty shoots with her, and we did about three cool movies with her.

Traci was a fun kid. She was full of life and loved attention—she loved showing off sexually and being a firecracker. You can see that in a lot of her films. She had a pretty vivid sexual life. She used to talk about things she did, the usual sort of sexual shenanigans—aircraft, sex in funny places.

TRACI LORDS (JANUARY 14, 1985): Who gives the best head? In my experience, I would say, probably men. Do I get off on giving head? Yeah, but it depends on my mood. Sometimes I'm exceptional—but sometimes there's times I don't want to do it—and it shows.

CHRISTY CANYON: Then one day I arrived at work, and there were video cameras everywhere. I called Jim South to find out what the hell was going on. He said, "Darlin', I told you it was a video shoot. . . ."

There was no way I would have ever done it had I known. But he pressured me, and I thought to myself, "Five hundred dollars! Gosh, I can pay this off and that off. . . ."

I hated it! Everything on the set was dirty. And afterwards I felt real dirty. The scene was with Ron Jeremy. Yuck! It was really tough. I had just turned eighteen, and I had only been with a few guys in my personal life.

HUMPHRY KNIPE: I directed two movies with Traci. One was called *Lovebites,* and the other was a piece of rubbish called *Miss Passion—*

which was a cheap video, but she did a scene with Ginger Lynn. Traci did her best work with Greg Dark. Traci did a lot of stuff—I don't know how many hundreds of feet of film.

GINGER LYNN: Back then it was such a small industry that we were all pretty tight—everybody hung out with everybody. But Traci was never in the group. She would go off with a person one-on-one, but she never fit into "the gang."

TRACI LORDS (JANUARY 14, 1985): I don't have a problem with any of the other girls. I like a lot of them a lot. I don't have any jealousies at all. I receive vibes—bad ones—from them. I get twinges of jealousy from other girls because, you know, they're like, "Why should Traci make so much money?"

CHRISTY CANYON: After the shoot I called Jim South and told him that it had been the worst experience of my entire life. Jim said, real calmly, "You know, darlin', you're already booked to do a scene tomorrow. After that, if you don't like it, I won't get you any more work."

I thought, "Okay, I'll do one more, and that's it."

I got there, and it was like 180 degrees different. It was for Paradise Visuals, and the producer was a guy that I ended up having a relationship with. All the really good people were there—Traci, Ginger, Peter North, Tom Byron. I really found myself getting into it.

TRACI LORDS (JANUARY 14, 1985): I like boy/girl a lot better than I like girl/girl. I like girls a lot—but there's very few in the business that I wanna be with. I like Ricki Blake. And I like Ginger Lynn. That's about it on girls.

GINGER LYNN: I worked with Traci in five or six scenes, and the scenes were wonderful because my dislike for her was so extreme that on camera it came across as chemistry.

TOM BYRON: I'd walk into a restaurant with Traci feeling like the king of the world. Everyone would be looking at her like, "What the fuck is she doing with that dork?"

It made me feel good, but I think I was more in love with the idea of being in love with her. I mean, we hung out, we did drugs, we fucked, and I said, "I love you, Krissy."

She said, "I love you, too, Tommy," but I don't know if you'd really call it love. But at that time, I definitely thought it was.

TRACI LORDS (JANUARY 14, 1985): How many men have I slept with? I'd say about five hundred. Women? About two hundred. Had I gotten together with women prior to going into the business? Yeah. Have I ever been in love with a woman? No.

GINGER LYNN: You know how you can look at some people and kind of see through them? Traci had this look in her eyes—or rather a void—that scared me.

CHRISTY CANYON: Traci and Ginger hated each other.

TOM BYRON: There was something about Traci that was very distant. She would start talking and cut herself off in the middle of a sentence because obviously she had a lot of things that she couldn't talk about.

GINGER LYNN: Traci made me nervous. She could be extremely cruel. I didn't find her attractive. I instinctually had a bad feeling about her.

HUMPHRY KNIPE: Traci wasn't any less forthcoming than anybody else. It was all irrelevant. She came from somewhere, you know? She didn't discuss her past. We just did movies with her.

TRACI LORDS (JANUARY 14, 1985): There's a part of me—the "Traci Lords" part—that's rude, spoiled, and bitchy. But I have to protect myself. Like if I say, at 3:30 in the morning, "I'm leaving after this scene, whether you like it or not," everyone may think, "What a bitch!" But they'd like to do the same thing—only they can't get away with it.

There are maybe two girls in the past three or four years who get what I get paid: Ginger Lynn and Raven. No one else.

GINGER LYNN: On *The Grafenburg Spot* we had a motor home that would take us from location to location, and Traci fucked the entire crew in between filming. And I never once—and back in those days I did drugs— saw her do a drug. I never saw her do anything that she was forced into doing. She seemed to enjoy herself.

TOM BYRON: I mean, we did drugs together, but she was always on the set on time, you know? She was very professional and always knew her lines. As a matter of fact, on that movie *What Gets Me Hot* she had to read a page-long monologue, and she did it in one take, okay? I can't see how anybody that's whacked out on drugs is gonna be able to do that. She was a consummate professional, which is why she was paid as well as she was and worked as often as she did.

I mean, she had to ask for days off because everybody wanted her. She could have worked every single day.

RUBY GOTTESMAN: Traci Lords—a strange thing. I got to meet her, and I took her to Texas, and we became good friends. She came to see me all the time.

Matter of fact, one day I was takin' lunch—and Traci comes over to the office, and someone on the intercom says, "Your wife is waitin,'" and

Traci gets all undressed—like naked. Just kiddin' around, that's the way Traci was.

Traci was on drugs, but she knew what she was doing. Absolutely.

RON JEREMY: Traci was getting a thousand dollars a day before anybody else. And then she went to a few thousand a day.

TRACI LORDS (JANUARY 14, 1985): Christy Canyon raised her rate to a thousand dollars a day, and no one used her so she had to go back down to seven-fifty. But I'm way beyond that now. I make a thousand for a video, and fifteen hundred for film. How far do I want to go? I want to keep on going until I drop to number two—and then I quit.

HUMPHRY KNIPE: Traci would've been very happy to be a movie star, but to be an actress you have to have the voice. Without it, you're dead. Traci's got the nasty, bratty look down cold. But not the voice.

CHRISTY CANYON: People would always say to me, "You're right up there with Ginger and Traci," like it was supposed to be a big thing. But I didn't think of it like that. I just thought, "I'm having a good time. It's fun, and I'm making the same money as them." I guess I was young and naive.

TRACI LORDS (JANUARY 14, 1985): What am I doing with the money? Investing. I'm buying a condo in Palos Verdes. I already own a house in Redondo Beach. And I have a Corvette and a Trans Am.

What's the wildest thing I've ever done sexually? I'd say fuck my boyfriend on the hood of my Corvette—at night, in public—on the Pacific Coast Highway, overlooking all of L.A.

It was offscreen, and it was my boyfriend. He was a really good lay.

TOM BYRON: She was living in Redondo Beach with a guy named Tommy—this surfer dude, this little, pretty boy. When Traci and I were on the set of *Sister Dearest*—you know, one of those incest things—it was real late at night, and we were just kind of like commiserating, when all of a sudden she goes, "Tommy's spending all my money. He treats me like shit; he just dented my car. I gotta get away from this guy."

I said, "Well, what's the problem? Come stay with me."

She says, "I can't."

I go, "What do you mean you can't? I'll pick you up. I'm not scared of this guy. I'll wipe the floor with him. You come stay with me."

She goes, "I can't. He knows too much about me. He's holding something over my head."

I was just like, "Well, whatever. You got my number. You know where I live. You got a place if you need it."

RARE CANCER SEE

Outbreak Occurs Amor

California—8 Died Ins

A DISEASE'S SPREA
PROVOKES ANXIET

Mysterious Illness Mos
omosex

Part 9: THE
PARTY'S

Gay Men To Drug Use
Heterosexuals And AID
New Data Examine

Syringes Also Involved In AIDS Trans
DRUG ABUSERS TRY TO CUT AIDS RIS
60 Percent Who Use Needles in New York Are Infected by

"This is a battle against disease, not against
fellow Americans… [But] AIDS education, o
any aspect of sex education, will not be value
neutral… Final judgment is up to God."

AIDS is the wrath o

N 41 HOMOSEXUALS
Men in New York and
2 Years First Appears
AIDS Spreads Pain and Fe
Among Ill and Healthy Alik
New Fear on Drug Use
nd AIDS; Top Officia
Voices New Fear on D

OVER

1984–1987

xperts Say Deaths Will
limb Sharply; Forecast
ases leads to compariso
agan to Back AIDS Plan Urging Youths to Avoid Sex
DS Worry Alters Sex Habits, St
OW CONTAGIOUS IS AIDS'

Headlines from *New York Times* and *Los Angeles Times*, 1984–1987.

The Porn Marriage
NEW YORK CITY/LOS ANGELES
1984

TOM BYRON: Teddy Snyder was a guy I worked for doing loops. He owned a company called VCX—had a partner named Bobby Genova. He was always a nice enough guy to me.

FRED LINCOLN: Christ, I couldn't tell you how many films I did for Teddy Snyder. When I was working for him, Ted would shoot, and Bobby Genova was his tote guy. Teddy and I were best buddies.

TOM BYRON: The very first time I worked with Traci Lords on film was for Teddy Snyder. It was called *Tracie Lords*—before, you know, the "official" spelling. It was a collection of loops.

Did Teddy direct it? *Direct*. No. You know, Teddy paid for it, and he was on the set. But Jason Russell filmed the thing—he was the cinematographer with his little sixteen-millimeter camera. Ted was just there.

SHARON MITCHELL: Very few of the connected guys were chick-fuckers. Usually they'd only get a porn girl to come out if it was a setup for information—a business thing, you know? "Let's put pussy in front of him, and we'll get what we want. After all these girls work for us." And any favor that was asked of us was complied with instantly.

I was asked to do a favor once or twice.

TIM CONNELLY: Teddy Snyder was about six foot two, wore cowboy hats and cowboy boots and a lot of gold. Weighed about 225. Big guy with a big gut—but hard fat, you know, not sloppy fat. Looked like he could kill you with a snap of his wrist. And he was like a cocaine cowboy.

Pouring sweat all the time. Real tough guy. And he liked to fuck the girls.

SHARON MITCHELL: One night Teddy Snyder knocked on my bedroom window, asked me to come down the fire escape, get into a car, and make a movie in the middle of the night as entertainment for certain people. I went, "Sure." I knew who these people were. I was getting paid. As far as I was concerned, it was just a movie.

FRED LINCOLN: When I first came out to Los Angeles, I wasn't getting any work, so Teddy gave me a contract to do a music video for Ginger Lynn. He paid me five hundred bucks and gave me a Porsche. And they never asked me to do a thing—except to plan this video.

ERIC EDWARDS: Teddy was the first guy I worked for. He was cool back then: My only complaint was—when he wanted a girl to do an anal, for example, he would say, "Hey, I'll give you another ten dollars."

Teddy had all this gold dripping off his neck; he bragged about crashing his airplane and then buying a new one. So I would go up to him and say, "Ted, come on, give her some more money, for Pete's sake!"

FRED LINCOLN: Teddy Snyder and Bobby Genova spent, like, a million dollars on Ginger's music video. It was supposed to be a legitimate thing—like what Andrea True did—but it never even came close because they didn't like the way Ginger sang. So they got somebody else, and they wanted her to sing while Ginger mouthed the words.

I said, "Wait a minute, guys. Let's say it's a success? The real singer's not gonna be quiet! She's gonna say, 'Hey! That's me singing!' And then we're gonna look like fuckin' idiots!" That's when I backed out.

TOM BYRON: Teddy got a kick outta me. I mean, a lot of those connected guys did. You know, "Ah, look at this fucking kid. He did a cum shot, hit the fuckin' wall, this fuckin' guy. Look at the big, fuckin' prick on this fuckin' kid ova hea'."

That's why I got to hang out at all their parties—I was nonthreatening. The girls who were there were for those guys. I didn't move on any of the girls. I just sat there.

I was just like, "Mr. Sabatoni, how you doin'? Oh, is that coke? Sure, I'll do a line. Thanks."

And they'd bust my balls. I was kinda like fucking Spider from *Goodfellas.* "Spider, go get me the fuckin' drink, Spider!" But I'd never tell them to go fuck themselves—so I never got shot in the foot.

All that coke that we used to snort over at fucking Bobby's—I heard it came from Henry Hill. Yeah, it was *Goodfellas* coke.

BOBBY GENOVA: Henry Hill was a good friend of mine.

TOM BYRON: I'm a big fan of the *Godfather* movies and all that other shit. I mean, I'm half-Italian, you know what I'm saying? I'm *one* of those guys. I admire that "code of honor" kind of thing. I mean, sometimes the line gets distorted or whatever, but when it comes to keeping a secret, I believe in that. I admire that. But Teddy, ahhh . . .

FRED LINCOLN: Teddy Snyder and Bobby Genova were makin' money. They had a plane. Were they fucking in the plane? No, Bobby just wanted to learn how to fly, ha, ha, ha. Bobby was a strange guy, still is.

TIM CONNELLY: You'd drive out to some industrial park in the middle of nowhere, and these high-level guys—Teddy and Bobby—are in a fucking Quonset hut running their little empire, doing blow, and fucking skanky little girls from San Bernardino.

TOM BYRON: Teddy used to have these little coke orgies or whatever—because I think he liked to videotape guys fucking his wife, Sharon.

Sharon had red hair—wasn't that long. White skin, pretty face. She was skinny because she did a lot of coke. That's about it. She was pretty friendly, but she didn't come on that strong to me. Marc Wallice was fucking her. Probably Paul Thomas. I don't know anyone else.

FRED LINCOLN: When Teddy first met Sharon, she was a member of the "horse set." She could've went to the moon! But she went along with Teddy's degenerate ways—so she gave up her career, thinking Teddy was going to take care of her.

PHIL VANNATTER (LAPD DETECTIVE): Sharon Snyder was sort of the outcast of her family. They were not happy with her lifestyle.

TOM BYRON: I woulda fucked her. I dunno, Sharon Snyder was a very sexual person. I mean, that might have been because she was full of coke—but she came on to a lot of people.

She probably made a couple of flirtatious passes at me, but I didn't really pick up on it. I mean, she was the wife of the guy who was paying my bills, so I wasn't gonna go there.

And Teddy definitely had a violent streak. I knew he was connected, but I wasn't scared of that; back then everybody was connected. But I'd heard stories about Teddy, you know? Paul Thomas told me that Teddy once fucking put a gun in his mouth and threatened to blow his fucking head off—and I think Marc Wallice said the same thing. You know what I'm saying? I'd heard Ted had done, like, scary things.

Plus, he did a lotta coke. So, you know, guns and coke . . . I kept a respectful distance.

PHIL VANNATTER: I saw a videotape of Sharon—several months pregnant—having oral sex with another man. This is the kind of people they were. Anybody who would film his pregnant wife having sex with somebody else has got to be a sick puppy.

To Be or Not to Be?

LOUISVILLE, KENTUCKY
1984

PAT LIVINGSTON: I just didn't want to go on. I didn't want to go on as Pat Salamone, and I didn't want to go on as Pat Livingston.

I just saw my life totally coming apart and Salamone was part of that, Vick and the family were part of that, the job was part of that. Everything was just . . . I just wanted to stop. So did I take a .357 Magnum down and look at it that week? You bet I did. I was sitting on the edge of the bed staring at it.

BILL KELLY: At the time MIPORN went into operation, pornography was a four-billion-dollar-a-year business—and by the time the operation was over, porn was about an eight-billion-dollar industry.

So we had absolutely no permanent effect on interstate transportation of obscene matter at all.

PAT LIVINGSTON: I can't remember whether I spun the cylinder or opened the cylinder. I had such a feeling of hopelessness, and no alternative other than to just end it. I wasn't able to think rationally.

NANCY LIVINGSTON: Vickie called me on a Friday night, just hysterical. She couldn't talk to me over the phone, so I went to pick her up. That's when she told me and my mother that she'd found the gun.

Vickie asked Michael if Daddy had taken his briefcase upstairs with him.

Michael, who was very perceptive, said, "Yeah, Mom, are you thinking what I'm thinking? He has a gun in there."

Pat was in the bedroom with the gun, and I think they wrestled with it. She took it away from him. It had four bullets in it.

PAT LIVINGSTON: I hadn't slept in three or four days, and I had worn myself down. That Friday I asked Vick to stay home, then, very shortly after, I wished she had gone. I wanted to be by myself and do what I wanted to do, and she wouldn't let me out of her sight. But eventually I left because I had an excuse to go see Dr. Riddick.

VICKIE LIVINGSTON: Pat had an appointment at Dr. Riddick's at five. He was procrastinating about leaving, then he finally left about 4:15. About 5:15 Riddick called me and wanted to know if Pat had left yet. That's when he told me that Pat had talked to him about suicide.

PAT LIVINGSTON: I just drove down the road to Shelbyville, toward Dr. Riddick's place, going very slow. Then I turned back to St. Matthews, past the police department and Bacon's, just kind of meandering, wandering. I didn't have any direction. I didn't know where I was going. I thought about going to Dr. Riddick's. But I didn't. I should have.

VICKIE LIVINGSTON: I was real scared. I tried to get into Pat's briefcase to look for his service revolver, but I didn't know the combination. I ran upstairs to check and see if the big gun was there—and it was—but Riddick was talking about the car and all this other stuff.

PAT LIVINGSTON: I ended up in Seneca Park, out by Route 64, where the golf course is. Then I got back on Route 64, drove through downtown. Then I went 10 to 15 miles into Indiana. Then I turned around, came back, and crossed the bridge back into Louisville.

I got off at the Grainstead exit, which is kind of near Riddick's office. I thought I might be going there. But then I got back on 64 again. I drove back over the bridge into Indiana. A couple of times along the way, I stopped the car and just sat there.

BILL KELLY: I was misquoted in one of the *Miami Herald* articles where I said, "Agents didn't use to have mental problems. They just went out and shot themselves."

It sounds cruel, but what I meant was this: Back in the old bureau, you never heard about a guy that had psychological problems. Nobody was getting psychiatric treatment that I ever heard of.

PAT LIVINGSTON: I thought about a lot of ways to kill myself. I thought about doing it the same way my uncle had done it—just going off the bridge. That seemed like a nice, easy way of doing it. I thought about using the gun.

BILL KELLY: Obviously it was happening to some guys, but instead of going to get help they'd take a service revolver and blow their brains out. That's what I meant—but it was sort of twisted around to make it look like I was suggesting that Pat should have shot himself. I wrote him a letter and said, "Pat, that is *not* what I meant."

PAT LIVINGSTON: Then I came back home and saw my brother-in-law Denny's car here. I just came in the kitchen, and Vick was on the phone to Riddick or somebody, and I heard her say, "He's here."

Denny was standing there, and Vickie's friend was standing there. I sat down in the chair. A dining room chair. People talked, and I just didn't say anything.

Then they asked if I wanted to go to the hospital, and I went.

BILL KELLY: I would have kicked Pat's tail from here to Butte, Montana, for the incident in Bacon's Department Store, but I would not have fired him. We had a tragedy on our hands. I was one of the few people that supported him before the bureau, saying, "I knew this case from the beginning, and I think that the bureau should have accepted some responsibility for his condition."

It was a shame. His life was destroyed, and so was his family's.

GRID

NEW YORK CITY/LOS ANGELES
1984–1985

SHARON MITCHELL: Marc Stevens was nine and a half inches—but we used to call him Mr. Ten-and-a-Half. At that length, does it really matter?

Marc was wonderful and flamboyant. We appeared in a couple of the same movies, but we never directly worked together. But I did work with Marc's dance troupe. We used to paint ourselves all odd colors—mostly silver and gold—and do dance shows. It was very popular, and it was fun.

ANNIE SPRINKLE: I met Marc Stevens at Leonard Curtman's studio, and I fucked him right away. Marc fucked girls, but he was totally gay—he had relationships with guys.

Marc and I became very good friends. We lived down the hall from each other for a good ten years—at Twenty-seventh and Lexington. I was in apartment 11, he was in 11B.

SHARON MITCHELL: Marc was a rather successful pimp for a while. He worked out of the same building where Annie Sprinkle had the Sprinkle Salon—a very nice building right off Gramercy Park. Marc had a stable of girls, but he'd call in for specialty stuff.

I only worked for Marc for about a day—ha, ha, ha—because I was a really bad hooker. I never liked sex that much to begin with, and at least in the porn movies I had my choice of people to be with. I mean, here comes somebody that you wouldn't have sex with if you weren't getting paid, and they want to do things to you with no camera around. I was just like, "*Whoa*. Why?!" So I wasn't very good at it, ha, ha, ha.

TIM CONNELLY: The first time I heard about anything AIDS-related was when Marc Stevens brought it up. He said, "There's something going down in the Village that seems to be, like, much bigger than what's normally going down in the Village—people are getting really sick and dying."

ANNIE SPRINKLE: Marc Stevens said, "Have you heard about this gay cancer thing?"

I laughed and said, "Gay cancer?!" I just thought that was hysterically funny.

Marc said, "No, really. Gay cancer."

I was like, "Yeah, *right*." But then I started hearing bits on the news about GRID: Gay Related Immunodeficiency Disease.

SHARON MITCHELL: I was up at Fred Lincoln's apartment kicking coke when I had a fucking kidney shutdown or something. Fred took me to the hospital, and they gave me whatever it is they give you.

So I'm in this complete stupor, and when I open my eyes the first people I see are Larry Levine, Al Goldstein, Fred Lincoln, and Ron Jeremy. They're all standing around the bed wearing fucking masks—because they thought I had GRID.

I went, "Oh my God! *Fuck!*" I thought I was dead, and I was having some sort of flashback thing—you know, "I've seen the light. . . . and it's *Ron Jeremy!*"

It turned out it was just fucking too much coke, you know? Which could have been gay-related, I'm sure.

HENRI PACHARD: I was in New York when I first heard about AIDS. What I started to hear was the question "Am I spreading something?"

I thought, "Am I a death merchant?"

That was a serious moral question for me for a while. Then it became "If they want to protect themselves they should, and if they don't wanna protect themselves, I'm not gonna."

My biggest fear was not so much about the ability to shoot these movies, but that they were going to be regulated by the Health Department, like when they shut down the bathhouses in all the major cities. Yet, why don't they shut down pornographers? Violating their First Amendment rights?

Bullshit.

ANNIE SPRINKLE: Did AIDS alter my life? Oh, totally, radically, drastically. It was like we'd had this big, fabulous orgy party, and then suddenly it ended. People were in the hospital; people were dying. There were funerals. It felt like we had gone to war.

TIM CONNELLY: Everybody thought it was the amyl nitrate. You'd be out at a club, having a drink—and it's really loud and crowded—and somebody would hand you a bottle of amyl nitrate. It was just a cheap high, a lot of people did it. So when the *Village Voice* did an article about the connection between amyl nitrate and Kaposi's sarcoma, I had to read it. But by the time I was done I wasn't buying their theory.

ANNIE SPRINKLE: Of course we fucked in the hospitals. I'd wear my nurse's outfit, and we'd play with dildos. I had sex with one guy the week before he went in for his spinal tap and then again when he came out. Because I figured, whatever "IT" was—if all these guys had it, I must have it.

HENRI PACHARD: This was 1984. We didn't have enough information. We discovered that AIDS was beginning to spread among drug users and homosexuals. So if you were a Haitian homosexual needle-using drug addict, then there was a good chance you would contract this failure in your immune system.

So we all thought, "It can't be me. I'm straight. I only do coke; I don't do needles, and she doesn't, either. So we're both cool."

TIM CONNELLY: The first person I knew who had it was a porn director named Robert. I worked in a bunch of his movies—he directed both gay and straight films. Robert was really sick when we did *Brooke Does College*. He just looked terrible. I tried to rub his shoulders because he said he ached all over—but he said he didn't want to be touched. Even being touched hurt him.

GLORIA LEONARD: God, there was a time—around 1985, 1986—I went to six funerals in four weeks. Among the first was Chuck Vincent and a guy I worked with, Wade Nichols; he also worked under the name Dennis Parker. I could go on and on.

ANNIE SPRINKLE: How could I not have AIDS, when all the people I was having sex with were getting really sick and losing their eyesight and becoming demented?

When you visited them in the hospital, you'd have to wear a mask and gown. But I'd just take all of that off. And you didn't know if you could touch them, but I did anyway. I just thought, *"I'm not going to stop touching my friends and lovers, you know?"*

TIM CONNELLY: Robert lived in this beautiful high-rise apartment on Fifty-seventh Street. He was always funny and happy—just the coolest guy in the world. He would have pajama parties. We'd all go over to his place on Saturday night in our pajamas and drink and eat and do whatever—stay up all night. It was just great fun.

When he got sick he moved out to California to be with his mom. So when Kelly and I came out, we went to visit him in this hospital down in Venice. He had lost all this weight, and he had these giant black sores all over him. We had to wear masks and suits because his lesions were festering. That was my first real awareness of the mortality of the disease.

He was saying it was Kaposi's sarcoma; I guessed it was AIDS.

ANNIE SPRINKLE: My hemorrhoids saved my life—because I'm sure I would have gotten AIDS if I had had more anal sex. I mean, my pussy was made of iron at that time. You could do anything to it. My pussy was invincible.

I was also into macrobiotics, doing a lot of seaweed. Maybe it was that; maybe it was just pure luck. I mean, God knows, I had a lot of sex with a lot of people with AIDS. Drank their piss. Had their Crisco-covered hand go from their butt to my pussy—all that.

You know, it made me think—maybe it was a miracle. An absolute miracle.

BUD LEE: I don't think anybody in our business has been infected with HIV from another human being. You know why? I think it's what they do when they're not working. It's their lifestyle.

ANNIE SPRINKLE: During this big AIDS crisis, I became really involved with the healing circle. Probably half the people there had AIDS; the other half were people really affected by AIDS or who didn't know if they had it. Most of us hadn't been tested.

GLORIA LEONARD: Did people really try to alter their behavior? No, they stuck their heads in the sand, essentially.

TIM CONNELLY: The only people I knew who had it were gay, and the only people who seemed to talk about having it were gay. So at that point—as crazy as it sounded—I thought maybe it was created by somebody who hated gay people. Because it just didn't make sense any other way. I mean, if it was just because they have anal sex, why weren't straight people getting it?

And somehow maybe they gave it to a gay guy, and gay guys only have sex with gay guys. We weren't hearing about gay women getting it.

ANNIE SPRINKLE: I had never cried before—you know, until AIDS hit. Then suddenly it was like a lifetime of tears and sadness. I suddenly felt the human condition for the first time.

JOHN WATERS: It's truly a taboo to fuck without rubbers in a gay movie, and even if you did, they wouldn't distribute it. But in straight movies they don't—and that shocks me because that's how you get AIDS, plain and simple.

BUD LEE: Every one of our movies should have condoms in them. What educational-minded person in their right mind is going to advocate unsafe sex between consenting adults? Not one. So for us to look legitimate—to hide behind that banner—we have to allow condoms. But we also have to temper it with freedom of choice among the talent.

TIM CONNELLY: When I heard that Tony Taylor had AIDS, that's when I realized it was bigger than the gay community.

Tony was a guy I met at Show World; he lived with Kelly and me for a while. He was a big, strapping, black guy from the Upper West Side, whose mother raised him alone. Tony was extremely articulate; he looked like Sidney Poitier. But then Tony got into drugs real bad, and he got AIDS.

Even though Tony was a sex worker, there was no question in my mind—there's no way he ever had gay sex. It was obvious he'd gotten it from a needle.

ANNIE SPRINKLE: At a certain point, Marc Stevens started doing so many drugs that I stopped hanging out with him. Then he started selling crack out of his apartment, and he had all these guys from Honduras with guns hanging around.

He had a gorgeous penthouse apartment—with views and decks—and they made it like this *cave*. All the windows were covered with black paper and the washer and dryer were being broken into all of the time.

SHARON MITCHELL: Marc was bisexual. You know how some people are gay for pay? I think Marc was *straight* for pay.

ANNIE SPRINKLE: Marc was really into coke for a long time. And then crack, and then he went through an angel dust phase.

One night one of Marc's crack guys crawled along the ledge of our apartment building and came in through my window. I woke up, and this guy was feeling my legs. I thought, *Holy Jesus*. That was pretty scary. But I killed him with kindness and got him to leave.

I was pissed off at Marc after that—he knew I lived there. So we didn't see each other for about six months after that—and all that time he was dying.

TIM CONNELLY: At that point I started feeling like I had to get out of this business. I'm in a relationship, and I'm having indiscriminate sex with strangers—on camera, you know? Whoever I fuck that day, I don't even know. I mean, I'd always try to find out who I have to work with in the hope that I might be able to say: "Well, if these are the choices, can I have this one?"

But you never ultimately have control over who you work with, you know?

ANNIE SPRINKLE: Marc wasn't particularly out about having AIDS. I saw him before he died, and it was just a really sad ending. He was frothing at the mouth; he must have weighed eighty pounds. Nobody was caring for him, and he wouldn't go to the hospital. And of course as soon as he died everything was stolen.

SHARON MITCHELL: Marc died of AIDS. It was slow and painful, and it involved a lot of freebase—a lot of drugs.

ANNIE SPRINKLE: Marc's mother had jumped out a window, so I think Marc always thought he would commit suicide, too. And in a way he did. I would say that smoking crack was a way of committing suicide.

HUMPHRY KNIPE: What happened to the sexual revolution? It caught AIDS and died.

Pimping and Pandering

LOS ANGELES
1985

BOBBY ELKINS: Hal Freeman was a bar-supply salesman. When I owned the Lemon Twist Lounge, he was my man. All my juices and all my bar stuff came from Hal.

Well, one day Hal comes in and says, "Look, my cousin Sam Lebowski and I are going to make these booths for peep shows. And we're gonna make loops for the booths." Hal was making rubber goods—dildos and stuff. So Hal says, "Come on over."

So I sold the bar to twin brothers. But one of the twins was AWOL from the army, and they put down like $40,000 for the bar, and the ABC Agency comes to me and says, "The bar can't go through. He's AWOL from the army, and you're going to have to stay here." So I said to Hal, "I'll be over, as soon as I get this thing with the bar cleared up."

PAUL FISHBEIN (FOUNDER OF *ADULT VIDEO NEWS*): Hal Freeman was a big guy, heavyset, sort of balding, had a big army tattoo on his forearm. Hal was a big presence, with a bellowing voice; he commanded attention when he walked into a room. He was one of those guys with a lot of bravado but actually had a big heart, you know?

BOBBY ELKINS: Hal and Sam were building rubber cocks; they hooked up to bicycle pumps as penis enlargers, ha, ha, ha. And then they were building peep-show booths, slapping them together out of plywood, a coat of paint. They were shit.

After I sold the bar, I kind of got my feet wet with Hal and Sam and then one day Hal says to me, "Why don't you be a salesman, and sell this stuff?" Which I did. And I helped them in other ways. Hal had sold a guy in Denver twenty of the peep-show booths, and the guy stiffed him. He owed him something like ten thousand dollars. Hal says, "Will you go up there and get my money for me?" That sounded exciting, so I go to Denver.

PAUL FISHBEIN: I was working out of my apartment in Philadelphia, putting out the *AVN Newsletter.* Hal called me from the set in San Francisco. At the time nobody was shooting in L.A. because of the ongoing pimping and pandering cases there.

Hal told me, "I got these beautiful girls here. I want you to come out and cover the movie." So I flew out from Philadelphia, in an ice storm, to cover this movie, *Layover.*

BOBBY ELKINS: I walk into the shop in Denver, and this guy has got two topless broads shining shoes in the corner.

I says, "I'm here for Sam and Hal Freeman. You owe them money. Why don't you pay them?"

He goes, "Whaa? Whaa?" So I call Hal and say, "Hal, this guy don't want to pay you."

Hal says, "Let me talk to him."

Hal talks to him, and I still can't get nothing out of him. So I tell Hal, "The only way I'm going to get the money back is to give him an okie-dokie." I says, "Hal, let me fuck him."

So I start telling the guy about eight-millimeter stuff, and he wants the stuff—he needs a hundred, two hundred pieces—so I tell him they're eighteen bucks a piece, and I need eighteen hundred.

PAUL FISHBEIN: It was the first time I was ever on an adult film set. I was fascinated. People were having sex in front of me, and they were filming it.

I met Paul Thomas, and he talked to me a lot. I interviewed everybody. I was really naive at the time, and Hal was like really pushing for the publicity. It turned out to be the first "On the Set" piece *AVN* ever ran. *And* I was an extra in the movie.

BOBBY ELKINS: This guy ain't paying Hal, and he's buying eighteen hundred bucks' worth of stuff from me, so me and this sharp dago kid get a trunk—one of those steel lockers. Then we fill it with peat moss and lock it up.

Then we meet at the airport, we're gonna make the switch at the airport. He turns over the eighteen hundred. I give him the locker. He goes, "Wait a minute. Let me open the thing. Let me make sure it's in there."

I start to run, and he follows me. But I give the eighteen hundred to the sharp dago kid.

Well, the guy from Denver calls the police, and they arrest me at the airport in Denver. The guy tells the cops, "We opened it, and it was just peat moss!"

I said, "So what do you want me to do? I got no money—I got nothing on me."

FRED LINCOLN: I was living in Ventura at the time, on the beach. Sharon Mitchell says, "Please—let me move in with you. I don't wanna start this heroin shit again. I wanna be straight. I wanna be okay."

BOBBY ELKINS: The cops lock me up. I walk into jail, and everybody has heard about the con man who put the peat moss in the trunk for eighteen hundred bucks. The head cop calls me in—Italian cop, good-looking—and says, "We know you fucked them, and we know he had the money—we saw the bank account. And you gave it to somebody."

I said, "I gave it to nobody."

I spend the weekend in jail, and I became a celebrity to all the *schvartzes* and Mexican kids because of that peat moss. When they let me out Monday morning, they said, "Take the first plane out, and never come to Denver again."

FRED LINCOLN: So we moved to a new place in Ventura, me and Mitch. She had a boyfriend, but Mitch and I've had flings off and on for twenty years; we've been buddies. Then Buck Adams and Amber Lynn come to the house, and Buck didn't have no place to live, so I let him stay there. Then Amber stayed. And they all started gettin' high, and I'm starting to do a lot of drinking.

I'm thinkin', this ain't workin' for me. Then Mitch got a new boyfriend—Buddy Love—and I didn't know it, but they're gettin' high together.

BOBBY ELKINS: Hal loved me for getting that money, even though it was only a quarter of what the guy owed him. That guy in Denver was greedy. The funny thing about life is, you cannot beat an honest man. An honest person is not greedy, and there's no way you can hurt an honest man.

Then Hal went into the video thing—Hollywood Video, right? I kind of liked Hal's videos. So I became a buyer, and I sold a lot of them to my clients.

FRED LINCOLN: Jesus, Amber Lynn was making so much money it was insane. She was the highest-paid girl on the dance circuit. She was making thirty-two thousand a week.

I told her, "You're making more than the entire Supreme Court! Whatsamatter with you? You can invest in real estate—buy bonds, stocks, whatever! You have a chance to reach an age where you don't have to worry about money!"

She said, "No, let's smoke it instead. That makes more sense."

What the fuck? What is wrong with you people?

LOS ANGELES TIMES, MAY 20, 1985: HARD-CORE SEX FILMS: DOES CASTING CONSTITUTE PANDERING?: "Cracking down on the city's $550-million-a-year adult film industry, the Los Angeles Police Department has taken the controversial step of arresting producers of hard-core sex films under the state's tough pandering law, which carries a three-year prison term."

PAUL FISHBEIN: The first time Hal Freeman was arrested was in 1983, the same year *AVN* started publishing. I didn't have anyone on the West Coast, so the stories came in by phone. I'm not even sure we covered his arrest. But Hal always said, "I'll fight this to the Supreme Court if I have to." There was never a doubt.

LOS ANGELES TIMES, MAY 20, 1985: HARD-CORE SEX FILMS: DOES CASTING CONSTITUTE PANDERING?: "The Los Angeles Police Department has sought pandering charges against six people connected with the adult film industry since 1983. To date, one prosecution has reached trial stage.

"The case involves Harold Freeman, an Encino filmmaker who is on trial in Van Nuys Superior Court in connection with the film 'Caught From Behind II.'"

BOBBY ELKINS: Hal Freeman never became big because he was always fighting the beef. What happens when you're fighting a beef? You think you can't expand because then you got a beef over a beef, then you're redoing a beef, you always got problems. So you stop making new stuff; you're not producing like you used to. That's what happens when you get in trouble. It all falls apart.

JERRY BUTLER (FORMER PORN STAR): Hal Freeman wanted to see me, so I drove to his office with Amber Lynn, Buck Adams, and Jessica Wylde. When we walked in for our appointment, Hal's daughter, Sherry, and his wife, Cynthia, looked at us as if we were animals in an exhibition. Then they took turns grilling us about our appointment with Hal. Here we were, in a business where we fucked our asses off so that people like them could make a lot of money, and they were whispering about us and giggling.

I'd had enough. "What the fuck is so funny? If you don't get off your ass and tell Hal I'm out here, I'll go berserk. And you won't like what you see."

They stopped laughing.

BOBBY ELKINS: Hal was married to a blond—a shiksa, right? He had a gentile daughter, too—looked like Hitler.

JERRY BUTLER: Hal called me inside immediately. He seemed pretty friendly, so I told him about the snot-nosed cunts he employed in his front office. He told me they were his wife and daughter, but I didn't apologize. "Hal, I can't say I'm sorry," I told him. "They treated us like animals."

He apologized—but in the next breath he asked me to do an anal scene for three hundred and fifty bucks, which is far below standard. I agreed, but on the day of the shoot, I never showed up. It was my way of getting back at him.

FRED LINCOLN: One day I was driving Amber Lynn back from the airport. She's coming back from Canada. We're talking about things—and Amber and I were fucking. So we're driving, and she said, "You know, I'd really like something to eat."

I had my little convertible, so I said, "You know, Amber, we can't leave the luggage because it's got no top." I said, "Let's drop by home."

So we dropped the luggage off, and I heard this thud from the closet. I looked inside, and Buck's in the fuckin' closet, dead. No pulse, no nothin'. God, I was so fuckin' mad. I start yelling, and Amber's freaking, she's screaming, "MY BROTHER!" I'm poundin' him on the chest. "You dumb son of a bitch. You wanna kill yourself, walk in front of a truck. What the fuck are you doin' in my closet?" I guess all that pounding brought him back to life; I mean all of a sudden he's breathin' again.

I mean, Buck did this over Janet Littledove, another porn star. Chrissakes—talk about a fuckin' moron.

JERRY BUTLER: Buck and Amber were adopted by their stepparents. Their biological mother died of cancer. They led a pretty shabby life in Orange County. They were rednecks—poor, white trash. Grew up stealing and driving fast cars. So I really clicked with Buck.

BUCK ADAMS: My sister, Amber Lynn, had been in the business maybe six months when a still photographer introduced her to an agent named Reb Sawitz. Now this was back in the days when male strippers were just crazy guys who ran around in their underwear, and I was making a little money doing that because I couldn't box anymore—I'd hurt my hand.

So Amber called me up and goes, "I'm doing movies, and they need a guy. You know, you can make three hundred and fifty bucks cash—like, now. You can work with one of my girlfriends, and she's really cute."

Which was an exceedingly huge lie—about the girl, not the money.

FRED LINCOLN: Buck Adams hung himself in my closet, but the bar broke, ha, ha, ha. So Buck comes back to life, but Amber's called 911. The cops show up, and Buck has all these outstanding warrants for child support. The cops are in the house and they pull out their guns. I don't even know if they had a warrant.

I said, "What the hell is goin' on here? All we need is an ambulance. This guy hurt himself."

The cops said, "No, he don't need no ambulance."

I finally calmed the cops down, calmed Amber down. I thought, "What am I doing with these fuckin' crazy people? Jesus."

You know what's wrong with Buck and Amber? You can never fuckin' believe anything they say, ha, ha, ha. If they say, "Nice day," then get your raincoat because it's probably storming.

JERRY BUTLER: I felt very brotherly toward Amber Lynn. Before doing *The Four-X Feeling* with her in New York, we were staying at the Edison Hotel. I was doing so much cocaine. Maybe the coke made me more intense, but Amber and I got into a pretty heavy conversation. I had never made love to her offscreen. That night she let me stay in her room.

We talked and talked, and she told me things about her childhood that I'd never known. Her mom had died at an early age, and her dad ran away.

I was very open with her, and I asked her to do something I felt very shy about. I let her take a hairbrush and stick it up my behind.

FRED LINCOLN: Fuck it that Buck and Amber had some trailer-park roots. Who cares about their childhood? Everybody blames their childhood for what they do when they're adults. How fuckin' stupid is that?

I knew Buck, knew he was high. But I like Buck; he was a good guy. Then things started to slip a little bit with Mitch, and she really panicked. And I said, "You know what, Mitch? I really can't be around drugs. That's why I left Tiffany Clark."

So after that little scene with the cops, I thought, "I should be living somewhere else." I actually left them the house.

VERONICA HART: You would never, ever film in Los Angeles because back then, there was a law called "pandering." They basically considered a paid performance of sex to be prostitution. According to them we were all whores—the guys, the girls, whatever. Basically they did not consider us actors and actresses; we were considered prostitutes because we were getting paid for sexual services. It didn't matter that the person we were having sex with was also getting paid—that we were both paid professionals.

FRED LINCOLN: Jamie Gillis calls me and says, "I'm going to San Francisco. Wanna rent my house in Hollywood?"

I said, "Lemme see it, Jamie. I'm lookin' to move." Because I couldn't stand the drive from Ventura anymore, fuckin' horrible.

Jamie's house was really nice; rent was like seven hundred fifty a month. I said, "Wow, this is cool. I'll take it." It was already furnished, so I just moved right in.

LOS ANGELES TIMES, MAY 20, 1985: HARD-CORE SEX FILMS: DOES CASTING CONSTITUTE PANDERING?: "'If I had been shooting in Los Angeles, you best believe I wouldn't be now,' said Les Baker, president of Gemini Film Corporation in Las Vegas, who films in the San Francisco area. 'Unequivocally, it has put a chill on the Los Angeles industry. No sensible person would stick his head into that meat grinder.'"

VERONICA HART: The only place really in California that was safe to shoot was in San Francisco, where nobody gave a shit. You had to be fucking in public or running around without your clothes on for them to get upset. The HoJo's in Marin County was our big hideout there.

SHARON MITCHELL: There were a couple of cops in Hollywood who were really keeping tabs on where the shoots were and chasing after us. Because there was no such thing as a permit, we couldn't shoot. They used to scan footage and recognize the palm trees as Los Angeles and track down the location.

FRED LINCOLN: I met this production manager, Patty, at Reb Sawitz's office. Reb told me she was good. Up to that point, I'd never used a production manager; I'd always done everything myself, but I liked it. Patty got me back with this producer in New York. Best movie I ever made was with him.

SHARON MITCHELL: The cops tracked *Backside to the Future* down to Zane Entertainment—the Zacari brothers. They thought the easiest way to prosecute was the pandering law; they wanted to prove that having sex with people in front of a camera wasn't any semblance of a performance. If you're getting paid for sex, it must be prostitution, so the producers must be panderers, and this must be stopped. Okay, which is a little roundabout. But they were very serious, very storm-trooper-like.

FRED LINCOLN: Then, all of a sudden, the word is out that I couldn't work for this guy anymore. I was done for. I said, "I gotta sit down and talk to him because something's wrong."

He says, "Wow, you went a hundred thousand dollars over budget."

I said, "Wait. What over budget? I never *touched* the budget. We had a seven-day shoot, and I shot in seven days. I *never* go over budget."

The guy took some money and told our backers it was my fault. So he and I had a fallin' out. But I met Patty when she was workin' for him.

SHARON MITCHELL: I'm at my home in Ventura one day, and I had this big, six-foot-long picture of me. So I put a line of cocaine from the shoes to all the way to the top. I'm going in the bathroom, and I'm getting high. I'm shooting a thing of dope, and I'm having a good time. I'm snorting a little, and I'm naked, taking Polaroids. I took Polaroids of everything back then. I'm entertaining some friends, playing poker, and having a good time. That's what life's about, right?

Then I get a knock on the door. I was very friendly with the Ventura Police Department at that time; the local cops liked me because I was a porn star. I gave 'em porn movies, and I was fun to talk to.

But this cop says, "You know, you're going away for a while. You better bring a toothbrush." I'm still loaded, so I'm thinking, "What the fuck do I need a toothbrush for?"

FRED LINCOLN: I had to have a sit-down with DiBe—Robert DiBernardo. He believed me. Of course he did—I'm from the old school. I don't fuck with nobody. I make a deal; I do it. I mean, that's the way I was brought up.

Anyway, Patty and I ended up getting married.

SHARON MITCHELL: They brought me to Ventura County and told me there's a warrant out for my arrest because I didn't appear in a court case. I acted like I'd conveniently forgotten, but really I'd just put it in a pile. I was loaded; I had more important things to do.

FRED LINCOLN: Just pandering—that's all these cops did. They went everywhere; they went to San Francisco, and they got Paul Thomas in Oakland. But they didn't bust P.T. They busted Patty, my wife, because she had the money. She was paying everybody, so they assumed she was the producer. And P.T. didn't say nothin', ha, ha, ha. Thanks, P.T.

I was in Florida. Patty called me up—she was in a complete panic, man—and Joey Perpara bailed her out. If it was Frisco Vice that busted them, or Oakland Vice, I would say okay. But it was these same two guys from L.A.—Conte and the other guy.

***LOS ANGELES TIMES*, MAY 20, 1985: HARD-CORE SEX FILMS: DOES CASTING CONSTITUTE PANDERING?:** " 'We tell them that they are part of an investigation involving pandering and prostitution,' Lieutenant Conte said. 'We make them fully aware they are a suspect in a prostitution case and tell them we're trying to identify the main serious offenders—the producers and still photographers.' "

FRED LINCOLN: It was bad, man. These guys would follow you—that's how I know there was a rat involved. Patty and I used to shoot at this ranch in Valermo, up by San Francisco. I mean, you rode twenty miles on the guy's property before you even got to the house. So it's not like somebody saw us and reported us, you know? And these cops came right to the door!

SHARON MITCHELL: They arrested everyone on that shoot, *Backside to the Future,* and scared them. I mean, these are young kids. They're saying, "We're going to take away your birthday presents if you don't say that you got paid *money! FOR SEX!!*" So these kids are saying, "Oh! He *did* pay me!!!" so they can go. Me, I knew this was harassment. I knew that this had something to do with obscenity. I was going to stand my ground and make a statement; that's just where I come from. So I knew I was going to be doing time for a while.

FRED LINCOLN: These cops were busting everybody everywhere. Scaring the shit out of people. Telling the girls they're going to jail for twenty years to get them to testify. These cops, Conte and the other one, were following people everywhere. People were ratting us out. I don't know who, but I've heard rumors—John Holmes, Jim South. . . .

LOS ANGELES TIMES, MAY 20, 1985: HARD-CORE SEX FILMS: DOES CASTING CONSTITUTE PANDERING?: "'These young ladies who appear in these pictures normally come through modeling agencies,' said Dave Friedman, head of Entertainment Ventures, which he described as the 'oldest exploitation film company in the United States.'

"'Contrary to the beliefs of our enemies, such as Citizens for Decency and Morality in Media, we do not coerce or kidnap these ladies for appearances in our movies. We use tried and true performers.'"

SHARON MITCHELL: They brought the investigator up to interview me there. The cop that headed the investigations wasn't a bad guy; he was reasonable because he had so much background on you that you kind of had to respect him. But this was another guy, who they'd hired to do sort of a bad-movie version of an interrogation with, with the lightbulb swinging overhead, you know: "And where were you on the night of . . ."

FRED LINCOLN: I mean, how the fuck could two LAPD vice cops be busting people outside of Los Angeles? What are they doing in Oakland? It's not even their jurisdiction.

I don't know how they got away with that shit because we used to go to San Francisco because San Francisco did not bother us. San Francisco would give us a permit.

LOS ANGELES TIMES, MAY 20, 1985: "Beverly Hills attorney Richard Chier is defending Marc and Tina Marie Carriere, an Indiana couple accused of pandering for hiring actresses to appear in an adult film they produced.

"Chier said one 21-year-old woman was followed by vice officers to her Huntington Beach home after performing in a film in Coldwater Canyon.

"'She's married and has a child,' Chier said, noting that the husband knew nothing of his wife's participation in such a film. 'She was not a hooker. She was a happily married woman who did this as a vocation. They (police) then went into her house when she wasn't home, knowing she wasn't home. Can you imagine if you were home and police said they were the vice squad and wanted to talk to your wife? She came home, and they said they were going to expose her unless she cooperated and signed a statement. They put words in her mouth.'"

FRED LINCOLN: There was one girl—I forget her name, but she was a really pretty girl, blond—that everybody said was a rat. That was when I first came out here. About 1984 or 1985. She told me that these cops told her they were going to put her away for twenty years, and she didn't know what to do.

Come on, you take a nineteen-year-old girl, stick her in a holding pen with hookers, and then tell her she's going to be there until she's forty—that's pretty powerful shit.

These girls aren't street girls. A lot of people think they are, but they're not. You know, a lot of them are just kind of like oversexed girls who like to be seen.

LOS ANGELES TIMES, MAY 20, 1985: "'They told me if I didn't cooperate they would arrest me for prostitution,' said Susan Hart, a Canoga Park adult-film actress whose family does not know she appears in hard-core films. They said, 'You don't want a record, do you?'"

SHARON MITCHELL: This cop was asking me, "What are you going to do when it all runs out?" He's popping his Ps, spitting in my face. "How do you like not being a manicured porn star? Huh?! *And you've just been here for a day and a half!* Who's paying you? Who directed that movie? And how much money did you get?"

I wasn't feeling very good, but I was still a smart-ass. I said, "You know, I make so many movies, I forget. But a bottle of champagne and a dozen roses would be extraordinarily helpful in helping me remember!"

***LOS ANGELES TIMES*, MAY 20, 1985:** "'I was really scared,' Hart said. 'I didn't want to go to jail. We went to a Burger King, and they asked me questions about others in the business, when they were going to shoot and where they lived.'"

SHARON MITCHELL: I just made the cop fucking crazy. Suze Randall sent big bouquets of flowers, like, "Don't give in, Mitch!!" to the Ventura County Women's Pig Farm, where they had me stashed for three days. Then they moved me to an L.A. County facility.

***LOS ANGELES TIMES*, MAY 20, 1985:** "Susan Hart, the name she goes by in the films, said in an interview that she was asked by Lieutenant Conte to sign a blank victim's report against one producer, which detectives later filled in.

"Lieutenant Conte denied Hart's allegation and said that she was shown the report after it was filled out and that she concurred in its statements."

FRED LINCOLN: I sat down and asked this lawyer, "How could it be pandering?"

He said, "Because they're actually fucking."

I said, "Well, I used to be a stuntman. I blew up buildings. Was I guilty of arson?"

"Whoa," he said. "That's different. That's a movie."

I said, "What the fuck do ya think we're doin'? We're making movies, too, you idiot!" I used to get so frustrated.

The lawyer said, "Well, you don't understand the law."

I said, "You know what? I'll tell ya what I *do* understand. You guys have gotten yachts with the money you've made from us. You don't want any of us to win because if we did, you'd have to go get a fuckin' job!"

SHARON MITCHELL: I think I ended up in the holding tank of Sybil Brand Women's Prison for a couple days. I was there for a while, and I guess it became clear that I wasn't going to say anything. And they needed everyone on the cast to say they'd been paid in order to prove their case. And Randy West and myself were the only two—probably the oldest—that didn't sell out. We just said, "No, no. I don't know. I don't remember."

***LOS ANGELES TIMES*, MAY 23, 1985:** "In a controversial test case, a Van Nuys jury found Harold Freeman, an Encino producer of hard-core sex films, guilty of pandering Wednesday, making him the first filmmaker convicted in California under a law that mandates a three-year prison sentence for hiring people to perform sex acts."

SHARON MITCHELL: I was kicking dope. I think they even offered me some balloons filled with heroin at one point. I said no because I was already three or four days into it. I figured I'd stick it out.

LOS ANGELES TIMES, MAY 23, 1985: "Prosecutors contended that women hired to perform in a 90-minute movie, 'Caught From Behind, Part II,' are prostitutes because they were paid to perform sex acts. Filmmaker Harold Freeman said throughout the six-day trial that the women were actresses.

"'We concluded that the acting was secondary and that the sex was primary,' jury foreman Joan Keller said after the verdict. 'The girls were hired for sex.'"

FRED LINCOLN: It was bullshit. People get seven years for murder and they're givin' us twenty years for pandering! If they did that to pimps, nobody would be a fuckin' pimp. Who's gonna be a pimp if you're gonna go away for twenty years?! Jesus!

Hal Freeman was the only one who fought this pandering thing.

LOS ANGELES TIMES, MAY 23, 1985: "'I will appeal and appeal and appeal until we get to the Supreme Court,' Freeman said.

"Freeman, 49, was arrested in October 1983, and charged with five counts of violating the state's 1982 'anti-pimp' law, under which anyone who procures another person to engage in sex is guilty of pandering.

"Freeman estimated that he has produced more than 100 full-length sex films since 1968."

SHARON MITCHELL: In court they wanted the director's real name, but they really wanted Zane's real family name. Their real family name was very long, and it ended with a vowel. I know from growing up in New York that you don't tell names like that.

TRICIA DEVERAUX (FORMER PORN STAR): Were the Zanes the same as the Zacari Family? Yeah.

FRED LINCOLN: Hal Freeman just pled not guilty, that was it. And he just kept appealing and appealing and appealing. Nobody supported anybody then.

LOS ANGELES TIMES, JULY 16, 1985: JUDGE GIVES LIGHT PENALTY TO PORNO FILM PRODUCER: "A judge Monday refused to impose a minimum three-year prison sentence on Harold Freeman, a producer of hard-core sex films who was convicted in May of pandering, and instead ordered the Encino man to spend 90 days in jail and pay $10,000."

PAUL FISHBEIN: I know people gave Hal money. Russ Hampshire gave him a bunch of money, but he didn't want anyone to know. It's not that Russ was afraid; he just didn't want people to think he was doing it for any other reason than to help Hal. Russ is one of those guys that came to everybody's aid. He wasn't looking for the kudos.

LOS ANGELES TIMES, JULY 16, 1985: JUDGE GIVES LIGHT PENALTY TO PORNO FILM PRODUCER: "Calling the minimum prison term required by law 'cruel and unusual punishment,' Van Nuys Superior Court Judge James Albracht also postponed imposition of the jail term and fine for Harold Freeman, pending appeal of the conviction.

"'This is a victory for me and other adult filmmakers,' a jubilant Freeman said as he left court."

FRED LINCOLN: Everybody was so afraid of this pimping and pandering law. I mean, it was one frightened industry.

LOS ANGELES TIMES, JUNE 29, 1985: POLICE RAID DISTRIBUTORS OF SEXUALLY EXPLICIT FILMS: "'Los Angeles police have conducted a series of raids this week at distributors of sexually explicit films,' said police and film company executives.

"Captain James Doherty, commander of the police department's administrative vice division, said the raids were part of an investigation that would start over the weekend. He would not say how many businesses would be searched. He said the results of the raids will be announced next week by Chief Daryl F. Gates."

Who Dropped the Dime on Traci?

LOS ANGELES
1986–1987

TIM CONNELLY: On New Year's Eve 1985, Traci Lords was launching her own company, TLC [Traci Lords Company]. So I ended up in the women's bathroom of some shithole club on Cahuenga with Traci and some other porn stars—and we were all doing cocaine. I can't remember the details of the conversation—but basically Traci really wanted to be in the *Directory of Adult Films*.

JIM SOUTH: Traci had started dating Stewart Dell, who'd been in the business, sort of as a producer, maybe a small-time director. He had more stories than Scheherazade.

TIM CONNELLY: Stewart and Traci had a lot of stuff in the works. They were about to go to France to shoot *Traci, I Love You*. Stewart was really smooth: about six feet, very thin, long hair, very Hollywood good-looking. He could have been a rock manager. He hitched his wagon to Traci Lords.

Stewart came from outside the business, and, he was going to take her beyond porn. He was into PR—the ultimate fast-talking huckster. And Traci was just this coked-up seventeen- or eighteen-year-old—who now decides she's gonna do Vivid Video one better.

TRACI LORDS: I've been thinking about going into makeup. And maybe producing my own films. A little of both. I want to do that in time—produce and direct my own movies.

I get a lot of jerks as directors. You get on set. They tell you how to fuck. They tell you when to scream. And I don't think that's right. I think for the best results, you should just be able to go with what you feel and act how you want to act.

What do I like most about the business? Getting paid for things I enjoy doing.

TIM CONNELLY: All of a sudden, Traci Lords went from being this petulant child/drug addict/porn star into someone who wants to take control of her own destiny. It seemed like a half-ditch attempt to mirror what Ginger Lynn was doing, except that—as Traci would be the first to point out to you—she was going to do it *BETTER!*

GINGER LYNN: I was talking to a friend I know. She liked Traci, but I kept telling her, "There's something I don't trust about her. Be careful."

TIM CONNELLY: Traci was going to be the contract star of her own company. Not only that—she was going to be the company president. Her grand scheme was to have the biggest, best porno company—all based on *her*. It was as if someone had told her, *If you make your own Barbie doll, you'll become a millionaire*, you know?

TOM BYRON: Traci told me, "I'm gonna be a legitimate Hollywood actress, and none of this porno shit's ever gonna matter." I was like, "Oh, sure, whatever, just let me rub your ass. . . ."

Then, literally days after her eighteenth birthday, the story broke.

HUMPHRY KNIPE: I came across Traci's story in the *Los Angeles Times*. There it was: She was underage. The breakfast I had, I threw up.

I've never felt so sick in my life because I knew what they could do to me. We were expecting the Feds to knock on the door any minute.

LOS ANGELES TIMES, JULY 18, 1986: SEX FILMS PULLED, STAR ALLEGEDLY TOO YOUNG. "Video shops and adult movie stores and theaters nationwide were pulling products featuring sex film star Traci Lords from their shelves Thursday because of an investigation by the Los Angeles district attorney's office into allegations that she was underage when she made most of her movies.

"Los Angeles police say that Lords, considered one of the top adult film actresses in the country, made 75 sexually explicit movies and videos before she turned 18 last May, and adult film industry officials are being advised to stop selling and showing her movies to avoid criminal prosecution."

HUMPHRY KNIPE: The story Traci told us was that she was in bed with her boyfriend when the Feds burst through the door and beat him up—whatever, roughed him up—and then dragged them both to jail. She said she had no idea who dropped the dime.

TRACI LORDS [FROM *UNDERNEATH IT ALL*, 2003]: "I tried to focus my eyes. The dim light from the aquarium cast a blue glow over the surreal creatures, lighting up the yellow FBI letters across their backs.

"'FBI!' I gasped, wondering if it was a hallucination. Had I died and gone to hell? I spoke to the blue men and demanded to know if this was a dream. Scott was dragged roughly to the floor and slammed facedown into the carpet when reality finally hit me.

"'Stop it!' I screamed as the armed men surrounded me and aimed their guns in my direction. I closed my eyes and waited for bullets to tear into my flesh. I felt sweat roll down my body.

"'GET THE FUCK OUT OF BED NOW!' I was ordered. My legs trembled as I tried to obey. My eyes darted around the room and took in their smirking faces as I was tightly handcuffed and led down the hallway and out the front door."

TOM BYRON: Once the news came out, it was the top story on every channel. I got twenty or thirty calls: "Oh, Tom, you must have known. I mean, you were *boyfriend and girlfriend. You must have known.*"

***LOS ANGELES TIMES*, JULY 18, 1986: SEX FILMS PULLED; STAR MAY HAVE BEEN A MINOR:** "'She's the hottest thing in the industry right now,' Los Angeles Vice Captain Jim Doherty said Thursday. 'She's a really big star, and everything she's done is against the law.'

"'Some people say, conceivably if the authorities wanted to push it through enough, they could make real inroads in closing the industry down,' one source told the newspaper."

TOM BYRON: When we first started going out, Traci had said, "Look, if someone calls me Nora, that's just a nickname. It's like a pet name—an inside kind of joke. Don't pay any attention to it." I said okay.

So when people called that day, I said, "Guys, I knew her as Kristie Nussman! I didn't know any Nora Kuzma!"

***LOS ANGELES TIMES*, JULY 18, 1986: SEX FILMS PULLED; STAR ALLEGEDLY TOO YOUNG:** "District attorney's investigators last Friday searched Lords' Los Angeles area home, the Sun Valley offices of Vantage International Productions, a major producer of adult films—and the Sherman Oaks offices of modeling agent Jim South, who is credited with discovering the actress in 1984."

JIM SOUTH: The cops walked in and said, "She's underage." I laughed and said, "Yeah, sure."

***LOS ANGELES TIMES*, JULY 18, 1986: SEX FILMS PULLED; STAR ALLEGEDLY TOO YOUNG:** "South said that Lords, on seeking employment, provided a California driver's license, a U.S. passport and a birth certificate, which stated her name was Kristie Nussman and gave her birth date as Nov. 17, 1962."

GLORIA LEONARD: Somehow Traci must have gotten a birth certificate, and parlayed that into a driver's license and ultimately a passport. And she certainly looked eighteen—honey, let me tell ya.

LOS ANGELES TIMES, JULY 19, 1986: SEX FILM STAR NOT FACING CHARGES, REINER SAYS: "Los Angeles County District Attorney Ira Reiner said Friday that his office is not planning to file criminal charges against sex film star Traci Lords."

CHRISTY CANYON: I never would have guessed that Traci was underage, but I did know she was a compulsive liar. One day she would say she was born in New York, the next week she was born in Las Vegas.

NEW YORK *DAILY NEWS,* JULY 19, 1986: PORN STARLET OFF HOOK: "'She may be a professional now, but she was a 15-year-old runaway when the pornographic film industry got ahold of her,' said District Attorney Ira Reiner. 'She was, I'm sure, grist for the mill as far as they were concerned.'"

GINGER LYNN: When I heard Traci was saying she was forced into the world of porn, I think I peed my pants, I laughed so hard.

LOS ANGELES TIMES, JULY 19, 1986: SEX FILM STAR NOT FACING CHARGES, REINER SAYS: "Reiner, however, says he would press charges against the pornographic filmmakers who employed Lords, if he could prove that they knew she was not yet 18."

BILL MARGOLD: There are an awful lot of Traci Lords titles out there. So when all hell broke loose, the industry immediately rushed to get rid of those tapes. Except that certain people thought they could make more money if they kept the tapes and sold them. And those people got busted.

LOS ANGELES TIMES, AUGUST 15, 1986: DISTRIBUTOR INDICTED OVER SEX VIDEOTAPE: "'A North Carolina video and magazine distributor has been indicted on a charge of the sexual exploitation of a minor for selling and distributing a videocassette that shows porn star Traci Lords engaging in sexual activity,' authorities said."

HUMPHRY KNIPE: The laws regarding child pornography are Draconian. So after we found out Traci was underage, everyone was going around in the middle of the night and dumping all the film into the deepest Dumpsters they could find—getting rid of whatever pictures we had of her. Pictures, porn, whatever it was, just destroy it. Because what was so terrifying was that even having a tape in your house was a felony.

LOS ANGELES TIMES, AUGUST 22, 1986: THE REGION: "Federal prosecutors have taken over the investigation of hard-core pornography films and videotapes starring Traci Lords. A spokesman for Los Angeles District Attorney Ira Reiner said the case was referred to the U.S. attorney because it transcends state lines and because under federal law, it only has to be proved that she was underage when the films were made.

"'Under state law,' he said, 'prosecutors would have to prove that those who hired her knew she was under 18.'"

TOM BYRON: Everyone was losing their minds. Bookstores had to pull all the Traci Lords titles and destroy them. Video companies had to take the Traci Lords masters they had and destroy them because they were now child pornography according to U.S. law. It was a completely devastating mess for the industry.

LOS ANGELES TIMES, OCTOBER 4, 1986: INVESTIGATION OF TRACI LORDS PORNOGRAPHY CASE EXPANDED: "Federal authorities are expanding the case of X-rated film star Traci Lords, to determine whether three other popular actresses were underage when they starred in sexually explicit movies, it was reported Friday.

"Federal subpoenas were issued Tuesday to five distributors, VCA, CBI, Caballero, Western Visuals and Paradise, seeking records relating to Traci Lords and [three other] actresses."

HUMPHRY KNIPE: We were all terrified. Greg Dark rang me every day, whispering, "Have you heard anything else?"

BILL MARGOLD: The cost of destroying those tapes? Multiple millions of dollars. It crippled people—temporarily.

GLORIA LEONARD: The case was made that she cost this industry millions of dollars because all the films had to be physically destroyed. If anything, she owed this industry. I mean, *she took the money.* Hello!?

She didn't repay anybody for the days she worked, you know? Not that that would've put a dent into what was ultimately lost, economically.

JIM SOUTH: First they indicted me for child pornography. The state law says that they have to prove you knew she was underage—which they absolutely could not do because nobody is stupid enough to give a girl that young work in pornography.

HUMPHRY KNIPE: Suze produced a Polaroid of Traci holding her ID. We Xeroxed it and sent it to everybody. It was because of that Polaroid that they decided there were not strong enough grounds to prosecute.

JIM SOUTH: We had a meeting in the judge's chamber after I was indicted.

They actually admitted that they believed I did not know. The charges were dismissed, and I breathed a sigh of relief, even though all the postponements had made the whole thing very expensive.

Then the federal government came along and reindicted me.

***LOS ANGELES TIMES*, MARCH 6, 1987: THREE IN TRACI LORDS SEX FILM CASE INDICTED:** "Sex film star Traci Lords' agent and two producers who allegedly propelled her to blue movie fame at the age of 16 were indicted by a federal grand jury in Los Angeles on Thursday in the first prosecution against commercial film producers under federal child pornography laws.

"James Marvin Souter Jr. (Jim South), 47, the man who allegedly hired Lords through his World Modeling Agency in 1984 for the film 'Those Young Girls' is charged with producers Ronald Rene Kantor, 40, and Rupert Sebastian Macnee, 39, with violating the federal law prohibiting the use of minors in sexually explicit films.

"The three men face a maximum of 10 years in prison and a $100,000 fine if convicted."

HUMPHRY KNIPE: You have no idea what teeth these child pornography laws have—they can put you in jail for ten years for each offense and you'll bloody rot. One roll of film—thirty-six pictures—can put you in jail for 360 years. Absolutely horrendous; no one would dream of doing it.

JIM SOUTH: They found a law called "strict liability," which says, if you get a minor work, it does not matter what kind of ID she has, or if both her parents confirm the age—you're guilty.

You cannot even introduce IDs as a defense. My attorney said, "It's unconstitutional, absolutely. But do you want to spend a hundred thousand dollars proving it?"

***LOS ANGELES TIMES*, MARCH 11, 1987: ARRESTS HINDER THE PRODUCTION OF SEXUALLY EXPLICIT FILMS, POLICE SAY:** "Police say they have temporarily blocked the hiring of hundreds of performers for sexually explicit films with arrests at two San Fernando modeling agencies in the past two weeks.

"James Marvin Souter (Jim South) of World Modeling was arrested for pandering on March 4 after sheriff's deputies raided the business and his Thousand Island home.

"In a separate case, he was indicted under federal child pornography statutes last Thursday for representing porn superstar Traci Lords when she was 16."

JIM SOUTH: They came after us like the Gestapo. It was unbelievable. They were really on a witch hunt. They were really looking hard.

LOS ANGELES TIMES, APRIL 1, 1987: MAN PLEADS GUILTY IN TRACI LORDS CASE: "James Marvin Souter (Jim South), the man who allegedly lured the teenage Traci Lords into performing sex acts on film, pleaded guilty Tuesday in Los Angeles federal court to procuring the future porn queen for one of her first blue movies when she was only 16."

JIM SOUTH: Tommy Byron, Boy Wonder, was dating her. I don't know for how long. But even *he* did not know she was underage, I guarantee it.

TOM BYRON: I don't know if people were mad at me after her real age came out; they probably were. I mean, a lot of people went out of business.

HUMPHRY KNIPE: Was she paying her mother off? Well, that wouldn't surprise me. I never met her mom. I don't know who turned her in—or whether she turned herself in.

TOM BYRON: I think Traci turned herself in because of something she said to me one day on the set of *Talk Dirty to Me III.* She said, "You know, I don't really worry about any of this shit because one day none of this is going to matter—I'm gonna be working for Paramount."

RUBY GOTTESMAN: What I think is, Traci told Stewart Dell she was underage. And when she reached eighteen, he made *Traci, I Love You* with her in France. She got a hundred thousand dollars for it. It was a setup.

JIM SOUTH: I really believe with all of my heart that Traci and Stewart were responsible for dropping the dime on Traci, to make her name absolutely huge. She hustled us.

TOM BYRON: Traci saying that she doesn't remember any of it, that she was on drugs—that's her PR people telling her to say that. She'd have to say that for her legitimate career. The world at that time was not ready to accept an unrepentant porn star.

I don't fault her for that, okay? I mean, she had to do what she had to do to get over—to get into the legitimate film business, which was really her ultimate dream to begin with. I think she had something to do with it. I think it was her plan from day one to turn herself in.

AL GOLDSTEIN: Traci Lords really deceived the industry. But because she denounced the business, Hollywood felt she was a victim, and she now does regular movies, like *Cry-Baby.*

But it's a shame. She blames pornography, but it was pornography that was the victim because she lied.

U.S. Department of Justice
Washington D.C. 20530

Attorney General's
Commission on Pornography

Final Report
1986

Part 10:

BACK-
LASH

The Meese Commission Report; United States Attorney General Edwin
Meese III with President Ronald Reagan

The Meese Commission

U.S.A.
1985–1987

GINGER LYNN: When I was making films with Traci, there were a lot of issues with the government and the Meese Commission. I know that the government and the IRS are in a position to do whatever they want, to whoever they want. And when I saw the photos of Traci that came out during that trial—the behind-the-scenes photos, taken during many, many, many films—I don't know how this possibly could have happened the way everyone claims it did.

TRACI LORDS [FROM *UNDERNEATH IT ALL*, 2003]: "The federal building in downtown Los Angeles wasn't as glamorous as I'd seen in the movies. A fat-faced man told me to sit in a yellow plastic chair in the center of the room and I did, crossing my legs extra tight.

"The fat-faced man stepped forward and introduced himself as Detective Rooker. He told me I was part of a sting operation that had something to do with a man named Meese and that they'd been gathering information on me for a while.

"I couldn't believe what I was hearing. 'YOU PEOPLE KNEW THE WHOLE TIME?' I went berserk.

"'Hey,' Rooker said, trying to calm me down. 'What are you crying for? Tomorrow we're all going to be famous. Isn't that what you want?'

"I just looked at him, not understanding. 'Famous for what?'"

GINGER LYNN: How did the government have photos from Traci's first movie? And if they knew, why didn't they stop it from the beginning? How did Traci get into this and have all the correct forms of ID if she was sixteen years old? I had a fake ID when I was sixteen. I cut the little piece out with a knife and then I put another number in, but anybody with half a brain can see that. But Traci's was a *real* ID—and everything was filled out the way it was supposed to be.

BILL KELLY: The Meese Commission was a follow-up to the original Attorney General's Commission of 1967–70, which was put together at the request of President Johnson. The original commission consisted of eighteen people, many of whom—especially the leadership—were members of the American Civil Liberties Union, which as you might imagine is not my favorite organization.

TRACI LORDS [FROM *UNDERNEATH IT ALL*, 2003]: "The FBI was relentless in its disruption of my life. After giving the initial statement at the federal building downtown and never being booked or read my rights, I had good reason to question authority.

"I couldn't walk outside my apartment without being stopped and served a subpoena to appear for prosecutions around the country, and I saw these prosecutors all over the news talking about the 'Traci Lords' case.

"There was no longer any doubt in my mind about why they wanted me to appear. It wasn't only because I was the most readily identifiable child in porn but also because wherever I went, the media followed."

GINGER LYNN: Not long after it all came out about Traci's age, there was a knock on my door, and two people read me my rights; one was a district attorney. I was asked to testify against adult film producers on Traci Lords's behalf. I refused.

BILL KELLY: That first commission handed in its two-million-dollar report to President Nixon in 1970, and they recommended that all obscenity laws in the United States—unless they involve children—be abrogated, wiped out. They said that pornography was not a large industry, had no real adverse consequences on people, and didn't even make a whole lot of money.

RICHARD NIXON (PRESIDENT OF THE UNITED STATES): So long as I am in the White House, there will be no relaxation of the national effort to control and eliminate smut from our national life—I totally reject this report.

BILL KELLY: President Nixon read that report, and do you know what he did with it? Put it straight in the circular file. In 1970, the porn business was making about four billion dollars. The report went through a vote in the Senate; only sixty-five senators voted—and sixty of them agreed with Nixon that it ought to be canned.

GINGER LYNN: The U.S. Attorney came in and said to me, "If you don't testify on Traci's behalf against"—there were sixty-some-odd film producers—"we will make your life difficult."

JIM SOUTH: Tommy Byron got a call from Channel Five News asking for an interview. I said, "Tommy, just listen to me. Don't do it. You're calling attention to yourself."

He went down to the Lamplighter restaurant to do the interview in the parking lot. I was there, and the guy turned the camera toward me, and I said, "Get the camera off of me!"

Well, a year later, Tommy was indicted for income tax evasion.

TOM BYRON: I went on television and shot my mouth off about the Meese Commission and the Los Angeles Vice Department. Which probably wasn't the smartest thing to do, but that's the kind of guy I am. I don't like to hold anything back. I don't like to bullshit anybody.

BILL KELLY: The Meese Commission was formed in 1985 and, in my opinion, they had a budget that was designed to fail. I don't think the Justice Department wanted a successful, or a comprehensive, report on pornography at that time because they only gave the Meese Commission four hundred thousand dollars.

GINGER LYNN: They showed me photographs from almost every single film Traci made. Photos taken from behind the bushes, taken from a car, taken from day one of her filming. Photos taken from the parking lot where I met her. These surveillance photos were going on from day fucking one. This was not an accident—I still don't believe she was underage.

So when I went before the grand jury, I got amnesia and I couldn't remember anything. They were pissed.

BILL KELLY: The Meese Commission didn't have any investigators to speak of. So about thirty of us—postal inspectors, FBI agents, me, and one or two other retired guys—volunteered to work for the commission for one year, free of charge. Which we did.

TOM BYRON: You gotta understand the political climate at the time. I mean, President Reagan was bowing down to every whim of the religious right. It was ridiculous. It spawned out of a bunch of holier-than-thou, do-gooder jerk-offs who thought they knew what was good for America. They wanted to deny Americans what they wanted—which was to take a video home and masturbate.

RONALD REAGAN (PRESIDENTIAL CANDIDATE, ADDRESSING THE DALLAS MORAL MAJORITY RALLY, OCTOBER 1980): I know this is a nonpartisan gathering—

and so I know you can't endorse me—but I only brought that up *because I want you to know I endorse you and what you're doing!*

LARRY FLYNT: Pornography has been a pet peeve of the religious right going all the way back to Anthony Comstock, who was the nation's first censor. And it's continued to remain as much in the Republican Party as the "right to life" has.

BILL KELLY: That's why the Meese Commission was so comprehensive—because of these volunteer federal officers, and I think several local guys in the LAPD, which has by far the best local investigative agency for obscenity in the United States. In fact, it's one of the only ones.

GINGER LYNN: Not long after I appeared before the grand jury, I got a knock on my door, and I was indicted. They were charging me with tax evasion.

TOM BYRON: The IRS basically did a six-year investigation of me; I guess they wanted to infiltrate the porno industry. My case boiled down to the fact that I had filed one return late and didn't file an extension.

So they charged me with tax fraud and tax evasion. It was a three-count indictment: two felony, one misdemeanor. I was facing twelve years in federal prison.

GINGER LYNN: When I went to fucking trial, and I saw the documents, it was the whole Traci Lords thing that did us in—Tom Byron, Harry Reems, and me. And we were three people who had helped her.

LARRY FLYNT: You must understand that the Meese Commission was the complete opposite of the Presidential Commission on Obscenity. The Meese Commission traveled the country basically interviewing victims. They were not using any scientific approach in their efforts to try to understand pornography or its effect on society.

JOHN WATERS: I love feminists like Ti-Grace Atkinson and Valerie Solanis; I was all for that. My favorite was Jenny Fope, remember her? The one that was named the head of NOW and then they found out she was wanted for murder? I'm a lesbian hag. I have no problem with any of that.

But when Andrea Dworkin and "Women Against Porn" came out—that's not my idea of a feminist; that's my idea of a right-wing censor. I hated all of them.

ANDREA DWORKIN [FROM "FINAL REPORT OF THE ATTORNEY GENERAL'S COMMISSION ON PORNOGRAPHY"]: "My name is Andrea Dworkin. I am a citizen of the United States, and in this country where I live, every year pictures are being made of women with our legs spread. We are called beaver, we are called pussy, our genitals are tied up, they are pasted, makeup is put on them to make them pop out of a page at a male viewer."

GINGER LYNN: I don't think that anybody ever intended—nor did they wish for—the adult industry to stop. They just wanted to make it *look* like they were stopping it. They make too much fucking money to stop it.

BILL MARGOLD: The Meese Commission and radical feminism were forced into an unhappy state of affairs. Both of them would go where anybody listened so they became this unholy alliance, dedicated to wiping out pornography. Obviously it failed.

I told them, "All you're doing is calling more attention to us," and it did, quite honestly. But the Meese Commission *wanted* to call attention to us—and by doing so they warned another generation not to watch us. And when you tell society they shouldn't watch us, they can't wait to go out and get us.

ANDREA DWORKIN: "Millions and millions of pictures are made of us in postures of submission and sexual access so that our vaginas are exposed for penetration, our anuses are exposed for penetration, and our throats are used as if they are genitals for penetration. In this country where I live as a citizen, real rapes are on film and being sold in the marketplace. And the major motif of pornography as a form of entertainment is that women are raped and violated and humiliated until we discover that we like it and at that point we ask for more."

GLORIA LEONARD: Andrea Dworkin and Catherine MacKinnon were the Osama bin Laden and Saddam Hussein of the so-called Feminist Movement. So radical, so over-the-top, you know? I mean, Dworkin considered penetration to be rape! I just laughed at them.

CATHERINE MACKINNON: If pornography is a part of your sexuality, then you have no right to your sexuality.

GLORIA LEONARD: No matter what you said, porn was *bad.* And of course the irony was, nine-tenths of those who radically pooh-poohed it had never even seen a goddamn porno movie!

I mean, nobody is drugged or dragged off the street to do this. In all my years in this business, I have never seen coercion. *Ever, ever, ever.* You always had the right to say, "No, I don't want to do this."

Including Linda Lovelace.

LINDA LOVELACE [FROM FINAL REPORT ON THE ATTORNEY GENERAL'S COMMISSION ON PORNOGRAPHY]: "During the filming of *Deep Throat,* actually the first day, I suffered a brutal beating in my room for smiling on the set. It was a hotel room and the whole crew was in one room, there was at least twenty people partying, music going, laughing, and having a good time. Mr. Traynor . . . started bouncing me off the walls."

BILL KELLY: In the book she allegedly wrote, *Inside Linda Lovelace*, Linda talked about how I used to harass her and threaten to yank her outta bed and put her on an airplane and put her before the grand jury in New York and all that. None of that is true. I never even saw the woman until we testified back to back before the Meese Commission in January 1986.

LINDA LOVELACE: "I figured out of twenty people, there might be one human being that would do something to help me. I was screaming for help, and I was being beaten. And all of a sudden the room next door became very quiet. Nobody, not one person, came to help me."

Disappearing DiBe

NEW YORK CITY
1986

BRUCE MOUW: Who was the greater power, Robert DiBernardo or Mickey Zaffarano?

There's no comparison: DiBe. If you put aside the porno stuff for a second, DiBe was very knowledgeable in labor racketeering. He controlled the Teamsters for the Gambino family for many years. So he was a rising star in the Gambinos—and very well respected by the other families.

BILL KELLY: After Gambino family godfather Paul Castellano and his bodyguard were murdered in front of Sparks Steak House in December 1985, John Gotti took over the Gambino family.

BRUCE MOUW: DiBe was very politically astute. He knew how to appease the bosses. And because he was a very wealthy man, Paul Castellano liked him, so they had a very close relationship.

He was very, very competent. He just got things done. And he was smarter than most of those other wise guys.

BILL KELLY: John Gotti didn't like Robert DiBernardo. I'm not sure, but I think it was because DiBe was Paul Castellano's man.

BRUCE MOUW: In early 1986, while John Gotti was in jail, his underboss, Frank DeCicco, was murdered in a car bombing. So they were looking for a new underboss. And the person who wanted to be underboss was Angelo Ruggiero, who was a captain at the time. Angelo was John's right-hand man, and his goal in life was to be John Gotti's underboss.

SAMMY "THE BULL" GRAVANO: I would see DiBe three, four times a week. We handled the construction, the unions. Did I ever hear him express views on who should replace Frank DeCicco as underboss? Yes, I did. His view was that I should be underboss. And it came up at a meeting with "Joe Pinney," myself, and Angelo. Angelo said that DiBe expressed an opinion that I should be underboss, and then he asked me if it was so. I said, "Yes."

SHARON MITCHELL: I met DiBe only once. I had to go get permission for money to make a movie because I was producing and directing. I think it was two hundred and fifty thousand, which was pretty standard then for a thirty-five-millimeter film.

So I was put in the back of a car, driven out to some godforsaken town on Long Island, and had a conversation with DiBe and some other old fuck. And they said, "You made a lot of money for us in the past. Okay, fine."

FRED LINCOLN: I wasn't friendly with DiBe. Nobody was. You just didn't talk to DiBe. He had nothin' to do with us. I just spoke to Teddy Rothstein and Andre D'Apice and I got along real good for a long time. Andre and I were good buddies. We'd probably still be partners if Andre hadn't gone to jail on MIPORN.

RUBY GOTTESMAN: They loved DiBe. He made 'em serious money. But then the people came to Gotti and said DiBe was talkin' bad about him, and that's why he got whacked. But they killed him for that? They shouldn't a killed this guy. This guy made 'em nothin' but serious money. I mean, DiBe had that whole pornography thing, and once he was gone, it was harder to make money. The mafia left the business. That was the only involvement: DiBe and Mickey Z.

JOHN GOTTI [FBI WIRETAP]: "DiBe, did he ever talk subversive to you? Never talked it to Angelo, and he never talked it to 'Joe Pinney'? I took Sammy's word that he talked about me behind my back. I took Sammy's word. I saw the papers and everything. He didn't rob nothin'. You know why he's dying? He's gonna die because he refused to come in when I called. He didn't do nothing else wrong."

BILL KELLY: At one point John Gotti ordered DiBernardo to come for a meeting, and DiBernardo ignored him. I understand that was the main reason he was killed. That, and the fact that DiBe was in line to move up; Gotti figured, "We better get rid of this guy, 'cause he's got too much clout."

BRUCE MOUW: Sammy "The Bull" Gravano and DiBernardo were actually very close friends. Gravano thought the world of DiBe. Sammy thought it was a bad idea to kill DiBe because they needed guys like DiBe to run the family and spread out things like labor racketeering to other businesses.

But Angelo Ruggiero started spreading stories that DiBe was talking behind John Gotti's back—that he wasn't a team player, and that he wanted to become boss of the family. So word got back to Gotti—and being the impulsive person he was, he said, "Kill him."

SAMMY "THE BULL" GRAVANO: Angelo came to me and told me that John Gotti sent out an order to kill DiBe. Angelo said that DiBe was talking behind his back, and there was another reason. . . .

BRUCE ELLAVSKY: Do I have any knowledge that Robert DiBernardo may have been cooperating with the United States Attorney's Office at the time of his disappearance? Hmmm . . .

I don't, but I probably wouldn't tell if I did.

ROGER YOUNG: Two things were behind the fact that DiBe got killed. One, I think, was too much publicity—too much going on where people know too much—and they were afraid he might roll to save his own skin.

Secondly, a lot of times they think, "They're getting too powerful. We can't trust them anymore. They might not be turning everything over to us—information and money."

SAMMY "THE BULL" GRAVANO: DiBe was just talking a lot and not meaning anything. He wasn't dangerous. It was something we could hold up on. But Angelo responded to me that this had to be done, that John was steaming. We already had a location to kill him, which was Tony Lee's mother's basement.

BRUCE MOUW: The hidden motive behind Angelo Ruggiero wanting Robert DiBernardo killed was the fact that he owed DiBe a ton of money. I think DiBe helped him buy his house in Cedarhurst, Long Island. So in one fell swoop DiBe gets killed, the way is cleared for Angelo to become under-boss—even though it never happened—plus he wiped out his loan.

SAMMY "THE BULL" GRAVANO: DiBe came in. He came downstairs. He said hello. He sat down. Then old man Paruta got up, and I told him to get DiBe a cup of coffee. He got up. In the cabinet there was a .38 with a silencer. He took the gun out, walked over to DiBe, and shot him twice in the back of the head. Me and Eddie picked him up and put him in the back room, locked it up. We left the office. We locked the office up, and I went and met with Angelo in the Burger King in Coney Island and told him it was done.

SHARON MITCHELL: DiBe was a very sweet guy. When they picked him up and took him for the ride, everyone looked at it as a big disservice. There wasn't an ounce of honor in that. I mean, why, because he didn't come in for a sit-down?

See, that's just where I come from in the school of pornography—from organized crime. For me it was ideal because I felt like these mobsters would protect me from anything. I wasn't attracted to them because they were dangerous or anything—but because they weren't. They were family guys; they were like my uncles. I felt safe with them.

BOBBY ELKINS: Everybody loved DiBe. But that's what I'm saying: If the mentality of the dagos was that they would kill DiBe because he was a big money earner, then they killed him because of their pride.

Gotti was an asshole. So was this little fucking stool pigeon Sammy the Bull. He was a piece of shit.

RICHARD ROSFELDER: They supposedly fed DiBe through a tree shredder.

BILL KELLY: We still don't know what happened to Robert DiBernardo's body. Somebody said, "He's having lunch with Jimmy Hoffa," and he probably is.

Conclusions

U.S.A.
1986-1987

GLORIA LEONARD: The radical feminists ended up as kind of odd bedfellows with the Christian right because they were basically espousing the same rhetoric. I used to debate the radical feminists all the time, at dozens and dozens of colleges and universities. Toward the end of one of our gigs, one of the so-called feminists with whom I used to debate actually hit on me, ha, ha, ha.

But I was asked to speak in front of the Meese Commission, and as luck would have it I wound up being very ill and was hospitalized. So I sent Veronica Vera down in my place. She did great.

VERONICA VERA: I had to think twice about it because there are parts of pornography I find stupid and silly. I didn't want be seen as representing some of the very misogynistic sleazy stuff. But I felt it was more important to stand up for free speech than to worry about being seen as defending stuff that I find distasteful.

I had sent them photos of myself in bondage because I thought this was really what they're concerned about. And accompanying the photos was a piece I had written, saying that pornography was a way to explore my own bondage fantasies, and I asked to read it.

Senator Arlen Specter said, "Okay, you can read it."

BILL MARGOLD: When the Meese Commission reared its empty head, we in the industry were told not to cooperate. That's the worst thing you can tell me. I said to the people around me, "Don't you want anybody to go there and tell the truth?"

"Oh, no. Don't cooperate—they'll go away."

I said, "If you don't tell them what the hell we do for a living, if you don't tell them what we're all about, then they're gonna make up their own stories."

KRISTIN STEEN: My instincts were sharp, but I made some serious mistakes, too. Back in 1969 or 1970, I agreed to do this one film—it was just supposed to be a very short, one-night thing. I was actually filling in for somebody who couldn't make it. I was supposed to be a body double. They got me on the set—it was a very small crew, and just me and one other actor. The scene was supposed to be in an airplane; the guy was supposed to try to touch me, and I was supposed to rebuke him.

It was just supposed to be a short, little, funny scene. He's supposed to get my three buttons open before I smack him. And that was it.

Well, we start shooting, and he gets the three buttons open, and I do my thing—and he doesn't stop. And I say, "Wait a second!"

He keeps going, and by now I'm trying to fight him off me, and he keeps going and the camera keeps rolling and I start to yell. I look around at the director, and all of a sudden I'm getting really, really scared, right?

He's on me, and he's in me, and he's . . . And I'm crying and screaming—and they're filming this, right?

VERONICA VERA: So I read, "I am the love object, waiting for you to enjoy me, to tie me up, to take pleasure from me. I'm the object of your desire, always open to your cock and your mouth. . . ." But when I was testifying, I got to this part about the cock in the mouth, and I thought, "Am I going to be able to say this?"

I stopped just before the word *cock,* and Specter had the text in front of him. I said, "Shall I go on, Senator?"

He said, "You certainly may."

So I finished up and said: "Always open to your cock and your mouth! Enjoy me, take pleasure from me, as you do, you'll understand by the purity of my surrender that you have become my captive, too."

Then I said, "Senator, I'm not a victim. I don't want to be considered a victim. I think that both men and women need to be free to explore their fantasies. I think otherwise it just makes it unfair that men or women have to feel guilty about exploring our fantasies."

VERONICA HART: The Meese Commission tried to get as many horror stories as they could, to validate the idea that people in the industry were victimized.

KRISTIN STEEN: Finally the camera stops, and the director comes over to me. I'm begging him, "*What the hell are you doing?! STOP THIS!*"

And he says, "Listen, the guys producing this film are really, really heavy guys, all right? They've paid a lot of money for us to get this, and I'm really sorry, but you're gonna have to go with it."

It was totally unbelievable to me. I'd never had any kind of experience like that. This was rape, and they were filming it. They turned the cameras on, and the guy had me pinned. . . .

That was the first time I had sex on camera.

NINA HARTLEY: What really irritated me about the Meese Commission and the radical right-wing feminists were the cries of "Women and Children! Women and Children!" As an adult female, I didn't appreciate somebody infantalizing me and portraying me as someone who needs protection from the big, bad phallus—or my own fantasies.

KRISTIN STEEN: So they finish, and the guy gets off me, and I'm crying. I'm completely in shock, freaking out, and they just walk away, right? But the cameraman is there packing up his stuff.

I don't know what the hell to do, so the cameraman takes pity on me. He comes over, puts a blanket around me, and says, "Listen, I'm really sorry. Can I take you home?" I can't believe this, but I believed he felt sorry, so I let him drive me home. I get home and I can't sleep and it's like four o'clock in the morning now. I stay up all night, and I'm freaking out.

VERONICA HART: This was a very frightening time for the porn business. It seemed like everybody was out to get pornographers, and you could actually go to jail for having produced or distributed or directed an adult video. There seemed to be a real witchhunt going on.

BILL MARGOLD: I'm not sure how I got to the Meese Commission. All I know is that I got this very strange call from this FBI man, Hagerty, chief investigator of the commission, and he says, "I hear you want to speak to the Meese Commission. What do you want to tell them?"

I said, "The truth."

KRISTIN STEEN: The next day I call my boyfriend, and he says, "What's the matter?" because I sounded really screwed up.

I said, "Well, I had this shoot last night. . . ."

So he drags it out of me, and he blows his top. He's furious. So he picks me up, and we go to the police station. And I said, "They're never gonna believe me!"

He says, "No, this is serious."

I said, "Well, I know it *feels* serious, but I don't know if *they're* gonna think it's serious."

But they did. They made out a report, and I gave their names. My boyfriend got me a lawyer, and we took them to court. I won about a hundred and fifty thousand dollars in a civil case against them. But they'd disappeared.

TOM BYRON: The Meese Commission said that pornography spawned violence against women. They cited all these biased reports of research they'd done with criminals, saying that criminals were inspired by pornography—which is so much bullshit. We inspire violent behavior no more than Freddy Krueger. I mean, we're doing movies, okay? We just happen to put a penis into a vagina, and that makes it bad?

KRISTIN STEEN: I had been raped on film. I don't know whatever happened to that; I mean maybe it was sold in South America. A few years later, when I was taking classes at NYU, I met some of those Women Against Pornography, and they wanted me to join them. But I didn't feel that my experiences with pornography were damaging to me. What was harmful to me was the violence perpetrated on me on that one occasion. So I didn't entirely agree with their premise; there were a few things I agreed with, but I couldn't blanket it. And I didn't want to go into attack mode.

JOHN WATERS: I think good pornography today is when the women are having as much fun as the men. I don't think all pornography is degrading to women at all, and some people I know are happy being in pornographic movies. Many are not.

But I would bet, if they ever did a survey, that 90 percent of porn stars were abused.

KRISTIN STEEN: I couldn't be a feminist because I'm not *against* anybody. I could be against child pornography—because children don't have a choice. And if I'd been abducted and raped as a child, and films were made, and pictures were taken, I would probably be very active in the movement. I have a child now, and I've educated her about certain rules—that you can say *no.*

BILL MARGOLD: The Meese Commission found some underground shit that somebody had made that had nothing to do with my business because I'm in the adult entertainment industry. This wasn't commercial stuff—it was underground mail-order crap. It wasn't sex; it was violence. It's seeing somebody with a cut-off tit or a hacked-up breast. That's what they thought was hard-core.

VERONICA HART: People love to see stories about how we're victimized. *I mean, obviously, how could a thinking, rational, sexually whole person choose this as a business?* You know, it's baloney—every business has their casualties. But the porn business—as much as any business—has some very smart, bright, well-balanced people working in it.

BILL MARGOLD: At one point, as an aside, I told them, "What you people believe is that we have sex with underage German Shepherds and then kill them. We don't have any time for that. Animals bite, and kids say no. Our stuff is between consenting adults. My job is to talk people out of this before they get into it. I don't want them to do anything that will hurt them."

TOM BYRON: I go on Cinemax and HBO, and I can't find a good movie to save my life. They're all soft porn—but that's okay. But as soon as you put a penis into a vagina, the rules change. The gloves come off; and all of a sudden you're branded a criminal, a detriment to society. You know, "We're gonna put you in jail for the rest of your life. You dirty, filthy pornographer, you."

BILL MARGOLD: As I was coming down from testimony, Barry Lynn of the ACLU came over to me and said, "I wish I could speak like that for those people, but I wear a suit."

And I realized at that point that the ACLU would sell us out in a heart-beat—that they have no use for the X-rated industry. Come fucking *on.*

KRISTIN STEEN: The Women Against Pornography were throwing the baby out with the bathwater. I think pornography has a place in our society—sex for money has a place in our society. Definitely.

Until people can have really honest, fulfilling relationships with each other, this is the way it's going to be. Pornography has always been there, and it always will. Until we're so evolved that we don't need to pay for it, or don't miss it, we're going to suffer from not having it.

I am not against pornography at all. I'm for it. I'm against people being used—and you can use people on either side of it.

LINDA LOVELACE: When I look back at all the feminists and Women Against Pornography—I kind of feel like they used me, too. Because when I came out and said what I said, you know, about being a victim, too, it supported everything they had been saying, and it was coming from the horse's mouth.

They needed me; that was good. But if I ever needed anything, they weren't really there. Between Andrea Dworkin and Kitty MacKinnon, they've written so many books, and they mention my name and all that, but financially they've never helped me out. They don't want me to do this or that, but they've never really helped me. When I showed up with them for speaking engagements, I'd always get five hundred dollars or so. But I know they made a few bucks off me, just like everybody else.

Christmas Eve with Lori and the Kids

WORTHINGTON ESTATES, OHIO/TERMINAL ISLAND PRISON, CALIFORNIA
1986–1987

RUBY GOTTESMAN: The MIPORN trial went on for years. And finally, when Norm Arno went to jail, they took everything from him. He got sentenced to five years on Terminal Island. Who gets five years for interstate transportation of obscene material? They picked on him because he had that big company, and they wanted to make an example of him.

TOMMY SINOPOLI: When Norm went to Terminal Island, VCX was the largest X-rated video company in the world, and it was a known fact that we started it together. I mean, I could have taken half the company, but after I spent a few hundred thousand dollars in court trying to get it back, I decided to just open up another company instead.

Did I ever call Lori and say, "Hey, this is half mine?" No. I didn't want those associations in my life. I don't think Lori Smith's elevator went all the way to the top. I don't think the lights were on in every room.

LORENE SMITH'S SANITY EVALUATION: "Ms. Smith stated that her husband, Norman, was convicted in the distribution of pornographic materials and incarcerated in the Federal Correctional System on such charges. At this time, she began to believe that she was 'the great prostitute,' a reference to a chapter in the Book of Revelations. She began to believe that her children were 'devils' and that she and her children must die."

RUBY GOTTESMAN: Norman made birthday parties for the kids. He'd hire a fire engine to come and take all the kids for rides up to the hills where he lived, you know? He was very nice with the kids.

But Lori, she was a wacko. She was completely out of it. And she had no use for me because she read, in the MIPORN wiretaps, that I said she was nothin' but a two-dollar whore.

Norm loved those kids. They were his whole life. I mean, the guy came alive when he saw those kids. When she killed the kids, that was the end of him. It was all downhill. And then they put her in an insane asylum.

LORENE SMITH'S SANITY EVALUATION: "Ms. Smith stated that once, while in a parking lot, she saw a car with a vanity license plate of an Eagle and interpreted it to mean that she should 'fly off a cliff.'

"She stated that as a result, she drove her Jaguar with her two children off of a cliff, but this, of course, did not result in the death of she or her children."

RUBY GOTTESMAN: Lori was drivin' a Jaguar or somethin', and she crashed it, fell down a cliff with the two kids in it. Maybe a hundred feet down, she went. And nobody got hurt. Imagine that!

LORENE SMITH'S SANITY EVALUATION: "Ms. Smith stated that she told hospital personnel that she lost control of her car, but that 'people knew' who she was and 'were trying to take my children away.' In a subsequent interview, Ms. Smith also indicated that while at the hospital, she attempted to drown her older son in a commode."

RUBY GOTTESMAN: I didn't visit Norm in Terminal Island—maybe I was mad at him at the time. Our friendship was hot and cold for a long time because of Lori. But I seen him right after that. I mean, he was terrible. He was drinkin' a lot and everything. He didn't shower; he didn't shave. He missed Lori and the kids; he was lonely.

LORENE SMITH'S SANITY EVALUATION: "Ms. Smith indicated that her 'delusions' persisted from September through May of 1985, and then ended. She stated that she 'became normal again and moved to Ohio, but in the back of my mind I still thought such things.'"

WORTHINGTON ESTATES POLICE DEPARTMENT SERGEANT LAWLESS (CRIME AGAINST PERSON CASE REPORT): "Approximately 3:35 P.M. Sheryl A. Lang and her husband, Gerard Lang, approached this officer and advised that they were concerned about the welfare of Mrs. Lang's sister, Lorene L. Smith, who lives at 6695 Hayhurst Street. I accompanied them to the Hayhurst address, and we checked around the house.

"Mrs. Lang stated she was willing to break into the house as we were getting no response at the door. I requested Lieutenant Hopkins to come to 6695 Hayhurst Street, and on his arrival we found a window unlocked on the northeast side of the house."

WEPD LIEUTENANT HOPKINS (CRIME AGAINST PERSON CASE REPORT): "Upon entering and unlocking the front door for Sergeant Lawless, a female voice called from the family room and said, 'Who's there?' I entered that room and identified myself as a police officer and asked Lori Smith if she was okay, and she said, 'Yes.' She was smoking a cigarette and watching TV. I asked if her kids were okay, and she said, 'No.'"

LORENE SMITH'S SANITY EVALUATION: "Ms. Smith indicated at 5:46 P.M. on Christmas Eve 1986, she took the children into the car in the garage and told them they were going to see their grandmother. As the car ran, one child, Jordan, complained of the smoke, and she had him come up to the front seat and sit with her. She said that after a period of time, the children lost consciousness.

"She then turned off the ignition of the car, got out of the car with the intention to open the garage door, but lost consciousness."

WEPD LIEUTENANT HOPKINS (CRIME AGAINST PERSON CASE REPORT): "I opened the southwest bedroom door and observed a small decomposed body in bed along the south wall. The body was covered to the neck with blankets and head exposed. I returned to the lower level and called for detective units.

"Upon Lieutenant Dayton's arrival, this officer and Sergeant Mauger located another small decomposed body in the southeast bedroom."

MIKE MAUGER (WEPD SERGEANT): Lori Smith's story to us was that she was getting ready to go somewhere for Christmas—that the children were outside in the garage, and apparently one of the children started the car. At the same time, somebody called, she got on the phone with them, started talking, and forgot about the children in the garage. She alleged the children succumbed to the carbon monoxide poisoning. She then took them upstairs to their beds and covered them up like they were normal sleeping children.

LORENE SMITH'S SANITY EVALUATION: "Ms. Smith stated that when she awoke, she found both children unconscious. She indicated that Jordan had expired and that Michael was comatose. She stated that she unsuccessfully gave Jordan mouth-to-mouth resuscitation.

"She stated that she took Michael and put him on her bed, wrapping him in an electric blanket. She stated she put on the movie *Flash Gordon* for him to watch, as that was his favorite movie, in the hope that this would revive him. She also indicated that she would feed him small amounts of potato soup via an eye dropper."

MIKE MAUGER: We went out to the garage. Normally, if there's carbon monoxide poisoning, the garage is dark—black. But it wasn't. And the first thing we did was look at the children to see if there was discoloration on the skin, but they had started putrefying. That's how bad they were.

The story of carbon monoxide didn't hold up because the chemical test we did showed no abnormal monoxide in the garage. What we believe was that she probably slowed their breathing by giving them some medication, and then smothered them. Possibly rolled pillows over their faces.

RUBY GOTTESMAN: When Lori killed the kids, Norm was devastated. He was, like, cryin' all day. I mean, I had to go sit with him. He was saying, "How could she do that to the kids?" All that shit.

COLUMBUS DISPATCH, JANUARY 13, 1987: FATHER RELEASED FROM PRISON FOR WORTHINGTON BOYS: "The father of two boys whose decomposing bodies were found last Tuesday in their Worthington home has been released from federal prison on a $100,000 bond so he can attend their funeral, Los Angeles officials said yesterday.

"Norman Arno, 59, of North Hollywood, California, was released Friday from a medium-security federal prison at Terminal Island, California. He has served four months of a five-year sentence for conspiracy to transport obscene materials across state lines."

MIKE MAUGER: I thought this might have been a major suicide plan—that she was going to kill the children and then kill herself. As time went on, we started hearing about Norm Arno being locked up. Apparently, she had money; I mean, there was no doubt that somebody was taking care of the household. Did anybody talk to Arno? I don't think they did. He may not have wanted to talk to us. I always thought that was really strange.

COLUMBUS DISPATCH, JANUARY 14, 1987: CON WANTS TO TAKE SONS' BODIES FOR CALIFORNIA BURIAL: "The father of two boys found dead in their mother's Worthington home is prepared to fight for what he believes is his right to take their bodies to California for burial, a Los Angeles attorney said yesterday."

MIKE MAUGER: We knew that Norm Arno came back here because we saw him. We knew he was doing federal time for pornography, so he probably did have somebody assigned to security, but I think he was a low-end security risk because it was Terminal Island, not some maximum-security prison.

COLUMBUS DISPATCH, JANUARY 18, 1987: JUSTICE DEPT. MEMO DETAILS DAD'S PORNOGRAPHY DEALS: "Arno, who was divorced from Ms. Smith in 1983, adamantly believes his ex-wife is innocent of any wrongdoing in the boys' deaths, one source said. The source said, 'They may not be together, but he still loves her.'"

MIKE MAUGER: We got Lori Smith indicted for murder, but they found her not guilty by reason of insanity.

The Last Chance

LOS ANGELES/MILAN
1988

LAURIE HOLMES (AKA MISTY DAWN, PORN STAR): I met John Holmes on the set of *Marathon* in San Francisco—I think it was early 1983. I didn't know what to think of him at first.

I thought, "Oh my God, John Holmes is going to be there!" I was nervous. I had driven up the coast with another L.A. guy, and when we got there he goes, "That's John Holmes in that limo!"

I went, "John Holmes! Oh no! Should I bring my gun?" John had just recently gotten out of jail. I think he got out in November, and I met him in January.

RON JEREMY: I worked with Misty Dawn, aka Laurie Holmes, before John did. Misty and I did one of the greatest scenes of all time, and when we were shooting it, she says, "I'm doing a scene with John Holmes next week. I'm all excited. I heard good things about him."

LAURIE HOLMES: I was immediately attracted to him. I walked up and said, "Hi, I'm Misty Dawn."

He kind of looked at me. I thought, "Well, he's kind of arrogant."

It was a different crowd in San Francisco than what I was used to. It was kind of a weird scene—I've never been on quite a set like that before. Some of the girls got a little jealous of me, tried to accuse me of stealing things out of the locker room. I said, "Everybody and their mother has been in here. Why are you looking at me?"

They were a rough crowd. They wanted to cut my face up or something. And John took me under his wing and said, "No! You leave her alone." Which made them really mad because then he locked me in his own dressing room.

BILL AMERSON: The first movie John made when he got out of jail was for Hal Freeman in San Francisco. That's where John met Laurie Rose. Laurie was known as Misty Dawn, the butt-fucking queen of the porno industry. That was her specialty—doing anal sex with a number of guys, one after the other.

She said to Bill Margold—who was on the set—"I really want to meet John. And I really want all that in my ass."

Bill told John. John thought it was amusing, thinking that it wasn't going to happen. But off camera it did happen. Laurie fell in love with him.

LAURIE HOLMES: I fell for him, and he fell for me. But he didn't let on that he really felt for me, which made me want him more.

John gave me his phone number back here in Los Angeles. He was living at Bill Amerson's house. I waited four or five days and then I called him. I went up to see him for a few minutes. I knew he liked young girls, so I, you know, dressed as the young girl.

BILL AMERSON: My first contact with Laurie was on my birthday. My wife had gone out of town to visit her relatives in Arizona. I was watching a boxing match, and there was a knock on the door. I opened the door and there was Laurie Rose—wrapped in a red ribbon.

I said, "John's room is the second door down that hallway."

Then John asked me if she could move in and be, like, his housekeeper and his maid, and I agreed.

LAURIE HOLMES: Everybody always concentrates on the mistakes John made and not the person himself. Yeah, he got into drugs. Yeah, maybe he stole a few things, got mixed up with the wrong people. But that was only a part of his life, a part of the person. John had a heart of gold. He was a great person. I mean, he was great to me. That's all I know.

BILL AMERSON: John liked Laurie because she could be *nasty*. That was his word. He said she was willing to try anything.

LAURIE HOLMES: I think John had an addictive personality. When he got into drugs, immediately he was addicted. He was addicted to scotch, that's for sure. I'm not sure if that was to wash down the drugs, or if he liked the taste, or whatever. Definitely addicted to sex, there's no denying that.

BILL AMERSON: Laurie would sit in his bedroom for two hours while he was in the bathroom doing drugs. She didn't like the fact that he used cocaine—she wanted him to just smoke pot—but I don't believe that she got him off drugs.

LAURIE HOLMES: A lot of people who worked with John felt he was a mystery man—reclusive. I mean, could you blame him? He didn't trust people very much. His thing was, "Friends will get you killed." With me anyway, it was, "If they can get ahold of you, they can get to me." That's the one thing I admired about John: I knew without a shadow of any doubt that he would have taken a bullet for me at any time. As a woman, that made me feel good.

So, no, he did not trust people. Maybe he did ham it up a little bit when it came to the other male actors. He liked to be a prima donna—he *was* a prima donna—maybe it was his right to be one.

BILL AMERSON: All of John's relationships were sexual. Even while Laurie was living with us he had a couple of mistresses—a producer and an actress.

LAURIE HOLMES: John had asked me to marry him back in the summer of 1983. We had gotten our own apartment. His whole plan was, "I'm getting older. I want to make a bunch of money and then I'm going to get out of the business, and we'll go away."

He had someplace picked out where we could get married and retire. But he would never tell me where it was, and I still don't know.

Then—I guess it was 1984—he came home and said, "I've got something to tell you. My divorce was final today. I know you didn't know I was married."

I go, "No, I didn't."

He goes, "Well, that's because there was no reason to bring it up. We've been estranged for years; and it's just one of those things. We finally went through it, and it was no big deal."

I said, "Oh, okay."

BILL AMERSON: John and Laurie got married because John found out that he was HIV positive. You see, John and I initiated HIV testing for performers in the adult industry.

Prior to shooting *Rocky X*, everyone had to take an HIV test. And to show the performers that we were really serious, John and I took the HIV test together. And we both came back negative.

About four or five months later we took another one. We were going to do it every six months because we wanted to show the industry that we weren't afraid of the tests and everything was okay.

LAURIE HOLMES: We lived in Encino for a long time. A typical yuck apartment, two bedrooms on Burbank Boulevard. Swimming pool, freeway behind us. Nothing special.

We watched a lot of movies. People think John Holmes was this big party animal—and I'm sure he was in his younger days—but he was just a homebody. We'd go to the mountains, parks, or movies, or whatever. He was a fine connoisseur of fine food or so he liked to portray himself. As long as he had his scotch and coffee it didn't matter.

BILL AMERSON: My test came back negative; John's test came back positive. I was with John at the doctor's office when the doctor informed him that he was HIV positive and explained that he could live another fifteen, maybe twenty years if he changed his lifestyle. The doctor told him to stop smoking, drinking, and doing drugs. Start taking vitamins and watching his diet. John—being as reactive as he was—immediately doubled his drug usage. Started smoking five packs of cigarettes a day. Drank a quart of scotch a day and just didn't give a shit about anything.

He knew he was going to die.

LAURIE HOLMES: John came back to the apartment in Encino, and he had that coldness about him, you know, that distance. He says, "I'm going to die." And then he drove off. Bill Amerson told me, "John tested positive."

Then he came back about half an hour later, and he was laughing about it. We took the rest of the day, went to the beach, and talked.

We didn't have any sex after that. He was protecting me. But in his mind, to never have sex again was like the ultimate punishment. You know, why even bother breathing?

RON JEREMY: The next thing you know, Laurie married him.

BILL AMERSON: One afternoon I got a phone call from John, who was obviously stoned. Appeared to be out of his mind.

He said, "I think I got married."

I said, "What do you mean?"

He said, "Laurie and I are in Las Vegas; and I think I got married a little while ago, but I'm not sure."

Well, John was up to taking fifty ten-milligram Valiums a day. Which should kill some people, but it didn't kill him. His cocaine elevated him so much that he needed that much Valium to come down.

It turns out they did, in fact, get married. Laurie had the idea that it was all a romantic thing. Laurie believed that John loved her. He may have told her that, but I never heard him.

TIM CONNELLY: When John came down with AIDS, everybody started thinking, How did he get it? Where did he get it? And we all knew he'd just gone to Europe, on this trip to go fuck all over Rome and Germany.

RON JEREMY: I had heard that John went to Italy knowing he had the virus. He couldn't really get a job in America; he did a gay movie here. He supposedly got the virus when he was in jail; his male lover supposedly died of it. So he went to Europe to work with Cicciolina—the Italian porn star who got elected to the Italian parliament.

I knew he fucked Cicciolina because she told me about it when I was in Italy years later. And that's kind of mean; that he knew he had it, and he went to work anyway.

CICCIOLINA: I had never met John Holmes; I didn't even know who he was. There was a production company, I don't remember the name, that had offices in Rome and in the United States, and they contacted me about a movie project involving some American talents. I agreed, and the day before production started they told me that I had to do this scene with this famous American actor that was hung like a horse.

TIM CONNELLY: The immediate suspicion was that John got HIV in Europe. But people who knew him a little better, who knew the history of him in the movies, knew he'd fucked this guy Joe Yale in the ass in a movie, and this guy was one of the first guys in gay porn to come down with AIDS and die. So he probably gave John the disease.

I immediately thought about intravenous drugs, transsexual hookers, you know. I mean, John Holmes was so out of his mind on drugs, and he fucked transsexual hookers. I mean, John was completely irresponsible in all areas of his life.

But I never really knew John to shoot drugs, and I wouldn't be surprised if somebody said that John would never touch a needle. I don't know, but I never saw needle marks, and he never went out of his way to hide his arms, you know what I mean?

RON JEREMY: I asked a friend of John's whether he'd known about the disease before going to Europe, and he said he did. So I said, "Why didn't you stop him from going?"

He said, "I couldn't."

I said, "Why didn't you call Italy and warn them what's coming across the ocean?"

CICCIOLINA: The first impression I had was that he was a very sad man, very kind. Very skinny and tall. He looked very sick, but I thought he had a flu or something. I mean, I had no idea what kind of disease he had. He was really, really skinny, but I didn't think he was seriously ill.

LAURIE HOLMES: After John was diagnosed, he really wasn't working on films or doing anything. Then he was offered this film in Europe, and he talked to me about it. It was a lot of money—money we could really use. Most of the actresses he was going to be working with were being flown out from here. The theory was that he had gotten AIDS from inside the business. He just figured, if they don't get it from me or they don't already have it, they're going to end up with it anyway—ignorance on AIDS was even within the business at that time. So he decided to do it.

We needed the money; he needed the money.

CICCIOLINA: My role in the movie was very brief; I only had to be on the set for about a day and a half. I just had to do a sex scene with him, but the fact that he wasn't feeling good caused a delay because he had serious problems getting an erection. When he finally got one, he could only stay hard for a short time, so we had to shoot the whole scene in just five minutes, and then edit it so that it looked longer.

TIM CONNELLY: The progression: Joe Yale, who fucked Holmes, gets AIDS. Then Lisa de Leeuw disappears, and we hear she has AIDS. Then John Holmes gets HIV, then AIDS. Then Lori Levine comes down with HIV and AIDS.

I mean, I don't know who gave what to who, but you have to wonder.

LAURIE HOLMES: We had started the John Holmes Relief Fund. Caballero, the movie company, gave me a thousand dollars; a few other people—Suze Randall, Annie Sprinkle, probably about ten people—gave money. Not many, though. John was very hurt. He felt like people had turned their backs on him. His whole attitude was, "God, I've made all these people all this money, and they won't return my phone calls."

TIM CONNELLY: I don't think it was indiscriminate sexual behavior among people in the adult film industry that gave John Holmes AIDS. I think it was irresponsible, drug-related behavior, addictive behavior patterns, and the way that carefree goes to careless. You get strung out on something, and then when you're on a bender for three days doing crack cocaine, the only thing that might get your dick hard is a couple of transsexual hookers and some heroin, you know?

No condom? *Fine.*

TOM LANGE (LAPD DETECTIVE): We knew Holmes was dying. The only reason we went to see him was that we felt it would be irresponsible if we didn't because he still had information that could have shed light on what happened with these murders, and you're not going to find out unless you go ask. Holmes had always played a game with us. He played a game his whole life, I think.

LAURIE HOLMES: I'd been tipped off that the cops were on the way. I cut out of work and got to the hospital fast. You never knew what state of mind John was going to be in; some days he was all there, and some days he thought Ronald Reagan was outside with a bomb.

I didn't want them to trick John into saying anything. John could have spun a whole tale on something that would have come down on someone else that wasn't true. I told him the cops were on the way, and I said, "Don't say anything. Just act like you're out of it, and I'll cover for you."

TOM LANGE: It was, quite frankly, a waste of time, but as responsible law enforcement officers following up on a very brutal quadruple murder, we had to at least try to see if on his deathbed he'd give us some information.

Of course he didn't. It was all nonsense.

LAURIE HOLMES: John moaned and groaned the whole time. About ten minutes later, Detective Lange turned to me and said, "What about you? Do you know anything?"

I said, "I don't know anything." I could just see John looking at me with that *shakes-head-no* look. I didn't know anything, and they would twist anything he would say, anyway. He was worried for me at that point.

TOM LANGE: We had to wheel Holmes out beneath a staircase. He was in quite a bit of agony. He wanted a cigarette, and he couldn't smoke in his room. So we got him a cigarette. He said, "You know, I always respected you guys, and I played a cop, and the LAPD is the greatest law enforcement outfit in the world." And on and on. It was a big stroke job.

He knew why we were there, and he wasn't about to answer any direct questions.

LAURIE HOLMES: They left disgusted. Oh, well.

CICCIOLINA: This was the time when I started my relationship with Jeff Koons, the famous American artist. He's like Andy Warhol; he makes art, like painting or sculptures, and he's very talented. He was courting me, and he knew I did this scene with John Holmes. So when John died, he called me from the States, and he asked me if I knew that John Holmes died of AIDS?

I said I didn't; they told me that the cause of his death was colon cancer. But Jeff told me that he'd been informed by friends in the hospital that the real cause was AIDS. So he faxed me the report from the hospital, and it really did read: Cause of Death—Related to HIV.

LAURIE HOLMES: John did get in touch with his brothers and sisters during his life but just toward the end. He sent his dog—our dog, Charlie—to his sister. His mother was trying to get him and his half brother, David, to make amends. John's mom had made a mistake and tried to rectify it later on. They were good people.

CICCIOLINA: I got really scared, but I went to take a test, and I was okay. Later that year Jeff and I got married in Budapest, and we went for our honeymoon in Germany, where we conceived our baby, Ludwig. Well, throughout our relationship, which lasted a couple of years, we both took tests every three or four months, and everything was fine. So I guess I'm fine.

LAURIE HOLMES: John didn't want a funeral. He was adamant about it. The funeral he did have wasn't really a funeral. He was cremated. I viewed his body before they put him in the oven. I put a picture of Jesus on his heart and watched them wheel him in.

I asked them, "Why is he green?"

They said, "That's the decay."

When we got his ashes, his mother and his half brother and I went around the islands on a boat out of Oxnard called the *China Clipper*, and I slept with John's ashes that night. I didn't want anybody to steal them. His brother David had drilled holes in the urn and put tape over them; around 4:30 or 5:00 that morning—before it got light—we all got up, peeled the tape off and tossed it over. We didn't say anything; our thoughts were inside us.

But you know, there was no funeral. I wasn't aware that a memorial service was going to be held until I heard it on the news, after the fact, you know?

Nobody invited his widow.

Jail

BALTIMORE/LOS ANGELES
1988–1989

TIM CONNELLY: I was making a movie in Sam Kinison's old house in the Hollywood Hills; Ron Jeremy was directing it. We'd been fucking all day and doing lines with Sam—off a mirror that had John Belushi's face on it—when we heard that the Hal Freeman conviction was overturned on appeal.

It's kind of ironic: There we were, in the middle of a shoot, when we found out that we could *legally* shoot, ha, ha, ha.

LOS ANGELES TIMES, AUGUST 25, 1988: SUPREME COURT EXONERATES FILM-MAKER OF PANDERING: "Pornographic filmmakers cannot be convicted of pandering for paying actors who engage in sex acts in movies, the California Supreme Court ruled today.

"Sexual acts in filmmaking are protected free speech rights, the court unanimously held in overturning the conviction of Hollywood filmmaker Harold Freeman on five counts of pandering in the film *Caught From Behind II.*"

BUD LEE: When Los Angeles County and the City of Los Angeles were defeated in their attempts to prosecute Hal Freeman on the grounds of pandering, that's what enabled us to move down from San Francisco. Because then, to make movies, all we had to do was buy insurance and get our insurance certificate to the permit office. Now we were the same as everybody else.

LOS ANGELES TIMES, DECEMBER 24, 1988: REJECTED LEGAL ASSAULT ON SEX FILMS APPEALED: "The district attorney's office is trying to revive a novel legal assault on pornography—rejected by the California Supreme Court in a case involving Hollywood sex filmmaker Harold Freeman—by appealing the case to the U.S. Supreme Court."

JOHN WATERS: I knew that Traci Lords was the top porno star at the time. I had never seen her in a movie, but I knew about her, and I knew about the scandal. That had just happened.

At the time I was casting *Cry-Baby*. It was my first Hollywood movie; I was with Universal, and it was actually the only time I had much power there—because *Hairspray* was perceived as a big hit. I had accidentally made a family movie.

GINGER LYNN: Not long after I had amnesia before the grand jury, the feds told me they were investigating me for tax evasion. So they kept their word—if I didn't help them, they would make my life difficult.

Well, I had always paid my taxes, so I wasn't worried.

TOM BYRON: Ginger's tax trouble started the same time mine did. First of all, her lawyer fucking *put her on the stand*. I never went to trial; I fucking pled out, you know?

JOHN WATERS: Suddenly all the studios want to see what I want to do. And all of them want to let me make *Cry-Baby*, right? So Imagine Films did *Cry-Baby*, with Brian Grazer producing. I told him I wanted to use Traci Lords, and he said, "Fine."

If I'd been any other director at Universal, they probably wouldn't have let me use Traci.

GINGER LYNN: I'd paid my taxes, so they spent five years—and I heard one man was paid a hundred thousand dollars per year—to watch every movie I'd ever made, to look at every layout, and read every interview. In those days, it wasn't mandatory that companies send 1099 tax forms to employees; they could send the records to the government. Most companies did; a few didn't. I ended up going to trial over two thousand and eighty-seven dollars and four cents—and they didn't want me to pay.

TOM BYRON: Ginger went on the stand and said that the reason she didn't keep her fucking files straight was because she was on coke all the time. And, "Oh, I'm the poor porn victim." Consequently she was found guilty and was subjected to the mandatory daily drug testing. But for her sentencing she hired my lawyer. She did thirty days' probation, and then she had to go to rehab. But she ended up going to jail because she came up dirty on the drug test.

GINGER LYNN: I was put on probation, and then some things happened—it was directly related to the entire fiasco, mess, charade—whatever the hell you wanna call it.

I ended up spending four months and seventeen days in federal prison. How was it? I have a lot more character now, ha, ha, ha—you thought I could lick pussy good before? You should've seen me after I got out of prison!

I was in with murderers and rapists and weapons dealers and drug dealers, you know? Two girls got knocked up while I was in there. I was the only other white girl there. I was fortunate enough to have several women who I did favors for, who took care of me and protected me. You know, you learn to assume the position very quickly. I was not raped. I was not injured.

But I saw a girl—who was a snitch—taken to a room by several girls; she was sodomized with a toilet brush, and one of her eyes was put out.

It was an experience I wouldn't wanna go through again.

JOHN WATERS: Traci read for me a couple times. She came in the first time looking great. She had on—very smart—no makeup, a pair of jeans, and a T-shirt. Traci looks mighty good in a T-shirt. But she's very quiet and very shy, the opposite of a porno star.

DAVE FRIEDMAN: I said to the attorney for the Adult Film Association, "We've got to strike back. This little broad [Traci Lords] fooled a lot of people. People are in real serious trouble now. How did she get a California driver's license? How did she get a passport using this phony ID? She is capable of a misdemeanor and a felony—using phony ID to get a passport and a license."

And the lawyer says, "Oh, well, we don't wanna turn her against us."

I said, "How much more damage can she do?"

Against my better judgment, I didn't go on the *CBS News* and say it. The lawyer talked me out of it.

RUBY GOTTESMAN: Now I stop sellin' Traci's movies; all the movies are comin' back from my customers. I'm gettin' back a couple thousand of her movies, right? I'm givin' 'em back to the manufacturers. And I had maybe a hundred left that I couldn't give back.

STEVE ORENSTEIN (RUBY GOTTESMAN'S PARTNER): I didn't really know Ruby Gottesman until he offered me a job. Jeff Levine, who I worked with at CPLC, went out on his own and was doing business with Ruby. Jeff called me and said, "Ruby's looking for someone to run his warehouse at X-Citement Video. I think you'd be good; if you're interested, give him a call." Ruby was running his company mostly out of his house; he wanted someone to run the warehouse and take over some of the buying—things like that.

RUBY GOTTESMAN: One day this Japanese guy comes in—his name was

Steve Suzuki, like the motorcycle. Nice American and everything. He says, "You got any, uh, Traci Lords movies?"

I says, "I got 'em, but I can't sell 'em to you. It's against the law."

He says, "Yeah, but I'm sending them to Hawaii—nobody'll know over there. Then they'll take 'em to Japan."

STEVE ORENSTEIN: When I got the phone call about Traci, I dunno, my reaction was probably just that we had to deal with it, whatever that meant—make a decision about what to do with the stuff because as innocent as it was at the time, we really didn't know what to do with it. The guys in Texas would return them, and the manufacturers wouldn't take them back.

So we'd say, "Well, put 'em upstairs with the defectives." And then along comes this guy, who says whatever he says to Ruby and convinces Ruby to sell them to him.

Remember, this was self-censorship. Nothing was coming down at this point, and everybody was pulling it from the shelves everywhere. And it wasn't some "taboo" product. It was normal product that was being sold up until yesterday.

RUBY GOTTESMAN: So I take Steve Suzuki upstairs, and I sell him a hundred movies, right? For cash. Then what happens is, he says nothing and leaves.

STEVE ORENSTEIN: Steve Suzuki was actually a customer for a year or two—undercover for the LAPD. And I guess when the Traci Lords thing came down, he was in a joint investigation with the FBI. And since he was already a customer, he just started asking for all these things everywhere he did business.

RUBY GOTTESMAN: Then I get the call where Suzuki says, "Yeah, I'll be there on Friday—just try to have as many Traci Lords movies as you can. I'll take them all."

And I hang up the phone, and I says, "This guy's a cop."

STEVE ORENSTEIN: I mean, I dealt with Steve Suzuki. That's why they indicted me, too. At one point Ruby asked me to go upstairs and help Steve, and I said no. Then Ruby went up there, and I guess I just thought, "I'm being out of line. I guess I'll go and do my job." Whatever. I don't know. It was like, "I guess I should go do it."

RUBY GOTTESMAN: So I get rid of all the Traci Lords movies. But, sure enough, they come on Friday and bust me. I was drivin' around, and I got a phone call, and a guy told me, "There's twenty FBI agents at the Denny's on the corner."

So I pulled in, and there's the FBI agents, lots of LAPD, and they're all over the place like I was the most wanted, right? They put me in handcuffs, and some guy comes over and says, "You know, Ruby, you're in big trouble."

STEVE ORENSTEIN: I wasn't even in the place when the cops showed up, so I don't know what they did. I got a call after they were in there, and I called the attorney, who said, "Don't go in. It's Friday—and they like to arrest everyone on Friday."

At this point they had already arrested Ruby, and that's really who they wanted anyway. So I just went to the office and turned myself in. Again, it's one of those usual things. They're surprisingly all nice and everything, asking questions about the movies and the girls and that sort of thing.

DAVE FRIEDMAN: When Ruby got involved with the Traci Lords thing, of course I took his side on it. Even though Ruby's a guy I don't think too much of.

STEVE ORENSTEIN: Part of my plea bargain was that I was supposed to testify against Ruby. But I was never called as a witness.

LOS ANGELES TIMES, JUNE 16, 1989: LORDS VIDEO AGENT CONVICTED OF CHILD PORNO CHARGES: "Holding that 'the law is designed to protect children until they are adults,' a federal judge Thursday convicted Van Nuys video distributor Rubin Gottesman of three child pornography charges stemming from the distribution of a trio of films in which teenage porn queen Traci Lords appeared."

GINGER LYNN: Was I thinking about Traci while I was in prison? Not so much. I tried to keep a very positive attitude and surround myself with my friends, and I did that by writing a lot of letters. And you can make two phone calls a day. I called my friends, my family, my attorney. At one point, I called the *Wall Street Journal*. Some things happened that were really ugly, and between *Hard Copy* and the *Wall Street Journal* I was out quicker than I thought I would be.

Everybody wanted to know, *Why?* You know, I'm a little porn star. I wasn't running the industry. I'm not some Mafia wife. I just fucked on film. I felt like the government's sacrificial lamb.

BILL MARGOLD: What I think saved us in the long run was that, lo and behold, *Penthouse* discovered that they'd shot Traci under the false identification, and *Penthouse* then pulled out the other piece of identification that Traci had used—a passport, which implicated the federal government. I don't think the government wanted to be implicated in child pornography—and if Tracy had fooled them, they were as culpable as we were. Their neck was on the block. So all of a sudden the Traci Lords thing started to lose its ferocity.

GINGER LYNN: The last three months in prison, I was in Gateway, which is a halfway house. There were seven women, and the rest of them were men. I got out during the day to go on jobs. I had an audition to act on *NYPD Blue*. I was there under a different name; no one in prison knows my name because the guys can get to you.

Anyway, I walked into the studio, and I saw Traci Lords sitting there.

Now, I'm in prison at the time. I'm only out to go to this audition. And my heart's beating so fast I can't stand up. I go up and get the script, and I'm reading through it, and there's one line that reads, "I wanna lick your lollipop."

I put the script back on the desk, walked out, and called my agent. I said, "I'm not doing this." It had nothing to do with that line about licking the lollipop, though. I was in shock that Traci was there.

My agent says, "Get back in there. Get the role first, then turn it down."

So I go back in, I audition, and they put me on hold—which means they want me for the role. Now, I've never had this happen in my career, ever. So I take the script back to prison, and I'm running my dialogue with my bodyguard, who picks me up every day and takes me back to this place in Echo Park. I'm working really hard on it—and eventually I go before Steven Bochco and the entire team for a second audition, and they say, "The role is yours."

For some reason, I was so hung up on the fact that I was doing time—and I was so angry at Traci—that I turned it down. I said, "You know what? I can't do this. I don't wanna say this line."

They said, "You know what? We'll take the line out." So that was kind of a little get-even for me—Traci didn't get the role, *I* got the role. . . . And I did it while I was in prison, ha, ha, ha!

Another Mob Hit?

LOS ANGELES
1989

TOM BYRON: Was it big news when Teddy Snyder got shot in front of his Rolls Royce holding the vial of coke? Oh, that was so poetic. Well, it made the newspaper.

LOS ANGELES TIMES, AUGUST 20, 1989: KILLING OF PORN PIONEER STILL BAFFLES POLICE, PEERS; INQUIRY AFFORDS RARE PEEK AT "PLAYPEN OF THE DAMNED": "Police say Snyder was found shot to death at 11:15 P.M. near his parked car at Blackhawk Street and Wilbur Avenue. He had been shot four times in the front of his body and five times from the rear. Three wounds bore gunpowder marks. Nearby witnesses reported hearing a loud argument before the shots.

"Law enforcement officers familiar with the case said details of the killing show that Snyder may have known his assailant and tried to run away as he was being shot.

"Sharon Snyder, now four months pregnant, said her husband had been trying to get out of the porn business because customers were not buying products anymore. 'Maybe people aren't as perverted as we thought,' she said."

PHIL VANNATTER (LAPD DETECTIVE): I didn't know who Teddy Snyder was until the Devonshire detectives—realizing they were dealing with a big-time pornographer—called us in. About eight to ten hours after the actual murder occurred, we took it over.

When we interviewed Sharon Snyder, she said she'd been doing laundry, and Teddy just disappeared; she didn't even know he was leaving.

TOM BYRON: I think Paul Thomas is the one who called me up and said, "Hey, hear about Ted Snyder? He just got fuckin' blown away."

I went, "Well, that's not surprising," ha, ha, ha. But that came with the territory, man. People were gettin' whacked all the time.

LOS ANGELES TIMES, AUGUST 20, 1989: KILLING OF PORN PIONEER STILL BAFFLES POLICE, PEERS, INQUIRY AFFORDS A PEEK AT "PLAYPEN OF THE DAMNED": "Amid the loose papers and frayed girlie posters of a bankrupt porn empire, Bob Genova telephoned a business acquaintance in Philadelphia with the latest news.

"'You hear what they did to my partner?' asked Genova, whose company had earned a reputation for B-movie porn.

"'They killed him,' he boomed in a nasal voice that echoed into the hallway outside his office, where a visitor waited to see him. 'It's hard to figure. I'm all by myself now. They're whittling me down.'

"Three weeks after Teddy Snyder's body was found punctured by nine bullets in a quiet San Fernando Valley neighborhood, the death of the balding pornographer with a taste for gold chains, leisure suits and luxury cars remains a mystery to police and to Snyder's colleagues in Los Angeles' billion-dollar adult film industry.

"There is no shortage of theories about his death."

PHIL VANNATTER: To me it didn't look like a mob hit because Teddy was shot numerous times, right out in the middle of the street. It wasn't in his front yard, it was on the other side of the Valley—on Blackhawk Avenue, in the Devonshire Division. He lived on one side of the Valley and was killed on the other. I said, "You know, I never heard of a mob hit where they machine-gunned somebody right in the street, in a prominent neighborhood, a nice neighborhood. Normally it's one or two shots to the head." And this guy was shot with what appeared to be an automatic weapon—just sprayed with it.

This homicide reeked of a drug deal gone bad.

BOBBY GENOVA: Nowadays there are so many drug deals that go awry.

LOS ANGELES TIMES, AUGUST 20, 1989: KILLING OF PORN PIONEER STILL BAFFLES POLICE, PEERS; INQUIRY AFFORDS RARE PEEK AT "PLAYPEN OF THE DAMNED": "One theory is that drugs were involved; he was regarded in the industry as a heavy user, and a vial of cocaine was in his hand when he was found dead on a Northridge street.

"A law enforcement investigator familiar with the case said the killing had the appearance of an organized crime–style hit. Court records show that the Northridge company Snyder founded, Video Cassette Recordings Inc., owed money to a company allegedly controlled by a man linked by federal prosecutors to an East Coast crime family. And VCR's offices have been searched as part of an ongoing investigation by a state and local law enforcement task force probing organized crime links to the porn business.

"However, many in the porn industry doubt that organized crime was involved in the killing. 'It's much ado about nothing,' Genova said.

"Whatever the reason for Snyder's death, Genova is shedding no tears for his partner, calling him a drug abuser and creep who did not care about their failing business."

PHIL VANNATTER: During our interviews we found out that Patty, Sharon Snyder's older sister, had apparently dated and almost married a capo in the Gambino family. My partner, Detective Kirk Mellecker, immediately jumped on that with blinders and said, "Oh my God. This has got to be a mob hit." But I thought it had to do with Teddy and Sharon's narcotics involvement or with Teddy's business in the Valley.

TIM CONNELLY: Once Teddy was at work all day with Bobby Genova, it was almost like they were *playing* mob, you know? They didn't seem like *real* mob. But there was a lot of stuff going on with those guys.

LOS ANGELES TIMES, SEPTEMBER 25, 1989: ALLEGED EAST COAST MOB FIGURE NAMED IN VIDEOTAPE FRAUD. "A man authorities describe as a New Jersey leader of an organized crime family has been charged with setting up a 'bogus' company in Chatsworth to defraud other firms out of more than $1 million worth of videotape and equipment, most of which was distributed by Los Angeles pornographers.

"Martin Taccetta, 38, of Florham Park, N.J., who federal and New Jersey authorities say is a prominent member of the Lucchese crime family, faces conspiracy and grand theft charges along with three alleged business associates. All four men are expected to be arrested today, district attorney's officials said."

BOBBY GENOVA: I knew I was a logical suspect. Two days after the shooting I walked into my warehouse and along comes this big Mercury Marquis. These two detectives came out and introduced themselves. They made an appointment to come over to my house at 7:00 P.M. on Friday evening.

These guys saw drugs, sex, Mafia, and thought they had a high-profile case. I knew their theory was cockamamie. They were bumbling and fumbling.

PHIL VANNATTER: Bob Genova wasn't really a lot of help, but I never felt he was involved. He seemed very upset by the fact that Teddy had been killed. And apparently they had made a lot of money together. *A lot of money.*

And Patty—Sharon's sister—was apparently the brains of the organization. I don't think Bobby Genova was very bright, to be honest. I think he was riding on Teddy's coattails.

LOS ANGELES TIMES, SEPTEMBER 25, 1989: ALLEGED EAST COAST MOB FIGURE NAMED IN VIDEOTAPE FRAUD. "The criminal complaint, filed late Friday in Los Angeles Superior Court, emerged from a three-year investigation into organized crime influence in the $1 billion local pornography industry, officials said. An undercover Los Angeles police officer at one point got a job at the company under investigation, Ollinor Video Products, Inc.

"One company that received tape from Ollinor was Video Cassette Recording (VCR), a Northridge-based producer and distributor of pornography videos. Ted Snyder, 47, co-founder of VCR was found shot nine times on a Chatsworth street on Aug. 1, 1989.

"No arrests have been made in the slaying."

Cry-Baby
BALTIMORE/LOS ANGELES/FT. WORTH, TX
1989–1990

JOHN WATERS: When Traci came to shoot *Cry-Baby*, she came with a gentleman that—I didn't know until much later—was involved with her in the porno business. And halfway through the film she bonded very heavily with the cast. This shoot was like rehab.

I mean, think about it: We had Susan Tyrell; Patty Hearst; Johnny Depp, who had just had some illegal incident; David Nelson; Iggy Pop, who was totally sober, you know? We played a game with the staff: Who *hasn't* been arrested? Everyone had a record.

So for the first time Traci felt like no one was judging her. I mean, we didn't care. I used to say to her, "The only problem was that you were too good of a porno star."

RUBY GOTTESMAN: So I pleaded not guilty and went to trial, which lasted about a year. They had three parts to the trial, and I won the first two, but on the third one they had Traci Lords waiting to testify—and her mother, who had testified in the two other cases.

My lawyer says, "A mother's a mother, and you can't make a mother look bad." So the mother came with her lies, like, "Such a nice girl she was . . ."

PATRICIA BRICELAND (MOTHER OF TRACI LORDS): We were living in Redondo Beach. My older daughter is Lorraine, she's 22; my next daughter is Nora, she's 20; I have a 19-year-old, Rachel; and a 17-year-old named Grace, G-R-A-C-E, Grace. And Nora lived with us up until she was—just right before her sixteenth birthday, when she did decide to leave home. . . .

When Nora was fifteen, she was a sophomore in high school, and she was at the age where girls get rebellious with their mothers. There was a strain between us. The move, that caused a lot of problems. I knew Nora was having a lot of problems. I knew she was concerned about money, and things were tough.

RUBY GOTTESMAN: We had a good relationship. Traci used me as sort of a confidant where she would come to me with her problems, and I would try to help her out. And Traci had a lot of problems. She had problems with her mother. She had a problem with drugs. She was having problems with producers not paying her the full amount of money she thought she was supposed to get. You know, just run-of-the-mill problems of someone working in the business.

PATRICIA BRICELAND: About a month after she left home, Nora came in and talked to me for a little while and took off again. She would come and see me for a couple of hours, and sometimes we would go out to lunch. I would say it continued like that from then up to the present time.

RUBY GOTTESMAN: Traci came to me one day in tears. She said she had an opportunity to go to London, England, for a modeling job, but she didn't have any money to go. And I couldn't believe it because she'd been working—she must have, at that time, made at least a hundred movies and was still working. I asked her where the money was? She just said, "I need this job. Could you lend me three thousand dollars?"

I asked when she was going to give it back, and she said she'd send it from London in thirty days. And she would call me in two weeks. I bawled her out. I told her she made a lot of money. What happened to all of it? But I finally gave her the money.

PATRICIA BRICELAND: Nora came for my other daughter's birthday party; she came for Christmas. She would spend a great part of the day here. We would talk about family relations.

She told me she was modeling, but she didn't tell me *where* she was modeling. I confronted her; she lied to me. She told me she was doing legitimate modeling. As it turned out, she was doing legitimate modeling, but she was doing other modeling, too.

RUBY GOTTESMAN: So Traci called me from London and told me the modeling job didn't work out and that she was coming home. And two weeks after that she came over and paid me back the three thousand—and then, besides that, offered to lend *me* money.

PATRICIA BRICELAND: I found that Nora seemed to be missing school without telling me. I didn't have any idea of what was going on.

But I heard rumors to the effect that Nora had been doing nude photography. So I confronted her with it.

RUBY GOTTESMAN: She was complaining about her mother. I told her, "You're old enough to do your own thing. You're not no baby. You're twenty years old. You should know better."

Does she look twenty to me on these box covers? You can't tell because of the makeup. Some she looks thirty; some she looks nineteen. She looks different in every picture. There is a hundred and twenty pictures where she looks different. It's the way they make her up.

PATRICIA BRICELAND: I told her that I heard rumors to the effect that she was involved in nude modeling, and she said it wasn't true.

I had heard such rumors when she was sixteen years old, yes, I had. Her sister, Lorraine, told me that she had friends who said they had seen Nora's picture in some magazines, but when I confronted Nora with that . . . she said it wasn't true.

I think she probably started doing the nude modeling—I think she got involved with these people—probably just before she left and began doing it very soon after she left.

RUBY GOTTESMAN: Traci worked her head off for two years, and she kept on telling me she wanted to make a lot of money and quit.

I says, "Quit now."

She said, "I can't. I don't have any money." But she said, "You watch. I'll come up with something."

PATRICIA BRICELAND: Eventually I did see some pictures, in *Penthouse*. And I confronted her with that. They were tastefully done, basically, but they were nude pictures.

RUBY GOTTESMAN: All of a sudden, I hear a rumor that Traci has her own company, TLC, Traci Lords Company. Then I heard that they'd produced a movie in Paris. And the day after this rumor started—that she'd just turned eighteen in June or something—this movie comes out, and it belongs to her.

PATRICIA BRICELAND: I think anyone can see just by looking at these pictures she went from a chubby little adolescent—although she had a nice figure—to a much more slender, more adult face.

Just looking at the pictures, you could see the change in the face, the cheekbones and the width of her face and the weight and the way it was distributed. She was pudgy at fifteen. People consider that voluptuous, but I consider it pudgy.

SHARON MITCHELL: They screened me to testify as a witness against Traci, and I said, "What? Can you tell the difference between a seventeen-year-old tit and an eighteen-year-old tit?"

They said, "Get her out of here."

RUBY GOTTESMAN: Caballero, which was probably in a state of receivership at that time, took over the movie—and as of last week they've sold a hundred thousand copies. I know for an exact fact that she got ten bucks for every copy that was sold in royalties. So she made her million dollars.

PATRICIA BRICELAND: I told Nora that if she didn't stop I would go to the police, and I would go to *Penthouse*. She told me that if I did, the people that she was involved with would kill her. I believed that could be possibly true, and so I only tried to keep the lines of communications open with Nora.

LOS ANGELES TIMES, **APRIL 27, 1989: DAUGHTER FEARED DEATH FROM MAKERS OF PORN FILMS, MOTHER TESTIFIES:** "Traci Lords, fearing for her life, pleaded with her mother not to reveal that she was underage when she made many of her films, the porn star's mother testified Wednesday.

"'She told me to keep my mouth shut or I would get her in terrible trouble,' Patricia Briceland said."

RUBY GOTTESMAN: So every other movie—in Traci's mind—became illegal. And in the law's eyes, too. So this movie, *Traci, I Love You*, which she made when she was of legal age, not only sold out, but I sold approximately six thousand pieces of this movie, more than any other movie in the history of my company. And it continues selling. I just bought fifty tapes yesterday. I buy fifty at least once a week. Got to buy them in fifties to get a discounted price. It's the only Traci Lords movie that's out there. And it just sells out. They don't rent it, they *buy* it.

STEVE ORENSTEIN: I don't think Traci Lords was a typical kiddie porn case, or what you'd think of as a child pornography case. When this came down about her being underage, people were shocked because she was very sexually aggressive on the sets. I mean, it was quite the opposite of her being a victim—she certainly wasn't someone getting taken advantage of.

JOHN WATERS: In *Cry-Baby* Traci played a sexpot—which is always the best way to rid yourself of an image, by playing it and making fun of it. That's what Johnny Depp did, too. He was on *Jump Street*, and he hated playing a teen idol, so I said, "Stick with us; we'll kill that." And we did—in the right way, you know?

LOS ANGELES TIMES, **OCTOBER 24, 1989: VIDEO PORN DISTRIBUTOR GETS ONE-YEAR SENTENCE:** "A Woodland Hills video distributor was sentenced to a year in prison Monday for selling videotapes of teenage porn actress Traci Lords in violation of child pornography laws.

"U.S. District Judge David V. Kenyon sentenced Rubin Gottesman, 56, to an additional term of three years' probation and fined his company, X-Citement Video, $100,000."

RUBY GOTTESMAN: The mother actually won the case, so when it came down I got one year. They recommended that I go to Boron Federal Prison in California, but the judge said, "No, you're a child pornographer, so you go to Forth Worth, Texas, where they have all the people like you."

But Fort Worth was nice—I mean, for a jail. It wasn't bad.

JOHN WATERS: During the making of *Cry-Baby*, the federal agents raided the set to make her come back to testify. Traci was terrified. I remember her sobbing—Patricia Hearst was comforting her—and Traci saying, "I'm so embarrassed."

I said, "Don't be embarrassed; everyone here's been arrested."

So I think we made her better. We rehabilitated Traci Lords.

STEVE ORENSTEIN: Why did I get five years' probation, and Ruby did time? Because I was silly, and I made a plea bargain. I mean, I had an attorney every day telling me to make a deal. Because it wasn't just the Traci Lords stuff, it was some bondage product as well, and that was potentially a problem. But that was dropped from the trial.

JOHN WATERS: Traci Lords fell in love with my best friend Pat Moran's son—who practically grew up on all of my sets, and who's now a very successful propmaster. So he and Traci had a big, very straight wedding in an Episcopal church in Baltimore.

RUBY GOTTESMAN: Once I was in jail, I got friendly with the cop in the dorm, and there were, like, two hundred and eighty guys on the floor. And they made me like an orderly. The cop was like a nice guy—he took a liking to me, you know? He'd bring in bagels for me, and shit like that. A nice guy, some Irish kid. And I was in charge, right?

JOHN WATERS: The day before the wedding, the priest asked Traci, "Have you been baptized?"

And she said, "Yes."

Later, Pat said, "You're half Jewish—you weren't baptized. Go over to John's, and he'll do it." See, I'd been ordained by Johnny Depp's lawyers to marry Johnny and Winona in the Universal Church. I talked him out of it because they were both too young. But I have these powers, so I'm legitimate, and I do happen to have a tabernacle. So I figured, "Well, come on over." And I played this record of castrated altar boys. I got all black tulips, and I wore all black.

Did she have to get naked or wear white robes? No, certainly not—we were doing the opposite of getting naked. We were wiping away males' defiant sexual behavior toward her, ha, ha, ha.

RUBY GOTTESMAN: One day, around lunchtime, I was supposed to be watchin' that nobody steals nothin'. My job was cleaning the phones—I'd disinfect the phones. So I'm hangin' around the phones, and here comes this redneck guy. There's a group of like twenty guys, and I recognize him to be one of them, with the tattoos and the beard and the hair—a redneck, you know?

He asks, "Your name Rubin Gottesman?"

Holy shit. I says, "Yeah, why?"

He says, "I'll be right back. Wait here."

Now I'm lookin' for the cop. There's no cop. The redneck comes over, and what is he bringin'? A four-year-old *AVN* with a story about me.

And he says, "Is this about you?"

I says, "Yeah."

He says, "I thought so." I became a hero. These guys, they'd come over and say, "Can we borrow the *USA Today*, just the sports section?" I says, "You can have the whole paper."

JOHN WATERS: I wiped away her sexual defiance, and I wiped away males' piggish behavior to her. And Traci started crying. She was scared, I think—because she didn't expect quite this much of a production when she came over. I took it dead seriously.

I think I splattered some holy water on Traci—Evian.

RUBY GOTTESMAN: They wanted my magazines. I was gettin' sent in, like, twenty porn magazines a month. But then they stopped at Christmastime. The government had, what's-his-name—Jesse Helmes—put somethin' on a rider that said, "No magazines with sexual things can be sent to federal prison." So no *Playboy*, no *Penthouse*, no nothin'. As a matter of fact, not even any pictures of your girlfriends, like, in bathing suits.

JOHN WATERS: They were married for quite some time, and they did break up, but they don't hate each other. I still see Traci. She came to the premiere of the new version of *Pink Flamingos* with me—and she said a really funny thing in the *Los Angeles Times* afterward. She said, "I didn't do anything *that* bad."

RUBY GOTTESMAN: Yeah, I got out of jail, but I had a very bad personal life. My oldest son got murdered in a drug thing. He was twenty-seven. He was meeting with a guy that owed him money—seven thousand—and the guy set him up with a robbery, and the robbery turned into murder. Some Israeli Mafia guys, I found out later.

He had over a million dollars in cash. They probably tortured him to find his money. I couldn't find a nickel. I have no money from him. And they took all his money, hit him on the head with a board, and he died. They found him in the trunk of a car after nineteen days. That was a terrible thing. And since I'm a pornographer, and he was drug dealer, the cops wasn't lookin' for no murderer.

BOBBY ELKINS: You know, it's really a horrible thing. Ruby's kid was really nice. I kind of liked him, even if his father was a jack-off.

After, the son started to sell dope and make some money. Some people say Ruby grabbed the money from his kid for a deal he was doing.

I don't know what happened, but they found his kid in a trunk of a car.

STEVE ORENSTEIN: I like Ruby. He's definitely a character, but I didn't realize he was crazy. I don't know if he's crazy, he's just . . . Ruby Gottesman had a reputation for how he dealt with people—vendors, let's say. Well, when we became partners, I started being treated like another vendor, so it didn't go too well.

The books were fine. It was just that payments weren't being made on time or at all. I'm sure I wasn't too happy about it. We were partners for about two years, and then we split up.

That's when I started Wicked Pictures.

Divorce: Porn Style

LOS ANGELES
1990–1991

TIM CONNELLY: When Teddy Snyder got murdered, nobody was surprised. The story going around—you know, the porn story, the inside story—was that he owed people money. He was in way over his head.

PHIL VANNATTER: I just looked at Sharon Snyder, and I knew she was a strung-out coke addict. She looked like hell. I know for a fact that she burned her nose out when she was with Teddy. And what we found out was, Teddy had been meeting Victor Diaz over on Blackhawk Avenue under the pretext of picking up some cocaine from him.

TOM BYRON: Marc Wallice had told me on a couple of occasions that Teddy had gotten a little out of hand and stuck a gun in his face.

Teddy liked to film his wife with other guys, having sex. I guess they were all coked out, and he would lose his mind, pull out a gun, and threaten them both.

PHIL VANNATTER: Bobby Genova told us about a diamond ring Teddy had, with "TED" spelled out in diamonds—and we were able to run that down to a jewelry store down in Dallas where Sharon had sold it after the murder. Sharon had reported it to us as stolen at the time of the murder. She had flown down to Dallas and sold this ring. She needed money, apparently, for coke.

TIM CONNELLY: Teddy Snyder was one of the worst cocaine addicts I've ever known. And I never saw him snort it, but I knew people who did—and these were guys that wouldn't come out of their offices all day, you know? They would go to work, and then stay in their office and snort coke. And I heard stories from them about Teddy buying ounces of coke every week.

PHIL VANNATER: I was looking into Sharon's background real strong, and one day I answered the telephone at the station and it was Dennis Fitzgerald calling from Fort Wanimi. We didn't know each other—I just happened to answer the phone. He says, "I have a guy up here talking about this big-time pornographer who was killed down in Los Angeles."

And I says, "You gotta be kidding? I got a big-time pornographer that was killed." We started talking, and this guy had been picked up for receiving stolen property. It was interesting because it fit in with what I was thinking already.

And this snitch Fitzgerald had was talking about another guy in Simi Valley, who was on federal probation for violation of the firearms act. He had manufactured some fully automatic weapons.

TOM BYRON: Paul Thomas told me about Teddy before I read it in the news. "Hey, did you hear about Ted Snyder? He got whacked."

I said, "Really? Well, that, you know, kind of makes sense, given the circles that he reputedly ran with."

Paul said, "Yeah, you know, they think it might have been his wife."

I said, "Really. Well, that sort of makes sense, too."

"Yeah, the guy, you know, he's kind of an asshole sometimes, you know, I mean he, you know, he threatened me with a gun a couple of times."

I said, "Oh, I heard that, too."

FRED LINCOLN: When Teddy was doing coke he wasn't logical no more—making Sharon fuck guys he brought over and he would videotape it. She was gorgeous! But Teddy never said for me to fuck her—I mean, I'd have kept her, you know? Everybody knew that about me in those days.

TOM BYRON: That was happening a lot in the early 1980s, you know? A lot of people turning up dead or missing. I mean, certain people ran this business back then—people that probably had a rap sheet or two; it wasn't the corporate, legitimate machine that it is now.

LOS ANGELES DAILY NEWS, JANUARY 28, 1990: RAID LED BACK TO SLAIN MAN'S WIFE, UNRELATED CASE SPURRED THE ARREST OF SPOUSE, FRIEND IN PORN MAKER'S KILLING: "When Theodore Snyder was shot and killed on a Northridge street last August, police said it looked like a mob killing out of the 'Untouchables'—he was hit nine times in a barrage from a machine gun."

PHIL VANNATTER: That snitch was a hanger-on with the Hell's Angels. He had long hair, was all buffed up from being in jail, and was wired on speed all the time. The sheriffs up there knew him well. They actually had a barricade situation with him, where they had to go in and get him out of this house with the SWAT team. You know, that kind of guy.

This firearm that Teddy was killed with—that snitch made the gun.

TIM CONNELLY: I only met Sharon Snyder once. She was probably good-looking in her heyday, which was probably in the mid to late seventies. And she was pretty strong; I think she really ran a lot of what was going on in Teddy's life, more than most people knew.

FRED LINCOLN: Sharon had been with Teddy for ten or fifteen years. Then she finally married him, and after like nine or ten months she got a divorce—because she wanted to get half the money.

Well, she goes to court and the judge notifies her that they'd be willing to give her, like, three years, so she's not entitled to anything. Oh God, she was devastated!

This girl was fucking *pissed!*

LOS ANGELES DAILY NEWS, JANUARY 28, 1990: RAID LED BACK TO SLAIN MAN'S WIFE: "In the end, the five-month probe led detectives right back to where they started—to Snyder's Woodland Hills home and his wife, Sharon.

"Last week, Sharon Snyder, 39, and an acquaintance, 47-year-old Victor Diaz of Reseda, were charged with the killing of Theodore Snyder in a plot to take over Snyder's estate."

PHIL VANNATTER: The snitch had told us that he had given Victor Diaz the gun, and had fired some shots into the floor of his house with it. So, with his permission, we went out to the house, recovered the ballistics evidence, and had it compared with the ballistics evidence from the murder. It was the same gun.

Apparently Diaz and this snitch were dealing dope together. That's how the guy met Sharon. In fact, he ended up with her mink coat as a trade for the gun. There wasn't one good person in this whole thing, including the victim. They all were a bunch of dirtbags.

FRED LINCOLN: Sharon gave Teddy's killer, Victor Diaz, a ten-thousand-dollar bill.

PHIL VANNATTER: That's where I started to put the whole thing together, when the snitch told me he had supplied the gun to Victor Diaz and that Diaz had told him that Sharon paid him with a ten-thousand-dollar bill.

So I asked Bobby Genova, "Did Teddy have a ten-thousand-dollar bill?" He said, "Yeah, he had it framed and hanging on his den wall."

Sharon was not a rocket scientist.

LOS ANGELES DAILY NEWS, JANUARY 28, 1990: RAID LED BACK TO SLAIN MAN'S WIFE: "Sharon Snyder promised Diaz $20,000 to kill her husband, and later gave Diaz a $10,000 bill from her husband's rare money collection as a down payment. . . . Diaz tried unsuccessfully to exchange the rare bill for smaller bills at a Ventura County bank, and it came to the attention of authorities, police said.

"The complaint also charges that Diaz bought a .38 caliber Mac II machine gun . . . on or about August 1, the day Theodore Snyder was killed. Police believe Diaz used the gun to kill Snyder.

"Snyder and Diaz are charged with murder, conspiracy to commit murder and special circumstances allegations that could mean the death penalty if they are convicted."

PHIL VANNATTER: Victor Diaz went to a preliminary hearing; then, when he went to superior court, he just pled guilty. And they worked out a deal for him to testify against Sharon.

I always felt Diaz was a real dirtbag—but I also felt that he'd been manipulated by Sharon. So I always thought she was more culpable in the murder. Because Victor Diaz would have never killed Teddy Snyder if it hadn't been for Sharon. The thought wouldn't have even crossed his mind.

FRED LINCOLN: Sharon Snyder got beat up real bad in jail by the other inmates. Why? I dunno, maybe they came on to her, and she said no. Was it payback for Teddy? Could've been. I mean, there's no question Teddy was connected.

The funny part is, Diaz got a letter in jail, supposedly from Sharon, telling him how sorry she was—she just felt so bad and if there was some way she could take it back, she would. Diaz wrote to his lawyer about it. But Sharon was a very tough woman—she might have had somebody else write the letter and put her name on it. But his lawyer brought the letter to court, like, "Ha! We got her!"

PHIL VANNATTER: Victor Diaz was horribly in love with Sharon. She had seduced him and told him that once Teddy was gone, they would be together all the time. Diaz was flattered because he's a big, fat, ugly Hispanic man, and when Sharon was cleaned up, she was halfway attractive. But otherwise, she was horrible looking, you know?

LOS ANGELES TIMES, AUGUST 17, 1991: INCRIMINATING LETTER IS NOT DEFENDANT'S, WITNESS SAYS: "A handwriting expert testified Friday that a Woodland Hills woman on trial for murder did not write a letter in which she purportedly admitted her role in the machine gun slaying of her pornographer husband.

"The letter was studied by Los Angeles police handwriting expert Phora Graigh, who testified that she compared samples of both Snyder and Victor Diaz, the confessed triggerman, and determined that neither of them wrote the letter.

'The letter was contrived by Diaz,' Alex R. Kessel, Snyder's attorney said. 'The bottom line is that he had someone do it. He had it prepared.'

FRED LINCOLN: They didn't get her.

LOS ANGELES TIMES, AUGUST 31, 1991: JURY ACQUITS WIFE IN 1989 SLAYING OF SEX-VIDEO MAKER: "The witness, Victor Diaz, 47, who admitted killing flamboyant sex-video producer Theodore J. Snyder, testified that he did it at Sharon Snyder's behest because he was in love with her, and she had promised to share the inheritance with him.

"In return for his testimony, Diaz, an admitted cocaine dealer, was allowed to plead no contest to second degree murder and has been promised a maximum sentence of seventeen years to life.

"Had she been convicted, Sharon Snyder could have been sentenced to life in prison without parole.

"After the verdict was read, Sharon Snyder smiled broadly for several minutes, then quickly left with bailiffs.

"Jurors said that Diaz's credibility plummeted when he said that Snyder had sent him a letter from jail implicating herself in the Aug. 1, 1989 slaying and pleading with him to 'take the whole rap for me.'"

PHIL VANNATTER: When Diaz got on the stand, he said, "Yes, I killed him because Sharon wanted me to. Yes, Sharon gave me a ten-thousand-dollar bill." But he wasn't real convincing with it. He actually said, "I still love her. I loved her then, and I love her now."

FRED LINCOLN: That's why it was thrown out.

PHIL VANNATTER: I asked the jury foreman, "How in the world could you not find this woman guilty with the evidence we put forward?"

And his only response was, "We hated Victor Diaz so much we didn't want to believe him. Yes, she's done some horrible things, but if we can't believe Victor Diaz, then we can't convict her." That was their whole feeling.

Sharon was going for sympathy. She was up-front: "Victor Diaz did this. I didn't have any hand in it." Even though we were able to show the connection with the payoff, the jury didn't buy it. I still don't know why.

I hated losing that case more than I did the O. J. Simpson case.

Sharon Snyder's attorney told me afterward, laughing, "You know, Sharon wants me to sue you."

And I said, "Well, let's get it on. I want to get all the evidence out again."

And he said, "Oh, no! I told her, let's let sleeping dogs lie."

Sharon wanted to sue me for false arrest because I arrested her, and she was found not guilty.

Everyone in this case was a space cadet.

SHARON MITCHELL: Sharon Snyder may have gotten out of jail, but she didn't get off. She lost half her face in state prison.

Part 11:
Fame & Misfortune

1990-1992

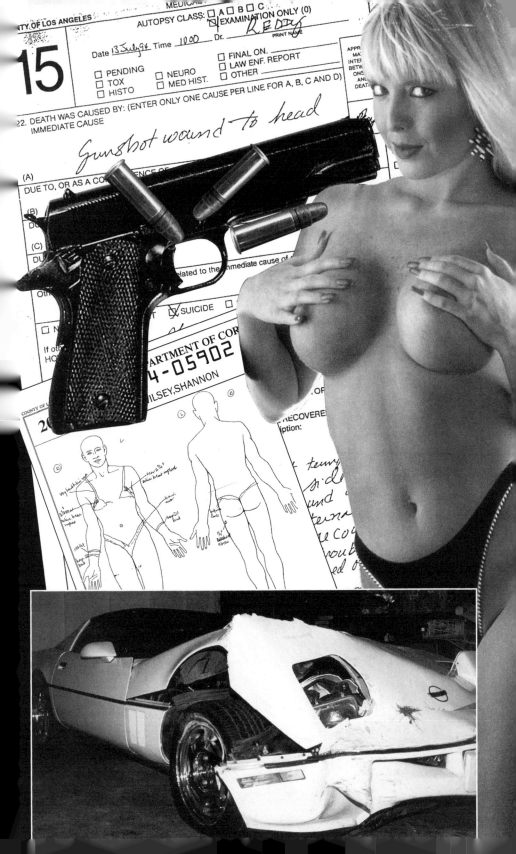

Left page: *Top:* Hunter Thompson (center) with the Mitchell brothers; *Bottom:* Savannah early *(left)* and late in her career.

Right page: *Clockwise from top left:* Savannah's autopsy report; Savannah; her car after accident.

Rock and Roll High School
LOS ANGELES
1990–1992

MICHAEL ALAGO (FORMER VICE PRESIDENT, ELEKTRA RECORDS): I had already signed Metallica to Elektra, and around 1990 I signed White Zombie to Geffen. I was hiring tons of escorts, and since I'm gay, all of the escorts were men from the porn industry. But I was with a buddy of mine at the Sunset Marquee, and we were all coked up, and somebody gave me Savannah's number. It was like a dare, almost. He said, "You're not gonna fucking call her and get her to do this?"

I said, "Man, I do this all the time with men. Let's just fuckin' do it."

So at midnight, we were all fucked up, and I called her, told her who I was, and this is what I did. I knew she was escorting, so could she come by?

BILL MARGOLD: Savannah was a somewhat attractive little blond marshmallow who came into the business in the early 1990s.

SAVANNAH: I started my career as a nude model. I've shot for a lot of magazines, *Hustler* and *Penthouse*, and most of the others. At first, I didn't know if I'd be taking my clothes off for a photographer, but after I did it, I thought it was really hot. It's kind of a sexual thing between the model and photographer; you make love to the camera. You know, the long lenses and the clicking, and I'm there moving around in different positions, showing him my pussy and tits, trying to turn him on.

Have I ever fucked a photographer after a session? I'm not saying.

MARC CARRIERE: With Savannah, I think we felt she was going to be big. I knew Savannah very well. I knew a lot about her problems; I knew her lifestyle. She was a pretty wild one.

MICHAEL ALAGO: I wish I could remember who I was with, but he was eating Savannah out while we were fucking her. You know, we just both took turns. We were surprised and amazed that we could get it up—because we were so coked up and drunk.

And, you know, I never fuck women. But Savannah was just fucking *genius,* you know? We bowed down to her, the way you bow down to certain people in life.

TOM BYRON: Savannah—*Savannahhhh!* Savannah was a very, very pretty girl—enjoyed cocaine immensely. People said she was a cold fuck. I didn't agree. I was one of the few people she would work with because I don't buy into that whole cold fish thing. To me it was a challenge to get some real emotion out of her. We played this game—I'd be fuckin' her, and I'd say, "Oh, that feels good."

And she'd say "No, it doesn't." Ha, ha, ha!

SAVANNAH: It's been said that when I'm having sex on camera, sometimes I look detached, almost as if I don't want to be there. That's just the way I am. I'm not a screamer or someone who likes to bounce and jump around a lot. I like to relax and feel it.

VERONICA HART: Savannah was gorgeous, but I don't think anybody would say that her sexual scenes were the hottest, or you know, she was the most into it.

SAVANNAH: I'm not into women. Yeah, I enjoy sucking cock, but it doesn't get me off or anything. Do I like guys coming on my face? YUCK! I don't see what's so hot about that—getting all that gooky stuff all over me. I don't mind so much on my tits or my stomach or my ass, but on the face, it makes me feel like I just blew my nose all over myself. That's not sexy. For me, anyway.

HENRI PACHARD: I suspected most of the women were in the business because they were really more frigid than they would let on. They weren't really capable of having an orgasm, and what better way to hide that than to become a porno star? You know, to act like you're really turned on and hot? I think the reason they don't have a good sex life is because they were abused as children, psychologically or sexually—probably sexually.

SAVANNAH: My boob job was a business decision. My manager at the time thought that I would be worth more money, and he paid for them, so why not? I think guys out there have this thing for big tits. It really helps. I almost doubled my daily fee after the operation. I like the attention. I like the way men flaunt all over me. I'm a natural show-off.

RON JEREMY: Savannah would laugh at girls less pretty than she was and make girls feel really bad. Then it occurred to me what I learned at school—that if you don't really love yourself, you're not gonna love other people, either. You have a hard time understanding emotion when your parents screwed you from ground zero.

But Savannah's dad was a lot smarter. He didn't try to blame the porn business because there was supposedly some abuse in the family before she got into porn.

MIKE WILSEY (SAVANNAH'S FATHER): When she was two years old, or less than two, her mom and I would play music on the stereo, and she'd just start dancing, you know, doing this cute little Indian dance. We'd just play our song over and over, just to watch her dance.

RON JEREMY: She never told me, but I know Savannah had a lot of problems with her father because it came out from friends of hers I knew. Her best friend and agent was Nancy Pera.

NANCY PERA: Savannah was signed as a contract girl about six months after I started working at Vivid. I directed her in quite a few movies—most of them were for Video Exclusives, Leisure Time—but the first ones I directed her in were for Vivid Video. Savannah and I got along; I was sort of her babysitter.

And anything that Savannah would do, [Vivid Video founder] Steve Hirsch would yell at me for. I always got in trouble because I was always with Savannah when anything was happening. And a lot of things happened.

PAM LONGORIA (SAVANNAH'S MOTHER): Everything I'm reading so far is just destroying me because there's so many lies being printed about her. In the *Los Angeles Times* it said she had an unhappy childhood and that she was molested as a child, which is not true. I always told her I loved her no matter what she was doing for a living. We never shunned her or nothing because of what she was—I mean, what her occupation was. I mean, we loved her unconditionally. And she knew it.

MIKE WILSEY: Me and her original mother had a lot of serious problems. I had a lot of remorse because of that—being angry with her mother—and Savannah suffered the consequences of my own selfishness. A man should love a child no matter what. I did, but reservedly. I wasn't here for her during most of her young years. I left her alone, and I think she grew up with a hole in her heart.

SAVANNAH [LETTER TO HER FATHER]: "You do not care about me and you never have. If you're 'there for me' then where were you 23 years ago? Where were you when I bounced from 'relative' to 'relative' because NO

ONE WANTED ME? Where were you when I was 17, going out with Gregg [Allman], a 42-year-old man? (Looking for the father I never had.) You are so fake and I will NEVER FORGIVE YOU.

"YOU THINK 'God' has—but if there is a God he sees the torture & pain I have been through since I was born and couldn't possibly forgive you! You will die knowing that YOUR 1ST BORN CHILD HOPES YOU ROT IN HELL WITH ALL THE PAIN I HAVE INSIDE—BECAUSE OF YOU!"

NANCY PERA: Savannah was in Texas visiting her family, and she had an autograph party scheduled in New Jersey at IBD—Frank Koretsky's store. I was going there to babysit her and make sure she showed up.

I met Savannah at the airport, and she came out and said, "I'm really sick."

I was motherly. "We'll get you some chicken soup. You're probably coming down with the flu or something."

Savannah said, "No, it's not that. It's drugs."

I asked, "What kind of drugs?" And finally she told me it was heroin.

BILL MARGOLD: I think a lot of Savannah's problems had nothing to do with the X-rated industry—they were more economically driven. Her childhood was not all that stable. And Savannah came to the industry with an awful lot of baggage, but for a while we gave her first-class trunks.

NANCY PERA: What are you going to do with an addict? You can't make them quit until they're ready to.

I liked Savannah, and here she is, sicker than a dog, and I'm thinking, *How are we going to make it to Frank Koretsky's open house tomorrow?* She's begging me, and I'm a sucker. So I finally agreed to go cop for her; then we got into a lot of trouble because we were a few minutes late.

BUD LEE: Savannah was a bitch, but the boss let her get away with a lotta shit.

Who was the boss? Steve Hirsch, who signed her to an exclusive Vivid Video contract in April 1991. She had arrived in the big time.

Steve actually said to me, "When I was in high school, I was the state wrestling champ in my class, but I was in the hundred-and-twenty-five-pound class, so the girls never even looked twice at me."

And then he goes, "Now I fuck all the cheerleaders."

NANCY PERA: When I got back to L.A., Steven Hirsch was livid. He said we took too long in the bathroom at lunch. I said, "She was putting on some makeup. *Jesus Christ.*" Anything we did, I got in trouble for.

When Savannah came in, I said, "We're in the doghouse, boy," because Steven had wanted to see her. And Savannah came out smiling. She said, "Well, he just gave me five grand."

He didn't say anything about it. But I would get reamed.

BILL MARGOLD: The only meeting I ever had with Savannah was at Jim South's office—she came in, called him a bunch of names, and then left. I said to him, "If she spoke to me like that, I'd throw her out."

And Jim said, "I can't do anything with her because she makes me money."

NANCY PERA: Steven Hirsch knew Savannah was doing drugs. He never said to me, "I know she's doing heroin," but he told me that he had put her through rehab in the beginning.

I asked Savannah about that later on, and she said that that was the biggest crock of shit, that he never sent her to any rehab.

JEANNA FINE: It was an XRCO show where I saw Savannah for the first time. Somebody pointed her out. She was in this red sequined biker jacket and her white hair and everything—and I thought, "God, she's just gorgeous."

Apparently she tried to talk to me—but I was kind of swamped at that point, so I didn't get a chance to talk to her.

NANCY PERA: Savannah never said, "I started having sex with Steven." *I* didn't even know if they were having sex because they had promoted this whole plot that Paul Thomas was having an affair with Savannah. So it wasn't until our first CES show in January, when I was sitting between Savannah and Steven, and Steven sort of tried to hold my hand accidentally—because he was reaching for Savannah's hand—that I started to suspect they were having an affair. And Jenny, Steven's girlfriend of fifteen years, was sitting right across the table from us.

BUD LEE: Savannah? I mean, your snot-nosed little fucking kid. She was eighteen, and somebody needed to turn her over on their fucking knee and spank her. Childish—ugh.

So I went the opposite route: I killed her with kindness. Found out what her favorite food was—deviled eggs—and had it for her on the set all the time.

NANCY PERA: A lot of people criticized Savannah for being spoiled and demanding. But Steven Hirsch let her get away with murder and then Savannah would get the blame.

JEANNA FINE: I honestly don't how we started being together. I just know that one day we were suddenly together, and then we were together constantly after that. It was probably one of my first real love affairs. Which was hard because I was also in a relationship with a man at that point, and they were both very demanding of my time—and jealous of each other.

I tried to bring the three of us together to live happily ever after. They looked beautiful together—and we had some great sex in the beginning— but it just didn't work. They were both children, basically.

TOM BYRON: I actually respected the fact that Savannah stood up for herself. People would say, "Oh, she's a bitch," and I'd just be like, "No, man, she just wants what she wants." I kinda went, "Oh, girl, man. You go!"

BUD LEE: Even though Steve Hirsch catered to rock stars, he'd rather hang out with the A&R people and people like that. He'd get all these guys from Sony and Columbia and Virgin and Mercury coming in to watch people film their scenes.

RON JEREMY: Did Savannah fuck a lot of rock stars? Yes. Was I there? Once, with Vince Neil. I wasn't there for Slash. I know *People* magazine reported that Savannah and Slash were messing around. They did it publicly, at a bar. I think she was giving him head. That's how I learned what *People* calls head—the "full tilt whoopie." So if you ever see "full tilt whoopie" in *People*, that's head.

SLASH: Was I arrested for having sex in public with Savannah? I wasn't actually arrested—it was the security people. But it wasn't my fault. She always used to like to be in a public place—that's when she got the horniest.

NANCY PERA: I mean, Slash had left the girl he had married for Savannah, but once they had that write-up in *People* his agent and managers and the other band members came down on him hard because they didn't like the press. I don't know why.

Slash was supposed to be taking Savannah to Hawaii, and he never showed up—never called or anything. Two days later he came by and got his stuff—he'd been sort of living with her—and that was it. Broke her heart.

Slash definitely, definitely, definitely broke Savannah's heart.

BRYN BRIDENTHAL (GEFFEN RECORDS PUBLICIST): Slash was totally and completely Savannah's fantasy.

NANCY PERA: His publicist may deny it, but Slash really hurt her. First off, I've seen them together. He used to send her flowers—these gigantic bouquets that would take up her whole kitchen counter.

RON JEREMY: Savannah and Slash had an off-and-on type of thing. They built it as this real big romance, but it was just like a side thing. I don't think Savannah was that foolish to think it was anything else.

NANCY PERA: What saddens me is that her sex-star status was the very reason these people were attracted to her—they'd probably never have given her the time of day otherwise—but it was also the very reason they'd ostracize her.

RON JEREMY: I introduced Savannah to Steve Pearcy from the band Ratt. They started messing around in the bathroom. I thought I was gonna get to watch, and then she excused me—it pissed me off. Savannah and Billy Idol went out only a few times. Gregg Allman and her—that wasn't my doing.

PAM LONGORIA: Savannah was a completely normal person until she got hooked up with Gregg Allman. She was sixteen or seventeen at the time. At first, I was proud that she had gotten a famous boyfriend.

JEANNA FINE: Savannah told me she was with her mom in a restaurant, and Gregg Allman was there. Savannah, or Shannon Wilsey—her real name— was fourteen or fifteen years old.

Shannon didn't know who Gregg Allman was, but her mom did—and she could see that Gregg was eyeballing her daughter. So her mom took her over and said, "This is my daughter, Shannon." And the rest is history.

KIRK WEST (ROAD MANAGER FOR THE ALLMAN BROTHERS BAND): Everybody knew she was young, but she told everybody she was eighteen. It was an intimate relationship; she traveled with Allman on and off for a couple years. She appeared in a Gregg Allman Band video, "Can't Keep Runnin'," as one of a group of cowgirls, and in 1989, in a bit part in a video for "Statesboro Blues."

MIKE WILSEY: She loved music; she loved rock stars. That's what she wanted to do—marry a rock star. And I figured that was what would happen.

JEANNA FINE: She used to say that Gregg had an elevator that went straight up to his penthouse, and he would leave her there—just way up above everybody—with no way to get back down. She said she felt like Rapunzel or Cinderella, just kind of separated from the world, living in this alternate universe.

KIRK WEST: I was on the road a good bit during 1987, 1988, 1989, and Gregg was not doing heroin. You get in that kind of position, people want to be your "friend," want to turn you on, and I have sat there personally and watched him turn those people away.

As for the pregnancy, none of us ever heard about that. I checked with members of the band and road crew on tour in the late 1980s, and no one recalled any paternity claims by her against Gregg Allman.

JEANNA FINE: I don't know whether Gregg was sober or not. There are stories that the first time she ever did anything was with him. But I've only heard her side, so I hesitate to lay any blame. But I do know Savannah would have discovered heroin with or without Gregg Allman.

I was in a similar relationship with an older man when I was her age. It was very exciting. He was a gambler and a drug dealer and had nice cars and a home of his own. So I understood how hard it was for her to be expected to move back into Mom's house afterward. She had a tattoo on her foot, between her ankle and her foot, that said, "Gregg," with a little heart.

NANCY PERA: She wanted to be somebody special, somebody important. She acted like a rebel, but she wanted everyone to love her, to respect her. And when they didn't, she would just act wilder.

VINCE NEIL: Savannah was the beginning of my descent into Hollywood Babylon.

JEANNA FINE: Savannah was the brattiest. I had such a hard time being with her in public; if I even tried talking to somebody else, she'd say, "Honey, I'm getting pissy."

That was her mantra. That meant I wasn't paying enough attention to her.

VINCE NEIL: Mötley Crüe's manager, Doug, called and fired me and told me not to speak with anyone in the band. That was it. What could I do after that kind of treatment? I had two choices: I could kill myself, or I could go to Hawaii with a stripper and get over it. I chose the latter.

I grabbed the first chick I could find, a porn star named Savannah, and took her to Hawaii.

RON JEREMY: Me and Savannah would cut to the front of the line at rock concerts; she'd be like, "Oh, all those other girls think they should get in before me?" Savannah had a bitchy attitude as far as that kind of thing went.

JEANNA FINE: Oh God, one time in particular, it was some big concert, and there were cameras all around, and Savannah was wearing shorts and this fringe jacket, and it was getting caught on everything—like everybody's dog collars and spiky things.

I mean, drinks are flying, cigarettes are getting knocked out of people's hands, and Savannah's not apologizing to anybody—she's just plowing through the crowd. And I'm walking behind her: "Oh, she's sorry," and "Oh, let me get that," and "Here's some money, buy yourself another drink."

Finally I caught myself, and I went, "What the fuck am I *doing?* When did I become her caretaker?"

VINCE NEIL: With the band out of my hair, I couldn't see any reason to stay sober, so we brought all the pills and coke we could carry with us. After staying up four days straight at the Maui Hilton, Savannah took one pill too many and dropped to the floor convulsing. I called an ambulance and followed her to the hospital.

I'd never seen anyone look so beautiful and innocent while lying overdosed in a stretcher.

MARC VERLAINE (EDITOR OF *EROTIC X-FILM GUIDE*): When I first met Savannah my immediate impression was that she was a professional party doll. She was in love with the scenes that rock stars and porn provided. In the rock world she was a supergroupie; in porn, she was a big fish in a small pond.

VINCE NEIL: When she got back to the hotel the next day, we picked up right where we had left off. But I was older and for some reason not only could I not get as fucked up as I used to, but I couldn't recover as quickly. By the time I returned to L.A. I was a mess. I flew to a clinic in Tucson to dry out. Savannah sent me a different porno picture of herself every day, until the "Sober Police" found my stash and busted me.

TOM BYRON: I almost fucked Savannah outside of work one time. Jeanna Fine, her boyfriend, and I were all sharing this big house in Hollywood, and we were having a coke party. I think Savannah wanted me, but there was this other girl, who looked more like a fucking pig, you know?

I wanted the fucking pig, man.

So I just kinda blew off Savannah. I just went upstairs with the fucking pig and did all kinds of vile shit to her. What was her name? I have no idea.

Then Jeanna mentioned that Savannah was a little offended. But dude, I'm coked out, you know what I'm saying? What the fuck? I ain't thinkin' right. Here's a pig that'll fucking tongue my ass for ten hours, you know what I'm saying?

And I couldn't have seen Savannah doing that, ha, ha, ha.

SAVANNAH [FROM *AVN* ACCEPTANCE SPEECH]: "If you don't love me, I'm sorry."

BILL MARGOLD: Savannah won an award from *AVN*—and, as insignificant as that may seem, she went up there and said, "I don't give a shit if you like me or not, I got this award."

Not the nicest thing in the world to say, but that was Savannah.

VINCE NEIL: By the time I completed treatment, Savannah was dating Pauly Shore.

RON JEREMY: I took Pauly Shore to the Free Speech Coalition dinner dance, which takes place at the Sheraton Universal Hotel every year. Pauly met Savannah at that show, and they became friends. And then I took Pauly to a little party upstairs. I knew a couple girls who might give him head.

So Pauly saw Savannah again some other time—and then Nancy Pera reintroduced them—but he met her the first time through me.

NANCY PERA: Savannah had been spending a weekend night over at Pauly's house once in a while because her dog and his dog got along. I don't know if there was anything sexual going on at the time.

Believe it or not, a lot of times she'd have guys spend the night and nothing would happen. It took me a while to find out, but she was afraid to be alone because of a stalker she had for a while.

HENRI PACHARD: Savannah was on a set one day and said, "Pauly and I share the same brain." And the writer—I think it was Raven Touchstone—asked, "Well, who's using it now?"

NANCY PERA: I suspect the stalker might have been someone she knew. At first I didn't believe her; I thought she was just paranoid, in that house up in the hills, you know?

Vince Neil talked somebody into lending her the gun.

Savannah had no concept of what a gun really was. She waved it around like a water pistol. She would come over to my house with her little knapsack bag, and she'd put the bag down, and the gun would fall out. And she slept with it under her pillow. She pointed it at me once, and I almost went ballistic.

RON JEREMY: Savannah liked Slash a lot, but I think Pauly Shore was the much stronger thing. Because Pauly was single.

Pauly let me know what was going on occasionally—and it wasn't totally monogamous. It was for a while; then it became a really strong friendship. Pauly would be seeing other girls, and Savannah was seeing other guys.

But Savannah told Pauly she wasn't working in porn anymore. Their relationship had gotten strong enough that he wanted her to stop doing guys—he must have been pretty serious if that's the case, you know?

Once I was on a location shoot with her, not far from where Pauly's home was. He had a beautiful home that he shared with his mom. And Savannah said, "Please, please, don't tell Pauly I'm here! Ron, I tucked my car way into the driveway so Pauly wouldn't see it."

I says, "I'm not a rat."

So I never did tell Pauly. But if he reads this, now he'll know.

TOM BYRON: I admire the strong women in the business—like Savannah. But the coke and shit—and she just spent money like water, you know, because she thought it was gonna go on forever. I mean, that's one thing about this business, it chews 'em up and spits 'em out, you know? A woman's longevity in this business is extremely limited.

HENRI PACHARD: Savannah was just trying to be something she's not—trying to be younger than she was, smarter, prettier—trying to be all these things and to get a little bit higher each time out. I suspect she was on heroin.

TOM BYRON: The prime target for this business will always be the lonely guy who wants to go into a video store and jerk off all over himself. So each time he goes in the video store, he wants something different, you know, "Who's the new girl?"

So unless a girl paces herself and saves her money, this business will eat her alive. Savannah was in over her head.

Tired

LAS VEGAS/LOS ANGELES
1991

ROGER YOUNG: What really amazes me is that when you hear about the Reuben Sturman case, what you're hearing about is the IRS case. As far as newspapers and TV news, they don't like to put in there that Reuben pled guilty to interstate transportation of obscene matter and racketeering. That was a big thing—and people don't understand that there was suspicion of jury tampering in that case because the first time we tried the case there were two females that hung the jury.

RICHARD ROSFELDER: There's probably never been a case that's even come close to the amount of time we spent on the Sturman case. From the early eighties through the day I retired, the IRS probably wished they never saw the case.

ROGER YOUNG: When the U.S. marshals transported Reuben Sturman, Ralph Levine was also in custody. Well, unfortunately they transported them together—in the backseat of a car, side by side. Here's a guy who's going to testify against Sturman; Reuben spit on him.

I mean, big mistake. Ralph really complained about it during pretrial preparation.

RICHARD ROSFELDER: When Reuben's wife, Naomi Delgado, walked into the courtroom at his tax trial wearing some kind of a fur outfit and a short skirt, my comment to the Strike Force attorneys was, "You'd think the defense lawyers would be smarter than to send her in looking like that."

ROGER YOUNG: Right before trial, Reuben comes over to me and asks, "How's your dad?"—not knowing that my dad had passed away.

I looked at Reuben and said, "He's doing great. He's better off than you and I."—meaning he's in heaven. Reuben didn't get it. He goes back, and the defense attorney leans over and whispers to him, "Roger's dad just passed away."

Reuben jumps up, runs right back over, puts his hand on my shoulder, and says, "Geez, I'm sorry. I didn't know. Your father was a fine man. He was honest. He did a good job. I had a lot of respect for him. I'm really sorry to hear that."

I'm thinking to myself, *Yeah, sure.* So I said, "Well, that's okay. Like I said, he's better off than you or I."

RICHARD ROSFELDER: I said, "That's about the dumbest thing I've seen going on today, other than Reuben snoring in his chair at the defense table." That was the depth of my perception.

Later it became apparent that she was dressed that way for a purpose. They were going after a juror—and Naomi ended up hooking up with him.

ROGER YOUNG: I think Reuben's biggest mistake was turning on his secretary of twenty years, Marjorie Rollins.

We spent a lot of time with her because she was so knowledgeable: She ran all his businesses, and kept the books and all the paperwork. She was a loyal employee. She thought the world of Reuben, and he took care of her pretty well financially—loaned her money when she needed it. Then Reuben got upset at her over something and fired her, after twenty years. That turned her.

Marjorie made us believe the old adage: "Hell hath no fury like a woman scorned."

RICHARD ROSFELDER: Reuben had literally hundreds of separate corporate entities. Marjorie Rollins testified that she'd just pull names out of the phone book, or some book she was reading, and, you know, they'd just create a president and a secretary/treasurer and put it down on paper.

Or they'd use people out of Reuben's Canadian operations, take their names and signatures, and make stamps. So when you were looking for a Roger Carlton or a Steven Baker—you know, if they existed at all, they were working in some warehouse up in Canada.

ROGER YOUNG: Rich Rosfelder said, "I'll bet you a month's paycheck you got jury tampering."

We were convinced something foul went on, and so were the other jurors. They were the ones who said, "Something's wrong here. There's no way these women can't find him not guilty."

RICHARD ROSFELDER: The amount of money that was being spent was pretty astronomical, and I think the risks were probably minimized through Sturman's efforts—the way that he defended the business operations.

I remain unimpressed with the suggestion that a lot of people make about Reuben Sturman: "It's a shame he didn't get involved in a more legitimate enterprise" or, "It's a shame that he didn't just pay his taxes."

I feel that Reuben—and the rest of the people who operated these businesses along with him—may have fared as well as they did financially because they were involved in an area that might attract the mob to a lucrative business operation. And by a lot of people's accounts, *did* attract the mob. They wanted their piece of the action.

ROGER YOUNG: When they came back with a hung jury, Sturman was all excited. He came over, looked at me, and said, "Nice try, kid."

I said, "It's not over."

He says, "What do you mean, it's not over?"

I said, "We're going to retry the case."

Of course the prosecutors said, "Roger's right. We're going to retry the case."

Sturman runs back to his attorneys and says, "Whaddya mean they're gonna retry? Didn't we win?"

RICHARD ROSFELDER: People knew that if they were going to go up against Reuben Sturman, he was going to put up a fight. I think he got used to winning those fights because he never lost.

That kind of became the trademark of his operation, you know—that he defended the people he supplied. He provided funds and lawyers . . . and may have changed the laws in the United States as a result.

ROGER YOUNG: After the hung jury, we were going to start trial again. Well, Sturman decides he's gonna accept the indictment straight up—he's going to plead guilty. He's not going to go to a second trial.

Why now? After fighting twenty years? He said he was tired. I was shocked.

That's not like him. That's out of character.

Reuben comes up to me in court after he pleads guilty and just says, "I'm through."

I asked, "What do you mean?"

He says, "I don't have anything to live for anymore. I'm just going to give up."

I think he was just waiting to die in prison.

Cain and Abel

LOS ANGELES/SAN FRANCISCO
1991

TOM BYRON: Jim Mitchell was a cool motherfucker. I worked for him only once, on a movie called *Grafenberg Girls Go Fishing*. We went out on a boat and had this big orgy in the fucking hull—the girls were being loaded down in a fish basket. And they had a fucking chef cooking fucking lobsters and steaks. It was one of the best fucking shoots I've ever been on. And fucking Jim and Artie had all the best fucking pot, man. We're all stoned—eating and fucking.

It was phenomenal.

MARILYN CHAMBERS: I loved the Mitchell brothers. They were like my brothers. What was the problem? Well, we were all doing coke. I mean, I was doing like ten theater shows a day. Grueling stuff—fist fucking, balls up my butt. I was just, *bhfoo!*

And, you know, when you're doing that stuff you don't eat a whole lot, ha, ha, ha. So I was a skinny little thing, and there was a lot of drugs and a lot of alcohol. It was just a mad scene, just, you know—mind-boggling. Made a lot of money, though. Those were the days.

BANA WITT (ARTIE MITCHELL'S GIRLFRIEND): I was never comfortable around Artie; he was so supercharged that I'd get breathless. As soon as I heard his voice, my heart would start racing; I'd have to pee. Almost a panic response. He was—so exciting, you know?

I was pretty good at pretending to be cool, not saying anything, but inside I didn't feel cool at all. I was just like, "Whoa, this is so heavy."

PATRICK COLLINS (PORNOGRAPHER): I loved the O'Farrell Theater. You could do a lot there, man. There were no windows; you could go stick the pussy in your face. It was a good time.

JACK BOULWARE: Jim was much more of the hands-on, day-to-day guy running the O'Farrell. Artie seemed a little aloof to me the few times that I saw him. They always had a bunch of other people around. But it was still a good time. They would invite people up to the theater and shoot pool and have a few Heinekens. But—as it happens with everybody who had a great time in the sixties and seventies—it can't last forever, you know?

BANA WITT: After I did my first sex scene for the Mitchell brothers, everybody was doing amyl nitrate, and I was lying on my back, and I said, "Hey, give me a hit."

So this girl spills the whole bottle up into my nose. I was epileptic at the time, and I just freaked. I started rushing. And the burning—it singed the membrane, you know?

MARILYN CHAMBERS: I broke up with Chuck Traynor around 1979 or 1980. And my boyfriend, Bobby—who was also my bodyguard—and I went to the O'Farrell Theater a bunch of times; that's when we got busted. I went out in the audience and let somebody touch me, and there happened to be a vice squad there. They were planning on arresting me anyway. Fortunately there were no drugs or anything like that, but Bobby did have a gun on him, which wasn't too good, ha, ha, ha. My arrest was the biggest news of the decade there, you know?

BANA WITT: That day, it just so happened Jim had asked for a gallon of water on the set. So he grabbed the water, and he started flushing my face with it. I thought, "You better call an ambulance." I was completely panicked; I thought I was gonna go into a big-time epileptic fit.

They put me in a spare room, and I laid down. After a while Artie came in to see how I was, and we started talking, and then we started fucking.

MARILYN CHAMBERS: The O'Farrell was packed the day after we were arrested. And they put the mayor's phone number up on the marquee—"Call Mayor Dianne Feinstein."

The Mitchells just had a great sense of humor. And all these reporters wrote articles, and I'm in jail with my fur coat and nothing else on, and they want to take pictures. I took a mug shot with every cop in the place, and they're going, "I'm really sorry we had to do this." And the next night they were all back enjoying the show.

BANA WITT: Sex is so great on amyl, and I had just had a megadose, but I was also potentially injured. Showed what a psycho Artie was, you know?

But we had absolutely fabulous sex. I mean, I was so high, and I was just hooked on Artie after that—for the rest of my life.

JACK BOULWARE: Journalists would come from all over the world, and the Mitchells had this policy of just inviting them in—so they knew they always had the media on their side. For a time, they even employed Hunter S. Thompson. He was working on a book called *Night Manager*, which never materialized. But there's a very nice photograph of Hunter in the theater with a cast on his leg.

BANA WITT: Hunter Thompson—that guy scared me so bad. He's so high-energy and narcissistic; he gives me the runs just being around him. And there was always so much coke around, so I was even more stressed.

ALEX CASTRO (SAN FRANCISCO CAB DRIVER): I was a driver for the Mitchell brothers, and one night I picked up Hunter Thompson at the theater, and it seemed like it was a party night.

He was going to do some sort of reading on Broadway, at a theater there. He was reading a book or something. And he was with this other guy who was a PR guy or something, and they had this huge bottle of champagne in my car. We went over to the reading, and of course there were a lot of literary types there.

BANA WITT: I didn't really know who Hunter was until Artie started hanging around with him. I hadn't read *Fear and Loathing*.

Artie said, "Oh, Hunter Thompson's down here, and I want him to meet the world's greatest poet, so you know, come on down."

So I get there, and of course there's just, like, *plates* of cocaine, so I did about ten lines. Well, I'm not so communicative on coke; when I do that much I stutter, and it's hard to talk. And Artie's like, "Recite some of your poetry for him."

ALEX CASTRO: Needless to say, they were kind of shocked when Hunter brought out all these dancers from the Mitchell brothers' theater onto the stage, and they started doing their thing—you know, seriously getting down.

Were the girls getting naked? They were getting more than that. . . .

BANA WITT: So I did a poem, and Hunter says, "Well, I wish I could write poems that good; I can't write poetry at all."

Artie's like, "Well, do another one," and so I did another one, but it just felt so weird.

ALEX CASTRO: Anyway, after the reading—or whatever it was—they went around North Beach, and as the night went on, they got pretty heated. And eventually the public relations gentleman said, "Let's call it a night."

Hunter didn't seem to like that very much. He ended up punching this guy out.

BANA WITT: I wasn't attracted to Hunter at all. He was so speedy, I couldn't imagine sleeping with him. The guy is just so wired, you can't even imagine him being *horizontal*—let alone relaxed and affectionate.

JACK BOULWARE: The Mitchell brothers were still very much prevalent in the San Francisco scene in the early 1990s, and they went out of their way to support younger artists and publishers. If somebody had a political cause and needed a space to throw a benefit, they would open up their theater. They weren't making films so much anymore, but they were definitely around.

MARILYN CHAMBERS: Artie got out of hand. As the years went by, the alcohol and the drugs consumed him. He would get really mean and angry, and Jim really had to take over the operation. A couple of times, Artie was not allowed in the theater. I think they came to a point where they were about to break up. Jim just didn't want to have anything to do with Artie because Artie was just impossible.

Eventually Artie's whole family—including his mom—begged Jim to help him; they wanted to get him to rehab. Artie would have none of it.

BANA WITT: Artie was very sadistic, but he had a totally gentle, sweet side. But when he was drunk he could be very emotionally cruel. So in the early years he played at keeping me strung out—which kept the sex just fabulous because I never saw him more than one night in a row and usually never more than five or six times a year, you know?

Over seventeen years, sometimes it was just two or three times a year, sometimes as much as a couple times a month; by the very end, it was several times a week.

TOM BYRON: The last time I ever saw Jim and Artie together was at an *AVN* Awards Show. I was cohosting, and I sang the opening number, "I Just Want to Make Love to You." Had my fucking Bon Jovi look on. I'm backstage, waiting to do my presenting thing, and Jim and Artie were presenting an award, and Artie was fucked up out of his fucking mind. Jim's going, "And the nominees are . . . And the winner is . . ."

Artie grabs the fucking envelope, rips it up, and says, "GUESS, MOTHERFUCKERS!"

Someone had to whisper to Jim and tell him the winner. It was really embarrassing.

BOB CALLAHAN (WRITER/JOURNALIST): One night I was out with Jim and Artie at a little party we had for a local boxer and a bunch of boxing writers. Artie was drunk and making an ass of himself, trying to pick a fight with this boxer.

Jim never showed his emotions much, but I could see he was heartbroken. He just looked at me and said, "God, it drives me nuts to see my brother like that. I built an empire with this guy, and now he's like a Telegraph Avenue street babbler. He doesn't even know how fucked up he is. He's got to get into a hospital."

TOM BYRON: Later, while the show was still going on, Artie came backstage and said, "Hey, Tom, c'mere. See that girl over there? That's my daughter, man. She really wants to fuck you."

I went, "Uhhhhhh, no, man, I'm already committed tonight. I already got something going on, you know?"

He goes, "Are you sure? 'Cause you could, man. She thought you were hot up there singing, man. Sh-sh-she really wants to fuck you."

I said, "Artie, man, how you doing? You doing all right?"

Artie goes, "Oh, yeah! *Yeah!* You wanna tootsie? Tootsie? Tootsie? You want zoozkie?"

I went, "No, man. I gotta go back onstage." That was the last time I saw him alive.

JACK BOULWARE: I threw a publishing party at a bar in San Francisco, and Jim Mitchell showed up with his girlfriend. He was a really nice guy. I bought him a drink, and we talked about smuggling Cuban cigars. That was really the first time I had ever chatted with him at any length.

Jim was very supportive. He was buying ads in a publication I was editing. He was just very enthusiastic and excited that people were still raising hell in San Francisco. Jim and Artie Mitchell were publishing a small anti–Gulf War newspaper called *The War News* and a bunch of sixties radicals were contributing to it.

TOM BYRON: Later on, I was looking for a fucking cigarette, and Jim handed me a Marlboro.

I said, "Thanks, man." I looked down; then I said, "Hey, Jim, how you doing?"

He goes, "Oh, good." Then he says, "Fuckin' Artie. That fuckin' Artie, man."

I said, "Yeah, all right, see ya later, Jim."

Those were the last words I ever heard from Jim Mitchell—"Fucking Artie!" Two months later Jim shot him.

MARILYN CHAMBERS: I think Jim went over there that night to scare Artie, but I think Art surprised him when he came down the hall. And Jim just started shooting. And the bullet ricocheted and went through his eye—and Artie was dead.

JACK BOULWARE: Two weeks later, I opened the newspaper and saw that Jim had killed his brother.

I was shocked. The whole city was shocked. They were such a part of the fabric of the city. I think people who lived here thought they'd always be around because they contributed so much local color to the city. They were fun-loving guys, you know? They weren't moody or weird or creepy porn people.

They were fun-loving porn people.

TOM BYRON: Oh, dude, man. Joey Silvera called me up and said, "Hey, hear the news, man? Artie got shot. I guess Jim did it."

I went, "What? Oh, *fuck!*"

Then I was like, "Oh, well. What are you gonna do?"

JACK BOULWARE: Tensions were clearly increasing between the two brothers. I don't know why. Does anybody really know why? Only Jim Mitchell knows why he would leave his office with a loaded .22, drive across the bay to his brother's house—which is dark, no lights on—bang on the door and start shooting.

Jim kills his brother and then walks away—he was trying to stick the rifle down his leg when the police caught him. I mean, that's what some people call "Okie Justice."

ROGER YOUNG: I wasn't too surprised when Jim shot Artie because I kind of followed their lifestyle and what they were doing. Again, I wish we'd gotten more involved. Because one of the Mitchells threw a birthday party for his daughter—Artie had them all in this spa together—and was accused of fondling one of the other girls. They were all underage—eleven or twelve. I was aware that there was something going on.

JACK BOULWARE: Jim was out on half a million dollars bail, and he continued to run the theater until his court date came up. Then he went to trial, and it was somewhat of a circus. People were covering it from a lot of different publications. And of course they found him guilty; they'd caught him red-handed.

MARILYN CHAMBERS: I went to visit Jim in prison, and he was a beaten man. I mean, it was a tragic mistake.

One of the reasons I went to visit him was that Robert DeNiro and I had sat down for, like, four hours, to talk about a movie. The book *The Bottom Feeders* had just come out, and Universal Studios wanted to do the Mitchell brothers' story. I was under contract to Universal as a consultant. I don't know if they sold it to Tribeca Films, but Tribeca was going to do it.

DeNiro was either going to direct it or play Artie and Jim's father. And when we met, DeNiro said, "Jim will not have anything to do with us." He said, "Unless I can talk to him, I really don't feel comfortable doing this because I don't want to do it above the waist. I want to do the whole story the way it is, but I need to know from Jim what his story was."

DeNiro asked, "Will you go talk to him?"

So I went to talk to Jim in prison.

Jim said, "I know why you're here, Mar. You know I love you, and I'm glad you came to see me, but I'm not interested."

JACK BOULWARE: Jim was given a six-year sentence, which means he served half of it, and now he's back running the business. I don't think he can go anywhere besides his home and the business—he's very restricted in where he can go in San Francisco—but he is back running the business.

MARILYN CHAMBERS: Jim said, "I don't care if it's DeShmiro or anybody else. I will not have anybody capitalizing on my family's tragedy, and that's it."

I felt stupid for bringing it up. I said, "Okay, fine. I understand. And I agree."

So I had to go back and tell DeNiro to forget it. Then Sean Penn was going to do it, and then they shot something in Canada with Charlie Sheen and Emilio Estevez for Showtime.

The Bombing
LOS ANGELES/PHOENIX/MILWAUKEE/CHICAGO
1991–1992

RICHARD ROSFELDER: Reuben Sturman was out on bond, and we saw an opportunity to create serious problems for him by telling the bookstores, "You send him money, you're going to prison."

By that time, we had developed serious credibility within the industry; Reuben needed to motivate the people to do what he said.

We, on the other hand, were motivating them to do what *we* said. I'd have IRS people go in and say, "Hey, you know, he owes us. Don't transfer any money to him, transfer it to us."

They'd say, "Well, geez . . ."

NAOMI DELGADO: I heard Reuben yelling at Mickey Feinberg. I really don't remember exactly what he said, but he was very upset. I could just hear Mickey saying, "But Reuben! But Reuben!"

TAMARA GREEN: My husband, Howard, owned and operated EWAP Incorporated and Book Cellar Incorporated—adult bookstores. When he died in June of 1990, I started looking through contracts. I found a lease agreement between the Hispano American Finance Company and the Book Cellar relating to the lease of peep-show booths.

I understood Hispano American Finance to be owned by a Reuben Sturman. Laura Murphy, who I hired as a controller, discovered it first and pointed out to me that for several months we had made double payments to the Hispano American Finance. At that point, I instructed Laura to stop making payments until we were caught up.

KEVIN BEECHUM (PORNOGRAPHER): In early December 1991, Mickey Feinberg came to my office in Northridge and asked if I knew anyone who would be willing to smash an adult bookstore in Phoenix for ten thousand dollars . . . half down and half when the job was finished.

I told him I didn't, but he kept asking, at least three or four times. So I talked it over with Jay Brissette because we were close friends; he had moved out to California when about seventy of us came out here from Bay City, Michigan.

Jay said he'd do it, so I told Mickey I had someone who would do the job.

TAMARA GREEN: Laura Murphy had several conversations with Reuben Sturman about the payments, and he, of course, kept insisting that they should be the double payments, and she kept insisting, no, we are paying according to the contract.

JAY BRISSETTE: Kevin told me we would be smashing up a few video machines, and he kind of put the crime as being malicious destruction. . . . They were peep-show machines, and bashing them would put them out of business for a day or two.

So I got some help—Donald Mares and Paul Mahn—and in late December 1991 we drove to Phoenix and stayed there for three days. On the first day we went into the store, Pleasure World and checked it out. It was just a salesperson behind a counter with video magazines, videocassette boxes—all types of items for sale—and a back room with approximately fifty peep-show booths.

TAMARA GREEN: Reuben told Laura, "The payments have to be as I have said, and if not it's going to be too late."

And Laura said, "Well, what does 'too late' mean?"

But there was never an answer to that.

JAY BRISSETTE: We decided we would go in separately at 6:00 or 7:00 the next morning—meet up after, when there would be no patrons there—and get into the back room, smash the machines, and then run out the exit door.

So the morning of the vandalization, we drove my truck, parked several blocks away, and walked to the store. We entered separately, just milled around, waiting for a few patrons to leave. We had baseball bats and hammers underneath our clothing.

Then we proceeded to the back room, smashing the machines, then ran out the door.

TAMARA GREEN: Michael Veto is the general manager of the Book Cellar, and after the vandalism, he and I talked about it. We decided that this could be a message that was being sent.

JAY BRISSETTE: On our way back to California, I contacted Kevin Beechum and told him the job was finished.

I received the final payment for the job from Kevin Beechum in mid-January 1992, and he said the people that were paying the money said I did a good job and gave me the balance of the money.

TAMARA GREEN: I was very frightened, and I didn't want any more violence, so we decided to make double payments again.

REUBEN STURMAN: Those people refused to pay me. And so we went into one of their stores and broke it up, to send them a message. Sure enough, they started paying me again. I thought that was very nice of them.

JAY BRISSETTE: I met Mickey Feinberg, by accident, at Kevin Beechum's office, in March of 1992. I was just talking to Kevin in his office, and Mickey walked in and asked if he could talk to Kevin in private. But Kevin said there was no need because I was the one doing the jobs. We all started laughing, and Mickey kind of said he thought so.

Then Mickey started going on about some more jobs, and Kevin kind of stopped the conversation and told him he didn't want no more of that talk going on in his office. Kevin said if we were going to talk about it, get out of his office. So I met with Mickey in the parking lot. Mickey told me he had a few more jobs in Cleveland and asked if I would be interested.

I said sure.

NAOMI DELGADO: Reuben was screaming over the telephone at Roy May, and Roy hung up the phone. After that call, Sturman said, "Roy doesn't know who he's fucking with, and he owes me money."

RICHARD ROSFELDER: We at the IRS and the Organized Crime Task Force created a serious dilemma for Sturman. Keeping the pressure on was part of our stategy, and it worked. It created problems for Reuben that we could have never envisioned. I mean, Reuben Sturman made some real bonehead moves.

NAOMI DELGADO: I know Reuben was upset with Roy because Roy wasn't paying him. He said he made several attempts to contact Roy but couldn't get through, and he said he was going to have Chuckie's legs broken. Chuckie is Paula's son. Paula Lawrence May, Roy's wife.

And Reuben said he knew that Paula had a house in Aspen and that he was going to have it blown up or something. I told him, "Please don't do this. I couldn't bear to live like this and worry about our daughter constantly."

JAY BRISSETTE: A few weeks later I met with Mickey Feinberg again, in a strip mall parking lot on Roscoe and DeSoto, in Canoga Park. It was just Mickey and myself in his car. He told me he had eight more jobs in Chicago and asked me if I would be interested, and how much I would charge.

I told him I would want ten thousand for each job. Mickey just said he would get back to me as soon as he heard something from his guy on what was going to happen.

We next met at Alphonso's, an Italian restaurant in Chatsworth. Again it was just Mickey and myself. Mickey told me his guy would pay seventy-five hundred for each job. He also told me he didn't get anything from the last job, and I told him I would pay him ten percent of whatever I made. I also told him I met this guy, Donald Mares, that knew something about bombs, and wondered if it would be all right to possibly use him on the next job. Mickey basically said he would leave it up to me.

NAOMI DELGADO: I first met Mickey at a party and then I would occasionally see him at a home on Weddington. I [spoke with him] maybe four or five, six times, just to say hello. [He and] Reuben—the two of them met in an office in the back portion of the house.

JAY BRISETTE: On April 13, me, Joe Martinez, Paul Mahn, and Donald Mares flew to Milwaukee, rented a car, and drove to Chicago. We stayed in a motel by O'Hare Airport. The next day, Tuesday, April 14, 1992, we had somebody go into each location and check it out. We had stink bombs—galvanized PVC pipe with stink vials inside—and we were going to put the bombs outside the stores by the coaxial cables. I figured it would blow up the cables and shut down all the video machines inside.

That night, Donny put everything together, and he went over how they worked with Joe and Paul. We decided we would go in two cars. Joe was going to do one. Paul was going to do two or three, and Donny was going to do the rest of them.

I dropped Joe Martinez off at Seventy-ninth Street and Cicero, and he took the bomb and placed it in the alley by the store. After I dropped him off I went to Camden Park and picked up Joe Martinez. It was approximately 8:00 P.M., and there was no one else around I knew.

CHICAGO TRIBUNE, AUGUST 27, 1993: PORN TRIAL JURY TOLD OF BOMB SCENE: "With rain fast approaching, Florence Clanton was hurrying out of a clothing store in the Rush Street area when she heard a loud bang and saw the windows of a passing car blow out and flames engulf the interior."

FLORENCE CLANTON: Immediately after the car passed there was a bolt of lightning. A few seconds later—BANG—all the windows blew out of the car. It was engulfed in heavy black smoke and flames.

The car continued to roll very slowly, and then I began to hear someone screaming, "OH, MY GOD, SOMEBODY HELP ME! SOMEBODY PLEASE HELP ME!"

The car banged a second time, and then it was engulfed in flames—and the screams became more intense.

CHICAGO TRIBUNE, **AUGUST 27, 1993: PORN TRIAL JURY TOLD OF BOMB SCENE:** "The driver, his head in flames, climbed out the window."

FLORENCE CLANTON: I yelled to him, *"Drop and roll—don't run!"* He stopped like he heard me. I said, "Get down so I can get your hair. *You've got to kneel down."*

He dropped down. He had on a gray coat, and I pulled the coat up over his head so I could smother his hair, just to pull him into me, so I could get the fire off of him. He laid on the ground and said, "Do I look okay? Am I all right?"

I said, "You look fine; you're okay."

But there was still screams coming from the car.

CHICAGO SUN-TIMES, **AUGUST 27, 1993: BOMB TESTIMONY OPENS EXTORTION TRIAL; WOMAN TELLS OF EFFORTS TO SAVE BLAST VICTIM:** "The auto had smashed into a utility pole and Donald Mares emerged, on fire from the waist up."

FLORENCE CLANTON: When I turned and looked back, the car slammed into the traffic light post in front of the Gap store—and out of the window comes the other guy, totally ablaze. All of his body—from his waist all the way up—was just on fire . . .

He was screaming, he was running, and I yelled to him, *"Don't run, just stop running—drop!"*

CHICAGO SUN-TIMES, **AUGUST 27, 1993: BOMB TESTIMONY OPENS EXTORTION TRIAL; WOMAN TELLS OF EFFORTS TO SAVE BLAST VICTIM:** "She chased him down as he ran, knocking him against the wall, trying to get his blazing nylon jacket off as it melted on him."

FLORENCE CLANTON: He kept running, and when I caught up with him I slammed him up against a building so I could gain control of him. When I got him up against the building, the blood just splattered all over the building, and he fell to the ground so I could roll him over. I tried to push him. I couldn't roll him over that good because he was on fire.

The driver of the car was a few feet away while I was trying to get the fire off the passenger's clothes. The driver was just sitting there. The passenger was saying, "Oh, my God, this is the worst I ever felt. I know I'm dying."

I told him, "You are not going to die."

He said, "It's okay, you can talk to me about dying. I know I'm going to die."

I told him, "Just shut up, you are not going to die, and you've got to listen to me. I've got to get all of your clothes off of you before they melt."

I told his friend to come and help me. He just looked at me for a moment and then crawled over to where his friend was and said, "Don't worry, I'll tell them it's not your fault." Then he said to me, "Don't worry about it; he ain't gonna make it. Just get out of here."

I said, "Hey, don't leave your friend!"

Then he got up, and he ran into a restaurant.

JAY BRISSETTE: About fifteen minutes later Paul Mahn showed up with facial cuts and it looked like his hair had been burned a little bit, and his expression was pretty frazzled. He said a bomb blew up in the car, and he had to leave Donny there, and Donny was in pretty bad shape.

FLORENCE CLANTON: After I got his shirt torn loose, I saw a four- to six-inch hole blown through his chest. He had a sucking hole, so I tuck the shirt and stuck it in the hole to try to stop the bleeding, and I wrapped the arm of the shirt the rest of the way. His arm was severed. So I thought maybe I could tie the shirt around to stop the bleeding, but he wouldn't hold still.

All his face was burned off—his hair, his eyebrows.

JAY BRISSETTE: I was pretty upset at the time and tried to collect my thoughts for a minute and decided I would call the car in stolen. We wanted to head back to Los Angeles, so we started driving back toward Wisconsin. We stayed at a motel that night then drove to the airport in Wisconsin, turned in the car, and bought new tickets to go back to Los Angeles. Me and Joe Martinez went together, and I left Paul Mahn with the remaining ticket.

Garth Cohen—the guy who was originally going to go but then backed out—picked us up at LAX. We dropped Joe Martinez off at his house and then went to a supermarket about a block away, and that's when I called my friend Kevin Beechum.

KEVIN BEECHUM: I'm fuckin' sittin' in my office in Northridge, and I'm sweatin' fuckin' bullets, and the phone rings and it's Jay. He's at Hughes market over here in Chatsworth. I'm like, "What the fuck are you doing?"

He said he was on fire; the bomb blew up in the car. I'm like, "Oh, fuck!"

Jay said, "I think Donny's dead."

I'm like, "Oh, shit." So I go pick him up and take him to my house in Chatsworth. And I call Mickey and tell him. He's like, "Oh, fuck."

I said, "Mickey, you said you'd get the lawyers; you'd pay the bail; you'd take care of the guys."

He said, "Don't worry. I'll see what I can do."

I ran to see my lawyer, Jim Henderson, and told him the story. Jimmy says, "Go sit tight until we hear something."

So me and Jay go back to my house, and as we're walking in we get a phone call from Little Joe saying that the FBI and the ATF are raiding his house. We're like, "Oh, fuck!" So we take off—but then we're like, where are we gonna go?

NAOMI DELGADO: I knew Russ Hampshire for about eight years or so. He's a friend of Reuben's. He's in the adult video business. Russ would come over to our house every Tuesday night for a card game.

RUSS HAMPSHIRE (OWNER OF VCA STUDIOS): Mickey Feinberg came to my office, asked me to close the door, and said that he was in trouble. He said he'd been asked to break up some stores in Chicago, and that an individual was killed with a bomb, and that it got back to him through Kevin Beechum.

Mickey said that Reuben Sturman had paid him fifty or sixty thousand dollars to do the job in Chicago. And they had him on a wire—but that he wasn't going to roll.

Mickey asked me to go see Sturman and tell him what happened and tell Sturman that he wasn't going to roll and that all he wanted was his legal bills and his family taken care of.

KEVIN BEECHUM: We hid out the whole weekend, and we're calling Mickey Feinberg. "Mickey, you've got to come up with the money—you've got to do something."

First he told me, "Go put your house up for the bail." I'm like, "Wait a minute! I'm not even supposed to be in this picture! This picture is between you guys; you gave them your word that you would fucking get the money."

Mickey finally tells us, "Fuck you, you're on your own."

I'm like, "Well, you're fucked."

He's like, "Fuck you!"

So now I'm pissed. I call Jimmy Henderson, and he says bring Jay here. So I do, and Jimmy says, "You guys are gonna go down if you don't cooperate. So fuck Mickey. If he's gonna screw us, we're gonna screw him back."

So Jay went there and cooperated with the FBI, and I did, too.

NAOMI DELGADO: In April 1992, Russ Hampshire came to see Reuben at our house. He asked to speak to Reuben, and they went outside to talk.

RUSS HAMPSHIRE: I asked him to step outside, and related the information that Mickey Feinberg had told me—that he just wanted to let Reuben know that he was not going to roll on him and that all he wanted was his legal bills paid for and his family taken care of. I told Reuben that they had Mickey Feinberg on a wire discussing whatever with Kevin Beechum.

Reuben said, "Oh, shit." He said to relate to Mickey that "I will definitely take care of his family and legal bills."

NAOMI DELGADO: I talked to Reuben afterward, and he said that Mickey had hired two guys, and one of the men was assembling a bomb, and it went off and killed him. Reuben said that he didn't know who these guys were—and these were people that Mickey had hired—and no one could point anything at Reuben. And he said that Mickey would go to jail for Reuben, if he would pay for Mickey's defense.

MARK PROSPERI (U.S. ATTORNEY): After Mickey Feinberg learns about the bombing, he goes to Russ Hampshire and says, "I want you to go talk to Reuben and tell him what happened," and that's exactly what he did. And then Hampshire becomes an intermediary between Feinberg and Sturman. And this time Reuben goes in there, and he checks for a wire and tells Naomi, "I don't want you to pay Feinberg any more than twenty-five thousand dollars."

NAOMI DELGADO: Later Mickey called, and he gave me directions to Russ Hampshire's office—he had set up a time—and we met. After I met with Russ, I met with Mickey Feinberg, in a screening room that was adjacent to Russ' office. Mickey said that one man who helped do the bombing had become a government witness, and he was going to finger Mickey. Mickey was going to need money for his defense.

KEVIN BEECHUM: Meanwhile, Mickey gets the money from Russ Hampshire from VCA. Mickey even collected some of the money from Reuben—and Mickey never gave us a fucking nickel. He came to my lawyer and gave him five hundred dollars, or five thousand, and I ended up having to pay Jim Henderson $140,000 to keep me out of it.

Mickey said, "I'm not going to cooperate. I never did nothing."

Then when he found out we were fucking him, he wants to cooperate. So he goes back to their men and says he's going to cooperate. But now it's too late; now he's facing fifteen to thirty years. Now he's *fucked*. He shoulda took the ten years. He would've been out by now.

NAOMI DELGADO: When Mickey said he would need money for his defense, I told him I would have to talk to Reuben about it. Then he said, "You're a very pretty woman, and you have a lovely child, and I wouldn't want anything to happen to you or your child."

I was frightened. I mean, I took it as a threat. So I told Reuben, and he told me that I would have to help Mickey if he needed it. I told him that Mickey was asking for twenty-five thousand dollars. Maybe he asked for more—I don't remember—but it ended up that I sent twenty-five thousand to his attorney.

CHICAGO TRIBUNE, SEPTEMBER 10, 1993: REPUTED PORN KINGPIN CONVICTED IN PLOT AGAINST ADULT BOOKSTORES: "Reuben Sturman, whom prosecutors described as the nation's largest distributor of hard-core pornography, was convicted Thursday of conspiring to send thugs to Chicago to damage several adult bookstores in an attempt to extort payoffs from their owner.

"A federal jury, though, acquitted Sturman of seven other counts related to the attempted bombings of the Chicago bookstores in April 1992. The jury convicted Sturman of conspiring to extort the Chicago owner through the use of force and violence. The jury, though, acquitted Sturman of involvement in the attempted bombings, apparently believing the hired men decided to escalate the violence without Sturman's knowledge."

RICHARD ROSFELDER: I think Reuben intended to scare some people, but I just didn't see him as the type of guy that would be intending to kill anybody. Because what happened in Chicago and Arizona was the result of one of those goofy bombers blowing himself up.

CLEVELAND PLAIN DEALER, SEPTEMBER 10, 1993: PORN KING CLEARED IN BOMBING CASE; MORE JAIL TIME DUE: "Pornography king Reuben Sturman was cleared of federal bombing charges yesterday but was convicted of other charges that could leave him in prison for the rest of his life.

"If Sturman had been convicted of the bombing charges, he would have faced a mandatory 30 years in prison because a man sent to Chicago last year to vandalize adult bookstores was killed when a bomb accidentally exploded in his lap.

"Sturman's sentence will now be determined by federal sentencing guidelines. He was convicted of conspiring to commit extortion and of separate charges that said he used threats of violence, but not bombs, to extort money from Roy May, who was buying several Chicago adult bookstores from Sturman."

RICHARD ROSFELDER: It appeared to me that he hired people to break up the bookstore and scare people and probably hired people to go up and plant bombs outside of bookstores and scare 'em there. I didn't really see it as anything more than that.

I didn't think Reuben was a killer.

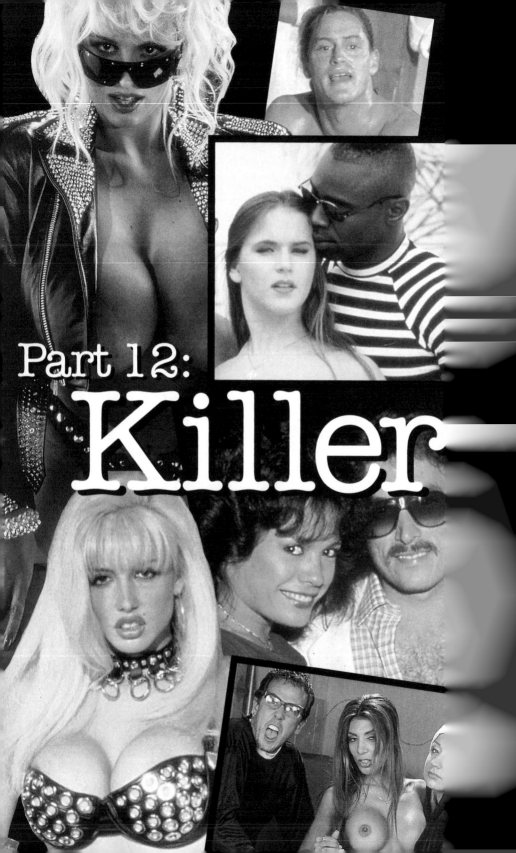

Part 12: Killer

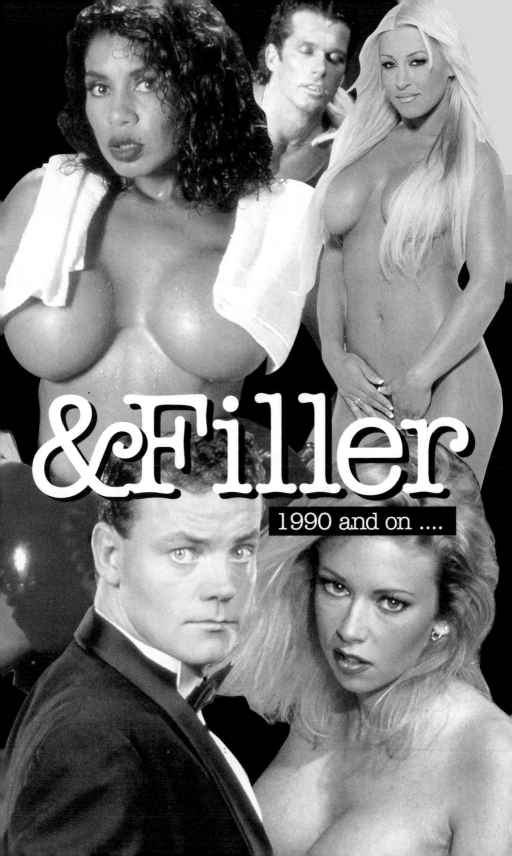

&Filler

1990 and on ....

Left page, *clockwise from top left:* Holly Body, Marc Wallice, Tricia Deveraux and Sean Michaels, Marc Carriere and Tina Marie, Lizzy Borden, unknown with Rob Black, Tiffany Lords.

Right page: *clockwise from top left:* Veronica Brazil, Cal Jammer, Jill Kelly, Jenna Jameson, John Wayne Bobbitt.

The Girls who Marc Built

LOS ANGELES/OGDEN, UTAH
1991–1993

TIM CONNELLY: I met Marc Carriere in 1985 at the CES show in Vegas. Marc and I met through Tina Marie, Marc's then-girlfriend—a big-breasted Samoan. Tina had one of the early 1980s tit jobs; fake tits were rare at that time.

Tina's big movie was *Star 84*, which Marc produced; she was also the star of *Firestorm*. Marc and Tina's relationship helped gain Marc entrée into the porno industry—being with Tina Marie made him okay.

RAY PISTOL: When Marc Carriere was starring Tina Marie, he had just brought out *Star 84*, and he was in town from Indiana. Tina was making an appearance in my store, signing autographs. Marc brought her over and hung around, and we just chatted about store business.

At that time I believe he had about five stores—a very nice guy, with a very good-looking wife. They were an engaging couple.

MARC CARRIERE: I found Tina Marie for the film *Star 84*. Tracked her down through Jim South, I believe. Jim and I had a parting of the ways soon after that. They got a little greedy. They wanted royalties—after they had already made the deal. My thing was, "You already made the deal. Let's talk about the next film."

That was the first big film that Bruce Seven, John Stagliano, and I worked on, and there was one thing that we all pretty much agreed upon: that the films should be mainly sex and be down and dirty.

JOHN STAGLIANO: Bruce Seven and I did Video Exclusive's first movie—which was Marc Carriere's first video production—which we're still owed five thousand dollars on. So you might want to mention that.

Video Exclusives still owes Bruce and me five thousand dollars. We think that Video Exclusives should pay up!

TIM CONNELLY: Marc came from the Midwest and was endlessly fascinated by the mail-order in all the magazines—you know, the X-Ray Specs advertisements, and things like that. So he went to a lot of the porn premieres, made a connection to *Hustler* and some of the other big magazines, and came up with some mail-order campaigns.

He used P.O. boxes for addresses—so his ads were all the same ads, though you would never know it. There were girl/girl ads, magazines, dildos, rubbers—whatever he could sell from Chicago to Michigan City and all points in between.

MARC CARRIERE: I didn't major in anything specific in college, just the usual courses. But what attracted me was this mail-order stuff. I thought, "What the hell could sell really well?" And then I thought, "Sex really sells."

ROSCOE JEFFERSON (PORN PRODUCER): Marc ran his mail-order business out of Indiana, with people he grew up with. Marc's brother, Brad, ran the company back there. Then Marc moved out to California and became a big porn producer. Marc and Brad talked constantly on the phone, from L.A. to Indiana. But Brad was getting a little disenchanted by the business. It was fun for him at first—but it was a lot of work. Brad didn't really have a taste for the business.

TIM CONNELLY: Marc quickly got a corner of the market. When he finally moved out to California, that's when we hooked up. He wanted to come up with a national campaign: "Porn for a Penny," a take-off on the record club concept. It was all about just getting somebody to give you their name; once you have their name, you can sell them whatever you want—and you can sell their name.

We learned that federal law said a mail-order company had thirty days to fulfill an order, or the company had to send a letter saying that they're back-ordered. If you're back-ordered, then you have another thirty days to either give them a cash credit or some other sort of fulfillment. So Marc immediately saw that as a ninety-day window. Within thirty days he would send out a postcard saying, "Your order is being processed. Due to the overwhelming response, we'll get to it as quickly as we can." Based on the responses he got for various offers, he figured out how to bulk-edit his mail-order requests. Then, in sixty days, they'd give you the choice of having a credit with their catalog or something else.

ROSCOE JEFFERSON: Rumor has it that there was money being kept in Marc's safes back in Indiana because a lot of people were sending cash in, and they weren't fulfilling those orders, they just kept them. But I don't know if that's true. If somebody decides he wants to buy the thousand porn scenes for $79.95, and he sends in a postal money order or cash, there's no real record of it. You can basically decide not to fulfill the order, as long as they send the payment by regular mail. They can go after you, but they can't prove it.

LOS ANGELES TIMES MAGAZINE, FEBRUARY 17, 1991: DEMAND IS STRONG, BUT POLICE CRACKDOWNS AND A SATURATED MARKET SPELL TROUBLE FOR ONE OF L.A.'S BIGGEST BUSINESSES: "Some of the wind has been taken out of Marc Carriere's bluster. His mail-order company was raided in October by federal agents, who took away four safes containing $548,409.15. He later was arrested on charges of tax evasion. The government said his income from 1986 to 1988 was 'substantially in excess' of the $2.96 million he claimed. He is awaiting trial."

ROSCOE JEFFERSON: Soon after that, Brad Carriere turned up dead.

On June 13, 1991, he committed suicide in the garage of his new home—which he was just about to move into, after marrying his childhood sweetheart. He sat in his car with the engine running and died of carbon-monoxide poisoning.

I saw Brad two weeks before his death; he was a happy guy. He was not threatened at all by the investigation. Figured that if they did have some trouble, that maybe somebody would have to go in.

SHARON MITCHELL: Apparently there was some family issue there, something about how Brad wasn't getting along with his wife. That whole Carriere thing was crazy, though. Those guys were pretty odd.

ROSCOE JEFFERSON: Did Marc talk about Brad's suicide? A little bit. He was very distant and cold. At the time, I was more concerned about Marc. I thought, "Marc would never do that. It's his *brother*." I never saw anything but an easygoing friendship between them.

But it was difficult because Marc's not the easiest guy in the world to talk to—very shut down. He leaves a lot of things unsaid—sentences trail off all the time. A lot of it's inference and innuendo.

RON JEREMY: Marc is a nice guy, but he hires tough guys as front people. Two editors tried to blackmail him, and so rumor has it that he sent a couple of black guys into the labs to threaten them. They didn't hit them, but they pushed them around and scared them. Marc's got the money and the power to do things like that—but he's only done it once that I've heard of.

SHARON MITCHELL: They were the beginning of this town's slide into oversaturation of the porn industry. And Ron Jeremy was right there with them—he'd jump on their fucking two-hundred-dollar-a-scene bandwagon.

That was the beginning of the end of any quality in the business. You can't compete with that much stuff that quick.

***LOS ANGELES TIMES MAGAZINE*, FEBRUARY 17, 1991: DEMAND IS STRONG, BUT POLICE CRACKDOWNS AND A SATURATED MARKET SPELL TROUBLE FOR ONE OF L.A.'S BIGGEST BUSINESSES.** "Others dispute the idea that it was Carriere who caused the price of an X-rated cassette to plunge from $100 a few years ago to as low as $5 today. Critics say he is just the industry's most swashbuckling price-buster, delivering an inferior product. Carriere doesn't spend much time worrying about what his competitors think of him. He is too busy planning his next move to out-flank his opponents in the flash wars."

MARC CARRIERE: Perry Ross offered to come and work for me and brought along the idea of doing to girls what he had done to Angela Baron. Which was: Find a girl, and do the whole plastic surgery trip. Make her a goddess.

Make our own goddesses. That sounded good to me.

TIM CONNELLY: Marc Carriere's movies were horrible. I told him that right away, and he knew it, so he opened up an office and started getting girls to be part of his "Killer and Filler" program.

MARC CARRIERE: I told Ron Jeremy that I wanted to make a one-day feature with six sex scenes and that we'd have to have one killer girl and the rest be filler. I think the first one was *California Blonds* then *Ebony Humpers*. Nobody was really doing those one-day-wonders back then.

RON JEREMY: I was the king of "Killer and Filler"—the technique of hiring that one girl who's on the box cover and shooting her in two or three scenes and then making two or three movies using her. Then the next day Marc would have me shoot the filler—the less expensive girls—and then we would have three movies. It was moviemaking conveyor-belt style.

MARC CARRIERE: Then Perry Ross was over at Jim South's office, and he bumps into this guy Rex Cabo. Perry said I had to meet Rex because he could bring a ton of girls down. So I met with him; he sounded like a fast talker, but he produced. He started bringing down girls by the busload.

TIM CONNELLY: Perry Ross ran Marc's place with an iron fist—while Rex Cabo brought in the girls. Being around either Rex Cabo or Perry Ross would send a chill up the spine of a normal person.

Today, Perry Ross is dead. He died from a mysterious drug overdose in Holland.

MARC CARRIERE: Every day these girls were coming in—ten a day—it was just incredible. Rex Cabo brought Savannah to us, Rikki Lee, Vivianna, et cetera. We would bring the girls up and assess them. We would decide if we were going to have work done on them, handpick them, and then do, like, twenty picture deals with them.

TIM CONNELLY: Marc was known for sending these girls off to Idaho—to Dr. Pearl. He'd call the doctor up and have him add more cc's of silicone or saline, so that the girls came out with monstrous breasts. Marc would pay the girls—ten thousand dollars, let's say. Then they'd come in and shoot five box covers in maybe two days, and then he'd get five scenes out of them or ten—two scenes for each video.

But he'd always shoot them for the box before they fucked because their tits would always come down a couple dings, visually, after a week in the Carriere Fuck Factory.

TREASURE BROWN (EXOTIC DANCER): Would Marc tell the surgeon to make the girls' tits bigger when they were already under? Yeah, that's completely true. And then Marc would tell them, "Don't worry! The saline's going to go down!"

It happened to one stripper, who had to have her boobs reduced. It was Dr. Pearl in Idaho. *Idaho!* This little hick town, and it's the epitome of boob jobs for porn stars!

They would fly these Pepperidge Farm country girls out from Indiana to Idaho, slap new tits on 'em, and then fly 'em off to Hollywood.

RAY PISTOL: It is funny to see somebody like Bunny Bleu go from bee stings to basketballs, you know?

TREASURE BROWN: Dr. Pearl did silicone when silicone was illegal—and it's far better. If you were questioning whether silicone was good or bad, he'd be like, "Look, this is a water balloon. This doesn't feel like a tit!"

I was like, "Oh, my God!"

Dr. Pearl was a little scary.

RAY PISTOL: Treasure told me she was sitting with a girl in Dr. Pearl's office, and she asked him, "Well, what if they break?"

Dr. Pearl's like, "They won't break!!"

Thump! Threw one of them up against the wall!

He said, "See?!"

JEANNA FINE: I was really scared when Dr. Pearl walked into the office because he looked like he had created himself. He kind of looks like the guy from *Poltergeist* with the black hat.

He came in and dropped his glasses; he was kind of stumbly. He was, like, seventy-something at that point. I was a little uncertain at that moment. And all his nurses were five feet tall and eighty years old. I thought, "Oh no, I'm not sure about this."

But he did fantastic work.

TIM CONNELLY: Marc was one of the first to make his product the "Big Mac of pornography." Vivid knew pretty early on that a good box cover could sell a movie, but Carriere took it to the extreme. He said, "Why don't we make it all about the box, and fuck everything else? Because all they really want is to see the girl on the box fuck."

So he'd get that girl, have a *Penthouse* photographer shoot her, and spend a lot of money on airbrushing. Then they'd pay the girl a flat rate and give her whatever she needed—a car, an abortion, the rent, whatever.

There was some heat in the industry about it. But the bottom line was that the girls didn't complain, you know? Because he really knew how to deal with them on a commercial level—and a lot of producers didn't.

MARC CARRIERE: I don't think you should get too involved with the girls. We have girls to this day who call at midnight looking for help. Even if we're not working with them anymore, we'll still help them out.

One girl came in and said she needed eight hundred dollars right away. For her rent or something. They were going to throw her out on the street. She said she would do a scene for us.

It took us seven months to get the scene out of her. We get burned more than they do.

Severed

MANASSAS, VIRGINIA
1993

JOHN WAYNE BOBBITT: I had been out with one of my best buddies, Robert Johnson. We'd spent a hard day at work unloading trucks at a warehouse, and we were really beat. So we went over to this club, Legends, where I sometimes worked as a bouncer. We had a few beers and a couple of shots. Then we went to three more clubs. We were just out girl-gazing. At 1:30 in the morning we ended up at Denny's and had coffee. But I was still exhausted when I got home, and that's it. I wasn't drunk, just exhausted.

LORENA BOBBITT: I went to bed, and I was awakened by the strong closing—the slam door, so I wake up. I look at the clock; it was maybe from 3:15, 3:30. I said if he have work today, and he said, "No, I went to bar." I went back to bed, and he slip by my side. I went to sleep.

LARRY FURST (PORN WRITER): On the early morning of June 23, 1993, ex-marine John Bobbitt came home from another night of heavy drinking in Manassas, Virginia, and climbed into bed with his Ecuadorean wife, Lorena. She claims he was drunk and abusive, pinning her to the bed and raping her.

LORENA BOBBITT: I feel like pull down to my underwears, and then he was on top of me again, and I wake up. I was like try to find out what is going on, and he grabbed my wrists and press down my hips. I felt like I couldn't breathe—his chest and right shoulder was on my face and my mouth. I said, "I don't want to have sex," and he wouldn't listen to me. He wouldn't let me go, and he started to pull down my underwears with his foot.

JOHN WAYNE BOBBITT: I remember laying down on the couch, then taking off my clothes, folding them up, and putting them on the ironing board. Before I fell asleep I remember doing something sexual with Lorena. I reached inside of her panties or something. She tried to get me erect again, but she couldn't because I'd been drinking.

LORENA BOBBITT: I tried to keep my legs closed, and I tried to keep my underwear on, but I couldn't. I only grabbed my right side with my three fingers and I hear a rip on my right-hand side of my underwear.

He took it off. He pulled my underwears down, and he force himself into me again. I was just crying. I tried to cry loud, but I couldn't breathe. It was hurting me. He hurt me. I feel like, I don't know, my vagina was ripping up or something.

JOHN WAYNE BOBBITT: But she'd had it all planned out already. The week before she'd threatened me with a knife, but she didn't point it at my dick. She knew exactly what she was doing when she sliced me. Believe me, it was premeditated.

LORENA BOBBITT: When he finished, I put my underwear on again. I was sitting in the bed, and I told him, why does he do this to me again and again and again? He pushes me away, says he doesn't care for my feelings. I went to the kitchen for a glass of water.

I was drinking the water trying to calm myself down—the only light that was on was the refrigerator light, and I saw the knife. I remember many things.

LARRY FURST: She severs his penis with a kitchen knife, flees the apartment, and then tosses the penis out of her car window.

LORENA BOBBITT: I don't remember cutting him. I was driving. I couldn't make a turn. I couldn't make a turn—my hands were busy—I tried to turn—but I couldn't because my hands were busy—and I just scream and I saw it—and I throw it out.

DR. DAVID BERMAN: The first question I asked was if they had found the severed part. At the time, they hadn't. Apparently, Lorena didn't know she was carrying it, and then when she realized she was, she rolled down the window and threw it out into a field. She went to her friends' house and told them where she threw it, and they called the police and the paramedics.

HOWARD PERRY: I'm a police officer with the City of Manassas Park, and I am a volunteer at the Yorkshire Volunteer Fire Department. We received a call in the early hours of June 23. We went to 8174 Peekwood Court, Apartment Number 5, the residence of John Wayne Bobbitt. We were looking for an extremity.

A penis.

We conducted a search of the apartment for half an hour. There was a large amount of blood on the bed leading to the bathroom, down the stairs, and to the parking lot. There was a butcher's block in the kitchen with some knives missing. The search was not successful.

JOHN WAYNE BOBBITT: All I could think was, "My wife cut me." I walked into the next room where my friend who was crashing at my place was sleeping and woke him up. I told him he had to take me to the hospital. He gets up and goes and brushes his teeth! I was holding myself to try to stop the bleeding.

Then I remember just going to the hospital. I had lost, like, half my blood. I never thought I would have my dick back again. I felt like I was in another world once I realized what had happened to me.

HOWARD PERRY: We left the apartment and proceeded to the intersection of Old Centerville Road and Maplewood Drive. We had received information that the penis was at that intersection. We recovered the penis. I picked up the penis and packed it in a clear plastic bag and packed it in ice. We got in the ambulance and proceeded to Prince William Hospital.

DR. DAVID BERMAN: It had to be *his* penis. You can't take it from a cadaver or anything like that. The body would reject it.

JOHN WAYNE BOBBITT: I waited at the hospital for two hours while they looked for it. I was lying there thinking the whole time, "My penis is gone!" That was all that was on my mind during those two hours.

DR. DAVID BERMAN: The penis was pretty white, all drained of blood, like a cadaver's penis. It was in a little baggie.

She cut it off at the bottom and left a little bit, about an inch. There are two main arteries at the base, and I had to repair and reattach those two major arteries along with two veins and two major nerves using microsurgery.

Microsurgery is fixing blood vessels and nerves under the microscope. Blood vessels that give the blood supply to the penis are a millimeter in size. People always ask, "How can you fix hundreds of thousands of blood vessels?" You only need to fix one or two main blood vessels, and the body will heal the rest. You connect them with very fine thread—finer than your hair.

JOHN WAYNE BOBBITT: Then the doctor told me how he could reattach it for me and that it would take two hours.

DR. DAVID BERMAN: It took nine and a half hours. But I'd never done one before so I was sort of learning as I went along. I went very slowly. Very carefully.

LARRY FURST: Lorena was arrested and charged with malicious wounding. It makes national headlines and women everywhere feel empowered by her act. Men grab for their crotches and think twice about pushing the old lady around after they've had a couple of drinks too many and want to tear off a piece late at night.

LORENA BOBBITT: I remember the put-downs and insults he told me. There were so many pictures in my head. I remember the first time he raped me. I remember how he did anal sex with me and hurt me. I remember when he told me about the abortion. I remember everything, everything.

JOHN WAYNE BOBBITT: A wife batterer? I was acquitted of that. Lorena tried to say that I raped her, but she couldn't prove it. She cut her own panties and that came out at my trial. And she tried to prove battery but there was no evidence. Actually it was the Commonwealth of Virginia that pressed charges because they thought I did something so terrible to her to make her do something so terrible. They were searching in the wrong area. Her feelings were hurt. She didn't want me to leave her. If she couldn't have me, she didn't want anyone to.

LORENA BOBBITT: I feel trapped. I don't know where to go. I don't know what to do. I was very scared of him. I didn't want him to rape me anymore. I didn't want him to hit me anymore. I did not want him to follow me and rape me.

JOHN WAYNE BOBBITT: Two weeks after the surgery, I woke up with a partial woody. I was in shock. Then I started wondering if I would ever have sex again. I called my mom up because I was so excited, and she got kind of mad at me. It was real exciting for me. The doctor had told me it might take two years.

DR. DAVID BERMAN: He actually got spontaneous erections early on, but they were only partial. It's a gradual process.

LARRY FURST: So the Bobbitts file for divorce, and John is charged with marital sexual assault. Lorena is found innocent by reason of temporary insanity.

She states it was an "irresistible impulse" that drove her to whacking off his wanger with their kitchen cutlery. John was later acquitted of his charges as well. Lorena's lawyer, Lisa Kemler, said, "This case was not about a penis. It's really about a life."

Bobbitt's reaction was typical for him. "You mean she got away with it?"

RON JEREMY: The John Wayne Bobbitt story was the most bizarre thing I'd ever heard in my entire life. A guy got his dick chopped off, it's thrown out the window of a car, and then it's refound and restuck on?

This is amazing. If you throw a hot dog out of a window, it ain't gonna be there an hour from now. Some dog's gonna eat it, or bugs are gonna crawl away with it, or a chipmunk's gonna get it. How do you throw a dick in a park and have it be there an hour later?

And what do the cops say when they're looking for it? You know, picture a bank robbery in progress: "Shut up, we're looking for a dick right now"?

But when I heard the story, I never thought that I'd be involved with John a year later.

LARRY FURST: After Bobbitt healed and Lorena faded from the public eye—declaring she hoped to lead a peaceful married life and raise a family—John moved to Las Vegas and started cashing in on his newfound celebrity.

JOHN WAYNE BOBBITT: I'm the very first man on earth who had his penis sliced off and then successfully reattached. The doctors tell me that I'm a first, a real medical miracle.

The Great Escape

CLEVELAND/BORON, CALIFORNIA
1992–1993

RICHARD ROSFELDER: I was having lunch with one of the editors of the *Cleveland Plain Dealer*, when I got paged and informed by the Strike Force that Reuben Sturman had escaped from prison.

I was surprised. I thought it was pretty cool. I mean, we had fought with the Sixth Circuit Court of Appeals over his bond—saying that he was a flight risk—and they basically disagreed. Then, when we charged him in the tax case, they reduced his bond from three million to a hundred thousand. It was total vindication of the position I took.

ROGER YOUNG: Reuben escapes from Boron Prison on Pearl Harbor Day, intentionally. Reuben Sturman never did anything that wasn't carefully planned out.

ORANGE COUNTY REGISTER, **DECEMBER 9, 1992: PORN KING FLEES:** "The head of an international pornography ring vanished from a federal prison camp in the Mojave Desert and may have fled the country," authorities said.

"'Reuben Sturman, 68, was missing at a 9 P.M. Monday bed check at the minimum security Boron Prison,' associate warden Jim Slade said Tuesday.

"Sturman was present at a 4 P.M. Monday head count at the camp.

"'The FBI, the U.S. Marshal's Service, the Kern County Sheriff's Department and other law enforcement agencies were searching for Sturman,' Slade said. He refused to say whether investigators had help in escaping. No other prisoners were reported missing."

CLEVELAND PLAIN DEALER, **DECEMBER 10, 1992: STURMAN MAY HAVE LEFT U.S.; AGENTS SAY PORNOGRAPHY CZAR HAD WORLDWIDE CONNECTIONS:** "Federal agents were worried Reuben Sturman might make a run for it before his sentencing hearing in June, so they kept a close eye on him. But the surveillance ended after marshals delivered him to a minimum-security prison camp near Boron, California, in the Mojave Desert.

"On Monday evening, six months after he arrived at the camp, which has no fences, Sturman walked away.

"'It was a surprise,' said George Rezny, chief of the IRS's Criminal Investigation Division in Cleveland. 'Our people did their job.'

"Authorities yesterday said Sturman might have fled the country and might be using international contacts and finances built up through his Cleveland-based pornography empire."

RICHARD ROSFELDER: I figured he'd be sitting on the beach over in Spain, sipping on whatever he was gonna be sipping on, and that at that juncture, the only question would be, "Who won?"

CLEVELAND PLAIN DEALER, DECEMBER 10, 1992: LOOKING FOR A RUBE: "At press time, Reuben Sturman hadn't been found. Authorities seeking Sturman are amazed at how he pulled off his escape—there's nothing near the prison but miles of sand and scraggly bushes. For now, those authorities say they have no idea where the 'porn czar' could be.

"Sturman has all the attractiveness of a reptile, and we root for his quick capture.

"Maybe they'll even make a film about his escape. Perhaps they'll call it 'From Behind the Jail Door.'"

RICHARD ROSFELDER: His Swiss accounts were never frozen, so he could've gone and gotten the money. He could have operated his businesses from there. I don't know why he didn't.

CLEVELAND PLAIN DEALER, DECEMBER 10, 1992: STURMAN MAY HAVE LEFT U.S.; AGENTS SAY PORNOGRAPHY CZAR HAD WORLDWIDE CONNECTIONS: "It is unclear whether authorities could get Sturman back if he did flee the country. The United States has extradition treaties with 103 countries, but the terms of those treaties differ as to what type of criminals they will hand over."

REUBEN STURMAN: I thought being in a big city was the easiest way to get lost. I figured if I stayed in Los Angeles and stayed away from everybody I knew there, I'd be fine.

RICHARD ROSFELDER: Why didn't he go to Switzerland? My guess—and it's pretty much a guess—would be that he wanted to be close to his daughter and that his wife wouldn't leave.

Naomi didn't want to relocate. His job was taking him elsewhere, and she wasn't interested in leaving.

REUBEN STURMAN: I couldn't stay away from my wife and child.

John Wayne Bobbitt Uncut

LAS VEGAS/LOS ANGELES
1993

RON JEREMY: Wet and Wild is a big giant water slide area in Las Vegas, and every year *Playboy* has a party there. So John Wayne Bobbitt's at this party, and so is LaToya Jackson, and it turns out that LaToya's husband is also managing John Bobbitt—Jack Gordon, with his son Aaron.

I had put a lot of celebrities in my movies. I had used Vince Neil in a girl/girl movie; I used Edie Williams in her first hard-core film; I had a football player do his first porno film for me. So I thought it would be fun for John Bobbitt to do a dialogue scene in my next girl/girl film.

LARRY FURST: Ron Jeremy was quick to say that it would be a tasteful, fully clothed, nonsex speaking role for John. Bobbitt, who had been languishing through his latest attempt at cashing in on his penis through stand-up comedy, saw this as a great opportunity to prove to the world and Lorena that he still had his manhood.

Aaron Gordon saw it as a way to cash in big-time on Bobbitt's severed penis. After all, the photos of John's bloody dickhead helped *Penthouse* magazine's lagging sales. Why not have it pay off again?

RON JEREMY: John Bobbitt knew who I was; he was a fan. He wanted to meet me, and he's saying, "What's it like fucking all those chicks?"

He was cute. He was all fast, and he was talking with these Vivid girls, and they were turning him down. He was trying to chase Janine Lindemulder all over the pool.

Was John smart? No. He has an attention span disorder, so he didn't come across as bright at all. But he's a sweet guy, very friendly. How can you not like a guy who's a big fan of yours?

JOHN WAYNE BOBBITT: Actually, the doctors told me to have sex as often as I can as part of my rehabilitation.

RON JEREMY: John had done nothing with his career up until that point. It would have been a year—he'd just turned down the Howard Stern show, showing his dick for fourteen thousand dollars or whatever.

So Cecil Watkins and I approached him about doing dialogue in an adult movie, and he goes, "Yeah, I'd like to do that." So we exchanged phone numbers.

Then Aaron Gordon showed up and says, "Yeah, it sounds good. We'll do it. We also heard that you do this show in Indiana."

Every year I host the Miss Nude Galaxy Pageant in Indiana. I've taken Malika Kinison, the Nelson Twins, Grandpa Munster (Al Lewis), Micky Kinison all there to cohost the show with me. Before me, Tim Allen from *Home Improvement* had done it.

JOHN WAYNE BOBBITT: After I got out of the marines I felt I was slated for something special. I'd done really well and had gone through advanced leadership training. I felt prepared to face anything that came my way in life. I mean, I was a marine. They taught us how to overcome anything.

RON JEREMY: So they said to me, "Tell you what, you pay John a thousand bucks to do the movie dialogue and then give him a thousand dollars to do the show. John wants to start doing some comedy."

I'm going, "He can barely talk in complete sentences. How's he gonna do comedy?"

When John tells people that he wants to do comedy, they laugh hysterically. "See, your comedy is working. But that's the biggest laugh you're ever gonna get." So he's gonna do comedy.

So I said, "Fine, he'll come host the show with me."

JOHN WAYNE BOBBITT: Comedy is harder than acting. Acting, you get chances to do it over again. But I'm not going to make a career doing dick jokes. One of the things I say is, "My name is John Wayne Bobbitt. Most of you know who I am. For those of you that don't, I'm the one that drove O. J. to the airport!" Ha, ha, ha.

I'm still getting the hang of it.

RON JEREMY: I get a call the next day from both Jack and Aaron Gordon saying, "We've changed our minds."

I ask, "Oh, can't do it?"

They say, "No—if he's gonna do porno, we want to do the whole thing—the whole nine yards."

I ask, "*What?*"

They say, "Everything. Fuck, the works."

I ask, "Are you sure he can do it?"

They go, "We know he can do it. He's been having sex with girls already."

I say, "Wow!"

JOHN WAYNE BOBBITT: I watched a lot of hard-core films because when I lived in Virginia, I owned a house and had a satellite dish and used to watch the Spice Channel. Lorena would always get upset when she discovered me watching those movies. She'd tell me she could dance for me if that's what I wanted or do the things those girls did.

RON JEREMY: Lipstik Video was mostly girl/girl and gay stuff; they don't really handle guy/girl stuff, and besides, it was way above what they could afford. So I hooked up the other company I'm very close to, Marc Carriere of Leisure Time. At that time, it was called Video Exclusives.

Marc's filthy rich and a very good friend of mine—covered my legal expenses when I was in jail. He's a stand-up guy, and so am I.

So I told Marc that John Bobbitt wants to do this thing. He goes, "Sounds great." So we got on Marc's plane and flew to Las Vegas to meet up with John Bobbitt, Aaron Gordon, and Jack Gordon at a restaurant at Caesar's Palace.

MARC CARRIERE: The reason Ron Jeremy brought that deal to me is that he has a strong sense of integrity. He could have gone to someone else with that deal, and he got a lot of shit for that. But he knows that by coming here, he could follow through with what he promised.

RON JEREMY: I was so excited to see John Wayne Bobbitt again—we got a picture, each of us holding a knife against our own crotches. He holds a knife on mine, I hold a knife on his. The waiters are going, "Oh, my God. Doesn't he hate jokes like that?" But John was a good sport. All the dick jokes, he didn't mind them at all.

And then they made a deal. Fifty thousand up front, thirty thousand upon completion of the movie. Then a big percentage—I think maybe fifty percent—after Marc Carriere recouped his money.

LARRY FURST: Leisure Time had just arranged to sell the Tonya Harding wedding night self-made porn tape through their giant mail-order division, and were eager to get Bobbitt on tape doing hard-core. The Gordons also reportedly dangled the carrot of perhaps getting LaToya to take some dick on-screen in the future.

RON JEREMY: So I got my day as a director. Other companies are pissed at me, including Arrow. Joe Garfinkel, my distant cousin, asked, "Why didn't you give the project to us, you scumbag bastard?" I said, "Look, Marc and I go back many, many years. Any other company would have simply thrown me a bone. Here's a finder's fee—get lost."

LARRY FURST: The production came together almost overnight. The crew was already calling him Forrest Gump behind his back and suffered through the first shots of the production, when John exhibited all the range of an air rifle. It didn't help that they picked a park in the flight line of Van Nuys airport to shoot exteriors during the busiest time of the day.

RON JEREMY: The shooting was very difficult.

LARRY FURST: Ron Jeremy instructed John Bobbitt in the famed "Hedgehog Pinch"—the technique Ron and other aging and/or failing fuck studs use to overstate their semi-erections. You grip the penis at the base and squeeze enough blood to stiffen the prick for the camera. Bobbitt followed instructions, almost hiding his dick between two fingers, Jasmine Aloha's two digits, and her ample lips.

JOHN WAYNE BOBBITT: How many cum shots did I do? It was four. It was something working with those three girls; I had never done anything like that before.

Some of this stuff was really hard to do—some guy with a camera is always right there, and there's the guys with the lights and the little thirty-five-millimeter cameras, too. I was melting from all the sweat.

Ron Jeremy really helped me; he's got a lot of experience. The producers, camera crew, and all the people were really professional, and we had a lot of fun.

RON JEREMY: I never admitted this before, but I might as well admit it now: We did use some medication at first.

John only got hard for one scene, where he worked with the same girl that was with the Heidi Fleiss documentary—Jordan St. James. She was the only girl he actually did a real hard-core scene with. With the other girls he needed a shot of Prostoglandin, which is an enzyme that gives you an automatic hard-on.

Did it work? Very well.

JOHN WAYNE BOBBITT: The nerves hadn't fully healed yet, so everything still felt different. Sometimes it's actually more intense, which makes it hard to do. But for the scenes I did in the movie it was pretty much under control.

CRYSTAL GOLD (PORN STAR): Let me go on record as saying that John Wayne Bobbitt can get his cock up very well. His cock is very useful, just like a normal man's dick. He gets very hard, and he came all over my tummy.

JOHN WAYNE BOBBITT: I'm not afraid of anything. Not after what I've been through. And I was fortunate enough to work with Jasmine Aloha. She got me comfortable, and it made it easy for me to lose my virginity in this area to her. She has a real Florence Nightingale complex, which I think is great. It really helped me a lot. I had this sort of posttraumatic stress disorder reaction to sex. But she and the other girls sure helped me through that situation.

JASMINE ALOHA (PORN STAR): I was dancing in Florida and had been in touch with Leisure Time about working for them. They called me up and wanted me to come in for this very special scene. I had no idea who the guy was at the time. They offered me good money, and I figured this would be good publicity for me so I decided to do it.

It took a really long time, but it was worth it in the end. John worked very hard the whole time and didn't quit for even a minute. John's also a nice guy. He amazed me with his abilities considering his situation. I have to give him a lot of credit.

RON JEREMY: *John Wayne Bobbitt: Uncut* would have been a really good fucking film, but the editor just screwed me royal. Never even looked at the editing notes. Did his own movie. Fucked me because I really did a good film. We got Lemmy from Motorhead to be the guy that discovers the dick in the park—lands on his foot. Motorhead—legendary band. And we had Vince Neil playing a bartender. And we reenacted Lorena Bobbitt with the knife.

JOHN WAYNE BOBBITT: Thinking of having it cut again was scary. You know, I never thought Lorena would do something like that. I certainly had some scary thoughts when I started doing my scene with Veronica Brazil. She asked me to stick my tongue in her mouth, and all I could think to say was, "Are you going to bite it off?"

VERONICA BRAZIL (PORN STAR): I played Lorena in the movie. I got the role because I'm a Latina and I'm very lucky and Marc Carriere likes me.

When I started to do the scene with John, I could tell he was very nervous. I told him that I wanted him to be passionate with me, and it was scaring him because I was showing him too much love. Even though I have to make like I'm cutting his penis off, you can't show that in an adult film. For me, the whole emotion is that I don't want him to ever be with anybody else again. I knew that if I killed him I would go to jail, but if I cut his dick off, I would probably get off. I think every woman can relate to that feeling.

And for me, I'm very jealous and possessive. I was shaking; my stomach felt very weird. I had the knife in my hand, and I wondered whether I would actually cut it off.

JOHN WAYNE BOBBITT: I'm pretty sure Lorena is upset. Veronica Brazil is from South America and so is Lorena. I think that is going to have an impact on her.

RON JEREMY: *John Wayne Bobbitt: Uncut* sold eighty thousand tapes worldwide. Biggest-selling film since *Deep Throat*. Marc Carriere actually got it screened at the Academy of Motion Pictures Arts and Sciences, and we gave the money toward Children of the Night, a benefit. We even had the party, I think, in the Steven Spielberg wing.

In fact, Eric Roberts came to the show, thinking it was a screening of *The Shawshank Redemption*. He sees it's a porn film and goes, "Oh my God." Starts walking out, but one of the photographers starts taking pictures of him, and Eric Roberts got so pissed that he punched one of the photographers. That was videotaped by *Hard Copy*—it shows the guy being a sore sport.

I had a lot of celebrities in that audience with me that night bigger than Eric Roberts. So Eric Roberts was being a big pussy.

Ding Dong, the Witch Is Dead

LOS ANGELES
1993–1994

BILL MARGOLD: Savannah was another overage juvenile delinquent that got caught up in the whirlpool of X. The performers need to be nurtured and worked with; they need to be taken and molded very slowly—like Seka or Marilyn Chambers—because fame is a barbed-wire treadmill. It's a very dangerous and vicious circle, and once you start feeling uneasy and fall off the center, you get chewed up anyway.

SAVANNAH: When I first got into the business, I was definitely a lot more bitchy than I am right now. And I'm glad I was because I've always gotten what I wanted, you know, as far as this business goes. I'm nice if you're nice to me.

JEANNA FINE: Me and Savannah had a falling out about a year before. You know, I've lost a lot of sleep over this, and I've had to come to some kind of peaceful place about it. She and I stopped talking, and I'd rather not go into why. She made an attempt to talk to me one time after that—at an award show—and I blew her off.

NANCY PERA: Jeanna and Savannah had broken up just after Savannah started at Vivid. Savannah would never talk about it, and I couldn't mention Jeanna to her. But Savannah finally said something about Jeanna having some drugs in Palm Springs, and they were doing heroin together, and Jeanna had the last of the heroin, and she wouldn't let Savannah have any. So Savannah left, and they never talked again. Of course, they tell a different story everywhere else.

RON JEREMY: Savannah was so unprofessional. She thought she had the whole world: "No one will ever fire me. I'm selling tapes." But she was too difficult to work with. She was the first girl in the history of the porn business to be fired from a company while she was still selling for them. That's unheard of. I mean, you could take a dump on the set, and we'd put up with it—as long as you were making money. But Vivid actually fired her. Paul Thomas couldn't stand it anymore.

NANCY PERA: Savannah got fired from Vivid right after she stopped being seen going out with Steve Hirsch. She said she just got bored with it and was sorry she started it in the beginning. Paul Thomas was sick of her. And one of the photographers called Steven and said he would never work with Savannah again because she'd walked out of a shoot.

Steven let her get away with murder; all the complaints would just roll off his back. Then, about a month after Savannah cut him off, he terminated Savannah's contract.

TOM BYRON: Savannah would be a little princess, you know? And she alienated people; she burned a lot of bridges. See, I didn't have to deal with her from a director's standpoint. I was just an actor. All I had to do was fuck her.

NANCY PERA: I became Savannah's "manager" after she left Vivid. Vivid would not give out Savannah's phone number to anyone, which stands to reason, so they started giving everyone my number. I started taking the messages, and I'd call her—and she was still on heroin, so if it was before noon she'd hang up on me. But eventually I'd get her, and we'd discuss it. She'd tell me what she wanted, what she'd do and how much she'd do it for, and I'd call them back. It just became a routine. I felt kind of motherly toward Savannah anyway.

RON JEREMY: After Vivid, she was able to tone down her bad behavior a little bit. Marc Carriere used her for a couple of jobs. John T. Bone used her for a *Starbanger* series—said she was a total angel. Very cooperative. I guess she wanted to prove a point—that Vivid should never have let her go.

JEANNA FINE: I ran for my life out of Hollywood. I had to get out. I moved down to San Diego. I got married and had a son, but I was still hearing things about Savannah. One night I said to my husband, "I'm going up to Hollywood next week, and I'm gonna find Shannon. I want to bring her here."

BUD LEE: Savannah had no respect for anybody. If she decided she'd rather not get out of bed this morning, she'd stay in bed—even if everyone on the set was waiting for her. The crews *hated* her.

And a lot of it was drugs—speed, heroin, cocaine. You know, whatever she could get.

RON JEREMY: Savannah would walk off the set in the middle of a shoot if there was a rock concert in town. She was doing a gig in Vegas right near the end—and this I heard right from the owner's mouth, Sam Ross, nice guy. She left the gig a few days early just because David Lee Roth was in town. She didn't even do the weekend crowd, which is the biggest one.

NANCY PERA: She met some asshole at the Paradise Club, and they kind of dated. He was married, and he was also seeing this older dancer with big tits—Venus Delight. Whenever Savannah danced at the club, they played footsie a little.

So Savannah and this guy were having dinner, and he said, "I got you tickets to see David Lee Roth Friday night." Savannah was all excited, but later on, when he was saying something about his wife, Savannah just said, "Why don't you just tell the bitch to shut up?" Well, he went ape-shit—said he wanted the tickets back. But Savannah went to the concert anyway.

The next day, Saturday, she went in to dance for the early show, and all her signs were down—she'd been replaced by Venus Delight. So Savannah got pissed off and drove back to Los Angeles.

For a while, it was just one thing after the other for Savannah. She'd call me in hysterics or come by my house every day.

RON JEREMY: Savannah totally screwed this club over, so naturally they held back her pay entirely. They were so mad, they just told her to get lost, get out, good-bye. The club owner said that out of the goodness of his heart he would have eventually mailed her a check for the work she did do because she had danced there Monday, Tuesday, Wednesday. But she destroyed him with his crowd when she skipped the weekend. I mean, they *advertise*.

NINA HARTLEY: Someone who knew Savannah very well said that she aspired to be a groupie. I mean, if you're looking for your sense of validation from people who cannot possibly provide it. . . . Hollywood just does not have a poor, young starlet's best interests at heart! Don't hold porn to a different standard from Hollywood. *Puh-leeze!*

VINCE NEIL: Savannah asked me to be her date to the *Adult Video News* awards. I told her I'd go with her but at the last minute blew her off for another girl.

NANCY PERA: I went out of town for a couple of days, and when I got back Savannah came over and said, "You told me you'd call me as soon as you got home!" I said, "I've only been home an hour or two. Geez." She'd just gotten a copy of the House of Pain video she was in. She played it for me twice; she was all jazzed. She was real cute. Then she said, "Well, I gotta run. I'll talk to you later." I saw she had a bottle of wine. I said, "Be careful, and put that in the trunk."

And she said, "Yeah, Mom. Sure." You know, that kind of attitude. The next time I heard from her was when she had the accident.

JEANNA FINE: I really feel that she just needed to hold a baby and change some diapers and be with regular people.

NANCY PERA: So I'm driving up to Savannah's house, and as I'm turning up off of Cahuenga, I see the paramedics at the bottom of the street. Then I see the fence she hit, and I said, "Oh, my God. This is serious." Everything kind of went into slo-mo. I pulled into her long driveway, and the housesitter is standing there—the guy who walked the dog. He had his white T-shirt pulled up into his mouth, chewing it.

He asked, "Who are you?"

I said, "I'm Nancy."

He said, "Oh, thank God you're here. Savannah just shot herself."

I said, "Oh, my God."

He said, "I just called 911."

And so I said, "They're down at the bottom of the hill—that's gotta be the fire truck—I'll go get them. They can't find the place."

BILL MARGOLD: Savannah committed suicide on July 11, 1994. Supposedly, the morning she died, she'd run into a fence and hurt herself a little bit and that was enough to push her over the brink.

VINCE NEIL: She disfigured herself in a car crash, went home, pulled out a Beretta, and shot herself in the head.

She had a lot of other problems in her life then, and I knew the reason wasn't because I stood her up—but I still felt terrible.

NANCY PERA: He said Savannah was still alive, so I just whipped the car around and went back down the hill to get the cops. The truck was coming up and the police car was behind it, and I said, "Follow me up." The cop wouldn't let me leave until I gave him my driver's license, which I threw at him. I turned around and led them up.

I hopped out before they had gotten parked or anything. I went running in, and the kid said, "She's over there." I looked, and I kept staring because he said, "nine-one-one said to put a blanket on her, and I couldn't find any, so I put towels." So here's this pile of towels, with this huge lake of blood around them. And I just lost it.

JEANNA FINE: My friend Chi Chi Larue called me crying and told me what happened. I just kind of instantly knew the second I heard his voice—he didn't even have to tell me.

NANCY PERA: I followed the gurney as they put Savannah into the ambulance. I tried to crawl in with her, but they wouldn't let me. Savannah gurgled something—they said she was trying to say something to me—but I just kept yelling, "Stay with us, Shannon!"

So they detained me. I mean, forty cops had already interviewed me, and by this time it was about three in the morning. Every time this one detective came through, I kept asking about Savannah, and he said, "She's stable. There's no news."

Finally he came back in. I said, "Well?" and he said, "She's passed away." This was, like, four or five in the morning. At six-thirty, they finally let me go. I thought she was dead.

TOM BYRON: Henri Pachard called me and said, "Hear about Savannah? She just shot herself."

I was like, "Awww, that sucks." I felt bad, but I was nothing more than a casual acquaintance. I fuckin' dunno, man—if you have a gun, and you're in the right frame of mind at the right time, you know what I'm saying? I mean, I think we've all been there.

NANCY PERA: About one o'clock on Monday afternoon, a reporter called me and said, "Why aren't you at the hospital?"

I said, "What do you mean? She's dead."

He said, "No, she's still alive." So I hung up on him and called the hospital. I thought she was going to be okay.

But when I talked to her dad, he wouldn't let me come down. I didn't know it, but they were just authorizing the hospital to pull the plug.

BILL MARGOLD: I was called at nine in the morning and told she was dead, when in fact she didn't die until eleven-thirty. And people—to be honest with you—were already celebrating her death. You know, "Hail, hail, the witch is dead."

Savannah was not loved—and she went out of her way not to be loved—by this business.

JEANNA FINE: She had broken her nose. The car was wrecked, and I know what was going through her mind. "Oh shit! How am I gonna get out of this? I have no money; I can't go make the money. The car is wrecked. They're gonna be pissed. I have to cancel the show. There's no way out."

But I really feel that when she pulled that trigger—she must have thought, right that second, "Oops," you know? Because Savannah could be so impulsively destructive, and then afterward she'd be like, "Hello! Why did I do that?"

HENRI PACHARD: Savannah blows herself away because she probably woke up and said to herself, "What's the big deal?"

And that's too bad. I mean, she never gave herself a chance, you know? Because she felt lonely and unloved? Fuck, man, I've felt lonely and unloved lots of times. But the last thing I'd do is off myself, you know? If you live to be over a hundred, you're gonna feel lonely and unloved because who the fuck loves anybody over a hundred? Nobody, ha, ha, ha.

BRYN BRIDENTHAL (PUBLICIST): I mean, Slash's reaction was sort of, "Savannah offed herself? That's too bad."

HENRI PACHARD: I never saw that much to her in the first place. Everyone's going crazy about this girl, Savannah. Big fucking deal; she looked to me like an old junkie—you know, with store-bought tits and long, straight, white hair. What's the big deal?

RON JEREMY: She just had a bloody nose, right? Well, put that together with drugs, being penniless, getting fired from a job. See, this I did learn in school—that when everything hits you at once, you start to feel like you have nowhere to go.

Savannah had a very bad social life. I mean, she had a friend at the time—a roadie for that band House of Pain—but the fact of the matter was, she had no money, and she must have known she'd fucked up.

So she's pissed off, gets into a car accident, and now her face is marked. Interesting, huh? Now she looks like all those girls she used to make fun of.

NANCY PERA: I mean, the postscript on this is horrible. Savannah's dad—whom she hated—ended up getting all of her stuff, and her mom tried to sue Gregg Allman for wrongful death because they wanted money.

TOM BYRON: I dunno—if Nancy Pera had gotten there before, or the House of Pain guy hadn't taken the dog out—circumstances beyond your fucking control. And Savannah was drunk, probably coked-out, heroin, whatever. Her nose is all broken; she's looking at her fucked-up face. She had no money. She's got this big dance gig she's not gonna be able to do. How's she gonna pay her rent? "OH, FUCK IT! BAM!"

If the gun hadn't been there, it wouldn't have happened. The industry didn't kill her. She killed herself.

HENRI PACHARD: I talked about it with a lot of people, but I never really talked one-on-one to any of the girls about why they got into the business. I suppose I was in my own form of denial. If I said, "Why are you doing this?" they might interpret that as, "Do you want me to quit and move in with you?" Because that happened a lot, ha ha ha. A lot of guys on both sides of the camera would get involved with a performer and make her stop being a performer—and they'd be only too glad to stop.

BILL MARGOLD: The day that she died is the day I said there'd be no more Savannahs.

Luckily, her death propelled an organization called PAW—Protecting Adult Welfare—into existence. I couldn't allow any more of these things to happen. Of course they have and they'll continue to because a lot of these people aren't prepared to come into the meat grinder of X—they're ground up, and they're not cared for.

To be honest with you, this is a business where the three most important letters should be H-U-G. You should hug these kids. But most people would sooner fuck 'em.

NINA HARTLEY: Not to make light of the deaths and other suicides as well, but I do not blame porn for their deaths—and who's to blame for suicide?

BILL MARGOLD: I'm really not interested in fucking these girls. I wanna hold them; I wanna protect them from themselves. Because they become famous so fast, and they don't know what fame's all about. They suck it up through their noses, they shoot it into their veins, they become polluted by it, they worry about it, and then, perhaps, they kill themselves over it because they're afraid their fame is going to dissipate. I think Savannah was a case of that.

VINCE NEIL: Most of the girls in her line of work are gold-diggers, but Savannah was never like that. She just wanted somebody to love her.

Caught

CLEVELAND/LOS ANGELES/CHICAGO
1993–1995

ROGER YOUNG: When Reuben Sturman escaped from Boron Prison, Richard Rosfelder and I were flown in to Los Angeles. We met with the federal marshals and brainstormed about all the relatives, all the associates, the money, who he knew, what was going on . . . everything.

REUBEN STURMAN: I would've been free and clear if I'd not gone to see my family. I just couldn't see myself leaving for Europe or Asia—I wouldn't want them to be on the run with me.

ROGER YOUNG: They caught Reuben in a hotel near Disneyland, with a loaded .45 and a briefcase with close to thirty thousand dollars next to his bed.

CHICAGO TRIBUNE, **APRIL 2, 1994: DEFENDANT CONVICTED IN EXTORTION ATTEMPT:** "After deliberating less than two hours Friday, a federal jury convicted Herbert 'Mickey' Feinberg of hiring four men to damage and bomb several Chicago adult bookstores in April 1992 in an attempt to extort payoffs for a powerful pornography distributor."

ROGER YOUNG: I asked Reuben, "When you fled Boron Prison on December seventh—Pearl Harbor Day—why didn't you go right to the airport? You know, you had a plan: People gave you the gun and the money. Why didn't you just take off?"

Reuben said, "Because that's the first place I thought you guys would be looking for me."

CHUCK BERNSTENE: Mickey Feinberg owed me eighteen thousand bucks; they told me to forget about it. Meaning, you know, walk away. Which I didn't take too well. I said, "I'm not happy about this."

But Mickey got his in the end. What happened? Conspiracy to commit murder. Yeah, and I think he's still in jail today.

CHICAGO SUN-TIMES, DECEMBER 10, 1994: EXTORTIONIST SENTENCED: "Herbert 'Mickey' Feinberg has been sentenced to 40 years in prison for his role in an extortion bombing scheme involving peep shows that resulted in the death of one man. Feinberg, 63, of Los Angeles was sentenced here this week to 30 years for the bombing charge and a 10-year sentence for extortion."

CHUCK BERNSTENE: So Mickey gets charged with conspiracy to commit murder and ends up doing life, ha, ha, ha.

CHICAGO SUN-TIMES, DECEMBER 10, 1994: EXTORTIONIST SENTENCED: "Feinberg and Reuben Sturman, the self-acknowledged godfather of pornographic peep shows, were accused of a 1992 plot of hiring thugs to blow up two Chicago adult bookstores because owners would not pay higher film rates."

ROGER YOUNG: When Reuben was caught I was flown to Chicago because he had convinced the FBI Strike Force that—for a deal—he would give them all this intelligence about organized crime and pornography. He was gonna lay it all out.

Turn, yeah.

RICHARD ROSFELDER: The bulk of my eighteen-year career in the IRS was spent on Reuben Sturman and Sturman-related cases.

ROGER YOUNG: I go with the Chicago case agent over to the holding cell where they had Sturman to pick him up.

Reuben says, "Hey, kid, what are you doing here?"

I said, "Well, heard you were gonna tell all."

He goes, "Thought I'd never see you again."

So we handcuff Reuben and take him over to the Strike Force offices at the Justice Department.

REUBEN STURMAN: Robert DiBernardo was one of my customers. I knew DiBernardo as a business acquaintance, not as a friend. He seemed to be a nice fellow.

ROGER YOUNG: I am convinced that Reuben was gonna try to scam a young Strike Force attorney and an agent who really didn't know all about him and his profile. That's why the agent said, "Roger, we better have you come in here."

So we sat and talked, went over the whole thing, and really nothing came up that we didn't already know. DiBe came up—oh yes, absolutely. And going to Fort Lauderdale for a sit-down with Ettore Zappi, and paying this debt he welched on to one of the Gambino stores.

REUBEN STURMAN: I didn't know Robert DiBernardo was in organized crime for the first ten years we did business. His two partners were Jewish. His first wife was Jewish. His second wife was Jewish. His kids went to Hebrew school. I really thought he was Jewish—until I had my eyes opened.

But that had nothing to do with me, anyway. Gotti's people shot him, and he disappeared from the face of the earth.

ROGER YOUNG: Reuben confirmed that DiBe was his contact in organized crime. He confirmed what Jimmy "The Weasel" Frattiano told me—that Sturman was already taken by DiBe.

Here's the wealthiest, most prolific producer/distributor of pornography in the history of the world—and none of the other families could really go after him because DiBe already claimed him, already had him under control.

RICHARD ROSFELDER: I spent the next three years, until I retired, investigating the escape, the jury tampering, the bribery, and put a lot more people in prison.

ROGER YOUNG: Reuben said, "It's too bad. I really liked DiBe. He was a nice guy."

I said, "Well, uh, you know, how'd it happen?"

He says, "Mob. Just the way they do things. That's their business."

NAOMI DELGADO: Reuben said he would lose the case without my help. He wanted me to offer a bribe of twenty-five thousand dollars to this one particular juror, and if the bribe didn't work, I should do whatever it took to sway him.

UNITED STATES COURT OF APPEALS FOR THE SIXTH CIRCUIT; FILED JULY 14, 1995: "In November 1989, near the end of Sturman's trial, defendant Naomi Delgado was observed in court staring at Hofstetter [a juror] and winking at him. During a recess at the trial, defendant sent Hofstetter a note, bearing a lipstick imprint, that invited him to join 'another person' at a suburban restaurant that evening."

NAOMI DELGADO: Reuben had never asked anything of me before. Never in my life. The juror was in the middle of the first row. I just remember looking over, and he was staring right at me.

CRAIG MORFORD (ASSISTANT U.S. ATTORNEY): We had a fifteen-year investigation, a ten-week trial, and it almost comes crashing down over dinner and drinks at the Pier W restaurant.

UNITED STATES COURT OF APPEALS FOR THE SIXTH CIRCUIT; FILED JULY 14, 1995: "Hofstetter went to the restaurant in hopes that the note had come from the 'sexy-looking woman' in court. He and the defendant had dinner that evening.

"During the meal, the defendant mentioned that she was with the Sturman party, but did not say she was Sturman's wife. Hofstetter stated that the defendant repeatedly mentioned the trial and insisted Hofstetter vote for Sturman's acquittal. After dinner, while Sturman's driver drove the two home, the defendant made physical advances to Hofstetter, which Hofstetter stated he rejected."

REUBEN STURMAN: I begged and pleaded with Naomi. I told her, "If I have a chance to get out of this, we've got to take it." I was willing to take that chance.

ROGER YOUNG: I don't know if an act was actually consummated.

UNITED STATES COURT OF APPEALS FOR THE SIXTH CIRCUIT; FILED JULY 14, 1995: "Hofstetter failed to inform the court or any other jurors about the contact with defendant. The jury subsequently voted to convict Sturman. This scheme remained secret until a secretary employed by defendant and Sturman informed the government in June 1992."

NAOMI DELGADO: The verdict was guilty on all counts. I felt totally responsible.

REUBEN STURMAN: Okay, I tampered with the jury. Very badly, in fact. They want me and everyone around me. I'm surprised they didn't indict my six-year-old kid. I beat these guys sixteen ways from Sunday, every one of them. They all hated me like poison because they could never win.

RICHARD ROSFELDER: There were also allegations that Reuben tried to bribe the judge. If Reuben thought he could have done himself any good by offering me a big bribe, he wouldn't have hesitated to try. But for some reason he just didn't choose to go that route.

REUBEN STURMAN: Rosfelder's a horrible man. He lied to the federal government. He lied to the Swiss government. He lied to everyone.

RICHARD ROSFELDER: Maybe Reuben figured it was kind of a battle between me and him. He may not have figured that if he could get the case derailed by dealing with somebody else, then he'd win.

ROGER YOUNG: I started on the Reuben Sturman case in December 1982. Then Sturman went away, was convicted in 1993. Escaped, and went back to prison, facing more charges. Now he had an escape from prison charge, trying to bribe a juror and trying to bribe a judge.

Things didn't look good for Reuben.

CLEVELAND PLAIN DEALER, MAY 29, 1995: LAWYER'S TRIAL TO STAR PORN KING STURMAN AS WITNESS FOR FEDS. "During his thirty years as the king of the pornography business, Reuben Sturman infuriated police, FBI agents and prosecutors with his arrogance and his ability to beat obscenity charges.

"But in a trial that opens tomorrow in U.S. District Court, Sturman will be the star witness for the prosecution.

"He is expected to testify that Cleveland attorney Sanford I. Atkin bilked him out of $550,000 by claiming he could bribe U.S. District Judge George W. White, who presided over Sturman's 1989 tax trial in Cleveland."

ROGER YOUNG: In all of Sturman's trials, I basically wanted to know, could he get to the judge? Because here you have somebody who, twelve different times in his career, was arrested for obscenity and was never, ever successfully convicted of interstate transportation of obscene matter.

CLEVELAND PLAIN DEALER MAY 29, 1995: LAWYER'S TRIAL TO STAR PORN KING STURMAN AS WITNESS FOR FEDS: "The FBI and Internal Revenue Service investigated Sturman's charges for nearly two years before indicting Atkin last fall on charges of obstructing justice, fraud, money-laundering and tax evasion.

"Atkin, 63, of Moreland Hills, has denied telling Sturman he could bribe White. In interviews and court filings, his attorneys have said the money Atkin got from Sturman was for legitimate legal fees. They contend Sturman hired Atkin to prepare a challenge to his tax conviction. The appeal was supposed to argue that Sturman's trial attorney, J. Michael Murray, made mistakes in his defense.

REUBEN STURMAN: I didn't think Sanford Atkin was much of an attorney.

CLEVELAND PLAIN DEALER, MAY 29, 1995: LAWYER'S TRIAL TO STAR PORN KING STURMAN AS WITNESS FOR FEDS: "Assistant U.S. Attorney Craig S. Morford and Michael Attanasio, a trial lawyer from the Justice Department's public integrity section, have said in court filings that the $550,000 that Atkins maintained Sturman paid him in legal fees is 'grossly disproportionate to the compensation he typically earned from bona fide clients.'

"'Reuben feels that he's been a victim in this,' said Adam Bourgeois, Sturman's Chicago-based attorney. 'Money was taken from him, and when he asked for it to be returned, the guy wouldn't give it back.'"

ROGER YOUNG: Oh, there's no question that Sturman gave the money to Atkin to try to get it to Judge White.

***CLEVELAND PLAIN DEALER*, JUNE 22, 1995: COURT NAILS LAWYERS FOR PORN KING:** "'I think we're finally at the end of the road,' said Assistant U.S. Attorney Craig S. Morford, who has spent much of his eight years with the U.S. Justice Department prosecuting Sturman and his associates."

REUBEN STURMAN: I was a businessman. I didn't see pornography as good. I didn't see it as bad. It was just a product to be sold. You want to know how the industry started? Well, you're looking at the person who started it. No one was anywhere near me. In the world. I was the biggest in the world, and there will never be another.

BILL KELLY: Reuben Sturman is deceased as of October 27, 1997, in federal prison in Manchester, Kentucky. Edward Joseph Wedelstedt is Reuben's successor on most of the businesses. He's probably the number one guy in the country.

If he's not, Kenny Guarino is. And if not Guarino, then it's Harry Virgil Mohney, who owns that Deja Vu chain of strip clubs—who's also a major pornographer. They're probably the top three guys in the country.

REUBEN STURMAN: I had a wonderful life. If I die tomorrow I'm going to die with a smile on my lips.

Waiting for Wood

LOS ANGELES
1995

HENRI PACHARD: I had returned from my thirty-fifth high school reunion when I showed up in Las Vegas for the VSDA show. Someone says, "Henri, there's a party goin' on in suite such-and-such."

So I went up to the party, and the place is packed with the porn industry. And this person yells out my name from all the way across this big hotel suite. "HENRI PACHARD, WHY DON'T YOU EVER CAST ME?"

It was Cal Jammer.

"You never call," I said, cleverly, instead of the truth: "You have dick problems." I didn't want to embarrass him.

TIM CONNELLY: Cal Jammer was about five foot eight, had light to medium brown hair—which he bleached blond a lot—and looked like a rugged surfer type with an acne-scarred face, like Jan-Michael Vincent.

Cal photographed real well up close because he looked a little pockmarked and tinted and a little ravaged from the sun. But you could tell he wasn't going to age well because of his features. But he had really beautiful blue eyes. Striking blue, sharp, with a gleam in them. And he had a decent body. He had that whole West Coast porn star look down.

But he was white trash, you know? I think he was from Valencia, California.

HENRI PACHARD: I'm known around the world as a very nice guy in the porno business; everybody likes Henri Pachard. So when Cal Jammer asked, "Henri, why don't you like me?" the answer was, "Because you don't wanna be liked, you asshole, or you wouldn't act the way you act."

How could he ask me such a humiliating question in front of a thousand other people? So he can hear, "Because you have a poor penis?"

TIM CONNELLY: When I met Cal, he was always comparing himself to other guys, and he'd try to make a point of stating what he thought his better performances were. Cal felt like he was always underestimated, and it seemed very obvious that he had no self-esteem.

HENRI PACHARD: I worked with Cal a couple times, and he was terrible. He had dick problems, and it was never his fault. When you're shooting video, the guy doesn't have a fluffer anymore—a person down there dedicated to sucking your dick to get you hard. You jock your dick up, and you stay there. I mean, like all the top-of-the-line guys, the pros, stay ready.

TIM CONNELLY: The problem with a guy like Cal Jammer was that when he gets into the business—because he's a new guy—people want to use him. But if you have an average-size cock, that's actually a small cock in the porn business. So eventually they always would rather hire the bigger cock. Doesn't matter if the guy looks retarded or acts retarded. If he's got the bigger cock, he's gonna get the gig.

HENRI PACHARD: A lot of the actors that can't get it up will get right up in your face and tell you how well they've double fucked some girl with some other guy, and it's usually a DP—a double penetration—which is the hardest thing to do for most male performers.

There's a little, thin piece of skin between a woman's vagina and her anus, and it heats up. You have to be able to feel it. Now DPs, we shoot a lot of them. But how many people in the world have DPs in their personal lives? I mean, I've had a lot of sex, but I can't raise my hand to this. I've never experienced a DP. I've never had the desire.

I don't think most men are physically able to do the old DP. It doesn't happen that much in the real world—it's a freak show. You can't get a good angle unless you get really close up—you know, stretch this, stretch that. If you can get ten good seconds of it, you're doing well. It's very sweaty and nasty, and it's very difficult to shoot.

TIM CONNELLY: Cal fucked like an eighteen-year-old kid, you know? He just seemed like a lemming, you know, running to the sea. It seemed like he was jack-rabbiting every time he fucked. No finesse. Later on, he got okay; he became a good model for stills.

HENRI PACHARD: So these guys complain that they don't get booked, but when it comes to DPs they do their own selling: "Let me tell you about the time me and this guy DP'd this girl!" And they're not lying—they probably *were* great. They got their dick in that girl's ass, and they were wonderful at it—because it felt so good to rub their dick against another guy's dick, and they didn't even know it.

I said, "I'm happy for you." I tell them they could be out making gay movies.

He'd say, "I don't do that."

I'd say, "All right."

I mean, this is an identity crisis they're in. They want me to feel sorry for them and give them money for their failures because they cannot accept their sexuality, and they're half my age. What am I gonna do, guide them? "Son, it's time you just accepted your proclivities. . . ."

That's not my job.

TIM CONNELLY: Cal met Adrianna Moore—who is now Jill Kelly—at a strip club in San Bernardino called the Tropical Lay. She was a stripper who was doing porno movies and some girl/girl stuff—she started around 1993 or 1994, and she was very selective about the work she did.

I found Jill very attractive. She hadn't had any of the surgery—the boob job, or the liposuction, or the nose job. Don't get me wrong, she's beautiful now. It's just that back then she looked very natural and real. She had this sort of doe-eyed innocence about her.

JILL KELLY: I was fifteen the first time I danced naked. I was nervous, but they, of course, thought I was of age. Then I broke up with my then-boyfriend because I was making money. So he called them up and told them. My name was Angel then; they said, "Angel, can you bring in your ID?"

I'm like, "Yeah, sure." Of course I never went back until years later when I was over eighteen—and they didn't even recognize me.

I did live sex shows with Tiffany Million in San Francisco at the O'Farrell Theater. Then, a year later, she called and told me she was doing adult, and said she wanted me to be her date to the awards show, which I did. And when I watched the porn stars come in, they had a line of people waiting for them. They didn't have to work and beg for dances every time. I thought, I could do that.

That's the weekend I met my first husband. His name was Cal Jammer.

TIM CONNELLY: Cal and Jill hit it off and started working together. Cal was trying to promote her as this girl he was with, who was now going to do other guys. When I ran into him at the *AVN* Awards in 1995, Cal acted like Jill was just this chick he was trying to help out.

I had just broken up with Kimberly Carson—after ten years—and it was the first time I was sort of back out in the field. And there I was in Las Vegas, and Jill was being a little flirtatious with me. And I thought, "Hey, I like her. She's not your typical porn star."

Cal was like, "Tim is the guy from Adam Film World, and he can really help you out." I made a point of saying that I'd seen her in some films, and I was interested in her and, you know, "Is she in, or is she out?" I was kind of curious about Jill—and Cal was sort of throwing her at me.

JILL KELLY: Me and Tiffany were gambling at one of those bars in Vegas. Cal was across the way, and he smiled at me. Later on Tiffany and I were at the bar, and I met him. I didn't even know he was an adult film star. It was like instant chemistry. It was kind of weird, you know? Cal was very sweet and kind of dorky, but you could tell he had a really good heart.

And of course he was going to help me get into the business, and you know, all that kind of good stuff.

HENRI PACHARD: I think there was an attraction that lasted about an hour with Jill and Cal. Cal was obsessed with her—but he'd gone through five other girls that he'd brought into the business. You know, "She only does scenes with me"—until eventually they would wise up and go work with everybody. Then Cal would find another girl.

He just ran outta girls.

TIM CONNELLY: When I started talking to Jill, I could feel there was a chemistry between us, at that moment—however fleeting or unimportant or unreal it was.

Then Cal started pulling me aside, saying, "Hey, you know, I don't know how to deal with this. You've been married to porn stars. I'm with her now, and I'm trying to help her out, but I don't know how I feel about her doing scenes with guys, and we're kind of together, and we're talking about getting married."

HENRI PACHARD: Who knows what happened? Jill Kelly's got a lot of money. What the fuck was she doing with this guy? She needed him like she needed a third tit.

JILL KELLY: Cal was a really supersweet guy, and later on I noticed that people took advantage of that fact. People would tease him, you know? Get real hard on him.

TIM CONNELLY: So I came up with some sort of therapy speech for Cal because I had just come out of therapy myself. He said, "Oh my God, you have no idea how much you've touched me. This is what I need to hear. Can I call you?"

I handed him my business card.

He said, "No, I have your office number. Can I call you at home?"

I asked, "For what?"

He said, "To talk about problems like this. You seem to know what to do. This is fucking my head up. I'm not getting any work, and I'm real jealous, and it's causing all this strain. We fight all the time."

JILL KELLY: Cal had a hard problem with, um, getting a hard-on. Of course, no one can stand that. It made it tough for him to get work, and it was tough on him emotionally—personally, you know? He was extremely insecure.

HUMPHRY KNIPE: I've seen a guy cry when he couldn't get it up. It's so humiliating. The whole set, everyone's sitting there: "Oh fuck, I wanna go home. I wanna get paid." The girl's humiliated because she can't get the guy up; she's worn her lipstick tube to the bone trying to get him hard. And the more worried he gets, the worse it gets.

I mean, if you don't have penetration and a cum shot, then you don't have a movie. It's a lot of pressure, and it can get pretty sordid.

Of course, this is before Viagra.

HENRI PACHARD: Cal liked feeling other guys' dicks alongside his. What's wrong with that? Is it such a bad thing that you feel you have to hide behind some stripper girlfriend who's gonna dump you in a minute? Why would someone set themselves up to fall like that?

JILL KELLY: After a month, Cal and I got married—which was the first mistake. I was twenty-one.

We were together for, gosh, like three months when I finally decided, "Okay, I'm ready to do movies." Because I'd been too chicken. Then Cal said, "I don't want you to."

Cal had always told me, "If you get into the business, you'll become a big star and forget about me." And I was so madly in love with him, I said, "That's impossible." Whatever. So I didn't get into the business.

But then I found out that he was cheating on me, off camera. That was the deal breaker. Because it's one thing when you're doing it for work and another thing to actually have some intimate time with somebody else.

TIM CONNELLY: Cal is saying all of this, and I just looked at him and said, "Look, dude, you can't have my home phone number. Call me at the office when you get back to town. I'll give you the number of my fucking therapist. I can't deal with these kinds of fucking problems."

Cal said, "That's what I needed to hear."

At that moment I look back at Jill Kelly, and she seemed to be completely shut down. I think because she realized whatever was happening at that moment was a little more than she could deal with, emotionally.

Cal never did call me.

JILL KELLY: I was okay with Cal doing movies, but the one thing I wasn't okay with was him lying to me. Because, you know, going out to dinner with somebody and holding their hand is more intimate than actually having sex with them. At least that's what I used to think.

So Cal and I were separated for a couple of months. Then we got back together, and it became even worse. Cal would make all these promises not to cheat and would never deliver. And I was supposed to stop my life and wait for him. I finally got tired of it, and I left him again.

RON JEREMY: I don't know why I can't forecast these things. They always told me in school how to look for the warning signs. I never saw it in Cal Jammer, that this guy was this unhappy—and that hurt me because I was kind of close to him.

JILL KELLY: Throughout our whole marriage—even in the beginning—Cal used to fake like he was going to kill himself. One time he was laying in the hallway with a gun—which wasn't even a gun; it was a pellet gun or a BB gun or something like that—and he was faking it. He pulled that stuff all the time.

TIM CONNELLY: People were like, "Wow, you were really harsh on Cal."

I was like, "Hey, fuck him! This self-serving asshole is just trying to promote some chick he's banging, and he's throwing her at me, and then all of a sudden he's jealous and insecure and defensive and worried and paranoid, and I throw out some low-level fucking therapy platitude at him, and suddenly he wants my home number and wants permission to call me twenty-four hours a day to talk about his 'issues.'"

I just thought the only thing I could do with a guy like that is give him the number of my therapist. Because there's no way I can fucking help him because he's just pissing me off because he's being a complete idiot.

He just seemed way too fucked up for me.

JILL KELLY: I'd been at the Sherman Oaks Galleria, and I was driving through Laurel Canyon. Cal was on the phone, going on and on. I'm the kind of person who is strong on the phone, but as soon as I see the person, I melt. So I knew I didn't want to see him. And he was like, "I'm coming over there right now."

By this time I was home. So I said, "No, I'm leaving."

Cal was like, "If you don't see me, you're going to find me dead on your doorstep." Of course, I was like, "Yeah, you know, *whatever.*" Called my mom, and called my best friend, and they were like, "Don't listen to him. He pulls shit like this all the time."

HENRI PACHARD: I'm a lousy fuck on camera, and I'm a lousy fuck *off* camera. What's the big deal? I'm not gonna kill myself over it!

But Cal wasn't getting enough bookings to keep up with his lifestyle. And poverty is just nature's way of telling a man he's in the wrong line of work. I mean, if you're broke all the time, it's time to change jobs.

JILL KELLY: I had never been scared of Cal, but for some reason—I don't know why—I was scared. And Buck Adams called me and said, "Get out of the house."

And I'm like, "Why?"

Buck was like, "He's coming there to kill you and kill himself."

And I was just like, I totally would never expect that. So I just acted like I wasn't there—because I didn't want to see Cal—because then I'd melt and say, "Whatever you want."

And then I heard this big crash. I thought it was a broken window.

But it was a gunshot.

TIM CONNELLY: Apparently Cal had called her on the cell phone; there was a trail of people Cal called on his way to Jill's. And when he got to her apartment, she wouldn't answer the door. I heard he was screaming at the window for her—and then he shot himself.

JILL KELLY: I waited a few minutes. Then, finally, I said, "Fuck it. I'm going out there." I locked my house up, walked down the steps, and there was Cal, lying in the gutter. It was sprinkling, and I'm just like, "Get up." And I laughed because I totally thought he was just like . . . I'm like, "Give me a break," you know?

Then, all of a sudden, you realize—when I first saw the blood, I thought it was from the magic store. And I saw part of his brain, and I thought it was, like, a chewed-up hot dog. But I went to nursing school, so I'm listening and looking for a pulse, and I felt nothing. I lifted up his sweater, thinking, "He can't hold his breath that long." Your mind just plays all these tricks on you.

RON JEREMY: Cal had always been insecure. But to go to his girlfriend's house and threaten to kill her and then blow his own brains out—why couldn't I have seen it?

JILL KELLY: The last thing Cal told me was, "It's the story of the boy who cried wolf." And I swear to God, I didn't know what that story was until after he died.

HENRI PACHARD: There was an awful lot of talk about Cal. There was a big article written about it in the *New Yorker* by this girl Susan Faludi. I still got her card somewhere. She interviewed me; she interviewed a lot of people. She was kind of cool, but she seemed really scared because she took her assignment so seriously. Anyway, Cal killed himself while she was in the middle of her story. Susan probably got a phone call from the *New Yorker*, "Write about this Cal Jammer kid. Randy Potes."

"Why?"

"The guy killed himself."

"So?"

"He was a porno actor."

"Cool."

"You know, just rewrite, change everything."

Then the whole article became about Cal's suicide, ha, ha, ha.

JILL KELLY: What about the rumor that I had a guy in the house? Oh, my God, that's the funniest thing in the whole fucking world. I swear on my life, I was the most loyal person—I'd had only slept with three guys in my whole life before then, but many girls. I'd heard rumors that I was a big swinger. It was so retarded. It was just insane to hear some of that shit.

There's so much that I will never, ever tell. I'll take to my fucking grave what really happened with Cal. Let them say whatever they want, you know?

TIM CONNELLY: Cal was like a lot of guys in the business. They're attracted to the girls in the business because they're very sexual, open, outgoing women. Then you connect with one of them, and you have something a little bit deeper, and suddenly they can't be a stripper; they can't be a porn star. I mean, I went through it myself.

JILL KELLY: Cal's cousin did not like me from the get-go. When we got married, she would ask about his ex-girlfriend right in front of me, you know? But she and his little brother came up to me at the funeral and said, "You know, Cal was bound to do it. If it wasn't with you, it was gonna be somebody else. It was just a matter of time." But most of Cal's family treated me like I was the reason he did it. And his family took everything that Cal and I worked for.

People in the industry were hard on me. And at that time, honestly, I was like a zombie. It was like I didn't care. All I cared about was making money and getting things for my family—because I was gonna kill myself. I couldn't live with the guilt. I was just making sure everybody was secure. It was really weird. But I guess the thing that helped me was that the harder people were on me, the more I tried.

HENRI PACHARD: Susan Faludi wanted to go to Cal's funeral. So I picked her up, took her to the funeral, and she met all these porno people—guys and girls and wannabes. You know, "Hey, let's go to Cal's funeral!"

The only reason I went was that Susan wanted to go. But about half of the industry was at that funeral, as if they felt some call. I mean, *all of a sudden.* Nobody particularly liked working with Cal because they knew it was gonna be a slow process. Yet they showed up, out of some kind of defiance. "We gotta do this—stand up and be counted for. This is one of our own."

There'd always been a girl that killed herself, but there'd never been a guy before. Maybe that's why all the guys showed up, from the beginners to the old veterans. It touched them close to home. It's interesting—that never came up.

I don't remember that being in the *New Yorker,* either.

Going to Extremes

LOS ANGELES
1996–1997

SHARON MITCHELL: I was practicing a gig at a local titty bar, making a few bucks. I liked performing at this club; I was really having a good time. It was run by some biker gang, and the bouncer would walk you to your car. So that night he walked me to my car, but I had forgotten my stash—I was still using dope. I went back in the club, and on the way out he said, "Do you want me to walk you out again?"

I said "No, that's okay."

And there was a guy out in the parking lot. He said, "Hey lady, do you want some money?"

He was from the Escondido nightclub down the street. He thought I was a hooker, you know? He knew my name and everything; he had seen the show.

TRICIA DEVERAUX (PORN STAR): I grew up in a small town a couple hours outside of Chicago. I was brought up very strict. I wasn't allowed to date. I wasn't allowed to go out with friends. I was very into my studies. I mean, I never rebelled as a teenager, ever. I did what I was supposed to do—when I was supposed to do it. I went to a private Catholic junior high. I was actually brought up being told that you should not have sex before marriage. Just the normal values of Midwestern life.

I went to college in the Midwest, too, and then finished my bachelor's degree out in Missouri. Then went to one year of medical school. I met Patrick in college, but he was never actually a sweetheart. I met him during a difficult point in my life, and he helped get me through it. So I got married to Patrick really young, before medical school—that was a mistake.

SHARON MITCHELL: I could tell this guy was kind of a wacko-crazed-fan type. He kept asking if I wanted money, and I said, "No, no."

Then he put his foot in between me and the car door. I figured, foot or no foot, I'm driving. I didn't think twice about it; I just drove away.

I went to the 7-Eleven—and the same guy approached me in the parking lot. And again, I didn't think twice about it. Why? Because I had to get in the fucking door to get a shot of dope in me. I knew I had one waiting at home.

Tunnel vision, right?

TRICIA DEVERAUX: Right before I started medical school, Patrick got a job as a bouncer in a strip club. I was like, "How could you do something like that?" I had never had any sort of exposure to stripping. One of my older sorority sisters had been a stripper, and her parents said what a horrible thing she did!

So I was very angry. But eventually I said, "Well, I want to see this place. I want to make sure this isn't some horrible, dingy sex club."

So Patrick brought me in to see it, and I got along really well with all the girls—the waitresses and dancers—and I ended up going there once in a while to visit Patrick. But I would talk to the girls instead.

SHARON MITCHELL: I get home—and this psycho crazed fan must have gotten in through the front door. I came in and closed the garage door, and as I walked up he pushed in behind me—attacked me—and this guy and I went at it for a while.

I fought this guy for fifteen minutes without a bell, you know what I mean? It was a real tussle. I just kept kicking stuff over; I thought if I broke enough things and made enough noise, someone would call the police. It was, like, three o'clock in the morning. He tried to rape me. He strangled me, broke my larynx, and broke my nose. Really fucked me up bad.

TRICIA DEVERAUX: Everybody at the strip club was always saying, "You should try out for the amateur contests! Why don't you do it?"

I'm like, "Oh my gosh!" I was really homely in high school. I was very plain. I never thought I was ugly, although at one point I was kind of chunky, had bad acne, braces—so definitely not pretty. Even at my best in high school, I was never pretty. Then I finally started to blossom a little bit in college, and by the time I walked into the strip club I was more the pretty-girl-next-door type.

554 The Other Hollywood

SHARON MITCHELL: Finally he hit me, and I passed out—I woke up choking on my own blood. I knew my throat had been broken, and I couldn't swallow. I said to myself, "Oh my God, this is it. I'm going to fucking die."

Then I thought, "This is fucked up, man. After all the shit I've done, I ain't going out because of this motherfucker!"

I rolled him over toward my weight pile and picked up a weight. It was pitch black; I was on the floor, and he was on top of me, strangling me—and I thought, *if I hit him, fine. If I hit me, fine.* At least I'll take myself out, you know?

TRICIA DEVERAUX: Eventually—it took a few months—I actually did the amateur contest, and I won. I probably danced to Metallica—I'm sure it was Metallica. I was really nervous, but I'd gotten to be really good friends with one of the bartenders, and he just told me, "Any time you get nervous just look over at me." I wore glasses back then, and when I took my glasses off to go onstage, I couldn't see him. But I looked back in his direction, and I knew he was there, and I just was like, you know, okay.

It actually helped not to be able to see the audience because I couldn't see them staring at me. I could see there were people there, but I didn't see their eyes focus on me, you know? And I could hear the applause. So I got all of the good things and none of the stuff that made me nervous, ha, ha, ha.

SHARON MITCHELL: That's a very odd place for a human being to be at—one of those do-or-die situations. It was one of those moments I've had in my life where I thought I'd rather—you could talk about it all the fuck you want, but I was confronted with a real life-and-death situation, and I wanted to live.

So I hit him on the head with the weight. Not a big thing, but enough to get him off me. Then there was a knock at the door—and it was the cops.

For once, I was really happy to see them.

TRICIA DEVERAUX: I thought, "I can do this—I can dance." But then I talked to my husband, and he didn't want me to be a stripper.

I said, "What? After you tell me how great a place this is? Was that just something you said to make me okay with the fact that you're working here?"

Patrick was like, "No, no, no!"

I said, "Well, then, I want to do this. You know, it's not like I have a lot of extra money. We're both college students; you know this would be good for the both of us."

He gave in. But he never worked there when I was working. He always hated it, and eventually he ended up quitting 'cause I got really good at stripping. I was never a hustler, so I didn't make tons of money. I enjoyed dancing, though, and the guys appreciated that I was nice to them.

SHARON MITCHELL: The cops took him away. I did the testimony on tape. Turns out the guy had murdered two other girls in different places in Southern California. He was a real serious nut. Just a bad, bad guy. A woman-hater. Hated me. Told the cops that he was trying to kill me, but I was too hard to kill.

But the cops were mad at me because I still had my stage clothes on because I was going to meet this guy I really liked. I knew what it looked like—it looked like a trick gone bad.

TRICIA DEVERAUX: I started thinking about doing porn when I saw all the feature girls come through the club—the porn stars that dance at clubs, for a week at a time, and make all this money.

Some of them weren't outrageously famous, but they were good dancers—people like Victoria Paris, Angela Barron, Tracy Lane. The main one that I just adored was Jeanna Fine, but the clincher was when Samantha Strong came out, and I hung out with her for the whole week. She was like, "Don't ever get your boobs done; I wish I hadn't gotten mine done." She was awesome.

Samantha, Jeanna Fine, and Victoria Paris had all given me their agents' addresses. So I started talking to my husband about doing porn, and, of course he wasn't thrilled by that either. Eventually I told him "You know, this is something I'm gonna do; if you don't like it I'm sorry."

SHARON MITCHELL: After some of the cops took away the crazy guy, this emergency service guy comes in, and he's a fucking novice. He's measuring my eyes with a flashlight.

I'm like, "Get that fucking thing away from me!"

He's like, "Officer, she's in shock."

So the cop comes over and says, "She's not in shock; she's a heroin addict."

I go, "Listen . . ." I could hardly talk. I said, "Listen man, don't you think I've had a hard enough time for one night?"

I don't know what it was, but he said, "Yeah, I do. I'm going to leave now, lady."

TRICIA DEVERAUX: Patrick and I were having problems; I was just not happy. So I told him, "You know, I'm gonna try out this porn thing. I might hate it. But I'm really gonna hate you if you tell me I can't do this. If that's the way you feel, we need to separate."

He didn't want to do that, so he decided to let me try it. I took some pictures and sent them to *Hustler,* for the Beaver Hunt thing, and they got accepted. At the same time, I made it to the national finals for the *Deja Vu* Stripper of the Year contest, and I won fifth in the nation. I was in medical school at the time, and I had to decide whether to allow my pictures to be published in the Stripper of the Year Contest. I had been doing everything very discreetly until then because I didn't want the medical school to find out.

But I let them publish the pictures, and I sent some to Jim South. Joey Silvera was at Jim South's office the day my pictures arrived, and he called me from there and asked me when I could come out to shoot.

I was like, "Oh my God!"

SHARON MITCHELL: After the guy attacked me, I was in full-on, posttraumatic shock. I kept seeing him coming over the balcony, seeing him in the rearview mirror. It was horrible. I went nuts. All I could do was shoot dope and shoot coke—and never enough of it. I just sat there propped up against a couch in my house, with a gun and a bunch of dope.

TRICIA DEVERAUX: I knew I liked being a bit of an exhibitionist with dancing. I didn't know if I would feel the same way about sex, but I was willing to give it a shot.

When I came out to L.A. and met Joey Silvera, I was attracted to him a little bit when I first saw him. He was a little older than what I was used to; I was twenty, and I think Joey was forty-three—twenty-three years older than me. But he was definitely an attractive person. He was just a sweetheart.

I still remember his dick was very pretty, ha, ha, ha. It was very nice looking, a nice shape—not too big, not too small—and mushroom-shaped. I mean, just exactly what I felt a dick should look like. Up until that point, I had only been with my husband, and I had only seen maybe three or four dozen porn movies, so those porn movies made up the other dicks I'd seen in my life, ha, ha, ha.

My first scene ended up being with Joey, on *Fashion Sluts 7.* Joey was the director, and he was the person I was with. It was very relaxed, and since he was the person I was with, that made me feel better. Then, when we were making love, Joey was like, "Do you do anal?" I didn't understand that there's this negotiating process in the porn business, where you hold out for a while to get more money, ha, ha, ha. I just knew I'd done it in my private life, so I said, "Oh, I'll do anal."

He said, "Okay, great. We're going to do an anal now, okay?"

I'm like, "Okay, sure."

I was nervous because a couple times in my private life it wasn't so easy to do anal, if I wasn't feeling relaxed. But Joey told me we could stop at any time; he really put me at ease. And it turned out great. If I hadn't been nervous I think I would have really enjoyed the sex.

SHARON MITCHELL: I had built up my production company again, but I was shooting dope, and I was very unhappy. I thought, "Aagh, this pesky work! Fuck! It gets in the way every time. I'll just deal dope!"

TRICIA DEVERAUX: After Joey, I started working with these two guys, Christopher Alexander and Bucky Malibu, who were the two shooting the *Nasty* series with Mr. Marcus. I got along really well with them, and after I went back to the Midwest to medical school they called me up.

They said, "We have this big production set up. One of the girls flaked, and we don't want to cancel the whole shoot, and we thought you'd be a good girl to be in it."

I'm like, "Oh, that's flattering."

He started describing it to me. "It would be fourteen guys and one girl. . . ."

Ha, ha, ha.

I said, "Well, I just need a little bit of time to think about it." The most I'd been with at that time was three guys for John Leslie, which included my first DP—double penetration.

So he said, "Well, if you could actually think about it really quick 'cause if you decide not to do it, we still have to find another girl."

I talked to my husband, and of course he doesn't want me to do it, but by that point he had already spent ten thousand dollars of my money on his stupid car. So I was like, "You know what? I don't care what he thinks. I'm gonna go do this."

SHARON MITCHELL: So I started dealing, and my old boyfriend calls me up: "Oh, I'm just out of jail, and I hear you're living in the neighborhood."

"No, you can't come over. No, no."

He whines a bit, right? So I let him come over.

I go, "Listen, this is really good stuff. You have to do just a little bit of it. . . ."

So he goes in the bathroom, locks the door, and the last thing I hear him say is, "God, that's good!"

Then I hear this *bang, crash, boom.* Obviously he'd OD'd; his head hit the sliding glass door on the shower. I'm pounding on the bathroom door. I open it up, he's blue—he's, like, *gray*—and I'm like, "Oh, man, this motherfucker!"

I was so mad at myself for letting this guy back in again. I thought,

"I'm going to roll him up in a fucking rug and put him in the goddamn Dumpster." They used to do that in the shooting galleries in New York. I had seen it more than once. And I was *there, you know?* I was there, man. But then I'm thinking he's too heavy—plus there's no rug.

TRICIA DEVERAUX: I flew out to L.A. for the shoot, but now it wasn't four-teen guys with one girl, but a bunch of guys with two girls. I was costar-ring with Chloe, one of the most popular stars in adult. I had worked with a couple of the guys before, but I met a lot of guys for the first time that day. Sean Michaels was one of them. He came up to me and said, "Tri-cia?"

"Yeah?"

"I just want to tell you that I masturbated to you."

Ha, ha, ha.

The story of the video was that I was going over to visit Chloe at her apartment complex, and she was trying to figure out how she was going to shave her bikini line. She was playing this real inhibited girl who couldn't get a date.

I'm like, "Well, you've got a lot of attractive guys in your complex," or something like that. Then I say, "Whoa, look at that," and I went outside and all these guys started hitting on me. Chloe looks outside the window, and I'm getting fucked and giving blow jobs, and I'm like, "Come on out! Come on out!"

It was group stuff, but it wasn't "Okay, this guy takes his turn, and that guy takes his turn." It was, like, four guys at a time with one girl, doing a DP, a hand job, and a blow job; sometimes it was one girl with one guy. Sean Michaels turned out to be a sweetie. We had to do more anal sex together because my pussy's really shallow, and his dick is so long it would actually hurt because he would just bottom out, you know? So I loved Sean Michaels.

I remember looking over at Chloe, and we'd be like, "WHOOOO!" Ha, ha, ha, like, "Okay, this is good sex. This is *overwhelming!*"

I made a lot of good friends on that shoot.

Then I had to go back to school.

SHARON MITCHELL: I'm looking at this ex-boyfriend dead on my floor, and I think, "Oh, fuck it!" So I start thumping on his chest; I give him mouth-to-mouth, the whole thing. I get the death rattle, and I get a pulse of, like, two. I mean, he was barely alive, but I got a pulse, so I call 911. Then I whip off all my clothes.

When the cops show up, I'm like, "Oh, hi Officer!"

They ask, "What's going on?"

I say, "Oh, these little balloons? I found those in his mouth."

They ask, "Oh yeah?"

After they bring him back to life with the Narcan, he sits up, and they say, "This woman saved your life, son. Aren't you lucky? Come on—we're taking you downtown."

TRICIA DEVERAUX: When I got back home, the medical school people had found out about me doing videos. It had been getting around school; I was hearing little rumors—the students would go on searches for my videos. I had a female lab partner who was so offended that she stopped talking to me.

Instead of confronting me about doing porn, though, the school chose to accuse me of cheating on a test.

I thought, "I'm not going to acknowledge cheating on a test I never cheated on." So I said, "If there's something else going on here, let talk about that."

The administrator said, "No, no, no, you cheated on a test."

I said, "No, I didn't."

He said, "No, no, no, we have evidence." The evidence was that 25 percent of my wrong answers were the same wrong answers as someone else sitting near me. Not the same person every time, either—one was from the person to the right, one from the person to the left, one from the person in front of me. It was ludicrous.

So I said, "You know what? Fuck you, I'm gonna go live a different life, where people aren't hypocritical." They ended up dismissing me, and I never fought it.

I was essentially blacklisted. It's not official, but when you get kicked out of a medical school, all the other medical schools know. And I couldn't tell them, "Well, yeah, I got kicked out, but it was because I was doing porn movies; you know, it's no big thing."

Ha, ha, ha.

SHARON MITCHELL: So they take my ex-boyfriend to the hospital and find out he has federal warrants.

He says, "I'll make you a deal."

So he turns me in for dealing dope. I swear to God. I'm down there on the bathroom floor, cleaning up the blood; I've just done a little speedball, and I'm still naked. The police don't even knock. It was just like, *boom!* The battering ram—the whole thing. They take me down there, and they're like, "We know you're loaded."

TRICIA DEVERAUX: What happened at medical school bothered me for a while, but luckily I had this exciting new life to concentrate on. So I left school and shot a couple more scenes; then somebody I had worked for recommended me to Rob Black because he was shooting in New York, and he needed to fly some girls there to shoot a video. It was his second video, *Cellar Dwellers,* and I flew out for that.

ROB BLACK: I had good talent in *Cellar Dwellers.* I actually had name people—Alisha Rio, Heather Lee, Steve Hatcher, Rick Masters. I flew all these people to Rochester, New York. And I had Tricia Deveraux. That's where I met Tricia.

TRICIA DEVERAUX: I talked to Rob on the phone quite a bit, making arrangements, and I thought, "His voice is really sexy." When I got to New York, I walked past him; Rob didn't recognize me; I was wearing sweats, my hair was up, my glasses were on, and he'd only seen me on a box cover. I turned around and started heading back, and he was like, "Whoa, that's her! That's her!"

SHARON MITCHELL: I borrow the bail money from the Hell's Angels, and I get bailed out on this beef, right?

I call my lawyer—who's an asshole like every other lawyer, but the guy had been my criminal drug lawyer ever since I started getting busted. He knew the drug laws; he was just a drug-criminal defense attorney. But the day that I was supposed to go to court, he called back; I didn't know it at the time, but that night his girlfriend had died. It was a bad scene. He must have been so freaked out—but he got up, didn't tell me about the dead girl, and brought me to court anyway.

TRICIA DEVERAUX: Rob said he was actually kind of impressed that I didn't show up all porned-out or anything. We just kind of hit it off. Then the night before my scene, I had a panic attack. So I knocked on his door at the hotel, and I was like, "I can't do it. I can't do it. I'm not going to get any sleep. I'm, you know, *gonna throw up!*"

Rob came to my room, and he held me all night. I fell asleep in his arms, and when I woke up the next morning he was still just laying in bed with me, with his clothes on.

I was like, "Oh, this is so sweet."

ROB BLACK: We fucked the night before Tricia's scene—so it wasn't tainted; then we fucked again right after her scene. But, you know, Tricia had taken a shower in between, ha, ha, ha.

TRICIA DEVERAUX: I think Rob and I hit it off partly because I was just separating from my husband—Patrick was too much of a pushover personality-wise, and we'd been having problems financially. And to see a person like Rob Black who was a go-getter and very assertive—I found that very attractive.

SHARON MITCHELL: When we get to the courthouse, my lawyer goes, "I don't think you better come into the courtroom. . . ." My name wasn't on the docket. This is my second strike, so I'm facing some ridiculous amount of time—like ten years. I'm thinking, "Why am I not on the docket? What's going on?" I'm sitting there waiting for my lawyer, thinking I'm going right to solitary confinement—with no nail polish—for the rest of my life.

TRICIA DEVERAUX: Rob had embezzled seventy thousand dollars from his dad over a period of time to shoot his first three videos. I think his Dad had put Rob in charge of the books—he trusted his son, you know?

ROB BLACK: When my dad, Dominic Zicari, started in 1968, he had, like, thirty bookstores—he worked a deal with Reuben Sturman. I was always told that my dad owned a dirty bookstore. That's what it was called: "A Dirty Bookstore." He sold pictures and videos of naked people.

As I got a little bit older, I was stealing product out of his warehouse to jerk off. I was, like, twelve years old.

My parents wanted me to go to college, so I went to Monroe Community College for about six months. In the fifth month I was sitting there going, "Why am I raising my hand? This is horrible."

So at the end of 1995, I had this vision—I wanted to start a porno company and call it Extreme Video. My Dad was like, "No, it's too hard. You'll never make it. We did it, and it didn't work. You can't do it from Rochester, you'd have to move to L.A." Blah, blah, blah.

I kept wanting to make porn, so I embezzled a lot of money from my Dad. "Embezzle" is a much better word than "steal," don't you think?

SHARON MITCHELL: I had gone to one of the district attorneys and talked to him in person—signed a few autographs; my lawyer had taught me how to play that card real well. Because boy, in a courthouse, they're all too happy to see "Miss Mitchell!"

So now, all of the sudden, my lawyer comes out of the courtroom and says, "The district attorney has decided to drop the case. It seems to him that you were in the wrong place at the wrong time. This guy planted stuff in your home."

The total lie I had told him had worked. I thought, "Oh man, my karma's going to kill me. I better get fucking clean. Now."

TRICIA DEVERAUX: Why didn't Rob just ask his dad for the money? I don't know. I can't explain most of Rob's actions, so I won't try. I mean, Rob's family, the Zacaris, are close—but it's not what's considered a normal family. In a normal family, a child wouldn't embezzle money from his father, ha, ha, ha.

Right after Rob's shoot, I received my official letter of dismissal from medical school, so I moved to Los Angeles and rented a house over in West Hills.

ROB BLACK: We were getting ready to release *Cellar Dwellers,* so we went to the VSDA show in Vegas to promote it; Missy and Tricia Deveraux signed autographs for me. We had these fliers where Tricia was on the back of an electric chair—it was some good shit.

But while I was there I get a call from my dad, who tells me that when I come back to town we've got serious problems. He had just opened up the checkbook, and I was, basically, just in so much shit. I was *fucked.* I just cringed—like when you fuck up in grammar school. I spent three more days in Vegas thinking, "I am so fucking dead."

SHARON MITCHELL: I thought, "Oh man, as much as I hate it, I got to get clean."

I mean, I'd tried to kill myself by overdosing—but I'd just wake up. I mean, there just wasn't enough dope on earth to kill my ass, you know? Probably because I sincerely didn't want to do it.

All those years I spent fucked up, I could go anywhere in the world with just like a day's worth of stuff and an ass-pocket full of cash, knowing I could cop anywhere.

But once I ran out in Niagara Falls, New York. I mean, there's snow up to your fucking tits in the winter in Niagara Falls. I can usually cop anywhere in the universe, but in Niagara Falls, in mid-winter, it's really hard. I mean, I'm good—but I ain't that fucking good.

So I thought, "Well, thank God there's Federal Express, you know?"

Because FedEx at the time couldn't X-ray anything because they were a private mail service. Now I think they can open anything. But at the time they couldn't. I had an account, needless to say, ha, ha, ha.

TRICIA DEVERAUX: I fell in love with Rob. He was exciting to me, and I was still excited for him and his ambitions. I wanted to help him out. But right after we got together, I got a job to go to France to shoot for Private for two weeks. I could tell Rob was a little bit upset. He said, "You don't need to do that, do you?"

And I said, "I don't *need* to, but I'd like to. This is a bonus—I'm working, plus I'm going to France!"

SHARON MITCHELL: So I call FedEx and say, "Listen! I'm a diabetic, and my fucking medicine is in this package I have coming! And if you don't get it to me I'm going to drop dead in about three hours, and it's going to be *on your ass*!" Then I hang up.

Now I have to go onstage—but I'm so sick I have to have my assistant wipe me off, I'm vomiting so much. I would do one number and smile and take a bow; then tell 'em to cut the lights before the next song, stick my head through the curtain, and vomit in a bucket. Then I'd turn around and smile and do another number. I thought, *"At this rate, I'm going to be dead tomorrow."*

I wake up the next morning in my hotel room and open the door to the balcony, and you can't even see it, there's so much snow. There had been another fucking blizzard overnight.

So I go out and ask, "Is there any mail? Did the mail come? I'm expecting a delivery."

They're like, "Oh, no. There's no post today, missy."

So I go back to bed, and I'm laying there dying when I hear this high-pitched sound: *eeeeeeeEEEEEE.* I look out the window, and it's a fucking snowmobile with a FedEx guy, with my package! Ha, ha, ha!

I think that was the best shot of dope I have ever done in my life.

ROB BLACK: I came back to Rochester, and my parents fucking yelled at me. It was one of those ultimatums—*Mow the lawn for the next ninety years! Get the fuck out if you think you're a tough guy! You're disowned!*

So I called Tricia up and said, "My parents threw me out, and I got no place to go. I'm gonna come out there with you."

TRICIA DEVERAUX: I was working in porn fairly consistently when I moved to L.A.—a couple times a week. I'd flown out to L.A. about five times at that point to make videos, and eventually I realized that if I was going to continue to do it, I needed to be out here for good.

So when Rob decided he wanted to move out here, I let him move into my house.

ROB BLACK: I got all my shit, and I moved in with Tricia and lived with her while she was still married. She was going to go through a divorce, but she was still married.

TRICIA DEVERAUX: Not even a month after he moved to L.A., I was in a story in *Adult Video News.* I said, "Oh, this is great! I'm starting to make it."

Rob said, "Let's see who's bigger from now on—you or me." He said it real serious. And this guy is madly in love with me? I was like, "What? Well, I don't know. Maybe it'll be me."

Rob was mad at me. That was his personality, and I was in denial.

SHARON MITCHELL: If that crazed-psycho fan, woman-hater, fucking guy hadn't tried to kill me, I wouldn't be here. He was like a Disciple of

Doom—there was death all around me, but he kept me alive, you know? I mean, I'm not even mad at him because he gave me my life back, ha, ha, ha. It was over. No more standing out in the middle of the street, looking at the sky, screaming, "COME ON MOTHERFUCKER! BRING IT ON!" You know, no more, "WELL GOD, STRIKE ME DEAD!"

So I checked into a detox. I was so bad they had to take me to the emergency room immediately.

TRICIA DEVERAUX: Rob was very possessive, which didn't really bother me at first because I'd never been in a possessive relationship before, so I didn't see what it could lead to. Then I started learning what that meant—that he didn't really want me doing anything that he wasn't a part of. I wasn't allowed to say anything bad about him. I couldn't question his perfection; if I did it was a betrayal.

Then the video *Bad Wives,* directed by Paul Thomas, ended up winning best film of 1996. I went up to Paul at a party Rob and I made an appearance at, and I said, "P. T., congratulations. I'm so happy for you."

Rob got mad at me and said, "What, I'm a piece of shit here?"

I asked him, "Rob, were *you* nominated for best film?"

He said, "No."

I said, "It's not like I'm congratulating someone who beat you in some category today."

He was like, "I don't care. That's just horrible, that you'd go and congratulate someone else."

That was the last straw—when I realized Rob was hopeless. I stepped back and looked at the whole picture and said, "Okay, there's a lot of things wrong with this. And none of it is me."

That's when I knew I had to break up with him.

SHARON MITCHELL: My life was just bisexual-weird-insanity. And heroin and more heroin. And jail sentences and more movies and traveling. And young girls. And then old men. I mean—I had this boyfriend that was, like, in his seventies. Fucking crazy, cranky, old fuck, right?

I'd see my little chickies, and then the older boyfriend would come over. One day, right before I get sober, I looked in the cabinet and there was Geritol and Lucky Charms, ha, ha, ha!

And a spoon of dope, you know?

TRICIA DEVERAUX: I was trying to break up with him, so I started using psychology against Rob. I'd ask, "What do we have in common?"

He'd ask, "What do you mean?"

I'm like, "We don't really have anything in common, other than, you know, listening to music. I mean, that's something for people to be friends about. What do we have in common to date about?"

Rob would never really have an answer. He'd just say, "I love you."

TIM CONNELLY: Rob loved Tricia Deveraux. He really felt this sort of incredible, deep, love-of-my-life, soul mate kind of connection with her.

SHARON MITCHELL: I went to school as soon as I got out of rehab. And I immediately excelled in school—superfast, right? Overachieving A's, super-ahead of the class, magna cum this and that. Took the graduate course first and then went backward. I got a scholarship all the way through to the master's.

I thought I would get as far away from the business as I could—and goddamn it, something drove me back, you know? And that's probably my redemption.

TRICIA DEVERAUX: Rob always told me that the one thing he could never forgive a girlfriend for was cheating on him. That's why he made me stop working with guys—because he thought that working with another guy would be cheating on him. I did a lot of girl/girl scenes for about six months.

Eventually, though, I slept with Rob's best friend. And I set it up so I knew he'd find out.

Rob's best friend was a guy from New York named Andy, who really didn't have anything to do with the porn business. So I started turning Andy against Rob. I said to him, "If Rob was such a good friend of yours, why does he treat you like shit all the time?" And he started to question Rob; finally he was like, "Well, you know what? I fucked your girlfriend."

That was what I was going for. I know it's manipulative, but I was at the point where I didn't know what else to do.

ROB BLACK: Tricia and I got into a fight at a party. She was being, like, a twat, so I sent her home. That's when she cheated on me with my best friend—this big, fat kid I brought out from New York. Then I broke up with her.

TRICIA DEVERAUX: I was afraid to leave Rob, but I figured, at the worst, he'd beat me a tiny bit—not like he'd kill me or anything. When he found out that Andy and I had slept together, Rob slapped me, really hard, once.

That was it. I was like, "Okay, that wasn't as bad as I was afraid it was gonna be." Ha, ha, ha.

SHARON MITCHELL: When all is said and done, heroin habit or no heroin habit, what have I been famous for? Fucking in front of a camera all my life? What the fuck? I don't want to go bed with that! I don't want to get in the fucking ground with that as my only accomplishment. I just think it's psychologically damaging. It follows you around like the plague for the rest of your life.

So when this HIV situation came up, since I was the one in school doing a term paper on HIV research, the board of directors at PAW—Protecting Adult Welfare—thought that I should handle it. Well, I quickly amassed information on testing—what kinds of tests were available—and I got information as fast as I could.

I'm just here to save lives. And get a little redemption out of it. And then maybe, I can go to heaven, you know?

TRICIA DEVERAUX: So I broke up with Rob; he got me fired from a job, but at least I got away from him. By the end of 1997 I was just doing some box covers to advance my dancing career, and doing less scenes. Everything was fine—that is, until I turned up HIV positive.

Celebrity Porn
LOS ANGELES/SEATTLE/LAS VEGAS/AMSTERDAM
1996–1997

EVAN WRIGHT (WRITER): There's really only one celebrity porn tape, and that's the Pamela Anderson and Tommy Lee video. There have been other celebrity scandal sex tapes, but the Pamela Anderson Lee video is the first one that was distributed over the Internet—that was actually *streamed* over the Internet.

TOMMY LEE: Pamela and I were chowing down on some dinner and flipping through television stations when we heard our names being mentioned on some news show. On the screen, there was a dude at Tower Video stocking the shelves with videotapes. And we knew just what they were.

RON JEREMY: Pam and Tommy Lee's first tape was stolen. I know that for a fact, and I know who stole it.

RAY PISTOL: An electrician walked out with the tape. I never asked his name; sometimes it's better not to know. But I do know the facts. He was in porn—kind of a hanger-on—and he did some work for Pam and Tommy, and they didn't pay him. So he just snooped around, found this tape, and said, "Well, I'll just get paid with this."

TOMMY LEE: Months earlier, we had taken a five-day houseboat trip on Lake Mead as a vacation. As usual, I brought along my video camera. We weren't trying to make a porno, just to document our vacation. We watched it once when we returned home then put it in our safe. The safe was a five-hundred-pound monstrosity hidden underneath a carpet in my studio control room in the garage, where we recorded part of *Generation Swine*.

RAY PISTOL: The electrician went to Milton Ingley and offered him the tape. Ingley was a porn director who owned a studio out there in the Valley.

TOMMY LEE: Pamela and I spent that Christmas in London while some work was being done on the house. Afterward, I finished recording in the basement and then dismantled the studio.

When the carpet was torn out, I saw nothing but empty space where the safe had once been. There were no broken locks or windows, so it had to have been an inside job. The only people with the keys were my assistant and the construction crew, which come to think of it, included an electrician who used to be a porn star and knew the porn business pretty well.

RON JEREMY: Milton Ingley had offered the Pam and Tommy Lee tape to everyone in the business. He asked me and Leisure Time first—because Marc Carriere had the John Wayne Bobbitt movie. Marc has so much money, plus Milton knew he had high-speed duplicating machinery. So he figured Marc should be the one to buy the Tommy Lee tape. But Marc Carriere said, "No, it's unethical. It was stolen, no release, no receipts. It's not fair."

TOMMY LEE: The way I figured it, they must have removed the safe with a crane, taken it back to one of their houses, and had it picked or blown open. They were probably after the guns and jewelry in there, but they also ended up with everything personal that was important to us—from family heirlooms to photographs.

RAY PISTOL: Milton Ingley didn't have any money, so he went to Butchie Peraino—and Butchie actually loaned him thirty thousand dollars to buy the Pam and Tommy Lee tape and to set up distribution. Butchie took Beta machines and camera equipment for collateral, in case he didn't get paid back. Then the tape was duplicated at LP Duplications.

Butchie *didn't* get fully paid back, so he wound up with the collateral equipment—plus some of his money. But not nearly as much as he was supposed to.

TOMMY LEE: I was so freaked out that I fired the assistant and sicced my lawyers on the construction company.

RON JEREMY: So Milton went to Europe and basically started it there. Then some guy pirated his tape, and then everyone pirated it. And then Seth Warshavsky from Internet Entertainment Group—who is a pretty conniving guy, but who's pretty smart—went legal with it.

TOMMY LEE: The next thing I knew, there was a porn peddler from a company called the IEG phoning me. He said that he had bought the tape and was going to broadcast it over the Internet.

RAY PISTOL: Milton came to me to work out how best to distribute it—which involved a dozen different sites, in a dozen different countries, so that even if they got a restraining order somewhere, you could just keep going on and on.

EVAN WRIGHT: The Internet is a natural for porn because of the anonymity. You don't have to go into the store and embarrass yourself by asking for your favorite big boob movie. You can just dial one up in the privacy of your own home.

RAY PISTOL: I wanted to spread the Pam and Tommy Lee tape on innumerable sites, but using ten different money points. Fuck—the Pentagon papers was my model! You shut this one down, it doesn't make a fuck, it's getting published over here!

I believe Seth Warshavsky was one of the money points—but there were others.

SETH WARSHAVSKY (PRESIDENT AND CEO OF INTERNET ENTERTAINMENT GROUP): We sold it at Tower Video and Wherehouse Video; we sold it pretty much in every major video store in the country. It was on pay-per-view; it was in hotel rooms. I think that's really one of the things that kind of helped legitimize porn.

JONATHAN SILVERSTEIN (IEG EMPLOYEE): I worked at IEG for close to two years, and over the course of that time IEG exploded in the media because of the Pamela Anderson tape.

RAY PISTOL: Instead of going with the multiple points, they used only about four, and they seemingly got ripped off at every point. But they did get some money out of it, I know that. I masterminded that deal, and then Milton Ingley screwed it all up.

EVAN WRIGHT: Twenty years ago it would have been hard for a Pamela Anderson Lee video to make it to the public because no one would have distributed it. But because of the Internet, it can be distributed worldwide, instantaneously, by anyone. There have always been celebrity scandals and celebrity sex, but now technology enables the public to find out about it much faster.

JONATHAN SILVERSTEIN: Seth was a marketing genius. His intention really wasn't to air the Pamela Anderson video on the Internet; he was only saying he was going to, for the publicity. He had a good PR firm; it was like a machine for him.

RON JEREMY: So the Pam and Tommy Lee tape was released out of Amsterdam into America. And because Pamela Lee mentioned it on the Howard Stern show, Seth Warshavsky tried to make a public domain issue out of it—and tried to take her to court to release the tape.

JONATHAN SILVERSTEIN: Seth figured that once he put out a press release, Pamela Anderson and Tommy Lee's attorneys would get an injunction so that Seth wouldn't be able to air the tape. Seth would save face: He wouldn't have to air the tape because legally he couldn't. Seth would just get all the publicity—and that would lead to a lot of traffic to ClubLove, Seth's website.

EVAN WRIGHT: There was a rumor put out by IEG that Pamela Anderson deliberately leaked the tape to revive a sagging career. That was completely false. I knew Pamela Anderson Lee and her husband, Tommy, from a prior story I did. They're actually very nice people. Believe it or not, Pamela Anderson Lee was very hurt by that sex tape. Even though it probably helped her career, there was no way Pamela or Tommy enjoyed that tape being put out.

TOMMY LEE: We had Pamela's lawyers send them a cease and desist order— but for some reason it didn't arrive on time. Our lawyers and managers advised us that the best way to minimize the damages was to sign a contract saying that—since the company had us by the balls—we would reluctantly allow a one-time Webcast so long as they didn't sell, copy, trade, or rebroadcast it.

We thought we had won. Hardly anyone would see the video on the Internet, and we could recover the tape and start over.

JONATHAN SILVERSTEIN: The day it all went down, it had been back and forth between Seth's lawyers and Pam's lawyers, and they were supposed to fax something over and they never did. So at some point Seth just said, "Fuck it. Air it."

That really exploded Internet Entertainment Group and turned Seth into the adult media mogul that he became. ClubLove was getting thousands of sign-ups a day. People were joining the site just to see this thing. Thousands of sign-ups a day is *huge*.

RON JEREMY: That's the thing with the Internet—it's a good thing to have in this world, but unfortunately it takes away a lot of privacy, right?

Some people claim that Pam said, "Might as well make money on it."

RAY PISTOL: Milton Ingley dropped two hundred of the Pam and Tommy tapes on me and said, "Here, do something with these." It wasn't my payment for anything; he just did it. He said, "Nobody's got these in the country, so do with them what you want to." I think I've got one left around here somewhere; the rest of them we sold for good money.

TOMMY LEE: Pamela and I were getting in fights all the time. Trying to have children, continue the careers that consumed us, make a new relationship work, and deal with the nonstop barrage of bullshit in the press was more of a challenge than we ever could have expected.

EVAN WRIGHT: Nobody believes me even though I probably know, better than anybody else, the background of that tape. I know that they did not want that tape put out.

We have this love-hate relationship with celebrities, but actually I knew Pam and Tommy, and they were hurt. It was a very hurtful thing.

TOMMY LEE: Then the judge in the case shut Pamela and me down on every privacy issue and allowed the sale of the tape because he ruled that the content was newsworthy. It pissed me off—because I don't ever want my kids to go to a friend's house and find a video in the VCR of their parents fucking.

SETH WARSHAVSKY: I didn't feel sorry for Pamela Anderson. She's a sophisticated woman. She's an actress. She's somewhat intelligent; she could be extremely intelligent. I just don't know her. But she was definitely surrounded by extremely competent counsel.

EVAN WRIGHT: That was the defense at IEG—the way they were able to put out the Pam and Tommy Lee video was because their lawyers argued that Pamela and Tommy had relentlessly publicized themselves anyway, talking about the sex tape and sex acts in explicit detail before IEG put out the tape. Celebrities are exhibitionists, too.

RON JEREMY: The Pam Anderson/Tommy Lee tape sold over a hundred and fifty thousand tapes.

TOMMY LEE: I finally broke down and watched the thing. I couldn't see the big deal; it's really just our vacation tape. There's only a little bit of fucking on there. That hasn't stopped Ron Jeremy, though, from trying to get me to make a fuck flick for him. I guess if my career as a musician ever fails, I can always be a porn star.

SETH WARSHAVSKY: I think the sex video was a phenomenal push for Pamela's career. I mean, if you do a search on Pamela Anderson, you'll see a couple hundred articles prior to the release of that video, and then thousands of articles after its release.

I think IEG really made Pamela the most talked about celebrity in the world.

JONATHAN SILVERSTEIN: Seth got press for other things, but the Pam and Tommy tape was really the launching pad because it got covered on *48 Hours* and Howard Stern. This was huge news—but all that did was bring other people out of the woodwork who had interesting and controversial material, too, you know?

TOMMY LEE: I tried to keep my cool after the drama. But it kept getting harder while the news kept getting worse. Then the Internet Entertainment Group started selling a tape of Brett Michaels from Poison with Pamela.

RON JEREMY: Now, where does this Brett Michaels and Pam Anderson tape come from all of a sudden? At one point, as far I as know, only three copies existed in this world. Actually, maybe four. Brett had one, Pam had one, Brett's friend had one, and I got one from a source that no one even knows about.

The tape is Brett Michaels and Pam having sex. I saw it early on, when very few people had ever seen it. But the Brett tape was made first; it goes back to 1991.

LARRY FLYNT: There were two videos involving Pamela Lee. One they said was stolen from their home. The other one was not stolen from their home, so that one could legally be sold anywhere.

So when it gets to the question of privacy—people should have privacy in their home. But if you're a public figure, you give up any right to privacy because you're there because of your profession or an act you committed. So if you don't want to give up your privacy, don't get into public life.

These guys who get on TV and harp about the paparazzi or somebody stealing videos? It goes with the territory. They can't have it both ways.

SETH WARSHAVSKY: I think it was a business decision on Pamela's part. Whether she thought it would further her career because of the publicity the video generated around her or whether she thought that it would be beneficial for her to look like a victim, I don't know. And to our surprise, Pamela sued us—after signing the agreement. So I never felt sorry for her.

EVAN WRIGHT: It's funny: Thirty years ago, when you talked about porn stars, they were strictly these infamous figures, like Linda Lovelace.

Today, Pamela Anderson Lee is basically a porn star. Rob Lowe was a porn star for a while. Then *Esquire* did an article a little while back where they had Jenna Jameson—a well-known porn star—posing next to her recipe for mashed potatoes.

RON JEREMY: Now, all of a sudden, this new tape is legal. Pam has to be behind it because Brett Michaels is very much against it. He went on the Howard Stern show saying he's against the tape, and he's gonna stop it, and he did. His lawyers did a court injunction and stopped the tape.

EVAN WRIGHT: I remember hearing this statistic, and I think it's true: In the late 1990s, NASA did live Webcasts of the streams of images from Mars. At about that time, the Pamela Anderson Lee video was also being streamed on the Internet. And I think more people were trying to watch close-up pictures of Pamela Anderson Lee's crotch than were watching the images of Mars.

SETH WARSHAVSKY: The Pamela Anderson and Tommy Lee video was the largest-selling adult video in history. It was really a perfect example of porn becoming more mainstream in America.

EVAN WRIGHT: I think a lot of people thought Pamela Anderson Lee looked really hot.

Outbreak

LOS ANGELES
1998

TRICIA DEVERAUX: I won an *AVN* Award for best girl/girl scene—and I enjoyed myself a lot in that scene. Then the next day, which was my birthday, I went back to Los Angeles and got an HIV test at the Norton Clinic.

That Friday, I got a call from Jim South saying that my HIV test had come back indeterminate.

SHARON MITCHELL: I roomed with Tommy Byron and Marc Wallice for a while in the San Fernando Valley when I first moved out here. Tommy Byron's great. He's very quiet and very clean. Very neat.

But Marc would sneak in and mess around in my underwear. I would open up my underwear, and it'd be all stretched out, you know? I couldn't wear it.

I mean, I knew it was Marc's kink, so eventually I just started buying larger underwear.

TRICIA DEVERAUX: So I ran out, got in my car, and drove to a clinic on Venice Boulevard. They opened the door and said, "We're closed."

I had been there before, and I said, "No, you don't understand! My test came back indeterminate!"

All of a sudden, this really nice, big, black lady just took me in her arms and said, "It's okay, honey. We'll take care of you."

And she pulled me inside and drew my blood, and they ran the ten-minute test, and it came back indeterminate again. So she called her supervisor and asked what to do.

SHARON MITCHELL: The Free Speech Coalition is a trade organization for adult entertainment manufacturers and producers, so they can provide legal defense education about laws and censorship in the United States. Somehow I got elected to the board of directors. Bad place to put a newly sober loudmouth chick that just wants to help the talent. I mean, I'm definitely not going to be a winner on this board, right?

TRICIA DEVERAUX: They drew my blood again, and they sent it out to a clinic that could do a DNA test over the weekend. Almost immediately, people were calling me and asking me if I was okay.

BILL MARGOLD: In 1997, I'd gotten Sharon Mitchell to be the AIDS matron—the HIV genealogist—although I'd already created the groundwork for genealogy as far back as 1993, with the first outbreak. So now Sharon Mitchell was going to be paid for doing this—which I didn't really mind, though up to that point nobody involved with PAW (Protecting Adult Welfare) had been paid.

SHARON MITCHELL: I quickly amassed information on what kinds of tests existed. I got information as fast as I could. I brought it back to the Free Speech Coalition board, and I said, "I need about thirteen thousand dollars to start this testing site."

BILL MARGOLD: Almost immediately, Sharon Mitchell wants to get paid more and more and more and more.

SHARON MITCHELL: Now, it just so happened that the Protecting Adult Welfare office had a sink—which is the only legal requirement to draw blood. And it was next to World Talent Modeling Agency. So I was given the grant—and as people were going in and out of World Modeling, I'd just grab them, draw their blood, and send them back out. They were like, "What! I've just been branded!" They were like cattle; they didn't really know what hit them. But that's the best way to start an industry standard for HIV testing.

TRICIA DEVERAUX: How did people find out? The Norton Clinic was instructed to call the agent if anything happened, so they called Jim South to have him contact me. I wish they would have contacted me first—at least give me a day to go and get the test again.

Apparently, Jim South called me from his office when there were other people there. So they knew he was calling Trish Deveraux to say that her HIV test was indeterminate. Unbelievable. He should have gone into a private room or something, you know?

Everybody was calling me: "Do you have AIDS? Are you going to die?"

I'm like, "Well, I'm waiting for another test result. Maybe it's a false positive."

MARC WALLICE: I was as big as I could be in this industry. Everywhere I went on the street, people would say, "Hey, Marc!" "You're that guy!" I was with Elegant Angel for a year. This was my first series, *Tails of Perversity*. My first shot.

TRICIA DEVERAUX: After the first positive DNA test, I wasn't really in denial, but I was like, "Maybe I'm really not HIV." It was just shock: "How could this happen?" I saw everybody's tests before I performed with them. I'd had sex with only two people outside of the adult business, and both times it was with a condom. And I don't do drugs. So I was just sitting there thinking, "I don't understand."

It was after the second positive that I started thinking, "Wow, I got this."

MARC WALLICE: Every film in the *Tails of Perversity* series got three and a half stars from *AVN* except the last one. It got four stars.

TRICIA DEVERAUX: Nobody knew where I got it. Then rumors started spreading. I gave Sharon Mitchell a list of everyone I'd had sex with for the previous six months. She said everybody on that list had to get a DNA test to prove that they didn't have HIV.

And the people who had been with me for less than one month before had to get a DNA test, wait a month, and get another one. So they were basically quarantined from the adult business.

MARC WALLICE: At Elegant Angel, we are the kings of anal sex. That's what people want. If you can get the majority of the scenes to be anal, why would you say no?

If there's a beautiful girl I want to see having sex, and she doesn't do anal, that's fine. I wouldn't turn a beautiful girl down that doesn't do anal over an okay-looking chick that will take it up the ass.

TRICIA DEVERAUX: I felt sorry for those people. I thought, *They can't work for a whole month because they had sex with me.* It was weird; I felt like I was now a potential infector. Nobody else became positive from me, but I still hurt those people; they were sitting at home going, "Do I have HIV? Can I ever work again?"

MARC WALLICE: I still give plenty before the anal ever happens. The anal just tops it off. Occasionally, like in the second to the last scene in *Tails of Perversity 4*, it's straight anal—"Let's not even fuck her pussy, except for the DP!"

TRICIA DEVERAUX: Most people were very sympathetic toward me. In fact, they had an industry-wide meeting at VCA about what was going to happen. Were companies going to start shooting with condoms?

In fact, I ran into Mr. Marcus there. He was one of the people quarantined because of me, and he was so nice to me.

MARC WALLICE: I've been making the best movies at Elegant Angel since Tom Byron left. I was all Patrick Collins had, until he hired Sean Michaels. I love the guy, but the truth is his movies fucking suck.

TRICIA DEVERAUX: I mean, I can understand it that people were saying, "Well, maybe she's doing drugs; maybe she's hooking on the side." But there was this person who said they saw me at a party shooting up heroin.

First of all, I don't go to parties. And second, I've never *seen* a person shoot up heroin, let alone shoot it up myself. So I thought, *How could a person say that?*

That was one of the main things that made me realize I just needed to get away. Because I knew that people were looking at me and wondering, "What did she do to get this? What did she do different from what we're doing?"

MARC WALLICE: I can't tell you the number of times I've been on a set where someone has had a test one, two, three, four days old, which is just a giveaway that they're faking the dates. I was one day over the deadline, so I changed the date. But I did *not* fake a test.

TRICIA DEVERAUX: I think I contracted HIV through Marc Wallice. Because when I looked at his test, I saw the name Mark Goldberg—which is his real name—and I saw negative for HIV next to his name. The name and the HIV screener was all I looked at.

Later, I saw a test from 1997, the same period when I worked with him—and it said he was a forty-four-year-old female named Mark Goldberg who was negative for HIV.

Marc Wallice was thirty-nine and a male.

BILL MARGOLD: With the outbreaks in 1998, Sharon Mitchell assumes command of the HIV testing. Then she decides that the world isn't big enough for the both of us and figures she'll squeeze me out of PAW—or at least remove me from the medical parts of PAW. Which, if I had capitulated, would have gutted me.

So I just decided to squeeze her out, by giving her an organization called AIM: Adult Industry Medical. I created it spontaneously. I told her, *Now you have your own business.* Emphasis on the word *business.* And more power to her.

TRICIA DEVERAUX: I worked for John Bond two different times—with Marc Wallice—in two weeks. So it was definitely one of those times. Most likely it was the second time: It was anal both times, but the first time was a facial. The second time he came on my ass after the anal sex.

So I thought, two to one, Marc had HIV at that point, came on my ass, and some of it got into my body.

SHARON MITCHELL: Every time someone would come up positive, we'd sit in a room and argue for three hours. After a couple of months we finally figured on a standard, and we implemented it through the Protecting Adult Welfare and the Free Speech Coalition.

That was when I started to lay the groundwork for my Adult Industry Medical connections.

TRICIA DEVERAUX: When Sharon Mitchell got my list, she went through it and supposedly everybody on it tested negative. I found out later that Marc Wallice had never gone in to get a test. He had called her and said, "Oh, no, I got a test. I'm fine."

For some reason I'll never understand, Sharon Mitchell apparently trusted Marc. She said, "Oh, okay, no problem." And she called me and said, "Everyone you've worked with is negative."

I was like, "Okay. Then where'd I get it from?"

SHARON MITCHELL: Tricia Deveraux came up positive on January 7, 1998. So we pushed away all the boxes and had an industry-wide meeting at VCA. I brought in some educators from around the local area, some doctors, people from UCLA and the AIDS Healthcare Foundation, and we decided that PCR-DNA was the best way to monitor for HIV.

TRICIA DEVERAUX: Then Brooke Ashley came up positive, and she turned in a list, and again Marc Wallice was on the phone saying, "No, I'm negative."

SHARON MITCHELL: Marc Wallice was HIV positive, and he was so ashamed that he went to any length to hide it. He went to anonymous testing centers—and at that time people were getting the ELISA test intermittently, like once a year, or every six months.

MARC WALLICE: Why did I prefer the clinic on San Fernando Road? Because it cost five dollars.

SHARON MITCHELL: PCR-DNA is the best test because it will not hide a positive reading if someone's on medication. Whereas it would on the ELISA RNA test—which is why we don't use that. The ELISA test is the antibody test, which has such a long window period.

There's too many partners—we found that out with Trish—that can be exposed in the six months that it takes to determine if there's antibodies to HIV. PCR-DNA tests are for the actual DNA of the actual HIV virus itself.

MARC WALLICE: Sharon Mitchell checked the code number of the March 1998 ELISA test, and it checked out. She called the lab. It matched. So it was not a faked test.

I gave PAW my last six or seven tests. One of them listed my age as forty-nine; some say thirty-seven, others thirty-eight, thirty-six. I never tell them my age.

TRICIA DEVERAUX: Then, within another two months, there was Kimberly Jade and a Hungarian girl named Caroline. And they all turned in lists, and Marc Wallice was on all of them.

SHARON MITCHELL: When Trish stepped up and gave me her list, I was in the right place at the right time to actually do something. It really became more and more clear as the fifth and sixth girl got HIV. The one common denominator name on all of their partner lists—that hadn't been tested, and had been indeed actively avoiding tests—was Marc Wallice.

TRICIA DEVERAUX: Eventually people started saying, "Well, where's Marc's DNA test?" And they asked Marc to go to AIM and get one, but he didn't want to.

SHARON MITCHELL: I thought to myself, "My God, what has this fucking society done to impact such shame on someone that they have to consider this diagnosis different from cancer?"

My thought was not, "What an evil son of a bitch." It was, "What the fuck can I do to make this different? What can I do to make my part of the world a little more functional, and a little more clear, and level the playing field?"

MARC WALLICE: I was doing great. Producing, directing, making more money than I'd ever made acting. The reason I stopped was that Patrick Collins started insisting that I get all these tests.

TRICIA DEVERAUX: Supposedly, Patrick had to bring Marc over to AIM, and Marc was crying.

MARC WALLICE: It was said that I had to be dragged into PAW to take my PCR test. That's bullshit. Fucking lying, asshole punks. I wasn't crying, and I wasn't dragged in there.

SHARON MITCHELL: I called Marc, and I called him, and I called him, and he actively avoided me. Finally I had to call his boss, Patrick Collins, who was in Budapest, and who has little tolerance for these things. Patrick's got a very booming voice; I think I must have heard him screaming in both ears that day, even though he was in Hungary.

So Patrick had his wife in L.A.—who was pregnant and had a baby in the backseat—go pick up Marc Wallice and bring him in for testing.

MARC WALLICE: I said, "Let's go in there and get this taken care of." I would've never gone in there if I knew I was positive. If anyone came to my house and dragged me, I'd fucking break their neck. They just kept making suggestions. I said, "Fine, let's go."

SHARON MITCHELL: We brought Marc to Dr. York's office in Mission Hills. Marc did not want to do it—he kept trying to get up and get out of it, you know, because it was apparent that he knew.

He had no visible signs of HIV. And, remember, Marc was an old drug user like the rest of us, so him looking a little thin and worn was not a big deal. His appearance wasn't a big issue, but his behavior was disturbing.

MARC WALLICE: If I knew I was positive, why would I ever have gone to PAW to take a test? Why wouldn't I just say, "Fuck you. I don't have to go there. And I'll just quit the business right now and direct." Wouldn't that have been much easier than going up there—knowing that I was going to come out positive?

SHARON MITCHELL: Everybody was trying to give him a break, but there was no way around it. I mean, there was a night where we had a general meeting at the Sportsman's Lodge, for industry only. That night, I was absolutely, 100 percent sure because I got Marc's results back, and he was avoiding me. He kept saying, "Do I have it or what?"

I said, "You have to come in so we can discuss your results."

And he wouldn't come in.

MARC WALLICE: Patrick Collins found out I was positive when he was in Europe. He kept telling Reuben Swift to call me, but I wouldn't take his calls. If Patrick wants to talk to me, he'll call me. Why does he keep sending his flunkies to call me?

TRICIA DEVERAUX: Was Marc Wallice in denial? I don't know. I actually do a little better just assuming that he is.

The adult industry came to the conclusion that he was the one who gave it to the four of us, although he denies it. He may have known or may have not. Probably he did.

SHARON MITCHELL: At AIM Healthcare, our release says that we have the right to disclose your results with or without your permission because there's so many partners in jeopardy.

So I had to go in and show his release test to Steven Hirsch, Steven

Orenstein, Jeffrey Douglas, Russ Hampshire, and everybody else. They said, "We've got to close the doors to the press and just make the fucking announcement."

And I did—and everybody went crazy. But once the reality was out—that HIV had hit the adult entertainment industry—it got compliance within that community pretty quick.

MARC WALLICE: I would never have gone up there if I had known I was positive. But nobody is listening to those points. They are just listening to the gossip which is saying that I knew I was positive for all these years because I had faked a test years ago.

TRICIA DEVERAUX: I have HIV no matter what, so I just have to let go. Every once in a while I think I'm gonna go ahead and prosecute Marc Wallice and put him in jail. But then I think, I've already put it to rest once. Why dig it back up again?

MARC WALLICE: I have no idea where I might have caught HIV. It had to be from the set. It couldn't have been at the awards show because I wasn't shooting any drugs or doing any street whores out there in Las Vegas.

I don't want to sound like an idiot, but maybe I had a nick on my balls from shaving. All the sweat and shit when you're doing a "cowgirl." All the sweat is dripping down there, and you got a little nick at the base of your dick.

Who knows? How can you prove that?

SHARON MITCHELL: I had the joy of having to tell Marc Wallice that he was HIV-positive. It was awful because I go back years with him—getting high and partying and just being a roommate and a brother, you know?

I discovered some very sad things. From his viral load, he appeared to have had it for quite some time.

MARC WALLICE: I suppose this will be the new thing on CNBC. I've seen people on TV say that they've done it purposefully. I saw it on *Geraldo* once—this black guy who was proud of being positive and infecting four hundred people.

This is nothing that has been proven yet. I don't know how they are going to prove it. It's not true.

SHARON MITCHELL: A viral load is the amount of a virus that is detected in your system. It's a measurement per two milliliters of blood of how much of the virus is in your blood. When I test someone and they come back positive on a PCR-DNA, I run a Sero conversion, and another couple different tests, including the viral load test. With that and a Western Blot, I can usually tell how long a person has had HIV.

MARC WALLICE: I hate to say it, but I'm going to laugh my ass off when the next person comes up positive that I haven't been involved with. I won't laugh for the person, but I will laugh for the idea that Marc Wallice infected the porn girls. Take that and stick it up your asses. And it's going to happen. *It's going to happen.*

SHARON MITCHELL: The PCR-DNA test turned out to be amazing because there has been absolutely zero spread of HIV in the adult industry—since Marc Wallice—because of the HIV monitoring system.

There have been people who have gotten HIV, and who might have brought it into the industry, but they haven't worked yet—because we've written all the policies for the companies that say you have to have a clean bill of health before you work.

I mean, it's happened where they're unzipping their flies, getting ready to have sex with a girl or two, and they call up going, "Hey, we're about ready to start a scene, where's the fax?"

And we're like, "Hold on, it's positive."

TRICIA DEVERAUX: Marc Wallice was basically blackballed from the whole industry except for a couple of companies. VCA believed his story—that he didn't know and that he was devastated. He didn't know what to do, so they took him in as an editor for a while. But eventually even VCA ended up firing him; now he's editing with a different company.

MARC WALLICE: I've got to start like a regular fucking piece of shit again. A six-dollar-an-hour job. I'm thinking of going to school to learn computers. I need something to do.

My mother can't keep giving me money anymore. I have one brother who's three years older. He's a fan. He doesn't know yet. Let him find out from the magazines.

I'm a big star to them. Little do they know.

BUD LEE: Marc Wallice is a little boy. Got bigger pants on him, like most of the people in our business. I like him a lot. He's a good kid.

SHARON MITCHELL: I also realized that the last movie I did was with Marc Wallice—without a condom. So telling him brought up a lot of things for me, too, which I had to set aside in order to do my job as a counselor.

TRICIA DEVERAUX: I talked to Simon Wolf, who was either owner or coowner of the company that hired Marc Wallice. I'm like, "Why is he editing for you? You know, he basically caused an HIV epidemic in the adult business."

Simon goes, "Well, that hasn't been proven, and he says differently, and I believe him."

MARC WALLICE: Now I walk around with my head down, trying to hide, thinking that everybody knows that I infected people with HIV because that's all they're going to read. What does my life hold now? A job at McDonald's in Utah?

BUD LEE: I got Marc Wallice a job after he was HIV-positive. Why? Well, a lot of us used to depend on the fact that Marc was a home-run king. He'd come on the set, get an erection, fuck as many women as you wanted him to, and he'd come when you asked him to do it. And he did that for us for fifteen years. Saved our asses again and again. We owe him. To make sure that he's gainfully employed in some way or fashion or another for the rest of his life.

As an industry, we owe him that.

SHARON MITCHELL: There's the question of where those other tests came from. Were they valid? Were they forged?

TRICIA DEVERAUX: I still laugh at how ironic it is that I wasn't doing anything outside of the business to get HIV. One of the reasons I came into the business was to explore my sexuality in this safe little community. And because one person betrayed that community, I got HIV.

SHARON MITCHELL: Was Marc bisexual? Probably, yeah. He had done some bisexual movies, so, you know, it happens that way. AIDS is in epidemic proportions in Los Angeles and in the United States. Why wouldn't it come into the porn business? Who knows what people do? The guys could be with other guys—and the girls could be shooting dope.

MARC WALLICE: I used to inject cocaine. About eight years ago, I used to shoot up with Sharon Mitchell and Barbara Holder, aka Aja. If I had it then, they have it, too. But I haven't done needles in seven years.

SHARON MITCHELL: I would do a shot five minutes before my scene. But I was a fanatic about using clean needles. I didn't fuck a lot of people. And I didn't fuck in the ass and all that.

MARC WALLICE: I don't fuck nobody outside the business. I've been doing that for seventeen years. Just because I worked with every person who's become positive, does that mean I'm the reason?

SHARON MITCHELL: It's easy for a woman to get it, and if a guy's exposed to it over and over again, it's easy for him to get it. You know there's high-risk categories. People who do pornography aren't uptight, you know? They're not executives. They have a lot of kink and a lot of shit going on.

TRICIA DEVERAUX: I haven't seen Marc Wallice since I found out he's the one. He didn't try to contact me. He tried to contact Brooke Ashley, and she basically told him to go die.

MARC WALLICE: I hear that Brooke Ashley is also pressing charges. I don't know how she can prove anything.

TRICIA DEVERAUX: Marc Wallice contacted John Stagliano after Brooke; I don't think he knew that John and I had been talking. Marc said, "What should I do?"

John's like, "Dude! You gave these girls HIV! I'm more worried about what's going to happen to them than I am about what's going to happen to you!"

Marc denied it. "No—I didn't know."

John was like, "I don't want to know you."

And that's basically how that ended up.

MARC WALLICE: When we're out together, even my mother says, "Marc, those people over there know you. You're a star."

I used to be a big, famous star. Now I'm a nobody.

JOHN STAGLIANO: Marc Wallice and I knew each other. We never went out socially or anything, but we both entered the performing end of the business in the very early eighties.

Before the controversy came about, he asked me to sell his movies and stuff. But we were never really friends, other than the fact that we would talk on sets. I shot him a lot of times in the 1980s, when I started the Buttman stuff.

But I haven't talked to Marc since 1996 or 1997.

DAVID AARON CLARK (PORN WRITER): People say John Stagliano changed everything when he did Buttman—when he took the camera off the tripod and squatted down and followed girls' butts around. But I think the real thing he did—that really grabbed people—was to use his work to feed his own lust.

JOHN STAGLIANO: People give me credit for inventing "gonzo porn" because a lot of people have imitated me. But Buttman was just an idea I had in 1989, after I had already started Evil Angel. I was thinking about two things: I wanted to shoot a buns fetish movie, and I wanted to do a movie where the camera was like part of the set, and I was in the movie as the cameraman, and girls could look right into the camera. I wanted to arrange it so the girls could be sexy right to the camera, which turned out to be very effective.

TIM CONNELLY: John Stagliano ended up living out the Book of Job—porn style. He lost his number-one actress and beloved but troubled girlfriend Krysti Lynn, whom he had been trying to help out of addiction and into a singing career.

JOHN STAGLIANO: I didn't meet Krysti Lynn until I was shooting her in San Diego. But I arranged to talk to her on the phone before that, through John Leslie, who had shot her in *Dog Walker* and *The Voyeur I*.

I told her I had seen her in some scenes, and I really wanted to shoot her. Yeah, I had a crush on her—yeah, sure.

BROCKTON O'TOOLE (PORN STAR): John was pretty serious about Krysti. He moved into the nicest place in Malibu, and she moved in with him. They shared a bedroom—the master bedroom.

JOHN STAGLIANO: I managed to make a date with Krysti the next time she came up from San Diego. We went out a few times, and she moved in with me about a month later.

We had a brief period where we were both really in love. Then it got difficult for me because she had a lot of emotional mood swings and stuff. So after about four months we continued to live together—but we weren't as intimate as we had been.

BROCKTON O'TOOLE: Krysti really wanted to have a family with him. And John was dragging his feet.

JOHN STAGLIANO: Krysti had been in treatment when she was younger; she had a lot of trouble as an adolescent—with her family and drugs and stuff like that. She just had a lot of energy, you know, and expected a lot out of life—and when she didn't get it, she'd get upset.

So she continued to live with me for another year without us being actual lovers.

BROCKTON O'TOOLE: They reached the point where John was going to underwrite a record contract for Krysti because she was a talented violinist and a very fine singer, and she wanted to see if she could make it as a pop singer. So they got some people out from Chicago, and, lo and behold, it turns out they want to work with her.

JOHN STAGLIANO: Krysti was supposedly going to meet Marky Mark, alias Mark Wahlberg, at some restaurant. She was at my house because we were supposed to look at a location the next morning for her music video. Krysti had recorded a song, which had been written by Prince and was produced by Ed Strickland, who had been working for Madonna's company. So we were producing a music video to go along with the song.

Krysti was all dressed up, and she was playing hard to get, and then Marky Mark's people didn't call back, so it was a memorable afternoon.

Krysti left, and she was going a hundred miles an hour on Los Virgines Road and lost control of the car and went off into a gully.

She died.

I never had anybody I was close to die before, so it was a little bit difficult.

BROCKTON O'TOOLE: John and I were out there when they found the vehicle. I went out there, and the highway patrol had already removed Krysti from the wreck and taken her away.

Krysti was found under the steering wheel. It was very sad. John was pretty torn up about it. So I have a feeling that the business down in Brazil would not have happened, if it hadn't been for this. I think he was punishing himself.

TRICIA DEVERAUX: Krysti had a friend in the car with her when they were both killed, and I think John felt responsible somehow.

BROCKTON O'TOOLE: John was torn up pretty badly. It was tough, but Krysti was driving, and she was at fault, no question about it. And there was this young girl, a secretary, who was also killed. Krysti was driving John's second car, so her family said to John, "What are you going to do about this?"

John had a meeting with the other girl's family, and he says "Let me talk to your lawyer."

The family went into another room. John said to the lawyer, "Well, what do you think?" The lawyer says, "Well, I think if you want to settle it right now, I think the family would agree to $250,000."

John said, "I'll write you a check. But I have to give it to the family myself. I want to tell them I'm sorry."

And he did—and told them not to worry about the funeral.

JOHN STAGLIANO: On the first anniversary of Krysti's death, I was feeling kind of bad about myself. The girlfriend I was with, I felt, didn't really love me; she didn't show affection, and I was not feeling good, a little bit bitter.

So I go down to Brazil.

TIM CONNELLY: John ended up on a suicide mission in South America, seeking out a Brazilian transvestite street hooker to violently fuck him up the ass without a condom, hoping to drown all his sorrows and guilt.

JOHN STAGLIANO: I'd been drinking a little bit, kind of enjoying being unhappy. Next thing I know I'm picking up this street "girl" and demanding to be fucked up the ass, so lost in my self-pity I don't care what happens.

I gamble, and I lose.

TRICIA DEVERAUX: John went down to Brazil, and he got HIV.

He knew right away that he'd done something he shouldn't have—the non-condom part for sure. So he started getting HIV tests.

JOHN STAGLIANO: I was real careful the next couple of months, getting tested all the time. I didn't think I'd gotten it because I really didn't think he'd taken the rubber off before he fucked me. But for six months I was worried, thinking I had to change my life.

And then I started thinking, "Man, I wish I could do it again. I'm not going to do it again. But I want to."

TIM CONNELLY: John, after being diagnosed HIV-positive, confessed his disease to a more-than-not ragingly homophobic industry, knowing full well the details of his infection would give his jealous detractors and business enemies poisoned fodder for the gossip market.

And with his courage he proved himself yet again to be of the rarest quality in the smut biz: an honest man.

JOHN STAGLIANO: You know, I am a little bisexual. I had sucked some guys' dicks in quarter peep shows and stuff like that, as a variety thing. But primarily, I guess, I'm heterosexual. I just personally don't worry so much what people think about me.

But, you know, admitting that I really wanted to get fucked in the ass, and might really like it, is not necessarily a socially acceptable thing for a straight man.

TRICIA DEVERAUX: I met John Stagliano because he called me—he had gotten HIV a year before I did. He said, "Well, you need to have someone to talk to who kind of understands a little bit about what it's like to have HIV. I could talk to you a little bit."

I said, "You know, that would be really nice." So we went out for a drink at a Mexican restaurant near my apartment. We hit it off immediately, as friends.

JOHN STAGLIANO: I really enjoyed shooting Tricia when she was working. The people in the business today are so much more sophisticated than they were, I think, ten years ago. So I just starting talking to Tricia after she got infected, and several months later we wound up getting together.

TRICIA DEVERAUX: John and I became really good friends, and then he had to go back down to Brazil to shoot a video. And he called me a couple times from Brazil, even though he barely knew me. I said, "This is costing you a fortune." He said, "Ah, don't worry about it."

Another time, he called me after he'd been drinking a little bit. I told him, "You know what? I think I just have to leave L.A. because everybody just thinks I'm this horrible drug user who was trying to infect them."

And John said, "Well, I know things are hard for you. But if you stay, maybe you could, you know—maybe it would be nice to have you around."

I just chalked it up to him being kind of drunk; I didn't think twice about it, and about a month later I went back to the Midwest, for a year and a half.

JOHN STAGLIANO: I grew up in Chicago; I have reason to go back to Chicago. So off and on for the next year I went back three or four times and saw Tricia there. Then she came back.

Yeah, we fell in love.

TRICIA DEVERAUX: We realized we liked a lot of the same things. We're both from the Chicago area—and our personalities are very similar, which was what really drew me to him right away because I'd bombed out on two relationships by going for two different extremes.

JOHN STAGLIANO: Tricia and I have a lot in common. We're both pretty much type-A personalities; we like the same music, rock and roll; and sexually we're very compatible.

TRICIA DEVERAUX: What do we tell critics who say we're only together because we both have HIV? I think that's why we started to get interested in each other. But if that was all there was, I think we would have broken up. We're both too strong-minded to stay with someone for that reason alone.

We've had a couple of hard times in our relationship because now that I'm out of porn as a performer I've always wanted my relationships off-camera to be monogamous.

John loves going to strip clubs; he loves hiring strippers to do private strip shows and things like that. And I was like, "Why do you need that?" John was always a very sexual person, so having HIV probably hit him a lot harder than it hit me. Because John was having casual sex, and he had to stop doing that.

JOHN STAGLIANO: I have girls dance for me sometimes—strippers—and when I've got their butts in my face I just play with them forever. I really get into focus, and I think, "Oh my God, what I had!"

In the last couple of months I've thought about how fucking incredible Krysti Lynn's butt was. I mean, I loved fucking Krysti from behind—it was the most incredible experience I ever had. I really enjoyed it, but I never appreciated it—not in the same way I appreciate the little things now.

TRICIA DEVERAUX: The decision to try to have a baby was difficult for John and me because of HIV. We didn't even know if it was even possible. Then we read a couple of articles about HIV-positive moms giving birth and the babies not having HIV. So we started talking to our doctors about it.

I asked the doctor, "Is all this just really good luck?" She said it was a protocol of several different things. The mom has to take HIV medication during pregnancy; I wasn't taking medicine yet, but I started when I was two months pregnant and took it all the way through the labor.

The doctor also said the baby would have to take HIV medicine for the first month after she was born. And I'd have to have a C-section because that would allow the doctors to control what would happen with the blood. She said, "If we do all those things, we'll have less than a 1 percent chance that your baby will have HIV."

Even then, we were worried: *What happens if she does?* But now it's clear that she still could have lived a normal life—and even if she didn't, there are worse things in life.

So we decided to try it.

The baby, Isabelle, is negative. And she's a really good thing for both of us.

JOHN STAGLIANO: I was getting fucked-up the other night watching porno movies. And I thought, this is how you write a movie: You set up this whole scenario where some guy's doing drugs, he's about to go too far and OD, and just before he does, he looks at the camera and says, *"Fuck you, people!* You live by a whole different standard than I do! I have this life in front of me that *inspires* me. Every one of you has done something at some point to fuck up your life—get a little too drunk, do too much cocaine. That's life, right? And you're judging *me?"*

I used to judge these people, and I never knew what was going on inside them.

You know, they're experiencing life in a certain way that I don't know about, but I need to know about. We want to push ourselves to experience life and to enjoy it: to be a race car driver, or do drugs, or get fucked in the ass and risk getting HIV—it's all the same fucking thing. Pushing yourself to experience life to its fullest necessarily involves risk. And if you sit in your room and never do anything—like my mother wanted me to do because she was worried that if I left the house I'd get hit by a car—you'll never know what life is like.

Maybe it's genetically programmed, like women holding back sex. We're genetically programmed to say, "Wait a second—*oh*, it feels good to go around that curve really fast, but I'm gonna crash."

You know, like Krysti Lynn did.

Source Notes

All quotes are from interviews with the authors, except for the following material quoted from other sources:

Prologue: *Roger Ebert:* "Russ Meyer: King of the Nudies," *Film Comment,* January–February 1973. *Ann Perry:* From interviews by Cass Paley. *Doris Wishman:* From Christopher J. Jarmick, *Senses of Cinema, Great Directors—a critical database,* September 2002. *Russ Meyer:* From interview by Roger Ebert, *Chicago Sun-Times,* February 16, 1969; from Russ Meyer as told to Adolph Albion Schwartz, *A Clean Breast* (Hollywood: Hauck Publishing Co., 2000).

PART ONE: THE SWORD SWALLOWER

1. The Turkey Raffle: *Linda Lovelace:* Some material from Linda Lovelace with Mike McGrady, *Ordeal* (New York: Citadel, 1980; Berkley, 1981), and interview with Eric Danville, © 2001. *Harry Reems:* From Harry Reems, *Here Comes Harry Reems* (New York: Pinnacle, 1975).

2. If You Can Make It There, You Can Make It Anywhere: *Linda Lovelace:* Some material from Linda Lovelace as told to Carl Wallin, *The Intimate Diary of Linda Lovelace* (New York: Pinnacle, 1974), and from *Ordeal. Harry Reems:* From *Here Comes Harry Reems.*

3. Vickie Killed the Nudie-Cuties: All original.

4. Rent: *Harry Reems:* From *Here Comes Harry Reems. Tina Russell:* From Tina Russell, *Porn Star: The Autobiography of Today's Most Exotic X-rated Actress* (New York: Lancer Books, 1973).

5. Doggie Style: *Linda Lovelace:* Some material from *Ordeal.*

6. Mary Had a Little Lamb: *Butchie Peraino:* From Nora Ephron, *Esquire,* February 1973. *Harry Reems:* From *Here Comes Harry Reems. Gerard Damiano:* From Al Goldstein, "Gerry Damiano Remembers Linda Lovelace: From Head to Eternity," *SCREW,* April 5, 1974. *Linda*

Lovelace: From *Ordeal* and Linda Lovelace, *Inside Linda Lovelace* (New York: Pinnacle, 1973).

7. "Do You Mind If I Smoke While You Eat?": *Harry Reems:* From *Here Comes Harry Reems* and Al Goldstein, "An Interview with Harry Reems: Superstud of the Silver Screen," *SCREW,* May 20, 1974. *Linda Lovelace:* From *Ordeal. Gerard Damiano:* From Al Goldstein, "Gerry Damiano Remembers Linda Lovelace," and "A Throat Is Born," *High Society,* undated article. *Carol Conners:* From interview with Earl Anthony, *Adam* Magazine.

8. SCREW-ed: *Chuck Traynor:* From *SCREW. Butchie Peraino:* From interview with Nora Ephron, *Esquire. Linda Lovelace:* from *Ordeal* and interview by Eric Danville. *Gerard Damiano:* From James Martin, "Gerard Damiano Interview," *Hustler,* March 1975. *Nora Ephron:* From Nora Ephron, *Esquire,* February 1973. *Harry Reems:* From *Here Comes Harry Reems. Fred Biersdorf:* From Ellen Farley and William K. Knoedelseder Jr., "Family Business" *Calendar/Los Angeles Times Sunday Magazine,* June 13, 1982. *Al Goldstein:* From "Al Goldstein: The *Playboy* Interview, *Playboy,* October 1974. *Sammy Davis Jr.:* From Sammy Davis Jr, with Jane Boyar and Burt Boyar, *Why Me?* (New York: Farrar, Straus, & Giroux, 1989).

9. Don't Count the Money, Weigh It: *Fred Biersdorf:* From Ellen Farley and William K. Knoedelseder Jr., "Family Business," *Calendar/Los Angeles Sunday Times Magazine. Chuck Bernstene:* From FBI wiretap. "Organized Crime Reaps Huge Profits from Dealing in Pornographic Films," *New York Times,* October 12, 1975.

PART TWO: PORNO CHIC

10. To Bowl or Not to Bowl?: *Jim and Artie Mitchell:* From Tony Crawley, "The Mitchell Brothers," *Game,* July 1976; William Rotsler, *Contemporary Erotic Cinema,* © 1973 by William Rotsler; Interview, *Club,* February 1976; Phyllis and Eberhard Kronhausen, "The People Behind the Green Door," *The Sex People* (Chicago: Playboy Press, 1975); and videotape interview, School of Erotology.

11. Size Matters: *Al Goldstein, Bill Amerson, Bob Chin, Bob Vosse, Sharon Holmes, Bunny Bleu, Annette Haven:* From interviews by Cass Paley.

12. Ebony and Ivory Snow: *Jim Mitchell:* From Interview, *Club,* February 1976. *Artie Mitchell:* From Tony Crawley, "The Mitchell Brothers," *Game,* July 1976.

13. Hair of the Dog: *Linda Lovelace:* From *Ordeal* and *The Intimate Diary of Linda Lovelace. Al Goldstein:* From "Al Goldstein: The *Playboy*

Interview." *Nick Tosches:* From Nick Tosches, "Arf? Arf, Arf, Arf! (Maybe)," "Openers," *Oui*, October 1973.

14. Automated Vending: *Reuben Sturman:* from Eric Schlosser, *Reefer Madness: Sex, Drugs and Cheap Labor in the American Black Market* (New York: Houghton Mifflin, 2003).

15. Trading Up: *Linda Lovelace:* From *Inside Linda Lovelace* and *The Intimate Diary of Linda Lovelace.* "Linda Lovelace Tries to Shed 'Deep Throat' Image for Miami Café Break-In": *Variety,* August 29, 1973. *Al Goldstein:* From *Playboy*, October 1974. "Roger Horrified as Porn Star Tries to Take Over Ann-Margret's Act": *Movie World,* May 1974. "Vegas Drug Bust": *People,* March 1974. "Milestones": *Time,* March 4, 1974.

16. The Devil in Miss Steinberg: *Harry Reems:* From *Here Comes Harry Reems.* *Gerard Damiano:* From Ken Gaul, "The Devil and Mr. Damiano," *Genesis,* September 1980; James Martin, "Gerard Damiano Interview," *Hustler,* March 1975; Kenneth Turan and Stephen F. Zito, *Sinema: American Pornographic Films and the People Who Make Them* (Praeger Publishers, 1974). *Linda Lovelace:* From *The Intimate Diary of Linda Lovelace* and *Inside Linda Lovelace. Annie Sprinkle:* From Annie Sprinkle, *Annie Sprinkle: Post-Porn Modernist* (San Francisco: Cleis Press, 1998).

17. Holmes v. Wadd: *Sharon Holmes, Bob Chinn, Bill Amerson, Bob Vosse, Dawn Schiller, Tom Blake:* From interviews by Cass Paley.

PART THREE: SHOW WORLD

18. Boxed Lunch: *Vanessa Del Rio, Annie Sprinkle:* Grady T. Turner with Vanessa Del Rio, Legs McNeil, and Annie Sprinkle, "Conversation Four: Porn," in *NYC Sex: How New York City Transformed Sex in America* (New York: Scala Publishers, 2002). *Serena:* Al Goldstein, "Daddy's Dirty Darling," *SCREW,* June 5, 1978.

19. The Ballad of Jason and Tina: All original.

20. Turnover: *Tiffany Clark:* Tiffany Clark, "Tiffany Clark's Lust at First Sight: True Confessions," *Partner,* undated article.

21. Plato's Retreat: *Al Goldstein, Patrice Trudeau, Josh Alan Friedman:* From Josh Alan Friedman, *Tales of Times Square* (New York: Delacorte Press, 1986; Feral House, 1993).

PART FOUR: FAMILY AFFAIRS

22. This Thing of Ours: *Operation Amore Report: Organized Crime and its Involvement in Pornography and Prostitution in the South Florida*

Area, Dade County Public Safety Department, Organized Crime Bureau, Vice Investigation Section, June 1977. Coroner's Report, Clark County, Nevada.

23. Memphis Backlash Blues: "Pornography on Trial," *New York Times Sunday Magazine,* March 6, 1977; *Harry Reems:* From *Here Comes Harry Reems;* "Eight Men Sentenced in Deep Throat Case," *New York Times,* May 1, 1977.

24. Deep Cover: *Pat Livingston, Bruce Ellavsky, Betty Jo:* Some material from interviews by Ron LaBrecque.

25: Nobody Does It Better: *Pat Livingston, Bruce Ellavsky, Dick Phinney:* Some material from interviews by Ron LaBrecque.

26. Looks Like We Made It: *Robert DiBernardo:* FBI wiretap. Operation Amore Report.

PART FIVE: PORN GOES BETTER WITH COKE

27. Down the Drain: *Al Goldstein, Patrice Trudeau:* From Josh Alan Friedman, *Tales of Times Square*

28. "Blow": All original.

29. Stayin' Alive: *Bruce Ellavsky:* From FBI wiretap (where indicated). *Al Bonanni, Bruce Ellavsky:* From interviews with Ron LaBrecque.

30. Seka to the Rescue: All original.

31. Johnny on the Pipe: *Annette Haven, Don Fernando, Richard Pacheco, Bob Vosse, Joel Sussman, Bill Amerson, Sheri St. Clair, Reb, Bob Chin, Bobby Hollander:* From interviews by Cass Paley.

32. Beauty and the Beast: *Lorene Smith's Sanity Evaluation:* Ohio Department of Mental Health, Central Ohio Psychiatric Hospital, Columbus, OH, November 1, 1989.

33. Falling Out: *Marty Bernbeck:* From FBI wiretap, 1979. *Pam Ellavsky:* From interviews by Ron LaBrecque.

34. St. Valentine's Day Massacre: *Fred Schwartz, Vickie Livingston:* From interviews by Ron LaBrecque. "55 Persons Indicted in Piracy of Films and in Pornography—FBI Investigation Called Biggest Attack Against Activities," *New York Times,* February 15, 1980. "Miami-Based FBI Investigation Breaks Up Porn Film Network," *Miami Herald,* February 15, 1980. *Artie Mitchell:* From videotaped interview, School of Erotology.

35. "Ordeal": "Mrs. Marciano Calls Herself 'A Typical Housewife'; The World Knew Her as Linda Lovelace," *People,* January 28, 1980. *Linda Lovelace:* From *Ordeal* and Linda Lovelace, *Out of Bondage* (New York: Berkley, 1987). "Now Here's A Switch Dept.": New York *Daily*

News, May 30, 1980. "A Strange Bedfellow for the War on Pornography": New York *Daily News*, June 8, 1980.

PART SIX: WONDERLAND AVENUE

36. The Godfather of Hollywood: *David Lind, Tracy McCourt:* From *The People of the State of California v. John Curtis Holmes, No. A374106. Jeanna Nash:* From divorce deposition. *John Holmes:* From Barbara Wilkins, "John Holmes: Murder, Sex, Drugs & Jail," *Hustler*, June 1983.

37. "It's Not Like You Said It Was Gonna Be": *David Lind, Tracy McCourt:* From *California v. Holmes. John Holmes:* From Barbara Wilkins, "John Holmes: Murder, Sex, Drugs & Jail," *Hustler*, June 1983.

38. Nobody Waved Hello: *John Holmes:* From Barbara Wilkins, "John Holmes: Murder, Sex, Drugs & Jail," *Hustler*, June 1983. *Susan Launius:* From *California v. Holmes. Frank Tomlinson:* From interviews by Cass Paley.

39. "Think This Will Fuck Up My Fourth of July Weekend?": *Tom Lange, Tom Blake:* From interviews by Cass Paley. *Linda Mitchell:* From *California v. Holmes.*

PART SEVEN: GETTING OUT

40. Method Acting: *Vickie Livingston, Michael Griffin, Fred Schwartz, Hope Johnson, Larry Powell:* From interviews by Ron LaBrecque.

41. On the Lam: *Dawn Schiller, Sharon Holmes, Tom Lange:* From interviews by Cass Paley.

42. Don't Embarrass the Bureau: *Vickie Livingston, Pat Livingston, Fred Schwartz, Nancy Livingston, Bill Brown:* Some material from Ron LaBrecque. "FBI Agent's Arrest May Hurt Porn Cases": *Miami Herald*, February 20, 1982. "FBI Boots Out MIPORN Undercover Agent": *Miami Herald*, May 15, 1982.

43. Grave's End: "Death of Mob's Porno King Takes Wraps off Gunmen": *Miami Herald*, February 27, 1980. *Bob Hanson:* Name changed (original interview). "2 Die, 1 Hurt by Shotgun," New York *Daily News*, January 5, 1982. "Two Slain and One Hurt in Mob-Style Shooting": *New York Times*, January 5, 1982. *Jay Dolton:* From confidential NYPD report. *Michael Croissant:* Farley and Knoedelseder, "Family Business," *Calendar/Los Angeles Times Sunday Magazine*, June 13, 1982. "Bystander Killed in Mob Shooting Was a Social Worker and Ex-Nun": *New York Times*, January 6, 1982.

44. The Trial: "Actor Arrested": Reuters International News, December 7, 1981. *Frank Tomlinson:* From interview by Cass Paley. "Holmes Ordered to Stand Trial": United Press International, February 2, 1982. "Holmes Found Innocent," United Press International, June 25, 1982. "Judge Ordered Holmes Released": Reuters International News, November 22, 1982. *Al Goldstein:* From "Al Goldstein: The *Playboy* Interview."

PART EIGHT: VIDEO VIXENS

45. Hooray for Hollywood!: *Michael London, Karen Applegate, Phillip Applegate, Bobby Hollander, Laurie Smith, Eddie Holzman:* Michael London, Calendar/*Los Angeles Times Sunday Magazine,* May 6, 1984.

46. Mr. Untouchable: "Reuben Sturman and Six Others Acquitted": *New York Times,* July 26, 1978. *Alan Dershowitz, Harold Lime:* From *Los Angeles Times,* 1995. *Reuben Sturman, Naomi Delgado:* From *Day One,* ABC News, July 20, 1995. Additional Reuben Sturman material from Eric Schlosser, *Reefer Madness.*

47: Shattered Innocence: *Karen Applegate:* Michael London, *Calendar/Los Angeles Times Sunday Magazine,* May 6, 1984. "A Porn Star's Suicide at 20 Leaves a Legacy of Shattered Innocence": *People,* March 14, 1988. "Shauna Grant Dead": *Film World Reports,* April 16, 1984.

48. Fast Forward: All original.

49. Club 90: All original.

50. Kristie Nussman: *Traci Lords:* From interview with Bob Ellison, *Adult Video News,* January 14, 1985, and Doug Oliver, "Traci Lords: Porn's Brightest Star Changes Orbit," *Hustler,* March 1986. *Christy Canyon:* From interview with Jeremy Stone, *Hustler,* © 1998 Tim Connelly. *Greg Dark:* From Doug Oliver, "Traci Lords: Porn's Brightest Star Changes Orbit," *Hustler,* March 1986.

PART NINE: THE PARTY'S OVER

51. The Porn Marriage: *Bobby Genova:* From the *Los Angeles* Times, August 20, 1989.

52. To Be or Not to Be?: *Pat Livingston, Nancy Livingston, Vickie Livingston:* From interviews by Ron LaBrecque.

53. GRID: All original.

54. Pimping and Pandering: *Jerry Butler:* Jerry Butler as told to Robert Rimmer & Catherine Tavel, *Raw Talent* (New York: Prometheus, 1990). *Buck Adams:* From interviews by Cass Paley. "Hard-Core Sex Films: Does

Casting Constitute Pandering?": *Los Angeles Times,* May 20, 1985. "Judge Gives Light Penalty to Porn Film Producer": *Los Angeles Times,* July 16, 1985. "Police Raid Distributors of Sexually Explicit Films": *Los Angeles Times,* June 29, 1985.

55. Who Dropped the Dime on Traci?: *Traci Lords:* From interview with Bob Ellison, *Adult Video News,* January 14, 1985, and Traci Lords, *Underneath It All* (New York: HarperEntertainment, 2003). *Christy Canyon:* From interview with Jeremy Stone, *Hustler,* © 1988 Tim Connelly. "Sex Films Pulled, Star Allegedly Too Young": *Los Angeles Times,* July 18, 1986. "Porn Starlet Off Hook": New York *Daily News,* July 19, 1986. "Sex Film Star Not Facing Charges, Reiner Says": *Los Angeles Times,* July 19, 1986. "Distributor Indicted Over Sex Videotape": *Los Angeles Times,* August 15, 1986. "The Region": *Los Angeles Times,* August 22, 1986. "Investigation of Traci Lords Pornography Case Expanded," *Los Angeles Times,* October 4, 1986. "Three in Traci Lords Sex Film Case Indicted": *Los Angeles Times,* March 5, 1987. "Arrests Hinder the Prosecution of Sexually Explicit Films, Police Say": *Los Angeles Times,* March 11, 1987. "Man Pleads Guilty in Traci Lords Case": *Los Angeles Times,* April 1, 1987.

PART TEN: BACKLASH

56. The Meese Commission: *Traci Lords:* From *Underneath It All. Richard Nixon, Andrea Dworkin:* Philip Nobile and Eric Nadler, *United States of America vs. Sex: How the Meese Commission Lied About Pornography* (Minotaur Press, 1986). *Ronald Reagan:* From taped remarks at Moral Majority rally, Dallas, Texas, October 1980. *Catherine MacKinnon, Linda Lovelace:* From the *Final Report of the Attorney General's Commission on Pornography,* 1986.

57. Disappearing DiBe: *Sammy "the Bull" Gravano, John Gotti:* From trial testimony as reproduced in Ralph Blumenthal, *The Gotti Tapes* (New York: Random House, 1992) and from Peter Maas, *Underboss* (New York: HarperCollins, 1997).

58. Conclusions: All original.

59. Christmas Eve with Lori and the Kids: *Lorene Smith's Sanity Evaluation:* Ohio Department of Mental Health, Central Ohio Psychiatric Hospital, Columbus, OH, November 1, 1989. *Sgt. Lawless, Sgt. Hopkins:* Worthington Police Department Police Report, Crime Against Person Case Report. "Father Released From Prison for Worthington Boys," *Columbus Dispatch,* January 13, 1987. "Con Wants to Take Sons' Bodies for California Burial": *Columbus Dispatch,* January 14, 1987. "Justice

Dept. Memo Details Dad's Pornography Deals": *Columbus Dispatch*, January 18, 1987.

60. The Last Chance: *Bill Amerson, Cicciolina, Tom Lange:* From interviews by Cass Paley.

61. Jail: "Supreme Court Exonerates Filmmaker of Pandering," *Los Angeles Times*, August 25, 1988. "Rejected Legal Assault on Sex Films Appealed," *Los Angeles Times*, December 24, 1988. "Lords Video Agent Convicted of Child Porno Charges": *Los Angeles Times*, June 16, 1989.

62. Another Mob Hit?: "Killing of Porn Pioneer Still Baffles Police, Peers; Inquiry Affords Rare Peek at 'Playpen of the Damned'": *Los Angeles Times*, August 20, 1989. "Alleged East Cost Mob Figure Named in Videotape Fraud": *Los Angeles Times*, September 25, 1989. *Bobby Genova:* From "Killing of Porn Pioneer Still Baffles Police, Peers," *Los Angeles Times*, August 20, 1989, and www.lukeford.com, July 1998.

63. Cry-Baby: *Patricia Briceland:* Testimony in Case CR8800295-01, *United States vs. Gottesman.* "Daughter Feared Death from Makers of Porn Films, Mother Testifies": *Los Angeles Times*, April 27, 1989. "Video Porn Distributor Gets 1-Year Sentence": *Los Angeles Times*, October 24, 1989.

64. Divorce: Porn Style: "Raid Led Back to Slain Man's Wife, Unrelated Case Spurred the Arrest of Spouse, Friend in Porn Maker's Killing": *Los Angeles Daily News*, January 28, 1990. "Incriminating Letter Is Not Defendant's, Witness Says": *Los Angeles Times*, August 17, 1991. "Jury Acquits Wife in 1989 Slaying of Sex-Video Maker": *Los Angeles Times*, August 31, 1991.

PART 11: FAME & MISFORTUNE

65. Rock and Roll High School: *Savannah:* From Russ Kregaen, "Savannah: Porn's Most Explosive Platinum Blonde Bombshell," 1992, and "Fast Forward: Savannah Opens Up," *Hustler Erotic Video Guide*, October 1993. *Marc Carriere:* From Tim Connelly, "The Entrepreneurs of Erotica, Part I: Marc Carriere," © Tim Connelly. *Vince Neil:* From Tommy Lee, Mick Mars, Vince Neil, and Nikki Sixx with Neil Strauss, *The Dirt* (ReganBooks, 2001). *Slash:* From interview with Joel McIver, *Record Collector*, February 2001. *Bryn Bridenthal, Pam Longoria, Kirk West, Mike Wilsey, Marc Verlaine:* From Peter Wilkinson, "Dream Girl," *Rolling Stone*, October 20, 1994, and Mike Sager, "Little Girl Lost," *GQ*, November 1994.

66. Tired: All original.

67. Cain and Abel: *Bob Callahan:* From John Hubner, *Bottom Feeders: From Free Love to Hard Core* (New York: Doubleday, 1992).

68. **The Bombing:** *Tamara Green, Jay Brisette, Naomi Delgado, Florence Clanton, Russ Hampshire:* From transcripts of *United States of America vs. Reuben Sturman.* "Porn Trial Jury Told of Bomb Scene": *Chicago Tribune,* August 27, 1993. "Bomb Testimony Opens Extortion Trial; Woman Tells of Efforts to Save Blast Victim": *Chicago Sun-Times,* August 27, 1993. "Reputed Porn Kingpin Convicted in Plot Against Adult Bookstores": *Chicago Tribune,* September 10, 1993. "Porn King Cleared in Bombing Case, More Jail Time Due": *Cleveland Plain Dealer,* September 10, 1993.

PART 12: KILLER AND FILLER

69. **The Girls who Mark Built:** *Mark Carriere:* www.lukeford.com. "Demand Is Strong, but Police Crackdowns and a Saturated Market Spell Trouble for One of L.A.'s Biggest Businesses," *Los Angeles Times Magazine,* February 17, 1991; Dick Howard, "The Entrepreneurs of Erotica, Part I: Mark Carriere," © Tim Connelly.

70. **Severed:** *John Wayne Bobbitt, Lorena Bobbitt, Howard Perry:* Peter Kane, *The Bobbitt Case: Transcripts of the Sex Trial That Shocked the World!* (New York: Pinnacle, 1994). *Larry Furst:* Larry Furst, "The Making and Raking of a Porn Stud: John Wayne Bobbitt Proves His Manhood and Shows the World How Smart He Really Is!," © 1999 Tim Connelly. *Dr. David Berman:* Rick Sandack, "The Third Degree: Dr. David Berman, Penis Attacher," *Chic,* March 1995.

71. **The Great Escape:** "Porn King Flees": *Orange County Register,* December 9, 1992. "Sturman May Have Left U.S.; Agents Say Pornography Czar Had Worldwide Connections": *Cleveland Plain Dealer,* December 10, 1992. "Looking for a Rube": *Cleveland Plain Dealer,* December 10, 1992. *Reuben Sturman:* From *Day One,* ABC News, July 20, 1995.

72. **John Wayne Bobbitt Uncut:** *Larry Furst, John Wayne Bobbitt, Crystal Gold, Jasmine Aloha, Veronica Brazil:* From Larry Furst, "The Making and Raking of A Porn Stud: John Wayne Bobbitt Proves His Manhood and Shows the World How Smart He Really Is!" © 1999 Tim Connelly. *Mark Carriere:* From Dick Howard, "The Entrepreneurs of Erotica, Part I: Mark Carriere," © Tim Connelly.

73. **Ding Dong, the Witch Is Dead:** *Savannah:* From "Fast Forward, Savannah Opens Up." *Vince Neil:* From *The Dirt* (ReganBooks, 2001). *Mark Carriere:* From Larry Furst, "The Making and Raking of A Porn Stud: John Wayne Bobbitt Proves His Manhood and Shows the World How Smart He Really Is!" © 1999 Tim Connelly. *Bryn Bridenthal:* From Peter Wilkinson, "Dream Girl," *Rolling Stone,* October 20, 1994.

74. Caught: *Naomi Delgado, Reuben Sturman:* From *Day One,* ABC News, July 20, 1995. "Defendant Convicted in Extortion Attempt": *Chicago Tribune,* April 2, 1994. "Extortionist Sentenced": *Chicago Sun-Times,* December 10, 1994. "In November 1989 . . .": *United States Court of Appeals for the Sixth Circuit,* court documents, July 14, 1995. "Lawyer's Trial to Star Porn King Sturman as Witness for Feds": *Cleveland Plain Dealer,* May 29, 1995. "Court Nails Lawyers for Porn King": *Cleveland Plain Dealer,* June 22, 1995.

75. Waiting for Wood: All original.

76. Going to Extremes: *Lizzy Borden:* Janelle Brown, "Porn Provocateur," www.salon.com, June 20, 2002.

77. Celebrity Porn: *Tommy Lee:* From *The Dirt* (New York: ReganBooks, 2002). *Jonathan Silverstein:* From *Los Angeles Times,* 1997.

78. Outbreak: *Marc Wallice:* From interview with Michael Louis Albo, *Hustler Erotic Video Guide,* September 1998; www.lukeford.com, © 1999 Luke Ford. *Tim Connelly, David Aaron Clark, John Stagliano:* David Aaron Clark and Tim Connelly, "Buttman in the High Castle: Rich, Famous, Talented & HIV-Positive: John Stagliano Has Looked into the Porn Abyss—& Allowed it to Look Back into Him," and "Buttman Opens Up About Every Aspect of His Life. And You Won't Believe What You Read!" © 2003.

Acknowledgments

Legs McNeil, Jennifer Osborne, and Peter Pavia wish to thank first and foremost: GILLIAN McCAIN and TIM CONNELLY.

Also: Bill Brown, Jane Hamilton, Dr. Sharon "Mitch" Mitchell, Tom Byron, Bill and Virginia Kelly, Dave Friedman, Nick Tosches, Josh Alan Friedman, Chuck Bernstene, Fred Lincoln, Kelly Nichols, Kelly Holland, Ruby Tuesday, Chloe, Dr. Annie Sprinkle, Roger Young, Ron Jeremy, the late Ron LaBrecque, Joan LaBrecque, Pat Livingston, Vickie Livingston, Nancy Livingston, Bruce Ellavsky, Pam Ellavsky, Ginger Lynn, Bill Margold, Eric Edwards, Gordon McNeil, Lucie Vonder Haar, Gloria Leonard, Georgina Spelvin, Marilyn Chambers, Roy Karch, the late Chuck Traynor, the late Linda Lovelace, Henri Pachard, Carol DiRenzy, Sharon Holmes, Dawn Schiller, Tricia Deveraux, Russ Hampshire, Ray Pistol, Treasure Brown, Paul Fishbein, Steve Hirsch, Steve Orenstein, Patrick Collins, Chris Cox, Cass Paley, Tom Lange, Bob Souza, Glen Souza, Nils Grevillius, Roy Karch, Kevin Beechum, Tommy Sinopoli, Eric Danville, Joel Steinberg, Wayne Clark, Lenny Camp, Johnny Keyes, Rebekah Poston, Rob Black, Lizzy Borden, John Stagliano, Ted Paramour, Phil Vannatter, Rhonda Jo Petty, Jeanna Fine, Nancy Pera, Veronica Vera, Candida Royalle, Tom Zupko, Nina Hartley, Al Goldstein, Al Ruddy, Ed Sharp, Al Bonanni, Tera Patrick, Evan Seinfeld, Seth Warshavsky, Jonathan Silverstein, Adam Glasser, Paul Dinin, Tempest Storm, Kitten Natividad, Bunny Yeager, Bob Rich, Edna Buchanan, Ed Horning, Dr. Carleton Riddick, Mike Mauger, Paul Thomas, Jerry Butler, Seka, Traci Lords, the late Robert "Dibe" DiBernardo, Sammy "The Bull" Gravano, the late Louis "Butchie" Peraino, the late Joe "The Whale" Peraino, the late Anthony Peraino Sr., Gerard Damiano, Harry Reems, the late Marc Stevens, the late Bobby Hollander, the late Teddy Gaswirth, the late Teddy Snyder, Bobby Genova, Marcella Cohen-Auerbach, Marc Carriere, the late Brad Carriere, Roscoe Jefferson, C. J. Laing, Sue Nero, Bud Lee, Michael Cirigliano, Michael London, Dave Hadley, Bill Amerson, Laurie Holmes, Jill Kelly, Leroy Griffith, Jim South, Daniel Metcalf, Dian Hanson, Christy Canyon, Jamie Gillis, Serena, Annette Haven, Rob and Rachel Rotten, Bobby Elkins, Amie Elkins, Bana Witt, Humphry Knipe, Suze Randall, John Waters, Roger Ebert, the late Russ Meyer, Ann Perry, the late Doris Wishman, Hugh Hefner, Vulture, Carol Conners, Nora Ephron, the late Sammy Davis Jr., Mark Prosperi, Fred Biersdorf, Phil Smith, Jim Mitchell, the late Artie Mitchell, Jack Boulware, Bob Chinn, Laurie Smith, Bob Vosse, Bunny Bleu, Heather Hunter, Joe Sarno, Larry Flynt, Steve Rudnick, Fred Schwartz, Tom Blake, Vanessa Del Rio, Tiffany Clark, the late Larry Levenson, the late Mickey Zaffarano, Patrice Trudeau, Larry Parrish, Bruce Kramer, Tony Bill, Kathy Jean, Dick Phinney, Bruce Mouw, Don Fernando, Richard Pacheco, Joel Sussman, Sheri St. Clair, Reb Sawitz, Marty Bernback, Tracy McCourt, the late John Holmes, Mike McGrady, Eddie Nash, Jeanna Nash, David Lind, Pete Hamill, Michael Alago, Mr. Marcus, Nadine Strossen, Jim Powers, Lorene Smith, the late Don Gilbert, Judge Richard S. Seward, Patti Harrison, Paul Hetrick, John J. Waltzer, David Clark, the late Nadia Childes, Kaylynn, La Tonya Underwood, Ralph L. Morgan, Alvine Nunes, Jennifer Oullette, Alan B. Andrews, the late Jimmy "The Weasel" Frattiano, Ed De Roo, Chi Chi Larue, Max Hardcore, Willie the Cameraman, Sean Michaels, Andrew Blake, Paul Camacho, Dawn Manners, Andrew Trentacosta, Handsome Dick Manitoba and Zoe, Arturo Vega, Mickey Leigh, Sandra Shulman, and last, but not least, Ruby Gottesman.

We would also thank the transcribers Nora Greening, Neil Colgrass, Natalie Butler, Mia, Crispin Kott, Skylaire Alfvegren, Heather Richardson, Pauline F. Holly, the Amazing Ed Webb, Jeff Guziak, and Adam Rehmeier.

For letting us excerpt parts of their own books or articles, we would like to thank the late Tina Russell, Harry Reems, Annie Sprinkle, Josh Alan Friedman, the late Russ Meyer, Suze Randall, the late Linda Lovelace, the late Ron LaBrecque, Jerry Butler, Eric Scholsberg, Michael London, Tim Connelly, and also *Adam Film World, Adult Video News, Hustler's Erotic Cinema,* the *Los Angeles Times,* the *Miami Herald,* the *New York Times, Playboy,* and *Screw.*

To our long list of investigators and reporters who helped in doing interviews and research, we would like to thank Stacey Asip (who is directing *Mrs. Dinsdorf,* with Legs producing), for her work on the MIPORN and *Deep Throat* chapters; Chris Cox, for his work on the John Holmes chapters; Eric Danville, for his work on the *Deep Throat* and Linda Lovelace chapters; Josh Alan Freidman, for his work on the Plato's Retreat chapters; Mary Greening, for her work on the sections concerning John Holmes, Teddy Snyder, and organized crime; Nils Grevillious, for his work on the John Holmes and organized crime chapters; the late Ron LaBrecque, for the MIPORN chapters; Michael London, for his work on the Shauna Grant chapters; Linda Marsa, for her work on the John Holmes chapters; Gillian McCain, for her work editing and copyediting the book; Shannon McNamara, for her work on the John Holmes chapters; Cass Paley, for his work on the John Holmes and general porn chapters; Peter Pavia, for ALL his work, especially the MIPORN, Reuben Sturman, Graves End, Norm Arno and Lori Smith, and the organized crime chapters; and, last but not least, to Jeff Roth for his overall research.

Legs McNeil would like to thank GILLIAN McCAIN for her undying love and support through the seven years of hell that has been this book. Gillian has been my best friend and has supported me through the worst. THANK YOU. Also my cowriters, Jennifer Osborne and Peter Pavia, for putting up with so much shit—mood swings, Xanax addiction, exacerbating frustrations, lack of money, and my constant perfectionism.

With all my love, thank you to the late SHANNON McNAMARA for spending five glorious months with me. All this is for you, baby.

To Kristina Berg, for all those late-night phone calls and loving encouragement; to Carol Overby; Mary C. Greening; Jim Marshall; Gary Kott, for all his words of wisdom over the years (even though he thinks I didn't listen to him); my big sister, Patrice Adcroft; and my big brother, John Holmstrom—for teaching me how to write and being an outstanding friend for more than thirty years, even when I didn't deserve it.

To Doris and Dick Goodwin for their loving support; Fred Zollo; and Bill Brown, for letting us take over his house in Coral Gables and listening to me whine. Also to Jane Hamilton for all her support and hiring me to write the Marilyn Chambers comeback movie, *Still Insatiable*.

Also to TIM CONNELLY for everything, Mickey Leigh, Carlotte Lesher, Mary Ann Walters, Steve Walters, Sharon Mitchell, Chloe, Steven Lampert (our computer expert), our MailBoxes Etc. man, W. T. "Doc" Maloney, Dr. Steven York, Dr. Robert Marantz and his late wife Joan, Dr. Mark Craig and his lovely wife Judy, Dr. Gary Brown, Bill Kelly, Bill Margold, Jay Cobe, Julia Murphy, Ali Morris, Katherine Garfield, Joan LaBrecque-Welles, Janus Johnson, Ginger Lynn, the late Don Gilbert, Fran Fried, Eric Rasmussen, and Kelly Holland for hiring me to write porn scripts during the bleakest moments of the book, Nica Ray, Bobby Miller, Ruby Tuesday, Tom Greening, Cynthia Lee Berryhill, Meredith Meyer, Amy Elkins, Tony Vick and his lovely wife Nancy, and my old friends— the late Joey Ramone, the late Dee Dee Ramone, and the late Johnny Ramone. Also to someone very special, who I was with the night before he died (with the wonderful Iris Berry): my thanks to the late Eliot Cohen. I still miss him every day (even though it was impossible to get him off the phone). Also my thanks to Julia and Simon, Roberta Bayley, Linda Marsa, and Richard Hyland—aka "Johnny Joyce"—the man in black. And to Margaret and Wayne Kramer, may they live happily ever after. Also to Mark "Fuckface" Groubert, may he find happiness wherever he is.

I'd also like to thank my family: Mrs. Ellen McNeil (who had a great time at Gillian's wedding and wants to go back to New Brunswick); my Aunt Margaret Clossick; my Aunt Mary Wilson; my Uncle Bill Clossick; my brother, Craig McNeil (author of *How to Ski the Blues and Blacks Without Getting Black and Blue*) and his lovely wife Amy; their two kids, Moira and Sean. Also my sister, Lauren Backman; her husband, Ken Backman; and their two daughters, Ainsley and Ashleigh Backman. And special thanks to my best male friend, Tom Hearn, and his wonderful wife Ann—and their two kids; Grady and Iris. Also to my real mom, Mrs. Diane Brown, who gave me my first job (she's still cleaning up the mess).

To my extended family, Mark McCain and his lovely wife, Caro, and Ann and Chris Evans, and Laura McCain-Jensen and her husband Peter Jensen, and the late Peter McCain and his lovely wife, Joyce McCain, and their two sons, Luke and John. Also to the late Marion "Billie" McCain— and especially to the late Harrison H. McCain, for his kind words to me in Chicago. Also thanks to Marilyn.

To my agents, editors, directors, publishers, producers, lawyers and accountants: Susan Lee Cohen, Jim Fitzgerald, Carol Mann, Fenton Lawless, Angela Ching-Kaplan, Eric Brown, Danny Feilds, Mick Farren, Alan Briesbart, John Aes-Nihl, Alan Arkush, Michael Alago, Handsome Dick Manitoba and his lovely wife, Henry Beck, Pat Carr, Ged Dunn, Hal Wilner, George Wendt, Chuck E. Weiss, Jack Walls, Daniel Rey, Mary Harron, Fran Pelzman, Mark Jacobsen, Floyd Mutrux, Emily Schlesinger, Brian Sweetie, Sandar Schulman, Arturo Vega, Adam Rifkin, Bill Bonnell, Benito Villa, Graydon Carter, John Gillies, Michael Hogan, Ed Dwyer, Bob Guccione Sr., Michael Kennedy, Jonathan Marder, Martha Thomases, Victor Bockris, Bob Foglenest, Tom Long, Neil Colgrass, Norman and Noris Mailer, Peter Alson, Tom Piazza, Sharon King-Hoag, Burt Kearns, Brett Hudson and Lisa Krone. Also to Gesila Freisinger and her lovely family, Jenny Muldar, Atheena Viscusi, Mara Hennessey and Mim Udovitch. Extra thanks to my accountant, Jimmy Keeny, for making sense of my receipts to the IRS for the last six years. And special thanks to the Pepsi Cola Company for convincing me to do a book on pornography.

To the folks at the St. Mark's Poetry Project: Ed Freedman, Wanda Phipps, and David Vogen. Also to the folks at Court TV—including Bonnie Dry, Mark Fichandler, and Frederica Broomfield, who did such a wonderful job promoting the television show. To our editor, the amazing Cal Morgan at ReganBooks, his assistant Marissa—and to Judith Regan herself, for taking a chance on us.

And very much love to the late Judy Conway-Greening, who died at home under the loving care of her daughters, Mary and Nora Greening, while I hid from the process, coward that I am.

Too many people died while this book was written, and my only hope is they not be forgotten.

Jennifer Osborne would like to thank the following: First and foremost, LEGS MCNEIL, my mentor and foxhole buddy, for taking a chance on me, for introducing me to Pete Pavia and Gillian McCain, and for being so willing to lend me everything, from your wisdom to clean socks (when necessary).

Special thanks to TIM CONNELLY for your love, support, insight— and for just putting up with me, even during my most "special" moods.

Special thanks to my family Nancy, Lee, Todd, Danielle, Kim, and Donna Osborne; Steve, Chris, Brian, Mike, and Stacy Barry; and Gramma Hoobler, for your love and encouragement, and for always understanding why my visits were going to come "next month" and never did.

Thanks to the friends who offered their support, patience, and humor throughout my time on this book: Wendy and Chris Campbell, Amanda Mendillo, William O'Donnell, J. Cobe, Kristina Berg, Anna and Kelly DeVine, and Scott and Renee Preston.

Also to Meredith Meyer, Ed Webb, Mitch, Tom Zupko, Axel Braun, Jen Blum, Mark Raskin, Dave and Jennie Gregory, Brian Lavelle, Andrew Wasser, Kim Williams, Louisa Achille, Mark Groubert, Karie Clark, Jeannie Cox, Carol Overby, Stacey Asip, Brian Martens, Gary Kott, Bill Brown, Callie Connelly, Mickey Leigh, Jordan Buky, Marty Hufford, and Mike Flynn, for supporting me and my sanity, in various ways, at various times.

And thanks to Eric Danville for introducing me to Legs McNeil.

Peter Pavia would like to thank: Drew Hubner and William Georrgiades, for being there at the beginning; John Gillies, for knowing a good story when he heard one; Bill Brown; Harold Price Fahringer; the incomparable Bill Kelly and his lovely wife, Virginia; Pat Livingston; Bruce Ellavsky; Gordon McNeill; Ed Sharpe; Marcella Cohen Auerbach; Robert Gibbons and his fine son, Robert; Anthony Marra; and a couple of NYPD guys who would prefer to remain nameless.

I would also like to thank Mike Dibble, Jimmy Gilroy, for his unflagging support, Michael Connery; my mother, Jeanne Pavia; Frances R. Bellave; my aunt and grandmother; and my wonderful wife, Ellen Harty, and the Princess of All Beautiful Girls, my daughter, Theresa, for their sacrifice and understanding. And, finally, I would like to thank my coauthors, Jennifer Osborne and Roderick Edward "Legs" McNeil, for their hard work and dedication. It appears on these pages.

Index

Note: References with page ranges may not be contiguous between pages; however, all pages in a range will have relevant references.

A

Adams, Tracey, 352
adult theater creation, 10
The Adventures of Lucky Pierre, 9, 10
AIDS/HIV, 574–90
  AIM Healthcare and, 577, 579, 580
  amyl nitrate and, 397–98
  Annie Sprinkle and, 396–401, 449
  Bill Margold and, 575, 577
  Gloria Leonard and, 398–99
  Henri Pachard and, 397–98
  John Holmes and, 448–51
  Marc Wallice and, 575, 576–84
  Sharon Mitchell and, 401, 566, 576–83
  Tim Connelly and, 396–401
  Tricia Deveraux and, 566, 574–84, 588
AIM (Adult Industry Medical), 577, 579, 580
Alago, Michael, 477–78
Allman, Gregg, 480, 483, 484, 535
Aloha, Jasmine, 527, 528
Amerson, Bill, 87–90, 132–33, 235–38, 445–47
An Adult Fair Tale, 150
Anderson, Pamela, 567–73
Apple, Danny, 355
Applegate, Colleen, 345–48, 360, 362
Applegate, Karen, 345, 361

Applegate, Phillip, 346
Arno, Norm, 175–79, 240–43, 245, 246, 250, 252, 255, 440–41, 443
Ashley, Brooke, 578, 584
Atkin, Sanford I., 541, 542

B

Babb, Kroger, 1
Bachelor Tom Peeping, 9
Baer, Max, 350–51
Beatty, Warren, 167, 184, 351–52
Beechum, Kevin, 498–99, 500, 503–5
Behind the Green Door
  at Cannes Film Festival, 96–97
  initial development, 84–86
  Ivory Snow box and, 95–96
  production/release, 92–98
Berman, Dr. David, 518–20
Bernback, Marty, 245–46
Bernstene, Chuck
  Al Nunes and, 248–50
  arrest, 255
  Lori Smith and, 242–43
  Mickey Feinberg and, 537–38
  Mickey Zaffarano and, 253, 332
  Norm Arno and, 75, 175–79, 240–43, 255
  Pat Livingston and, 248–50
  Perainos and, 75, 177, 179
bestiality movies, 47–51, 99–100

Betty Jo (ex-girlfriend of Pat
    Livingston), 197–98
Biersdorf, Fred, 72, 75, 76
Big Tom. *See* Blake, Tom (Big Tom)
Bill, Tony, 184–85, 187–88
Black, Rob, 560–66
blackmail trunk, 340–41
Blake, Tom (Big Tom), 134–37, 297,
    298, 299–300
Blasingame, James, 329, 330
Bleu, Bunny, 91
Bobbitt, John Wayne, 517–21, 524–29
Bobbitt, Lorena, 517–21, 524, 526, 528,
    529
bombing, 501–4, 537–38
Bonanno family, 175, 178, 199
Bonnani, Al, 219–20
boob jobs, 478, 511, 515–16, 555
Book Cellar, 498–500
Boreman, Linda, 31. *See also* Lovelace,
    Linda
Boulware, Jack, 84, 94, 492–97
Bovee, Lesllie, 90, 91
boxed lunch, 142
Brand of Shame, 11
Brazil, Veronica, 528–29
Briceland, Patricia, 462–65
Bridenthal, Bryn, 482, 535
Brissette, Jay, 499–501, 503
Brown, Bill, 196–98, 219–26, 245–49,
    251, 257–59, 261, 314, 328, 330
Brown, Treasure, 515
Bryanston Films, 180–82, 356
burlesque, end of, 10, 11. *See also* live
    burlesque
Butler, Jerry, 405–7
Buttman, 584
Buzzard, Caprice, 38
Byron, Tom, 361
    Ginger Lynn and, 367, 453
    IRS investigation, 428
    Marc Wallice and, 574, 577
    Meese Commission and, 438–39
    Mitchell brothers and, 491,
        494–96
    Savannah and, 478, 482, 485, 487,
        531, 534–35
    Sharon Mitchell on, 574
    tax problems, 453
    Teddy Snyder and, 389–91, 458–59,
        469–70
    Traci Lords and, 377–85, 389,
        416–17, 419, 421, 427–28

C

Camp, Lenny
    Bill Kelly on, 33, 64, 157–58
    Chuck Traynor and, 17–18, 33–34,
        58, 65
    Deep Throat and, 60, 64–65
    deep throat technique and, 32–33
    Jean Jennings and, 155, 156, 157
    underage girl bust, 157–58
Canyon, Christy, 381–85, 411, 418
Carnal Knowledge, 184
Caroll, E. Jean, 374
Carriere, Brad, 513
Carriere, Marc, 411, 511, 513, 514–16,
    526, 528, 529, 531, 568
Carriere, Tina Marie, 411, 511
Carson, Johnny, 70, 97
Cayman Islands, 196–98
Chambers, Marilyn
    arrest, 492
    Behind the Green Door and, 84–86,
        92–98
    Bill Margold and, 367, 530
    Chuck Traynor and, 115–20, 492
    drug use, 491
    getting started, 20–22, 24–29, 81–86
    Hefner, Lovelace and, 103
    Ivory Snow box and, 24, 25, 26, 83,
        95–97
    Johnny Keyes and, 92–94
    into legitimate acting, 115–20
    Mitchell brothers and, 491–92,
        494–97
    Resurrection of Eve and, 98
    Sammy Davis Jr. and, 119, 120
checkers, 176–77
Chier, Richard, 411
child pornography, 250, 251. *See also*
    underage girls
Chinn, Bob, 88–89, 132, 237–38
Cicciolina, 448–51
Clanton, Florence, 501, 502–3
Clark, David Aaron, 584
Clark, Tiffany, 161–62, 166, 168, 212,
    213, 215–18, 374, 407
Clark, Wayne, 192
Club 90, 371–76
cocaine
    John Holmes and, 237–39, 276–77,
        279
    Lori Smith and, 243
    NYC 1977–1978, 214–18

Plato's Retreat and, 212
Ruby Gottesman and, 200–203
See also drugs
Cochiaro, Frank, 219, 220, 221
Cohen, Marcella, 254, 314, 331
Collins, Patrick, 491–92, 577, 579, 580
Colombo, Joseph, family, 67, 68, 108, 178, 182, 186, 232, 234, 334–35
Connelly, Tim, xv
  AIDS/HIV and, 396–401, 447–49, 587
  Cal Jammer and, 543–50
  film vs. video and, 368–69
  Ginger Lynn and, 366–67, 370
  Hal Freeman conviction, 452
  Helen Madigan and, 143, 145, 146, 147–48, 149, 162–63, 164, 165, 212
  Jason Russell and, 154–55, 159, 160
  Jean Jennings and, 158–59
  Jim South and, 346, 366
  John Holmes and, 447–49, 585–87
  Kelly Nichols and, 164–67, 362, 364
  Marc Carriere and, 511–12, 514–16
  Plato's and, 212
  Rob Black/Tricia Deveraux and, 565
  Sam Kinison and, 452
  Sharon Mitchell and, 145
  Shauna Grant and, 359, 360, 362, 364
  Show World and, 143–44, 150, 400
  suitcase pimps and, 230
  Teddy Snyder and, 389–91, 460, 469, 471
  Tina Russell and, 159–60
  Traci Lords and, 415–16
Conners, Carol, 64–65
Coonskin, 181
Costello, Sean, 43, 44
Cox, Chris, 275–79, 289–90, 293
crime, interconnectedness of, 110
Croissant, Michael, 334
Cry-Baby, 421, 453, 462, 465, 466

D

Damiano, Gerard
  Annie Sprinkle and, 128–30
  Chuck Traynor and, 53–54, 56, 61, 63
  Deep Throat and, 54–57, 60–61, 63, 64, 65–66, 68, 70, 75–76, 122, 124

The Devil in Miss Jones and, 121–31
  Fred Lincoln and, 52–53, 59, 76, 121–22, 128–29, 131, 161
  Harry Reems and, 58, 61, 121, 184
  Linda Lovelace and, 53–54, 55–57, 60–61, 62, 63, 65, 130
  Perainos and, 53–54, 57, 66, 68, 75–76
  sexual liberation and, 130
D'Apice, Andre, 207, 219–23, 224–26
Dark, Greg, 380–81, 383, 419
Davis, Sammy, Jr.
  Chuck Traynor and, 99, 102, 111–12, 114, 119, 120, 268–69
  Deep Throat showing, 70–71
  Linda Lovelace and, 99, 111–12, 114, 266, 268–69
  Marilyn Chambers and, 119, 120
  Plato's and, 212
DeCavalcante crime family, 219
Deep Inside Porn Stars, 374–76
Deep Throat, 38, 52
  Arizona trial, 128–30
  financial bonanza, 74–77
  idea for, 56–59
  Memphis prosecution, 181–91
  Peraino family and, 67–68, 74, 75–76, 176–79
  production, 60–66, 67
  release, reviews, 67–73, 99
  See also Lovelace, Linda
deep throat technique, 32–33, 37–38
Del Rio, Vanessa, 141–42, 144
Delgado, Naomi, 358, 488–89, 505, 523, 539–40
DeNiro, Robert, 496–97
Denver con job, 403–4
Deroo, Ed, 369
Dershowitz, Alan, 191, 216
DeSalvo, Bobby, 177, 190, 355
DeSinzy, Pete, 7
Deveraux, Tricia, 552–66
  getting started, 552–58
  HIV ordeal, 566, 574–84, 588
  John Stagliano and, 586–89
  Marc Wallice and, 577–84
  medical-school blacklist, 559
  Rob Black and, 560–66
Deverell, Billy (William), 280, 283, 284–85, 286, 296
The Devil in Miss Jones, 121–31
Diaz, Victor, 469, 471–73

DiBernardo, Robert (DiBe)
   disappearance, 431–34, 539
   Ellavsky/Livingston and, 205–6, 207
   Feds pursuing, 199, 205–6, 207
   Fred Lincoln and, 409
   industry position, 106, 178–79
   John Gotti and, 431–34, 539
   Mafia connections, 106, 107,
      178–79, 199, 205, 220, 221
   Reuben Sturman and, 106, 107, 109,
      357, 538–39
Diles, Gregory, 284–85, 289, 291, 292,
   303
DiStephano Vince (Vinny), 355–56
dog movie, 47–51, 99–100
Dolton, Jay, 333–34
Donlan, James, 182, 187
DPs (double penetrations), 544–45
Dreyfuss, Richard, 212–13
drugs
   John Holmes and, 234, 235, 237–39,
      276–77, 281, 283, 287–88
   Linda Lovelace and, 117–18
   Marilyn Chambers and, 491
   Mitchell brothers and, 491, 492–93,
      494, 495
   Savannah and, 478, 481
   Sharon Mitchell and, 214, 216–18,
      237, 404, 409, 412–13, 552,
      555–65
   Wonderland robbery and, 284–86
   See also cocaine
Dworkin, Andrea, 428–29, 439

E

Ebert, Roger, 2, 7, 8, 9
Edwards, Eric
   Annie Sprinkle and, 129
   Arcadia Lake and, 147–48, 150
   Bernard's and, 159
   Deep Throat and, 59
   dog movie and, 20–22, 29, 37–38,
      45–46, 47–51
   Teddy Snyder and, 390
Elkins, Bobby, 179, 355–57, 402–6,
   434, 468
Ellavsky, Bruce
   family challenges, 244, 247–51
   industry infiltration, 195–98,
      199–200, 203, 204–7
   Mickey Zaffarano and, 255

   Pat Livingston arrests and, 219–20,
      224–25, 314
   publicity and, 257
   as sole MIPORN witness, 331
   team falling out, 244–51, 257, 261
Ellavsky, Pam, 247–49
Ephron, Nora, 69
The Erotic Adventures of Zorro, 11

F

Fallible, Billy, 9
Faludi, Susan, 550, 551
Federal Bureau of Investigation (FBI)
   Deep Throat investigation. See Kelly,
      Bill
   embarrassing, 314, 326–31
   forced to drop charges, 331
   infiltrating porn industry, 193,
      194–98, 199–203, 204–7
   undercover agents, 193, 194–98
   See also Ellavsky, Bruce; Livingston,
      Pat; other specific agents
Feinberg, Mickey, 498–99, 500–501,
   504–6, 537–38
feminist movement, 266, 267, 428, 429,
   435, 437, 438, 439
feminist pornography, 374
Fernando, Don, 233–34
Fine, Jeanna, 481–85, 530–31, 533–35
Fishbein, Paul, 402–3, 405, 413–14
Fitzgerald, Eddie, 193–94
flashing, 23
Flesh of the Lotus, 89
Flynt, Larry, 104, 106, 108, 110, 428,
   572
Frattiano, Jimmy "The Weasel," 106
Free Speech Coalition, 486, 574–75, 578
Freeman, Hal (Harold), 402–6, 413–14,
   445, 452
The French Peep Show, 7
Friedman, Dave
   casting/pandering and, 410
   Deep Throat and, 67, 69–70, 176–77
   early exploitation business, 1–4, 6–11
   FBI firing and, 331
   Norm Arno and, 176, 241
   Perainos and, 176–77
   Traci Lords and, 454, 456
Friedman, Josh Alan, 169–71
Furst, Larry, 517–18, 520–21, 524,
   526–27

G

Gambino family
  Colombos and, 178
  Danny Apple and, 355
  Ettore Zappi and, 107
  John Gotti and, 431–34, 539
  Mickey Zaffarano and, 175, 178, 199
  Patty Snyder and, 460
  Reuben Sturman and, 106, 107, 108, 439
  Robert DiBernardo and, 106, 107, 199, 205, 221, 431
Gaswirth, Teddy, 193, 194, 246–47, 255
Genova, Bobby, 389, 390, 391, 459–61, 469, 471
Gillis, Jamie
  C. J. Laing and, 145, 185
  Fred Lincoln and, 408
  getting started, 29, 43–44, 45
  Larry Levenson and, 168–69, 171
  Seka and, 231–32
  Serena and, 150–53, 162
  Sharon Mitchell and, 145–46, 159
  Show World and, 143
The Godfather, 180, 186, 361, 391
Godfather of Hollywood. *See* Nash, Eddie
Gold, Crystal, 528
Golde Coaste Specialties, 195, 200, 205, 206, 252
Goldstein, Al
  C. J. Laing and, 145
  Deep Throat and, 68–70, 71–73, 99
  dog movie and, 99–101
  on getting laid, 211
  John Holmes and, 87, 90, 339
  Larry Levenson bet, 170
  Sharon Mitchell and, 397
  Traci Lords and, 421
gonzo porn, 584
Gordon, Aaron, 524, 525-26
Gordon, Jack, 524, 525-26
Gottesman, Ruby
  Al Nunes and, 249
  arrests, 254–55, 456
  child porn conviction, 454–56, 462, 465–66
  FBI undercover agents and, 190, 199, 200–202, 204–6, 331
  helping FBI, 201–2, 204, 206
  jail, 465–67
  Lori Smith and, 241–42, 440–41, 443
  Mafia connections, 176, 178, 179, 256, 432
  Mickey Zaffarano and, 178, 256
  Norm Arno and, 175–76, 240–43, 440–41, 443
  Pat Livingston and, 331
  Perainos and, 176
  Rhonda Jo Petty and, 201–3
  Robert DiBernardo and, 178, 432
  selling illegal movies, 455, 465
  Steve Orenstein and, 454–56, 465–66, 468
  Traci Lords and, 384–85, 421, 454–56, 463–65
Gotti, John, 431–34, 539
Grafenberg Girls Go Fishing, 491
Grant, Shauna, 359–64
Gravano, Sammy "The Bull," 431–33
Green, Tamara, 498–500
GRID (Gay Related Immunodeficiency Disease), 397
Griffin, Michael, 312–13
Guarino, Kenny, 193–94, 542

H

Hamilton, Jane, xv
Hampshire, Russ, 413–14, 504–5, 581
Hanson, Bob, 332, 334–35
Harper, Valerie, 267
Harry the Pick, 316
Hart, Susan, 411, 412
Hart, Veronica, xv
  Best Actress nomination, 360
  California mid–80s, 407–8
  Club 90 and, 372–76
  Deep Inside Porn Stars and, 374, 375, 376
  Eric Edwards and, 148
  on Hollywood, 349
  Lenny Kurtman and, 230–31
  Meese Commission and, 436–37
  in *Pandora's Mirror*, 372
  Phil Donahue Show, 373–74
  porn life/industry, 352, 373–74
  pregnancy, 372
  Savannah and, 478
  Seka and, 230–32
  on video, 368–69

Hartley, Nina, 354–55, 437, 532, 536
Haven, Annette, 90–91, 233
The Head Mistress, 11
Hefner, Hugh
    Bunny Yeager and, 6, 11
    Chuck Traynor and, 101–3, 268
    Linda Lovelace and, 100–103, 268
    "orgy night," 101–2
Hell's Angels, 83, 470, 560
Hicks, Steve, 346, 351
High Priestess of Sexual Witchcraft, 37, 38
High Society, 214–15, 216–17, 350
Hirsch, Steve, 479, 480, 481, 482, 531, 580
Hollander, Bobby, 238–39, 347, 362
Holly, Lolly, 145
Hollywood
    Kelly Nichols in, 347–50, 351–52
    other Hollywood and, 345–53
    Rhonda Jo Petty on, 348, 350–51
    Sharon Mitchell on, 353
    Veronica Hart on, 349
Holmes, John
    acquittal, 337–40
    AIDS and, 448–51
    arrests, 134–36, 325, 336
    Bill Amerson and, 87–90, 132–33, 235–38, 445–47
    blackmail trunk, 340–41
    Dawn Schiller and. See Schiller, Dawn
    death, 451
    drug use, 234, 235, 237–39, 276–77, 281, 283, 287–88
    Eddie Nash and, 276–77, 279–82, 289–90, 291–92, 293, 302, 303–4, 336–38
    family/early background, 88–89, 316–21
    getting started, 87–91
    how he treated women, 90–91
    as informant, 136–37, 299–302, 336–40
    Johnny Wadd series, 89–90
    on the lam, 304–5, 315–25
    Laurie Holmes and, 444–51
    murder arrest, 298
    porn star perspectives of, 233–39
    protective custody, 300–302
    sizeable attribute of, 87–91
    theiving by, 318

Wonderland murders, 289–93, 297–305, 336–40, 449–50
Wonderland robbery, 280–82, 283, 284, 286, 289–90
Holmes, Laurie, 361, 444–51
Holmes, Sharon
    Dawn Schiller relationship, 134, 137
    destroying blackmail trunk, 340–41
    John Holmes background and, 88–89, 316–21
    John Holmes porn career and, 87–91, 132–34
    shutting John out, 340
    Wonderland murders and, 290–92, 298–304, 316–21, 337–41
Holzman, Eddie, 348
Hoover, J. Edgar, 77
Hopkins, Lt., 442–43
Horning, Ed, 311, 314, 328–30
Howard, Paul, 206

I

The Immoral Mr. Teas, 7, 8, 9
Inside Linda Lovelace, 100
Interstate Transportation of Obscene Materials (ITOM), 182, 183
Ivory Snow box, 24, 25, 26, 83, 95–97

J

Jameson, Jenna, 573
Jammer, Cal, 543–51
Jefferson, Roscoe, 512–13
Jennings, Jean, 155–60
Jeremy, Ron
    Cal Jammer and, 548–49
    Christy Canyon and, 382
    Ginger Lynn and, 366
    John Holmes and, 444, 447–48
    John Wayne Bobbitt and, 521, 524–29
    Marc Carriere and, 513–14
    Pam/Tommy Lee and, 567–68, 570–73
    Savannah and, 479, 482–84, 486, 530–32, 535
    Sharon Mitchell and, 397
    Traci Lords and, 382, 385
Johnson, Hope, 310–11

K

Karch, Roy, 228–30
Kelly, Bill, 3, 5, 6, 33
  agent psychological problems,
    394–95
  Bryanston Films and, 180–82
  connecting Mafia/porn, 76–77
  Deep Throat and, 64, 66, 67, 69,
    74–77, 177, 184, 186–87,
    189–90
  Dick Phinney, secrecy and, 200
  Joe Peraino hit and, 332–33
  John Gotti and, 431–32
  kiddie porn and, 250
  "kissing" incident, 243
  Lenny Camp and, 157–58
  losing indictments, 331
  Meese Commission and, 426–28,
    430
  MIPORN operation. *See* MIPORN
  Norm Arno and, 240
  Pat Livingston firing, 395
  Pat Livingston/Bruce Ellavsky and,
    204, 256, 259, 262
  porn reduction futility, 393
  Reuben Sturman and, 104, 106–7,
    108, 228, 358
  Robert DiBernardo and, 178,
    431–32, 434
  training undercover agents, 194–95
Kelly, Jill, 545–50
Kendrick, Walter, xv–xvi
Keyes, Johnny, 92–97
Kinison, Sam, 452
Knipe, Humphry, 367, 378–85, 401,
  416, 418–21, 547
Kramer, Bruce, 187–89
Kurtman, Lenny, 230–31
Kuzma, Nora, 417. *See also* Lords, Traci

L

La Rosa, Rose, 8, 10
Laing, C. J., 94–95
  Bernard's and, 159, 169
  getting started, 82–83
  Harry Reems and, 185, 191
  New York action, 145–47
  swing clubs and, 169
Lake, Arcadia, 147, 148, 150
Lange, Jessica, 347, 348

Lange, Tom
  arresting John Holmes, 324–25
  on Eddie Nash, 275
  tracking Holmes/Schiller, 321–25
  Wonderland murder investigation,
    295–96, 298, 300, 302–4, 449–50
Launius, Ron, 280, 283, 284–85, 286,
  296
Launius, Susan, 292, 295, 296
Leach, Robin, 350, 351
Lebowski, Sam, 402–3
Lee, Bud, 167, 359, 399–400, 452,
  480–82, 531, 582–83
Lee, Tommy, 567–73
legality, of porn, 52
Leonard, Gloria
  AIDS and, 398–99
  Annie Sprinkle and, 130, 373
  Club 90 and, 372–73, 376
  Deep Inside Porn Stars and, 376
  defending industry, 266–67
  film vs. video and, 368–69
  Ginger Lynn and, 370
  High Society publisher, 214–17
  John Holmes and, 234–35, 238–39
  Leonard Kurtman and, 231
  Linda Lovelace and, 267–68
  Meese Commission and, 429, 435
  phone sex business, 215–16, 217
  radical feminists and, 429, 435
  Reuben Sturman and, 356
  Robin Leach and, 347, 350–51
  Seka and, 229, 232
  Shauna Grant and, 359
  Traci Lords and, 418–19
Levenson, Larry, 168–71, 211–13
Levine, Ralph, 108
Lewis, Herschell Gordon, 6, 9
Lime, Harold, 356–57
Lincoln, Fred
  Amber Lynn and, 166, 404–7
  Bobby Genova and, 389–91
  Buck Adams and, 404, 406–7
  Butchie Peraino and, 36, 47, 52–53,
    122, 190
  cocaine and, 212, 214, 216–18
  Deep Throat and, 59, 73
  on *Deep Throat* income, 76
  on *Deep Throat* prosecution, 184
  The Devil in Miss Jones and,
    121–23, 124–29, 131
  early porn personalities and, 40,
    42–44, 46

Lincoln, Fred (*continued*)
  getting started, 26, 30, 36
  Ginger Lynn and, 390
  Harry Reems and, 184, 191
  Jamie Gillis, Serena and, 150–53, 408
  Jason/Tina Russell and, 154
  Jean Jennings and, 155–60
  Jerry Damiano and, 52–53, 59, 76, 121–22, 128–29, 131, 161
  Larry Levenson and, 168–69, 211–13
  Larry Parrish and, 184
  Lenny Camp and, 155–57
  Linda Boreman (Lovelace) and, 47, 73
  Melody Burlesque and, 142
  Mickey Zaffarano and, 178
  pandering busts, 409–14
  Patty and, 408–9
  Robert DiBernardo and, 178, 409, 432
  Seka and, 229–32
  SEX U.S.A. and, 52–53, 59
  Sharon Mitchell and, 227–32, 397, 404, 470
  Show World and, 143–44, 147–53
  Teddy Snyder and, 389–91, 470–71
  Tiffany Clark and, 161–62, 164, 166, 216–18
Lind, David, 280–81, 283–86
Linda Lovelace for President, 119, 120
live burlesque
  Melody Burlesque, 141–43, 145
  Show World, 143–44, 147–53
Living Venus, 8
Livingston, Nancy, 326–28, 393
Livingston, Pat
  arrests, 219–26, 310–14
  concluding investigation, 252–54
  dad's reaction/death, 326–28, 331
  as discredited witness, 331
  embarrassing FBI, 314, 326–31
  as emotionless shell, 328
  firing of, 329–31, 395
  industry infiltration, 194–95, 204–7
  losing control, 257–60
  Mickey Zaffarano and, 252–56
  reuniting with wife, 261–62
  shoplifting fiasco, 310–14, 326–31
  suicide consideration, 393–95
  team falling out, 244–51, 257, 261
  undercover training, 193, 194–95
Livingston, Vickie, 309–10, 312–14,

326, 327–28, 393, 394–95
London, Michael, 345–48, 360, 362–63
Longoria, Pam, 479, 483
Lords, Traci
  arrest, 416–17
  false IDs, 417–18, 425–26
  films destroyed, 418–19
  income, 385–86
  marriage, 466–67
  Meese Commission and, 425–30
  mother on, 462–65
  name origin, 378
  real name, 377
  Ruby Gottesman and, 384–85, 421, 454–56, 463–65
  self–description, 377–84
  sexual preferences, 380–83
  Sharon Mitchell and, 464
  successful charade, 377–85
  Tom Byron and, 377–85, 389, 416–17, 419, 421, 427–28
  underage revealed, 415–21
Lovelace, Linda
  Ann–Margret and, 112–13
  Anthony Peraino and, 59, 68
  attempting legitimate acting, 111–20
  beatings by Chuck Traynor, 60–61, 120, 268
  Butchie Peraino and, 54, 56, 57–58, 64, 71, 99, 100–101, 118–19
  David Winters and, 112–20
  Deep Throat and, 56–59, 60–66, 67–68, 71–73, 265–66, 429–30
  Deep Throat prosecution and, 185
  dog movie, 47–51, 99–100, 101
  drug arrest, 117–18
  Elvis Presley and, 116–17, 118
  feminist movement and, 266, 267, 439
  first pregnancy/adoption, 263–64
  fisting at Hefner's, 102
  Gerard Damiano and, 53–54, 55–57, 60–61, 62, 63, 65, 130
  giving deep throat, 55–56
  Hugh Hefner and, 100–103, 268
  Larry Marchiano and, 263, 264–65, 268, 269–71
  leaving Chuck Traynor, 114–15
  Meese Commission and, 429–30
  meeting Chuck Traynor, 15–19
  name origin, 66
  Ordeal book, 265–71
  on *Phil Donahue Show*, 266–67

polygraph test, 266
Sammy Davis Jr. and, 99, 111–12,
    114, 268–69
starting out, 15–19, 31–35
Women Against Pornography and,
    267, 439
Lowe, Rob, 572–73
Lucchese crime family, 460
Luros, Milton, 106, 108–9
Lustful Turk, 11
Lynn, Amber, 164, 404–7
Lynn, Ginger, 456–57
Fred Lincoln and, 390
getting started, 345, 346–51, 365–67
Meese Commission and, 425–29
music video, 390
peers on, 367–68, 369–70
in prison, 453–54, 456–57
Tom Byron and, 367, 453
Traci Lords and, 378, 383–84, 416,
    418, 425–26, 456–57
Lynn, Krysti, 585–86, 589, 590

M

MacKinnon, Catherine, 267, 429, 439
Madigan, Helen, 143, 145, 146, 147,
    148, 149, 162–63, 164, 165, 212
Mafia
Bonanno family, 175, 178, 199
Deep Throat and, 63, 67
FBI evidence against, 76–77
funding porn, 44–45, 76–77
gangland war, 332–35
John Holmes revealing, 301
Lucchese family, 460
Mickey Zaffarano and, 175–79, 199,
    206, 251, 252–56, 332
MIPORN and, 199
Norm Arno and, 175–79
peep show industry and, 106–10
Teddy Snyder murder and, 458–61
See also DiBernardo, Robert (DiBe);
    Gambino family; Peraino family;
    Peraino, Anthony, Sr.; Peraino,
    Butchie (Lou)
Mahn, Paul, 499, 501, 503
mail–order business
Bill Margold and, 438
Marc Carriere and, 512–13
Norm Arno and, 175–76
undercover, 196, 205–6

Mainer, Phil, 183
Marcell, Mike, 346
Marchiano, Larry, 263, 264–65, 268,
    269–71
Mares, Donald (Donny), 499, 501,
    502–3
Margold, Bill
AIDS, HIV and, 575, 577
Ginger Lynn and, 367
Jamie/Serena and, 152
John Holmes and, 233, 236
Meese Commission and, 429,
    435–36, 437–39
naming Seka, 229
Savannah and, 477, 480–81, 486,
    530, 536, 553–54
top three porn women and, 367
Traci Lords and, 418–19, 456–57
"Mary Had a Little Lamb," 57, 64
Mauger, Mike, 442–43
May, Roy, 500, 506
McCourt, Tracy, 281, 284–86
McGrady, Mike, 265–66
McMahon, Ed, 70
McNeil, Gordon, 199, 244, 251, 252,
    257–60, 309
Meese Commission, 425–30, 435–39
Melody Burlesque, 141–42, 145
Menning, Sam, 32, 33
Meyer, Russ, 3, 7, 8
Miller, Joy, 296
Million, Tiffany, 545, 546
MIPORN, 192–98, 199
arrests/indictments, 254–56
emphasis, 199
fictional TV story on, 309–10
futility of, 393
losing indictments, 331
undercover agents, 193, 194–98
undermined by agent arrest, 314,
    326–31
See also Ellavsky, Bruce; Livingston,
    Pat
Miss Passion, 582
Misty Dawn. *See* Holmes, Laurie
Mitchell, Linda, 294–95
Mitchell, Sharon, xv
AIDS, HIV and, 401, 566,
    576–83
AIM and, 577, 579, 580
arrests, 147–49, 409–10, 559–61
attempted murder of, 552–55
bestiality movies and, 51

Mitchell, Sharon (*continued*)
  Chuck Traynor and, 65–66
  dealing drugs, 557–61
  detox program, 564
  drugs and, 214, 216–18, 237, 397,
    404, 409, 412–13, 552, 555–65
  Fred Lincoln and, 227–32, 397, 404,
    470
  getting started, 22–27, 141–43,
    155–56
  Ginger Lynn and, 368
  Hollywood crowd and, 352–53
  Jamie Gillis and, 145–46
  John Holmes and, 234, 237–38
  Linda Lovelace and, 51
  Marc Carriere and, 513–14
  Marc Stevens and, 396, 400–401
  Marc Wallice and, 574, 578–83
  mid–seventies stardom, 141, 144–45,
    159, 214
  in Niagara Falls, 562–64
  organized crime and, 434
  pandering bust, 409–13
  Robert DiBernardo and, 433–34
  in school, 565–66
  Seka movie production, 227–32
  servicing movie customer, 156–57
  Sharon Snyder and, 473
  Shauna Grant and, 361
  Show World act, 147–48
  Teddy Snyder and, 389–90
  Tim Connelly and, 145
  Traci Lords and, 464
  Vanessa Del Rio and, 143, 144
  Warren Beatty and, 352
Mitchell brothers
  Bana Witt and, 491–94
  Behind the Green Door and, 84–86,
    94–97
  drugs and, 491, 492–93, 494, 495
  getting started, 81–86
  Ivory Snow box and, 95–97
  Jack Boulware and, 84, 94, 492–97
  Jim in prison, 496–97
  Jim killing Artie, 495–96
  Marilyn Chambers and, 491–92,
    494–97
  Mickey Zaffarano and, 256
  movie about, 496–97
  Tom Byron and, 491, 494–96
mob. *See* Mafia
Morgan, Chesty, 3
Mouw, Bruce, 205, 431–33

N

Nash, Eddie, 275–82
  Chris Cox and, 275–79, 289–90, 293
  Holmes giving up, 336–38
  murders, 290–92, 302, 303–4
  robbery, 280–82, 283, 284–86
  See also Wonderland Avenue gang
Nash, Jeanna, 278–79
Neil, Vince, 482, 484–86, 524, 528,
  532–33, 536
Nero, Susie, 159, 375, 376
Nichols, Kelly
  as Best Actress, 360, 361
  Club 90 and, 374–75
  on *Deep Inside Porn Stars*, 374–75
  Fred Lincoln and, 150
  getting started, 162–67
  Ginger Lynn and, 366, 368–70
  in Hollywood, 345, 347–50, 351–52
  revealing occupation to men and,
    373
  Serena and, 151
  Shauna Grant and, 359–64
  Tim Connelly and, 164–67, 362, 364
  Warren Beatty and, 351–52
Nicholson, Jack, 184
Nixon, Richard, 426
nudie–cuties
  early history, 8–11
  heyday, 11
  origin, 8
nudist camp movies, 1, 2, 6–7, 10
Nunes, Al, 248–50
Nussman, Kristie. *See* Lords, Traci

O

Operation Amore, 175, 192, 206. *See
  also* Kelly, Bill
Ordeal, 265–71
Orenstein, Steve, 454–56, 465–66, 468
O'Toole, Brockton, 585–86

P

Pachard, Henri
  AIDS and, 397–98
  Cal Jammer and, 543–44, 546–47,
    549–51
  changing perspective, 368–69

on DPs, 544–45
Savannah and, 486–87, 534, 535
Shauna Grant and, 360–64
on women porn stars, 366, 478, 536
Pacheco, Richard, 234
Page, Bettie, 5, 6
Palmer, Gail, 237
pandering crackdown, 405, 407–15, 452
Pandora's Mirror, 372
Parrish, Larry, 181–83, 185–89
Pastori, Henry, 334
Pearl, Dr., 515–16
peep show industry, 104–10
Pera, Nancy, 479–84, 486, 530–35
Peraino, Anthony, Sr.
    Deep Throat and, 58, 59, 63–64, 67
    Mafia connection, 67–68
    Memphis conviction, 190
    See also Peraino family
Peraino, Butchie (Lou), 36, 47
    Fred Lincoln on, 190
    Josh Alan Friedman and, 169–70
    Larry Levenson come bet, 170–71
    Linda Lovelace, *Deep Throat* and, 54, 56, 57–58, 68, 69, 71, 72, 76
    Memphis conviction, 190
    SEX U.S.A. and, 52–53
    Vince DiStephano and, 355–56
    See also Peraino family
Peraino, Joe, Jr., 332–33
Peraino, Joe "the Whale," 332–34, 356
Peraino family
    Bryanston Films, 180–82
    Deep Throat and, 67–68, 74, 75–76, 176–79, 180–91
    fear of IRS, 75
    Norm Arno and, 175–79
    Vince DiStephano and, 355–56
Perry, Ann, 2
Perry, Howard, 518–19
Petty, Rhonda Jo, 159, 200–203, 215, 348, 350–51
Phil Donahue Show, 265, 266–67, 373
Phinney, Dick, 200–201, 309–10, 331
phone sex business, 215–16, 217
"pickles and beaver," 2, 10
Pinney, Roy, 3–4, 432
Pistol, Ray, 54, 511, 515, 567–69, 571
A Place Beyond Shame, 229
Plato's Retreat, 168–71, 211
Playboy Mansion, 101, 103, 191

porn marks, 353
Pornography in Denmark, 52
Powell, Larry, 311–13
Presley, Elvis
    Linda Lovelace and, 116–17, 118
    Tempest Storm and, 7–8
prostitution
    Annie Sprinkle and, 372–73
    Chuck Traynor and, 18–19, 31
    Dawn Schiller and, 277, 280–81, 283, 319–20
    sluts vs. whores, 171
pubic hair, 2, 10

R

Randall, Suze, 351, 367, 378–80, 382, 412, 419, 449
Raw Ones, 10
Reagan, Ronald, 427–28, 450
Reb, 236
Reems, Harry
    C. J. Laing and, 185, 191
    Deep Throat and, 58–59, 62–64, 183, 185
    The Devil in Miss Jones and, 121, 123–24, 127
    Gerard Damiano and, 58, 61, 121, 184
    getting started, 20–21, 23–29, 38–45, 46
    legal defense fund, 184, 185
    Linda Lovelace and, 53, 54–56, 58–59, 62–63
    perjuring himself, 185
religious right, 216, 427, 428, 435
Resurrection of Eve, 98
Richardson, Barbara, 296
Rollins, Marjorie, 489
Room Eleven, 9, 10
Rosfelder, Richard, 354–58, 434, 488–90, 498, 500, 506–7, 522–23, 537, 538–40
Ross, Perry, 514–15
Rothstein, Teddy, 107, 204–5, 206, 207
Royalle, Candida, 371–74
Ruddy, Al, 180, 182, 186
Rudnick, Steve, 104–10
Russell, Jason, 38, 39–40, 44, 154–55, 160
Russell, Tina, 38–41, 44, 154, 159–60

S

Salomone, Pat. *See* Livingston, Pat
Savannah, 477–87, 530–36
  Bill Margold on, 477, 480–81, 486,
    530, 536, 553–54
  Bryn Bridenthal on, 482, 535
  Bud Lee on, 480–81, 531
  drug use, 478, 481
  father, 479–80, 483
  getting started, 477
  Henri Pachard and, 478, 486–87
  Jeanna Fine and, 481–85, 530–31,
    533–35
  Marc Carriere and, 515
  mother, 479, 483
  Nancy Pera and, 479–84, 486,
    530–35
  Nina Hartley on, 532, 536
  Pauly Shore and, 486–87
  preferences, 478
  Ron Jeremy on, 479, 482–84, 486,
    530–32, 535
  Slash and, 482–83, 486
  Steve Hirsch and, 479, 480, 481,
    482, 531
  suicide, 533–36
  Tom Byron and, 478, 482, 485, 487,
    531, 534–35
  Veronica Hart on, 478
  Vince Neil and, 482, 484–86,
    532–33, 536
Schiller, Dawn
  back home, 336–37
  Eddie Nash and, 276–77
  giving John up, 324–25
  John Holmes relationship, 133–37,
    280–81, 283–84, 287–88, 315–25
  on the lam, 304–5, 315–25
  prostitution and, 277, 280–81, 283,
    319–20
  as stripper, 338–39
  to Thailand, 337–39
  Wonderland murders and, 289,
    291–93, 296–305
School Girls, 181, 183
Schwartz, Fred, 252, 256–60, 314,
  329–31
Screw magazine, 68–69, 71–72, 99–100,
  170, 211
Seka, 167, 229–32
Serena, 143, 150, 151–53
SEX U.S.A., 52–53

Sextet, 31
sexual liberation, 130
Sharp, Ed, 330
Shore, Pauly, 486–87
Show World, 143–44, 147–53, 162,
  163, 164, 165, 231, 400
Silvera, Joey, 143, 360, 496, 556–57
Silverstein, Jonathan, 569–70, 572
Sinopoli, Tommy, 240–41, 255, 440
Size matters, 87–91
Slash, 482–83, 486
Smith, Laurie, 347, 360, 361–64
Smith, Lorene (Lori), 240, 241–43,
  440–43
Smith, Phil, 76, 192–93
Smith, Roger, 113
Smitty, 42–43, 44
Snyder, Sharon, 391–92, 458, 469,
  471–73
Snyder, Teddy, 37, 358–59, 389–91,
  458–61, 469–70, 471, 472, 473
Soltan, Zaris, 158
Sonny, Dan, 9
South, Jim
  business of, 346, 366
  Ginger Lynn and, 350, 365–66
  on Hollywood, 353
  Marc Carriere and, 511, 514
  Savannah and, 481
  Shauna Grant and, 359
  Tim Connelly on, 346, 366
  Tommy Byron and, 427
  Traci Lords and, 377–78, 381–83,
    415, 417–18, 419–21
  Tricia Deveraux and, 556, 574, 575
  underage allegations, 419–21
Souza, Bob, 280, 286, 294–96
Souza, Glen, 175, 178–79, 242
Spelvin, Georgina, 42
  The Devil in Miss Jones and,
    121–24, 126, 127, 130, 131
  getting started, 20–23, 28,
    37–41
  Mafia and, 44–45
Sprinkle, Annie
  AIDS and, 396–401, 449
  Deep Inside Porn Stars and, 375
  getting started, 124–31
  Gloria Leonard and, 130, 373
  live burlesque, 141–43
  Marc Stevens and, 396, 400–401
  Plato's Retreat and, 169
  prostitution and, 372–73

transitioning out, 372–73
Veronica Vera and, 371–72
St. Clair, Sheri, 236
Stagliano, John, 511–12, 584–89
Star Distributors, 206, 220
Stark, Ray, 27, 28
Starlet, 11
Steen, Kristin, 352, 436–39
Steinberg, Ellen. *See* Sprinkle, Annie
Steinberg, Joel, 222, 224–26
Steinem, Gloria, 266, 267
Stevens, Marc, 38, 39, 121–23, 143,
   147, 159, 160, 396–97, 400
Stinger, Maria, 4, 5
Storm, Tempest, 7–8, 23, 141
Streicher, Herbert. *See* Reems, Harry
Sturman, Reuben
   acquittal, 354–55
   Bill Kelly on, 104, 106–7, 108, 228,
      331, 358
   bombing by, 501–4, 537–38
   Book Cellar vandalism and,
      498–500
   caught, 537–42
   conviction, 540
   death, 542
   Dominic Zicari and, 561
   dropping charges against, 331
   Gloria Leonard on, 356
   investigation of, 356–58
   judge–bribing, 540–42
   jury tampering, 539–40
   Larry Flynt and, 104, 106, 108,
      110
   Mickey Feinberg and, 498–99,
      500–501, 504–6, 537–38
   Naomi Delgado and, 358, 488–89,
      505, 523, 539–40
   Nina Hartley on, 355
   peep show industry/connections,
      104–10
   porn store plot, 498–507
   prison escape, 522–23
   Robert DiBernardo and, 106, 107,
      109, 357, 538–39
   Sharon Mitchell and, 227
   tax evasion, 357–58, 488–90,
      498–500
suitcase pimp, 230
Sussman, Joel, 235
Suzuki, Steve, 455
The Sword Swallower, 68. *See also*
   Deep Throat

T

Taccetta, Martin, 460
The Texas Chain Saw Massacre,
   180–81, 182
Thar She Blows, 11
Thevis, Mike, 106–7
This Film Is All About . . . , 52
Thomas, Paul, 229, 391, 403, 409, 459,
   470, 481, 531, 564
Thompson, Hunter, 493–94
Tomlinson, Frank, 321, 322, 323, 325,
   336–38
Torchio, Junior, 176, 177
Tosches, Nick, 100
Trader Horny, 11
Traynor, Chuck
   Al Goldstein and, 100
   Anthony Peraino and, 58–59, 67, 68,
      74
   beating Linda Lovelace, 60–61, 120,
      268
   Bunny Yeager and, 3, 5, 31–32
   Butchie Peraino and, 36, 54, 57–58,
      66, 67, 68, 71, 74, 101, 118–19
   Carol Conners and, 65
   David Winters and, 111–15, 118–19
   Deep Throat and, 56, 60–61, 62–63,
      65, 70–72, 74
   Deep Throat prosecution and,
      186
   deep throat technique and, 33
   divorce, 119
   dog movie and, 47–50, 100–101
   Gerard Damiano and, 53–54, 56, 61,
      63
   getting started, 4–6
   Harry Reems and, 61–62
   Hugh Hefner and, 101–3, 268
   Larry Marchiano and, 263–65
   Lenny Camp on, 17–18, 33–34, 58,
      65
   Linda Lovelace leaving, 114–15
   Linda Lovelace relationship decline,
      111–16
   making Linda Lovelace, 66, 112
   Maria Stinger and, 4–5
   Marilyn Chambers and, 115–20, 492
   marrying Linda Lovelace, 37
   meeting Linda Lovelace, 15–19
   Ordeal accusations, 268–69
   Perainos and, 67, 68, 74
   as pimp, 65–66

Traynor, Chuck (*continued*)
    prostitution and, 18–19, 31
    recruiting girls, 37
    Sammy Davis Jr. and, 99, 111–12,
        114, 119, 120, 268–69
    starting film career, 31–35
Traynor, Linda. *See* Lovelace, Linda
Trudeau, Patrice, 171, 211
turkey raffle, 18

U

underage girls
    Jean Jennings, 155–60
    Jim South and, 419–21
    John Holmes and, 135–36
    Lenny Camp conviction for, 157–58
    Sharon Mitchell, 155
    Traci Lords. *See* Lords, Traci
undercover agents, 193, 194–98

V

Vannatter, Phil, 391–92, 458–61,
    469–73
Vera, Veronica, 371–72, 374–76,
    435–36
Verlaine, Marc, 485
Veze, Bob, 346, 347
Vickie, deep throat and, 32–33
Video Vixen, 370
videos
    films vs., 368
    power of women and, 366
Vincent, Chuck, 164–65, 230
Vonder Haar, Lucie, 244–45
Vosse, Bob, 90–91, 133, 235–37
Vulture, 32–33

W

Wadd, Johnny. *See* Holmes, John
Wakerly, Bruce. *See* Ellavsky, Bruce
Wallice, Marc, 391, 469, 574, 575,
    576–84
Warshavsky, Seth, 568, 569, 570,
    571–73
Waters, John, 1–2, 52, 70, 399, 428,
    438, 453–54, 462, 465–67
Wedelstedt, Edward Joseph, 542

Wilsey, Mike, 479, 483
Wilsey, Shannon. *See* Savannah
Winters, David, 112–20
Wishman, Doris, 2–3, 7
Witt, Bana, 491–94
Wolf, Peter, 169
Wolfe, Bob, 29, 39, 47–50, 54
Women Against Pornography, 267, 428,
    438, 439
Wonderland Avenue gang
    Eddie Nash and, 275–82, 289–90,
        291–92
    John Holmes and, 280–82, 283, 284,
        286, 289–93
Wonderland murders, 290–92
    Eddie Nash and. *See* Nash, Eddie
    finding bodies, 294–96
    investigation, 294–305
    John Holmes and, 289–93, 297–305,
        336–40
    robbery instigating, 280–82, 283,
        284–86
Woods, Bambi, 144
World Modeling. *See* South, Jim
Wright, Evan, 567, 569–73

Y

Yeager, Bunny
    Bill Kelly on, 3, 5, 6
    Carol Conners and, 65
    Chuck Traynor and, 3, 5, 31–32
    Deep Throat and, 58, 70
    early days, 2–4, 5–7
    Hugh Hefner and, 6, 11
    modeling agent, 3–4
    movies, 7, 9–11
    photographer, 3–5, 6
Yelvington, James, 329, 330
Yontz, Dorothy. *See* Seka
Young, Roger, 104–10, 356–58, 433,
    488–90, 496, 522, 537–42

Z

Zaffarano, Michael (Mickey), 175–79,
    199, 206, 251, 252–56, 332
Zappi, Ettore, 107
Zelda, Miss, 6
Zicari, Dominic, 561
Zuraw, Veronica, 333, 335